T0365128

THE GREATEST AND DEADLIEST HURRICANES OF THE CARIBBEAN AND THE AMERICAS

The Stories Behind the Great Storms of the North Atlantic

Wayne Neely

Foreword by Michel Davison

THE GREATEST AND DEADLIEST HURRICANES OF THE CARIBBEAN AND THE AMERICAS

THE STORIES BEHIND THE GREAT STORMS OF THE NORTH ATLANTIC

iUniverse books may be ordered through booksellers or by contacting:

iUniverse
1663 Liberty Drive
Bloomington, IN 47403
www.iuniverse.com
1-800-Authors (1-800-288-4677)

A satellite image of Hurricane Katrina in the Gulf of Mexico on August 28, 2005. Katrina was a large, powerful, deadly and very destructive Category 5 hurricane that made landfall over Louisiana. Image courtesy of NOAA-The National Hurricane Center.

ISBN: 978-1-5320-1151-1 (sc)
ISBN: 978-1-5320-1152-8 (hc)
ISBN: 978-1-5320-1150-4 (e)

Library of Congress Control Number: 2016920243

Print information available on the last page.

iUniverse rev. date: 12/19/2016

TABLE OF CONTENTS

DEDICATION

In memory of Dr. Myles Munroe: you may be gone, but your legacy lives on forever… RIP.

To my recently deceased Uncles: Glenwood and Theophilus Neely.

To my grandmother, the late Joanna Gibson: you were and continue to be my life-long inspiration.

To Mr. Les Brown, who at a conference held here in the Bahamas, through his own unique way and method reminded me: 1) "Pass it on"; 2) "It is important how you use your down time"; 3) "Someone's opinion of you doesn't have to become a reality"; and 4) "In the time of adversity, expand!" To the late Dr. Myles Munroe, who always reminded me to: 1) "Die empty!" 2) "Pursue your purpose!" 3) "Purpose is when you know and understand what you were born to accomplish. Vision is when you see it in your mind and begin to imagine it!"; and 4) "Maximize your potential." I listened to them, and this book is the end result. Thank you, Mr. Les Brown and Dr. Myles Munroe, for your invaluable contributions to my life.

A hurricane is like a half glass of water: it is up to you to determine whether it is half-full or half-empty. If you look at the damage and destruction caused by the hurricane, then you are looking at the glass as half-empty. But if you look at the ultimate purpose of a hurricane on this Earth, then you are looking at the glass as half-full. My goal is to get more people to look at and appreciate the hurricane as a half-full glass of water.

"I don't count my sit-ups. I only start counting when it starts hurting. That is when I start counting, because then is when it really counts. That's what makes you a champion." Lesson to learn: the victories only truly count when they take the most effort. Push yourself by celebrating the ones that made you work for it... Muhammad Ali.

Wilbur Wright: "No bird ever soars in a calm wind, but it is the strong winds that propel us to greater heights." Lesson to learn: it is the same thing as soaring in the height of adversity that propels us to even greater heights to overcome our obstacles in life.

According to scientists, the bumblebee's body is too heavy and its wing span much too small. Aerodynamically, the bumblebee cannot or shouldn't be able to fly. However, no one ever told the bumblebee that, and for some strange reason it just keeps flying, going against odds of all logical explanations or rational thinking. Lesson to learn: when you don't know your limitations, you go out and surprise even yourself. In hindsight, you wonder if you had any limitations. The only limitations a person has are those that are self-imposed. Don't let education or life challenges put limitations on you.

PREFACE

The ten costliest catastrophes in the North Atlantic within the last one hundred years all have been natural disasters—seven of them hurricanes—and all have occurred since 1989, a period including, ironically, what the United States Government at one point dubbed "the decade for natural disaster reduction." Called the greatest storms on the planet, hurricanes are phenomenal, yet menacing features of the tropical North Atlantic Ocean, causing immense physical, social and economic upheaval. As people continue to build on and develop coastal areas, sadly society's liability to hurricanes will dramatically increase, regardless of changes in the environment. This book addresses these key issues, providing a detailed examination of hurricanes with respect to both climate and society. It covers everything from historical data sets and hurricane statistics used in forecasting and documenting societal vulnerability to hurricanes. Special attention is given to the major North Atlantic hurricanes, particularly those great storms that made landfall somewhere within the various countries of the North Atlantic. Scientists in the fields of meteorology, climatology, geography, history, economics, as well as decision makers in government, the private sector and industry will find this book an invaluable reference tool and the ideal handbook for anyone interested in hurricanes in general, their impressive capabilities and their great impact on the region.

The diverse cultures of the region have been shaped as much by hurricanes as they have been by geography, economics, diplomacy, commerce, or the era and legacy of colonial rule. Hurricanes have carved devastating paths across the region for centuries — and they continue to wreak havoc despite vast improvements in the technology to predict and prepare for these storms. Take Christopher Columbus, for example: - in June of 1495, during his Second Voyage to the New World, he encountered a "whirlwind" as he referred to it, so strong that "it plucked up by the roots…great trees" and "beat down to the bottom of the sea three ships which lay at anchor." The local Indians, he wrote, called "these tempests of the air...Furacanes." "Furacanes" was a mistranscription of Huracán, the Taíno word for a powerful storm of wind and rain under the control of a supernatural god.[1] All the Indian groups in the region had a similar word, and the Spanish quickly adopted them in their descriptions of these powerful storms that routinely battered their early settlements.

Recently, scores of people were killed (a total of 233 persons, both direct and indirect) when Hurricane Sandy plowed across Cuba, Hispaniola, the Bahamas, and other Caribbean nations, leaving thousands more homeless. It then went on to devastate the Eastern Seaboard of the United States. Hurricane Sandy (also unofficially known as "*Superstorm Sandy*") was the deadliest and most destructive hurricane of the very active 2012 North Atlantic hurricane season, as well as the second-costliest hurricane, right behind Hurricane Katrina, in the United States hurricane history. Classified as the eighteenth named storm, tenth hurricane and second major hurricane of that year, Sandy was a Category 3 storm at its peak intensity when it made landfall in Cuba. While it was a Category 2 hurricane off the coast of the Northeastern United States, the storm became the largest North Atlantic hurricane on record (as measured by diameter, with winds spanning 1,100 miles). Damage estimates from this storm amounted to over $75 billion, a total surpassed only by Hurricane Katrina of 2005, with damage totals of over $125 billion.[2]

That is what hurricanes do. They stop the world—your world, when they choose to come your way. They are among the most powerful, most mysterious forces on Earth, and they have been terrorizing people along the shores of the Atlantic Ocean, the United States, the Caribbean Sea, and the Gulf of Mexico for centuries. It is undeniable that the world today is going through a transformation of sorts with regards to powerful natural disasters like these hurricanes. Every year, most of the countries within this region, especially those in the tropical areas, experience hurricanes with different categories, speeds, and intensities. Yet for all their fury, hurricanes begin their lives as fragile weather systems far from the towns and cities where they devastate and make their names famous.

Consider this a hurricane can pack a mind-boggling amount of power. The heat energy released by a hurricane equals 50 to 200 trillion watts—or about

---

1 Matthew Mulcahy, *Hurricanes and Society in the British Greater Caribbean, 1624-1783,* (Baltimore, The Johns Hopkins University Press, 2006), pg. 14.

2 *http://www.aoml.noaa.gov/hrd/tcfaq/costliesttable.html.* Retrieved: 10-11-2015.

the same amount of energy released by exploding a 10-megaton nuclear bomb every 20 minutes.

With this stored up power, a hurricane can release it to cause significant damage and create destruction for many months or even years to follow in certain places. Some may even cause millions or even billions of dollars' worth of property damage in just one single country, state or city. Even the most highly technological advanced cities and countries around the region cannot control the awesome power of nature when it comes to hurricanes.

One might wonder which cities and countries around the region did the most intense hurricanes hit, how strong, deadly and impactful they were? What would happen if they were to hit today with the same intensity, and what would be the present-day cost when inflation is factored in? How many persons died in the Great Hurricane of 1780-the deadliest hurricane of the North Atlantic, or the Great Galveston Hurricane of 1900-the deadliest hurricane in US history, and which islands were impacted by these storms? This book will seek to provide comprehensive answers to these and many other thought-provoking questions and provide a full and unbiased viewpoint of the most destructive, deadliest and strongest hurricanes ever faced by residents of the North Atlantic. This book will seek to examine these questions and come up with this list or gallery of mega-storms.

For many residents of the North Atlantic, the big question that seems to be on everyone's mind before and during hurricane season is: how active will the season be? Will it impact their country, and how severe will it be? Every storm is different, but one of the ways to answer these questions is to explore the hurricane history of the region. Here, you'll find diverse profiles of storms that this region will never forget. For many of the storms, I've gathered a vast amount of storm data from the National Hurricane Center database reports, personal recollections from a vast array of individuals who experienced some of the more recent storms, newspapers reports, individual country climatological data reports, ships log reports, national archives and various libraries' storm reports from around the region and other ways to make this book as compelling, accurate, and reader-friendly as possible.

Hurricanes are called the greatest storms on the planet, and for very valid reasons; hurricanes of the North Atlantic often cause tremendous social and economic upheaval in parts of Canada, Bermuda, the United States, Central America, the Bahamas and the Caribbean. Sadly, with the increasing development of these coastal areas, the societal impact of these storms will likely increase. Thankfully, our ability to track and monitor these storms has advanced tremendously, thereby significantly reducing the death toll over coastal locations around the region. This book provides a comprehensive and detailed analysis of North Atlantic hurricanes and what they mean to and how they have impacted our society. It is intended to be used as an intermediary between hurricane climate research and the users of hurricane information. Topics include the climatology of tropical cyclones in general, and those of the North Atlantic in particular, focusing on the region's significant landfalling storms, and societal vulnerability to hurricanes, including analysis of hurricanes in the social and economic sciences of the region.

The study of weather is quite an amazing subject and is something that we are affected by everyday of our lives - a heavy snowstorm at a major airport that delays or cancels a flight; a sudden and unexpected afternoon thunderstorm that ruins a family picnic, a heavy flooding on a main highway that disrupts our driving pattern or be it a hurricane that forces us to evacuate our homes and move into a shelter. We rarely stop to give it any special thought until extreme weather events like hurricanes ruin the plans that we have for our daily lives. Humans are immensely fascinated by the weather, particularly extreme weather events such as hurricanes. Whether it be their powerful winds, terrible flooding, massive storm surge or the great destruction that these powerful storms bring to our lives, region or worldwide - we often stand in awe of these majestic storms of nature called hurricanes.

I wanted to fill this book with as much facts and information about hurricanes as possible with a hope and desire that when you reach the end of this book, you will become empowered with the knowledge and understanding of these great storms and see them for their ultimate purpose on this Earth. I went to great lengths to ensure the accuracy of the facts, discussions, and varied databases of hurricanes included in this book. However, hurricanes can invite distorted views from those directly or indirectly affected, and from the public at large. So even though I checked and re-checked dates, data, statistical reports with other sources and knowledgeable persons in the field of meteorology, climatology, history, geography and others, this book may still contain some inadvertent possible errors, and if that is the case, I do apologize, because it is not my goal to misrepresent or mislead you the reader in anyway, shape or form.

Most people are familiar with a hurricane's coastal impacts: storm surge, high winds, and heavy rain. Most hurricanes begin to rapidly weaken once they encounter land. The sustained winds steadily decline as the storm runs out of fuel—namely, warmth and moisture extracted from the upper ocean. Occasionally, however, the damage and devastation don't just end up only along the immediate coast, but inland as well. Although defining hurricanes and their place in history is somewhat subjective, loss of life and property damage provide objective measures, along with the event's significance as it relates to weather records. Hurricanes have always accounted for a great deal of death and destruction, and as populations continue to move into coastal areas prone to these dangerous storms, it seems as if we will inherently become more vulnerable to the dangers associated with hurricanes.

The broad area around the Earth known as the tropics, in the region 23½° north and south of the equator, experiences one of nature's greatest wraths called 'hurricanes'. In fact, about two-thirds of all tropical cyclones form between 10° and 20° north and south of the equator annually. These natural disasters called hurricanes every year take a great toll on our lives and the way we live them. Natural disasters such as hurricanes are never simply natural events, but rather they are connected to human interactions with the environment. Disasters become defined as such only when they strike and significantly impact human communities. Their impact has as much to do with the context in which they strike as with the physical forces that give rise to them. Social, economic and political conditions determine the extent of damage brought about by the hazards of hurricanes, the effects on different communities within society, and the response by both individuals and official institutions.

People all over the world are affected by a variety of weather conditions, and this region is no exception. In this region, we have our share of droughts, frontal systems, tornadoes, floods and hurricanes that affect our lives on a daily basis. People depend on the weather in many different ways. Farmers depend on the rains to water their crops, sailors count on the strong winds to fill their sails, and tourists take advantage of the sunshine for a great vacation. Yet the weather at times is anything but dependable or predictable. The Earth's atmosphere is always in constant turmoil, a chaotic brew of gases and water kept in constant motion by the sun's energy. Sometimes this energy is unleashed with sudden and unexpected savagery, especially with hurricanes, which can turn our islands or countries within the region into a wasteland of rubbles. However, thanks to meteorologists, our ability to predict where chaos might strike next is now better than ever. Yet a hurricane remains one of the deadliest of the natural forces at work on our planet.

When it comes to the impact and dangers associated with hurricanes, our responses invariably contain this guilty triple-take of excitement, shame and pity, and we feel we have to suppress our sense of exhilaration when a hurricane strikes a landmass in this region. Because of my background in meteorology and geography, I have other responses as well; all too frequently, I can see that a hurricane disaster was foreseeable, whereby measures could have been taken either to escape from it or to prevent it from happening in the first place. I hope the reader will develop that same sense while reading this book. It is very easy to understand why disasters like hurricanes happen. It was all too easy in past centuries to portray hurricanes as chaotic; unforeseen and unforeseeable. People were actively encouraged especially by spiritual leaders, to think of them as acts of punishment by a revengeful god or the Almighty God for something they had or not done. Thankfully, the twentieth century brought about a greater increase in our understanding of the way the world around us works. We now have to accept the fact that many hurricane disasters are – and increasingly will be – foreseeable. Some historic hurricane disasters could have been foreseen, and avoiding action could have been taken.

Many hurricane disasters are the result of powerful natural forces, but there is also a human element in play that makes the disaster much worse. For example, the hurricane season of 2008 was the cruelest ever experienced in Haiti. Four storms--Fay, Gustav, Hanna, and Ike--dumped heavy rains on the impoverished nation. The rugged hillsides, stripped bare of 98% of their forest cover thanks to deforestation, let flood waters rampage into large areas of the country. Particularly hard hit was Gonaives, the fourth largest city. "According to reliefweb.org, the rains from 2008's four storms killed 793, left 310 missing, injured 593, destroyed 22,702 homes, and damaged another 84,625. About 800,000 people were affected--8% of Haiti's total population. The flood wiped out 70% of Haiti's crops, resulting in dozens of deaths of children due to malnutrition in the months following the storms. Damage was estimated at over $1 billion, the costliest natural disaster in Haitian history. The damage amounted to over 5% of the country's $17 billion GDP, a staggering blow for a nation so poor."[34]

The mudslides that happened in Haiti from these storms were produced by heavy rains and loose layers of rock and soil lying on steep mountain sides – entirely a natural phenomenon – but the disaster was made far worse by people who misguidedly built settlements on the valley floors and deforested the mountainside, and by misguided authorities who turned a blind eye to these activities. When it comes to hurricanes and man, you will notice that throughout this book there is this insidious partnership between destructive

---

3 *www.reliefweb.org*. Retrieved: 11-11-2014.

4 *https://www.wunderground.com/hurricane/haiti.asp*. Retrieved: 11-11-2014.

natural processes and environmentally insensitive human behavior. There is an element of subjectivity, of value judgement, when we use the words 'hurricane disaster.'

In this book, you will witness the full brunt of nature's fury as some of the greatest, deadliest and strongest storms in the history of the North Atlantic come alive. Witness the rage of Hurricane Andrew over Florida in 1992 or the flood waters of Hurricane Mitch as it battered several countries in Central America in 1998. Furthermore, you will indeed witness many of the major historic hurricanes firsthand and their destructive aftermaths. When massive hurricanes like Andrew and Mitch threaten the region, it is up to the experts at the National Hurricane Center (NHC) in Miami to tell us when and where they will make landfall. Predicting storms of these magnitudes is a very tricky and stressful thing. One wrong calculation could leave millions of unsuspecting people directly in a storm's deadly path. In this book, you will also learn what it takes for a hurricane to develop, strengthen or dissipate, and find out how today's advanced technology is improving the science of hurricanes, and learn about the most active and interesting North Atlantic hurricane seasons on record.

Weather is the general term for the constantly changing atmospheric conditions that occur at a particular place and time. It is simply a result of the physical interactions between wind, sunshine, air, and water within our atmosphere. Hurricanes are among the most memorable of all of these weather phenomena. Perhaps one of the biggest challenges that many governments in this region face is how to adapt to and deal with the costly damages, repercussions, and destruction caused by these powerful forces of nature called hurricanes. A lot of time, money and effort are put into studying these powerful storms, with a hope of lessening the impact that they have on our daily lives and society as a whole, but then when all is said and done in most cases, nature always seems to have the upper hand.

This book examines North Atlantic hurricanes with respect to both climate and society. My purpose is a comprehensive reference for users of hurricane information. Users include geographers, meteorologists, climate scientists, economists, and decision makers in government and industry, particularly those involved in the urban planning, disaster relief, and insurance fields. The emphasis is on physical models to explain statistical relationships of hurricane activity with respect to weather and climate events. The better people are informed, the better they can prepare for the next big storm. This book is written in a way whereby it can be used as a college or university student textbook, or quite simply for the 'armchair' meteorologist who basically wants to find out general information about a specific hurricane and the impact it had on a particular island or country within this region.

This book has several main themes. Firstly, it begins with a general description of hurricanes, including an examination of historical data sets and a presentation of various hurricane statistics. Secondly, details on the origin, naming, track and meteorological history of some of the major hurricanes of the North Atlantic are presented. Thirdly, this is followed by the North Atlantic hurricane records most closely linked to people and society. Special focus is given to major or notable hurricanes, landfalling hurricanes and the analysis of cycles, trends, and return periods. Finally, the last theme is based on societal vulnerability to hurricanes. This book is my attempt to present the various historical hurricane records of the North Atlantic in a clear, precise, comprehensive, and original manner. The reader will decide if I have succeeded or not.

Taking readers from the voyages of Christopher Columbus to the devastation of Hurricanes Andrew, Mitch, Katrina, Sandy, Joaquin, and Matthew this book will look at the ethical, cultural, political, and economic challenges that hurricanes posed to the region's indigenous populations and the diverse European peoples who ventured to the New World to exploit its riches. I will describe how the United States provided the prototype for responding to environmental threats when it emerged as a major superpower and began to exert its influence over the Caribbean in the nineteenth century, and how the region's governments came to assume greater responsibilities for prevention and relief from hurricanes. Furthermore, a new light will be shed on recent catastrophes like Hurricanes Katrina, Mitch, Andrew and Sandy by framing them within a long and contentious history of human interaction with the natural world in this region. Spanning more than five centuries and drawing on extensive archival research in Europe and the Americas, *The Greatest and Deadliest Hurricanes of the North Atlantic* emphasizes the continuing critical role of race, social inequality, and economic ideology in the shaping of our responses to natural disasters.

FOREWORD

Tropical cyclones are one of the most damaging meteorological systems in nature, capable of producing and sustaining strong damaging winds for a prolonged period of time. They can spawn tornadoes that can add to the destructive force of these titans of nature and result in tidal waves that can easily overcome the defenses of the smaller islands in the Bahamas chain. But of high concern to our meteorologists at the Weather Prediction Center International Desks-NCEP) are the heavy rains that often associate with these cyclones. A track correction of 50-100 nautical miles can result in a totally different outcome, with a storm moving farther out to sea "only" dumping five to ten inches, while one closer to land can result in rainfall amounts in excess of 20 inches of nearly continuous rainfall in less than a day.

For their location, the Bahamas and the nation islands of the Caribbean are at the vanguard of what these brutes of nature are capable of doing, and every year they remind us all what they are capable of doing. As a new generation, modern day meteorologists have benefited from advances in computer science and numerical weather prediction, and we can provide better forecasts than what we were able to do just a decade ago. But we still have a lot to learn from previous events, so we don't make the same mistakes time after time. Knowledge and clear understanding on how past events unfolded have the power of helping the meteorological community to save lives.

As part of the learning process, there is the need to document what these brutes of nature are capable of doing. This is a hard task when trying to record the impact of an event that took place many decades ago, prior to the age of meteorological satellites, weather RADAR and super computers. Wayne Neely, unfazed by the challenge, has made this book a quest to document these systems before they are forgotten or get lost in the annals of history. This book will be a very welcome addition to the library of any history buff and meteorologists who want to learn from the past.

I have known Wayne for five years, and I consider him a very dear and loyal friend (please don't tell him I said that). He is a proud Bahamian, a native of Andros Island, who represents his nation with much pride and carries the flag with honor. The love for his country carries over to his work, and this book is a labor of love that only a most trusted friend can do. He has firsthand knowledge of the devastating effects of hurricanes, most recently during last year's Hurricane Joaquin that devastated the central Bahamas. When you have gone through, what they have gone through, you want to make sure you learn from your experience. Resistance is not futile, but not learning from history is futile at its worst.

Michel Davison
Lead Forecaster and Chief Coordinator of Administration at NCEP's International Desk of the U.S. National Oceanographic Atmospheric Administration

Michel Davison is a U.S. National Weather Service meteorologist with the Weather Prediction Center of the National Centers for Environmental Prediction (NCEP). Since 1993, he has been the lead forecaster and chief of the International Desks, training hundreds of meteorologists from Central America, the island nations of the Caribbean and South America on the proper application of numerical weather prediction models and modern techniques.

This has led to improvements in weather forecasting capabilities, in particular in the area of quantitative precipitation forecasting. *"He is one of the world's foremost experts on tropical meteorology, and I had the distinct pleasure of training under his great leadership and guidance, and I can truly say it was an honor to learn from him and his vast and expansive knowledge of tropical meteorology."* *Wayne Neely*

AUTHOR'S NOTE

Over the last 26 years of my life as a professional Bahamian meteorologist, hurricanes and their impact on my country of the Bahamas and the region as a whole have led me to write ten books on hurricanes. These books have allowed me to procure some of the best meteorologists in the business to write the foreword for me, from Bryan Norcross (Ph.D.), Hurricane Specialist at the Weather Channel; the late Herbert Saffir, co-creator of the Saffir-Simpson Hurricane Wind Scale; Phil Klotzbach (Ph.D.), from Colorado State University; the late Professor William Gray, from Colorado State University. Steve Lyons (Ph.D.), former Hurricane Specialist at the Weather Channel and now meteorologist in charge of the San Angelo National Weather Service Office in Texas, Chris Landsea (Ph.D.), Science and Operations Officer at the National Hurricane Center; and Kerry Emanuel (Ph.D.), Professor of Meteorology at Massachusetts Institute of Technology (MIT). This book is no different with Michel Davison, lead Forecaster and Chief Coordinator of Administration at Weather Prediction Center, NCEP's (the National Centers for Environmental Prediction) International Desks of the U.S. National Oceanographic Atmospheric Administration. This was done not only to add credibility to these books, but also to show the importance of hurricanes and their great impact on the lives of people of all walks of life here in this region and worldwide.

INTRODUCTION

Pearl Buck once said that, "If you want to understand today, you have to search yesterday." Most of the tropical cyclone information contained in this book is derived from the USA's National Hurricane Center (NHC) in Miami, the governing body which tracks, monitors and forecast all hurricanes for the entire region. One of the lesser-known but important functions of the United States National Hurricane Center is to maintain a historical hurricane database that supports a wide variety of uses in the research community, private sector, and the general public. This database, known as HURDAT (short for 'HURricane DATabase'), documents the life cycle of each known tropical or subtropical cyclone. In the North Atlantic basin, this dataset extends back to 1851. The HURDAT includes 6-hourly estimates of position, intensity, cyclone type (i.e., whether the system was tropical, subtropical, or extratropical), and in recent years also includes estimates of cyclone size. Currently, after each hurricane season ends, a post-analysis of the season's cyclones is conducted by NHC, and the results are added to the database.

The 2005 North Atlantic hurricane season was the most active North Atlantic hurricane season on record, shattering numerous records. The impact of the season was widespread and ruinous with an estimated 3,913 deaths and record damage of about $159.2 billion. During this season, numerous records were broken as there were 28 storms (27 named and 1 unnamed), of which 15 became hurricanes and 7 became major hurricanes. The most catastrophic effects of the season were felt on the United States' Gulf Coast, where a 30-foot storm surge emanating from Hurricane Katrina caused devastating flooding that destroyed most structures on the Mississippi coastline; subsequent levee failures in New Orleans, Louisiana caused by the storm crippled the city. Additionally, Hurricane Stan in combination with an extratropical system caused deadly mudslides across Central America, with Guatemala being hardest-hit. The 2005 season was the first to observe more tropical cyclones in the Atlantic than the Western Pacific; on average, the latter experiences 26 while the Atlantic only averages 12. This event was repeated in the 2010 season; however, the 2010 typhoon season broke the record for the fewest storms observed in a single year, while the 2005 typhoon season featured near average activity.

In 2012, Hurricane Sandy ravaged the Eastern Seaboard of the United States and in 2005 Hurricane Katrina nearly wiped Louisiana off the map. Furthermore, Hurricane Mitch brought chaos and destruction to many Central American countries in 1998. Yet, despite all of these recent gigantic hurricane events, we still behave as if natural disasters like hurricanes are outliers. Why else would we continue to build multi-million homes and businesses along the hurricane prone coastlines in this region routinely ravaged by these hurricanes? Unfortunately, hurricanes devastations within this region are much more common than we realize. Our increasing numbers of these storms exposes us to increasing risks, by taking us behind the scenes of the underlying dynamics that causes them. By understanding what causes these intricate evolutionary changes within the Earth's atmosphere, (which begins with just a mere thunderstorm cloud and with organization and growth it could morph into a major Category 5 hurricane), and only when this process is fully understood, we can begin to understand the dynamics of natural disasters like hurricanes.

The Atlantic dataset was created in the mid-1960s, originally in support of the space program to study the climatological impacts of tropical cyclones at Kennedy Space Center. It became obvious a couple of decades ago, however, that the HURDAT needed to be revised because it was incomplete, contained significant errors, or did not reflect the latest scientific understanding regarding the interpretation of past tropical cyclone data. Charlie Neumann, a former NHC employee, documented many of these problems and obtained a grant to address them under a program eventually called the Atlantic Hurricane Database Re-analysis Project. Chris Landsea, then employed by the NOAA Hurricane Research Division (HRD) and now currently the Science and Operations Officer at the NHC, has served as the lead scientist and program manager of the Re-analysis Project since the late 1990s.

Over the past two decades, Landsea, researchers Andrew Hagen and Sandy Delgado, and some local meteorology students have systematically searched for and compiled any available data related to each known storm in past hurricane seasons. This compilation also includes systems not in the HURDAT that could potentially be classified as tropical cyclones. The data are carefully examined using standardized analysis techniques, and a best track is developed for each system, many of which would be different from the existing tracks in the original dataset.[5]

Recently, Katrina one of the region's most recent notable and deadly hurricanes, taught the United States a significant and very valuable lesson of what can go wrong when a major hurricane makes impact with a densely populated city. The results were devastating, because in most cases when mankind clashes with the brunt-force of nature, somehow nature always seems to have the upper-hand or the 'trump-card' so to speak in the battle. Katrina was a very powerful and deadly storm. The strong prevailing wind gusts ripped the roof of the New Orleans Superdome, revealing long, narrow strips that flew through the air allowing the torrential rainfall and strong gusty winds to enter into the building unabated, thousands of people were camped on the playing field, the tiers of seats, and in the raw cement corridors. It was not comfortable for these storm victims because many of them were soaked and shivering. Unfortunately, the worst was still yet to come. Hurricane Katrina had battered the outskirts of Miami, and now it was making a beeline for the city of New Orleans—destroying the city and setting the stage for massive flooding. New Orleans, a huge swath of southern Louisiana, and the entire Mississippi coast would be left in ruins.

There is a ritual of sorts that goes on in the islands and countries of the North Atlantic every year when folks get wind of the news that a big storm is brewing somewhere within this region. Windows are boarded up, boats are dry-docked and grocery stores and hardware stores are picked clean of anything that might come in handy in the unlikely event that a massive hurricane hits. What keeps people going through the annual routine of prepping for the next 'big one' in these vulnerable coastal locales? It is that many have seen a real, live hurricane or two, and they know the kind of serious destruction these storms can cause. From the 16th-century hurricanes that ravaged the Caribbean to the devastating blow issued by Sandy in 2012, history is replete with stories of the wreckage and ruins that comes along with a major storm.

Hurricanes are the most powerful storms on Earth; the hurricane is an awe-inspiring feature of tropical weather. Accounting for a relatively small percentage (approximately 12%) of global tropical cyclone activity, hurricanes of the North Atlantic have a tremendous impact on the people and economies of the region. When measured in terms of past loss of life and property damage,

---

5 *https://noaanhc.wordpress.com/2016/02/11/solving-the-jigsaw-puzzle-of-hurricane-history*. Retrieved: 14-02-2016.

hurricanes rank near to or at the top of all natural hazards, rivaling major earthquakes. Despite significant reductions in the number of deaths from hurricanes, economic costs of hurricanes affecting the region have increased exponentially. As significant economic development continues on islands and shorelines of the region, it stands to reason that our vulnerability to hurricanes will rise at an increasing or alarming rate, regardless of the changes to the climate.

The North Atlantic hurricane season officially begins on June 1st and continues through November 30th. Although the number of tropical storms and hurricanes typically peaks during August and September, it is important to remember that residents of this region can be impacted by tropical weather systems any time during the six-month-long season. During this time, the coastal areas of the North Atlantic come under the threat from the ferocious winds and floodwaters of hurricanes that form somewhere in the Atlantic Ocean basin. In 2005, one of the most devastating storms ever to hit U.S. soil, Hurricane Katrina, all but destroyed parts of New Orleans as the surging ocean waters it pushed to land overtopped the city's protective levees, inundating a vast region, displacing millions of residents and killing 1,836 people. In 1780, the deadliest hurricane of the North Atlantic killed over 22,000 persons in the Caribbean, notably the countries of, Barbados, St. Lucia, Martinique and St. Eustatius.

Wind speed, costs, deaths, intensity and width are some of the ways to define the greatest and deadliest hurricanes of the North Atlantic. If using wind speed, intensity or width as the definition, it is necessary to explain whether the measurement was recorded at landfall or was the highest measurement recorded in the hurricane's life cycle. The largest loss of life from a hurricane is often caused by the storm surge and flooding, rather than the sustained winds. Do not underestimate a lower category hurricane, because many of the top deadliest or greatest hurricanes in the region's history were not Category 5 hurricanes at landfall. It is a common misconception that a lower category hurricane is less of a threat than a higher category hurricane. For example, Hurricane Katrina was the costliest hurricane in United States history, and yet it was only a Category 3 hurricane when it made landfall in Louisiana in 2005.

The Great Labor Day Hurricane of 1935 was the strongest and most intense hurricane to make landfall in the United States in recorded history. The second tropical cyclone, second hurricane, and second major hurricane of the 1935 North Atlantic hurricane season, the Great Labor Day Hurricane was the first of three Category 5 hurricanes at landfall that the United States endured during the 20th Century (the other two being 1969's Hurricane Camille and 1992's Hurricane Andrew). Hurricane Andrew was the only Category 5 hurricane to make the list of the top five costliest hurricanes to strike the United States. Category 5 hurricanes are extremely rare and in fact, only six times—in the 1932, 1933, 1960, 1961, 2005, and 2007 hurricane seasons—has more than one Category 5 hurricane formed. Only in 2005 have more than two Category 5 hurricanes formed, and only in 2007 has more than one made landfall at Category 5 strength. Hurricanes of such intensity are somewhat infrequent in the North Atlantic basin, occurring only once every three years on average, and landfalls by such storms are even scarcer. Thirty-three Category 5s have been recorded in the North Atlantic basin since 1851, when records began. Only one Category 5 has been recorded in July, eight in August, eighteen in September, four in October, and one in November. There have been no officially recorded June or off-season Category 5 hurricanes.

Between 1924 and 2015, 33 hurricanes were recorded at Category 5 strength. No Category 5 hurricanes were observed officially before 1924. It can be presumed that earlier storms reached Category 5 strength over open waters, but the strongest winds were not measured. The anemometer, a device used for measuring wind speed, was invented in 1846. However, during major hurricane strikes the instruments as a whole were often blown away, leaving the hurricane's peak intensity unrecorded. For example, as the Great Beaufort Hurricane of 1879 struck North Carolina, the anemometer cups were blown away when indicating 138 mph.[6]

A reanalysis of weather data is ongoing by researchers at the National Hurricane Center who may upgrade or downgrade other North Atlantic hurricanes currently listed at Categories 4 and 5. For example, the 1825 Santa Ana hurricane is suspected to have reached Category 5 strength. Furthermore, paleotempestological research aims to identify past major hurricanes by comparing sedimentary evidence of recent and past hurricanes strikes. For example, a "giant hurricane" significantly more powerful than Hurricane Hattie (Category 5) has been identified in Belizean sediment, having struck the region sometime before 1500. Officially, the decade with the most Category 5 hurricanes is 2000–2009, with eight Category 5 hurricanes having occurred: Isabel (2003), Ivan (2004), Emily (2005), Katrina (2005), Rita (2005), Wilma

---

6 James E. Hudgins, *Tropical cyclones affecting North Carolina since 1586* (PDF). (National Weather Service Office Blacksburg, Virginia. National Oceanic and Atmospheric Administration, 2000). Retrieved: 05-07-2015.

(2005), Dean (2007), and Felix (2007). The previous decades with the most Category 5 hurricanes were the 1930s and 1960s, with six occurring between 1930 and 1939 (before naming began) and again between 1960 and 1969 (Ethel, Donna, Carla, Hattie, Beulah, and Camille).[7]

Seven Atlantic hurricanes—Camille, Allen, Andrew, Isabel, Ivan, Dean and Felix—reached Category 5 intensity on more than one occasion; that is, by reaching Category 5 intensity, weakening to a Category 4 or lower, and then becoming a Category 5 again. Such hurricanes have their dates shown together. Camille, Andrew, Dean and Felix each attained Category 5 status twice during their lifespans. Allen, Isabel and Ivan reached Category 5 intensity on three separate occasions. However, no Atlantic hurricane has reached Category 5 intensity more than three times during its lifespan. The November 1932 Cuba hurricane holds the record for most time spent as a Category 5 (although it took place before the satellite or reconnaissance era so the record may be somewhat suspect).

Another hurricane called Hurricane Camille of 1969 had the highest sustained winds of 190 mph at landfall ever recorded in a North Atlantic hurricane when it struck the Mississippi Coast. Hurricane Camille was the third and strongest tropical cyclone and second hurricane during the 1969 North Atlantic hurricane season. It reached this milestone near the mouth of the Mississippi River on the night of August 17. Estimates put sustained winds around 190 miles per hour, but the true speed will never be known because the weather recording equipment was destroyed at landfall. Camille was the second strongest U.S. landfalling hurricane in recorded history (by central pressure), second only to the Great Labor Day Hurricane of 1935, but it holds the distinction of having the strongest winds. It was also the first modern Category 5 hurricane to ever receive a person's name when making landfall in the United States.

Hurricanes Mitch and Katrina are grim reminders of hurricanes devastating and deadly potential. Hurricane Mitch which struck several Central American countries in 1998, was the most powerful hurricane and the most destructive of the 1998 North Atlantic hurricane season, with maximum sustained winds of 180 mph. The storm was the thirteenth tropical storm, ninth hurricane, and third major hurricane of the season. Along with Hurricane Georges, Mitch was

---

7 Mccloskey, T; G Keller, *5000-year sedimentary record of hurricane strikes on the central coast of Belize*. Quaternary International 195 (1-2): pgs. 53–68, 2009. Retrieved: 05-07-2015.

the most notable hurricane in the season. At the time, Hurricane Mitch was the strongest North Atlantic hurricane observed in the month of October, though that record has since been surpassed by Hurricane Wilma of the 2005 season. This hurricane matched the fourth most intense North Atlantic hurricane on record (it has since dropped to seventh). Hurricane Mitch was the deadliest North Atlantic hurricane since the Great Hurricane of 1780, displacing the Great Galveston Hurricane of 1900 as the second-deadliest hurricane on record. Nearly eleven thousand people were confirmed dead, and almost as many reported missing. The hurricane and the subsequent flooding caused extreme damage, estimated at over $6.2 billion (1998 USD). Mitch caused such massive and widespread damage that Honduran President Carlos Roberto Flores claimed it destroyed over fifty years of progress in the country.

The costliest hurricane ever recorded in the North Atlantic was Hurricane Katrina, the most recent, costliest hurricane was Hurricane Sandy, which struck the coastlines of Jamaica, the Bahamas, Cuba and North Eastern United States, causing $75 billion in total cost (2012 USD) in late October 2012. Katrina was the costliest natural disaster, as well as one of the five deadliest hurricanes, in the history of the United States. The storm is currently ranked as the third most intense United States landfalling tropical cyclone, behind only the Great Labor Day Hurricane of 1935 and Hurricane Camille in 1969. Overall, at least 1,836 people died in Katrina and subsequent floods, making it the deadliest United States hurricane since the Great Okeechobee Hurricane of 1928. Later, Hurricane Ike in 2008 and Hurricane Sandy in 2012 caused more damage than Hurricane Andrew, but both were far less destructive than Katrina. All of these highlighted storms will be mentioned in great detail in future pages of this book.

Whether they are called hurricanes in the North Atlantic, typhoons in the western Pacific or cyclones in the Indian Ocean, great damage and destruction can result wherever they strike land. These storms develop under different conditions than the everyday storm—they're also far less predictable. Despite the fact that hurricanes strike hardest in coastal areas, development and population growth along the coastal areas continue to rise at a rapid rate. For example, in the United States, there are approximately 45 million permanent residents living on or along the coastal shorelines. During holidays, weekends, and in the summer, the population in some coastal areas increases ten- to a hundred-fold. Even though 80 to 90 percent of the population living in storm-prone areas has never experienced the core of a hurricane, a disaster, if not a catastrophe, is waiting to happen with every hurricane season. It's only a matter of time.

The focus of this book is not the hurricanes themselves, but on a grander scale of how people, governments, and societies have responded to them. These hurricanes in this book will begin when Europeans first arrived in the Caribbean in 1492, but modern meteorological and scientific studies indicate that hurricanes had visited the region of the North Atlantic for many millennia before the Pleistocene epoch, when Homo sapiens arose as a species, and long before peoples inhabited the Americas. While, of course, these natural phenomena were not 'labelled' as disasters, so long as human lives were not at risk, the sub-field of paleotempestology (the study of ancient storms and weather) and hundreds of modern post-hurricanes studies have shown that the great storms have tremendous effects on flora and fauna, water resources, landscapes, coral reefs, nesting sites, and species survival.

This book will showcase some of the greatest and deadliest hurricanes of the North Atlantic. The North Atlantic basin encompasses the waters between North and Central America and the continents of Europe and Africa, and includes the Caribbean Sea and the Gulf of Mexico. Eighty-five to ninety percent of them originate between 20°N and 20°S latitude. Furthermore, the storms discussed in this book will present a set of normal and extreme statistics as gathered by various storms over several hundred years or more. The statistics include average frequencies, mean intensities, seasonal cycles, geographic distributions of origin, and so on. The set of hurricane statistics is placed against the backdrop of climate conditions around the region and worldwide. Global climate anomalies are offered as explanations to the variations in hurricane activities in the North Atlantic basin.

The main breeding grounds for hurricanes are the tropical waters of the North Atlantic basin. In this case, hurricanes are most likely to develop where the oceans are at their warmest and the dynamics of the surface and the upper levels of the atmosphere are ideal for their formation. As a matter of fact, more than 50% of the North Atlantic tropical cyclones reach hurricane intensity, and the strongest of these are the Cape Verde type storms. Many persons in this region and worldwide perceive the North Atlantic Ocean basin as a prolific producer of hurricanes because of the significant publicity these storms generate in the media and elsewhere. However, in reality, the North Atlantic basin is generally a marginal basin in terms of hurricane activity. Every tropical ocean except the South Atlantic and southeast Pacific contains hurricanes; several of these tropical oceans produce more hurricanes annually than the

North Atlantic. For example, the most active ocean basin in the world is the Northwest Pacific, which averages 17 hurricanes per year. The second most active is the eastern North Pacific, which averages 10 hurricanes. In contrast, the North Atlantic mean number of hurricanes is 10 named storms, 6 hurricanes and 2 major hurricanes. For example, the North Atlantic hurricane season officially starts June 1st and ends November 30th, but most tropical storms and hurricanes form between August 15 and October 15. The peak of the North Atlantic hurricane season is September 10.

The first chapters serve as an introduction to hurricanes. Included in these chapters are definitions and descriptions of the salient features of these powerful tropical cyclones. The environmental conditions conducive to their growth and development are also examined. This book describes climatological features of the North Atlantic hurricane activity from data archived over the past century and more. Specifically, the focus is hurricane activity relevant to planning and mitigation strategies in the North Atlantic basin. In terms of climatology, hurricanes are strongest in late summer because of three favorable conditions- warm water, weak wind shear, and cyclonic disturbances which are optimum in late summer. In particular, water temperatures peak in late summer, which seems paradoxical because the longest day is in June. However, the days are still longer than nights until fall, therefore the water is still accumulating heat into late summer. The monsoon troughs are most active in late summer as well, and the large-scale circulation patterns favor weak wind shear in late summer.

Hurricanes, as defined by the World Meteorological Organization (WMO) and the National Oceanic and Atmospheric Administration (NOAA), are tropical cyclones—a warm-core, non-frontal synoptic-scale cyclone, originating over tropical or subtropical waters with organized deep convection and a closed surface wind circulation about a well-defined center—in the Atlantic, Caribbean Sea, Gulf of Mexico, or eastern Pacific, in which the maximum 1-minute sustained surface winds exceeds 64 kts (74 mph) or greater. Please note that the following storms in this book are not exhaustive and do not include every single notable storm in the region's history. Typically, if a hurricane has caused significant damage to a particular location, its name is requested to be retired either by the country or countries affected or by the region the system affected. The costliest hurricane ever recorded in the North Atlantic was Hurricane Katrina, which struck the coastline of Louisiana in August 2005, causing over $125 billion dollars in property damage. The second and most recent hurricane on that list is 'Super Storm' Sandy, which struck the coastlines of Jamaica, Cuba, the Bahamas and northeast United States, causing over $75 billion in total cost in late October 2012.

To give you some idea of the strength and devastation associated with these storms of the North Atlantic, this book will provide a wide-ranging listing of some of the most memorable hurricanes since pre-colonial times. These storm rankings or listings of these great and deadly hurricanes of this region are based on tracking or documenting hurricanes dating back to as far as 1494. Keep in mind that when viewing this list, it must be noted that Florida, the Bahamas and the Western Caribbean get most of their hurricane action due to the vulnerability or location of these countries at all 6 months of the hurricane season. Take the Bahamas, for instance, which on average gets brushed or hit by a hurricane once every three years and gets hit by a major hurricane once every 12 years. There are three Bahamian islands ranked in the top 10 impacts from tropical systems of all cities, islands and countries in the North Atlantic Basin, and they are Andros, Abaco and Grand Bahama. This is because the Bahamas, and especially these afore-mentioned islands, are affected by the four different types of hurricanes impacting the region, whereby some other countries are only impacted by one or two of the different types of hurricanes impacting the region. Take, for instance, Barbados which is basically only affected by the Cape Verde - type hurricanes.[8]

Florida, jutting like a thumb into the sea between the sub-tropical Atlantic and the Gulf of Mexico, is the most exposed of all the states within the United States to hurricanes therefore, they experience many more storms than any of the other states. Florida is one of the most common spots in the region to get hit by a hurricane during the time period from June to November. In an average year, they experience at least 3-4 hurricanes in a typical hurricane season. At least one of those will be a major hurricane. Miami, Florida, is one of the most frequently hit places in the continental United States, for tropical systems. Hurricanes typically will be most frequent towards the beginning of the fall semester in August and September. The list of Florida hurricanes encompasses approximately 488 tropical or subtropical cyclones that affected the state of Florida. More storms hit Florida than any other U.S. state, and since 1851 only eighteen hurricane seasons passed without a known storm impacting the state. Tropical cyclones have affected Florida in every month of the year with

---

8 Wayne Neely, *The Great Okeechobee Hurricane of 1928-The Story of the Second Deadliest Hurricane in American History and the Deadliest Hurricane in Bahamian History,* (Bloomington, iUniverse, 2014), pg. xvi.

the exceptions of January and March. Nearly one-third of the cyclones affected the state in September, and nearly three-fourths of the storms affected the state between August and October, which coincides with the peak of the hurricane season.

In the North Atlantic, tropical cyclone data extend back to 1851. The storm tracks and intensities have been carefully examined, reviewed and reconstructed using all available data sources. There are certainly gaps and missing storms in the first 115 years of the database (pre-satellite era), but the record is as complete as possible based on ship reports and land-based observations. So one period of record from which we can create and define a hurricane database climatology is from 1851 to the present. In December 1966, the first geostationary weather satellite was launched into orbit and provided regular complete coverage of the Atlantic basin. This was a significant advancement for detecting and monitoring tropical cyclones. The record definitely becomes more reliable and complete from this point on, so another useful climatology on hurricane activity to construct is from 1967 to the present. There's another way you could look at it — by NOAA's defined climatic period from 1981 to 2010, the "climate normal". Every 10 years, NOAA officially changes its baseline climatology to reflect the past three decades of observations. In 2021, the climate normal will change to 1991 to 2020, but until then, we use 1981 to 2010.

The Mid-Atlantic coast does get many brushes and recurvatures, as well as back door extra-tropical storms. The eastern Caribbean has only July, August, September, and to a lesser extent October as main threats per month from hurricanes. While the number of casualties from these storms has gone down over the years, the costs associated with the damage caused by these storms have risen tremendously. That has resulted from more people in record-breaking numbers building along the coastline, and more expensive homes and businesses are also located there.

Every year, hurricanes make landfall in many of the islands or countries of the North Atlantic. Have you ever wondered what year experienced the greatest number of storms? What was the costliest or deadliest storm in this region's history? How about the oddest storm track or the longest-lived hurricane? In this book, I will examine the threat of these freaks of nature called hurricanes by looking back at all aspects of these hurricanes in our region's history. An extensive international, regional and national dataset on hurricane tracks and intensities, compiled by the National Hurricane Center and other governing bodies, were used to examine all the occurrences of tropical cyclones spanning across the North Atlantic region from 1494 to the present- day season. The term "tropical cyclone" includes all named systems, including tropical storms and those in the post-tropical phase, but excludes tropical depressions. However, our region can experience periods or years of inactivity, and vice -versa. For instance, in the 1929 hurricane season, there were only 3 named storms that year. On the other hand, the 2005 record breaking year for hurricanes saw 28 storms (27 named storms and 1 unnamed storm) in the North Atlantic and the 1933 season, with 21 named storms came in second on this list.

Our region's level of activity is probably best described as episodic, with frequencies in-line with the well-known Atlantic Multi-Decadal Oscillation (AMO). The AMO describes a cyclical rise and fall of North Atlantic basin hurricane activity on time scales of 20-30 years, tied to intrinsic (natural) modes of climate variability. Hurricane track is influenced by several factors, but fundamentally on the strength and position of the mid-Atlantic Ridge – a sprawling, subtropical dome of high pressure across the central and western Atlantic. The ridge establishes a broad-scale, clockwise circulation that wheels embedded hurricanes westward across the Atlantic, then re-curves them toward the north. If, in a given season, the ridge lies close to the U.S. mainland, storms are repeatedly steered into the Bahamas and the eastern states of the United States. When displaced farther east, most storms will re-curve harmlessly over the open Atlantic Ocean. Historically, hurricanes or their remnants have approached our region from every compass direction, including the north. By far, the most common trajectory of a hurricane, and especially the Cape Verde- type storm, is it initially moves from the east, moving westwards into the Atlantic, followed by a northwestward track through the Caribbean, and then a northerly to northeasterly track over the USA.

Every single hurricane tells a unique story, some of them good, but most of them bad, because in many cases they leave behind widespread devastation. Each hurricane is unique and different, and no two hurricanes are alike, just like the fingerprints on our hand. What I have done in this book was to research them and capture as many of these stories related to hurricanes as humanly possible, and then say what made them so unique in the annals of the North Atlantic hurricane history. Let's take Hurricane Wilma (the strongest North Atlantic hurricane on record), for example; it is one of the more notable storms within this region. On October 19, 2005, Hurricane Wilma's lowest central pressure dropped to 882 mbar (26.05 inches Hg) (beating Hurricane Gilbert in 1988, the prior record holder, which had a central pressure of 888 mbar), the lowest sea-level pressure ever observed in a North Atlantic hurricane, according to National Hurricane Center in Miami. Peak winds reached 185 mph while the slow moving storm churned over the Yucatan Peninsula.

Besides having unsurpassed intensity, Wilma is also remembered for its rapid intensification and massive size. It was part of the record breaking 2005 North Atlantic season, which included three of the six most intense North Atlantic hurricanes ever observed (along with #4 Rita and #6 Katrina), Wilma was the twenty-second storm, thirteenth hurricane, sixth major hurricane, fourth Category 5 hurricane, and second-most destructive hurricane of the very busy 2005 hurricane season. A tropical depression formed in the Caribbean Sea near Jamaica on October 15 and intensified into a tropical storm two days later, which was named Wilma. After heading westward as a tropical depression, Wilma turned abruptly southward after becoming a tropical storm. Wilma continued intensifying and eventually became a hurricane on October 18. Shortly thereafter, extreme and record breaking intensification occurred, and in only 24 hours, Wilma became a Category 5 hurricane with winds of 185 mph. As a result, Wilma is ranked among the top ten costliest hurricanes ever recorded in the North Atlantic and the fifth costliest storm in United States history.

While Hurricanes Sandy, Katrina, Mitch, Wilma and Andrew are some of the most remembered of these recent swirling storms — their names are now infamous — they are certainly not alone in causing significant death and destruction to areas of the North Atlantic. This book will present some of the strongest, most damaging and deadly hurricanes to ever affect the North Atlantic basin, including the United States, Caribbean and Central America. It is not an exhaustive list and does not include every single notable storm in the history of the North Atlantic. The information on these storms is gathered and provided by the National Hurricane Center and the National Weather Service in the United States, various weather offices, archives, museums and libraries across the region.

Hurricanes are not just hurricanes but they bring with them a wide-ranging collection of hazardous weather conditions including high winds, torrential rainfall, coastal storm surge flooding and erosion, inland flooding, tornadoes and very high ocean waves. However, in keeping with the framework of balance, without tropical weather systems and storms, many parts of the region would lose out on a significant part of summertime rainfall. In fact, about 60% to 70% of the annual rainfall in the Bahamas is directly related to tropical cyclones.

Interest in the weather is a pervasive and continuing human attitude, and the old saying "Everybody talks about the weather..." is a truism that originates from this interest. The weather affects us all at one time or the other. But we rarely stop to consider its causes until extreme weather conditions such as hurricanes and floods inconvenience us in some way or the other or place our lives in danger in some shape or form. Every other day, hurricanes, floods, droughts and other weather conditions make the headlines nationally and internationally as they bring tragedy to thousands of people. News accounts of hurricanes have made these disasters familiar to everyone, and television has brought vivid pictures of those events into our homes and our lives. They are a reminder of the power of the forces of nature that generate the weather, which most of us have thankfully experienced only in a less dreadful guise.

The weather is one of those things we cannot control, and so the best we can do is to study it carefully so that we can be forewarned about what it will bring, with a view to lessening the impact that it has on our daily lives. Few things in nature can compare to the destructive forces of hurricanes. This is because hurricanes are capable of completely destroying coastal areas with sustained winds of over 157 miles per hour, intense areas of rainfall, and massive storm surges of over 25 feet in height. In fact, during its life cycle, a hurricane can expend as much energy as 10,000 nuclear bombs. The term hurricane is derived from the ancient Indian word 'Huracán', a god of evil recognized by the Taínos and Maya Indians. In other parts of the world, hurricanes are known as typhoons in the western Pacific and China Sea area, in Bangladesh, Pakistan, and India they are known simply as cyclones without a name, and in Australia as Willy-Willies.

When we hear about hurricanes, we tend to think of the more recent ones that have affected us. We have mental images of destroyed buildings and uprooted trees, massive flooding, flipped over cars, and a sense of loss for the hurricane victims. The definition of hurricane is easily understood: a tropical cyclone with high wind speeds of more than 74 miles per hour. Severe flooding, high wind speeds, tornadoes and huge storm surges and torrential downpours are to be expected from a fully developed hurricane. To kick off our list of top hurricanes, we will take a look back at some of the greatest storms to impact the region over the many years of their occurrences.

Hurricanes are marvels of nature that strike fear in the hearts of humans, with their terrifyingly strong winds, high seas and torrential rains. Hurricanes are the most dangerous and unpredictable of all the natural forces at work on our planet. Earth's chaotic atmosphere can strike at random with little or no warnings, and with devastating consequences. Today, tragedies are rare, thanks in part to weather satellites, Doppler radars, televisions, computers, radios and special airplanes called Reconnaissance Aircrafts. They report the progress of each hurricane, so ships have ample warnings to keep well away from them, and persons on land have adequate time to batten down or evacuate from these deadly storms. On the land, these warnings are valuable in saving lives. They can't prevent the force of the strong winds, floods, the torrential rainfall and the accompanying storm surge from destroying crops, boats, homes and businesses worth millions of dollars each year, but they can and do save lives with the early warning systems provided to the general public by meteorologists.

Here in this region, no island or country can be considered entirely free from these wraths of nature. For example, Hurricane Ivan in September 2004 damaged over 90 per cent of Grenada's housing stock, and probably half of those in the Cayman Islands. It destroyed 50 percent of St. Lucia's banana crop and 20 percent of St. Vincent's bananas. In fact, it is estimated that as many as nine Caribbean countries have suffered death and damage from Ivan alone during the 2004 hurricane season. Trinidad, normally considered to be outside the hurricane belt because of its nearness to the equator, had a freak storm in 1933, which destroyed coconut plantations and oil installations in the south of the island.

Barbados, which was relatively storm- free for the first half of the last century, suffered a major blow from a hurricane in 1955, which went on to wreck Grenada. In addition, there was Hurricane Lenny, which had a very strange and unusual west to east movement in mid-November of 1999, and on that track it went on to hit the west coast of Barbados. It caused millions of dollars in damage to the normally sheltered zone on the western shores of Barbados. Then there was Hurricane Gilbert, which until Wilma of 2005 (882mbar) had the lowest central pressure reading of any hurricane in this region of 888mbar (26.17 inches). This hurricane went on to totally devastate the country of Jamaica, bringing its economy to a virtual standstill for almost two years after the storm.

Finally, there was Hurricane Catarina (officially it is called Cyclone Catarina, because the term cyclone is the southern hemispheric term for hurricane - but for uniformity, I will use the term 'hurricane'), which even though it did not occur in the North Atlantic, it amazed and baffled meteorologists from every corner of the Earth. It formed on the east coast of Brazil on March 26, 2004, killing 3 persons and leaving 2,000 homeless in its wake. Before then, there was a long held belief or rule of law, so to speak, that it was impossible or near impossible to have a hurricane forming off the east coast of Brazil, because the dynamics of the atmosphere and oceans wouldn't and couldn't support it. There are thousands of books written about the location of hurricanes and where they can or can't form, and eastern Brazil has always been a 'no formation' zone. Now, thanks in part to Hurricane Catarina in 2004, these books have to be edited or re-written to reflect this change that Hurricane Catarina brought about in the scientific community.

It is the coming of summer to the northern hemisphere that ushers in conditions that spawn tropical storms and hurricanes. The movement of the sun—which is not really movement, of course, but a positional shift relative to Earth caused by the planet's year-long orbit—brings the peak power of solar radiation northward. The sun's track moves first to the equator, and from the sun's position over the equator in late March its apparent movement is northward to the Tropic of Cancer in late June, (23.5° north latitude), when it begins to retreat southward again in July, and August. Behind this solar track, the sea and air grow significantly warmer, and the polar airflows make a steady retreat.

This northward shift of the sun brings the season of tropical cyclones to the northern hemisphere. This means it is time to look seaward, along our coasts. This is as true for Asia as it is for the United States and the Caribbean. Over the western Pacific, the tropical cyclone season is never quite over, but varies greatly in intensity. Every year, conditions east of the Philippines send a score of violent storms howling toward Asia, but it is worse from June through October. Southwest of Mexico, eastern Pacific hurricanes develop during the spring, summer, and fall. Most of these will die at sea as they move over colder ocean waters. But there are destructive exceptions when storms occasionally curve back toward Mexico and the southwestern United States, bringing flooding rains.

Along the U.S. Atlantic and Gulf coasts, the Caribbean and Central America, the hurricane season lasts from June through November. Early in this season, the western Caribbean and Gulf of Mexico are the principal areas of origin. In July and August, this spawning center begins to shift eastward, and by early September a few storms are being born as far east as the Cape Verde Islands, off Africa's west coast. Again after mid-September, most storms begin in the western Caribbean and Gulf of Mexico.

In an average year, more than 80 to 100 disturbances with hurricane potential are observed in the North Atlantic, and on average only twelve of these reach the tropical storm stage, and only about six mature into hurricanes, and three into major hurricanes. For the National Hurricane Center - the governing body for studying, monitoring and tracking hurricanes in this region - the hurricane season means another hazard from the atmosphere, at a time when tornadoes, floods, and severe storms are also playing seasonal havoc elsewhere in the region. However, not all will be severe, and not all will necessarily touch land. Late August and September are considered the months with the most numerous and most violent storms, mainly because the waters of the Caribbean are warmer and the atmosphere is more conducive to development of these storms.

This book will present a summary of the greatest and deadliest hurricanes of the Caribbean and the Americas. Prior to this publication, we often heard and debated about hurricanes that affected this region in a general way, but never before have they been documented in such a comprehensive, informative and entertaining way. There are those who will argue that I missed out a particular storm, over-emphasized or neglected another, but these storms are in my opinion are some of the most memorable storms to affect this region. You can feel free to agree or disagree with me on any of these choices. This book, however, seeks to provide invaluable information on both historical and recent hurricanes to affect the North Atlantic. My main goal here is to provide a historical and educational perspective of these great hurricanes and help document what made them, in my humble opinion, unique and memorable. It is written in a non-technical and non-scientific language when and where possible, so that the average reader can understand and appreciate what made these storms so great in the archives of the North Atlantic hurricane history. I hope that you enjoy learning about these hurricanes, as I have enjoyed researching and presenting them to you.

This book will attempt to answer some of the major questions that arise from the interest of hurricanes. Its emphasis will be placed on understanding them, and by that I mean providing the reader with the physical attributes of these amazing atmospheric storms known as hurricanes. As such, its purpose is twofold, first, to give the reader a deeper appreciation of the physical attributes of these storms and what makes them work; and second, to impart a historical awareness of these storms and how they affected life in general in the countries affected. In the process of communicating this understanding, a considerable amount of descriptive information about the structure and dynamics of hurricanes will be presented. This book is targeted to the general reader who is interested in knowing when and where tropical cyclones have affected this region, and the magnitude of the damage inflicted by these hurricanes.

CHAPTER ONE

The history behind the word 'hurricane' and other tropical cyclones' names

"The worst storms of all the world's seas are those of these islands and coasts," wrote Bartolomé de Las Casas in his log-book (1561), responding to his experiences with several hurricanes on the island of Hispaniola.[9] The forces of nature, such as deadly hurricanes, have shaped the lives of people from the earliest times. Indeed, the first 'meteorologists' were priests and shamans of ancient communities. Whatever lifestyles these ancient people followed, they all developed beliefs about the world around them. These beliefs helped them to explain how the world began, what happens in the future, or what happened after a person died. The world of spirits was very important. Those people, who became noted for their skills at interpreting signs in the world around them, became spiritual leaders in their communities.

All religions and different races of people recognized the power of the weather elements, and most scriptures contain tales about or prophecies foretelling great natural disasters sometimes visited upon a community because of the sins of its citizens. Ancient peoples often reacted to the weather in a fearful, superstitious manner. They believed that mythological gods controlled the weather elements, such as winds, rain and sun, which governed their existence. When weather conditions were favorable, there would be plenty of game to hunt, fish to catch, and bountiful harvests. But their livelihood was at the mercy of the wild weather, because fierce hurricanes could damage villages

---

9 Stuart, B. Schwartz, *Sea of Storms-The History of Hurricanes in the Greater Caribbean from Columbus to Katrina*, (New Jersey, Princeton University Press, 2015), pg. 1.

of flimsy huts, destroy crops and generate vast floodwaters that could sweep away livestock.

In times of hurricanes, food shortages and starvation were constant threats, as crops failed and game animals became scarce when their food supplies dried up due to a hurricane. These ancient tribes, as you will see later, believed that their weather fortunes were inextricably linked with the moods and actions of their gods. For this reason, they spent a great deal of time and effort appeasing these mythological weather gods. Many of these ancient tribes tried to remain on favorable terms with their deities through a mixture of prayers, rituals, dances and sometimes even human sacrifices. In some cultures, such as the Aztecs of Central America, they would offer up human sacrifices to appease their rain-god, Tláloc. In addition, Quetzalcoatl, the all-powerful and mighty deity in the ancient Aztecs society whose name means 'Precious Feathered Serpent', played a critical role; he was the creator of life and controlled devastating hurricanes. The Egyptians celebrated Ra, the sun god. Thor was the Norse god of thunder and lightning, a god to please so that calm waters would grace their seafaring expeditions. The Greeks had many weather gods; however, it was Zeus who was the most powerful of them all.

The actual origin of the word 'hurricane' and other tropical cyclone names was based on the many religions, cultures, myths, and races of people. In modern cultures, 'myth' has come to mean a story or an idea that is not true. The word 'myth' comes directly from the Greek word 'mythos'(μύθος), whose many meanings include, 'word', 'saying', 'story', and 'fiction'. Today, the word 'myth' is used any and everywhere, and people now speak of myths about how to catch or cure the common cold. But the age-old myths about hurricanes in this book were an important part of these people's religions, cultures, and everyday lives. Often-times, they were both deeply spiritual and culturally entertaining and significant. For many of these ancient races, their mythology was their history, and there was often little, if any, distinction between the two.

Some myths were actually based on historical events, such as devastating hurricanes, or even wars, but myths often offer us a treasure trove of dramatic tales. The active beings in myths are generally gods and goddesses, heroes and heroines, or animals. Most myths are set in a timeless past before recorded and critical history began. A myth is a sacred narrative in the sense that it holds religious or spiritual significance for those who tell it, and it contributes to and expresses systems of thoughts and values. It is a traditional story, typically involving supernatural beings or forces or creatures, which embodies and provides an explanation, aetiology (origin myths), or justification for something such as the early history of a society, a religious belief or ritual, or a natural phenomenon.

The United Nations' sub-body, the World Meteorological Organization estimates that in an average year, about 80 of these tropical cyclones kill up to 15,000 people worldwide and cause an estimate of several billion dollars' worth of property damage alone. Hurricanes, typhoons and cyclones are all the same kind of violent storms originating over warm tropical ocean waters and are called by different names all over the world. From the Timor Sea to as far as northwestern Australia, they are called cyclones, or by the Australian colloquial term of 'Willy-Willies', from an old Aboriginal word (derived from whirlwind). In the Bay of Bengal and the Indian Ocean, they are simply called Cyclones (an English name based on a Greek word meaning "coil", as in "coil of a snake", because the winds that spiral within them resemble the coils of a snake) and are not named even to this day.

They are called 'hurricanes' (derived from a Carib, Mayan or Taíno/Arawak Indian word) in the Gulf of Mexico, Central and North America, the Caribbean and Eastern North Pacific Oceans (east of the International Dateline). In the Indian Ocean all the way to Mauritius and along the Arabian Coasts, they are known as 'Asifa-t'. In Mexico and Central America, hurricanes are also known as El Cordonazo, and in Haiti they are known as Taínos. While they are called Typhoons [originating from the Chinese word 'Ty-Fung' (going back to as far as the Song (960-1278) and Yuan (1260-1341) dynasties) translated to mean 'Big or Great Wind'], in the Western North Pacific and in the Philippines and the South China Sea (west of the International Dateline) they are known as 'Baguios' or 'Chubasco'(or simply a typhoon). The word Baguio was derived from the Philippine city of Baguio, which was inundated by a typhoon in July 1911, with over 46 inches of rain in a 24-hour period. Also, in the scientific literature of the 1600s, including the book *Geographia Naturalis,* by geographer Bernhardus Varenius, the term whirlwind was used, but this term never achieved regional or worldwide acceptance as a name for a hurricane.

In Japan, they are known as 'Repus', or by the more revered name of a typhoon. The word "taifū" (台風) in Japanese means typhoon; the first character meaning "pedestal" or "stand"; the second character meaning wind. The Japanese term for "divine wind" is kamikaze (神風). The kamikazes were a pair or series of typhoons that were said to have saved Japan from two Mongol invasion fleets under Kublai Khan, who attacked Japan in 1274, and again in 1281. The latter is said to have been the largest attempted naval invasion in history, whose scale was only recently eclipsed in modern times by the D-Day invasion by the Allied forces into Normandy in 1944. This was the term that was given to the typhoon winds that came up and blew the Mongol invasion fleet off course and destroyed it as it was poised to attack Japan.

On October 29, 1274, the first invasion began. Some 40,000 men, including about 25,000 Mongolians, 8,000 Korean troops, and 7,000 Chinese seamen, set sail from Korea in about 900 ships to attack Japan. With fewer troops and inferior weapons, the Japanese were far outmatched and overwhelmed and were sure to be defeated. But at nightfall, just as they were attacking the Japanese coastal forces, the Korean sailors sensed an approaching typhoon and begged their reluctant Mongol commanders to put the invasion force back at sea, or else it would be trapped on the coast and its ships destroyed at anchor by this typhoon. The next morning, the Japanese were surprised and delighted to see the Mongol fleet struggling to regain the open ocean in the midst of a great typhoon. The ships, sadly, were no match for this great storm, and many foundered or were simply dashed to bits and pieces on the rocky coast. Nearly 13,000 men perished in this storm, mostly by drowning. This Mongol fleet had been decimated by a powerful typhoon as it was poised to attack Japan.

With the second storm, even as Kublai Khan was mounting his second Japanese offensive, he was waging a bitter war of conquest against southern China, whose people had resisted him for 40 years. But finally, in 1279, the last of the southern providences, Canton, fell to the Mongol forces, and China was united under one ruler for the first time in three hundred years. Buoyed by success, Kublai again tried to bully Japan into submission by sending his emissaries to the Japanese, asking them to surrender to his forces. But this time the Japanese executed his emissaries, enraging him even further and thereby paving the way for a second invasion. Knowing this was inevitable, the Japanese went to work building coastal fortifications, including a massive dike around Hakozaki Bay, which encompasses the site of the first invasion.

The second Mongol invasion of Japan assumed staggering proportions. One armada consisted of 40,000 Mongols, Koreans, and Chinese, who were to set sail from Korea, while a second, larger force of some 100,000 men were to set out from various ports in south China. The invasion plan called for the two armadas to join forces in the spring before the summer typhoon season, but unfortunately the southern force was late, delaying the invasion until late June 1281. The Japanese defenders held back the invading forces for six weeks until on the fifteenth and sixteenth of August, history then repeated itself when a gigantic typhoon decimated the Mongol fleet poised to attack Japan again.

As a direct result of these famous storms, the Japanese came to think of the typhoon as a 'divine wind' or 'kamikaze' sent by their gods to deliver their land from the evil invaders. Because they needed another intervention to drive away the Allied forces in WWII, they gave this name to their Japanese suicide pilots as nationalist propaganda. In the Japanese Shinto religion, many forces of nature are worshipped as gods, known as 'kami', and are represented as human figures. The Japanese god of thunder is often depicted as a strong man beating his drum. The Japanese called it kamikaze, and the Mongols never, ever returned to attack Japan again because of their personal experiences with these two great storms. In popular Japanese myths at the time, the god Raijin was the god who turned the storms against the Mongols. Other variations say that the god Fūjin or Ryūjin caused the destructive kamikaze. This use of *kamikaze* has come to be the common meaning of the word in English.[10]

Whatever name they are known by in different regions of the world, they refer to the same weather phenomena as a 'tropical cyclone'. They are all the same severe tropical storms that share the same fundamental characteristics, aside from the fact that they rotate clockwise in the southern hemisphere, and counterclockwise in the northern hemisphere. However, by World Meteorological Organization International Agreement, the term tropical cyclone is the general term given to all hurricane-type storms that originate over tropical waters. The term cyclone, used by meteorologists, refers to an area of low pressure in which winds move counterclockwise in the northern hemisphere around the low pressure center and are usually associated with bad weather, heavy rainfall and strong wind speeds.

A tropical cyclone was the name first given to these intense circular storms by Englishman Captain Henry Piddington (1797-1848), who was keenly interested in storms affecting India and spent many years collecting information on ships caught in severe storms in the Indian Ocean. He would later become the president of the Marine Courts of Inquiry in Calcutta, India. He used the term tropical cyclone to refer to a tropical storm that blew the freighter 'Charles Heddles' in circles for nearly a week in Mauritius in February of 1845. In his book *'Sailor's Hornbook for the Laws of Storms in All Parts of the World,'* published in 1855, he called these storms cyclones, from the Greek word for coil of a snake. He called these storms tropical cyclones because it expressed sufficiently what he described as the 'tendency to move in a circular motion'.

---

10 Kerry Emanuel, *Divine Wind-The History and Science of Hurricanes*, (Boston, Oxford University Press, 2005), pgs. 3- 5.

The word cyclone is from the Greek word 'κύκλος', meaning 'circle' or Kyklos, meaning 'coils of the snake', describing the rotating movement of the storm. An Egyptian word 'Cykline', meaning to 'to spin', has also been cited as a possible origin. In Greek mythology, Typhoeus or Typhōn was the son of Tartarus and Gaia. He was a monster with many heads, a man's body, and a coiled snake's tail. The king of the gods and god of the sky and weather, Zeus, fought a great battle with Typhoeus and finally buried him under Mount Etna. According to legend, he was the source of the powerful storm winds that caused widespread devastation, the loss of many lives and numerous shipwrecks. The Greek word 'typhōn', meaning 'whirlwind', comes from this legend, another possible source for the origin of the English word 'typhoon'. The term is most often used for cyclones occurring in the Western Pacific Ocean and Indian Ocean. In addition, the word is an alteration of the Arabic word, tūfān, meaning hurricane, and the Greek word typhōn, meaning violent storm and an Egyptian word 'Cykline', meaning to 'to spin'.

The history of the word 'typhoon' presents a perfect example of the long journey that many words made in coming to the English Language vocabulary. It traveled from Greece to Arabia to India and also arose independently in China before assuming its current form in our language. The Greek word typhōn, used both as the name of the father of the winds and a common noun meaning 'whirlwind, typhoon', was borrowed into Arabic during the Middle Ages, when Arabic learning both preserved and expanded the classical heritage and passed it on to Europe and other parts of the world. In the Arabic version of the Greek word, it was passed into languages spoken in India, where Arabic-speaking Muslim invaders had settled in the eleventh century. Thus, the descendant of the Arabic word, passing into English through an Indian language and appearing in English in forms such as touffon and tūfān, originally referred specifically to a severe storm in India.

The modern form of typhoon was also influenced by a borrowing from the Cantonese variety of Chinese, namely the word 'Ty-Fung', and re-spelled to make it look more like Greek. 'Ty-Fung', meaning literally 'great wind', was coincidentally similar to the Arabic borrowing and is first recorded in English guise as tuffoon in 1699. The Cantonese tai-fung and the Mandarin ta-feng are derived from the word jufeng. It is also believed to have originated from the Chinese word 'jufeng', 'Ju' can mean either 'a wind coming from four directions' or 'scary'; 'feng' is the generic word for wind. Arguably, the first scientific description of a tropical cyclone and the first appearance of the word jufeng in the literature are contained in a Chinese book called *Nan Yue Zhi*

(Book of the Southern Yue Region), written around A.D. 470. In that book, it is stated that "Many Jufeng occur around Xi'n County. Ju is a wind (or storm) that comes in all four directions. Another meaning for Jufeng is that it is a scary wind. It frequently occurs in the sixth and seventh month (of the Chinese lunar calendar; roughly July and August of the Gregorian calendar). Before it comes, it is said that chickens and dogs are silent for three days. Major ones may last up to seven days, and minor ones last one or two days. These are called heifeng (meaning black storms/winds) in foreign countries."[11]

European travelers to China in the sixteenth century took note of a word sounding like typhoon being used to denote severe coastal windstorms. On the other hand, typhoon was used in European texts and literature around 1500, long before systematic contact with China was established. It is possible that the European use of this word was derived from Typhon, the draconian Earth demon of Greek Legend. The various forms of the word from these different countries coalesced and finally became typhoon, a spelling that officially first appeared in 1819 in Percy Bysshe Shelley's play 'Prometheus Unbound'. This play was concerned with the torments of the Greek mythological figure Prometheus and his suffering at the hands of Zeus. By the early eighteenth century, typhon and typhoon were in common use in European literature, as in the famous poem 'Summer', by Scottish poet James Thomson (1700-1748):

> *"Beneath the radiant line that grits the globe,*
> *The circling Typhon, whirled from point to point.*
> *Exhausting all the rage of all the sky,*
> *And dire Ecnephia, reign."*[12]

In Yoruba mythology, Oya, the female warrior, was the goddess of fire, wind and thunder. When she became angry, she created tornadoes and hurricanes. Additionally, to ward off violent and tropical downpours, Yoruba priests in southwestern Nigeria held ceremonies around images of the thunder and lightning god Sango to protect them from the powerful winds of hurricanes. When these storms are over Senegal in West Africa, near the Cape Verde Islands, the Senegalese pray to the sea gods that give and take away life for protection from these storms. The elders of this nation chant supplications

---

11 Kerry Emanuel, Divine Wind-The History and Science of Hurricanes, (Boston, Oxford University Press, 2005), pgs. 18-21.

12 Ibid, pg. 21.

and toss a concoction of wine, grain, milk and water into the waves; priests cut a cow's neck and let it bleed into the surf, then throw its limbs into the water. They do all of this in hopes of appeasing the fickle, exacting sea and obtaining a quiet summer without storms.

In ancient Egyptian legend, Set was regarded as the god of storms. He was associated with natural calamities like hurricanes, thunderstorms, lightning, earthquakes and eclipses. In Iroquois mythology, Ga-oh was the wind giant whose house was guarded by several animals, each representing a specific type of wind. The Bear was the north wind, who brought winter hurricanes, and he was also capable of crushing the world with his storms or destroying it with his cold air. In Babylonian mythology, Marduk, the god of gods, defeated the bad-tempered dragon goddess Tiamat with the help of a hurricane. When the other gods learned about Tiamat's plans to destroy them, they turned to Marduk for help. Armed with a bow and an arrow, strong winds, and a powerful hurricane, Marduk captured Tiamat and let the hurricane winds fill her jaws and stomach. Then he shot an arrow into her belly and instantly killed her and then became the lord of all the gods.

The Meso-American and Caribbean Indians worshipped many gods. They had similar religions based on the worship of mainly agricultural and natural elements gods, even though the gods' names and the symbols for them were a bit different. People asked their gods for good weather, lack of hurricanes, abundant crops and good health or for welfare. The main Inca god was the creator god Viracocha. His assistants were the gods of the Earth and the sea. As farming occupied such an important place in the region, the 'Earth mother' or 'Earth goddess' was particularly important. The Aztecs, Mayas, Taínos and other Indians adopted many gods from other civilizations. As with the Mayans, Aztecs and Taínos, each god was connected with some aspects of nature or natural forces, and in each of these religions, hurricanes or the fear of them and the respect for them played a vital part of their worship. The destructive power of storms like hurricanes inspires both fear and fascination, and it is no surprise that humans throughout time have tried to control these storms. Ancient tribes were known to make offerings to the weather gods to appease them. People in ancient times believed that these violent storms were brought on by angry weather gods. In some cultures, the word for hurricane means 'storm god', 'evil spirit', 'devil', or 'god of thunder and lightning'.

The word 'hurricane' comes to us via the early Spanish explorers of the New World, who were told by the Indians of this region of an evil god capable of inflicting strong winds and great destruction on their lives and possessions.

The natives of the Caribbean and Central America had a healthy respect for hurricanes and an uncanny understanding of nature. In the legends of the Mayan civilizations of Central America and the Taínos of the Caribbean, these gods played an important role in their Creation. According to their beliefs and myths, the wicked gods Huracán, Hurrikán, Hunraken, and Jurakan annually victimized and savagely ravaged their homes, inflicting them with destructive winds, torrential rainfall and deadly floods. These natives were terrified whenever these gods made an appearance. They would beat drums, blew conch shells, shouted curses, engage in bizarre rituals and did everything possible to thwart these gods and drive them away. Sometimes they felt they were successful in frightening them off, and at other times their fury could not be withstood, and they suffered the consequences from an angry weather god. Some of these natives depicted these fearsome deities on primitive carvings as a hideous creature with swirling arms, ready to release his winds and claim its prey.

There are several theories about the origin of the word 'hurricane'; some people believe it originated from the Caribbean Taíno-Arawak speaking Indians. The Taínos were the indigenous inhabitants of the Bahamas, Greater Antilles, and some of the Lesser Antilles – especially in Guadeloupe, Dominica and Martinique. The Taínos ("Taíno" means "good" "people"), unlike the Caribs (who practiced regular raids on other groups), were peaceful seafaring people and distant relatives of the Arawak people of South America. The Taíno society was divided into two classes: Nitainos (nobles) and the Naborias (commoners). Both were governed by chiefs known as caciques, who were the maximum authority in a Yucayeque (village). The chiefs were advised by priest-healers known as Bohiques and the Nitaynos, which is how the elders and warriors were known.

It is believed that these Indians named their storm god 'Huracán', and over time it eventually evolved into the English word 'hurricane' that we are familiar with today. Others believed that it originated from the fierce group of cannibalistic Indians called the Caribs, but according to some historians this seems like the least likely source of this word. Native people throughout the Caribbean Basin linked hurricanes to supernatural forces and had a word for these storms, which often had similar spellings, but they all signified death and destruction by some evil spirit, and the early European colonial explorers to the New World picked up the native names.

Actually, one early historian noted that the local Caribbean Indians, in preparation for these hurricanes, often tied themselves to trees to keep from being blown away from their strong winds. According to one early seventeenth-century English account, Indians on St. Christopher viewed 'Hurry-Cano' as a "tempestuous spirit." These ancient Indians of this region personalized the hurricane, believing that it was bearing down on them as punishment by the gods for something they had done-or not done. In fact, the entire Mesoamerican religions recognized and respected the duality of forces so that the gods of wind could in their benevolent form bring rains for the crops. On the other hand, in their malevolent aspects were destroyers of homes and milipas, bearers of misery and death. These days, there is more science and less superstition to these powerful storms of nature called hurricanes. Yet we humanize hurricanes with familiar names, and the big ones become folkloric and iconic characters, their rampages woven into the histories of the regions' coastal towns and cities.

Another popular theory about the hurricane's origin is that it came from the Mayan Indians of Mexico, who had an ancient word for these storms, called 'Hurrikán' (or 'Huracán'). Hurrikán was the Mayan god of the storm. He was present at all three attempts to create humanity, in which he did most of the actual work of creating human beings under the direction of Kukulkán (known by the Aztecs name Quetzalcoatl) and Tepeu. Unlike the other Creators, Hurrikán was not heavily personified by the Mayans and was generally considered to be more like the winds and the storms themselves. In the Mayan language, his name means "one-legged". The word hurricane is derived from Hurrikán's name. Hurrikán is similar to the Aztecs god Tlaloc.

In Mayan mythology, 'Hurrikán' ("one legged") was a wind, storm and fire god and one of the creator deities who participated in all three attempts of creating humanity. 'Hurrikán' was the Mayan god of big wind, and his image was chiseled into the walls of the Mayan temples. He was one of the three most powerful forces in the pantheon of deities, along with Cabrakán (earthquakes) and Chirakán (volcanoes). He also caused the Great Flood after the first humans angered the gods. He supposedly lived in the windy mists above the floodwaters and repeated "Earth" until land came up from the seas. In appearance, he has one leg, the other being transformed into a serpent, a zoomorphic snout or long-nose, and a smoking object such as a cigar, torch holder or axe head, which pierces a mirror on his forehead.

Actually, the first human historical record of hurricanes can be found in the ancient Mayan hieroglyphics. A powerful and deadly hurricane struck the Northern Yucatán in 1464, wiping out most of the Mayan Indian population of that area. According to Mayan mythology, the Mayan rain and wind god Chac sent rain for the crops. But he also sent hurricanes, which destroyed crops and flooded villages. The Mayans hoped that if they made offerings to Chac (including human sacrifices), the rains would continue to fall, but the hurricanes would cease. Every year, the Mayans threw a young woman into the sea as a sacrifice to appease the god Hurrikán, and a warrior was also sacrificed to lead the girl to Hurrikán's underwater kingdom. Also, one of the sacrifices in honor of this god was to drown children in wells. In some Maya regions, Chac, the god of rain and wind, was so important that the facades of their buildings were covered with the masks of Chac. In actual fact, at its peak it was one of the most densely populated and culturally dynamic societies in the world, but still they always built their homes far away from the hurricane-prone coast.

By customarily building their major settlements away from the hurricane-prone coastline, the Mayan Indians practiced a method of disaster mitigation that, if rigorously applied today, would reduce the potential for devastation along coastal areas. The only Mayan port city discovered to date is the small-to-medium sized city of Tulum, on the east coast of the Yucatán Peninsula, south of Cancun. Tulum remained occupied when the Spaniards first arrived in the sixteenth century, and its citizens were more prepared for the storms than for the Spaniards. As the many visitors to these ruins can see, the ceremonial buildings and grounds of the city were so skillfully constructed that many remain today and withstand many hurricanes.

The Indians of Guatemala called the god of stormy weather 'Hunrakán'. Of course, the Indians did not observe in what period of the year these hurricanes could strike their country; they believed that the devil or the evil spirits sent them whenever they pleased. Their gods were the uncontrollable forces of nature on which their lives were wholly dependent, the sun, the stars, the rains and the storms. On the islands of the Greater Antilles-Cuba, Jamaica, Hispaniola, and Puerto Rico -the Taíno people preferred to plant root crops like yucca, potato, malanga, and yautia because of their resistance to wind and to mitigate storm damage. It didn't take the Spanish and other European colonists to the Caribbean long to realize that the root crops preferred by the Taíno Indians were well adapted to a hurricane-prone environment, a lesson that was later learned by slaves and slave -owners throughout the region.

The Taínos were generally considered to be part of the Taíno-Arawak Indians, who traveled from the Orinoco-Amazon region of South America to Venezuela and then into the Caribbean Islands of the Dominican Republic, Haiti, Bahamas, Jamaica, Puerto Rico, and as far west as Cuba. Christopher Columbus called these inhabitants of the Western Hemisphere 'Indians' because he mistakenly thought he had reached the islands on the eastern side of the Indian Ocean. The word 'Taíno' comes directly from Christopher Columbus, because they were the indigenous set of people he encountered on his first voyage to the Caribbean, and they called themselves 'Taíno', meaning "good" or "noble," to differentiate themselves from their fierce enemies-, the Carib Indians. This name applied to all the Island Taínos, including those in the Lesser Antilles. These so-called Indians were divided into innumerable small ethnic groups, each with its own combination of linguistic, cultural, and biological traits.

Locally, the Taínos referred to themselves by the name of their location. For example, those in Puerto Rico referred to themselves as Boricua or Borinquen, which means 'people from the island of the valiant noble lords' or La tierra del altivo Seor. Their island was called Borike'n, meaning 'great land of the valiant noble lord.' The Spaniards changed it to Puerto Rico. Those occupying the Bahamas called themselves 'Lucayo' or 'Lucayans', meaning 'small islands or island people.' The name "Lucayan" is an Anglicization of the Spanish Lucayos, derived in turn from the Taíno Lukku-Cairi (which the people used for themselves), also translates to "people of the islands", (the Taíno word for "island", cairi, became cayo in Spanish and "cay" in English [spelled "key" in American English]). Although the Taínos are extinct as a separate and identifiable race or culture, they are alive in the region in their vocabulary, music, and beliefs.

Another important consequence of their navigation skills and their canoes was the fact that the Taínos had contact with other indigenous groups of the Americas, including the Mayas of Mexico and Guatemala. What is the evidence to suggest that the Taínos had contact with the Mayan culture? There are many similarities between the Mayan god 'Hurrikán' and Taíno god 'Huracán', also similarities in their ballgames and similarities in their social structure and social stratification. Furthermore, the Meso-Indians of Mexico also flattened the heads of their infants in a similar fashion to the Island based Taínos and their relatives.

In the 1930s, the Smithsonian Institute excavated a Chosen, Florida burial mound. On one distinct level of the Chosen mound, the graves of small-boned, short people with elongated heads were found, reminiscent of the Maya and very different from the tall, large-boned Calusas race in Florida. The Maya, a trading society, had trade routes that ran from Venezuela and Bacatá (Bogotá) to the Bahamas. Emeralds that could only come from the Chivor mines in Columbia were found in Mexico. On an expedition to conquer the Incas, Francisco Pizzaro intercepted an oceanic raft from Peru heading north to Costa

Rica. A trade link or influence connecting Lake Okeechobee and the Meso-American Mayas was a real and intriguing possibility. One canoe dredged up in Boca Raton area in 1957—made out of a cypress tree trunk—was forty-six feet long. It was an ocean canoe, one that would take thirty people and trade goods to the Bahamas or Cuba. During the Spanish colonial period, it was not unusual for Calusa traders to make the two-day canoe trip across the Florida Straits to barter with their brethren in Cuba.

The Taíno Indians believed in two supreme gods, one male and the other female. They also believed that man had a soul and that after death he would go to a paradise called 'Coyaba', where the natural weather elements such as droughts and hurricanes would be forgotten in an eternity of feasting and dancing. In the Taíno Indians culture, they believed in a female zemí (spirit) named Guabancex-the Lady of the Winds, who controlled hurricanes, among other things-but when angered, she sent out her two assistants Guataubá (an assistant who produced hurricane winds) and Coatrisquie (who caused the accompanying floodwaters) to order all the other zemís to lend her their winds, and with this great power she made the winds and the waters move and cast houses to the ground and uprooted trees.

Representations of Guabancex portrayed her head as the eye of the storm, with twisting arms symbolizing the swirling winds. The international symbol that we use today for hurricanes was derived from this zemí. The various likenesses of this god invariably consist of a head of an indeterminate gender with no torso, two distinctive arms spiraling out from its sides. Most of these images exhibit cyclonic (counterclockwise) spirals. The Cuban ethnologist Fernando Ortiz believes that they were inspired by the tropical hurricanes that have always plagued the Caribbean. If so, the Taínos discovered the cyclonic or vortical nature of hurricanes many hundreds of years before the descendants of European settlers did. How they may have made this deduction remains a mystery to this day.

The spiral rain bands so well known to us from satellites and radars were not officially 'discovered' until the meteorological radar was developed during World War II, and they are far too big to be discerned by eye from the ground. It is speculated that these ancient people surveyed the damage done by the hurricane, and based on the direction by which the trees fell, concluded that the damage could only have been done by rotating winds. Or perhaps they witnessed tornadoes or waterspouts, which are much smaller phenomena whose rotation is readily apparent, and came to believe that all destructive winds are rotary. They also believed that sickness or misfortunes such as devastating hurricanes were the works of malignant or highly displeased zemís, and good fortune was a sign that the zemís were pleased. To keep the zemís pleased, great public festivals were held to propitiate the tribal zemís, or simply in their honor. On these occasions, everyone would be well-dressed in elaborate outfits, and the cacique would lead a parade beating a wooden drum. Gifts of the finest cassava were offered to the zemís in hopes that the zemís would protect them against the four chief scourges of the Taínos' existence: fire, sickness, the Caribs, and most importantly devastating hurricanes.

The language of the Taínos was not a written one, and written works from them are very scarce. Some documentation of their lifestyles may be found in the writings of Spanish priests, such as Bartholomew de Las Casas in Puerto Rico and the Dominican Republic during the early 16th century. Some of the Taíno origin words were borrowed by the Spanish and subsequently found their way into the English Language and are modern day reminders of this once proud and vigorous race of people. These words include: avocado, potato, buccaneer, cay, manatee, maize, savanna, guava, barbacoa (barbecue), cacique (chief), jamaca (hammock), batata ("sweet potato"), Tabacú (tobacco), caniba (cannibal), canoa (canoe), Iguana (lizard), and Huracán or huruká (hurricane).

Interestingly, two of the islands in the Bahamas, Inagua and Mayaguana, both derived their names from the Lucayan word 'Iguana.' Bimini (meaning "two small islands" in English), another island in the Bahamas, also got its name from these Indians; however, most of the other islands in the Bahamas and the rest of the Caribbean were also given Indian names, but they have been changed over the many years and centuries by various groups of people who settled or passed through the Bahamas or other Caribbean islands. For example, in the Bahamas the Lucayans called the island of Exuma-Yuma, San Salvador was called Guanahani, Long Island was called Samana, Cat Island was called Guanima, Abaco was called Lucayoneque, Eleuthera was called Cigateo, Rum Cay was called Manigua and Crooked Island was called Saomere. Christopher Columbus, when he came to the Bahamas and landed on Guanahani, he renamed it San Salvador, Manigua, he renamed it Santa Maria de la Concepcion, Yuma, he renamed it Fernandina, Saomete, he renamed it Isabella, and the Ragged Island chain he renamed Islas de Arenas.[13] However, for the early Spanish explorers, the islands of the Bahamas were of no particular economic value, so therefore they established only temporary settlements, mainly to transport the

13 Peter Barratt, Bahama Saga-The Epic Story of the Bahama Islands, (Bloomington, AuthorHouse, 2006), pg. 51.

peaceful Indians to be used as their slaves in East Hispaniola and Cuba to mine the valuable deposits of gold and silver and to dive for pearls.

Jurakán is the phonetic name given by the Spanish settlers to the god of chaos and disorder that the Taíno Indians in Puerto Rico (and also the Carib and Arawak Indians elsewhere in the Caribbean) believed controlled the weather, particularly hurricanes. From this we derive the Spanish word Huracán, and eventually the English word hurricane. As the spelling and pronunciation varied across various indigenous groups, there were many alternative names along the way. For example, many West Indian historians and indigenous Indians called them by the various names, including Juracán, furacan, furican, haurachan, herycano, hurachano, hurricano, and so on. The term makes an early appearance in William Shakespeare's King Lear (Act 3, Scene 2). Being the easternmost of the Greater Antilles, Puerto Rico is often in the path of many of the North Atlantic tropical storms and hurricanes that tend to come ashore on the east coast of the island. The Taínos believed that Juracán lived at the top of a rainforest peak called El Yunque (literally, the anvil, but truly derived from the name of the Taíno god of order and creation, Yuquiyú), from where he stirred the winds and caused the waves to smash against the shore.

In the Taíno culture, it was said that when the hurricane was upon them, these people would shut themselves up in their leaky huts and shouted and banged drums and blew shell trumpets to keep the evil spirits of the hurricane from killing them or destroying their homes and crops. Boinayel and his twin brother Márohu were the gods of rain and fair weather, respectively. Guabancex was the non-nurturing aspect of the goddess Atabey who had control over natural disasters. Juracán is often identified as the god of storms but the word simply means hurricane in the Taíno language. Guabancex had two assistants: Guataubá, a messenger who created hurricane winds, and Coatrisquie who created floodwaters. According to Taíno legend, the goddess Atabei first created the Earth, the sky, and all the celestial bodies. The metaphor of the sacred waters was included because the Taínos attributed religious and mythical qualities to water. For example, the goddess Atabei was associated with water. She was also the goddess of water. Yocahú, the supreme deity, was also associated with water. Both of these deities are called Bagua, which is water, the source of life. This image of water as a sacred entity was central to their beliefs. They were at the mercy of water for their farming. Without rain, they would not be able to farm their conucos.

These Indians prayed to the twin gods of rain and fair weather so that they would be pleased and prayed to these gods to keep the evil hurricane away from their farms and homes. To continue her (Atabei) work, she bore two sons, Yucaju and Guacar. Yucaju created the sun and moon to give light and then made plants and animals to populate the Earth. Seeing the beautiful fruits of Yucaju's work, Guacar became jealous and began to tear up the Earth with powerful winds, renaming himself Jurakan, the god of destruction. Yucaju then created Locuo, a being that was an intermediate between a god and a man, to live in peaceful harmony with the world. Locuo, in turn, created the first man and woman, Guaguyona and Yaya. All three continued to suffer from the powerful winds and floods inflicted by the evil god Jurakán. It was said that the god Jurakán was perpetually angry and ruled the power of the hurricane. He became known as the god of strong winds, hence the name today of hurricane. He was feared and revered, and when the hurricanes blew, the Taínos thought they had displeased Jurakán. Jurakán would later become Huracán in Spanish and Hurricane in English.

The origin of the name "Bahamas" is unclear in the history of these islands in the West Indies. Some historians believe it may have been derived from the Spanish word 'baja mar', meaning lands of the 'shallow seas', or the Lucayan Indian word for the island of Grand Bahama, ba-ha-ma meaning 'large upper middle land.'[14] The seafaring Taíno people moved into the uninhabited southeastern Bahamas from the islands of Hispaniola and Cuba sometime around 1000-800 A.D. These people came to be known as the Lucayans. According to various historians, there were estimated reports of well over 20,000 to 30,000+ Lucayans living in the Bahamas at the time of world famous Spanish explorer Christopher Columbus' arrival in 1492. Christopher Columbus' first landfall in the New World was on an island called San Salvador, which is generally accepted to be present-day San Salvador (also known as Watlings Island) in the southeastern Bahamas. The Lucayans called this island Guanahaní, but Columbus renamed it San Salvador (Spanish for "Holy Saviour").[15]

Unfortunately, Columbus' discovery of this island of San Salvador is a very controversial and debatable topic among historians, scientists and lay people alike. Even to this day, some of them still suggest that Columbus made his

14 Ashley Saunders, History of Bimini Volume 2, (Nassau, New World Press, 2006), pgs. 5-9.

15 Ibid. pgs. 6-9.

landfall in some other island in the Bahamas, such as Rum Cay, Samana Cay, Cat Island, and some even suggested he landed as far south as the Turks and Caicos Islands. However, it still remains a matter of great debate and mystery within the archeological and scientific community. Regrettably, that question may never be solved, as Columbus' original log book has been lost for centuries, and the only evidence is in the edited abstracts made by Father Bartolomé de las Casas, a 16th-century Spanish historian, social reformer and Dominican friar. He became the first resident Bishop of Chiapas, and the first officially appointed "Protector of the Indians". His extensive writings, the most famous being *A Short Account of the Destruction of the Indies* and *Historia de Las Indias*, chronicle the first decades of colonization of the West Indies and focus particularly on the atrocities committed by the colonizers against the indigenous peoples, some of them Lucayan Indians brought to Hispaniola from the Bahamas, which eventually resulted in the genocide of these Indians.

Arriving as one of the first European settlers in the Americas, he initially participated in, but eventually felt compelled to oppose, the atrocities committed against the Native Americans by the Spanish colonists. In 1515, he reformed his views, gave up his Indian slaves and encomienda, and advocated, before King Charles V, Holy Roman Emperor, on behalf of rights for the natives. In his early writings, he advocated the use of African slaves instead of Natives in the West-Indian colonies; consequently, criticisms have been leveled at him as being partly responsible for the beginning of the Transatlantic slave trade. Later in life, he retracted those early views as he came to see all forms of slavery as equally wrong.

In the Bahamas, Columbus made first contact with the Lucayans and exchanged goods with them. The Lucayans-a word that meant 'meal-eaters' in their own language, from their dependence upon cassava flour made from the bitter manioc root as their staple starch food-were sub-Taínos of the Bahamas and believed that all of their islands were once part of the mainland of America but had been cut off by the howling winds and waves of the hurricanes, and they referred to these storms as huruká. The Lucayans (the Bahamas being known then as the Lucayan Islands) were sub-Taínos who lived in the Bahamas at the time of Christopher Columbus' landfall on October 12, 1492. Sometime between 1000-800 A.D., the Taínos of Hispaniola, pressured by over-population and trading concerns, migrated into the southeastern islands of the Bahamas. The Taínos of Cuba moved into the northwestern Bahamas shortly afterwards. They are widely thought to be the first Amerindians encountered by the Spanish.

The Lucayan Indians had a form of self-government where the Cacique was the leader of the village who had many wives and was responsible for the governing of the village (such as, when to plant or harvest certain crops). These Indians lived by inter-island and intra-island trade. The main or stable food in their diets were, yam, cassava(yucca), beans, maize, and pumpkins. A bread was made from cassava and a wine called kasira was made from fermented cassava juice. A ball game called batos was also played. The Lucayans were polytheists, their male god was called Yocahu and their female goddess, Atabeyra. Their lesser gods were called Zemis.

Early historical accounts describe them as a peaceful set of people, and they referred to themselves as 'Lucayos,' 'Lukku Kairi' or 'Lukku-Cairi', meaning 'small islands' or 'island people' because they referred to themselves by the name of their location. The Lucayans spoke the Ciboney dialect of the Taíno language. This assumption was made from the only piece of speech that was recorded phonetically and has been passed down to us. Las Casas informs us that the Taíno Indians of the Greater Antilles and Lucayans were unable to understand one another, 'here'(in Hispaniola), he wrote "they do not call gold 'caona' as in the main part of the island, nor 'nozay' as on the islet of Guanahani(San Salvador) but tuob."[16] This brief hint of language difference tends to reinforce the theory that the Bahamian Islands were first settled by people coming from eastern Cuba of the sub-Taíno culture.

Before Columbus arrived in the Bahamas, there were about 20,000 to 30,000+ Lucayans living there, but because of slavery, diseases such as smallpox and yellow fever (to which they had no immunity), and other hardships brought on by the arrival of the Europeans, by 1517 they were virtually non-existent. As a matter of fact, when Spanish Conquistador Ponce de Leon visited those islands in 1513 in search of the magical 'Fountain of Youth,' he found no trace of these Lucayan Indians, with the exception of one elderly Indian woman. These Indians of the Caribbean and Central America lived in one of the most hurricane prone areas of the Earth; as a result, most of them built their temples, huts, pyramids and houses well away from the hurricane prone coastline because of the great fear and respect that they had for hurricanes.

Many early colonists in the Caribbean took solace by displaying a Cord of Saint Francis of Assisi, a short length of rope with three knots with three turns apiece, in their boats, churches and homes as a protective talisman during

16 Peter Barratt, Bahama Saga-The Epic Story of the Bahama Islands, (Bloomington, AuthorHouse, 2006), pg. 51.

the hurricane season. Various legends and lore soon developed regarding Saint Francis and his connection with nature, including tropical weather and hurricanes. According to tradition, if these residents untied the first knot of the cord, winds would pick up, but only moderately. Winds of 'half a gale' resulted from untying the second knot. If all three knots were untied, winds of hurricane strength were produced. Today, some descendants of African slaves in the West Indies still tie knots in the leaves of certain trees and hang them in their homes to ward off hurricanes.

Similar accounts also emerged from encounters with the Carib Indians. In old historical accounts, these Indians were referred to by various names, such as, 'Caribs,' 'Charaibes,' 'Charibees' and 'Caribbees', and they were a mysterious set of people who migrated from the Amazon jungles of South America.[17] They were a tribe of warlike and cannibalistic Indians who migrated northwards into the Caribbean in their canoes, overcoming and dominating an earlier race of peaceful people called the Taínos. While Columbus explored all parts of the West Indies, his successors colonized only those parts inhabited by the Taíno Indians, avoiding the Carib inhabited islands because they lacked gold, but most importantly because the Carib Indians were too difficult to subjugate. Ironically, the region became known as the Caribbean, named after these fierce Indians.

Their practice of eating their enemies so captured the imagination of the Europeans that the Caribbean Sea was also named after these Indians. The English word 'cannibal' is derived from the term 'Caniba', used by the Taínos to refer to the Caribs eating the flesh of their enemies. Their raids were made over long distances in large canoes and had as one of their main objectives to take the Taíno women as their captives, wives and slaves. While on the other hand, the captured Taíno men were tortured and killed and then barbecued and eaten during an elaborate ceremony because it was believed that if they did this, they would obtain their enemies' personal power and control their spirits.

The French traveler Charles de Rochefort wrote that when these Caribs Indians heard the thunder clap, they would "make all the haste they can to their little houses and sit down on low stools about the fire, covering their faces and resting their heads on their hands and knees, and in that posture they fall a weeping and say…Maboya is very angry with them: and they say the same

[17] Ashley Saunders, History of Bimini Volume 2, (Nassau, New World Press, 2006), pg. 14.

when there happens a Hurricane."[18] In fact, the early French comments about hurricanes often noted that the information about them had been acquired from the Carib Indians of the Caribbean. In the seventeenth-century works of Catholic Fathers Du Tertre and Labat and probably-Huguenot Rochefort, the hurricanes appear as a feature of life in the islands and a sign of God's power and justice, but all of these authors also expressed a curiosity about the specific nature and natural causes of the storms. Labat, for instance, stated that the calm before the storm, the cloud formations, the erratic movement of birds, and the rising sea level as signs of a storm's approach, and noted from his personal experience on Guadeloupe the damage that a hurricane could cause.[19]

The Caribs were terrified of spilling fresh water into the sea because they believed that it aroused the anger of hurricanes. They had no small stone gods but believed in good and powerful bad spirits called 'Maboya', which caused all the misfortunes of their lives. They even wore carved amulets and employed medicine men to drive the evil Maboya away. When a great and powerful storm began to rise out of the sea, the Caribs blew frantically into the air to chase it away and chewed manioc bread and spat it into the wind for the same purpose. When that was no use, they gave way to panic and crouched in their communal houses, moaning with their arms held over their heads. They felt that they were reasonably safe there because they fortified their houses with corner posts dug deep into the ground. They also believed that beyond the Maboya were great spirits, the male sun and the female moon. They believed that the spirits of the stars controlled the weather. They also believed in a bird named Savacou, which was sent out by the angry Maboya to call up the hurricane, and after this task was finished, this bird would then be transformed into a star.

The power and danger of hurricanes was no less important to the Caribs. They also recognized the destructive nature of hurricanes and believed the evil spirits or Maboya caused them. They, like every other Indian group, feared hurricanes but recognized their seasonal nature and integrated them into the rhythm of their year, and especially into their cycle of vengeance and war against their archenemies, the Taínos. Each year when the constellation of Ursa Minor, also known as the 'Little Dipper,' appeared in the Caribbean sky following the summer solstice, it signaled to the Caribs the approach of their

---

18 Matthew Mulcahy, Hurricanes and Society in the British Greater Caribbean, 1624-1783, (Baltimore, The Johns Hopkins University Press, 2006), pg. 35.

19 Labat, Nouveau voyage aux Isles de l'Amerique, pgs. 165-66, http://gallica.bnf.fr/ark:/12148/bpt6k114024q. Retrieved: 10-10-2014.

raiding season. They called this constellation, "the canoe of the heron," and its reoccurrence each year around the middle of June signaled the opening of the season when, following the stormy months of July, August, and early September (the peak of the present day hurricane season), their own canoes were launched. The Carib raids against the Taínos for women, food, and captives, and later against the Europeans, were carried out principally from late September to December after the passage of the peak of the hurricane season. These patterns continued for almost a century after the Europeans arrival in the Caribbean. Caribs raids against Puerto Rico lasted until the early seventeenth century despite Spanish counterattacks against the Caribs' home islands of Dominica and Guadeloupe.

According to noted English Historian John Oldmixon of the late 1600s and early 1700s, he reported that the Carib Indians excelled in forecasting hurricanes. Writing about a hurricane that occurred in 1740 on the island of St. Christopher he said: "Hurricanes are still frequent here, and it was some time since the custom of both the English and French inhabitants in this and the other Charibbees-Islands, to send about the month of June, to the native Charibbees of Dominica and St. Vincent, to know whether there would be any hurricanes that year; and about 10 or 12 Days before the hurricane came they constantly sent them word, and it was rarely failed."[20]

According to Carib Indians 'Signs or Prognosticks,' a hurricane comes "on the day of the full change, or quarters of the moon. If it will come on the full moon, you being in the change, then observe these signs. That day you will see the skies very turbulent, the sun redder than at other times, a great calm, and the hills clear of clouds or fogs over them, which in the high-lands are seldom so. In the hollows of the Earth or wells, there will be great noise, as if you were in a great storm; the stars at night will look very big with Burs about them, the north-west sky smelling stronger than at other times, as it usually does in violent storms; and sometimes that day for an hour or two, the winds blows very hard westerly, out of its usual course. On the full moon you have the same signs, but a great Bur about the moon, and many about the moon, and many about the sun. The like signs must be taken notice of on the quarter-days of the moon."[21]

---

20 John Oldmixon, "An Early Colonial Historian: John Oldmixon and the British Empire in America-Journal of American Studies Vol.3 (August, 1741-2nd ed.)," Cambridge University Press, London, pgs. 113-123. Retrieved: 11-10-2005.

21 John Oldmixon, "An Early Colonial Historian: John Oldmixon and the British Empire in America-Journal of American Studies Vol.3 (August, 1741-2nd ed.)," Cambridge University Press, London, pgs. 113-123. Retrieved: 11-10-2005.

According to several elderly Carib Indians, hurricanes had become more frequent in the recent years following the arrival of the Europeans to the Caribbean, which they viewed as punishment for their interactions with them. In fact, as early as the 1630s, English colonists reported that Carib Indians knew when storms would strike by the number of rings that appeared around the moon: three rings meant the storm would arrive in three days, two rings meant two days and one ring meant the storm would arrive in one day. Of course, the connection between such signs and the onset of hurricanes was indeed a very unreliable way to predict the onset of hurricanes. The Carib Indians, while raiding islands in the Caribbean, would kill off the Taíno men and take the Taíno women as wives and mothers to their children. Actually, when the Europeans came to the Caribbean, they surprisingly found that many Carib women spoke the Taíno language because of the large number of female Taíno captives among them. So, it is speculated that a word like 'hurricane' was passed into the Carib speech, and this was how these fierce people learned about the terror of these savage storms. Native Indians of the West Indies often engaged in ritual purifications and sacrifices and offered songs and dances to help ward off hurricanes.

Some European observers sought to record the signs the Indians used. The Spanish Augustinian Father Iñigo Abbad y Lasierra, in his 1788 account of Puerto Rico, noted that the Indians had read certain signs as a premonition of a hurricane's approach, such as a red sun at sunrise and sunset, a strong odor from the sea, the sudden change of the wind from east to west. However, not every European observer was convinced of the Indians' abilities at prediction. Father Jean Baptiste du Tertre, a Jesuit priest who wrote from experience in the French islands in the mid-seventeenth century, noted that many settlers believed that the Indians could predict the arrival of hurricanes, but that in fact, since the storms came in the same period each year, it was natural that sometimes their predictions were correct, even though they had no special knowledge or ability to truly predict these storms.

By the mid-seventeenth century, the reading of the 'natural signs' was no longer a skill exclusively reserved to the indigenous Indians population of the islands or to the mariners. It had become a region wide knowledge, a necessary skill practiced by all. Generally, as time progressed, colonist observations and mariners' experiences were joined with the clues learned from the indigenous peoples and developed into a kind of local wisdom on each island of the signs to look for. Indians had observed the behavior of certain birds and fish, and the colonists learned from them. Father Jean-Baptiste Labat, a French Dominican, in his description of the French islands in the seventeenth century, noted that on approach of a hurricane, the birds instinctually exhibited certain uneasiness and flew away from the coast for shelter inland or to another location in the Caribbean until the storm had passed. Furthermore, other signs and behavior were also observed with the crickets, cicadas, toads and frogs, as they all disappeared before the passage of a hurricane.

An Aztec myth tells that when the gods created the world, it was dark and cold. The youngest of the gods sacrificed himself to create a sun. But it was like him, weak, dim and feeble. Only when more powerful gods offered themselves did the sun blaze into life and shine brightly on them. However, there was one disadvantage, and that was that these gods needed constant fuel, human lives, and the Aztecs obliged. They offered tens of thousands of human sacrifices a year just to make sure that the sun rose each morning and to prevent natural disasters such as devastating hurricanes from destroying their communities and villages. Tlaloc was an important deity in Aztecs religion, a god of rain, fertility, and water. He was a beneficent god who gave life and sustenance, but he was also feared for his ability to send hurricanes, hail, thunder and lightning and for being the lord of the powerful element of water. In Aztecs iconography, he is usually depicted with goggle eyes and fangs. He was associated with caves, springs and mountains. He is known for having demanded child sacrifices.

The Aztecs god Tezcatlipoca (meaning Lord of the Hurricane) was believed to have special powers over the hurricane winds, as did the Palenque god Tahil (Obsidian Mirror) and the Quiché Maya sky god Huracán. The Aztecs god Tezcatlipoca was feared for his capricious nature, and the Aztecs called him Yaotl (meaning 'Adversary'). Tonatiuh was the Aztecs Sun god, and the Aztecs saw the sun as a divinity that controlled the weather, including hurricanes and consequently, all human life forms. The Aztecs of Mexico, in particular, built vast temples to the sun god Tonatiuh and made bloody sacrifices of both human and animal to persuade him to shine brightly on them and in particular not send any destructive hurricanes their way and to allow prosperity for their crops. When they built these temples, they were constructed according to the Earth's alignment with the sun, but most importantly they were always constructed with hurricanes in mind and away from the hurricane-prone coastline.

The Aztecs people considered Tonatiuh the leader of Tollán, their heaven. He was also known as the fifth sun because the Aztecs believed that he was the sun that took over when the fourth sun was expelled from the sky. Mesoamerican creation narratives proposed that before the current world age began, there were a number of previous creations. The Aztecs' account of the five suns or world ages revealed that in each of the five creations, the Earth's inhabitants found a more satisfactory staple food than eaten by their predecessors. In the era of the first sun, which was governed by Black Tezcatlipoca, the world was inhabited by a race of giants who lived on acorns. The second sun, whose presiding god was a serpent god called Quetzatzalcóatl, was believed to be the creator of life and in control of the vital rain-bearing winds, and he saw the emergence of a race of primitive humans who lived on the seeds of the mesquite tree.

After the third age, which was ruled by Tláloc, in which people lived on plants that grew on water, such as the water lily, people returned to a diet of wild seeds in the fourth age of Chalchiúhtlicue. It was only in the fifth and current age, an age subject to the sun god Tonatiuh that the people of Mesoamerica learned how to plant and harvest maize. According to their cosmology, each sun was a god with its own cosmic era. The Aztecs believed they were still in Tonatiuh's era, and according to their creation mythology, this god demanded human sacrifices as a tribute, and without it he would refuse to move through the sky, hold back on the rainfall for their crops and would send destructive hurricanes their way. It is said that some 20,000 people were sacrificed each year to Tonatiuh and other gods, though this number, however, is thought to be highly inflated either by the Aztecs, who wanted to inspire fear in their enemies, or the Spaniards, who wanted to speak ill of the Aztecs. The Aztecs were fascinated by the sun, so they worshiped and carefully observed it and had a solar calendar second only in accuracy to the Mayans.

It was Captain Fernando de Oviedo who gave these storms their modern name when he wrote, "So when the devil wishes to terrify them, he promises them the 'Huracán,' which means tempest."[22] The Portuguese word for them is Huracao, which is believed to have originated from the original Taíno word Huracán. The Native American Indians had a word for these powerful storms, which they called 'Hurucane', meaning 'evil spirit of the wind.'

When a hurricane approached the Florida coast, the medicine men of the North American Indians worked frantic incantations to drive the evil hurricane away. There's a folklore that the Seminole Indians can mystically sense a storm well ahead of time by watching the sawgrass bloom. These Indians of Florida were actually the first to flee from a storm, citing the blooming of the Florida Everglades sawgrass. They believed that only 'an atmospheric condition' such as a major hurricane would cause the pollen to bloom on the sawgrass several

---

22 *http://hrsbstaff.ednet.ns.ca/primetl/school/juan/hurricanesheets.html.* Retrieved: 11-10-2005.

days before a hurricane's arrival, giving the native Indians an advanced warning of the impending storm. Black educator Mary McLeod Bethune repeated a story that these Indians were seen leaving several days before the storm, saying, "Follow Indian, Indian no fool, going to dry land, big water coming." One has to wonder if the Seminoles, like other Indians of the region, had a 'sixth sense' when it came to hurricanes.

Many other sub-culture Indians had similar words for these powerful storms, which they all feared and respected greatly. The Quiche people of southern Guatemala believed in the god Huraken, for their god of thunder and lightning. For example, the Galibi Indians of Dutch and French Guiana called these hurricanes Yuracan and Hyroacan, or simply the devil. Other Guiana Indians called them Yarukka, and other similar Indian names were Hyrorokan, aracan, urican, huiranvucan, Yurakon, Yuruk or Yoroko. As hurricanes were becoming more frequent in the Caribbean, many of the colonists and natives of this region had various words and spellings, all sounding phonetically similar for these powerful storms. The English called them 'Hurricanes', 'Haurachana', 'Uracan', 'Herocano', 'Harrycane', 'Tempest', and 'Hyrracano.' The Spanish called them 'Huracán'and 'Furicane', and the Portuguese called them 'Huracao', and 'Furicane.' The French had for a long time adapted the Indian word called 'Ouragan', and the Dutch referred to them as 'Orkan.' These various spellings were used until the word 'hurricane' was finally settled on in the English Language. Among the Caribbean, Central and North American peoples, the word 'hurricane' seems to have always been associated with evil spirits and violence.

After his first voyage to the New World, Columbus returned to Isabella in Hispaniola with seventeen ships. Columbus' settlers built houses, storerooms, a Roman Catholic Church, and a large house for Columbus. He brought more than a thousand men, including sailors, soldiers, carpenters, stonemasons, and other workers. Priests and nobles came as well. The Spaniards brought pigs, horses, wheat, sugarcane, and guns. Rats and microbes came with them as well. The settlement took up more than two hectares. At the time, some estimated the Taíno Indian population in Hispaniola to be as high as one million persons. They lived on fish and staples such as pineapple, which they introduced to the Spaniards. The food that they provided was important to the Spaniards. Describing these Indians, Columbus said that there were no finer people in the world. In March 1494, Columbus' men began to search, with Taíno Indians, in the mountains of Hispaniola for gold, and small amounts were found. In June 1495, a large storm that the Taíno Indians called a hurricane hit the island. The

Indians retreated to the mountains, while the Spaniards remained in the colony. Several ships were sunk, including the flagship, the *Marie-Galante.*

Christopher Columbus, on his first voyage, managed to avoid encountering any hurricanes, but it wasn't until some of his later voyages that he encountered several hurricanes that disrupted these voyages to the New World. Based on his first voyage before encountering any hurricanes, Columbus concluded that the weather in the New World was benign: "In all the Indies, I have always found May-like weather," he commented. Although sailing through hurricane-prone waters during the most dangerous months, he did not have any serious hurricane encounters on his early voyage. However, on his final voyages, Christopher Columbus himself weathered at least three of these dangerous storms. The town of La Isabella was struck by two of the earliest North Atlantic hurricanes observed by Europeans in 1494 and 1495. Columbus provided the earliest account of a hurricane in a letter written to Queen Isabella in 1494. In this letter, he wrote, "The tempest arose and worried me so that I knew not where to turn; Eyes never behold the seas so high, angry and covered by foam. We were forced to keep out in this bloody ocean, seething like a pot of hot fire. Never did the sky look more terrible; for one whole day and night it blazed like a furnace. The flashes came with such fury and frightfulness that we all thought the ships would be blasted. All this time the water never ceased to fall from the sky...The people were so worn out, that they longed for death to end their terrible suffering."[23]

The extensive shallow banks and coral reefs in the vicinity of most Caribbean islands present hazards to navigation that were immediately appreciated by the Spanish explorers. These dangers were compounded by violent tropical storms and hurricanes that appeared without sufficient warning and by the unseaworthy character of vessels that had spent months cruising in shipworm-infested waters. Despite the explorers' exercising what must have seemed like due caution, there is an extensive list of shipwrecks. Columbus himself lost nine ships: *Santa María,* which was wrecked near Haiti on Christmas Eve on his first voyage; *Niña* and three other vessels at La Isabella in 1495; and the entire fleet of his fourth voyage-*Vizcaina* and *Gallega* off the coast of Central America in 1503, and *Capitana* and *Santiago* in Puerto Santa Gloria, Jamaica, 1504. However, as early as June of 1494, the small town of Isabella, founded by Columbus on Hispaniola, became the first European settlement destroyed by a hurricane. The Spaniards who accompanied Columbus on his four voyages to the New World

---

23 *http://www.fascinatingearth.com/node/311.* Retrieved: 11-10-2005.

took back to Europe with them a new concept of what a severe storm could be, and naturally, a new word of Indian origin. It seems that the Indian word was pronounced 'Furacán' or 'Furacánes' during the early years of discovery and colonization of America. Peter Martyr, one of the earliest historians of the New World, said that they were called by the natives 'Furacanes,' although the plural is obviously Spanish. The Rev. P. du Tertre, (1667) in his great work during the middle of the seventeenth century, wrote first 'ouragan', and later 'houragan.'

After 1474, some changes in the Spanish language were made. For instance, words beginning with 'h' were pronounced using the 'f consonant.' The kingdoms of Aragon and Castile were united in 1474, before the discovery of America, and after that time some changes in the Spanish language were made. One of them involved words beginning with the letter 'h.' In Aragon, they pronounced such words as 'f'. As Menéndez Pidal said, "Aragon was the land of the 'f', but the old Castilian lost the sound or pronunciation," so that Spanish Scholar Nebrija (Nebrija wrote a grammar of the Castilian language and is credited as the first published grammar of any Romance language) wrote, instead of the lost 'f', an aspirated 'h.' Menéndez wrote concerning the pronunciation of the word 'hurricane' and its language used by Fernando Colón, son of Christopher Columbus, "Vacillation between 'f' and 'h' is very marked predominance of the 'h.' And so, the 'h' became in Spanish a silent letter, as it still is today."

Father Bartholomew de Las Casas, referring to one of these storms, wrote: "At this time the four vessels brought by Juan Aguado were destroyed in the port (of Isabella) by a great tempest, called by the Indians in their language 'Furacán.' Now we call them hurricanes, something that almost all of us have experienced at sea or on land..."[24] Las Casas, outraged by the brutal treatment of the Indians on Hispaniola, declared that the wrath of the hurricane that struck Hispaniola was the judgment of God on the city and the men who had committed such sins against humanity. All other European languages coined a word for the tropical cyclone, based on the Spanish 'Huracán.' Gonzalo Fernandez de Oviedo (Oviedo y Valdes, 1851, Book VI, Ch. III) is more explicit in his writings concerning the origin of the word 'hurricane.' He says: "Hurricane, in the language of this island, properly means an excessively severe storm or tempest; because, in fact, it is only a very great wind and a very great and excessive rainfall, both together or either these two things by themselves."

---

24 José C. Millas, *Hurricanes of The Caribbean and Adjacent Regions 1492-1800*, (Miami, Edward Brothers Inc/Academy of Arts and Sciences of the Americas, 1968), pg. xi.

Oviedo further noted that the winds of the 'Huracán' were so "fierce that they topple houses and uproot many large trees."[25]

Even in the English language, the word 'hurricane' evolved through several variations. For example, William Shakespeare mentioned it in his play 'King Lear', where he wrote "Blow, winds, and crack your cheeks! Rage! Blow! You catracts and hurricanes, spout till you have drench'd out steeples, drown'd the cocks!" Girolamo Benzoni, in 1565 in his Book History of the New World, mentioned his encounter with a hurricane in Hispaniola, which at the time he referred to as 'Furacanum.' "In those days a wondrous and terrible disaster occurred in this country. At sunrise such a horrible, strong wind began that the inhabitants of the island thought they had never seen or heard anything like it before. The raging storm wind (which the Spaniards called Furacanum) came with great violence, as if it wanted to spit heaven and Earth apart from one another, and hurl everything to the ground...The people were as a whole so despairing because of their great fear that they run here and there, as if they were senseless and mad, and did not know what they did...The strong and frightful wind threw some entire houses and capitals including the people from the capital, tore them apart in the air and threw them down to the ground in pieces. This awful weather did such noticeable damage in such a short time that not three ships stood secure in the sea harbor or came through the storm undamaged. For the anchors, even if they were yet strong, were broken apart through the strong force of the wind and all the masts, despite their being new, were crumpled. The ships were blown around by the wind, so that all the people in them were drowned. For the most part the Indians had crawled away and hidden themselves in holes in order to escape such disaster."[26]

As stated earlier, Christopher Columbus did not learn on his first voyage, the voyage of discovery, of the existence of such terrible 'tempests' or 'storms.' He had the exceptional good fortune of not being struck by any of them during this voyage. The Indians, while enjoying pleasant weather, had no reason to speak about these storms to a group of strangers who spoke a language that they could not understand. Naturally, Columbus did not say one word about these awful storms in his much celebrated letter *"The Letter of Columbus on the Discovery of America."* However, on his second voyage things were quite different.

---

25 Ibid. Pg. xi.

26 Benzon, G. History of the New World Vol. 21, (London. Hakluyt Society, 1837).

After arriving on November 3, 1493, at an island in the Lesser Antilles that he named Dominica, Columbus sailed northward and later westward, to Isabella Hispaniola, the first city in the New World, at the end of January 1494. Then in June of that year, 1494, Isabella was struck by a hurricane, the first time that European men had seen such a terrible storm. Surely, for the first time they heard the Taíno Indians, very much excited, extending their arms raised upward into the air and shouting, "Furacán! Furacán!" when the storm commenced. We can indeed say that it was that moment in history when the word 'hurricane' suddenly appeared to the Europeans. Columbus was not at that time in Isabella because he was sailing near the Isle of Pines, Cuba. So, his companions of the ships 'Marigalante' and 'Gallega' were the first white men to hear these words, which were of Indian origin and about a phenomenon of the New World. Knowledge of 'Furacanes,' both the word and the terrifying storms it described, remained limited to Spanish speakers until 1555, when Richard Eden translated Columbus' ship report and other Spanish accounts of the New World, making it the first time it appeared in the English vocabulary.

In October of 1495, probably in the second half of the month, another hurricane struck Isabella, which was much stronger than the first. It finally gave Columbus, who was there at the time, the opportunity of knowing what a hurricane was and of its destructive abilities. It also gave him the opportunity of hearing the Indians shouting the same word with fear and anxiety on their faces, on the account of these terrible storms of the tropics, which they believed were caused by evil spirits. Christopher Columbus would later declare that "nothing but the service of God and the extension of the monarchy would induce him to expose himself to such danger from these storms ever again."[27] 'The Nińa' was the only vessel that was the smallest, oldest and the most fragile at the time, but amazingly it withstood that hurricane. The other two ships of Columbus, 'The San Juan' and 'The Cordera' were in the harbor and were lost or badly damaged by this hurricane. Columbus gave orders to have one repaired and another ship known as 'India' constructed out of the wreck of the ones that had been destroyed, making it the first ship to be built in the Caribbean by Europeans.

In 1502, during his fourth voyage, Columbus warned the Governor Don Nicolas de Orvando of Santo Domingo of an approaching hurricane, but he was ignored; as a result, a Spanish treasure fleet set sailed and lost 21 of 30 ships with 500 men. Columbus had a serious disagreement with the bureaucrats

---

27 Ivan Ray Tannehill, Hurricanes-Their Nature and History, (New Jersey, Princeton University Press, 1950), pg. 141.

appointed by Spain to govern the fledgling colonies in the Caribbean to extract gold, pearl and other precious commodities from the native Indians. Among the more unfriendly of these exploiters was Don Nicolas de Orvando, the Governor of Hispaniola, with whom Columbus had been forbidden to have any contact by the request of his Spanish sovereigns. But as Columbus approached Santa Domingo, he recognized the early signs of an approaching hurricane, such as large ocean swells and a veil of cirrostratus clouds overhead. Concerned for the safety of his men and ships, he sent a message to Governor Orvando, begging him to be allowed to seek refuge in Santa Domingo Harbor.

Columbus had observed that the Governor was preparing a large fleet of ships to set sail for Spain, carrying large quantities of gold and slaves, and warned him to delay the trip until the hurricane had passed. Refusing both the request and the advice, Orvando read Columbus' note out loud to the crew and residents, who roared with laughter at Columbus' advice. Unfortunately, the laughter was very short-lived, and Orvando's ships left port only to their own demise when 21 of the 30 ships were lost in a hurricane between Hispaniola and Puerto Rico. An additional four of them were badly damaged, but fortunately they were able to return to port, where they, too, eventually sunk. Only one ship, the *Aguja*, made it to Spain, and that one, no doubt to Orvando's intense distress, was carrying what little remained of Columbus' own gold.

Meanwhile, Columbus, anticipating strong winds from the north from this hurricane, positioned his fleet in a harbor on the south side of Hispaniola. On June 13, the storm hit with ferocious northeast winds. Even with the protection of the mountainous terrain to the windward side, the fleet struggled. In Columbus' own words, "The storm was terrible and on that night the ships were parted from me. Each one of them was reduced to an extremity, expecting nothing save death; each one of them was certain the others were lost."[28] The anchors held only on Columbus' ship; the others were dragged out to sea, where their crews fought for their lives. Nevertheless, the fleet survived with only minimal damage. Almost 18 months later, Columbus returned to Santo Domingo, only to discover that it had been largely destroyed by the hurricane.

When the Europeans first attempted to create settlements in the Caribbean and the Americas, they quickly learned about these storms. As time passed and these settlers learned more about their new homeland, they experienced

---

[28] National Geographic Magazine, A Columbus Casebook-A Supplement to Where Columbus Found the New World. (Washington, National Geographic Society, 1986), pgs. 62-64.

these storms on such a regular basis that they became accustomed to them. Eventually, they began calling them equinoctial storms, as the storms would normally hit in the weeks around the period of the fall equinox, which in the northern hemisphere occurs in late September.

By the 1590s, about a hundred ships a year were sailing from Havana for Seville, most of them leaving in July and August before the height of the hurricane season. The storms usually came in the late summer just as the harvest of sugar and a number of other crops had ended. Thus, there was always a danger of substantial losses after a year of investment and labor. The felling of maize fields was always a risk. Root crops like yucca and potatoes had better resistance to the wind and water, but too much moisture rotted them in the ground. Not only were current crops, but the seeds for the next year was also vulnerable.

In 1546, the judge Alonso López de Cerrato wrote from Santo Domingo that the island had never been so prosperous when it was struck by three hurricanes which decimated the island which left no trees, sugarcane, maize, yucca, or shacks (bohíos) standing. Similar conditions occurred in Cuba, when a powerful hurricane in 1692 struck western Cuba and destroyed all of the seed and plantings of plantains, yucca, and maize on which they had to rely on to feed themselves. The problems with these storms were more exacerbated on the smaller islands of the Caribbean when a hurricane struck them, because real starvation would set in, especially when overconcentration on export or cash crops had already placed foodstuffs in short supply, even under normal circumstances. Portable water sources were often fouled by brackish water from the storm, and food became a major problem. In the first days after a hurricane, there were plantains, guanabana, and other edible fruits that had fallen to the ground, but these soon were consumed or rotted, and then hunger would set in.

English explorers and privateers soon contributed their own accounts of encounters with these storms. In 1513, Juan Ponce de León completed the first recorded cruise along the Florida coast and came ashore near present-day St. Augustine to claim Florida for Spain. Famous for his unsuccessful search for the magical 'Fountain of Youth,' he might have discovered Florida earlier had it not been for the ravages of hurricanes. In August of 1508, he was struck by two hurricanes within two weeks. The first drove his ship onto the rocks near the Port of Yuna, Hispaniola, and the second left his ship aground on the southwest coast of Puerto Rico.

Soon after Hernando Cortés found treasures of gold and silver in the newly discovered lands of the West, expeditions to retrieve the riches of the New World for Spain began in earnest. In 1525, Cortés lost the first ship he sent to Mexico in a severe hurricane, along with its crew of over seventy persons. Famous English Explorer Sir John Hawkins wrote his own encounters with these storms. Sir John Hawkins wrote that he left Cartagena in late July 1568 "Hoping to have escaped the time of their stormes...which they call Furicanos."[29] Hawkins did not leave soon enough, and he and his ships were bashed by an "extreme storme", as he referred to it, lasting several days.

Failure to leave Havana on time was, as one commander put it in 1630, was to "tempt God," by placing the treasure-laden fleets at risk to losses from the storms. However, the very regularity and predictability of the system also made the fleets vulnerable to corsairs (sometimes referred to as 'buccaneers') and foreign rivals, who would simply just lay in wait off the Florida Keys or the Bahamas in the natural deep water channels, knowing and strategically waiting until the silver-laden fleet would appear and simply attack them at this vulnerable time. Losses to corsairs or rivals were usually of individual ships, whereas the destruction caused by hurricanes at sea were more generalized, but together these maritime risks sometimes produced disastrous results not only for ships and men, but for Spanish policy as well. In 1624 three more galleons were lost, along with over a million pesos belonging to private individuals and about another half million belonging to the Royal Treasury. The New Spain fleet left Veracruz too late in 1631 and was caught by a hurricane, losing its flagship and all its silver off Campeche. In addition, the Dutch captured a whole fleet off Matanzas, Cuba, in 1628. With these disruptions of trade and the flow of silver to the royal treasury, it was difficult for Spain to finance its domestic commitments, its foreign policy, imperial responsibilities.[30]

English Explorer Sir Francis Drake encountered several major hurricanes while sailing the dangerous seas of the Americas and the Atlantic Ocean, and in most cases these encounters changed the course of West Indian and American history. Sir Francis Drake, who traveled the seas of the globe in quest of glory and valuable loot, nearly lost his ships in the fleet on the Outer Banks of Carolina. One of his most famous encounters was with a major hurricane that occurred while he was anchored near the ill-fated Roanoke colony in present day North Carolina in June of 1586. His ships were anchored just off the banks while he checked on the progress of Sir Walter Raleigh's colonists on Roanoke

---

29 Matthew Mulcahy, Hurricanes and Society in the British Greater Caribbean, 1624-1783, (Baltimore, The Johns Hopkins University Press, 2006), pgs. 14-15.

30 Stuart, B. Schwartz, Sea of Storms-The History of Hurricanes in the Greater Caribbean from Columbus to Katrina, (New Jersey, Princeton University Press, 2015), pgs. 36-39.

Island. The hurricane lasted for three days, scattering Drake's fleet and nearly destroying many of his ships. There was no greater thorn in the side of the Spaniards than Francis Drake. His exploits were legendary, making him a hero to the English but a simple pirate to the Spaniards, and for good reasons because he often robbed them of their valuable treasures. To the Spanish, he was known as El Draque, "the Dragon"; "Draque" is the Spanish pronunciation of "Drake." As a talented sea captain and navigator, he attacked their fleets and took their ships and treasures. He raided their settlements in America and played a major role in the defeat of the greatest fleet ever assembled, the "Spanish Armada."

No other English seaman brought home more wealth or had a bigger impact on English history than Drake. At the age of 28, he was trapped in a Mexican port by Spanish war ships. He had gone there for repairs after an encounter with one of his first major hurricanes at sea. Drake escaped, but some of the sailors left behind were so badly treated by the Spanish that he swore revenge. He returned to the area in 1572 with two ships and 73 men. Over the next fifteen months, he raided Spanish towns and their all-important Silver train across the isthmus from Panama. Other English accounts reported ships damaged or lost in storms characterized by extreme wind and rain, some of which were definitely hurricanes. The English (including Drake and Hawkins) had a great respect for hurricanes, to such an extent that as the hurricane season was understood to be approaching, more and more pirates went home or laid up their ships in some sheltered harbor until the last hurricane had passed and was replaced by the cool air of old man winter.

Probably those that first discovered the period of the year in which hurricanes developed were Spanish priests, officers of the navy or army, or civilians that had lived for a long time in the Caribbean. After living a considerable time in the Caribbean, like 60-100 years, Spanish officials and settlers were by the time no strangers to the natural disasters of the New World. They had already experienced many hurricanes, and in some way their explanations of these hurricanes were consistently providential, and even so they were considered normal within divine purpose. But despite their acceptance of God's will as a primary cause for these hurricanes, there were always a practical and a political aspect to their perceptions, and to their responses as well.

By the end of the sixteenth century, they should have already known the approximate period that these hurricanes occurred. The Roman Catholic Church knew early on that the hurricane season extended at least from August to October because the hierarchy ordered that all of the churches in the Caribbean say a special prayer to protect them from these deadly hurricanes.

The prayer that had to be said was: 'Ad repellendas tempestates,' translated to mean 'for the repelling of the hurricanes or tempests.' It was also ordered that the prayer should be said in Puerto Rico during August and September and in Cuba in September and October. This indicates that it was known that hurricanes were more frequent in those islands during the months mentioned. Eventually, West Indian colonists, through first-hand experiences with these storms, gradually learned that hurricanes struck the Caribbean within a well-defined season. Initially, those early colonists believed that hurricanes could strike at any time of the year, but by the middle of the seventeenth century most of them recognized that there was a distinct hurricane season. This was because the hurricanes simply occurred too frequently within a particular time period for them to remain strange and unusual in their eyes. Numerous letters and reports written by colonists specifically discussed the period between July and October as the 'time of hurricanes.'

One case in point, by the 1660s the dangers of the storms were known well enough that advertisements in Europe to attract colonists to Suriname highlighted the fact that this colony was more fertile than other lands in this region, and moreover free of the dangers of hurricanes (which they called 'Orcanen') which are all too common in other parts of the North Atlantic. Interestingly enough, the Dutch had originally believed that Curaçao was also free from hurricanes as well, but that hope was dashed when a very destructive hurricane in October of 1681 proved them wrong and decimated the island.[31]

The geography of hurricanes challenged the concept of these storms as 'national judgments or divine favor' by which God spoke to a specific group of people or country. Individual storms routinely struck various islands colonized by different European powers. For example, in 1707 a hurricane devastated the English Leeward Islands, the Dutch Islands of Saba and St. Eustatius, and the French Island of Guadeloupe. In 1674, a Dutch attack on the French Islands was thwarted by a hurricane, which also caused significant damage in the English Leeward Islands and in Barbados. Guadeloupe, Martinique, and nearby Antigua were located on the same or nearby geographical boundary (16-17°N) that made them vulnerable to the Cape Verde type storms, which forms in the far eastern Atlantic and traverse the wide and expansive Atlantic Ocean and then increase in energy and destructive abilities as they move westward into the eastern most Caribbean countries of the Lesser and Greater Antilles.

---

31 Stuart, B. Schwartz, *Sea of Storms-The History of Hurricanes in the Greater Caribbean from Columbus to Katrina,* (New Jersey, Princeton University Press, 2015), pg. 52.

The French islands were hit by a pretty destructive hurricane in 1635, the first year of their settlement, Guadeloupe averaged a strike every ten years or so in the seventeenth century. Along with Martinique and St. Christopher, it was devastated again in August 1666, at which time an English fleet attacking the island under the command of Lord Willoughby was caught and lost. Between 1699 and 1720, four heavy storms struck the island, and it then suffered other intense periods between 1738 and 1742 (four strikes) and 1765 and 1767 (three strikes). Martinique also was often hit, suffering from the ravages of hurricanes in 1680 and 1695, with great loss of life and damage to shipping in its harbors, and then was periodically visited by storms in the eighteenth century.

The presence of hurricanes made colonists question their ability to transform the hostile environment of the Caribbean and by extension their ability to establish successful and stable societies here. But hurricanes raised other questions as well: What caused them? What forces gave rise to such powerful and dangerous storms? For some-probably a significant majority during the first several decades of the seventeenth century-they believed that these storms came directly from the hands of God. They interpreted hurricanes as 'wondrous events' or 'divine judgments' for human sins. Others linked hurricanes to various natural processes, including shifting wind patterns. The explosion of various natural processes, including shifting wind patterns, the explosion of various chemicals in the atmosphere, and the celestial movement of the planets and stars.

Gradually, the colonists and their governors learned from their first-hand experiences with these storms and therefore adapted to them. First, they learned to avoid shipping during the hurricane season to prevent losses. Second, they insured their ships and cargoes against the loss inflicted on them by hurricanes. Third, they would often spread the cargo among a number of ships to mitigate the losses by having several vessels instead of just one ship. Fourth, they encouraged their slaves to plant root crops, which were less susceptible to losses from a hurricane. Finally, they would avoid the purchase of new slaves until after the hurricane season had passed.

CHAPTER TWO

The Naming of Hurricanes

North Atlantic Tropical Cyclone Names

2016	2017	2018	2019	2020	2021
Alex	Arlene	Alberto	Andrea	Arthur	Ana
Bonnie	Bret	Beryl	Barry	Bertha	Bill
Colin	Cindy	Chris	Chantal	Cristobal	Claudette
Danielle	Don	Debby	Dorian	Dolly	Danny
Earl	Emily	Ernesto	Erin	Edouard	Elsa
Fiona	Franklin	Florence	Fernand	Fay	Fred
Gaston	Gert	Gordon	Gabrielle	Gonzalo	Grace
Hermine	Harvey	Helene	Humberto	Hanna	Henri
Ian	Irma	Isaac	Imelda	Isaias	Ida
Julia	Jose	Joyce	Jerry	Josephine	Julian
Karl	Katia	Kirk	Karen	Kyle	Kate
Lisa	Lee	Leslie	Lorenzo	Laura	Larry
Matthew	Maria	Michael	Melissa	Marco	Mindy
Nicole	Nate	Nadine	Nestor	Nana	Nicholas
Otto	Ophelia	Oscar	Olga	Omar	Odette
Paula	Philippe	Patty	Pablo	Paulette	Peter
Richard	Rina	Rafael	Rebekah	Rene	Rose
Shary	Sean	Sara	Sebastien	Sally	Sam
Tobias	Tammy	Tony	Tanya	Teddy	Teresa
Virginie	Vince	Valerie	Van	Vicky	Victor
Walter	Whitney	William	Wendy	Wilfred	Wanda

Information Courtesy of NOAA-National Hurricane Center

For as long as people have been tracking and reporting hurricanes, also known as tropical cyclones, they've been struggling to find ways to identify them. Until well into the 20th century, newspapers and forecasters in the Caribbean and the Americas devised names for storms that referenced their time period, geographic location or intensity or some other distinguishing factor. It's a funny thing, this naming of storms. We don't name tornadoes, blizzards, or frontal systems. It would seem silly, but we do name our hurricanes. On the opposite corners of our stormy planet, meteorologists name their cyclones, too (although with sometimes more meaningful or symbolic names).

Hurricanes are the only weather disasters that have been given their own iconic names, such as Hurricanes Sandy, Andrew, Gilbert, Katrina, Camille or Mitch. No two hurricanes are the same, but like people, they share similar characteristics; yet, still they have their own unique stories to tell. The naming of storms or hurricanes has undergone various stages of development and transformation. Initially, the word 'Hurricane' accompanied by the year of occurrence was used. For example, 'the Great Hurricane of 1780', which killed over 22,000 persons in Martinique, Barbados and St. Eustatius. Another example was 'the Great Storm of 1703', whose incredible damage of the British Isles was expertly detailed by Robinson Crusoe's author, Daniel Defoe. The naming scheme was later substituted by a numbering system (e.g. Hurricane #1, #2, #3 of 1833 etc...); however, this became too cumbersome and confusing, especially when disseminating information about two or more storms within the same geographical area or location.

For the major hurricanes of this region, they were often named after the particular country or city they devastated. This was especially true for severe hurricanes, which made their landing somewhere in the Caribbean or the Americas. Three notable examples were: first, 'the Great Dominican Republic Hurricane of 1930', which killed over 8,000 persons in the Dominican Republic. The 1930 Dominican Republic Hurricane, also known as 'Hurricane San Zenon', is the fifth deadliest North Atlantic hurricane on record. The second of only two known tropical cyclones in the very quiet 1930 North Atlantic hurricane season, the hurricane was first observed on August 29 to the east of the Lesser Antilles. The cyclone was a small but intense Category 4 hurricane.

Next was 'the Pointe-à-Pitre Hurricane of 1776', which devastated the country of Guadeloupe and killed over 6,000 persons and devastated its largest city and economic capital of Pointe-à-Pitre. The 1776 Pointe-à-Pitre hurricane was at one point the deadliest North Atlantic on record. Although its intensity and complete track is unknown, it is known that the storm struck Guadeloupe on September 6, 1776, near Pointe-à-Pitre, which is currently the largest city on the island. At least 6,000 fatalities occurred on Guadeloupe, which was a higher death toll than any other known hurricane before it to hit that country. The storm struck a large convoy of French and Dutch merchant ships, sinking or running aground 60% of the vessels. The ships were transporting goods to Europe.

Finally, 'the Great Nassau Hurricane of 1926', which devastated the city of Nassau in the Bahamas during the 1926 North Atlantic hurricane season. The Great Nassau Hurricane of 1926, also known as 'the Bahamas-Florida Hurricane of July 1926' and 'Hurricane San Liborio,' was a destructive Category 4 hurricane that affected the Bahamas at peak intensity. Although it weakened considerably before its Florida landfall, it was reported as one of the most severe storms to affect Nassau in the Bahamas in several years until the Great Lake Okeechobee Hurricane of 1928, which occurred just two years later. Approximately 258 persons died in this storm in the Bahamas.

In some cases, they were even named after the holiday on which they occurred, for example, 'the Great Labor Day Hurricane of 1935.' The Great Labor Day Hurricane of 1935 was the strongest tropical cyclone during the 1935 North Atlantic hurricane season. This compact and intense hurricane caused extensive damage in the Bahamas and the upper Florida Keys. To this day, this hurricane is the strongest and most intense hurricane on record to ever have struck the United States in terms of barometric pressure. Furthermore, it was one of the strongest recorded hurricane landfalls worldwide. It was the only hurricane known to have made landfall in the United States with a minimum central pressure below 900 mbar; only two others have struck the United States with winds of Category 5 strength on the Saffir-Simpson Hurricane Scale (originally called the Saffir-Simpson Hurricane Scale (now called the Saffir-Simpson Hurricane Wind Scale) included typical storm surges expected for each category). It remains the third-strongest North Atlantic hurricane on record, and it was only surpassed by Hurricane Gilbert (888 mbar) in 1988 and Hurricane Wilma (882 mbar) in 2005. In total, at least 408 people were killed by this hurricane.

In some cases, they were named after the ship which experienced that particular storm. Three notable examples were: 'Antje's Hurricane of 1842', 'the Racer's Storm of 1837' and 'the Sea Venture Hurricane of 1609.' In 1842, a North Atlantic hurricane that ripped off the mast of a boat named *Antje* became known as Antje's Hurricane. A westward moving hurricane, nicknamed Antje's Hurricane after a schooner of the same name that was dismasted by the storm. The cyclone moved across the Florida Keys on September 4. It continued westward across the Gulf of Mexico, hitting between Matamoros and Tampico, Mexico. Its unusual westward movement, also seen by a hurricane in 1932 and Hurricane Anita in 1977, was due to a strong high pressure system to its north.

The 1837 Racer's Storm was a very powerful and destructive hurricane in the 19th century, causing 105 deaths and heavy damage to many cities on its 2,000+ mile path. The Racer's Storm was the 10th known tropical storm in the 1837 North Atlantic hurricane season. The Racer's Storm was named after the British war ship *HMS Racer,* which encountered the storm in the extreme northwest Caribbean on September 28th. Another example was 'the Sea Venture Hurricane of 1609.' On July 28th of 1609, a fleet of seven tall ships, with two pinnaces in tow carrying 150 settlers and supplies from Plymouth, England, to Virginia to relieve the starving Jamestown colonists, was struck by a hurricane while en route there. They had been sent by the Virginia Company of London to fortify the Jamestown settlement. Sir George Somers' mission was to resupply the six hundred or so pioneers who a year before had settled in the infant British colonial settlement of King James' Town, situated in one of the estuaries south of the Potomac River.

The ship *Sea Venture* was grounded at Bermuda, which for some time was called Somers Island after the ship's captain, Admiral Sir George Somers. After being struck by this hurricane, the Sea Venture sprung a leak and everyone on board worked frantically to save this ship and their lives by trying to pump the water out of the hull of the ship. They tried to stem the flow of water coming into the ship by stuffing salt beef and anything else they could find to fit into the leaks of the ship. After this proved futile, most of the crew simply gave up hope, falling asleep where they could, exhausted and aching from their relentless but futile efforts. But just as they were about to give up and face the grim reality that they would be lost to the unforgiving Atlantic Ocean, they spotted the island of Bermuda. Somers skillfully navigated the floundering Sea Venture onto a reef about half a mile to the leeward side of Bermuda. They used the ship's long boat to ferry the crew and passengers ashore.

The passengers of the shipwrecked Sea Venture became Bermuda's first inhabitants, and their stories helped inspire William Shakespeare's writing of his final play 'The Tempest', making it perhaps the most famous hurricane in early American history. "And another storm brewing," William Shakespeare wrote in 'The Tempest.' "I hear it sing in the wind."[32] Most of those venturing to the New World had no knowledge of the word or the actual storm. The lead ship, the three-hundred-ton *Sea Venture,* was the largest in the fleet and carried

[32] *http://www.william-shakespeare.info/shakespeare-play-the-tempest.html.* Retrieved: 03-06-2013.

Sir Thomas Gates, the newly appointed governor of the colony, and Sir Georges Somers, admiral of the Virginia Company.

It is interesting to note that Shakespeare did not name his play 'The Hurricane.' He actually did know the word "hurricano" because it appears in two earlier plays, King Lear and Troilus and Cressida. Maybe he recognized that such a title would be confusing and unfamiliar to most of his audience, so he chose a more familiar word 'The Tempest', instead. Though the island was uninhabited, Spaniards had visited Bermuda earlier and set ashore wild pigs. The shipwrecked passengers fed on those wild pigs, fish, berries and other plentiful game on the island. Although they yearned to stay on that island paradise, they managed to make two vessels *'Patience'* and *'Deliverance'* out of what was left of the Sea Venture, and ten months later they set sail for Jamestown. However, some persons remained on the island and became the first colonists of that island, including Admiral Sir George Somers, who initially left with the other Jamestown passengers but eventually returned and died on that island. To this day, Bermuda still celebrates 'Somers' Day' as a public holiday.

In some instances, hurricanes were named after important persons within this region; one such storm was the 'Willoughby Gale of 1666.' The word 'gale' during these colonial times was often interchanged with the word 'hurricane', but they often meant the same thing-a hurricane and not the official term we now use today for the definition of a 'meteorological gale.' This storm was named after the British Governor of Barbados, Lord Francis Willoughby, who lost his life aboard the flagship *Hope* along with over 2,000 of his troops in his fleet in this hurricane. He was appointed Governor of Barbados by Charles II in May of 1650 and attempted to negotiate the strained politics of that island, which also experienced a division between the Royalists and Parliamentarians. His last act on behalf of the English Crown came in July 1666, when having learned of the recent French seizure of St. Kitts, he formed a relief force of two Royal Navy Frigates, twelve other large vessels (including commandeered merchant ships), a fire ship, and a ketch, bearing over 2,000 men.

Lord Willoughby had planned to proceed north to Nevis, Montserrat, and Antigua to gather further reinforcements before descending on the French. Leaving Barbados on July 28th, his fleet waited for the French just off the coast of Martinique and Guadeloupe, where he sent a frigate to assault the harbor and ended up capturing two French merchant vessels on August 4th. This success could not be exploited, however, as that night most of his force was destroyed by a strong hurricane, including the flagship *Hope*, from which Willoughby drowned during the storm. This hurricane occurred in 1666 and was a very intense storm which struck the islands of St. Kitts, Guadeloupe, and Martinique. The fleet was actually caught by surprise by this hurricane after leaving Barbados en route to St. Kitts and Nevis to aid the colonists there to help battle against the French attacks. After the storm, only two vessels from this fleet were ever heard from again, and the French captured some of these survivors. All of the vessels and boats on the coast of Guadeloupe were dashed to pieces. For a period in the late seventeenth century, some colonists referred to especially powerful and deadly hurricanes as "Willoughby Gales."

Personal names were also used elsewhere in this region, for example, 'Saxby's Gale' which occurred in Canada in 1869 and was named after a naval officer who was thought to have predicted it. The Saxby Gale was the name given to a tropical cyclone that struck eastern Canada's Bay of Fundy region on the night of October 4–5, 1869. The storm was named for Lieutenant Stephen Martin Saxby, a naval instructor and amateur astronomer who, based on his astronomical studies, had predicted extremely high tides in the North Atlantic Ocean on October 5, 1869, which would produce a massive storm surge in the event of a storm. The hurricane caused extensive destruction to port facilities and communities along the Bay of Fundy coast in both New Brunswick and Nova Scotia, as well as Maine, particularly Calais, St. Andrews, St. George, St. John, Moncton, Sackville, Amherst, Windsor and Truro. Much of the devastation was attributed to a 2-metre storm surge created by the storm, which coincided with a perigean spring tide; the Bay of Fundy having one of the highest tidal ranges in the world. The Saxby Gale storm surge produced a water level that gave Burntcoat Head, Nova Scotia, the honor of having the highest tidal range ever recorded. It is also thought to have formed the long gravel beach that connects Partridge Island, Nova Scotia, to the mainland.

The storm (which pre-dated the practice of naming hurricanes) was given the name 'Saxby' in honor of Lieutenant Stephen Martin Saxby, Royal Navy, who was a naval instructor and amateur astronomer. Lt. Saxby had written a letter of warning, published December 25, 1868, in London's 'The Standard' newspaper, in which he notes the astronomical forces predicted for October 5, 1869, which would produce extremely high tides in the North Atlantic Ocean during the height of hurricane season. Lt. Saxby followed this warning with a reminder published on September 16, 1869, to 'The Standard', in which he also warns of a major 'atmospheric disturbance' that would coincide with the high water level at an undetermined location. Many newspapers took up Saxby's warning in the coming days.

In a monthly weather column published October 1, 1869, in Halifax's 'The Evening Express,' amateur meteorologist Frederick Allison relayed Lt. Saxby's warning for a devastating storm the following week. Despite the warning, many readers throughout the United Kingdom, Canada, Newfoundland and the United States dismissed Saxby since there were frequent gales and hurricanes during the month of October. The fact that the high tides occurred throughout the North Atlantic basin was unremarkable and astronomically predictable, except for their coinciding with the hurricane that struck the Gulf of Maine and Bay of Fundy to produce the devastating storm surge. Lt. Saxby's predictions were considered quite lunatic at the time. Some believed that his predictions were founded upon astrology, which was not the case.

Another example was 'the Daniel Defoe Hurricane of 1703', which occurred in November of 1703 and moved from the Atlantic across to southern England. It was made famous by an obscure political pamphleteer, Daniel Defoe. It was six years before he wrote the world famous book *'Robinson Crusoe.'* At the time the hurricane struck, he needed money, so the storm gave him the idea of collecting eyewitness accounts of the storm and publishing them in a pamphlet. He printed and sold this pamphlet under the very strange and exceptionally long title of *'The storm or collection of the Most Remarkable Casualties and Disasters which happened in the late Dreadful Tempest both by Sea and Land.'* In total, around 8,000 sailors lost their lives, untold numbers perished in the floods on shore, and 14,000 homes, 400 windmills and 16,000 sheep were destroyed. Some of the windmills burned down because they turned so fast in the fierce winds that friction generated enough heat to set them on fire. The damage in London alone was estimated to have cost £2 million (at 18th century prices).

An additional example was 'the Benjamin Franklin Hurricane of October 1743,' which affected the Northeastern United States and New England, brought gusty winds and rainy conditions as far as Philadelphia, and produced extensive flooding in Boston. This was the first hurricane to be measured accurately by scientific instruments. John Winthrop, a professor of natural philosophy at Harvard College, measured the pressure and tides during the storm passage. This storm wasn't particularly powerful, but it was memorable because it garnered the interest of future patriot and one of the founders of the United States, Benjamin Franklin, who believed the storm was coming in from Boston. He was wrong because it was actually going to Boston. From this information, he surmised that the storm was traveling in a clockwise manner from the southwest to northeast. Putting two and two together, Franklin concluded that the low pressure system was causing the storm to move in this manner.

One aspect of the Earth's general circulation is that storms are not stationary; they move, and in somewhat predictable ways. Until the mid-eighteenth century, it had been generally assumed that storms were born, played out, and died in a single location and that they did not move across the Earth's surface. Benjamin Franklin had planned to study a lunar eclipse one evening in September 1743, but the remnants of this hurricane ruined his evening. This was a big disappointment to him, because he had been looking forward to the lunar eclipse that this storm had obscured. His curiosity aroused, Franklin gathered additional details about the storm by reading the Boston newspapers and learned that the storm had moved up the Atlantic seaboard and against the surface winds. He learned that this hurricane struck Boston a day later, sending flood tides sweeping over the docks, destroying boats, and submerging waterfront streets. In the succeeding months, he collected additional reports from travelers and newspapers from Georgia to Nova Scotia and satisfied himself that at least in this part of the world, storms have a tendency to take a northeasterly path up the Atlantic Coast. Thus, science took the first step toward a basic understanding of hurricanes and their movements.

Benjamin Franklin is also popularly known for his off-the-wall weather experiment years later, where during a thunderstorm, in 1752, he carried out a dangerous experiment to demonstrate that a thunderstorm generates electricity. He flew a kite, with metal objects attached to its string, high in the sky into a thunderstorm cloud (cumulonimbus). The metal items produced sparks, proving that electricity had passed along the wet string. After discovering that bolts of lightning were in fact electricity, with this knowledge Franklin developed the lightning rod to allow the lightning bolt to travel along the rod and safely into the ground. This discovery by Franklin is still used even to this day all over the world. A year later, after Benjamin Franklin's famous kite flight, Swedish physicist G.W. Richmann conducted a similar experiment following Franklin's instructions to the letter, and as fate would have it, he was struck by lightning, which killed him instantly. Sailing home from France on the fifth of September, 1789, after his great years as a U.S. Ambassador, Benjamin Franklin experienced a storm that may have been the same storm that devastated Dominica. He was eighty years old and suffering from "the Stone" but was busy observing the temperatures of the sea water, which would eventually lead to his discovery of the Gulf Stream.

Finally, there was the 'Alexander Hamilton Hurricane of 1772,' which he experienced growing up as a boy living in the Caribbean on the island of St. Kitts in the Leeward Islands. This was an extremely powerful and deadly hurricane. He later on in life became the confidential aide to George Washington, and his greatness rests on his Federalist influence on the American Constitution as much as on his financial genius as the first United States Secretary of the Treasury. Today he is featured on the United States ten-dollar bill, and he is one of two non-presidents featured on currently issued United States bills. The other is Benjamin Franklin, who is found on the United States $100 bill. A westward moving hurricane hit Puerto Rico on August 28. It continued through the Caribbean, hitting Hispaniola on August 30, and later on Jamaica. It moved northwestward through the Gulf of Mexico and hit just west of Mobile, Alabama, on September 4th. Many ships were destroyed in the Mobile area, and its death toll was very severe. In Pensacola, it destroyed most of the wharves. The most devastation occurred in the vicinity of Mobile and the Pasca Oocola River. All shipping at the Mouth of the Mississippi was driven into the marshes; this included the ship 'El Principe de Orange', from which only 6 persons survived.

This storm was famously described by Alexander Hamilton, who was living on the island of St. Croix at the time and wrote a letter about it to his father in St. Kitts. The letter was so dramatic and moving that it was published in newspapers locally on the island and first in New York, and then in other states, and the locals on St. Kitts raised enough money to have him brought to America to receive a formal education to make good use of his intellectual abilities. This was because this letter created such a sensation that some planters of St. Kitts, in the midst of the hurricane devastation, took up a collection to send him to America for better schooling because they saw in him great potential. By 1774, he was a student at King's College, now Columbia University, in New York. On St. Kitts, the damage was considerable, and once again many houses were flattened, and there were several fatalities and many more injuries. Total damage from this storm alone was estimated at £500,000 on St. Kitts. The second storm struck just three days later, causing even more significant damage to the few remaining houses on this island already battered and weakened by the previous storm in 1772.

Several claimants have been put forth as the originators of the modern tropical cyclone 'naming' system. However, it was forecaster Clement Lindley Wragge, an Australian meteorologist who in 1887 began giving women's names, names from history and mythology and male names, especially names of politicians who offended him, to these storms before the end of the 19th century. He was a colorful and controversial meteorologist in charge of the Brisbane, Australia, government weather office. He initially named the storms after mythological figures but later named them after politicians he didn't like. For example, Wragge named some of these storms using biblical names, such as Ram, Raken, Talmon, and Uphaz, or the ancient names of Xerxes and Hannibal.

Wragge even nicknamed one storm Eline, a name that he thought was reminiscent of "dusty maidens with liquid eyes and bewitching manners." Most ingeniously, he gained a measure of personal revenge by naming some of the nastiest storms with politicians' names, such as Drake, Barton, and Deakin. By properly naming a hurricane, he was able to publicly describe a politician (perhaps a politician who was not too generous with the weather bureau appropriations) as "causing great distress" or "wandering aimlessly about the Pacific." By naming these storms after these hated politicians, he could get a degree of revenge on them without suffering any repercussions from them. During his last days in office, he fought with the Australian government over the right to issue national forecasts, and he lost and was fired in 1902.

For a while, hurricanes in the West Indies were often named after the particular Saint's Day on which the hurricane occurred. As Christianity took hold in the West Indies, the naming system of storms here in the Caribbean was based on the Catholic tradition of naming these storms with the 'Saint' of the day (e.g. San Ciprian on September 26th). This system for naming them was haphazard and not really a system at all. Powerful hurricanes hitting especially the Spanish speaking islands of the Caribbean got Catholic Saints' names. According to Historian Alejandro Tapia, the first hurricane to be named with the Saint of the day was the 'Hurricane of San Bartolomé', which devastated Puerto Rico and the Dominican Republic on August 24th and 25th of 1568. The earlier tropical cyclones were simply designated by historians' years later after their passages.

One example of a great storm named after a Saint of the day was 'Hurricane Saint Felipe I', which struck Puerto Rico on September 13, 1876. Another example was 'Hurricane Saint Felipe II', which occurred, strangely enough, on the very same date 52 years later on September 13, 1928. Another hurricane, which was named the 'Hurricane of Saint Elena', struck Puerto Rico on August 18, 1851, and caused massive casualties. Then there was the 'Hurricane of Santa Ana' (in English, Saint Anne), which struck Puerto Rico and Guadeloupe on July 26, 1825, the date of the feast in honor of the Mother of the Blessed Virgin, which killed over 1,300 persons. In addition, there was the 'Hurricane of Saint

Ciriaco', which killed 3,369 persons in Puerto Rico on August 8, 1899, (feast day of Saint Cyriacus) and remains one of the longest duration tropical storms (28 days) to hit the Caribbean or anywhere in the world.

The tradition of naming storms after the Saint of the day officially ended with Hurricane Betsy in 1956, which is still remembered as the 'Hurricane of Santa Clara.' However, years later with the passage of Hurricane Donna in 1960, the storm was recognized as the 'Hurricane of San Lorenzo.' At this time, only the major hurricanes were given names, so most storms, especially the minor storms before 1950 in the North Atlantic, never received any kind of special designation. This is why this hurricane in 1929 was never named but was simply referred to as 'The Great Bahamas Hurricane of 1929.' The word 'Great' simply meant that the hurricane was a powerful storm and that it had sustained winds of 136 mph or greater and a minimum central pressure of 28.00 inches or less.

Later, latitude-longitude positions were used. At first, they listed these storms by the latitude and longitude positions where they were first reported. This was cumbersome, slow, open to errors and confusing. For example, a name like 'Hurricane 12.8°N latitude and 54.7°W longitude' was very difficult to remember, and it would be easy to confuse this storm with another that was seen two months later but almost at the same location. In addition, this posed another significant problem in the 1940s, when meteorologists began airborne studies of tropical cyclones and ships and aircrafts communicated mainly in Morse code. This was fine for the letters of the alphabet, but it was awkward at dealing with numbers because it was slow and caused confusion among its users.

In this region, these early storms were often referred to as gales, severe gales, equinoctial storms, or line storms. The latter two names referred to the time of the year and the location from which these storms were born (referring to the Equatorial line). Gauging the strength and fury of a seventeenth or eighteenth-century storm was quite a difficult task, because at the time these colonists had no means of measuring the wind speeds of a hurricane. Contemporaries recognized a hierarchy of winds ranging from 'a stark calm' to 'a small Gale' to 'a Top-Sail Gale' to 'a fret of wind' and 'a Tempest.' These terms were later replaced by the word 'hurricane', but such terms offered little help in interpreting the power of hurricanes or differentiating lesser strength tropical storms from hurricanes.

Experience has shown that using distinctive names in communications is quicker and less subject to error than the cumbersome latitude-longitude identification methods. The idea was that the names should be short, familiar to users, easy to remember, and that their use would facilitate communications with millions of people of different ethnic races threatened by the storm. This was because a hurricane can last for a week or more and there can be more than one storm at a given time, so weather forecasters starting naming these storms so that there would be absolutely no confusion when talking about a particular storm. Names are easier to use and facilitate better communications among individuals and meteorologists with language barriers within the same geographical region, such as within the Caribbean, Central America and North America.

The first U.S. named hurricane (unofficially named) was Hurricane George, which was the fifth storm in 1947 season. George had top winds of 155 mph as it came ashore around mid-day on September 17th, between Pompano Beach and Delray Beach. The second hurricane unofficially named was Hurricane Bess (named for the outspoken First Lady of the USA, Bess Truman, in 1949). The third storm was nicknamed by the news media 'Hurricane Harry', after the then president of the United States Harry Truman. United States Navy and Air Force meteorologists working in the Pacific Ocean began naming tropical cyclones during World War II, when they often had to track multiple storms. They gave each storm a distinctive name in order to distinguish the cyclones more quickly than listing their positions when issuing warnings.

Towards the end of World War II, two separate United States fleets in the Pacific lacking sufficient weather information about these storms were twice badly damaged when they sailed directly into them, resulting in massive causalities. Three ships were sunk, twenty-one were badly damaged, 146 planes were blown overboard, and 763 men were lost. One of the results that came out of these tragedies was the fact that all U.S. Army and Navy planes were then ordered to start tracking and studying these deadly storms so as to prevent similar disasters like those ones from occurring again. During World War II, this naming practice became widespread in weather map discussions among forecasters, especially Air Force and Navy meteorologists, who plotted the movements of these storms over the wide expanses of the Pacific Ocean.

Using the convention of applying 'she' to inanimate objects such as vehicles, these military meteorologists, beginning in 1945 in the Northwest Pacific, started naming these storms after their wives and girlfriends. However, this practice didn't last too long, for whatever reason, but my guess is that those women rejected or took offense to being named after something that was responsible for so much damage and destruction. Another theory was that this practice was started by a radio operator who sang, "Every little breeze seems to whisper Louise" when issuing a hurricane warning. From that point on, that particular hurricane and future hurricanes were referred to as Louise, and the use of female names for hurricanes became standard practice.

An early example of the use of a woman's name for a storm was in the bestselling pocketbook novel *Storm*, by George R. Stewart, published by Random House in 1941, which has since been made into a major motion picture by Walt Disney, further promoting the idea of naming storms. It involved a young meteorologist working in the San Francisco Weather Bureau Office tracking a storm, which he called 'Maria,' from its birth as a disturbance in the North Pacific to its death over North America many days later. The focus of the book is a storm named Maria, but pronounced 'Ma-Rye-Ah.' Yes, the song in the famous Broadway show 'Paint Your Wagon' named "They Call the Wind Maria" was inspired by this fictional storm. He gave it a name because he said that he could easily say 'Hurricane Maria' rather than 'the low pressure center which at 6pm yesterday was located at latitude seventy-four degrees east and longitude forty-three degrees north', which he considered too long and cumbersome. As Stewart detailed in his novel, "Not since at any price would the Junior Meteorologist have revealed to the Chief that he was bestowing names-and girls' names-upon those great moving low-pressure areas." He unofficially gave the storms in his book women names such as Lucy, Katherine and Ruth, after some girls he knew, because he said that they each had a unique personality. It is not known whether George Stewart was indeed the inspiration for the trend toward naming hurricanes, which came along later in the decade, but it seems likely.[33]

By 1947, tropical cyclones developing in the North Atlantic were named by the United States Army Air Force in private communications between weather centers and aircraft using the phonetic alphabet. This practice continued until September 1950, when the names started to be used publicly after three hurricanes (Baker, Dog, and Easy) had occurred simultaneously and caused confusion within the media and the public. Over the next 2 years, the public use of the phonetic alphabet to name systems continued before at the 1953 Interdepartmental Hurricane Conference it was decided to start using a new list of female names during that season, as a second phonetic alphabet had been developed. During the active but mild 1953 North Atlantic hurricane season,

---

[33] George R. Stewart, (1941) Storm, (USA, University of Nebraska Press, 1941), pgs. 5-31.

the names were readily used in the press, with few objections recorded; as a result, the same names were reused during the next year, with only one change: Gilda for Gail. Over the next 6 years, a new list of names was developed ahead of each season, before in 1960 forecasters developed four alphabetical sets and repeated them every four years. These new sets followed the example of the typhoon names and excluded names beginning with the letters Q, U, X, Y, and Z, and keeping them confined to female names only.

In 1950, military alphabet names (e.g. Able, Baker, Charley, Dog, Easy, Fox etc.) were adopted by the World Meteorological Organization (WMO), and the first named Atlantic hurricane was Able in 1950. The Joint Army/Navy (JAN) phonetic Alphabet was developed in 1941 and was used by all branches of the United States military until the promulgation of the NATO phonetic alphabet in 1956, which replaced it. Before the JAN phonetic alphabet, each branch of the armed forces used its own phonetic alphabet, leading to difficulties in inter-branch communications. This naming method was not very popular and caused a lot of confusion because officials soon realized that this naming convention would cause more problems in the history books if more than one powerful Hurricane Able made landfall and caused extensive damage and death to warrant retirement. This was because hurricanes that have a severe impact on the lives or the economy of a country or region are remembered for generations after the devastation they caused, and some go into weather history, so distinguishing one storm name from another is essential for the history books.

The modern naming convention came about in response to the need for unambiguous radio communications with ships and aircrafts. As air and sea transportation started to increase and meteorological observations improved in number and quality, several typhoons, hurricanes or cyclones might have to be tracked at any given time. To help in their identification, in 1953 the systematic use of only regular women names w used in alphabetical order, and this lasted until 1978. 1953's Alice was the first real human-named storm. At the time, they named them after women because these meteorologists reasoned that people might pay more attention to a storm if they envisioned it as a tangible entity, a character, rather than just a bundle of wind. But the use of only women names eventually was rejected as sexist, and forecasters finally went with both male and female names. Beginning in 1960, four semi-permanent sets of names were established, to be recycled after four years. This list was expanded to ten sets in 1971, but before making it through the list even once these sets were replaced by the now familiar 6 sets of men and women names.

This naming practice started in the Eastern Pacific in 1959, and in 1960 for the remainder of the North Pacific. It is interesting to note that in the Northwest Pacific Basin, the names, by and large, are not personal names. While there are a few men and women names, the majority of the Northwest Pacific tropical cyclone names generally reflect Pacific culture, and the names consists of flowers, animals, birds, trees, or even foods, while some are just descriptive adjectives. In addition, the names are not allotted in alphabetical order but are arranged by the contributing nation, with the countries being alphabetized. For example, the Cambodians have contributed Naki (a flower), Krovanh (a tree) and Damrey (an elephant). China has submitted names such as Yutu (a mythological rabbit), Longwang (the dragon king and god of rain in Chinese mythology), and Dainmu (the mother of lightning and the goddess in charge of thunder). Micronesian typhoon names include Sinlaku (a legendary Kosrae goddess) and Ewiniar (the Chuuk Storm god). Hurricanes in the central Pacific have name lists for only four years and use Hawaiian names.

There were some exceptional hurricanes which became both a hurricane and a typhoon during its lifespan. Hurricane Genevieve, also referred to as Typhoon Genevieve, a notable example was the fourth-most intense tropical cyclone of the North Pacific Ocean in 2014. A long-lasting system, Genevieve was the first one to track across all three northern Pacific basins since Hurricane Jimena in 2003. Genevieve developed from a tropical wave into the eighth tropical storm of the 2014 Pacific hurricane season well east-southeast of Hawaii on July 25. However, increased vertical wind shear caused it to weaken into a tropical depression by the following day and degenerate into a remnant low on July 28. Late on July 29, the system regenerated into a tropical depression, but it weakened into a remnant low again on July 31, owing to vertical wind shear and dry air. The remnants redeveloped into a tropical depression and briefly became a tropical storm south of Hawaii on August 2, yet it weakened back into a tropical depression soon afterwards.

Late on August 5, Genevieve re-intensified into a tropical storm, and intensified into a Category 1 hurricane on the next day when undergoing rapid deepening because of favorable environmental conditions. Early on August 7, Genevieve strengthened into a Category 4 hurricane, shortly before it crossed the International Date Line and was reclassified as a typhoon, also becoming the thirteenth named storm of the 2014 Pacific typhoon season. Late on the same day, Genevieve reached maximum intensity, when it was located west-southwest of Wake Island. The typhoon crossed 30°N at noon on August 10 and weakened to a severe tropical storm soon afterwards, because of unfavorable sea surface temperatures and expanding subsidence. Genevieve weakened into a tropical storm on August 11 and a tropical depression the following day, as its deep convection diminished.

In the North Atlantic Basin in 1979, gender equality finally reached the naming process of hurricanes when thousands of sexism complaints written to the WMO and feminists groups in the USA and worldwide urged the WMO to add men's names; hence, both men and women names were used alternately, and this practice is still in use today. That year would also herald the practice of drawing up a list of names in advance of the hurricane season, and today an alphabetical list of 21 names is used. Hurricane Bob was the first North Atlantic storm named after a man in the 1979 hurricane season; however, it was not retired (it would eventually be retired in the 1991 hurricane season). Hurricane David was the second storm named after a man, and it was the first male storm to be retired in the North Atlantic Region. This was due to the great death toll and substantial damage it inflicted to the countries of Dominica, the Dominican Republic and the Bahamas during the last week of August and the first week of September in 1979.

Since 1979, the naming list now includes names from non-English speaking countries within this region, such as Dutch, French and Spanish names, which also have a large presence here in the Caribbean. This is done to reflect the diversity of the different ethnic languages of the various countries in this region, so the names of Spanish, French, Dutch, and English persons are used in the naming process. The names of storms are now selected by a select committee from member countries of the World Meteorological Organization that falls within that particular region of the world, and we here in the Caribbean come under Region IV for classification purposes. This committee meets once a year after the hurricane season has passed and before the beginning of the new hurricane season to decide on which names to be retired and to replace those names with a new set of names when and where necessary. As of Joaquin of 2015, 80 tropical cyclones have had their names retired in the North Atlantic basin.

The practice of giving different names to storms in different hurricane basins has also led to a few rare circumstances of name-changing storms. For example, in October of 1988, after Atlantic Hurricane Joan devastated Central America, it proceeded to move into the Pacific and became Pacific tropical storm Miriam. Hurricane Joan was a powerful hurricane that caused death and destruction in over a dozen countries in the Caribbean and Central America. Another example was Hurricane Hattie, which was a powerful Category 5 hurricane that pounded Central America on Halloween during the 1961 North Atlantic hurricane season. It caused $370 million in damages and killed around 275 persons. Hattie is the only hurricane on record to have earned three names (Hattie, Simone, Inga) while crossing into different basins twice. Hattie swept across the Caribbean and came ashore in the town of Belize City, British Honduras (now called Belize), on October 31st. It was a strong Category 4 hurricane at landfall, having weakened from a Category 5 hurricane just offshore. After making landfall, its remnants crossed over into the Pacific and attained tropical storm status again under the name Simone. In a remarkable turn of events, after Simone itself made landfall, its remnants crossed back over to the Gulf of Mexico, where the storm became Tropical Storm Inga before dissipating. However, it is debatable whether Inga in fact formed from the remnants of Simone at all.

It is interesting to note here that the letters Q, U, X, Y, and Z are not included in the hurricane list because of the scarcity of names beginning with those letters. However, in other regions of the world, some of these letters are used; for example, only "Q" and "U" are omitted in the Northeastern Pacific Basin. When a storm causes tremendous damage and death, the name is taken out of circulation and retired for reasons of sensitivity. It is then replaced with a name of the same letter and of the same gender, and if possible, the same language as the name being retired (e.g. neither Hurricane Irene in 2011 nor Hurricane Katrina in 2005 will ever be used again). The list includes one tropical storm, Allison of 2001, which caused billions in damage from its heavy rains.

The name used the most, at least with the same spelling, is Arlene (seven times), while Frances and Florence have been used seven and six times, respectively. However, considering different spellings of the same name, Debbie/Debby has been used seven times, and Anna/Ana has been used eight times. The first name to be called into use five times was Edith, but that name hasn't been used since 1971. After the 1996 season, Lilly has the distinction of being the first 'L' name to be used three times, while Marco is the first 'M' name to be used more than once. The name Kendra was assigned to a system in the 1966 hurricane season, but in post-season analysis it was decided it had not been a bona fide tropical storm. This storm marked the birth of reclassification of storms in the post-hurricane season (Hurricane Andrew was a storm that was reclassified from a Category 4 hurricane to a Category 5 hurricane in the off-season).

In only five years (2005, 1995, 2010, 2011,2012) have names beginning with the letter 'O' and beyond been used, but there have been several other years in which more than 14 storms have been tracked, such as: 1887-19 storms, 1933-21 storms, 1936-16 storms, 1969-18 storms, 1995-19 storms, 2005-28 storms, 2010-19 storms, 2011-19 storms and 2012-19 storms. The 2010 Atlantic hurricane season has been extremely active, being the most active season since 2005. It must be noted that the 2010, 2011 and 2012 seasons tie the record with the 1995 North Atlantic hurricane season and the 1887 North Atlantic hurricane season for the third most named storms (19). Furthermore, 2010 also ties the record with the 1969 North Atlantic hurricane season and 1887 for the second most hurricanes (12). The 2012 Atlantic hurricane season was the third most active season, tied with 1887, 1995, 2010, and 2011. It was an above average season in which 19 tropical cyclones formed. All nineteen depressions attained tropical storm status, and ten of these became hurricanes. Two hurricanes further intensified into major hurricanes. The first three of these years were well before the naming of storms began, but 1969 requires an explanation. This was early in the era of complete satellite coverage, and forecasters were still studying the evolution of non-tropical systems (sub-tropical) into warm-core, tropical-type storms. Several systems that year were not named as tropical because they began at higher latitudes and were initially cold-cored.

Formal classification of subtropical (hybrid type) cyclones and public advisories on them began in 1972, and a few years later a review was made of various types of satellite images from the late 60s and early 70s, and several of these systems were included as tropical storms. In fact, two of the storms added in 1969 were hurricanes, so 1969 now stands as having 12 hurricanes. Today, subtropical storms are named using the same list as tropical storms and hurricanes. This makes sense because subtropical cyclones often take on tropical characteristics. Imagine how confusing it would be if the system got a new name just because it underwent internal changes. There is no subtropical classification equivalent to a hurricane. The assumption is that once a storm got that strong, it would have acquired tropical characteristics and therefore be called a hurricane, or it would have merged with an extratropical system in the North Atlantic and lost its name altogether. For example, on October 24, 1979, a subtropical storm briefly reached hurricane strength as it neared Newfoundland, Canada. It quickly combined with another low-pressure system, but it was never named.

Whenever a hurricane has had a major impact, any country affected by the storm can request that the name of the hurricane be 'retired' by agreement of the World Meteorological Organization (WMO). Prior to 1969, officially, retiring a storm name actually meant that it cannot could not be reused for at least 10 ten years, to facilitate historic references, legal actions, insurance claim activities, etc.and so forth and to avoid public confusion with another storm of the same name. But today these storms are retired indefinitely, and if that happens, it is replaced with a storm's name with the same gender because the retired storm often becomes a household name in the region or countries it affected. The practice of retiring significant names was started in 1955 by the United States Weather Bureau, after hurricanes Carol, Edna, and Hazel struck the Northeastern United States and caused a significant amount of damage in the previous year. In 1977, the United States National Oceanic and Atmospheric Administration passed control of the naming lists to the WMO Region IV Hurricane Committee, who decided that they would retire names at their annual session when required. Since the formal start of naming during the 1947 North Atlantic hurricane season, an average of one storm name has been retired each season, though many seasons (most recently 2009) have had no storm names retired. The most recent tropical cyclone to have its name retired was Hurricane Joaquin, which caused severe flooding in the Bahamas in 2015.

When that list of names is exhausted, the Greek Alphabet (Alpha, Beta, Gamma, Delta, Epsilon, Zeta, Eta, Theta, Iota, Kappa and Lambda) is used. It must be noted that so far this list has only been used once in either the Pacific or the North Atlantic Basins, which was in the North Atlantic hurricane season of 2005. It is important to note here that there were a few subtropical storms that used the Greek Alphabet in the 1970s, but they were really not truly tropical in nature. There was Subtropical Storm Alpha of 1972, which was a pre-season storm that made landfall in Georgia, and then there was Subtropical Storm Alfa in 1973, which briefly threatened Cape Cod but stayed out to sea. The 22nd named storm of a particular year when the naming list is exhausted would be Tropical Storm Alpha. Additional storms, if needed, would be named Beta, Gamma, Delta, and so on.

Several extremely rare weather events occurred in the 2005 North Atlantic hurricane season. First was the fact that Tropical Storm Alpha formed, which was moderately strong tropical storm that made landfall in the Dominican Republic killing nine persons and then over Haiti, killing 17 persons before being absorbed by Hurricane Wilma's large circulation. This was notable because it was the first tropical storm to be named with the Greek Alphabet in the North Atlantic basin after the list of hurricane names was exhausted. Second, at the time it was thought that Alpha was the twenty-second storm of the season, and so was the storm which broke the 1933 season's record for most storms in a single season. However, in post-hurricane season analysis it was revealed that there was also a previously unnoticed subtropical storm, on October 4, which made Alpha the twenty-third storm of the season.

Finally, the WMO Region IV Hurricane Committee (the governing body for hurricanes of the North Atlantic) after the 2005 North Atlantic season faced a serious dilemma, similar to that of the early 1950s with the naming of a storm after the military alphabet. Alpha caused significant damage and deaths over Haiti and the Dominican Republic that warranted this storm name to be retired, but just like the early 1950s, they realized that this storm would cause confusion in the record books if the primary list is once again exhausted and another tropical storm or hurricane named Alpha forms. So this committee decided to retire the name 'Alpha of 2005' rather than just the Greek Alphabet 'Alpha' so that should this situation occur again, the name 'Alpha' can be reused again.

A majority of the costliest Atlantic hurricanes in recorded history have peaked as major hurricanes. However, weaker tropical cyclones can still cause widespread damage. Both tropical storms Allison in 2001 and Matthew in 2010 have caused in total over several billion dollars in damage the former of which accounted for a higher damage total. Due to their excessive damage, the names of tropical cyclones accruing over $1 billion in damage are often retired by the World Meteorological Organization. However, this is not always the case. Hurricane Juan in 1985 was the first hurricane to cause over a billion dollars in damage and not be retired; its name was retired on a later usage in 2003 that did not cause over a billion in damage. Since Juan, five tropical cyclones that caused over a billion in damage were not retired, the most recent of which being Hurricane Isaac in 2012.

The first hurricane to cause over $1 billion in damage was Hurricane Betsy in 1965, which caused much of its damage in southeastern Louisiana. Four years later, Hurricane Camille slightly exceeded Betsy's damage total after affecting similar regions, becoming the second tropical cyclone to cause as much damage. After the 1960s, each decade saw an increase in tropical cyclones causing at least a billion in damage over the last, due to increasing urban development and population located on or near the vulnerable hurricane prone coastlines. In the 1970s, four hurricanes caused over a billion in damage; the costliest of which was Hurricane Frederic, which caused $2.3 billion in damage, particularly in the southeastern United States. The following decade featured seven hurricanes causing in excess of a billion in damage. In the 1990s, nine tropical cyclones accrued more than a billion in damage. Seventeen tropical cyclones in the 2000s caused in excess of $1 billion in damage. Both the 2004 and 2005 seasons had five billion-dollar hurricanes apiece, the most of any season on record. Hurricane Ivan caused at least a billion dollars in damage in three separate countries. Thus far in the 2010s, seven tropical cyclones have amounted to over $1 billion in damage, including the recent Hurricane Matthew in 2016 which up to press time of this book amounted to $8.1 billion in the countries impacted by this Category 5 hurricane.

If a storm forms in the off-season, it will take the next name on the list based on the current calendar date. For example, if a tropical cyclone formed on December 29th, it would take the name from the previous season's list of names. If a storm formed in February, it would be named from the subsequent season's list of names. Theoretically, a hurricane or tropical storm of any strength can have its name retired; retirement is based entirely on the level of damage and deaths caused by a storm. However, up until 1972 (Hurricane Agnes), there was no Category 1 hurricane that had its name retired, and no named tropical storm had its name retired until 2001 (Tropical Storm Allison). Allison is one of only three tropical storms to have their names retired without ever having reached hurricane strength. This is at least partially due to the fact that weaker storms tend to cause less damage, and the few weak storms that have had their names retired caused most of their destruction through heavy rainfall rather than winds.

While no requests for retirement have ever been turned down, some storms such as Hurricane Gordon in 1994 caused a great deal of death and destruction but it was still not retired, as the main country which was affected, Haiti did not request retirement. Hurricane Gordon in 1994 killed 1,122 persons in Haiti, and 23 deaths in other nations. Damage in the United States was estimated at $400 million, and damages in Haiti and Cuba were severe. Despite the tremendous damage caused, the name 'Gordon' was not retired and was reused in both the 2000 and 2006 North Atlantic hurricane seasons. Since 1950, 77 storms have had their names retired. Of these, two (Carol and Edna) were reused after the storm for which they were retired but were later retroactively retired, and two others (Hilda and Janet) were included on later lists of storm names but were not reused before being retroactively retired. Before 1979, when the first permanent six-year storm names list began, some storm names were simply not used anymore. For example, in 1966, 'Fern' was substituted for 'Frieda,' and no reason was cited.

In the North Atlantic basin, in most cases, a tropical cyclone retains its name throughout its life. However, a tropical cyclone may be renamed in several situations. First, when a tropical storm crosses from the Atlantic into the Pacific, or vice versa, before 2001 it was the policy of National Hurricane Center (NHC) to rename a tropical storm that crossed from the Atlantic into the Pacific, or vice versa. Examples included Hurricane Cesar-Douglas in 1996 and Hurricane Joan-Miriam in 1988. In 2001, when Iris moved across Central America, NHC mentioned that Iris would retain its name if it regenerated in the Pacific. However, the Pacific tropical depression developed from the remnants of Iris was called Fifteen-E instead. The depression later became Tropical Storm Manuel. NHC explained that Iris had dissipated as a tropical cyclone prior to entering the eastern North Pacific basin; the new depression was properly named Fifteen-E, rather than Iris. In 2003, when Larry was about to move across Mexico, NHC attempted to provide greater clarity: "Should Larry remain a tropical cyclone during its passage over Mexico into the Pacific, it would retain its name. However, a new name would be given if the surface circulation dissipates and then regenerates in the Pacific."[34] Up to now, it is extremely rare for a tropical cyclone to retain its name during the passage from the Atlantic to the Pacific, or vice versa.

Second, storms are renamed in situations where there are uncertainties of the continuation of storms. When the remnants of a tropical cyclone redevelop, the redeveloping system will be treated as a new tropical cyclone if there are uncertainties of the continuation, even though the original system may contribute to the forming of the new system. One example is the remnants of Tropical Depression #10 reforming into Tropical Depression #12 from the 2005 season, which went on to become the powerful and deadly Hurricane Katrina. Another example was a storm that had the most names, as stated earlier; in 1961, there was one tropical storm that had three lives and three names. Tropical Storm Hattie developed off the Caribbean Coast of Nicaragua on October 28, 1961, and drifted north and west before crossing Central America at Guatemala. It re-emerged into the Pacific Ocean on November 1st and was re-christened Simone. Two days later, it recurved back towards the coastline of Central America and crossed over into the Atlantic via Mexico, re-emerging into the Gulf of Mexico as Inga.

---

34 *www.nhc.noaa.gov/archice/2003/dis/al172003.discuss.016.shtml.* Retrieved: 11-12-2012.

CHAPTER THREE

The anatomy of a hurricane

A cross-sectional view into a hurricane

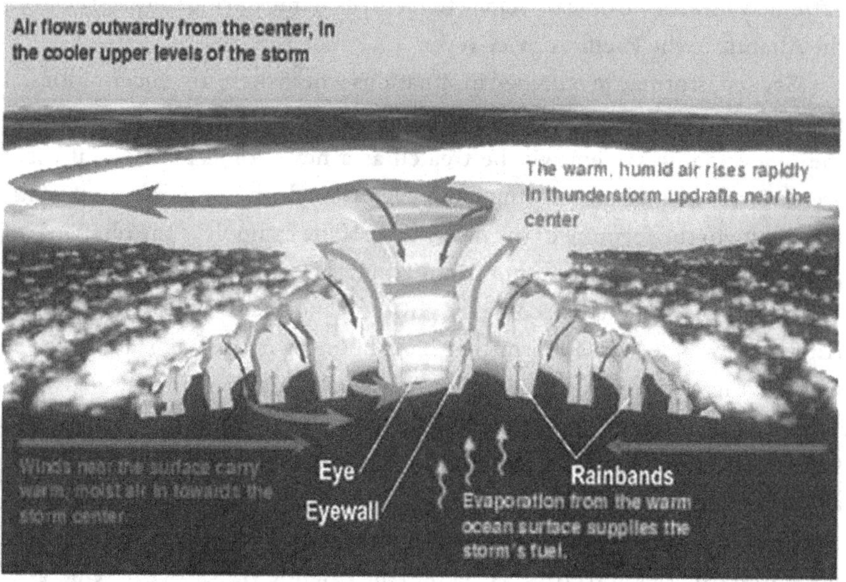

(Courtesy of The Comet Program)

A tropical cyclone is a powerful storm system characterized by a low pressure center and numerous severe thunderstorms that produce strong winds and flooding rainfall. A tropical cyclone feeds on the heat released (latent heat) when moist air rises and the water vapor it contains condenses. They are fueled by a different heat mechanism than other cyclonic windstorms, such as nor'easters, European windstorms, and polar lows, leading to their classification as "warm core" storm systems. A fully developed hurricane is a vast heat engine. It has the power of 400 of the largest nuclear bombs, and enough energy to match the United States' electricity consumption for six months. The power comes from clusters of thunderstorms held together by winds into huge rings hundreds of miles across within the tropics. The term 'tropical' simply refers to both the geographic origin of these systems, which forms almost exclusively in tropical regions of the Earth, and their formation in maritime tropical air masses.

A hurricane consists of a mass of organized thunderstorms that spiral in towards the extreme low pressure of the storm's eye or center. The most intense thunderstorms will have the heaviest rainfall, and the highest winds occurring outside the eye, in the region known as the eyewall. In the eye itself, the air is warm, winds are light, and skies are generally clear and rain-free but can also be cloudy to overcast. When a hurricane reaches land, it begins to run out of energy. Yet it is here that it causes the most destruction. Long before the main storm arrives, coasts are battered by huge waves stirred up by the winds. Winds circulates anti-clockwise, and so these waves are largest on the right side of the hurricane at the front—the right front quadrant.

A hurricane is a rotating, organized system of clouds and thunderstorms that originates over tropical or subtropical waters and has a closed low-level circulation. Hurricanes forming between 5 and 30 degrees' north latitude typically move towards the west. Sometimes the winds in the middle and upper levels of the atmosphere change and steer the hurricane towards the north and northwest. When hurricanes reach latitudes near 30 degrees north, they often move northeast. The official hurricane season for the Atlantic Basin (the Atlantic Ocean, the Caribbean Sea, and the Gulf of Mexico) is from 1 June to 30 November. The peak of the season is from mid-August to late October. Captain George Nares, a nineteenth century Scottish naval officer and polar explorer, was always on the lookout for hurricanes. "June-too soon," he wrote. "July-stand by; August-look out you must; September-remember; October-all over." Whatever you think about the dynamics of hurricanes-two things can be said about them, and that is they are very unpredictable and extremely destructive.

Hurricanes evolve and decay from weather anomalies through defined stages. Tropical storms are loosely defined as a warm-core system, non-frontal, low pressure large weather system with a well-defined counter clockwise wind rotation that form over tropical or subtropical waters. This distinguishes them from thunderstorms and tornadoes. No one should ignore the potential for damage, loss of life and instability of a hurricane; however, if not ignored there is sufficient warning to casually pack and fly to another continent if so declined. Hurricanes are the same weather systems as typhoons in the Pacific and cyclones in the Indian Ocean. If north of the equator they spin in the counter clockwise direction. The direction of spin is due to the earth's rotation called the "Coriolis effect"(it was initially called the 'Coriolis force' but that has been changed to the 'Coriolis effect' because no 'force' is involved) named after Gaspard-Gustave Coriolis, a French physicist. Air and water, if flowing in a vertical direction like in a sink, a whirlpool or twister acts like kind of an axis of the Earth and rotates around it.

The amount of deflection depends on the air's speed and its location of latitude. It is almost zero in slow moving air and increases to the square of the speed. As to the deflection in respect to latitude, it is zero at the equator and maximum at the Earth's poles. This is a very simplification of the spiraling winds as the many other 'forces' such as friction with the Earth's features, radiation, condensation and evaporation. The warm, moist air cools releasing moisture as it rises into the cooler upper atmosphere. This air column is the eye wall; however, some moisture falls (descending air) to the inside creating a clear area or eye. The tightness or how compact the columns are situated will be depended on the surface resistance or tension and many other forces. This causes an "eye" to appear when conditions are correct if viewed from above. Generally, the smoother the surface and stronger the forces, the more distinct the eye will be.

Hurricanes, tornadoes, whirlpools, etc., are vertical spiraling circular or elliptical columns. The outer winds can be distorted from a circle by an uneven surface area, as when part of the hurricane is over land and the other over water, or from the side or shear pressures of upper level air. A term often heard relating to tropical storm and hurricane development is vertical shear. In the case of a hurricane, strong upper level wind currents at or near the center of the hurricane or the potential hurricane will shear or cut off the tops, thus preventing a "chimney" for vertical convection.

The direction of movement will be the total of all the forces applied. The space above the Earth's surface is full of high and low pressure areas, with huge rivers of wind being attracted, pushed and deflected by each other. It is a three-dimensional space with many pressure areas in multiple vertical and horizontal layers. These are in a constant state of change vertically and horizontally, shifting, turning, building, decaying, etc. These are the steering and shaping forces for the huge storm system, which is itself a complex and multifaceted pressure area called a storm, hurricane or whatever. To make the process even more complex, winds of all the low pressures areas spin in the counter clockwise direction, and winds of the high pressure area spin in the clockwise direction. The jet streams and wind rivers twist and turn, rise and lower through the pressure mazes.

Wind is air movement between areas of two different atmospheric pressures and flows from the high pressure to the low pressure. These pressures are generally measured in "inches of mercury"; however, the meteorologists prefer to use "millibars", which is used internationally. One millibar (mbar) equals 0.02953 inch; however, 0.03 will be close enough for general use. At sea level, normal pressure is 29.29 inches of mercury or 1013 mbar. When the center pressure decreases, there is a finite time delay for the winds to increase throughout the hurricane. The eye is not necessarily cylindrical, as it may be elongated by many forces; i.e., as it may be wider at the top in stronger hurricanes and is called the "stadium effect."

In the eye, or chimney, the pressure drops rapidly and the temperature rises at even a steeper rate. That is the chimney or eye of the hurricane. The low pressure chimney pulls in warm, moist air from hundreds of miles around the hurricane to fuel the hurricane. The warm moist air is carried thousands of feet up the chimney, where it is released in cold, dry air to form clouds of moisture. Round and round, and up and down the transfer of energy perpetuates the heat engine or the cyclone generator. A visible eye usually forms when winds reach about 74 mph. Most people are familiar with a whirlwind, but the huge size of a hurricane disguises the whirling appearance, except when viewed from above.

Generally, the first phase of a potential hurricane referred to as "tropical disturbance." It will have no to very little organization at this time. It will still not have much organization when referred to as a "tropical wave", which looks as a "wave" on the weather charts. It will catch the eyes of forecasters if the wave becomes well-defined. If conditions are favorable, the "wave" will strengthen even more, coupled with other factors, and may result in circular component. If the winds strengthen to 39 mph (34 kts), it is defined and reported as a tropical depression and it is referred to as a tropical storm when wind speeds range from 49 mph to 74 mph. Not all waves become tropical depressions and simply drift or disappear in the river of wind called the trade winds.

In some months, these will be coming off the coast of Africa in what is called the "tropical convergence zone" and drift slowly towards the Caribbean, the Bahamas and North and Central America. In June and October, many form in the western Caribbean and are steered northward towards Florida. In reality, the atmosphere is a dynamic spatial mass of varying pressure cells and rivers of air currents of varying moisture content and varying stability. In most instances, the earlier and later hurricanes tend to be shorter in duration - June and November 8 days, and August and September 12. However, deadly hurricanes can occur anytime in the hurricane season. They are classified as follows:

- **Tropical Disturbance**: The birth of a hurricane, having only a slight circulation or perturbation in the easterlies with no closed isobars around an area of low pressure. Tropical disturbances commonly exist in the tropical trade winds at any one time and are often accompanied by clouds and precipitation.
- **Tropical Depression:** A tropical cyclone with maximum sustained winds of 38 mph (33 knots) or less. If sustained winds increase to at least 20 knots, a disturbance is upgraded to a tropical depression. Surface wind speeds vary between 20 and 34 knots, and a tropical depression has at least one closed isobar that accompanies a drop in pressure in the center of the storm.
- **Tropical Storm:** A tropical cyclone with maximum sustained winds of 39 to 73 mph (34 to 63 knots), a tropical depression is upgraded to a tropical storm and the storm becomes more organized. Tropical storms resemble the appearance of hurricanes due to the intensified circulation.
- **Hurricane:** As surface pressures continue to drop, a tropical storm becomes a hurricane and it has maximum sustained winds of 74 mph (64 knots) or higher. A pronounced rotation develops around the central core as spiral rain bands rotate around the eye of the storm. The heaviest precipitation and strongest winds are associated with the eye wall. In the western North Pacific, hurricanes are called typhoons; similar storms in the Indian Ocean and South Pacific Ocean are called cyclones.
- **Major Hurricane:** A tropical cyclone with maximum sustained winds of 111 mph (96 knots) or higher, corresponding to a Category 3, 4 or 5 on the Saffir-Simpson Hurricane Wind Scale.

The nature of hurricanes varies with their age, size and position, but the following features generally characterize most fully developed hurricanes:

- They are tropical, meaning that they are generated in tropical areas of the ocean near the equator.

- They are cyclonic, meaning that their winds swirl around a central eye. Wind direction is counterclockwise (west to east) in the northern hemisphere and clockwise (east to west) in the southern hemisphere.
- They are low-pressure systems. The eye of a hurricane is always a low-pressure area. The lowest barometric pressures ever recorded have occurred inside hurricanes.
- The winds swirling around the center of the storm have a sustained speed of at least 74 mph.

Size:

In the Caribbean, the average diameter of a well-developed hurricane is between 100 to 500 miles, but some have reached diameters of 800 miles. The diameter of the eye, or calm center, of a well-developed hurricane is on average between 10 to 20 miles across. The size of a typical tropical cyclone can vary considerably, depending on the extent of the wind fields and rain fields.

Speed:

Hurricanes generally move at speeds of less than 15 miles per hour. In The Atlantic, the average hurricane moves about 3,000 miles in its average nine-day life. However, some hurricanes last three weeks and travel 10,000 miles. For example, tropical Storm Ginger in 1971 spun around the open ocean for 28 days in the Atlantic.

Winds:

The fierce winds which blow in an anti-clockwise direction around the center of the central calm in the northern hemisphere may reach 100 to 200 mph. Wind speeds are the greatest near the surface around the central calm, or eye. The force of the wind can quickly decimate the tree population, down power lines and utility poles, knock over signs, and may be strong enough to destroy some homes and buildings. Flying debris can also cause damage, and in cases where people are caught outdoors, injuries and death can prevail. When a hurricane first makes landfall, it is common for tornadoes to form which can cause severe localized wind damage. In most cases, however, wind is a secondary cause of damage. Storm surge is normally the primary cause. The right front quadrant is strongest side of the hurricane, this is the area where there is positive convergence, in this quadrant the winds are typically the strongest, the storm surge is highest, and the possibility of tornadoes is the greatest. The right side of a hurricane is the strongest side because the wind speed and the hurricane speed-of-motion are complimentary there; meaning on this side the wind blows in the same direction as the storm's forward motion. On the left side, the hurricane's speed of motion subtracts from the wind speed.

The Mean Sea Level Atmospheric Pressure:

In the tropics this varies by only about 0.3%, but during the passage of the central low pressure of a hurricane, it may fall by 5% or 10% below the average of 29.2 inches or 989 mbar.

Clouds:

The solid cumulonimbus or rain clouds, which surround the core, which makes up the main part of the hurricane, may extend for a radius of 100 miles around the eye and reach heights of 40,000 to 50,000 feet. Within the eye, the sky is generally clear and rain-free.

Rainfall:

The torrential rains that normally accompany a hurricane can cause serious flooding. Whereas the storm surge and high winds are concentrated near the eye, the rain may extend for hundreds of miles and may last for several days, affecting areas well after the hurricane has diminished. An average of 10 to 15 inches of rain falls over coastal areas during the passage of a well-developed hurricane, but over 20 inches have been recorded, and rain may fall at the rate of one inch an hour. In twenty-four hours, a record of 29.6 inches fell at Adjuntas in Puerto Rico in 1928, and that is a record that still stands even to this day. Furthermore, Hurricane Camille during a six-hour period dumped over 760 millimeters (30 inches) of rainfall over central Virginia, drowning 109 persons in the process with flash flooding.

Sea:

Violent hurricane winds may produce storm surges of up to 45 feet high at sea, and storm surges of over twenty feet may crash against shores at speeds of up to 40 mph. A long swell may move outwards from the eye of hurricanes for more than 1,000 miles. These long swells are often the first visible signs of an approaching hurricane and are known as the 'storm surge.'

Eye:

An area at the center of the hurricane of clear skies that can also have scattered to broken to even overcast clouds. Within the eye, the winds are light, the surface pressure is very low and there is almost no rain, and it can have a diameter of 20 to 40 miles across. The eye is the warmest part of the hurricane and has the lowest pressure reading.

Eyewall:

Adjacent to the eye is the eyewall, a ring or wall of intense thunderstorms that whirl around the storm's center and extend upward to almost 15 km above sea level. Within the eyewall, we find the heaviest rainfall and the strongest winds. This is the most dangerous part of the hurricane, and the winds in this area may blow over 157mph, gusting up to 225mph in severe storms. The winds spiral in a counterclockwise direction into the storm's low-pressure center. The eye is the calmest part of the storm because the strong surface winds converging towards the center never actually reach the exact center of the storm, but instead form a cylinder of relatively calm air.

Spiral Bands:

Long bands of rain clouds that appear to spiral inward to the eyewall, these are called spiral rain bands or feeder bands and can be hundreds of miles across. Surface winds increase in speed as they blow counterclockwise and inward toward the center. These bands become more pronounced as the storm intensifies and are fed by the warm oceans.

The Height:

A hurricane may be as much as 9 miles (15km) high. This is equal to almost twice the height of Mount Everest, the highest mountain on Earth.

Storm Surge:

A storm surge, also called a hurricane surge, is the abnormal rise in sea level accompanying a tropical cyclone. The height of the storm surge is the difference between the observed level of sea surface and its level in the absence of the storm. The storm surge is estimated by subtracting the normal or astronomical tide from the observed or estimated storm tide. The greatest danger to life from an approaching hurricane is the storm surge. Hurricanes have a vacuum effect on the ocean. The water is pulled toward the hurricane, causing it to 'pile up' like a small mountain. A mound of water forms under the center of a hurricane as the intensely low pressure draws water up. Over the ocean, this mound of water is barely noticeable, but builds up as the storm approaches land. The surge's height as it reaches land depends upon the slope of the ocean floor at the coast. The more gradual the slope, the less volume of sea there is in which the surge can dissipate, and further inland the water is displaced. This dome of water can be up to 40 to 60 miles long as it moves onto the shoreline near the landfall point of the eye. A cubic yard of sea water weighs approximately 1,700 pounds, and this water is constantly slamming into shoreline structures, even well-built structures get quickly demolished. Storm surge is responsible for over 75% of the entire hurricane related deaths and injuries.

Tropical Waves:

A migratory wave-like disturbance in the tropical easterlies. Tropical waves occasionally intensify into tropical cyclones. They are also called Easterly Waves.

Tropical Disturbance:

A discrete tropical weather system of apparently organized convection - generally 100 to 300 miles in diameter - originating in the tropics or subtropics, having a non-frontal migratory character, and maintaining its identity for 24 hours or more. Disturbances associated with perturbations in the wind field and progressing through the tropics from east to west are also known as easterly or tropical waves.

Tropical Depression:

An organized system of clouds and thunderstorms with a well-defined circulation and maximum sustained winds of 20 to 33 knots.

Tropical storm:

An organized system of strong thunderstorms with a well-defined circulation and maximum sustained winds of 34 to 63 knots. At this point, the storm is given a name.

Hurricane:

This the term used in North America and the Caribbean to describe a severe tropical cyclone with a well-defined circulation and having winds in excess of 64 knots (74mph) and capable of producing widespread wind damage and heavy flooding; Beaufort scale numbers 12 through 17.

Hurricane season:

The part of the year having a relatively high incidence of hurricanes. The hurricane season in the North Atlantic runs from June 1 to November 30.

Hurricane Warning:

A warning is given when it is likely that a hurricane will strike an area within 36 hours. At this point, residents should have completed the necessary preparations for the storm.

Hurricane Watch:

A hurricane watch indicates that a hurricane poses a threat to an area within 48 hours and residents of the area should be prepared.

All Clear:

All Clear simply means that the hurricane or tropical storm has left the affected area and all the Alerts, Warnings, and Watches are lifted, but the residents in that area should exercise extreme caution for downed power lines, debris, fallen trees, flooding etc.

Other Hurricane Effects:

Tornadoes:

Tornadoes may form especially in the spiral rain bands of a hurricane as it moves onshore. The changing wind speeds with height act like a huge twisting mechanism, thus allowing the possibility of tornado formation.

Flooding Rainfall:

Rainfall is a very real threat from a land falling hurricane. Hurricane Andrew and Floyd caused tremendous flooding across many Bahamian Islands after they made landfall. This is especially true if the hurricane stalls over a region, raining itself out. For example, during the passage of Hurricane David over the Bahamas in 1979, Crooked Island reported a whopping total of 13.04 inches during this storm, while other islands reported similar amounts.

Damaging Winds:

Damaging winds will accompany any hurricane, no matter what category it is. A hurricane by definition has winds of at least 74 miles per hour. This wind speed alone is enough to cause damage to poorly constructed signage and knock over some trees and other vegetation. Obviously, the stronger the hurricane (higher winds), the more potential there is for wind damage to exist.

Lightning and Hail:

Lightning and hail are less frequent occurrences during hurricanes than other severe weather events like thunderstorms. Lightning is more frequent during a typical afternoon thunderstorm because there are more factors present that promote lightning development. The same reason generally holds true concerning hail during a hurricane. There will be some lightning during a hurricane, but some of the 'flashes' will actually be electric transformers exploding or power lines sparking sending an eerie glow in the sky.

CHAPTER FOUR

The impact of the major hurricanes on the Caribbean, North and Central America during the early to late colonial era and how they impacted the history of the region.

People didn't appreciate the politeness of hurricanes until scientists developed the technology to monitor and track them. Until recently, there were no enhanced satellite images, no planes to fly into the hurricane's eye and no weather radars to monitor their intensity. The Taíno Indians described the hurricane's warning signs to Christopher Columbus, and he listened to them and on at least one occasion this knowledge saved Columbus' fleet from a watery grave. West Indies residents eventually came to know that hurricanes were likely to strike during August and September. They would watch closely for the signs: a hazy sun, a light drizzle, an upswing of the winds, rising sea levels, and some even watched the erratic inland flight of the magnificent frigate bird, known on some islands as the hurricane bird. But the telltale signs didn't always appear to tell their story.

Estimating the strength and the fury of an early colonial era storm was very difficult because colonists had no means of measuring wind speed. Contemporaries recognized a hierarchy of winds, starting with 'a stark calm' to 'a small gale' to 'a top-sail gale' to 'a fret of wind' and 'a tempest'—later replaced by the word "hurricane"—but such terms are very subjective and varied from island to island or from one storm to the next and offer very little help in interpreting the power of hurricanes or differentiating lesser tropical storms from hurricanes. Furthermore, increased development of the built environment over time meant that the potential for damage, even from minor storms, increased as well, making damage estimates a questionable foundation for judging the power of storms.

Hurricanes are annual, seasonal threats in the North Atlantic region. Most storms develop in the eastern Atlantic Ocean off the West African Coast and are known as Cape Verde type hurricanes, although some arise within the Gulf of Mexico, the Bahamas or the Caribbean Basin itself as you will s later. In most of these cases, the storms originate in the region where the northeasterly and southeasterly trade winds converge, generally between 5 and 20 degrees north of the equator. Each year, hundreds of tropical depressions spin up over warm waters worldwide. But more is needed for a depression to grow into one of Earth's most powerful and menacing storms. Besides the warm ocean temperatures, the depression needs lots of warm, moist air to feed on and light winds in the upper atmosphere or in other words, weak vertical wind shear. These high level winds also matter and is a critical factor in determining whether the storm will grow or dissipate. Strong differences in wind direction and strength at different heights in the atmosphere, known as wind shear, can pull a tropical system apart, dissipating its energy. On the other hand, high wind shear plays a key role in tornado formation, including tornadoes that form over land as a hurricane dissipates.

The wind speed of hurricanes ranges from 74 miles per hour, the minimum speed separating hurricanes from tropical storms, to in excess of 157 miles per hour, the base for today's definition of a Category 5 storm on the Saffir-Simpson Hurricane Wind Scale. In addition to pounding winds and driving rains, the most dangerous element of hurricanes is often the storm surge, floodwaters that can exceed twenty feet in height. In most years, on average roughly twelve tropical storms develop in the region, about six of which become hurricanes and three major hurricanes, but the number can vary considerably from one or two to more than twenty.

Hurricanes sometimes move up the eastern seaboard of the United States and strike the mid-Atlantic and New England states, or a westward movement into the Caribbean and then over Central America of the United States. They are most common and most destructive, however, among the islands of the Caribbean Basin and the low-lying coastal areas of the South Atlantic coast of North America and along the Gulf of Mexico. Although individual locations can go for years, even sometimes decades, between major storms, it is a rare year that some part of the Greater Caribbean is not hit, and several hurricanes can strike within a short period. Jamaica, for example, endured five hurricanes in seven years in the early 1780s. South Carolina experienced two major storms within two weeks in September 1752. In the 1933 hurricane season, 21 storms developed in the North Atlantic, and that was only recently surpassed in the record breaking 2005 hurricane season, which saw a record 27 named storms and one unnamed storm during that year.

Hurricanes were an entirely new phenomenon for colonists in the seventeenth century. Although Western Europe occasionally experienced storms of great intensity, such events did not compare to the frequency or ferocity with which hurricanes struck the Caribbean, the Bahamas, Central and North America. These storms quickly became a defining character or the element of life in the region, and shared risks from them linked the early U.S. colony of South Carolina and the West Indies into a well-defined hurricane zone in the eyes of contemporaries. Early colonist Edmund Burke during this era, for example, wrote that Carolina "is the only one of our colonies upon the continent which is subject to hurricanes." The great naturalist Mark Catesby likewise stated that South Carolina represented the edge of the hurricane zone. Hurricanes ended in Carolina, according to Catesby, with "Virginia not having often much of it."[35]

Colonists got their first taste of the power of the storms nine months after establishing a permanent settlement on St. Christopher (St. Kitts) in early 1624. These initial settlers erected a small fort and a few rudimentary dwellings and planted some tobacco and provision crops, but "upon the nineteenth of September came a 'Hericano' and blew it away." The relative lack of physical development limited the economic damage from hurricanes in the early years of settlement. Finding adequate provisions and shelter concerned early colonists on St. Christopher far more than calculating the value of their lost tobacco, and the same was true for other colonists in the early decades of settlement.[36] The devastation from hurricanes meant food, clean water, adequate shelter were often in short supply for weeks, sometimes months, resulting in difficult conditions. Following two hurricanes in 1681, one St. Christopher planter noted that the storms had occasioned a "sickly and scarce time" on the island. Colonists who survived the 1722 hurricane in Jamaica were "reduced to great extremity for want of water, provisions, and other necessaries." Such shortages and the lack of adequate shelter made the island "very sickly" and claimed

---

35 Matthew Mulcahy, Hurricanes and Society in the British Greater Caribbean, 1624-1783, (Baltimore, The Johns Hopkins University Press, 2006), pg. 19.

36 Ibid, pg. 10.

numerous lives. One Jamaica planter noted that water following the 1780 storm "stinks horribly & tastes very nauseous."[37]

That changed with the emergence of sugar and rice plantations in the mid-seventeenth century (sugar) and early eighteenth century (rice). Sugar plantations represented large and complex economic enterprises by the standards of the day. In addition to the fields and labor needed to grow the sugar cane crop, producing sugar itself required mills, boiling houses, curing houses, trash houses, storehouses, and distilleries to crush the canes, transform the liquid into sugar or rum and prepare it for shipment to markets in Europe or North America. At the end of the seventeenth century, Sir Dalby Thomas estimated the cost of establishing a one hundred-acre plantation at £5,625: £1,250 for fifty slaves and almost £4,000 for "Land, Houses, Mills, Vessels &c., All other Tools and Implements." Edward Long estimated the capital value of a three-hundred-acre Jamaica plantation in the 1770s at £10,017: land and crops were valued at £2,970 sterling, one hundred slaves at £3,570, the sugar works and equipment at £2,463, and sixty cattle at £1,014. These investments created substantial profits and made sugar planters the wealthiest colonists in all of British America. Profits were greatest at the start of the sugar revolution in the middle of the seventeenth century, but successful plantations in the mid-eighteenth century still generated annual returns of roughly 10 percent, depending on the particular island.[38]

Eighteenth-century rice production involved smaller, but still significant capital investments. Hurricanes also had a dramatic effect on this crop as well. Planters and their slaves generally grew rice on swampy lands along the rivers that cut across the coastal low country. To do so, they cleared and drained the land and constructed a series of embankments, ditches, and reservoirs to control the flow of water from nearby freshwater rivers and streams. Later, planters constructed even more elaborate systems of embankments, canals, trunks, and floodgates to take advantage of the rising and falling of tidal rivers in order to flood their fields. Irrigated fields boosted production, but whether

---

37 Matthew Mulcahy, *Hurricanes and Society in the British Greater Caribbean, 1624-1783,* (Baltimore, The Johns Hopkins University Press, 2006), pg. 1.

38 Thomas, *An Historical Account of the Rise and Growth of the West-India Colonies*, pg. 18; Edward Long, *History of Jamaica* (London, 1774) quoted in Sheridan, Sugar and Slavery, pgs. 264–65; on sugar production, Dunn, *Sugar and Slaves*, pgs. 188–223; on profits, see J. R. Ward, *"The Profitability of Sugar Planting in the British West Indies 1650–1834,"* Economic History Review 31 (May 1978): Pgs. 197–213.

planters employed freshwater reservoirs or tidal flows, such environmental manipulation was costly.

Simply clearing an acre of land cost roughly eight shillings and six pence. One estimate from the later part of the eighteenth century suggested that draining the fields and building the necessary infrastructure cost an additional £1 to £4.20, making it far more expensive than other types of farm operations on the mainland. Establishing and operating a rice plantation also required a significant amount of labor. Contemporaries generally agreed that between thirty and forty laborers were required for successful rice production. One observer stated that, including the cost of purchasing slaves, £2,476 was necessary to establish a two hundred-acre low country plantation. Although less profitable than sugar, rice still created great fortunes: probate inventories indicate that nine of the ten richest men in mainland North America on the eve of the Revolution were low country planters.[39]

Colonists got their first taste of the power of the storms nine months after establishing a permanent settlement. Hurricanes posed several similar threats to the sugar and rice plantations of the region. First, the storms regularly laid waste the valuable crops themselves. Sugar grew on a staggered fourteen to eighteen-month schedule: canes were planted between September and January for the harvest the following February through June. Hurricanes struck a few months before the start of the harvest, greatly damaging the mature canes. "The canes and other objects of culture are the first to be blown away" by the storms, which left the "surface of the earth . . . truly bared." "Whole fields of sugar canes [were] whirled into the air, and scattered over the face of the country," wrote one observer. "The cane fields appear as if a roller had passed over them," noted another. Although planters attempted to salvage whatever

---

[39] Morgan, P. (1998) *Slave Counterpoint: Black Culture in the Eighteenth-Century Chesapeake and Lowcountry* (Chapel Hill, 1998), Pgs. 37, 147–58; Chaplin, *An Anxious Pursuit*, Pgs. 227–76; Mart Stewart, *"What Nature Suffers to Groe,"* Pgs. 87–116; Hilliard, S. (1975) *"The Tidewater Rice Plantation: An Ingenious Adaptation to Nature,"* in Geoscience and Man, vol. 12: Coastal Resources, ed. H. J. Walker, Baton Rouge, Pgs. 57–66; Russell Menard, *"Slavery, Economic Growth, and Revolutionary Ideology in the South Carolina Lowcountry,"* in The Economy of Early America: The Revolutionary Period, 1763–1790, eds. Ronald Hoffman et al. (Charlottesville, Va., 1988), pg. 265.

they could, under or overripe cane had little value, and unless crushed quickly, was almost worthless.[40]

Hurricane season overlapped with the actual harvest season for rice. As Henry Laurens [a wealthy South Carolina planter and merchant] indicated, the storms routinely flooded rice fields, often ruining the year's crop. "Ye violence of the rain and wind" accompanying a 1724 hurricane resulted in flooding that "damnified some of the Indian corn and rice" in South Carolina. Henry Laurens reported, "The ripe Crops of Rice have suffer'd very much all along the Sea Coast" from a 1769 hurricane. "Rotten rice, dead Hogs, Calves poultry, rats & insects, are enough to make a well man sick," one Georgia overseer wrote following a hurricane in the early nineteenth century. The Charleston merchant John Guerard noted that what little rice survived the September 1752 hurricanes proved almost worthless. "A great deal pounding away to powder," Guerard wrote of the rice, "which is a natural consequence by its being so long weather beaten & lying in the water which to be sure softened the grain and causes it to moulder away under the force of the Pestle."[41]

During the initial decades of colonization, hurricanes generated shared misery among colonists in the West Indies and elsewhere. All colonists struggled to find adequate provisions and to rebuild their small and simple settlements following various storms. But the development of plantation agriculture – particularly sugar in the West Indies and rice along the Carolina coast – and the transition to large-scale African slavery beginning in the mid-seventeenth century transformed the impact of hurricanes. Among white colonists, increased wealth from plantation agriculture led to greater social and economic stratification – which meant increased differences in housing, resources, and access to credit, all of which influenced vulnerability and experiences with storms. Following the 1675 hurricane in Barbados, for example, numerous small farmers who lacked the resources to rebuild were forced to sell their land

---

40 American Husbandry: Containing an Account of the Soil, Climate, Production and Agriculture of the British Colonies (London, 1775), vol. 2, pg. 114; Charlevoix, A Voyage to North America, vol. 2, pg. 291; John Stewart, A View of the Past and Present State of the Island of Jamaica (Edinburgh, 1823, repr. 1969), pg. 44; Beckford, Descriptive Account of the Island of Jamaica, vol. 1, pg. 130.

41 Governor Nicholson to the Duke of Newcastle, 25 Aug. 1724, CSPC, pg. 214; Laurens to Henry Bright & Co., 21 Sept. 1769, Papers of Henry Laurens, vol. 6, pg. 140; Roswell King, quoted in Stewart, "What Nature Suffers to Groe," pg. 138; John Guerard to William Jolliffe, 29 Dec. 1752, Guerard Letterbook, SCHS; Chaplin, An Anxious Pursuit, pg. 241–42.

to wealthier sugar planters, furthering the process of land consolidation into the hands of elites. The hurricane that struck Jamaica on October 3, 1780, stripped many poor whites of what few resources they had, and many suffered from "great distress and sickness," and were "reduced to beggary." A second hurricane struck Barbados seven days later and killed numerous British colonists, but as the governor noted, "fortunately few People of Consequence are among the number." The wealthiest West Indian planters were able to flee the region altogether, becoming absentees in England and managing their estates from afar. Their properties remained vulnerable to destruction by storms, but they resided safely in what one called a "more favored climate."

Hurricanes also caused extensive damage to the elaborate infrastructure needed to grow and process the crops. Sugar plantations, with their windmills, boiling houses, and other buildings, were particularly vulnerable to damage. "Furious Hurricanes," Sir Dalby Thomas wrote at the end of the seventeenth century, "not only does the Crops an Injury, but sometimes tumbles down and Levels their Mills, Work-Houses, and strongest Buildings." One traveler to the region wrote that, during storms, "windmills are swept away in a moment; their works, their fixtures, the ponderous copper boilers, and stills of several hundred weights are wrenched from the ground, and battered to pieces." Losses from a 1733 hurricane in Montserrat included thirty of the thirty-six mills on the island, "the other six... much shatter'd, having lost their Veins and Round Houses," along with significant damage to "most of the Boiling-Houses, and the Sugar in them, which was considerable." In the low country, the storms often damaged or destroyed the complex series of gates and embankments used to control the flow of water onto rice fields. Henry Laurens wrote that on one of his plantations, one-third of his rice lands "suffer'd by salt water breaking over the Banks," damaging the fields during a 1769 storm.[42]

In addition, hurricanes routinely claimed the lives of African slaves whose labor generated the wealth of the colonies. Many slaves died during the storms, crushed beneath falling buildings or drowned in rising floodwaters. Others perished in the weeks following the storms due to a lack of adequate food and shelter or to disease associated with such shortages. African slaves comprised the poorest and most vulnerable members of these plantation societies during

---

42 Thomas, An Historical Account of the Rise and Growth of the West-India Colonies, pg. 20; Charlevoix, A Voyage to North America, pg. 291; [Rev. Robert Robertson], A Short Account of the Hurricane that pass'd thro' the English Leeward Islands (London, 1733), pgs. 11–12; Laurens to John Rutherford, 13 Oct. 1769, Papers of Henry Laurens, vol. 6, pgs. 159–60.

the seventeenth and eighteenth centuries, and hurricanes took an especially heavy toll on slave populations. Although exact numbers are hard to calculate given incomplete records, it is clear that hurricanes routinely killed hundreds, and sometimes thousands, of slaves.

Two hundred slaves perished during a 1722 hurricane in Jamaica when the slave ship *Kingston* sank. The October 10, 1780, storm killed at least 2,000 slaves in Barbados: some records suggest that the slave population decreased by over 5,000 between 1780 and 1781, and one observer stated that most perished in the storm or from storm-related causes. After sweeping across Barbados, the storm moved north through the Lesser Antilles. A hurricane in 1822 in South Carolina claimed the lives of hundreds of slaves who found themselves trapped in the low-lying Santee Delta, miles from higher ground and with no shelter.

In 1924, a particularly severe hurricane smashed into the northern half of Montserrat around midnight, when most of the residents were sleeping peacefully. A couple of hours later, 36 people were dead and half of the population was left homeless. It is quite fair to say that the people of this region have developed a deep respect for the power of hurricanes from the early colonial times even up to this day. Many hurricanes have left an important and indelible mark on the region's history. Even Christopher Columbus on his first voyage managed to avoid encountering any hurricanes, but it wasn't until his later voyages that he encountered several hurricanes that disrupted some of his voyages to the New World.

English explorers and privateers soon contributed their own accounts of encounters with these storms. Famous English explorer Sir John Hawkins wrote his own encounters with these storms. Sir John Hawkins wrote that he left Cartagena in late July 1568 "Hoping to have escaped the time of their stormes… which they call Furicanos." Hawkins did not leave soon enough, and he and his ships were bashed by an "extreme storme" as he referred to it, lasting several days.[43] English explorer Sir Francis Drake encountered a major storm while anchored near the ill-fated Roanoke Colony in the United States in June 1586. The Roanoke Colony, also known as the Lost Colony, established on Roanoke Island, in what is today's Dare County, North Carolina, was a late 16th-century attempt by Queen Elizabeth I to establish a permanent English settlement. The enterprise was originally financed and organized by Sir Humphrey Gilbert, who drowned in 1583 during an aborted attempt to colonize St. John's,

[43] Matthew Mulcahy, Hurricanes and Society in the British Greater Caribbean, 1624-1783, (Baltimore, The Johns Hopkins University Press, 2006), pg. 14.

Newfoundland. Sir Humphrey Gilbert's half-brother, Sir Walter Raleigh, later gained his brother's charter from the Queen and subsequently executed the details of the charter through his delegates Ralph Lane and Richard Grenville, Raleigh's distant cousin. The final group of colonists disappeared during the Anglo-Spanish War, three years after the last shipment of supplies from England. Their disappearance gave rise to the nickname "The Lost Colony." To this day, there has been no conclusive evidence as to what happened to the colonists.[44]

Other English accounts reported ships damaged or lost in storms characterized by extreme wind and rain, some of which were definitely hurricanes. The English had a great respect for hurricanes, to such an extent that as the hurricane season was understood to be approaching, more and more pirates went home or laid up their ships in some sheltered harbor until the last hurricane had passed and was replaced by the cool air of old man winter.

Increasing knowledge about the geographic boundaries of the hurricane zone was matched by the gradual realization that the storms were seasonal. Writers in the first decades of colonization thought they could strike at any time of the year. For example, English colonist John Taylor wrote in 1638 that it was "uncertain" when a hurricane might hit the Caribbean because it had no definite time period in days, months or years for them to occur. Probably those that first discovered the period of the year in which hurricanes developed were Spanish priests, officers of the Navy or Army, or civilians that had lived for a long time in the Caribbean. By the end of the sixteenth century, they should have known already the approximate period that these hurricanes occurred. The Roman Catholic Church knew early on that the hurricane season extended at least from August to October because the hierarchy ordered that all of the churches in the Caribbean had to say a special prayer to protect them from these deadly hurricanes and the prayer which had to be said was: 'Ad repellendas tempestates', translated to mean 'For repelling of hurricanes or tempest.' It was also ordered that the prayer should be said in Puerto Rico during August and September and in Cuba in September and October. This indicates that it was known that hurricanes were more frequent in those islands during the months mentioned.

The hand of God could send the winds or stop them. The early Spanish Catholics had been the first in the Caribbean to wonder about the relationship of these hurricanes to God's ultimate design, or if He would use His powers

---

44 Charter to Sir Walter Raleigh March 25, 1584, University of Groningen.

to send the hurricanes or to protect against them. The people of other nations and faiths who followed them were no less concerned. West Indian colonists through first-hand experience with these storms gradually learned that hurricanes struck the Caribbean within a well-defined season. Initially, those early colonists believed that hurricanes could strike at any time, but by the middle of the seventeenth century most recognized that there was a definite and distinct hurricane season. This was because the hurricanes simply occurred too frequent within a particular time period for them to remain strange and unusual in their eyes. Numerous letters and reports written by colonists specifically discussed the period between July and October as the 'time of hurricanes.'

British colonists in the Caribbean during the seventeenth and eighteenth centuries responded to hurricanes with a day of public fasting and prayer during the hurricane season or after a major hurricane had passed. This was done to give God thanks for delivering them from danger and saving their lives during the passage of the hurricane. By the 1680s, fast days and thanksgiving ceremonies had become prescribed events in several colonies. Alternate Fridays during the months of August, September, and October were designated fast days in St. Christopher in 1683. That tradition continued in the Leeward Islands into the eighteenth century. The local minister in Nevis wrote in 1724 that "the last Fridays in the months of July, August, and September were to be observed as days of fasting, that being the season of the year which we call 'Hurricane Time' 3rd Thursday of October as a day of thanksgiving every year when there has been no Hurricane." A very destructive storm struck the island of St. Croix on October 25, 1791, "the very day, on which, by rule of the island, our churches return thanks yearly, in case no hurricane has happened." On the island of St. Lucia, local residents sang the 'Miserere mei Dues' at the beginning of the hurricane season and a 'Te Deum' at the end of the hurricane season. This switch to set, fixed fast days suggested that hurricanes had ceased to be strange or unusual events and had become expected during specified months of the year.[45]

This also occurred in other Caribbean countries as well, because in Cuba and Puerto Rico, praying to God for His divine intervention for protection against these storms became part of the liturgy. On Danish St. Croix and St. Thomas, special prayers were offered on June 25 at the beginning of the season, and then again on October 25 at its end. The commander of the Dutch part of

---

45 Matthew Mulcahy, *Hurricanes and Society in the British Greater Caribbean, 1624-1783,* (Baltimore, The Johns Hopkins University Press, 2006), pg. 48.

Saint Maarten (St. Martin) in 1749 ordered a day of prayer in thanks for being spared military attacks and to ask God to continue to offer divine protection to them against hurricanes and to also thank Him for being spared from any military attacks. Such prayer days became a regular habit or occurrence for them each year. For example, a governor's order of July 1793 noted that the dangerous part of the year-the hurricane season approached, and they must fear the 'punishing hands' of God because of their 'sins and iniquities.' *The Gazette Officiale de la Guadeloupe*, after describing the damages caused by a powerful and devastating hurricane in 1825, ended its report noting: "We finish this distressing narration of the island's disaster by expressing the shared sentiments of respect for the Sovereign-Arbiter of all things that these disasters inspire. Thus we say, the same blow struck country and city, the houses, palaces, the Tabernacle, young and old, rich and poor, painful proof by which providence wished to recognize our submission to His decrees."[46]

As stated before, increasing knowledge about the geographical boundaries of the hurricane zone was matched by the gradual realization that storms were seasonal. Over time, the relative balance between a 'natural' or 'theological' explanation of the storms by the colonists in the Caribbean changed, but even when hurricanes were perceived as some 'nature' driven phenomenon rather than divine punishment or diabolical action, God's intervention was called upon as a protective force. Writers in the first decades of colonization believed that these storms could strike at any time. John Taylor wrote in 1638 that it was "uncertaine" when a hurricane might strike, "for it had no certaine or set times of either years or days for the coming of it." A pamphlet advised travelers to arrive in the region before August or else they would encounter "The hurricanes, as they call them, which are certain violent and contrary winds that doe terribly infest the Atlantic and Indian Seas all winter long, from September to March."[47]

By the end of the 1650s, colonists had learned the seasonal boundaries of hurricanes from Carib Indians. Charles de Rochefort wrote with assurance in the early 1660s that hurricanes came "in the months of July, August, or September: at other times there is no fear of it." At some point this information became a local Caribbean mariner's proverb: "June too soon, July stand by,

46 Gazette Officiale de la Guadeloupe, 31st July, 1825, pg.42. Retrieved: 12-11-2014.

47 *http://www.shakespearesengland.co.uk/category/weather/circles fringed the moon*. Retrieved: 12-11-2014.

August look out you must, or September remember, October all over."[48] The seasonality of hurricanes did little to alleviate the fear they inspired, and colonists remained on edge throughout these months. Increased experience did not make hurricanes any less terrifying, but it did make them appear less as heavenly divine judgments from the Almighty God or from the evil spirits and more as part of the natural world. However, residents never knew if a late afternoon thunderstorm during the summer months might foreshadow a terrible hurricane.

The presence of hurricanes made colonists question their ability to transform the hostile environment of the Greater Caribbean, Central and North America, and by extension their ability to establish successful and stable societies in this region. But hurricanes raised other questions as well. What caused them? Are they from God, and if not, then what forces gave rise to such powerful and deadly storms? How can they be prevented? When and where should the colonists prepare for them? Colonists who struggled to make sense of hurricanes during the seventeenth century drew on a variety of intellectual paradigms and traditions. For some, probably a significant majority during the first several decades of the seventeenth century believed that these storms came directly from the hands of God. They interpreted hurricanes as "wondrous events," divine judgments for human sins.

Others linked the storms to various natural processes, including shifting wind patterns, the explosion of various chemicals in the atmosphere, and the celestial movement and alignment of the planets and stars. For example, the Dominican Father Jean-Baptiste Labat, arrived in Martinique in 1695, having observed everything on his voyage which he set down in his vivid narrative, *'Memoires des Nouveaux Voyages Faits Aux Isle de l'Amerique.'*[49] He was certain that hurricanes were caused by either the movement of the Earth around the sun or the sun around the Earth. "Or this compression and rarefaction of the air is the cause of the winds. They are not here," he announced firmly, "by accident." Whatever interpretation they advanced, all agreed with one seventeenth-century commentator that, "So General a Conspiracy of the Winds....which

---

48 Rick Schwartz, Hurricanes and the Middle Atlantic States, (USA, Blue Diamond Books, 2007), pg. 60.

49 J.B. Labat, *Nouveau voyage aux isles de l'Amérique: contenant l'histoire naturelle de ce* (1695)pg. 1.

so much disorders the Frame of Nature, must necessarily proceed from some very extraordinary cause."[50]

Explanations for hurricanes remained diverse throughout the seventeenth and eighteenth centuries, and colonists continued to debate their possible causes, effects and the meaning of the destruction that accompanied them. Hurricanes remained 'Acts of God,' but unlike early interpretations of the storms as special providences sent by God in response to specific human transgressions. By the turn of the century, colonists increasingly viewed hurricanes as part of God's general providence, arising from fixed natural processes observable to humans. By the middle decades of the eighteenth century, some even argued that the storms were beneficial, increasing rainfall, especially for plantation field crops such as sugarcane, coffee, rice, cotton, tobacco, and even clearing the air of dust and pollutants. These shifting interpretations of hurricanes and the operations of the natural world more generally mirrored intellectual changes in England during this period, but colonists' ideas about hurricanes remained grounded in their specific experiences.

Hurricanes were entirely new to the Europeans, Western Europe had occasionally experienced great storms, but they were no match to the frequency or ferocity with which these powerful hurricanes struck the Greater Caribbean. The storms routinely swept across the colonies, destroying fields and crops, leveling plantations, cities, and towns, disrupting shipping and trade, and causing widespread devastation and death among the colonists. Although other catastrophes such as earthquakes, volcanoes, droughts, and epidemics (such as Cholera and Yellow Fever) threatened colonial settlements throughout the region at various times, it was hurricanes that generated the most fear among the colonists because of the great potential for destruction and death.

The effects of these storms, moreover, extended beyond the colonies themselves. The plantation colonies of the Greater Caribbean, North and Central America formed the 'brightest jewels' in the crown of the English, French, Spanish and Dutch Empires. They produced exotic staple crops (such as tobacco, coffee, rice, corn, cotton and sugar cane) that fed the appetites of consumers on both sides of the Atlantic and generated a tremendous amount of wealth, not only for colonial planters and plantation owners, but for the mother countries as well. Despite repeated destruction from hurricanes (and other calamities), these crops reaped tremendous rewards, and successful

---

50 Matthew Mulcahy, *Hurricanes and Society in the British Greater Caribbean, 1624-1783,* (Baltimore, The Johns Hopkins University Press, 2006), pg. 33.

sugar, rice, coffee, cotton and tobacco planters and merchants quickly became the wealthiest of all the colonists in the region. It is important to note that hurricanes did play some role in the shift away from sugar on some islands in the region, but only at the end of the nineteenth century. Likewise, hurricanes contributed to the decline of rice production in the coastal low-country of South Carolina, but not until the 1890s.

A series of storms struck the final blows to an industry already shaken by the physical devastation and societal changes caused by the U.S. Civil War. The devastation caused by these powerful hurricanes in this region thus reverberated throughout the Caribbean, the Americas and Europe. The loss of crops by hurricanes often drove up the cost of sugar for coffee and tea drinkers and thus, raised the price of agricultural goods in Europe. The physical damage caused by the storms increased demand in the colonies for everything from provisions to building supplies to finished crafts and furniture, and North American and European merchants and artisans rushed to supply the need. As a result of these storms, the merchants and ship captains tried to schedule voyages to the region before or after the hurricane season had passed to avoid the threat.

European migrants to the New World came with hopes of recreating, or improving on, the world they had left behind, but everywhere they settled, the physical environment forced them to change some of the attitudes, beliefs, and practices that had characterized their lives in Europe. As many historians have suggested, new weather patterns and conditions, different geographies, and unknown plants and animals to say nothing of new peoples, cultures, religion and new social relationships-all required colonists to adapt to or change some of their basic cultural practices and ideals. This dynamic relationship between the environmental conditions colonists encountered and cultural ideals and institutions they brought with them shaped colonization efforts in all parts of the Caribbean, North and Central America.

In the Greater Caribbean, hurricanes played a major role in the process of encounter and accommodation. The devastation accompanying hurricanes tested colonists' notions of improvement and that their faith could transform the New World into a world they could conquer and tame. The frequency of these storms made them question prevailing interpretations of the causes of such disasters. Hurricanes affected economic prospects, routinely caused significant short-term losses for most planters, and complete devastation for others. The destruction of houses and other buildings required rethinking familiar European building styles and practices. The frequent damage from hurricanes reinforced trade connections to merchants in Europe and North America, who supplied vital credit, provisions, and building supplies in the wake of these disasters. Thus, in a variety of ways large and small, hurricanes shaped the mental and physical world of colonists during the seventeenth and eighteenth centuries.

Hurricanes also shaped the lives of the African slaves who made up the majority of the population in the West Indies. Hurricanes were new to the Africans, as well as Europeans, and the storms caused particular hardships for slaves because most of them lived in substandard houses or huts and had never experienced hurricanes before they had made their voyage to the New World. Unfortunately, existing historical accounts and documents, all written by colonists or travelers, gave only brief glimpses of slaves' experiences before, during and after hurricanes. Africans, like English colonists, had little experience with hurricanes, although tornadoes are frequent in West Africa, and it seems likely that slaves made some connection between the two. Charles Leslie suggested that eighteenth-century slaves in Jamaica worshipped "two gods, a good and a bad one." According to Leslie, "The evil god sends storms, earthquakes, and all kinds of mischief."

The Jamaican pen keeper Thomas Thistlewood noted that slaves in Westmoreland Parish connected the 'bad weather' and subsequent 1780 hurricanes to burial of a local merchant named Cholman: "The negroes say him (Cholman) and the devil were playing cards together, which occasioned the storm."[51] Such evidence suggests that some slaves may have viewed the storms as divine punishment, while others saw them as hazards created by a devil figure. It seems probable that African attitudes about hurricanes gradually evolved along with Europeans ones over the seventeenth and eighteenth centuries, although what form that evolution took place is not entirely clear.

Slaves almost certainly learned to read the skies for signs of coming hurricanes and shared with English colonists a general sense of the hurricane season, but few colonists commented on African attitudes or knowledge about storms or how they affected life on the plantation for slaves. When they did, such comments were often negative. One visitor to Jamaica in the early nineteenth century, for example, wrote that slaves considered hurricanes, "indications of the divine wrath, as punishments inflicted by heaven on the human race for their crimes and impiety; they have no idea of their arising from natural causes; the

---

[51] Matthew Mulcahy, <u>*Hurricanes and Society in the British Greater Caribbean, 1624-1783,*</u> (Baltimore, The Johns Hopkins University Press, 2006), pg. 54.

necessary war of elements is to them an incomprehensible doctrine." The slaves, he claimed, "did not look much to natural causes and remote consequences."[52]

As planters learned about the seasonality of these storms and the signs associated with an approaching hurricane, they took what steps they could to mitigate the risks to their plantations. Sugar cane in the fields remained the most vulnerable to these storms, but sugar planters did their best to ensure that the previous year's crop was milled, processed, and shipped long before the start of hurricane season. Hurricanes, of course, did not respect international political boundaries, because major storms routinely struck Spanish Florida and Spanish, French, Dutch, and Danish colonies in the West Indies. A 1707 hurricane, for example, leveled the English Leeward Islands, the Dutch islands of Saba and St. Eustatius, and the French island of Guadeloupe. Although most shared basic characteristics with their British neighbors mainly slavery and plantation agriculture-important differences in cultural, legal, political, and religious systems distinguished the colonies, which influenced both the impact of the storms and how colonists recovered from them.

On July 28, 1609, a fleet of seven tall ships, with two pinnaces in tow carrying 150 settlers and supplies from Plymouth, England to Virginia to relieve the starving Jamestown colonists, was struck by a hurricane. They had been sent by the Virginia Company of London to fortify the Jamestown settlement. Some of the ships were damaged, while others were destroyed and part of the fleet was grounded at Bermuda, which for some time was called 'Somers Island', after the ship's captain, Admiral Sir George Somers. He claimed the island for the British Crown and vowed to return, which he did and later died on that island. When he discovered Bermuda, he wrote that when something loomed up ahead, he thought at once that it was the "dreadful coast of the Bermudas...enchanted and inhabited with witches and devils...and wondrous dangerous rocks and unspeakable hazard of ship wreck... And that the rather they be so terrible to all that ever touched on them, and such tempest, thunders and other fearful objects are seen and heard about them that they be called commonly, the devils islands, and are feared and voided of all sea travelers alive, above any other place in the world. Yet it had pleased our Merciful God, to make even this hideous and hated place both the place of our safety, and means of deliverance..."[53]

---

52 J., Stewart, (1808) An Account of Jamaica and its Inhabitants, by a Gentleman, Longtime Resident in the West Indies, (London, 1808) pg. 33.

53 C. Knight, *Pictorial Edition of the works of Shakespeare Vol II*, (London, England, George Routledge and Sons, 1867), pg. 393.

After being struck by this hurricane, the *Sea Venture* sprung a leak and everyone on board worked hard to save this ship and their lives by trying to pump the water out of the hull of the ship. They tried to stem the flow of water coming onto the ship by stuffing salt beef and anything else they could find to fit into the leaks of the ship. After this proved futile, most of the crew gave up hope, falling asleep where they could, exhausted and aching from their relentless but futile efforts. But just as they were about to give up and face the grim reality that they would be lost to the unforgiving Atlantic Ocean, they spotted the island of Bermuda. Somers skillfully navigated the floundering *Sea Venture* onto the reef about half a mile to the leeward side of Bermuda. They used the ship's long boat to ferry the crew and passengers ashore. The passengers became Bermuda's first inhabitants, and their stories helped inspire William Shakespeare's writing of his final play 'The Tempest', making it perhaps the most famous hurricane in early American history. Most of those venturing to the New World had no knowledge of the word or the actual storm.

The lead ship, the three hundred-ton *Sea Venture,* was the largest in the fleet and carried Sir Thomas Gates, the newly appointed governor of the colony, and Sir Georges Somers, Admiral of the Virginia Company. When passengers on the ship the Sea Venture encountered that hurricane, no one actually knew to call this storm a hurricane. "For mine own part," wrote one passenger, William Strachey, who had been appointed Secretary to the Deputy Governor of Virginia, "I had been in some storms before, as well as upon the coast of Barbary and Algiers in the Levant...Yet all that I had ever suffered gathered together might not hold comparison with this."[54] Strachey's account of the storm and the settlers' journey on Bermuda served as the source of William Shakespeare's 'The Tempest.' It is interesting to note that Shakespeare did not name his play 'The Hurricane.' He actually did know the word "hurricano" because it appears in two earlier plays, King Lear and Troilus and Cressida. Maybe he recognized that such a title would be confusing and unfamiliar to most of his audience, so he chose a more familiar word 'The Tempest' instead.

Though the island was uninhabited, Spaniards had visited Bermuda earlier and set ashore wild pigs. The shipwrecked passengers fed on those wild pigs, fish, berries and other plentiful game on the island. Although they yearned to stay on that island paradise, they managed to make two vessels out of what was left of the *Sea Venture,* and ten months later they set sail for Jamestown. Although

---

54 Matthew Mulcahy, *Hurricanes and Society in the British Greater Caribbean, 1624-1783,* (Baltimore, The Johns Hopkins University Press, 2006), pg. 15.

most of the colonists moved on to Virginia the next year, some remained there and colonized Bermuda. The island still celebrates Somers Day each July 28, and Bermuda's coat of arms features the wreck of the Sea Venture, one of the ships lost in this storm.

Had it not been for a hurricane, France, rather than Spain, might have claimed Florida in 1565. The French lost their bid to control the Atlantic coast of North America when a 1565 hurricane dispersed their fleet, allowing the Spanish to capture France's Fort Caroline near present day Jacksonville, Florida. The Spaniards at St. Augustine massacred the French colonists at Fort Caroline, ensuring Spanish control of east Florida. The Spaniards at the time considered the French encroachment on the U.S. mainland a threat to the Spanish shipping routes on their return trips to Europe, which adhered closely to the peninsular coastline. If France had been able to grasp and maintain control of the Atlantic seaboard, it is impossible to imagine what the history of the United States of America would have become had it not been for that hurricane; and it is safe to say that one hurricane on the American mainland drastically changed the course of American history.

The 1500s were a time of great religious chaos in France, and many of the French Protestants, known as the Huguenots, were persecuted. One of the leaders of the Huguenots was a French Admiral called Gaspard de Coligny. At the peak of the turmoil, Coligny selected the mariner Jean Ribaut to establish a New World colony for the Huguenots. Ribaut began his journey in 1562, arriving on May 1 at the mouth of what is today known as the St. John's River. Forty-nine years after Ponce de Leon had lay claim to 'Pascua Florida' for Spain, Ribaut erected a stone monument inscribed with the French coat of arms, declaring the territory the possession of the King of France. He then sailed north, establishing a colony he called Charlesfort (Paris Island), South Carolina, returning to Dieppe in July with the intention of sending settlers and supplies back to Charlesfort.

Finding the Huguenots and Catholics at war, Ribaut had to flee to England with the intentions of getting a fleet of ships and some supplies for his New World colony, but to his surprise he was imprisoned in the tower of London, suspected of planning to steal English ships. When aid was not forthcoming, the 28 Charlesfort colonists rebelled against and killed their commander and, abandoning the settlement, returned to France in a ship of their own construction. Meanwhile, Admiral Coligny sent Ribaut's lieutenant, René Goulaine de Laudonniére, to Florida with a group of colonists. Arriving at the entrance of the St. John's River, and assisted by the Timugua chief Athore, they built a fortified settlement named Fort Caroline, in honor of the French King Charles IX.

Living at Fort Caroline was very difficult because the French had great difficulty adapting to the local climate and swampy terrain, and after less than a year they abandoned the settlement and returned to France. By this time, the English had released Ribaut, who was then sent by Coligny to Fort Caroline with a supply of seven ships and about six hundred new colonists. He met Laudonnniére's party just as they were getting ready to sail. At the same time, a fleet under the command of Admiral Pedro Menéndez de Avilés was on its way with the mandate to destroy the French at Fort Caroline and reclaim the territory for the country of Spain.

Menéndez had set sail from Spain with a total of 11 ships, but this fleet encountered a hurricane and six of the ships were destroyed. After briefly confronting the French fleet at Fort Caroline, Menéndez regrouped at St. Augustine. Ribaut and his team decided to attack St. Augustine. On September 19th, 1565, he set sail with 400 men for the battle, leaving about 250 soldiers at Fort Caroline. Being outnumbered by the French, the Spaniards would surely have succumbed to the French invasion had it not been for that hurricane. The French fleet while en route was overtaken and ravaged by a strong hurricane and was wrecked some distance south of St. Augustine with very little casualties.

Suspecting that Menéndez would try and attack the already weakened guarded Fort Caroline, Ribaut and his battered men attempted to make their way there. Outside St. Augustine, they encountered a small contingent from Menendez's force. Menéndez managed to convince the French into surrendering, promising to spare their lives, but proceeded to kill all of them, including Ribaut. None of Ribaut's men had any idea that Menéndez had already attacked and killed most of the inhabitants of Fort Caroline. As a result of the battle, the Spanish later built Fort Matanzas (Spanish for 'massacre') at the site of the murder of Ribaut and his men.

In early 1624, a small group of colonists led by Sir Thomas Warner landed on the island of St. Christopher (now called St. Kitts), one of the Leeward Islands in the northeastern Caribbean. They immediately set about securing their possessions, and over the next several months they built a small fort, built a few rudimentary dwellings, and planted some tobacco and provisional crops. Their initial effort of building this colony proved to be a disaster and was very short-lived. On the 19th of September of that year, a powerful hurricane came ashore and wiped it all away. To make matters worse, two years after they had rebuilt their infant colony, a second powerful storm swept across the island. The hurricane in August of that year killed seventy-five persons and sank five ships. One of the colonist, John Smith reported that the hurricane "blew down all our houses, tobacco and two drums (were thrown) into the air we know whither, drove two ships on shore that were split; all our provisions thus lost, we were very miserable."[55]

The colonists, Smith recalled, scavenged in the "wilde woods" for food, and they struggled to survive until the next June, when sea turtles came ashore, providing some welcome relief and a variety to their diet. Warner, Smith, Somers and other English colonists who traveled to the West Indies and North America in the seventeenth century expected the physical environment to present obstacles, but one thing they were not prepared for was the frequency and ferocity of these Atlantic hurricanes and tropical storms. Colonists at first worried about how tropical heat, humidity, diseases, earthquakes, and drought would affect them, but hurricanes quickly became the region's most feared and number one natural disaster.

The 1609 and the 1624 hurricanes were not the first hurricanes the English had encountered in the New World. Early privateers had learned about these powerful storms during the sixteenth century while cruising in the region in search of Spanish treasure laden fleets. In 1640, a hurricane partially destroyed a large Dutch fleet apparently poised to attack Havana, Cuba. Another naval disaster occurred in 1666 to Lord Francis Willoughby (the British Governor of Barbados whose life was also lost in this storm) and his fleet of seventeen ships and nearly 2,000 troops. The fleet was caught in a hurricane after leaving Barbados en route to St. Christopher and Nevis to aid colonists against French attacks. Only a few vessels were ever heard from again, and the French captured some of the survivors. For a period in the late seventeenth century, some colonists in the Caribbean referred to especially powerful and deadly storms as "Willoughby Gales." The 1640 and 1666 events secured, more or less, control of Cuba by the Spaniards and Guadeloupe by the French.

The great damage from a hurricane in 1667 was beyond the scope of many Englishmen, and a pamphlet entitled '*Strange News from Virginia, being a true relation of the great tempest in Virginia,*' was published, describing the devastation from this storm. Here's an excerpt from this pamphlet, as follows: "Neither did it end here, but the trees were torn up by their roots and in many places the whole woods were blown down, so that they cannot go from plantation to plantation.

55 *Awnsham* Churchill, A Collection of Voyages and Travels, Volume 2, (Hong Kong, Asian Educational Services, 1782), pg. 361.

The sea (by the violence of the winds) swelled twelve feet above its usual height, drowning the whole country before it, with many of the inhabitants, their cattle and goods, the rest being forced to save themselves in the mountains nearest adjoining, where they were forced to remain many days in great want."[56]

More damage is described by a letter written from the Colonial Secretary Mr. Thomas Ludwell to Lord Berkeley: "This poor country...is now reduced to a very miserable condition....on the 27th of August followed the most dreadful Harry Cane that ever the colony groaned under. The night of it was the most dismal time I ever knew or heard of, for the wind and rain raised so confused a noise, mixed with the continual cracks of falling houses....The waves were impetuously beaten against the shores and by that violence forced and as it were crowded the creeks, rivers and bays to that prodigious height that it hazarded the drowning of many people who lived not in sight of the rivers, yet were forced to climb to the top of their houses to keep themselves above water...the nearest computation is at least 10,000 houses blown down."[57] The storm is believed to have created the peninsula of Seawell's Point and Willoughby Spit in modern-day Norfolk, Virginia. Other reported damages included the destruction of an early fortification under construction at what is known today as Old Point Comfort. At least 75 persons were reported to have died in the storm. Matters were made much worse with nearly two weeks of rain following the landfall of the 'Harry Cane,' including a possible visit from a smaller hurricane which would have extended the period of rain.

In 1696, a party of Quakers sailing from Jamaica to Philadelphia was caught in a hurricane and shipwrecked in the middle of the night on what is now Jupiter Island, to the north of Palm Beach, Florida. That event and the hardships the travelers endured during the remainder of their journey were described by one of them, Jonathan Dickinson, after whom a Florida state park is now named. This hurricane is only known because it turned a routine sea voyage into an epic overland journey. Other storms are remembered because of the scale of the damage they caused. In 1099, for example, a hurricane moving through the English Channel produced a storm surge that killed 100,000 people then, which would be equivalent to the loss of 1 million today-approximately equivalent to the entire present-day population of Dallas, Texas. Quite apart from the innumerable personal tragedies such disaster represents, it would have caused

---

56 D. Ludlum, *The Weather Factor*, (Boston, Springer Pub., 1984), pg. 15.

57 D. Healey, *Great Storms of the Chesapeake*, (Charleston, The History Press, 2012) pg. 22.

major economic disruption, producing a shortage of labor leading to wage rises over a large area.[58]

Hurricanes also caused great devastation to agriculture, shipping and trade industries of the West Indies and North America. A severe hurricane in 1724 destroyed most of the colonists in South Carolina's supply of Indian corn and rice. Hurricanes also caused extensive damage to the elaborate infrastructure needed to grow and process the crops. Sugar plantations, with their windmills, boiling houses, curing houses, and other buildings, were particularly vulnerable. For example, a powerful hurricane in 1733 destroyed thirty of the thirty-six windmills on the island of Montserrat. The French settled the Gulf coast only at the beginning of the eighteenth century, but colonists there soon had their own experiences with hurricanes. A 1722 storm destroyed thirty-four houses, the church, and the hospital in New Orleans. Another major hurricane damaged the city in 1779. One survivor wrote, "More than half of the town was stripped of its covering, many houses thrown down in town and country, no ship or vessel of any kind was seen on the river the next morning. The river which at this season is low was forced over its banks and the crops which were not yet collected, disappeared from the face of the Earth."[59]

Then, as now, commentators struggled to find adequate words to describe the power of a hurricane. One colonial governor simply reported to his superiors in London that, "To describe the hurricane is impossible." A seventeenth-century colonist recalled that the "terror" of the storm "was such that I thought it was the Emblem of Hell & the last dissolution of all things." After surviving a 1772 hurricane in the West Indies, a young Alexander Hamilton wrote that the noise accompanying a storm would "strike astonishment into Angels." Everyone agreed that hurricanes were "the most terrible calamity to which they are subject from the climate."

In addition, hurricanes destroyed ships and port facilities, both essential for shipping crops to the markets throughout to the United States and Europe. For example, during the 1675 hurricane in Barbados, twelve ships in Bridgetown's Harbor (most of them loaded with sugar) were destroyed by this hurricane. The 1752 hurricanes in South Carolina destroyed the wharves and warehouses along the Cooper River that functioned as the colony's hub for trade and

---

58 Michael Allaby, Hurricanes, (New York, Infobase Publishing, New York, 2003), pg. 131.

59 D. Ludlum, Early American Hurricanes, 1492-1870, (Boston, Springer Publishers, Boston,1963), pgs. 60-66.

commerce. These storms tore roofs off city warehouses, which in turn ruined a great deal of rice and other goods stored in them and caused over £10,000 in losses. This storm forced Jacob Motte, the public treasurer of the colony, to declare bankruptcy. This storm left Motte unable to pay back a number of loans that he had made to himself from the public treasury to finance his rice and navel stores. He was then forced to transfer his entire estate-including the plantations, slaves, and household furniture to a board of trustees appointed by the Council and Assembly.

The reverberations from bankruptcies and defaults after hurricanes helped reshape the economic landscape of the colonies of North America and the West Indies, particularly in the sugar islands. Overall, hurricanes aided the process by which, during the seventeenth and early eighteenth centuries, land in many of the sugar colonies came to be dominated by wealthier planters and larger plantations. They were in a better position to recover or burrow money to rebuild from the merchants in Europe after these hurricanes had passed.

Absenteeism among West Indian planters is often the subject of great debate and much speculation, but absentees were more common in the Greater Caribbean than elsewhere in the British America, and hurricanes were one of the main reasons why this happened. Many wealthy plantation owners, gracious of this new-found sugar wealth, left their termite-ridden plantation houses, their fields, their hordes of slaves, to overseers and agents, and moved away from the hurricane plagued West Indies and went back to Europe, where they spent their new-found sugar money among the extravagances of Paris, Bath and London. Hurricanes posed several similar threats to the sugar and rice plantations of the region. In fact, everything about the production of sugar was dependent on hurricanes, and hurricanes set the schedule for the entire year.

First, the storms regularly laid waste to the valuable crops themselves. Sugar cane grew on a staggered fourteen- to eighteen-month schedule, and the sugarcanes were planted between late September or early October (after the hurricane season), and January for the harvest the following February through June. Hurricanes struck a few months before the start of the harvest, greatly damaging the mature canes. Second, hurricanes also influenced another important aspect of the business of sugar and rice production, and that was shipping. Everyone involved in the production and sale of sugar and rice crops had keen interest in getting them safely to various markets. That meant making sure that the vessels transporting the crops arrived in the colony or departed the colony long before the hurricane season. It is important to note that shipping in the region never came to a complete halt, but it did slow down tremendously during the late summer months, as ship captains attempted to fill their cargo holds and left for Europe and North America before the peak of the hurricane season. In addition, some ship captains avoided certain ports such as Barbados, because they feared that they were particularly vulnerable to the Cape Verde type hurricanes.

Hurricanes routinely claimed the lives of African slaves whose labor generated the wealth of the colonies, and whose labor was necessary for every detail of sugar production. Many slaves died during the storms, crushed beneath falling buildings or drowned in the rising floodwaters. Others perished in the weeks following the storms from starvation due to a lack of adequate food supply and shelter or to the diseases associated with such shortage such as Cholera. Some hurricanes even claimed the lives of slaves held on ships before they were unloaded and sold. For example, some two hundred slaves perished in 1722 when a hurricane sank the slave ship *Kingston* that had recently arrived in Jamaica. As a result of this and other similar disasters, many slave ships merchants were warned against having their slave cargos arrive in the late summer months because they would face the risk of having the hurricanes destroy them.

Jamaica and Barbados struggled for several years to recover from the powerful and deadly hurricanes in 1780. Sugar production was already in decline, and as a result of the American Revolution, it dropped even further in 1781. Sugar imports into England from the islands did not return to pre-hurricane levels until 1783. Rum exports to Europe, by extension, provided additional evidence for the loss of agricultural productivity. Barbados shipped 2,527 hogsheads of rum in 1780, but exports significantly declined to just over 500 hogsheads in 1781 after the Great Hurricane of 1780. It remained under 1,000 hogsheads until 1784, when the colony shipped 3,315 hogsheads to England. So, it took Barbados almost four full years for trade to recover fully from the Great Hurricane of 1780. Hurricanes also affected rice production in South Carolina. For example, the 1724 Hurricane contributed to a steep drop in exports of well over £1.5 million pounds of rice (from approximately £8.6 million to £7 million). The loss from two successive hurricanes in the fall of 1752 was particularly severe. The number of barrels of rice shipped from the colony dropped from over 82,000 barrels in 1752 to just over 37,000 barrels in

1753. Planters recovered quickly, and production reached record levels by 1754 (93,000 barrels).[60]

In addition, the hurricane also wiped away the pine trees used in the production of turpentine and naval stores. For example, one planter alone estimated that he lost over £10,000 worth of trees. The storms destroyed provisional crops just as much as they did damage to sugar and rice fields, creating widespread shortages. Plantain was a major source of food for slaves in the island colonies, and these trees were especially hard hit by the storms. The delicate trees and their fruit suffered significant damage in even minor storms; major storms often uprooted them completely. However, it is important to note here that assessing the impact of such destruction on plantation production is difficult. This was especially true for the seventeenth century, when systematic record keeping was less developed and what records that were kept were often destroyed by later hurricanes. More complete and reliable records were only started to be kept in the early eighteenth century.

Scarcities existed to some extent after most major hurricanes during the seventeenth and eighteenth centuries. The worst crisis emerged during the American Revolution, when the combination of several major hurricanes and the elimination of trade with North American suppliers brought widespread suffering, malnutrition and death to thousands of slaves in Jamaica and Barbados. The storms destroyed their main locally grown food, plantains, while the American Revolution eliminated their source of imported supplies. Slaves often suffered food shortages in the wake of major hurricanes, but they faced especially harsh conditions in the 1780s, when the combination of several devastating hurricanes and the political crisis of the American Revolution left Jamaica and Barbados with little food and very few options for relief. The war severed relations between the rebellious mainland and the loyal West Indian colonies, eliminating the islands' neighboring and best source of food supply.

The war ended in 1783, but trade between the islands and the new United States remained restricted. The consequences of that separation proved disastrous when two powerful hurricanes struck Jamaica and Barbados less than a week apart in early October 1780. Thousands of slaves died during the storms, most crushed beneath falling buildings or drowned in the storm surge, but others perished in the following weeks and months from inadequate food supply, contamination and diseases, and all faced shortages and difficult

---

60 Matthew Mulcahy, *Hurricanes and Society in the British Greater Caribbean, 1624-1783*, (Baltimore, The Johns Hopkins University Press, 2006), pg. 74.

conditions for a long time. At least two thousand slaves perished in Barbados during the October 10, 1780, storm, and perhaps an equal number of whites. Many slaves died during the storm, but others died in the following days and weeks from injuries, starvation caused by inadequate or lack of food supplies, contaminated water, disease, or some combination of all of these factors. A committee from the Jamaican Assembly conducted an official investigation and found that at least 15,000 slaves (out of a population of 256,000) perished as a result of the five hurricanes to hit Jamaica from 1780 to 1800. Some slaves certainly died from causes unrelated to the hurricanes, but numerous accounts, public and private, suggested that hundreds and possibly thousands died from hardships caused by these storms and by the loss of trade with North America.[61]

Throughout the seventeenth and eighteenth centuries, hurricanes routinely leveled houses, churches, towns, and plantations. The widespread devastation forced colonists to re-evaluate some of their basic ideas about construction. Beginning in the middle decades of the seventeenth century, many residents tried to erect buildings they hoped would better withstand powerful hurricanes. To get away from pirates and from the winds and the terrible storm surge, many houses were moved from the seacoast inland, up mountain slopes, leaving only the ruins of some ancient ports to recurring destruction. All the houses were built to a much higher and more rigid standards designed to support the powerful winds and waves of a hurricane. The most significant adaptations included reducing their height and altering the materials used in construction. In fact, some colonists also built hurricane houses to shelter them in the midst of a storm. In the Bahamas, for example, some of these hurricane houses were built on many of the Out Islands and were constructed with very sturdy materials and a roof extending all the way to the ground and built with no walls, and in the late 1700s, 1800s and early 1900s they worked remarkably well and served their purpose.

In the early days of colonization in the Caribbean, the majority of the houses were poorly built and very flimsy, little more than wood and thatch, which were just mere playthings for a hurricane's powerful winds. The islanders had to learn how to build hurricane shelters and hurricane-proof homes. These shelters were triangular structures made of thatch, around ten feet square at the base and eight feet high. A log in the center of the shelter was set deep in the soil, and lianas, woody vines, were used to latch the roof to nearby trees. During

61 Matthew Mulcahy, *Hurricanes, Poverty, and Vulnerability: An Historical Perspective*, (Baltimore, The Johns Hopkins University Press, 2006), published on: June 11, 2006.

the storm, the neighbors crowded into the shelters. As the hurricane's winds whipped them about, they shared strong hot coffee served in coconut shells and ate potato-like vegetables served heaped atop a palm branch. When the winds were especially bad, the men pressed an oxen yoke against the windward wall to support it. Halfway through the storm, after the eye had passed and the winds changed directions, the men would brace the opposite wall. When the storm was over, they ventured outside to check the damage.

Architectural adaptations were most pronounced in the island colonies and least visible in South Carolina. As a matter of fact, despite several major storms in the eighteenth century, South Carolinians made relatively few adjustments to hurricanes, reflecting both different social and environmental conditions in the mainland colony and different perceptions of the danger from the storms. England underwent something of a revolution in house building during the seventeenth century, moving from 'medieval modes of design' to a 'Renaissance style.' As a result, many of these changes made their way into the buildings in the Caribbean. Important characteristics of this new style included more use of bricks and stones and increased building heights of three to four stories. Wealthy colonists incorporated many of these innovations into their own buildings beginning in the later decades of the seventeenth century. In the major port cities, colonists constructed three and four story structures modeled on English urban dwellings. Strong winds and storm surges often damaged or destroyed all sorts of buildings in the colonies, but 'English style' structures seemed especially vulnerable.

Colonists in Jamaica discovered that the dwellings built by Spanish before the English conquest in 1655 often withstood the worst storms while their own structures crumbled. So as a result, many colonists took steps to reduce their vulnerability to these storms, and the most important and notable change was to reduce the building structures from three and four stories to just one and two stories. Changes to the height of buildings occurred gradually over time, but by the middle of the eighteenth century lower dwellings had become a distinguishing feature of these islands architecture because colonists came to believe that low-profile roofs offered the best defense against hurricanes. After major experiences with hurricanes, many of the roofs were hipped rather than gabled, which colonists believed offered more resistance to the strong winds. Both roof forms were common in the colonies in the seventeenth and eighteenth centuries, but experience with hurricanes often forced colonists to abandon gables in favor of hipped roofs. In addition to changing the roofs of their dwellings, some colonists altered their designs, such as making the eastern end of the house circular to be better suited to the hurricane's strong winds. Timber served as the primary building material throughout the region during the early seventeenth century.

As the population grew and plantation agriculture expanded, colonists exhausted local supplies and increasingly relied on shipments of wood and building materials from the mainland colonies. Timber remained important throughout the eighteenth century, but beginning in the 1660s, many who could afford it turned to brick and stone for buildings, in part because they believed that such materials could better withstand hurricanes. The Rev. Robert Robertson in Nevis advocated the use of brick and stone after a 1733 hurricane, noting "such buildings would prove a better security against storms than any we can make of Timber."[62] In addition, colonists gradually learned to cover their windows with strong shutters and to secure them and the doors with sturdy latches, hinges, and bolts. Bolting doors and windows before a storm provided greater security for the structures, according to Robertson, because once a door had been blown, open the wind enters, it fills the house and displaces the entire building by compromising the building structure.

Many colonists believed that the combination of informed design, sound materials, and common sense precautions would provide some security against the storms, although they knew that ultimately such efforts offered only minimal protection against these powerful storms. In addition, some colonists constructed special storm shelters, or 'hurricane houses', which families could flee to during a major storm. In Charleston, South Carolina, repeated destruction from hurricanes and fires over the course of the eighteenth century contributed a great deal to the city's physical layout and growth. After the storms, officials ordered many of the streams, creeks, and ponds that flowed through the city to be filled in to allow for more construction. Streets were widened and extended across the peninsula. South Carolina officials also took advantage of the hurricanes' devastation to redesign and improve the city's defenses. The new fortifications that stretched around the city's southern point were four feet higher than the previous defenses, which not only strengthened Charleston militarily, but offered increased protection against the swelling seas that flooded the city during major storms.

These storms quickly became a defining characteristic of the region, distinguishing it from other parts of the world, and most important, from Europe

[62] Matthew Mulcahy, Hurricanes and Society in the British Greater Caribbean, 1624-1783, (Baltimore, The Johns Hopkins University Press, 2006), pg. 125.

itself. Hurricanes were more than environmental markers, but these storms also raised troubling questions about the relationship between European cultures to the New World nature. Colonists arrived with a preconceived notion that they could transform the wilderness of the New World into an orderly, productive, and settled landscape. But these 'New World' hurricanes forced them to adjust their expectations about how colonial society would develop over time and helped shape a distinct mentality among all who settled there.

Many migrants also hoped to escape the devastation routinely brought about by hurricanes in the West Indies. One report to the Carolina Proprietors in London suggested that the new colony would have no trouble finding recruits in the islands, since many in Barbados and Antigua "would willingly come off and transport themselves farther from the terrible 'Hurry Caines' that cometh every year and destroy their houses and crops." Another stated that "many (were) removing from Antigua weary of Hurricanes."[63] Hopes of escaping hurricanes in South Carolina were dashed several years after the English arrived. In early September 1686, a "hurricane wonderfully horrid and destructive" swept along the coast, destroying the fragile houses, fences, and fields of the early colonizers. "The whole country seems to be one entire map of devastation," wrote one survivor. "The greatest parts of our houses are blown down and still lie in their ruins, many of us not having the least cottage to secure us from the rigor of the weather."[64] Another major storm struck in 1700, killing ninety-seven people, most of them sailors on board the Scottish ship *Rising Sun* anchored in the port. Thirteen years later, the storm surge of another hurricane drowned at least seventy people and did significant damage to forts, houses, and plantations throughout the colony, and one estimate stated the loss at £100,000. Hurricanes and lesser tropical storms remained frequent visitors to the colony throughout the eighteenth century.

---

63 Matthew Mulcahy, *Hurricanes and Society in the British Greater Caribbean, 1624-1783,* (Baltimore, The Johns Hopkins University Press, 2006), pg. 125.

64 Ibid., pg. 19.

CHAPTER FIVE

Some important or pivotal events that impacted and changed the science of tracking, monitoring, and forecasting hurricanes

The atmosphere surrounding our planet Earth sustains life and affects our lives in innumerable ways. It contains life-supporting oxygen and limits the effects of radiation from the sun. Hurricanes are a result of the physics and chemistry of the atmosphere and their interactions with the landforms and oceans of Earth. Over the last 100 years, scientists have gathered a wealth of information about hurricanes, but there is still much that is not yet understood. Even though they're large enough to see and track from space, hurricanes can be surprisingly difficult to predict. Fortunately, over the years, advancements in weather-related technology have drastically improved the tracking, monitoring, and understanding of the dynamics of hurricanes, thereby saving many lives.

Weather is the state of the atmosphere at a particular place and time as described by variations in cloudiness, humidity, precipitation, pressure, temperature, visibility, and wind. The way in which these elements shape the weather is a complicated one, but still a very fascinating story. Weather is a dynamic force, and we are only beginning to understand how it works. We live in the atmosphere, the large parcel of air that surrounds the Earth. Weather is what's happening at the bottom of the atmosphere, mostly in a layer that is seven and a half miles thick called the Troposphere ('Tropo' originating from a Greek word meaning 'change'). This pattern of weather, repeated over many years, constitutes the climate of a particular region. Obviously, different areas of the world have different climates. In equatorial regions, the weather is always warm, and usually wet. Deserts are dry, and polar regions are cold. The different climate regions result partly from the sun, which shines more strongly at the tropics than elsewhere.

Throughout history, mankind has always been in awe of the ever-changing nature of the weather and climate of our Earth. Ancient civilizations considered natural disasters to be the work of the gods and did any and everything to appease them into sending good weather their way. Even to this day, the weather still plays an important role in our lives and the way we live it. It affects many of the things that we do, from the clothes we wear and the food we eat to where we live and how we travel. As a result, the weather is of great interest to people everywhere, from meteorologists, the scientists who study it in great depth, to the average person on the street going about their everyday lives. Whereas, climate is the historical record and description of average daily and seasonal weather events over a long period of time-the average weather over decades. On a planetary scale, winds, temperature, and pressure govern the Earth's climate. All three of these driving forces result from unequal solar heating of the Earth. In short, the Earth's almost unlimited variety of climates stems from variations in the amount of solar radiation striking the Earth. The word 'climate' comes from the Ancient Greek word 'Klima,' meaning 'inclination' (which refers to the elevation of the sun above the horizon) and it reflects the importance early scholars attributed to the sun's influence on the Earth's weather and climatic patterns.

At tropical latitudes, the sun's rays strike nearly perpendicular to the Earth's surface. This delivers an intense amount of solar radiation per unit area and is the main reason for the consistently warmer temperatures at tropical latitudes and therefore this area becomes a breeding ground for hurricanes, which benefits greatly from this intense heat. The opposite is true at the poles, where the sun's solar radiation strikes the Earth at an angle, spreads over a larger area, and diffuses its energy. Since solar radiation at the poles is far less intense per unit area than near the equator, the poles receive less heat. This simple process of heating of the Earth forms one of the basic principles of our understanding of the weather and climate on this Earth and the overall the dynamics of hurricanes.

We live in an age of scientific and technological explosion, amid a world of recent discoveries and advancements that have fundamentally altered almost every aspect of our daily lives. Sometimes we need to step back and evaluate the changes brought on by technological advancements and make sure we understand the ramifications those changes have brought about in our world today. The technology of today has given us things undreamed of in times gone by, such as satellites, radars, computers, telephones, televisions and others. The rapid pace of these advancements has made our world more complicated, threatening to outrun our ability to make sense of the changes that confront us. Technology by itself is neither good nor bad, however the main questions we must ponder are, how can we control it and apply it to our lives? Weather forecasting is the application of current technology and science to predict the state of the atmosphere for a future time and a given location.

The history of weather forecasting goes way back in time; however, the various techniques used have changed significantly since then. The first 'meteorologists' were the shamans and priests of early communities, whose tasks involved appeasing the gods, who, it was believed, controlled all natural phenomena, including the weather. The reputations of these mediators, and sometimes their very existence, depended upon their success in bringing good weather. Today, weather forecasts are made by collecting as much data as possible about the current state of the atmosphere (particularly pressure, temperature, rainfall, humidity and wind) and understanding of atmospheric processes through meteorology to determine how the atmosphere changes over time and place in the future. However, the chaotic nature of the atmosphere and incomplete understanding of the processes that go on within them means that forecasts become less accurate over long periods of time. The invention of the synoptic weather chart in 1819 has been credited to H.W. Brandes, a professor at the University of Breslau; weather maps at first were drawn from observations gathered by mail. The circulation of the winds in these cyclonic storms was clearly depicted on these first weather maps, which revolutionized the infant field of meteorology at the time.

The ability to forecast the weather is as ancient as the first primitive man who prayed for rain, or the fervent wish to bring down heaven's wrath on 'thine own enemy.' In days of old, the task was left to a tribe's sorcerer or druid. Shamans shook rattles at the heavens to conjure up rain; witch doctors threw dried chicken bones into the air to end a drought; wizards mumbled sacred words and burned magic dust to make their enemies die of thirst; and medicine men danced around totem poles invoking magic to smite the tribe's enemy with a bolt of lightning. Even Moses had no problem about asking God to visit upon his enemies the worst of suffering, and his God was ruthless and vengeful.

Many people's livelihoods, and indeed their very own lives, are strongly influenced by the weather. In ancient times, people had very little idea how the weather worked, but somehow they realized that clouds were composed of water and air, but they could not figure out where the wind came from and did not understand the sun and its influence on the Earth's climate. Many believed that the gods made the weather, so weather mythology is often associated with religion. Others relied on guesses based on simple observations of plants, animals, or the sky to make a forecast. Many ideas and observations were handed down from generation to generation as old sayings or stories, and some are quite reliable, but most of them in the majority of the cases were simply off the mark. But only when we understand fully how the weather works can we predict it with pin-point accuracy.

The science of weather began in ancient Greece, when philosophers tried to explain what caused the weather. Some ideas were correct, but they did not test their theories, so in fact they were often wrong. In ancient Greek mythology, they included several gods who were believed to personify and control all things celestial and terrestrial, including the weather. One of their gods was Zeus, who was ruler of the heavens and controlled the clouds, rain, and thunder. Many persons in the past have tried to predict what the weather would be like a day or a season in advance.

Ancient Egypt was a perfect cradle for civilization, where the weather was almost always sunny and warm and the River Nile supplied water for irrigation. This meant, however, that Egyptian communities, which were well established by 3500 BC, depended almost totally on the Nile for their prosperity. The Egyptians tried to use the movements of the stars as a guide to the annual rise and fall of the river, as well as the extent of its periodic flooding. This dependence on the Nile and the heavens found expressions in two powerful gods-Ra (sometimes referred to as 'Re') and 'Osiris.' The Egyptians believed that the Sun god Ra controlled the heavenly bodies (hence the weather), traveling across the sky in his solar boat each day and returning through the underworld. Osiris, on the other hand was regarded as both the ruler of the dead and the source of fertility for the living-he controlled the sprouting of vegetation and the annual flooding of the Nile.

Great rivers also supported the civilizations that emerged around 3500 BC on the flood plains of the lower Tigris and Euphrates rivers in Mesopotamia, and later in the Indus Valley in the Indian subcontinent. Although these great cultures depended greatly on rivers, their mythologies indicated that rain and hence forecasting the weather was also very important. For example, the chief god of the Babylonians-whose kingdom in southern Mesopotamia prospered from 2100 to 689 BC-was 'Marduk', originally god of the thunderstorms, but ultimately god of the atmosphere, hence god of the weather. The Babylonians tried to predict the short-term changes in the weather based on astronomical observations, and the appearance of clouds and their patterns and optical phenomena such as haloes. In the Vedic religion of ancient India, 'Indra', god of the rain and storms, was among the most important deities. In early northern European cultures, the Norse god Thor was thought to be all powerful. His name originated from the Germanic word for thunder, and he was usually represented as a great warrior carrying a large hammer, which symbolized a thunderbolt.

In the Bible, two famous 'weather forecasters' who received prominent mention in the Old Testament were Joseph and Noah. In the book of Genesis, it was in Egypt that Joseph accurately made one of the most famous long-range forecasts of all time. He interpreted the Pharaoh's dream (which involved seven fat cows and seven thin cows) and successfully predicted that the dream meant that there will be seven good years, which would be followed by seven years of famine, and he recommended that they store up grain during the prosperous times to get them through the seven years of famine. That advice is still relevant in drought prone areas back then as it is now. In the biblical account of Noah and the Great Flood, God gave Noah the warning of the impending Great Flood and instructed him to build an ark to save himself and his family. Therefore, with a little help from divine instructions, Noah was able to predict the 'apocalyptic flood.'

In about 340 BC, philosopher Aristotle (380-322 BC) described weather patterns in his book or treatise *'Meteorologica'*, which was an attempt to describe everything of a physical nature in the sky, air, sea, and Earth, including all known weather phenomena. This first text-book on atmospheric science had some interesting notions, such as "hurricanes are caused by evil winds falling upon good winds with a resulting moral conflict." In fact, it was Aristotle who gave us the word 'meteorology' for the scientific study of weather.[65] Philosophers Aristotle and Theophrastus (372-287 BC) were among the first people to try to explain scientifically how the weather works. They lived about 2,400 years ago in ancient Greece and wrote about clouds, hail, storms, and snow formation, and more unusual phenomena, such as sun haloes.

After Aristotle retired, his pupil Theophrastus continued his work. His book entitled *'On Weather Signs'* gives some 80 different signs of rain, 50 of storms, 45 of wind, and 24 of fair weather. Some were fairly reliable-for example: "whenever there is fog, there is little or no rain." This is often correct because fog generally occurs with stable weather near the center of a high pressure area

[65] *http://www.scienceforums.com/topic/20297-climategate/page-3.* Retrieved: 04-11-2014.

where there is very little or no precipitation. Others were simply off the mark, "If shooting stars are frequent, they are a sign of either rain or wind; and the wind or rain will come from the quarter whence they proceed." Their ideas were not challenged until about 2,000 years later.

An ancient Maori myth describes how the god of thunder and lightning, Tawhaki, went up into the sky disguised as a kite. Maori priests believed they could predict the weather by watching how kites, which they flew in Tawhaki's honor, moved across the sky. In other cultures, such as in the Solomon Islands, a figurehead is attached to the front of a canoe before the men went out to sea, and it is believed that this figurehead is able to ward off dangerous hurricanes at sea or is able to protect them should they ever encounter a powerful storm, and this ancient belief has been handed down from generation to generation in this culture. According to ancient records, the Chinese were predicting weather at least as far back as 300 BC. Ancient methods of weather forecasting usually relied on experience to spot patterns of events. For example, they noticed that if the sunset gave a particularly red sky, then the following day brought fair weather.

In the United States before the National Weather Service, determining what tomorrow's weather would be like was mainly part guesswork, part superstition, and part understood, observation. People made out what weather was to come was by the shape of goose bones, groundhog shadows, the aching of once broken bones, the thickness of squirrel fur, a plague of woolly bear caterpillars, and the high honking of wild geese flying south at night over frosted rustling cornfields. To kick a cat in the dark meant rain, and if a groundhog on February 2 came out and saw his shadow, it meant that there'll be six more weeks of winter.

To ward off violent and tropical downpours, Yoruba priests in southwestern Nigeria held ceremonies around images of the thunder and lightning god 'Sango', and it is a long held belief that this was exported to the Caribbean with the African slave trade. In many West African nations, the elders would chant supplications and toss a concoction of wine, grain, milk, and water into the waves; priests would cut the cow's neck and let it bleed into the surf, then throw its limbs into the waters; and people would bang on drums and throw money into the water. They did all of this with the hope and the desire of appeasing the fickle, exacting sea and obtaining a quiet summer. These experiences accumulated over the generations to produce weather folklore. However, not all of these predictions proved reliable, and many of them have since been found not to stand up to rigorous statistical testing.

In the 17th century, in Renaissance Italy, the first meteorological instruments were developed to measure changes in air temperature, atmospheric pressure, and humidity. It was in Italy, around 1600, that the great mathematician and astronomer Galileo Galilei (1564-1642) made the first weather thermometer, or as he called it the 'thermoscope', and it was really a very inaccurate instrument. Some 40 years later, Galileo's secretary-turn-assistant Evangelista Torricelli, made the first practical barometer for use in measuring atmospheric pressure. He filled a glass tube about 4 feet long with mercury and inverted the open end into a dish of the same liquid. Torricelli noted that much of the mercury remained in the tube instead of going into the dish and that the space above the mercury in the tube was a vacuum. He concluded that the mercury column was being supported by air pressure and that variations in the height of the column were caused by actual changes in atmospheric pressure.

As a result of this experiment, it was French scientist and philosopher Blaise Pascal (1623-62) who realized that these changes in atmospheric pressure might be related to changes in the weather, and this paved the way for the use of the barometer in weather forecasting. Pascal was also the first to discover and demonstrate that air pressure decreases with height. The first really successful thermometer was one made by German Physicist Daniel Fahrenheit (developer of the Fahrenheit temperature scale) in 1709 using alcohol, followed in 1714 by the mercury thermometer. This scale was calibrated on three points-the temperature of a mixture of water, ice, and common salt (0°F); the freezing point of water (32°F); and the temperature of the human body (assumed to be 96°F). In 1742, Anders Celsius, a Swedish astronomer, introduced a scale that set zero as the boiling point of water and 100 degrees at the freezing point. This 'upside-down' scale was designed to avoid negative temperatures in winter. In 1745, the scale was reversed by Swedish scientist Carolus Linnaeus (1707-78). It is this scale that is known world-wide today as the Celsius scale.

This period marked the rebirth of using advanced meteorological instruments for the studying and forecasting of the weather. The barometer was developed in the middle of the seventeenth century, and members of the Royal Society began sending the instruments to the correspondents in the West Indies by the 1670s-earlier, apparently, than the instruments appeared in North America-sometimes with the express purpose of gathering information on hurricanes. Sir Peter Colletion sent several barometers to Barbados in 1677 in order "to examine whether they would be of any use for the foretelling the seasons and mutations of the weather as they are found to do here, especially concerning hurricanes." Ralph Bohun speculated in 1671 that "there might be excellent use made of the barometer for predicting of hurricanes," based on accounts of its use by "a person of quality" who lived near the sea and who had observed movement in the instrument before storms. Some early accounts indicated that this might indeed be the case. A report to the Royal Society in the 1680s stated that "Quicksilver" in barometers in Barbados did not react "unless in a violent storm of hurricane."[66] The use of barometers, however, was not widespread, nor was their results viewed as trustworthy. Barometers were expensive, and even those who had the instruments had trouble using or understanding them. During the early years of sea exploration, no practical scientific instruments were in use so sailors at sea depended upon the sun, the stars and the compass.

In the eighteenth century, several meteorological networks were set up under the patronage of learned societies such as the Royal Society in Britain, the Académie des Sciences in France, and Mannheim Meteorological Society in Germany. A request in 1723 by James Jurin, secretary of the Royal Society, resulted in observations being received from England, continental Europe, North America, and India. In 1730's observation networks were set up in Siberia by scientists involved in Vitus Bering's Great Northern Expedition. The most significant of the early networks was that established by the Mannheim Society. From 14 stations in 1781, the network gradually grew to include 39 observations in Russia, Europe, Greenland, and North America. The society closed in 1799, but by then it had established procedures that were to prove invaluable when synoptic forecasting emerged in the nineteenth century.

The two men most credited with the birth of forecasting as a science were Sir Francis Beaufort (created the Beaufort Wind Scale) and his protégé Robert Fitzroy (developer of the Fitzroy Barometer). Both were influential men in British Naval and Governmental circles, and though ridiculed by many at the time, their work gained scientific credence, and was accepted by the British Navy and formed the basis for all of today's weather forecasting knowledge. The first weather instruments-a barometer, thermometer, hydrometer and a rain gauge-were introduced in America as forecasting weather instruments. Beginning in 1731 at Charleston, one of the most hurricane prone cities located on the U.S. mainland by a Scottish physician, Dr. John Lining and he believed that the weather was the cause of epidemics.

---

66 Matthew Mulcahy, Hurricanes and Society in the British Greater Caribbean, 1624-1783, (Baltimore, The Johns Hopkins University Press, 2006), pgs. 52-54.

One of the great pioneering 'self-taught scientists' was William Redfield who was a Connecticut saddle and harness maker by profession. He is credited as being one of the first persons to take an important first step towards our understanding of hurricanes. While traveling around Connecticut by foot (because he couldn't afford a horse) after a strong hurricane which hit in September of 1821, he noticed that some trees and most cornfields in some areas were blown down and were actually pointing towards the northwest, while those only a few miles away were pointing to the southeast. He gathered more information about the storm from other places along the East Coast and concluded in an article in the 'American Journal of Science' in 1831 that: "This storm was exhibited in the form of a great whirlwind."[67]

Redfield's detailed observations and logical presentation convinced others in the United States and elsewhere that he was on the right track. Following his lead, they began the work of understanding hurricanes that continues to this day. It was not until the invention of the telegraph in 1837 by Samuel F.B. Morse that the modern age of weather forecasting began. Before this time, it was not possible to transport information about the current state of the weather any faster than a steam train or by boat. These forms of weather dissemination would have been impossible and very useless to make an accurate synoptic weather forecast in a timely manner based on those observations. However, the telegraph allowed reports of weather conditions from a wide area to be received almost instantaneously. This allowed synoptic forecasts to be made by knowing what the weather conditions were like from station to station and country to country.

In 1843, the U.S. Congress appropriated $30,000 for the construction of a telegraph line from Washington to Baltimore. It was completed in 1844 and from that time on, the success of the electromagnetic telegraph was assured. From these early efforts it was apparent that movements of storms could be followed from day to day on the weather map with information received from across the country via telegraph. In 1848, the Smithsonian Museum organized a network of weather observers across the United States and its territories. However, it wasn't until 1868 and 1869 when two storms on the Great Lakes in the United States sank or damaged more than 3,000 vessels and claimed the lives of some 530 persons that led to a Resolution of Congress, which President Ulysses S. Grant signed into law in 1870, that established the nation's first official weather service, the meteorological division of the Signal Service-popularly

67 J. Espy, The Philosophy of Storms, (Boston, Freeman and Bolles, 1841), pg. 210.

known as The Weather Bureau, which relayed data twice daily to Washington by telegraph.

Timeliness was lacking for effective hurricane tracking because of the lack of wireless communications. With the invention of the telegraph, hurricane warning stations were established throughout the West Indies with the main center in Kingston, Jamaica. The first detailed studies of the nature of hurricanes in this hemisphere begun before the American Civil War by a group of poverty-stricken Jesuit scientists in Havana, Cuba who began to track and monitor hurricanes of the Caribbean. The Director of 'The Royal College of Bélen, Observatory' was headed by Father Antonio Cobre, a mathematician and physicist and upon his death was replaced by Father Benito Viñes and then Father Gangoite, gave classes in practical science training in daily observations. They aroused an overwhelming demand for weather information from the hurricane-conscious people of the Caribbean, United States and mainland Europe.

Today, the U.S. National Weather Service is one of the world's best-known weather Agencies because of the work it does with the forecasting of the major weather events such as hurricanes and tornadoes. However, it was not always so popular, especially in its early years of existence. The first incarnation of the National Weather Service was founded in the wake of the Civil War, as an agency in the Army Signal Service Corps. Its main mission was to take observations at military stations and to warn of storms on the Great Lakes and on the Atlantic and Gulf Coasts. From its inception, the agency earned a reputation for the corruption of its personnel and the unreliability of its weather forecast. For example, in 1881 William Howgate, the chief financial manager of the agency, was arrested for embezzling a quarter of a million dollars. To give an idea of the magnitude of his crime, consider that during this time the U.S. military budget was about forty million dollars. Howgate was tried and convicted, only to escape a year later. Other servicemen in stations around the country were investigated throughout the 1880s and fired in large numbers for reckless neglect. It was discovered that one man had sold his station's weather instruments to pay off a gambling debt, while another had converted his office into a photography studio for nude models.

Moreover, the agency's weather predictions were frequently and dangerously wrong. Consider this, on March 12, 1888, the New York station's forecast called for "fair weather"; instead of fair weather, New York got the powerful Blizzard of '88' which dumped an amazing 21 inches of snow on the city and killed four hundred people throughout the northeast. The scandal and the unreliability of the organization were far too great for it to continue as it was. As a result, in 1891, the Army Signal Service Corps' weather service portfolio was removed from the Department of War and given a new home in the civilian Department of Agriculture by the Congress of the United States. It was named the Weather Bureau: It would not be called the National Weather Service until 1970. During the years leading up to 1900, the Weather Bureau's servicemen took regular measurements of such atmospheric conditions as temperature, wind speed and direction, air pressure, rainfall, and cloud conditions. They transmitted their findings from one station to another by telegraph.

Battling negative public opinion and the sheer newness of their science, the early weathermen paved the groundwork for an organization that today predicts weather effectively and saves the lives of hundreds perhaps thousands of persons on a yearly basis. The National Weather Service is the sole United States official voice for issuing warnings during life-threatening weather situations, such as hurricanes, floods and tornadoes. The United States Weather Bureau played a vital part in the history of modern day weather forecasting. In 1902, Cunard ships at sea began to receive U.S. Weather Bureau forecasts by wireless telegraph. In 1903, the Wright Brothers before their historic flight consulted with the U.S. Weather Bureau to prepare for their flight. By 1910, the Weather Bureau was sending out weekly forecasts for agricultural planners.

With the advent of aviation industry, this demanded more sophisticated means of tracking and forecasting the weather, and it also provided an unprecedented tool for observing it. In 1918, the Weather Bureau began to send out forecasts to military and air-mail flights. By 1931, the Weather Bureau was operating regular observation flights, marking the end of the era of kites in weather observation. The close links between aviation and meteorology led President Roosevelt to transfer the Weather Bureau to the Department of Commerce in 1940. In 1943 a hurricane forecast center was established in Miami, Florida. In 1955 Miami office of the U.S. Weather Bureau was designated the primary hurricane warning center responsible for coordinating all forecasting and warnings issued for hurricanes in the Atlantic. In 1955 the Congress increased the Weather Bureau's funding in response to the disasters of Hurricanes Carol, Edna and Hazel in 1954 and Hurricanes Connie and Diane in 1955. The extra funds not only paid for hurricane research, but also accelerated work on computer forecasting and the purchase of a computer.

The Weather Bureau's budget in 1953 was $27.5 million in total and today, President Obama's fiscal year 2015 discretionary budget request for NOAA, the National Oceanic and Atmospheric Administration, totals $5.5 billion.

This is $174 million over the 2014 enacted budget, an increase of 3.2 percent.[68] In 1957 after they had gotten their computer and established the Hurricane Research Project, the Weather Bureau's budget was $57.5 million, more than double as a result of these hurricanes. The main reasons for the steep drop in hurricane-related deaths since 1960s was due to the introduction of weather satellites and radars to warn residents of some impending hurricane-related danger such as, the storm surge, the strong winds or the torrential rainfall. In addition to increased funding in the area of meteorology, educating the public about hurricanes and the dangers or hazards associated with them, and more emphasis being placed on preparing and evacuating people from hurricane-prone areas also played a significant role in reduction the deaths related to these storms.

The National Weather Service's National Hurricane Center has since moved to Coral Gables, Florida. There, the latest computer technology and most sophisticated atmospheric weather programs are run on high speed 'super' computers. Their job is to predict a hurricane's size, intensity, movement, and storm surge. The Center issues a hurricane watch if it is determined that the hurricane will hit a certain area within 24 to 36 hours. A hurricane warning is issued if the storm is forecast to hit a particular area within 36 hours or less, whereas, a hurricane watch is issued if the storm is forecast to hit a particular area within 48 hours or less. The development of computers, radars, satellites in the 1950s and onward has given meteorologists even greater means for analyzing and predicting weather patterns. In 1977, the last weather observation ship was sent back to port; its job is now done entirely by satellites.

Advance notice of weather events like devastating hurricanes gives people time to prepare, and to evacuate if necessary. Though forecasting is an imperfect science, and weather will often change its course at the last minute, weather forecasting saves lives since it allows disaster management officials to call for evacuation. For example, during Hurricane Andrew in August 1992, the death toll was surprisingly low because most residents had been sufficiently warned and evacuated by the time Hurricane Andrew hit South Florida. Today, with modern technology, meteorologists can predict where disasters might strike next with far greater accuracy than yesterday's forecast, thereby saving many lives in the process. Great progress was made in the science of meteorology during the 20th century, which allowed greater understanding of meteorological

---

68 *http://www.noaanews.noaa.gov/stories2014/20140313_budget_statement.html.* Retrieved: 04-11- 2014.

processes that takes place within the Earth's atmosphere with severe weather events such as hurricanes, tornadoes and thunderstorms.

The idea of numerical weather prediction was presented by Lewis Fry Richardson in 1922. However, computers fast enough to complete the vast number of calculations required to produce a forecast before the event had occurred did not exist at that time. It was not until the 1970's that numerical weather prediction models became operational in meteorological forecasting agencies around the world. Numerical weather prediction models are computer simulations of the atmosphere. They take the analysis as the starting point and evolve the state of the atmosphere forward in time using the understanding of physics and fluid dynamics. The complicated equations which govern how the state of a fluid changes with time require supercomputers to solve them. The output from these models provides the basis understanding of our daily, weekly or monthly weather forecasts for severe weather events such as hurricanes, frontal systems or thunderstorms.

Traditional observations made at the surface of atmospheric pressure, temperature, wind speed, wind direction, humidity, precipitation are collected routinely from trained observers, automatic weather stations or buoys. The World Meteorological Organization acts to standardize the instrumentation, observing practices and timing of these observations worldwide. Stations either report hourly in weather reports, or every three to six hours in intermediate or synoptic weather reports. Additionally, information about the temperature, humidity and wind above the surface are found by launching a radiosonde (weather balloon) high up into the earth's atmosphere. Data from these weather balloons up to the tropopause are usually transmitted back to the surface.

For centuries, weather observing tools consisted of the human eye and the various human senses. Only within the last six centuries has the rudimentary technology of weather observation been developed. The rain gauge, barometer, anemometer, hygrometer and thermometer were all invented in the centuries between 1400 and 1700. These instruments, which were improved upon through the years, remain basic observing tools of meteorological offices around the world and its network of cooperative observers today. However, with the advent of the telegraph system in the 1840's, the ability of meteorologists to simultaneously make weather observations at many widely dispersed stations, develop near real-time maps of weather systems, and then predict the future course of observed weather phenomena experienced a quantum leap. Suddenly, meteorologists were able to chart the course of a weather phenomenon on a near continent-wide basis. Since that time communications have drastically improved with the development of radio and telephone, new observing systems such as radar and satellites have evolved, and ever more powerful computing systems have become available to the meteorologist. Concurrently, this has led to improved communications with the public and in particular, vastly improved warning capabilities which, in turn, resulted in saving many more lives in the process.

This section highlights the story of some of these major improvements and how the capabilities of meteorologists to observe, predict, and communicate has evolved through time. In 1898, President McKinley stated he was more afraid of hurricanes than of the Spanish Navy. President McKinley is quoted as having remarked at the time of the Spanish-American War that more warships had gone to the bottom of the sea in storms than under the fire of enemy fleets. Commenting on the Spanish-American War of 1898, President William McKinley's concern about these hurricanes translated to a revamped United States hurricane warning service, forerunner of today's National Hurricane Center in Florida, the governing body for monitoring and tracking hurricanes of the North Atlantic. Although the Army Signals Corps, beginning in 1873, had been attempting to issue storm warnings, there was no tracking of hurricanes in the United States until 1890. Following a bad storm in 1899, a more comprehensive system was established during McKinley's Administration. In 1898, he ordered that the Weather Bureau set up a hurricane warning system in the Caribbean. Following the deadliest hurricane in U.S. history, which hit Galveston, Texas and killed over 8,000 persons, the U.S. Weather Bureau began making three-day hurricane forecasts and by 1935, a full hurricane warning system was in place.

In March 1889, war was avoided between the United States and Germany by a tropical cyclone. Throughout the late nineteenth century, various western countries contended for control of the South Pacific islands. One of the many island groups under dispute was Samoa. Between 1847 and 1861, Great Britain, United States, and Germany all laid claims to the territory and established diplomatic missions there in that country. Part of their strategies involved siding with local tribal chiefs and arming them to fight rival chiefs supported by rival western nations. Late in 1888 a German naval force took the native chief of the Samoans away and set up another king in his place. The natives rebelled and in one of the collisions, twenty-two German soldiers were killed. The Germans retaliated by shelling a native village and accidentally destroying properties of some American citizens. An American flag which was raised by an American citizen to protect his property was torn down and burned. Secretary of State

Thomas Bayard protested, so American warships were ordered to Samoa to protect the rights of American citizens there.

On March 16, 1889, there were, one British, three German and three American warships in the harbor at Apia, Samoa. With relations between the two countries in this state of strain, a powerful hurricane approached Apia. The British warship *'Calliope'* moved from the inner harbor into the heart of the hurricane and amazingly survived. The remaining warships of the United States and Germany and also six merchant ships were destroyed on the reefs, sent to the bottom ocean or beached by the hurricane. Sadly, a total of 150 sailors lost their lives to this storm. However, while the hurricanes raged all of the hostile parties became friends and many acts of heroism were recorded. The natives came to the rescue of both American and German sailors. The Navy Department expressed appreciation of the courage of the natives, especially to Chief Seumanu, a native leader, and suggested that he be presented with a double banked whaleboat with fittings and that his men be justly rewarded. In this case, the hurricane brought peace temporarily, but at a heavy cost.

After this storm, it caused the Germans and the Americans to resolve their differences peacefully. The hurricane hastened action to settle differences in the congress and the Treaty of Berlin in 1889 has been credited with being responsible, indirectly, for the founding of a modern navy of the United States, because it made the United States realize that it was a 'major power' in the world, which required a larger navy to curb other aggressive countries. In the words of Robert Louis Stevenson: "Thus in what seemed the very article of war, and within a single day, the sword arm of each of the two angry powers was broken: their formidable ships reduced to junk, the disciplined hundreds to a horde of castaways. The hurricane of March 16 made thus a marking epoch in world history; directly and at once it brought about the congress and Treaty of Berlin; indirectly and by a process still continuing, it founded the modern navy of the United States."[69]

It may seem a bit unusual, but the first reconnaissance flight into a hurricane was an unplanned and unauthorized flight based on a simple bet. To monitor and track the development and movement of a hurricane, we rely on remote sensing by satellites and radars, as well as data gathered by reconnaissance aircrafts (or sometimes called Hurricane Hunters). The reconnaissance aircraft was major advancement in the field of meteorology. The reconnaissance aircraft flying into

---

69 Ivan Ray Tannehill, Hurricanes-Their Nature and History, (New Jersey, Princeton University Press, 1950), pg. 133.

the eye of a hurricane has been a great success for both meteorologists and the public at large. This idea of flying into hurricanes to gather vital information about hurricanes was also a recent development. On July 27th 1943, during the height of World War II, brave pioneers Major Joseph P. Duckworth a flight instructor and navigator Ralph O'Hair took an AT-6 aircraft from the United States Bryan Air Force Base in Texas without permission. They did this simply to find out what it was like to fly inside the eye of a hurricane that was nearing Galveston Texas at the time, which they did with remarkable success.

At the edge of the storm, the small plane rocked violently in the strong winds, driving rain enveloped it and dark clouds blotted out the sun. As Duckworth pressed on, the hurricane force winds tossed the plane up and down and sideways like a roller coaster ride. Suddenly the plane was surrounded by the calm of the eye. Above blue skies and below was the Texas landscape. Then the dark clouds closed in and powerful winds raged and seized the plane from the opposite direction as they exited the storm. When they got back from the trip their senior officer, Lieutenant William Jones Burdick complained bitterly not because they removed an USAF aircraft without permission but because he had not been taken along on the trip, so Major Duckworth was forced to take him back up with him on a second trip into the eye of the hurricane where Burdick performed some visual and written observations and so hence the first and second reconnaissance trips into a hurricane were performed on that day.

Major Duckworth later received the Air Medal of Honor for that flight of his by the United States Government. You may be surprised to learn that this first intentional flight into a hurricane was not carefully planned mission but was a spur of the moment decision based on a bet to Major Joseph Duckworth by the British airmen who were also on the base at the time. The British airmen laughed and made fun of the American AT-6 aircraft because they believed that it was a frail and inferior aircraft and couldn't be relied on in severe weather, such as thunderstorms or hurricanes. Major Duckworth vigorously defended the high quality workmanship of the aircraft and his instrument flying techniques because he believed that with proper training a pilot could fly in any kind of weather including a hurricane. So he bet them to prove the quality workmanship of this aircraft, he bet them that he would fly this aircraft into the eye of the hurricane in the Gulf of Mexico at the time and return safely and the bet was accepted by the British airmen. Major Duckworth had long firmly believed that no weather was unflyable when the pilot was competent in instrument flying techniques.

In his report, Duckworth later stated, "The only embarrassing episode would have been engine failure, which, with the strong ground winds, would probably have prevented a landing, and certainly would have made descent via parachute highly inconvenient."[70] And no one on that base was more competent or experienced than Joseph P. Duckworth to fly in such weather. Major Duckworth needed a navigator. Across the table sat the only navigator at the airfield that morning: Lieutenant Ralph O'Hair. Duckworth asked O'Hair to volunteer to accompany him on this risky, unsanctioned flight into the hurricane. O'Hair was shocked at the invitation but agreed out of the respect he had for Duckworth's skill as a pilot. "There was no one in the Air Force who could have ordered me to do that; I love life too much." O'Hair later recalled.[71] Neither Duckworth nor O'Hair ever repeated their flight into a hurricane, but they certainly proved it could be done.

This spur of the moment flight opened new research doors into learning about the dynamics and anatomy of hurricanes and what makes them work. Furthermore, as a result of this flight, on August 7, 1944, the U.S. War Department created the first Weather Reconnaissance Squadron. This unit was activated three weeks later, although it wasn't until February 1945 before enough men and aircraft could be assembled to form an operational flight. The reconnaissance aircrafts are members of the 53rd Weather Reconnaissance Squadron/403rd Wing, based at Keesler Air Force Base in Biloxi, Mississippi. Today, NOAA hurricane-hunter planes, and similar propeller-driven models flown by a special Air Force unit out of Mississippi, are flown directly into storms with sustained winds of 155 mph or higher. Since 1944, the United States Department of Defense (which oversees the U.S. Military) has been the only organization to fly into tropical storms and hurricanes to help warn civilians as well as military personnel of approaching storms. However, it wasn't until 1954, when Hurricanes Carol, Edna, and Hazel swept up the eastern coast of the United States (Hazel went directly over Washington, D.C.), that policymakers finally took hurricane threats seriously enough to finance research into hurricanes. They did this with the hope and desire of improving the overall scientific understanding of hurricanes, with a view to lessening the significant damage inflicted and the great death toll associated with these storms.

---

70 *http://www.chicagotribune.com/sns-hc-history-1943-story.html.* Retrieved: 04-11-2014.

71 D. Florin, Mega Disasters: The Science of Predicting the Next Catastrophe, (New Jersey, Princeton University Press, 2010), pg. 78.

During this era, the U.S. Reconnaissance Aircraft fleet was considerably improved. For example, one of the major discoveries of the reconnaissance aircraft missions flying into hurricanes was finding out that the minimum threshold temperature for a hurricane to form is 26.5°C (80°F) and below that threshold temperature they found out that hurricanes simply won't form. In fact, when a reconnaissance aircraft makes a trip into a hurricane, one or two of the airplane seats are often reserved for hurricane researchers or other hurricane specialists studying hurricanes (such as doctorate students in meteorology).

Since 1965, the reconnaissance aircraft team has used the C-130 Hercules and the WP-3D, two very sturdy turboprop planes. The only difference between the WC-130 plane and the cargo version is the specialized, highly sensitive weather equipment installed on the WC-130. The team can cover up to five storm missions per day, anywhere from the mid-Atlantic to Hawaii. While the WC-130 aircraft is better than jets for flying around in hurricanes at relatively low altitudes, it can't do two important jobs for researchers and the National Hurricane Center. Meteorologists want to find out more about what goes on at the top of a hurricane, more than 40,000 feet above the Earth's surface. It is believed that measurements there should answer some questions about why hurricanes strengthen or weaken unexpectedly. Also, new computer models could do a better job of predicting where a hurricane is heading, if meteorological data was available for winds high above the Earth's surface or oceans for thousands of square miles around the storm.

To fill in these lack of meteorological data gaps, in 1996 NOAA purchased a Gulfstream IV business jet and turned it into a research airplane. It can fly up to 45,000 feet and go more than 4,600 miles without refueling. However, the jet won't fly directly into the most turbulent parts of the hurricane as the WC-130s and the WP-3Ds will continue doing. Pilots and researchers flying in the jet will have the satisfaction of knowing they're gathering vital information that will help produce better hurricane forecast and save lives in the process. These airplanes are relatively very safe and the only plane to be lost in a hurricane in the North Atlantic was a Navy P-2V, which disappeared in Hurricane Janet in the central Caribbean Sea in September, 1955, with all eleven crew members believed to have perished. However, three Air Force planes have been lost flying into Pacific typhoons in more than 50 years of such flying.

When a reconnaissance aircraft is set to fly into a tropical storm or hurricane, it is ready for a long mission. Most commonly, one plane will be in the air for up to 11 hours. These aircrafts gather vital information about wind speed and direction, temperature, humidity, and barometric pressure within the storm. As they fly into a hurricane, they drop special parachute borne weather sensors called dropwindsondes into the storm. These sensors measure the storm's characteristics such as pressure, temperature, humidity, wind speed and direction and the messages are sent back to the plane and this information is important because it provides a detailed look at the storm's structure. By combining the data obtained by multiple dropwindsondes, computer models can reconstruct the environment both inside and outside a hurricane, identifying conditions that feed or sap its strength or steer it in a particular direction. As a result, a five-day forecast is just as accurate today as a three-day forecast was 15 years ago.

The information gathered from the hurricane is relayed back to the National Hurricane Center in Miami, Florida, where it is interpreted and distributed to international, national and local governments and organizations, meteorological offices and news media. The National Hurricane Center predicts the hurricane's movement and intensity using various weather models and The National Hurricane Center and the affected countries issues hurricane watches and warnings in the storm's path. This modern system (tracking, early detection, warnings) has greatly reduced the loss of life during a hurricane. Several other tools are used to monitor hurricanes and they include ships, weather buoys, radiosonde, automated and manned surface observing stations, satellites and radars.

We take for granted the low death tolls in hurricanes nowadays, but sadly this wasn't always the case, and we actually have the invention of satellite technology for this. For example, there was The Great Galveston Hurricane of 1900 which killed over 8000 persons in the State of Texas alone. In 1928 there was a storm over Florida near Lake Okeechobee, which killed at least 2,500 persons in Florida alone and at least 4,118 persons in the United States and the Caribbean combined. Then there was Hurricane Flora in 1963 which killed 7,193 in the Caribbean and Florida. Today, the death toll from these hurricanes has significantly declined and often times you can count them on one or two hands. Unfortunately, the damage to homes, boats and other personal property have significantly increased mainly because a lot more persons are now living on or near the coast. Certainly, one can't compare the loss of a loved one to the loss of a house, boat, car, or other personal properties, because you can replace those things but you can't replace a human life.

Modern weather forecasting depends on gathering, assessing and disseminating millions of observations and measurements of atmospheric conditions, constantly recorded at the same time all over the world. No single system of measurements or instruments can give meteorologists a complete picture, so information is fed in from a wide range of sources. Most important are the many land-based weather stations, from city centers to remote islands. Ships and radio signals from drifting weather buoys and ships report details of conditions at sea. Weather balloons and specially equipped airplanes take measurements up through the atmosphere, while in space weather satellites constantly circle the Earth, beaming back real-time pictures of cloud and temperature patterns.

Today, it is difficult to imagine what it was like to live during the 1700s, 1800s and early 1900s during a hurricane in this region. Meteorologists are now able to track and monitor a hurricane from its inception as it comes off the African coast as a tropical wave or disturbance and then eventually progress into a full-fledged hurricane as it travels along a designated route within the region. We take this for granted and often times never stop to realize the importance of modern technology, such as satellites and radars, and man's overall advancement over the last 50 to 75 years within the meteorological arena. In 1954, a hurricane was detected by camera on a Navy rocket and this convinced the U.S. Government of the utility of weather satellites. Furthermore, it also helped convinced this government that spending such a large sum of money for acquiring the use of satellite technology for weather forecasting would be worth it in the end. In addition, it would ultimately reduce the overall devastation and significantly reduce the great death toll from these hurricanes by providing advanced warnings.

The satellite, which now allows meteorologists to track these storms from the time they come off the African coast until they make landfall somewhere within the region, wasn't available for use until on 1st April, 1960. This was accomplished with the launching of the polar orbiting satellite TIROS 1(Television Infrared Observation Satellite). This satellite which was crude by today's standards, but its TV images did reveal a high degree of organization to the Earth's weather and cloud systems that surprised many atmospheric scientists. This technological advancement revolutionized the field of meteorology in such a way that no other meteorological instrument had ever done before. This led to a much more improved and refined weather forecast.

When the first weather satellite was launched into orbit the operators were rewarded almost instantaneously, because a few days after its launching, the satellite discovered a previously unreported typhoon in the South Pacific just east of Australia. Since the launch of TIROS, no hurricane or typhoon has gone undetected. Furthermore, the value of satellites was made clear to the public too, when in September of 1961 satellite images of Hurricane Clara led to the evacuation of more than 350,000 persons from their homes along the Gulf Coast-the largest mass evacuation in the United States at the time. The improvement in the warning of severe tropical storms alone has probably paid for the investment in meteorological satellites many times over.

Satellites do not look into the heart of a hurricane because that work is still being done by reconnaissance aircrafts. They show changes in the size of the eye and also inside the entire storm itself, to determine if the eye is growing bigger or smaller, if the storm is weakening or strengthening. Most important, satellites can show with pin-point accuracy the location of a storm, record its speed and direction closely. In addition, with the introduction of satellite technology, it also answered a lot of meteorological questions and put forth many new theories on the dynamics of hurricanes, which ultimately resulted in the saving many lives in the process. Today, with our sophisticated early detection and warning systems, there are minimal deaths from hurricanes, however damages to homes and properties are often increased not because of these early warning systems, but simply because more persons are now living on or near the coast.

There are two types of weather satellites, one is the Geostationary satellites which always remain fixed in the same spot high above the equator, about 21,600 miles (36,000 km) out in space. There are five of these types of satellites altogether, providing an almost complete picture of the globe (except for the two poles) every half hour. Then there are the polar-orbiting satellites which circle the Earth in strips from pole to pole. They provide a continuously changing and more detailed weather picture from closer to the Earth's surface. Increasingly, data from weather satellites are being used due to their (almost) global coverage.

Although their visible light images are very useful for forecasters to see development of clouds, little of this information can be used by numerical weather prediction models. The infra-red (IR) data however can be used as it gives information on the temperature at the surface and cloud tops. Individual clouds can also be tracked from one time to the next to provide information on wind direction and strength at the clouds steering level. Polar orbiting satellites provide soundings of temperature and moisture throughout the depth of the atmosphere. Compared with similar data from radiosonde balloons, the satellite data has the advantage that coverage is global, however the accuracy and resolution is not as good.

Today, we can turn on our radios, computers and televisions and get up to the minute weather reports and track these storms 24 hours a day. Prior to these inventions, residents throughout the region got little or no warnings, mass confusion and a high death toll from these storms. Today, in meteorology every available technology is utilized, ranging from satellites, orbiting high above the Earth's surface, to manned and unmanned weather-observing stations on remote islands, weather radars, weather-observing ships, drifting buoys makes sure that no hurricane goes undetected. Once identified, advisories and warnings are regularly and meticulously prepared, and then rapidly dispatched around the world. Using a wide range of communications technology, these messages are sent to all threatened communities and ships at sea. The use of the internet is becoming an increasing popular source of hurricane warnings, but radio and television broadcasts are still the public's preferred source of information.

With the success of satellite and radar technology, these inspired nations to cooperate in the collection of data. In 1961, President John F. Kennedy invited other countries to join the United States in developing an international weather prediction programme. Although, this was at the height of the Cold War, 150 countries, including Russia, responded positively, and the World Weather Watch was created under the auspices of the World Meteorological Organization (WMO) in 1963. Under the scheme, members of the WMO exchanged data from their networks on a regular basis, thus facilitating the preparation of global weather charts. The resulting data clarified our understanding of global weather patterns and allowed scientists to refine existing weather forecast based on numerical models and weather forecast in general.

In the field of meteorology, there are now all types of different weather instruments to measure the different types of weather elements in the hurricane such as, anemometers, barometers, hygrographs, thermometers, rain gauge, and radiosonde weather balloons just to name a few. Today we take those things and other modern amenities for granted and often never reflect back to a time when they weren't invented yet. For example, the weather satellite and weather radar have improved and modernized the field of meteorology significantly and to such a point that it was quite difficult for me as a meteorologist to imagine what it would be like without these two important weather forecasting tools. The satellite on the other hand, like the radar was also a recent discovery, and this allowed meteorologists to track these storms with much greater accuracy. The satellite allowed meteorologists to actually now see the origins of a hurricane from its birth on the African Coast or in the Caribbean to its death anyway along the North American coast, in the Atlantic Ocean, in the Caribbean or Latin America. It also allowed the meteorologists to understand and study these storms with greater accuracy and in significantly greater details resulting in a much-improved weather forecast and saving many lives in the process.

Watching menacing hurricanes bear down on populated coastal communities raises a fundamental question: Can we stop or modify these powerful storms? As crazy as the idea may sound, scientists have tried to do just that -- and failed. But does that mean it's an idea that can't work? Maybe we will never know. The scientific successes of World War II, with such successes as the development of radar and the atomic bomb, led to the feeling that science could accomplish anything, maybe even find a way to modify or destroy hurricanes. Efforts in storm modification go as far back as the late 1940s when Dr. Irwin Langmuir began exploring the idea of using silver iodide crystals (dry ice) to weaken storms such as hurricanes. In 1947, he gathered together a team of scientists from General Electric, and brought his idea to fruition with 'Project Cirrus.' The highlight of this effort occurred on October 13, 1947 when Langmuir and his team had a Navy plane fly into a hurricane off the coast of Georgia, and drop a payload of silver iodide crystals into it.

The hope of using silver iodide crystals was to release energy from the storm's inner core and thus weaken the hurricane itself. It was originally considered a success. After the cloud seeding had taken place, the hurricane suddenly changed direction, and made landfall near the coastal city of Savannah, Georgia. The public blamed the seeding, and Irving Langmuir claimed that the reversal had been caused by human intervention and Project Cirrus was cancelled. As a result of this storm's reversal, several lawsuits were threatened. Only the fact that a system in the 1906 season had taken a similar path, as well as evidence showing that the storm had already begun to turn when the cloud seeding began, ended the litigation. This disaster set back the cause of seeding hurricanes for eleven more years. However, about a decade later, a scientist named Mook recognized that the storm's sudden change in direction was not caused by the seeding, but rather the upper level steering winds in the vicinity of the hurricane. Nevertheless, Langmuir's work had generated some enthusiasm. This enthusiasm was particularly strong among officials in the United States Government.

In the years following Langmuir's experiment, a number of powerful hurricanes made landfall in the United States. They included Carol, Edna, and Hazel in 1954, and the first billion-dollar hurricane, Hurricane Diane in 1955. All four of these storms were Category 4 strength on the Saffir-Simpson

Hurricane Wind Scale, and caused extensive damage from Florida all the way up to New England and even Canada. In response to these devastating storms, President Dwight Eisenhower appointed a Presidential Commission to investigate the idea of storm modification. Despite the lack of enthusiasm for the idea, the US Congress extended the life of this special committee for another two years in 1956, and by the end of the decade there were scientists that were ready to take another stab at attacking hurricane modification.

There were many ideas that were brought up in this commission and one of the ideas was to drop an atomic bomb at the center of the hurricane to break it up but this idea didn't get very far because it was felt that it would be futile effort because scientists determined that it would be like trying to stop a freight train by placing feathers on the tracks. "Because a mature hurricane of moderate strength and size releases as much condensation heat energy in a day as the fusion energy of about 400 hydrogen super bombs," Robert and Joanne Simpson wrote in a report to the 'Project Stormfury Advisory Panel', a scientific body formed in 1964 to try to find hurricanes' ''Achilles' heel.'' At the time Robert Simpson (Simpson, who eventually went on to co-develop the hurricane classification system known as the Saffir-Simpson Hurricane Wind Scale along with Herbert Saffir) was head of the U.S. Hurricane Research program and Joanne was one of the world's leading tropical weather researchers.

Simpson later went on to become Director of the National Hurricane Center. She at her last post was the chief scientist for meteorology at NASA's Goodard Space Flight Center in Greenbelt, Md. "In the face of this gargantuan machine," the Simpsons said in 1964, "man's puny resources do not allow the brute force, head-on, or trial-and-error approaches."[72] So that idea was eventually scrapped. Joanne Simpson said the only idea other than cloud seeding and the atomic bomb that had much merit was to spread a thin film on the ocean to reduce evaporation, thus reducing the amount of humid air available to fuel the storm and such films are used on some reservoirs. But, Simpson said, the idea wasn't practical for hurricanes first because of the sheer size of the land or sea area involved would make this virtually an impossible proposition and second, because you can't "recognize which clouds are going to develop (into a hurricane), and you can't go around coating the sea every place." By the time scientists know where a storm is beginning, the winds are

---

72 *Williams, J. (2005)* *Stormfury attempted to weaken hurricanes,* *USATODAY.com.* Retrieved: *05-05-2006, http://usatoday30.usatoday.com/weather/hurricane/wstormfury.html.*

strong enough to break up the film. Money that could be spent on trying to find ways to weaken hurricanes would be better spent on building stronger houses in areas that hurricanes hit, Simpson said. "If the money that people might invest in another Stormfury or whatever was invested in enforcing building codes, it's a heck of a lot better investment."[73]

In 1961, the National Oceanic Atmospheric Administration (NOAA) scientists made an attempt to modify the weather that produces hurricanes. In an experiment called Project Stormfury, researchers seeded the clouds in hurricanes with silver iodide crystals to increase precipitation within the storm and to slow down the hurricane's rotating winds. Initially, it appeared to work, although in the end the researchers could never prove whether the results stemmed from the cloud seeding or from natural events. But since the program's demise in 1983, weather modification research has essentially come to a halt in the United States but is still carried on in some countries in SE Asia, like Thailand.

Some researchers, including Dr. Robert Simpson who was also the former Director of the National Hurricane Center in Miami at the time, believed that a hurricane's weakness might be its internal heat engine. A hurricane draws most of its energy from latent heat, released as water vapor as rising air condenses to form clouds and rain. At low levels, warm, moist air spirals over the tropical sea toward the storm's center, carrying great quantities of heat, fueling the storm. The hypothesis of storm modification was based on movement of a figure skater. Just as a spiraling figure skater gains momentum by moving her arms in toward her body, the air spiraling inward from the outer fringes of the hurricane drives up wind speeds as the air gets closer to the center. The highest winds are mainly found at the inner fringes of the storm's eye wall. At the eye wall, air is carried upward and spirals away from the center of the hurricane as the outflow layer at the top of the storm. Researchers thought that if they could cause this spiraling air to spread farther from the center of the hurricane, it would be like extending the arms of the ice skater. They turned to the work of the late Bernard Vonnegut, brother of novelist Kurt Vonnegut. In 1946 he discovered that silver iodide could be used to "seed" clouds. If the silver iodide were dropped in clouds of "super cooled" water -- water that is colder than 0 degrees Celsius but is not frozen -- it would turn the water to ice crystals that would fall as snow. In summer, the snow would melt on the way down to become rain.

[73] Ibid.

The Project Stormfury hypothesis was to seed the first rain band outside the wall of clouds surrounding the eye. The seeding would cause super cooled water droplets to turn into ice, which releases heat. That heat would cause the clouds to grow faster, pulling in air that would otherwise reach the wall of clouds around the eye. With its supply of air cut off, the old eye wall would fade away, and a second eye wall would grow outside the first. Because it would be wider than the original eye wall, the air spiraling into it would be slower. There were several guidelines used in selecting which storms to seed. The hurricane had to have a less than 10 percent chance of approaching inhabited land within a day; it had to be within range of the seeding aircraft; and it had to be a fairly intense storm with a well-formed eye. The primary effect of these conditions was to make possible seeding targets extremely rare.

The hypothesis was first tested in 1961 in the eye wall of Hurricane Esther about 400 miles just to the north of Puerto Rico. The hurricane stopped growing and even showed signs of weakening by about 10%. The following day the aircraft returned to seed, but the seeding canisters fell outside the eye wall, and the storm showed no changes. Still, the results were encouraging. When Hurricane Beulah showed up August 23, 1963, Project Stormfury was ready with 10 airplanes. Again, the results were encouraging. Finally, in 1969, Project Stormfury was going to have a significant test case. It was on the heels of Hurricane Camille barreling down on the Gulf Coast region of Mississippi and Alabama when Hurricane Debby was seeded on five occasions over the two-day period of August 19-20, 1969. Each time the storm was seeded, sustained winds were reduced significantly. The maximum wind speed decreased from near 115 mph to about 80 mph, a reduction of about 30%. The hurricane was left alone for the next 24 hours, and the maximum winds returned to nearly 115 mph. After a repeat of the seeding, the maximum wind speed weakened to about 98 mph, a reduction of about 15%. Such reductions in wind speed are significant because the force exerted by the wind is proportional to the square of the wind speed (a wind speed of 100 mph exerts four times the force of a wind speed of 50 mph).

Small incremental changes in the wind speed can have dramatic effects especially on coastal communities. A speed reduction of 10% to 15%, for example, would result in a 20% to 30% reduction in the force of the wind. Part of the wind speed reduction after seeding was probably caused by influences of large-scale weather patterns outside the hurricane. But analyses strongly suggested that significant reductions could be attributed to the seeding. Still, there was no consensus on routinely seeding major hurricanes. In 1963, the Project Stormfury team was able to conduct tests on Hurricane Beulah, but with only marginal success. Then, in 1965, the team considered seeding Hurricane Betsy, but due to the close proximity to Puerto Rico and other Caribbean islands, fear of lawsuits and the storm's erratic motion, the team did not go through with it, and Betsy ended up hitting the Bahamas and South Florida and causing millions of dollars in damage. Betsy was the last major hurricane to make a direct hit on South Florida before 1992 when Hurricane Andrew devastated Homestead, Florida.

Ultimately though, Project Stormfury was cancelled in 1980 since the team was unable to clearly ascertain whether or not the seeding efforts were really causing storms to weaken, or the systems just became victims of the environment around them, because researchers found that unseeded hurricanes often undergo the same structural changes that were expected from seeded hurricanes. In reality, it was also determined that most hurricanes do not contain enough super cooled water droplets for cloud seeding to be effective. However, the work done did bear some positive results as forecasters and scientists alike were able to learn a great deal about hurricanes from their research, and it has helped them improve forecasting accuracy because the observational data and these storms lifecycle research generated by Project Stormfury helped improve meteorologists' ability to forecast the movement and intensity of future hurricanes.

In the end Project Stormfury came to a halt because they were getting great opposition from meteorologists, environmentalists and others because they raised some fundamental questions about this project and argued that we should not tamper with 'nature' or the natural environment, because in the end the Earth itself will suffer. The reality is that hurricanes serve a very useful purpose on this earth and to try and alter these storms natural balance as deadly and destructive as they may seem may result in unforeseen climatic changes. Their main purpose on this Earth is to transfer, heat from the equator to the poles and in the end that is simply what the hurricane is doing. The Earth and its environment are like the rivets on an airplane holding it together. Sadly, destroying or altering the hurricane's environment and natural life cycle is like removing those rivets on the plane one by one. Sooner or later there is going to come a point in time, when you have removed so many rivets that it will eventually compromise the integrity and the structure of that airplane. The same can be said of the planet Earth with modifying or altering the climate of this planet. In other words, the Earth is like a spider web where every strand supports and relies upon every other strand. If you put stress or pressure on any one segment, it will be felt all across the web. Take away even one strand, and the whole web gets weaker. If you take away more than a few, the entire web may collapse. Well, hurricanes are like the strand on the spider's web or the rivets on a plane, removing them could compromise the entire Earth and I think in the end those scientists came to realize this point.

There have been numerous other techniques that have been considered over the years to modify hurricanes, such as seeding clouds with dry ice or Silver Iodide, cooling the ocean with cryogenic material or icebergs, changing the radiational balance in the hurricane environment by absorption of sunlight with carbon black, exploding the hurricane apart with hydrogen bombs, and blowing the storm away from land with giant fans, etc. As carefully reasoned as some of these suggestions are, they all share the same shortcomings, and that is they fail to appreciate the incredible size and power of tropical cyclones. For example, when Hurricane Andrew struck South Florida in 1992, the eye and eyewall devastated a swath 20 miles wide. The heat energy released around the eye was 5,000 times the combined heat and electrical power generation of the Turkey Point nuclear power plant over which the eye passed. The kinetic energy of the wind at any instant was equivalent to that released by a nuclear warhead.

Perhaps if the time comes when men and women can travel at nearly the speed of light to the stars, we will then have enough energy for brute-force intervention in hurricane dynamics. Attacking weak tropical waves or depressions before they have a chance to grow into hurricanes isn't promising either. About 80 of these disturbances form every year in the Atlantic basin, but on average only about 6 become hurricanes in a typical year. There is no way to tell in advance which ones will develop. If the energy released in a tropical disturbance were only 10% of that released in a hurricane, it's still a lot of power, so that the hurricane police would need to dim the whole world's lights many times a year. Perhaps someday, somebody will come up with a way to weaken hurricanes artificially. It is a beguiling notion. Wouldn't it be wonderful if we could do it? Maybe we will never know. Perhaps the best solution is not to try to alter or destroy the tropical cyclones, but just learn to co-exist with them.

Since we know that coastal regions are vulnerable to the storms, building codes that can have houses stand up to the force of the tropical cyclones needs to be enforced. The people that choose to live in these locations should be willing to shoulder a fair portion of the costs in terms of property insurance - not exorbitant rates, but ones which truly reflect the risk of living in a vulnerable region. In addition, efforts to educate the public on effective preparedness need to continue. Helping poorer nations in their mitigation efforts can also result in saving countless lives. Finally, we need to continue in our efforts to better understand and observe hurricanes in order to more accurately predict their development, intensification and track.

It is interesting to note that the first weather radar was discovered by 'accident' during the Second World War. The word 'radar' is an acronym for 'Radio Detection And Ranging.' The meteorological radar provides information on precipitation location and intensity. This helped weather stations to anticipate hurricanes, fronts, thunderstorms and tornadoes. Additionally, if Doppler radar is used then wind speed and direction can be determined within the cell or structure of the storm. The use of radar to detect storms began at least as early as August, 1943. The radar was first introduced during the Second World War for civil aviation purposes.

The United States Government used the radar as a means to track and monitor the US, allies and enemy airplanes, but something unusual happened during this war. The pilots and the radar technicians realized that whenever it rained, the radars were often what they referred to as 'useless' because they showed the areas of severe or significant weather on these radars in what they referred to as '*Ghost Echoes.*' These radar technicians at the time considered this to be a real nuisance for them, simply because they never really cared too much about these weather events on their primitive radar screens. Furthermore, they also didn't care about the location of precipitation or other severe weathers events such as snowstorms or thunderstorms, but simply the location of the allies and the enemy aircrafts.

After the war, they were left with surplus of radars and it was only then that the idea came to them that they should use the radar as a weather forecasting tool. Simply because the radar actually showed areas of disturbed weather on the radar screen with such clarity that they realized that it could be an excellent weather forecasting tool. They modified the conventional air traffic radar and hence the weather radar was born.

Nowadays, there are more advanced radars in use like the Doppler radar which is like the conventional radar in the sense that it can detect areas of precipitation and measure rainfall intensity. But a Doppler radar can do more because it can also measure speed of precipitation movement, wind speed and direction inside the cloud, and the height of cloud tops. This actually gives the weather observer a three-dimensional cross-sectional view into a cloud, a thunderstorm cell, a hurricane or even tornado funnel and gather vital information that can lead to saving many lives in the process. They can also help to understand these weather systems with greater accuracy leading to a much more improved and refined weather forecast.

As stated earlier, radar technicians had noticed what they called "ghost echoes" on their relatively primitive scopes but did not realize at first that they were caused by thunderstorms. Later they did, and these U.S. Army and Navy meteorologists soon learned how to use the radar to follow other types of storms and they later developed better techniques of detection. During this period there was a hurricane that came relatively close to the State of Florida which allowed these radar technicians to track this storm by the use of radar. But the massive size and structure of the September 15th storm, and its closeness to the radar station, resulted in some striking observations of the hurricane.

Throughout the period when the hurricane was near Florida, the general shape of the disturbance and precipitation patterns were plainly seen on the radar. When the hurricane was relatively close enough to the radar station, and the center only a few miles away, the radar revealed the eye of the storm, the calm area in the center, the height of the clouds surrounding the eyewall of the hurricane, and the lack of echoes proved that there was no precipitation within its center. These opened new doors into the understanding of the structure and dynamics of hurricanes which in turn led to improved weather reports and forecasts which ultimately saved lives in the process. Today, all over the world, the radar is an essential tool for analyzing and predicting the weather because the equipment is capable of detecting and tracking thunderstorms, frontal activities, tornadoes, hurricanes, and other severe weather events.

CHAPTER SIX

The dynamics and climatology of North Atlantic hurricanes

Hurricanes are from the family of giant spiraling super storms called 'tropical cyclones' that can unleash more than 2.4 trillion gallons (9 trillion liters) of rainfall a day. These same tropical storms are known as cyclones in the northern Indian Ocean and Bay of Bengal, and as typhoons in the western Pacific Ocean. These low pressure systems are fed by energy from the warm seas. If a storm achieves wind speeds of up to 38 miles an hour, it becomes known as a tropical depression. A tropical depression becomes a tropical storm, and is given a name, when its sustained wind speeds top 39 miles an hour. When a storm's sustained wind speeds reach 74 miles an hour it becomes a hurricane and earns a category rating of 1 to 5 on the Saffir-Simpson Hurricane Wind Scale.

Hurricanes are enormous heat engines that generate energy on a staggering scale. They draw heat from warm, moist ocean air and release it through condensation of water vapor (latent heat) in thunderstorms. Hurricanes spin around a low-pressure center known as the "eye." Sinking air makes this 20- to 30-mile-wide area notoriously calm. But the eye is surrounded by a circular "eye wall" that hosts the storm's strongest winds and rain. A tropical cyclone is a rapidly rotating storm system characterized by a low-pressure center, strong winds, and a spiral arrangement of thunderstorms that produce heavy rain. Depending on its location and strength, a tropical cyclone is referred to by names such as hurricanes, typhoons, tropical storms, cyclonic storms, tropical depressions, and simply cyclones.

Tropical cyclones typically form over large bodies of relatively warm water. They derive their energy through the evaporation of water from the ocean surface, which ultimately recondenses into clouds and rain when moist air rises and cools to saturation. This energy source differs from that of mid-latitude cyclonic storms, such as nor'easters and European windstorms, which are fueled primarily by horizontal temperature contrasts or what meteorologists refer to as 'baroclinic instability.' The strong rotating winds of a tropical cyclone are a result of the conservation of angular momentum imparted by the Earth's rotation as air flows inwards toward the axis of rotation in what meteorologists refer to as a 'barotropic atmosphere.' As a result, they rarely form within 5° north and south of the equator. A hurricane is a huge storm, because it can be up to 600 miles across and have strong winds spiraling inward and upward at speeds of 75 to 200 mph. Each hurricane usually lasts for an average of a week or more, moving 10-20 miles per hour over the open ocean. Tropical refers to the geographical origin of these systems, which form almost exclusively over tropical seas. Cyclones refers to their cyclonic nature, with winds blowing in a counter-clockwise flow and the flow occurring in the opposite direction of circulation is due to the Coriolis effect.

In addition to strong winds and rain, tropical cyclones are capable of generating high waves, damaging storm surge, and tornadoes. They typically weaken rapidly over land where they are cut off from their primary energy source. For this reason, coastal regions are particularly vulnerable to damage from a tropical cyclone as compared to inland regions. Heavy rains, however, can cause significant flooding inland, and storm surges can produce extensive coastal flooding up to 25 miles from the coastline. Though their effects on human populations are often devastating, tropical cyclones can relieve drought conditions. They also carry heat energy away from the tropics and transport it toward temperate latitudes, which may play an important role in modulating regional and global climate. Furthermore, they also act as the earth's filter system by cleansing the air of toxins and pollutants out of the atmosphere.

Worldwide, tropical cyclone activity peaks in late summer, when the difference between temperatures aloft and sea surface temperatures is the greatest. However, each particular basin has its own seasonal patterns. On a worldwide scale, May is considered the least active month, while September is the most active month. November is the only month in which all the tropical cyclone basins are active. The statistical peak of the North Atlantic hurricane season is September 10. The North Atlantic hurricane season is the period in a year when hurricanes usually form. However, it must be noted that there have been several hurricanes over the years that have not been fully tropical which are categorized as subtropical depressions and subtropical storms with a few occurring outside the months dedicated to the regular hurricane season. The most active season was 2005, during which 28 tropical cyclones formed, of which a record 15 became hurricanes. The least active season was in 1914, with only one known tropical cyclone developing during that year. On the other hand, the Northeast Pacific Ocean has a broader period of activity, but in a similar time frame to the Atlantic. The Northwest Pacific sees tropical cyclones year-round, with a minimum in February and March and a peak in early September. In the North Indian basin, storms are most common from April to December, with peaks in May and November. In the southern hemisphere, the tropical cyclone year begins on July 1 and runs all year-round encompassing the tropical cyclone seasons, which run from November 1 until the end of April, with peaks in mid-February to early March.

Most hurricanes start life as areas of disturbed weather and thunderstorms in the tropics or as meteorologists often say, 'areas of deep convective activity.' Many of these disturbances, or tropical waves, produce little more than heavy rains and strong gusty winds. But if conditions are ideal, a tropical wave succeeds in spinning into a complete circle of winds rotating around an area of low air pressure at its center, it's given the name tropical depression. When a depression's peak sustained winds reach 39 miles per hour (34 knots), it's called a tropical storm and the system is given an assigned name. As a tropical system strengthens, its winds spiral inward, concentrating moisture near the center. This spiraling, a result of Earth's rotation, can't happen near the equator. To benefit from the curving winds produced by the Coriolis effect, a storm needs to be at least 5°N or 5°S or 300 miles north or south of the equator.

When a tropical disturbance organizes to the point where it's sustained wind speeds top 34 knots (39 miles per hour), it's known as a tropical cyclone. In the North Atlantic, the system is given a name. But various parts of the world use a variety of terms once a tropical cyclone packs winds of at least 65 knots (74 mph) in a particular "basin" (an oceanic region where these storms occur). Around the Caribbean, the Bahamas, North and Central America, they're called hurricanes. That's the source of the name used in the North Atlantic Ocean, Caribbean Sea, Gulf of Mexico, and Northeast Pacific Ocean. In the Northwest Pacific, the same powerful storms are called 'typhoons.' In the southeastern Indian and southwest Pacific Oceans they're called 'severe tropical cyclones.' In the North Indian Ocean, they're called 'severe cyclonic storms,' while in the Southwest Indian Ocean; they simply keep the name 'tropical cyclone.'

Hurricanes that make Category 3 status on the Saffir-Simpson Hurricane Wind Scale (winds of at least 96 knots or 111 mph) are labeled 'intense hurricanes.' If a typhoon hits 132 knots (150 mph), it becomes a 'super typhoon.' When a system weakens below hurricane strength, it is typically reclassified as a 'post-tropical cyclone.' This was the case with Hurricane Sandy in 2012 just before landfall. In order to reduce confusion, the National Weather Service introduced a new policy in 2013 in which hurricane warnings may be continued even after a storm has technically become post-tropical.

Whatever you call them, these monster storms are the most powerful atmospheric phenomena on Earth. Hurricanes gather energy from water vapor in the atmosphere stretched for hundreds of thousands of square miles across the warm ocean water of the tropics. The storms themselves can bring heavy rains and gale-force winds blowing 38 to 73 miles per hour across an area the size of Louisiana. Hurricane-force winds can extend 50 miles or more from the storm center. According to NOAA's National Hurricane Center, the average hurricane eye—the still center where pressure is lowest and air temperature in the upper atmosphere is highest—stretches 30 miles across, with some growing as large as 120 miles wide. The eye typically shrinks as a hurricane intensifies, sometimes narrowing to less than 10 miles in width. Eventually, a new eye may form around the old one; hurricanes often weaken during this transition but can intensify again as the new eye contracts. Hurricane intensity is categorized on different scales around the world, however in the North Atlantic basin, the strongest storms, equivalent to Category 5 on the Saffir-Simpson Hurricane Wind Scale, have sustained winds that exceed 157 miles per hour (135 knots).

In order to grow, hurricanes need plenty of warm, moist air to form showers and thunderstorms, along with winds that don't change direction much with height, which allows the central circulation to develop undisturbed. If these atmospheric conditions are right, then hurricane strength is dictated largely by the presence or absence of deep, warm ocean water. As winds strengthen, more water evaporates, releasing energy stored in the warm seas. Size does not determine intensity. Some of the most destructive hurricanes to hit the region, including Hurricane Andrew in 1992, extended over a relatively small area.

The term tropical cyclone is a family of low pressure systems and is the broad term for a non-frontal synoptic scale low-pressure system that forms over tropical or sub-tropical waters with organized deep convection and a well-defined cyclonic surface wind circulation. They are given different names depending on where they are located around the world. In the North Atlantic they are called hurricanes. Its energy source is mainly derived from evaporation and sensible heat flux from the warm oceanic waters around the world. These energy sources are achieved and maintained through latent heat of condensation and fusion in convective clouds concentrated near the cyclone's "warm-core" center.

Cyclogenesis is the development or strengthening of cyclonic circulation in the atmosphere (a low pressure area). Cyclogenesis is an umbrella term for at least three different processes, all of which result in the development of some sort of cyclone. Before tropical cyclogenesis and development can occur, there are several precursor environmental conditions that must be in place. It must be noted that having these conditions in place is necessary, but not sufficient, as many disturbances that appear to have favorable conditions do not develop. The beginning of life for any hurricane is a pre-existing disturbance, an area of low pressure, over the tropical ocean. For cyclogenesis to occur there must be a pre-existing near-surface disturbance with sufficient vorticity and convergence. Tropical cyclones cannot be generated spontaneously. To develop, they require a weakly organized system with sizable spin and low level inflow. However, several other ingredients are also required for a system to become a hurricane. In setting the stage for a hurricane formation, there must be several environmental conditions in place for that hurricane to form and thrive. Having a pre-existing disturbance is not the only ingredient necessary for a hurricane to form. This disturbance must be located in an environment that is favorable for development.

Conditions necessary for hurricanes to form and thrive:

- A sea surface temperature (SST) of at least 26.5°C (80°F) down to a depth of about 300 feet, to provide the system with a constant supply of warm, moist air to maintain its growth and development.
- A vertical temperature profile in the atmosphere that cools enough with height to support thunderstorm activity.
- Sufficient water vapor in the middle of the troposphere. Even over the tropical oceans, dry air sometimes exists in the middle of the troposphere, and this dry air suppresses thunderstorms, preventing tropical depression formation. The more humid the air in the troposphere, the less the disturbance will have to moisten the air (via evaporation from the sea surface) in order for cyclogenesis to occur.

- Sufficient distance from the equator for the Coriolis effect (deflection of an object to the right of motion in the northern hemisphere due to the Earth's rotation is called the 'Coriolis effect') to be significant, usually at least 300 miles. Closer to the equator, the Coriolis effect is too weak, therefore, it is difficult to establish cyclonic rotation here. In other words, for tropical cyclogenesis to occur there is a requirement for non-negligible amounts of the Coriolis effect to provide for near gradient wind balance to occur. Without a significant Coriolis effect, inflow into the low pressure center is not deflected to the right (to the left in the southern hemisphere) and the partial vacuum of the low is quickly filled.
- Low values of vertical wind shear from the surface of the earth to the upper troposphere (about 8 miles up). For reasons that still remain unclear or only partially understood, wind shear inhibits the development of tropical systems. Some research shows this may be due to the injection of dry air into the storm system. Low values of vertical wind shear between the 850 and 200 mbar levels of the atmosphere must be present for cyclogenesis to occur. Vertical wind shear is the magnitude of wind change with height. Large values of vertical wind shear disrupt the incipient tropical cyclone and can prevent genesis, or, if a tropical cyclone has already formed, large vertical shear can weaken or destroy the tropical cyclone by interfering with the organization of deep convection around the cyclone center.
- Low level convergence and upper level divergence air-flow to allow a free flow of warm, moist air throughout the system. In other words, an atmosphere which cools fast enough with height such that it is potentially unstable to moist convection. It is the precipitating convection typically in the form of thunderstorm complexes which allows the heat stored in the ocean waters to be liberated for tropical cyclone development.

Whatever their size or strength, long-lived hurricanes normally weaken after they come ashore and encounter the land. The land surface creates drag and the vital oceanic heat source disappears. The high winds of the hurricane gradually weaken and spread over a larger area. As the hurricane moves inland, the friction with the land surface acts to increase the flow of air toward the hurricane center and weakens it. This creates a greater inflow of air toward the lowest pressures and this in turn leads to rising surface pressures in a process known as 'filling' and a weakening of circulation within the storm. Surface friction may also alter the movement of hurricanes at landfall. Initially there will be a difference in frictional effects between the portion of the storm over land and the portion over the water. The greater friction over land will lead to greater inflow toward the center and a corresponding increase in mass and pressure in the right-front quadrant which will cause the storm to jog to the left. More important for dissipation is the fact that over land the hurricane is removed from its source of heat and moisture (the ocean) that fuels the convection.

Without the rapidly rising air near the storm center, the hurricane weakens. In general, the decrease of maximum wind speed after landfall is proportional to the storm's intensity. The more intense the circulation around the eye as the storm approaches the coast, the quicker it will weaken over land. Hurricanes typically loose hurricane intensity within 12 hours of landfall, but powerful storms can remain at hurricane intensity for greater than 24 hours after landfall. Observations and model simulations indicate that hurricanes can maintain strength or even intensify when moving over swampy land.

Also, the frictional effects on surface winds can help create the wind shear needed to spawn tornadoes. One hurricane can produce dozens of tornadoes as it moves ashore. But the worst hurricane damage is often the result of a storm surge that causes coastal flooding. For example, along parts of the Mississippi coast, the surge from Hurricane Katrina in 2005 was over 28 feet above mean sea level, putting it among the highest surges ever recorded in the United States. Large waves on top of a storm surge cause even more damage. Surge risk varies depending on the strength and structure of a given hurricane as well as geography and tidal cycles along the coast where it strikes.

Although Superstorm Sandy fell just below hurricane strength several hours before its center reached southern New Jersey in October 2012, Sandy was an extremely large system, and it struck near high tide. As a result, the storm pushed huge amounts of water into the New York and New Jersey coastlines, producing a catastrophic storm surge that set records in several places. Originally, the Saffir-Simpson Scale (now called the Saffir-Simpson Hurricane Wind Scale partly because of this factor) included typical storm surges expected for each category. In the case of Sandy and several other recent hurricanes, storm surges have been higher than the levels once assigned to each Saffir-Simpson category. The categories have been revised so that they now refer only to wind speed, and the National Hurricane Center is moving toward new ways of depicting the threat from storm surge, including storm surge watches and warnings that will be distinct from hurricane watches and warnings.

The Saffir-Simpson Hurricane Wind Scale measures the amount of wind damage caused by hurricanes. The speed of the wind determines the category of the storm. Categories range from 1 to 5. Currently, the Saffir-Simpson Hurricane Wind Scale takes into account only wind speed. Since its development in 1971, it has gone through a few modifications. An earlier version used storm surge and central pressure as well as wind speed to determine damage. This scale was known as the Saffir-Simpson Hurricane Scale. Storm surge in some hurricanes produced larger or smaller surges that placed them in different categories than what their sustained winds would categorize them as. According to NOAA, to avoid public confusion, the scale was modified to only categorize wind speed and its predicted damage. The Saffir-Simpson Hurricane Wind Scale is a 1 to 5 rating based on a hurricane's sustained wind speed. This scale estimates potential property damage. Hurricanes reaching Category 3 and higher are considered major hurricanes because of their potential for significant loss of life and damage. Category 1 and 2 storms are still dangerous, however, and require preventative measures.

The Saffir–Simpson Hurricane Wind Scale, classifies hurricanes of the North Atlantic that exceed the intensities of tropical depressions and tropical storms – into five categories, each distinguished by the intensities of their sustained winds. To be classified as a hurricane, a tropical cyclone must have maximum sustained winds of at least 74 mph (64 knots) (Category 1). The highest classification in the scale, Category 5, is reserved for storms with sustained winds exceeding 156 mph (136 knots [this was recently changed in 2012 from 155 mph or greater to over 156 mph]). The classifications can provide some indication of the potential damage and flooding a hurricane will cause upon landfall.

Officially, the Saffir–Simpson Hurricane Wind Scale is used 'only' to describe hurricanes forming in the North Atlantic Ocean and northern Pacific Ocean east of the International Date Line. Other areas use different scales to label these storms, which are called "cyclones" or "typhoons", depending on the area. There is some criticism of the Saffir-Simpson Hurricane Wind Scale for not taking rain, storm speed, and other important factors into consideration, but the defenders of this scale say that part of the goal of the scale is to be straight forward and simple to understand. On average there are about 70 to 110 named tropical cyclones per year across the world, including about 40 to 60 that reach hurricane strength. This range has held remarkably steady within the last 40 years.

Within each basin, the numbers often vary more dramatically than the global average. In part this is due to ocean-atmosphere cycles such as El Niño and La Niño. Because they affect where showers and thunderstorms develop, these cycles can suppress hurricane activity in one basin while enhancing it in another. During El Niño years, the Atlantic tends to be less active than usual, while parts of the central and northeast Pacific are typically busier than usual. While the long-distance effects are not exactly opposite during La Niña events, there is a tendency for more activity in the Atlantic than the Pacific. El Niño events increase the wind shear over the Atlantic, producing a less-favorable environment for formation and decreasing tropical activity in the North Atlantic basin. Conversely, La Niña causes an increase in activity due to a decrease in wind shear.

Even though the total number of tropical cyclones around the world holds fairly steady, some years are more active than others. Of all the hurricanes that build over the North Atlantic each year, only a small fraction of them would ever make it to the individual countries at hurricane strength. However, the total number of hurricanes swirling across the North Atlantic remains unusually high. In recent years, we've seen several hurricanes and tropical storms strike in unfamiliar places. This could be a result of improved monitoring (i.e. widespread use of satellites, radars, the computer and the internet to track and monitor storms), 24-hour constant news and weather coverage, regional changes in ocean temperatures and upper-air circulation (perhaps linked to global warming in some cases), natural variability, or all of the above. The South Atlantic had been considered free of tropical cyclones—that is, until March 2004, when a very mysterious and unusual hybrid storm later dubbed Hurricane Catarina made landfall in Brazil. Since 2011, the Brazilian Navy Hydrographic Center has started to use the same scale of the North Atlantic Ocean for tropical cyclones in the South Atlantic Ocean and assign names to them which reach 35 knots (40 mph).

In 2005, in the North Atlantic basin, there was a record breaking 28 storms which formed that year (the prior record was the 1933 hurricane season which recorded 21 named storms that year). In October 2005, Vince became the first tropical storm ever recorded in Spain. In the Arabian Sea, Gonu became a Category 5 in June 2007—that region's strongest tropical cyclone on record. After weakening, Gonu brought unprecedented damage from rain, wind, and flooding to parts of Oman and Iran. Although the Bay of Bengal has seen the world's deadliest tropical cyclones on record (notably Cyclone Bhola which struck Bangladesh in 1970 killing up to 500,000 persons making it the world's deadliest tropical cyclone), most of these strike India and Bangladesh, while the coast of Myanmar tends to experience only weaker cyclones. The catastrophic Cyclone Nargis, which struck Myanmar in May 2008, appears to be the first major cyclone (Category 3 strength or higher) ever recorded in the populous Irrawaddy Delta. More than 138,000 people died in the storm and its aftermath.

In the tropical latitudes, tropical storms and hurricanes generally move westward with a slight tend toward the north, under the influence of the subtropical ridge, a high pressure system that usually extends east-west across the subtropics. South of the subtropical ridge, surface easterly winds (blowing from east to west) prevail. If the subtropical ridge is weakened by an upper level trough, a tropical cyclone may turn poleward and then recurve, or curve back toward the northeast into the main belt of the westerlies. Poleward (north) of the subtropical ridge, westerly winds prevail and generally steer tropical cyclones that reach northern latitudes toward the east. The westerlies also steer extra-tropical cyclones with their cold and warm fronts from west to east.

In the North Atlantic there are four different types of hurricanes that influence us in some way or the other. The first is the Cape Verde type hurricane which as its name suggests originates off the African Coast in the vicinity of the Cape Verde Islands. This type initially moves in a westerly direction and then in a west-northwest to a northwesterly track as it makes its way through the Caribbean. The Cape Verde Islands is an archipelago about 400 miles off the West African Coast and are volcanic in nature. It was colonized by Portugal in the fifteenth century and became an independent country in 1975. At one point in their history these islands served as an outpost station for the movement of African slaves on the 'Middle Passage' to the Americas. Cape Verde-type hurricanes are those North Atlantic basin tropical cyclones that develop into tropical storms fairly close (<600 miles or so) of the Cape Verde Islands and then become hurricanes before reaching the Caribbean.

This type of hurricane forms over the Atlantic mainly during the early part of the season- late June thru mid-September months but some have formed as late as October, when the easterly waves are most dominant and prominent features in the Caribbean region. The numbers range from none up to around five per year - with an average of around 2. These hurricanes are usually the largest and most intense storms of the season because they often have plenty of warm, expansive, open ocean over which to develop before encountering land. A good portion of Cape Verde storms are large, some setting records. Most of the longest-lived tropical cyclones in the North Atlantic basin are Cape Verde type hurricanes. While many move harmlessly out to sea, some move across the Caribbean Sea and Gulf of Mexico, becoming damaging storms for many Caribbean nations, Central America, Mexico, Bermuda, the United States, and occasionally even as far north as Canada. Research projects since the 1970s have been launched to understand the formation of these storms.

At the beginning and the middle of the hurricane season, storms also tend to form near the Bahamas and this type has come to be known as 'Bahama Busters', according to world-renowned Professor William Gray. An example of this type was Hurricane Katrina in 2005, which formed just east to the Bahamas and moved initially westward and then northwestward into the Gulf of Mexico and then over Louisiana. After leaving the Bahamas, this type of hurricane tends to rapidly intensify over the very warm Loop Current in the Gulf of Mexico, posing significant danger to the Gulf Coast states impacted by this hurricane. These states include the coasts of Texas, Louisiana, Mississippi, Alabama, and Florida.

Then there is the Gulf of Mexico type, which as it names suggests, originates in the Gulf of Mexico and travels westward, northwestward or northward in most cases from its inception and mainly influences Central America, and the Gulf Coast States of the United States. Then there is the western Caribbean type, which forms during the early and late parts of the hurricane season and forms in the most favored location near the Gulf of Honduras mainly in May and June and mid-September thru late November. The formations of these cyclones are due in part to the seasonal movement of the Inter-Tropical Convergence Zone, also known as the equatorial trough. From its inception, this type of hurricane seems to take a northward movement, which normally takes a track over the island of Cuba and into the Bahamas, the severity of which is influenced by how long the cyclone remains over the mountainous terrain of Cuba.

In this region, the climatology does serve to characterize the general properties of an average season and can be used as one of many other tools for making forecasts. Most storms form in warm waters several hundred miles north of the equator near the Inter-Tropical Convergence Zone from tropical waves. Storms frequently form in the warm waters of the Gulf of Mexico, the Caribbean Sea, and the tropical North Atlantic Ocean as far east as the Cape Verde Islands, the origin of strong and long-lasting Cape Verde-type hurricanes. Systems may also strengthen over the Gulf Stream off the coast of the eastern United States, wherever water temperatures frequently exceed the minimum threshold temperature of 26.5 °C (80°F) during the late summer months.

Vertical wind shear is a term used to describe the changes in horizontal winds between two levels in the atmosphere. Wind changes in horizontal winds between two levels in the atmosphere. Wind changes can arise from changes in speed and changes in direction. Decrease in wind shear (strong wind shear tends to tear the storm apart, inhibiting its growth, and vice-versa) which from July to August contributes to a significant increase of tropical activity. An average of 2.8 North Atlantic tropical storms develops annually in August. On average, four named tropical storms, including one hurricane, occur by August 30, and the first intense hurricane develops by 4 September. The peak of the hurricane season occurs on 11th September and corresponds to low wind shear and the warmest sea surface temperatures. The month of September sees an average of 3 storms a year. By September 24, the average North Atlantic season features 7 named tropical storms, including 4 hurricanes. In addition, two major hurricanes occur on average by 28 September. Relatively few tropical cyclones make landfall at these intensities.

The favorable conditions found during September begin to decay in October. The main reason for the decrease in activity is increasing wind shear, although sea surface temperatures are also cooler than in September. Activity falls markedly with 1.8 cyclones developing on average, despite a climatological secondary peak around 20 October. By 21 October, the average season features 9 named storms with 5 hurricanes. A third major hurricane occurs after 28 September in half of all North Atlantic tropical cyclone seasons. In contrast to mid-season activity, the mean locus of formation shifts westward to the Caribbean and Gulf of Mexico, reversing the eastward progression of June through August. Wind shear from these westerlies increases substantially through November, generally preventing cyclone formation.

On average, one tropical storm forms during every other November. On rare occasions, a major hurricane occurs. The few intense hurricanes in November include Hurricane Lenny in mid-November 1999, Hurricane Kate in late November 1985 (the latest major hurricane on record), and Hurricane Paloma in early November 2008. Hurricane Paloma of 2008 was the third-strongest November North Atlantic hurricane on record. It was a late season hurricane, setting several records for its intensity and formation. Paloma was the third most powerful November hurricane on record in the Atlantic Basin, behind only a 1932 hurricane and 1999's Lenny. It also marked the first time that at least one major hurricane formed in every month of the hurricane season from July to November, with only June not having a major hurricane this season.

Although the hurricane season is defined as beginning on June 1 and ending on November 30, there have been several off-season storms. Since 1870, there have been 32 off-season cyclones, 18 of which occurred in May. In the same time span, nine storms formed in December, two in April, and one each in January, February and March. During five years (1887, 1953, 2003, 2007, and 2012), tropical cyclones formed in the North Atlantic Ocean both during or before May and during December. In 1887, four storms occurred outside the season, the most in a single year. High vertical wind shear and low sea surface temperatures generally preclude tropical cyclone formation during the off-season. Tropical cyclones have formed in all months. Three tropical cyclones existed during the month of January, two of which formed during late December: the second Hurricane Alice in 1954/1955, and Tropical Storm Zeta in 2005/2006. The only hurricane to form in January was a Category 1 hurricane in the 1938 season. A subtropical storm in January also began the 1978 North Atlantic hurricane season. The strongest storm outside the hurricane season, Hurricane Able in 1951, attained Category 3 status on 21 May and ranks as the earliest intense hurricane on record.

List of some notable North Atlantic Hurricane Records

With all the aforementioned information taken into consideration, let's take an extensive look at some of the most "fascinating facts" of the major historical records for tropical cyclone activity throughout the North Atlantic basin:

- The season in which the most tropical storms formed on record was the 2005 North Atlantic Hurricane (28). That season was also the one in which the most hurricanes formed on record (15).
- The 2005 North Atlantic season had the most major hurricanes on record (7). The 1950 North Atlantic season was once thought to have more, but a re-analysis showed that several storms were weaker than thought, and thus the record is now held by the 2005 season.
- The least active season on record since 1944 (when the database is considered more reliable) was the 1983 North Atlantic hurricane season, with one tropical storm, two hurricanes, and one major hurricane. Overall, the 1914 North Atlantic season remains the least active, with only one documented storm.
- The most intense hurricane (by barometric pressure) on record to form in the North Atlantic basin was Hurricane Wilma (2005) (882 mbar).
- Hours to go from a tropical storm to a Category 5: 16 hours - 70mph to 155mph – Hurricane Wilma in 2005.

- Maximum pressure drop in 12 hours: 90+mbar – Wilma in 2005.
- Maximum pressure drop in 24 hours: 98mbar – Wilma in 2005 - 1200 UTC October to October 19.
- First storm named after a Greek letter: Alpha - 1972 (It should be noted that the Alpha that formed in 1972 was sub-tropical, whereas the Alpha that formed in 2005 was truly tropical).
- Most rapid intensification in a 24-hour period: Wilma 2005 October 17 - 98mb (previous record: Super Typhoon Forrest 1983 - Western Pacific - 92mbar).
- The largest hurricane (in gale diameter) on record to form in the North Atlantic was Hurricane Sandy (2012), with a gale diameter of 1,100 miles.
- The longest-lasting hurricane was the San Ciriaco's Hurricane of 1899, which lasted for 27 days and 18 hours as a tropical cyclone.
- The longest-tracked hurricane was Hurricane Faith, which traveled for 6,850 miles as a tropical cyclone.
- The most tornadoes spawned by a single hurricane was 127 by Hurricane Ivan (2004 season).
- The strongest landfalling hurricane was the Great Labor Day Hurricane of 1935 (892 hPa).
- The deadliest hurricane was the Great Hurricane of 1780 (22,000 fatalities).
- The deadliest hurricane to make landfall on the continental United States was the Galveston Hurricane in 1900, which may have killed up to 12,000 people.
- The most damaging hurricane (adjusted for inflation) was Hurricane Katrina of the 2005 season, which caused $125 billion in damage (2005 USD).
- The quickest forming hurricane was Hurricane Humberto in 2007. It was a minimal hurricane that formed and intensified faster than any other tropical cyclone on record before landfall. Developing on September 12, 2007, in the northwestern Gulf of Mexico, the cyclone rapidly strengthened and struck High Island, Texas, with winds of about 90 mph early on September 13.
- Total number of tropical cyclones (includes subtropical storms): 1446 (an average of about 12 named storms, 6 hurricanes and 3 major hurricanes).
- Total number of hurricanes: 853

1) Total number of "major" hurricanes: 308
2) Total number of tropical cyclones by the month:

a) September = 492
b) August = 366
c) October = 294
d) July = 110
e) June = 83
f) November = 65
g) May = 21
h) December = 10
i) April = 2
j) March = 1
k) February = 1
l) January = 1

Note: These statistics are reflective of the month in which tropical cyclones initially achieved tropical storm or sub-tropical storm intensity.

Total number of hurricanes by the month:

a) September = 332
b) August = 225
c) October = 161
d) July = 54
e) November = 41
f) June = 32
g) May = 4
h) December = 4
i) March = 1
j) Others = 0

Total number of major hurricanes by month:

a) September = 148
b) August = 87
c) October = 51
d) July = 10
e) November = 7
f) June = 4

g) May = 1
h) December = 0
i) Others = 0

While the number of storms in the North Atlantic has slightly increased since 1995, there is no obvious global trend. The annual number of tropical cyclones worldwide remains about 87 ± 10. However, the ability of climatologists to make long-term data analysis in certain basins is limited by the lack of reliable historical data in these basins, primarily in the southern hemisphere. In spite of that, some hurricane experts claim that there is some evidence that the intensity of hurricanes is increasing. Kerry Emanuel, an Atmospheric Science Professor at Massachusetts Institute of Technology (MIT), stated, "Records of hurricane activity worldwide show an upswing of both the maximum wind speed in and the duration of hurricanes. The energy released by the average hurricane (again considering all hurricanes worldwide) seems to have increased by around 70% in the past 30 years or so, corresponding to about a 15% increase in the maximum wind speed and a 60% increase in storm lifetime."[74] At the time, Emanuel theorized that increased heat from global warming was driving this trend; however, some argue that Emanuel's own research in 2008 refuted this theory. Others contend that the trend does not exist at all, but instead is a figment created by faulty readings from primitive 1970s-era measurement equipment. Vecchi and Knutson (2008) found a weakly positive, although not statistically-significant trend in the number of North Atlantic tropical cyclones for 1878–2006, but also a surprisingly strong decrease in cyclone duration over this period.[75]

On May 14, 2014, the journal *Nature* published a peer-reviewed submission from October 2013 by James P. Kossin, Kerry A. Emanuel, and Gabriel A. Vecchi that suggests that a poleward migration exists for the paths of maximum intensity of tropical cyclone activity in the Atlantic.[76] The focus of the report is on the latitude at which recent tropical cyclones in the Atlantic are reaching

---

74 Emanuel, Kerry (January 2006*), wind.mit.edu/~emanuel/anthro.html-"Anthropogenic Effects on Tropical Cyclone Activity."* Retrieved: 25-03-2015.

75 Vecchi, Gabriel A.; Knutson, Thomas R. (2008). *On Estimates of Historical North Atlantic Tropical Cyclone Activity*. *Journal of Climate* 21 (14): 3580–3600.

76 Kossin, James P., Emanuel, Kerry A, and Vecchi, Gabriel A., *The poleward migration of the location of tropical cyclone maximum intensity*, The Journal Nature, pgs. 509, 349–352 (15 May 2014) doi:10.1038/nature13278, received 21 October 2013 accepted 21 March 2014 published online 14 May 2014.

maximum intensity. Their data indicates that during the past thirty years, the peak intensity of these storms has shifted poleward in both hemispheres at a rate of approximately 60 km per decade, amounting to approximately one degree of latitude per decade.

Atlantic storms are becoming more destructive financially, since five of the ten most expensive storms in United States history have occurred since 1990. According to the World Meteorological Organization, "recent increase in societal impact from tropical cyclones has largely been caused by rising concentrations of population and infrastructure in coastal regions."[77] On the other hand, Pielke *et al.* (2008) normalized mainland U.S. hurricane damage from 1900–2005 to 2005 values and found no remaining trend of increasing absolute damage. The 1970s and 1980s were notable because of the extremely low amounts of damage compared to other decades. The decade 1996–2005 has the second most damage among the past 11 decades, with only the decade 1926–1935 surpassing its costs. The most damaging single storm is the Great Miami Hurricane of 1926, with $157 billion of normalized damage.

Often in part because of the threat of hurricanes, many coastal regions had sparse population between major ports until the advent of automobile tourism; therefore, the most severe portions of hurricanes striking the coast may have gone unmeasured in some instances. The combined effects of ship destruction and remote landfall severely limit the number of intense hurricanes in the official record before the era of hurricane reconnaissance aircraft, satellite and radar technology. Although the record shows a distinct increase in the number and strength of intense hurricanes, therefore experts regard the early data as suspect.[78] Christopher Landsea *et al.* estimated an undercount bias of zero to six tropical cyclones per year between 1851 and 1885, and zero to four per year between 1886 and 1910. These undercounts roughly take into account the typical size of tropical cyclones, the density of shipping tracks over the Atlantic basin, and the amount of populated coastline.[79]

---

77 *A summary Statement on Tropical Cyclones and Climate Change* (Press release). World Meteorological Organization. Retrieved: 04-12-2006.

78 Neumann, Charles J. *1.3: A Global Climatology-Global Guide to Tropical Cyclone Forecasting.* Bureau of Meteorology.

79 Chris Landsea, et al. *The Atlantic hurricane database re-analysis project: Documentation for the 1851–1910 alterations and additions to the HURDAT database.* In Murname, R. J.; Liu, K.-B. *Hurricanes and Typhoons: Past, Present and Future.* (New York: Columbia University Press, 2004), pgs. 177–221.

The number and strength of Atlantic hurricanes may undergo a 50–70 year cycle, also known as the 'North Atlantic Multidecadal Oscillation' (AMO), Nyberg et al. reconstructed Atlantic major hurricane activity back to the early eighteenth century and found five periods averaging 3–5 major hurricanes per year and lasting 40–60 years, and six others averaging 1.5–2.5 major hurricanes per year and lasting 10–20 years. These periods are associated with the AMO. Throughout, a decadal oscillation related to solar irradiance was responsible for enhancing/dampening the number of major hurricanes by 1–2 per year.[80]

Although it was more common since 1995, a few above-normal hurricane seasons occurred during the period of years from 1970 to 1994. Very destructive hurricanes struck frequently from 1926 to 1960, including many major New England and Florida hurricanes. Twenty-one Atlantic tropical storms formed in 1933, a record only recently exceeded in 2005, which saw 28 storms. Tropical hurricanes occurred infrequently during the seasons of 1900 to 1925; however, many intense storms formed during 1870 to 1899. During the 1887 season, 19 tropical storms formed, of which a record 4 occurred after November 1 and 11 and strengthened into hurricanes.

Few hurricanes occurred in the 1840s to 1860s; however, many struck in the early 19th century, including an 1821 storm that made a direct hit on New York City. Some historical weather experts say these storms may have been as high as Category 4 in strength. These active hurricane seasons predated satellite coverage of the North Atlantic basin. Before the satellite era began in 1960, tropical storms or hurricanes went undetected unless a reconnaissance aircraft encountered one, a ship reported a voyage through the storm, or a storm hit land in a populated area. The official record, therefore, could miss storms in which no ship experienced gale-force winds, recognized it as a tropical storm (as opposed to a high-latitude extra-tropical cyclone, a tropical wave, or a brief squall), returned to port, and reported the experience.

Since the reliable record keeping of tropical cyclone data within the North Atlantic Ocean began in 1851, there have been 1,505 systems of at least tropical storm intensity, and 879 of at least hurricane intensity. Though a majority of these tropical cyclones have fallen within climatological averages, prevailing atmospheric conditions occasionally lead to anomalous tropical systems, which at times reach extremes in statistical record-keeping, including in duration and intensity. The scope of this list is limited to tropical cyclone records solely

---

80 Nyberg, J.; Winter, A.; Malmgren, B. A. Reconstruction of Major Hurricane Activity. *Eos Trans. AGU* 86 (52, Fall Meet. Suppl.): Abstract PP21C–1597, (2005).

within the Atlantic Ocean north of the equator and is subdivided by their reason for notability. Climatologically speaking, approximately 97 percent of tropical cyclones that form in the North Atlantic develop between the defined dates of season.

Though the beginning of the annual hurricane season has historically remained the same, the official end of the hurricane season has shifted from its initial date of October 31. Regardless, on average once every few years a tropical cyclone develops outside the outside the limit of the season. From 1851 to the present day, there have been 66 tropical cyclones in the off-season, with the most recent being Hurricane Alex in 2016. The first tropical cyclone of the 1938 North Atlantic hurricane season, which formed on January 3, became the earliest forming tropical storm and hurricane after reanalysis concluded on the storm in December 2012. In 1951, Hurricane Able became the earliest forming major hurricane – a tropical cyclone with winds exceeding 115 mph – after it reached the equivalent of Category 3 intensity on the Saffir-Simpson Hurricane Wind Scale on May 21. Though it developed within the bounds of the North Atlantic hurricane season, Hurricane Audrey in 1957 became the earliest developing Category 4 hurricane on record after it reached the intensity on June 27. The earliest-forming Category 5 hurricane, Emily, reached the highest intensity on the Saffir-Simpson Hurricane Wind Scale on July 17, 2005.

Though the official end of the Atlantic hurricane season occurs on November 30, the dates of October 31 and November 15 have also been historically marked as the official end date for the hurricane season. December, the only month of the year after the hurricane season, has featured the cyclogenesis of 15 tropical cyclones. Tropical Storm Zeta in 2005 and Hurricane Alex in January, 2016 were the latest tropical cyclones to attain tropical storm intensities as they did so on December 30 with regards to Zeta and January with regards to Hurricane Alex in 2016. However, the second Hurricane Alice in 1954 was the latest forming tropical cyclone to attain hurricane intensity. Both Zeta and Alice were the only two storms to exist in two calendar years – the former from 1954 to 1955, and the latter from 2005 to 2006. No storms have been recorded to exceed Category 1 hurricane intensity in December.

In 1999, Hurricane Lenny reached Category 4 intensity on November 17 as it took an unprecedented west to east track across the Caribbean; its intensity made it the latest developing Category 4 hurricane, though this was well within the bounds of the hurricane season. Hurricane Hattie (October 27-November 1, 1961) was initially thought to have been the latest forming Category 5 hurricane ever documented, though reanalysis indicated that a devastating hurricane in 1932 reached such intensity at a later date. Consequently, this made the hurricane the latest developing tropical cyclone to reach all four Saffir–Simpson Hurricane Wind Scale classifications past Category 1 intensity. The figures below show the zones of origin and tracks for different months during the hurricane season. These figures only depict average conditions. Hurricanes can originate in different locations and travel much different paths from the average. Nonetheless, having a sense of the general pattern can give you a better picture of the average hurricane season for your area.

Tropical cyclone climatology by the month:

Total and average number of tropical storms by the month (1851–2011)

Month	Total	Average
January — April	5	<0.05
May	18	0.1
June	82	0.5
July	114	0.7
August	362	2.3
September	555	3.5
October	323	2.0
November	87	0.5
December	16	0.1

(Courtesy of NOAA/NHC FAQ)

June

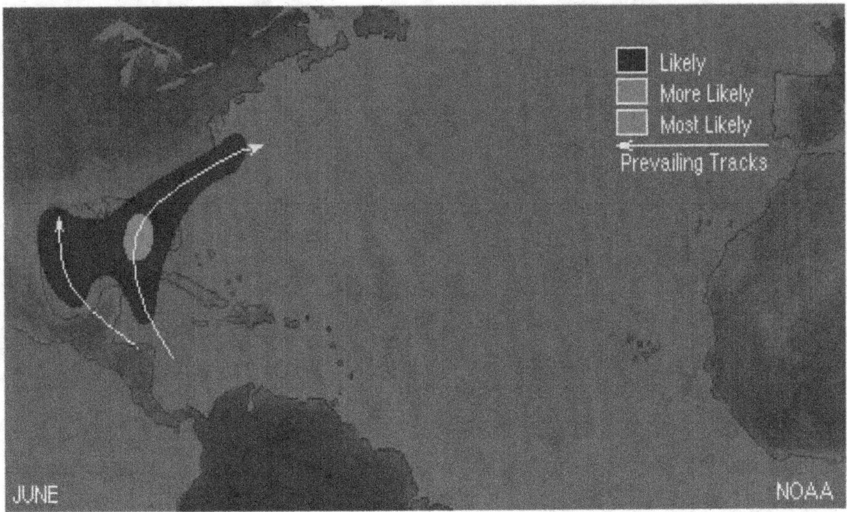

(Typical locations and tracks in June for tropical cyclones of the North Atlantic (Image courtesy of NOAA-NHC).)

The beginning of the hurricane season is most closely related to the timing of increases in sea surface temperatures, convective instability, and other thermodynamic factors. Although June marks the beginning of the hurricane season, generally little activity occurs during the month, with an average of one tropical cyclone every two years. Tropical systems usually form in the Gulf of Mexico or off the east coast of the United States. Those that originate in the Gulf of Mexico or the western Caribbean Sea will have a shorter lifespan, simply as a result of their proximity to land. A hurricane traveling in almost any direction out of the Gulf of Mexico will eventually encounter land and dissipate. Since 1851, a total of 81 tropical storms and hurricanes formed in the month of June. During this period, two of these systems developed in the deep tropics east of the Lesser Antilles. Since 1870, three major hurricanes have formed during June, most notably Hurricane Audrey in 1957. Audrey ranks as the earliest forming Category 4 hurricane in the Atlantic basin. Audrey attained an intensity greater than that of any Atlantic tropical cyclone during June or July until Hurricanes Dennis and Emily of 2005. The easternmost forming storm during June, Tropical Storm Ana in 1979, formed at 45°W.

July

(Typical locations and tracks in July for tropical cyclones of the North Atlantic (Image courtesy of NOAA-NHC FAQ))

Not much tropical activity occurs during the month of July, but the majority of hurricane seasons see the formation of one tropical cyclone during July. By July, the areas of hurricane formation move eastward to include the western Atlantic between 10-20°N and the tropical central Atlantic between 10-20°N. From an average of Atlantic tropical cyclone seasons from 1944 to 2015, the first tropical storm in half of the seasons occurred by 11 July, and a second formed by 8 August. Formation usually occurs in the eastern Caribbean Sea around the Lesser Antilles, in the northern and eastern parts of the Gulf of Mexico, in the vicinity of the northern Bahamas, and off the coast of The Carolinas and Virginia over the Gulf Stream. Storms travel westward through the Caribbean and then either move towards the north and curve near the eastern coast of the United States or stay on a north-westward track and enter the Gulf of Mexico. Since 1851, a total of 105 tropical storms have formed during the month of July. Since 1870, ten of these storms reached major hurricane intensity. Only Hurricane Emily of 2005, the strongest July tropical cyclone in the Atlantic basin, attained Category 5 hurricane status during July, making it the earliest Category 5 hurricane on record. The easternmost forming storm and longest lived during the month of July, Hurricane Bertha in 2008 formed at 22.9°W and lasted 17 days.[81]

---

[81] USDC and NOAA/NHC _Historical Climatology Series 6-2 Tropical Cyclones of the North Atlantic Ocean 1851-2006,_ (2009) pg. 213.

August

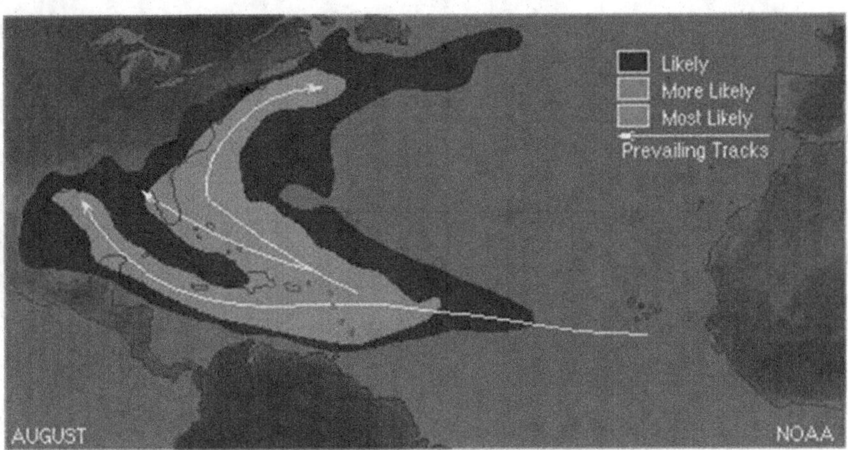

(Typical locations and tracks in August for tropical cyclones of the North Atlantic (Image courtesy of NOAA-NHC))

Decrease in wind shear from July to August contributes to a significant increase of tropical activity. In August, the points of origin are considerably more numerous, with many of them concentrated in the western and central North Atlantic. Most of the storms forming during this month are the Cape Verde type hurricanes. Hurricanes that move to higher latitudes over the central and western North Atlantic rapidly lose their intensity as they make a transformation to an extra-tropical cyclone. These hurricane-initiated or hurricane-enhanced extra-tropical cyclones may last for weeks as they traverse large distances across to Europe and beyond. An average of 2.8 Atlantic tropical storms develops annually in August. On average, four named tropical storms, including one hurricane, occur by August 30, and the first intense hurricane develops by 4 September.

September

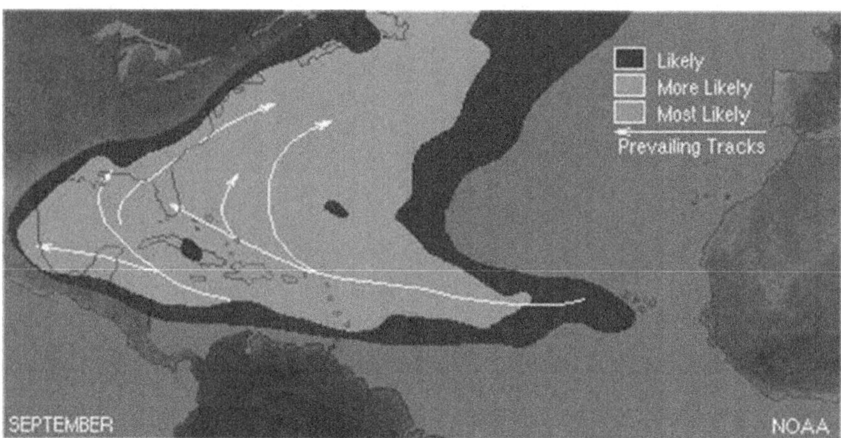

(Typical locations and tracks in September for tropical cyclones of the North Atlantic (Image courtesy of NOAA-NHC.))

The peak of the hurricane season occurs in September and corresponds to low wind shear and the warmest sea surface temperatures. The month of September sees an average of 3 storms a year. By 24 September, the average Atlantic season features 7 named tropical storms, including 4 hurricanes. In addition, two major hurricanes occur on average by 28 September. Relatively few tropical cyclones make landfall at these intensities.

October

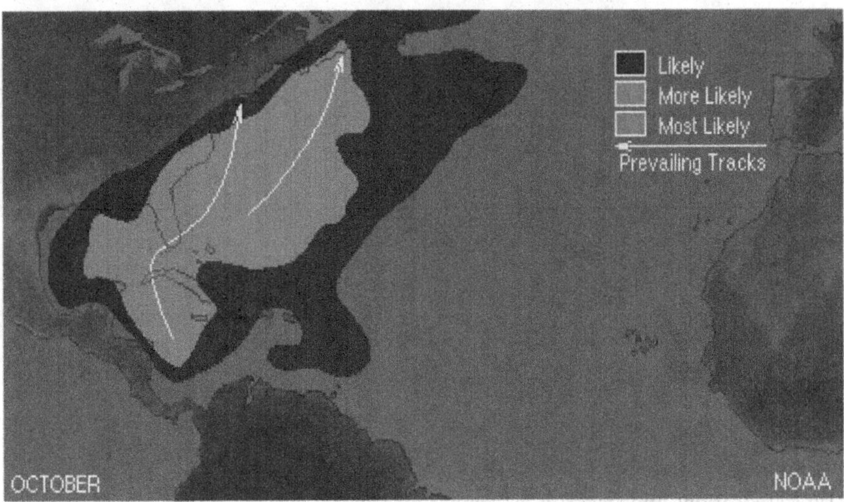

(Typical locations and tracks in October for tropical cyclones of the North Atlantic (Image courtesy of NOAA-NHC))

The favorable conditions found during September begin to decay in October. The main reason for the decrease in activity is increasing wind shear, although sea surface temperatures are also cooler than in September. As a result of these factors, most hurricanes tend not to form over the central and eastern tropical Atlantic. Activity falls markedly with 1.8 cyclones developing on average despite a climatological secondary peak around 20 October. By 21 October, the average season features 9 named storms with 5 hurricanes. A third major hurricane occurs after 28 September in half of all Atlantic tropical cyclone seasons. In contrast to mid-season activity, the mean locus of formation shifts westward to the Caribbean and Gulf of Mexico, reversing the eastward progression of June through August.

November

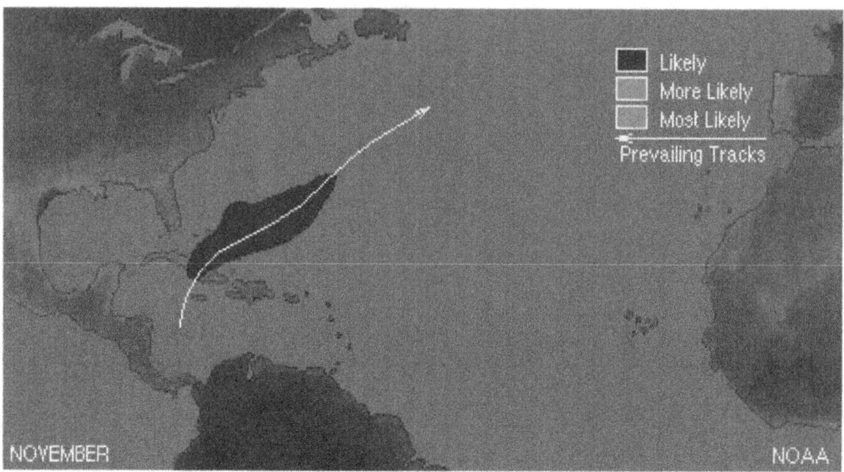

(Typical locations and tracks in November for tropical cyclones of the North Atlantic (Image courtesy of NOAA-NHC))

Wind shear from westerlies increases substantially through November, generally preventing cyclone formation. On average, one tropical storm forms during every other November. On rare occasions, a major hurricane occurs. The few intense hurricanes in November include Hurricane Lenny in mid-November 1999, Hurricane Kate in late November 1985 (the latest major hurricane on record), and Hurricane Paloma in early November 2008.

CHAPTER SEVEN

An investigation of the historical hurricane activities in the North Atlantic

The diverse cultures of the Caribbean and the rest of the region have been shaped as much by hurricanes as they have by diplomacy, commerce, or the legacy of colonial rule. In this wide-ranging work on the history of the greatest and deadliest hurricanes of the region, in this and other upcoming chapters this book will examine just how these varied countries have responded to the dangers of hurricanes. Furthermore, this book will show how these destructive storms have influenced the region's history, from the rise of plantations, to slavery and its abolition, to migrations, racial conflict, and even war.

Since explorer Christopher Columbus first sailed the Caribbean Sea, catastrophic storms have been recorded to hit this area of the North Atlantic, sinking ships, destroying homes and killing thousands of people. Even if today's equipment and weather monitoring satellites can predict the direction of a hurricane and estimate its intensity, humans are still not immune to the disaster brought by hurricanes. The hazardous and powerful forces of hurricanes are not to be ignored: the wind can reach impossible speeds and be the main cause of destruction, while intense rainfall and huge waves can cause floods, beach erosion and sink even a big ship. The highest intensity that a hurricane can reach is known as a Category 5 hurricane on the Saffir-Simpson Hurricane Wind Scale. Unfortunately, such disastrous storms occur every several years in the North Atlantic, and their feared names are not something to underestimate or ignore.

Throughout the late 1400s through to the early to mid-1800s in the era of conquest and colonization of the Caribbean, North and Central America, the hurricanes were a definite and dangerous limiting factor. It was a presence that shaped the Spanish, and later, other European actions and strategies within this region. Much of the early history of the Spanish conquest and colonization of the New World and some of its distinctive stories and characters were formed or influenced by these great and powerful storms.

Hurricanes have been affecting the North Atlantic for centuries, and since there is no known way to prevent them, we can expect that they will continue to affect these countries and islands for years to come. Today, it can be said that every island or country within this region has experienced the direct effects of at least one hurricane or has had a disturbance in the island's weather conditions due to a hurricane passing nearby. Historically, the islands and countries which have suffered the least due to these natural disasters are Barbados and Trinidad and Tobago, as they are the most easterly islands in the Windward Islands chain and tends not to be in the direct path of most hurricanes affecting the region because of their nearness to the equator and out of the typical route for hurricanes. Furthermore, places like Aruba and Bonaire rarely feel the forces of these monster storms for the same reason. Hurricane Andrew in 1992, Hurricane Mitch in 1998, Hurricane Sandy in 2012, and Hurricane Katrina in 2005 are perhaps some of the most recent enduring and memorable destructive hurricanes to hit the region.

Hurricanes played an important role during the European exploration and colonization of the Caribbean and the Americas. New settlements were established, battles were lost and geography was changed by these monster storms. During the sixteenth, seventeenth and eighteenth centuries, hurricanes posed some great and unique challenges for the colonists in the Caribbean and the Americas. These storms quickly became the most feared aspect of their physical environment, destroying staple and cash crops and provisions, leveling plantations, cities and towns, disrupting shipping and trade, and resulting in major economic losses for colonial residents and native inhabitants.

During the sixteenth and seventeenth centuries, hurricanes making landfall somewhere in the Caribbean and the coast of North America may have gone unreported because of the dispersed character of colonial settlements in the region. By the eighteenth century, settlements were more uniformly distributed throughout the Caribbean and the increased use of the sea-lanes provided a higher likelihood of storms being detected and reported. With the coming of the Europeans, written records, first in meticulous Spanish and then English, began but generally only storms that sank ships or devastated colonial settlements were recorded. The quantitative record of Atlantic hurricanes began in 1851 and actually started to be reliable just before the turn of the 20th

Century. The historical record of hurricane activity in this region before the late 1800s is sadly deficient.

Prior to the use of the Saffir-Simpson Hurricane Wind Scale, it was difficult to speak comparatively about hurricanes and their effects, although people have always (if inaccurately) done so. Reports from governors, colonists and observers in the seventeenth and eighteenth centuries often made reference to the memory of elderly residents who might say that a particular storm was "worse than the hurricane of 1866," or "more frightening than the one in 1780." During this era, that kind of anecdotal accounting, along with records of losses and deaths, was all that governments and societies could gauge a storm's effects. Thankfully, today the Saffir-Simpson Hurricane Wind Scale now allows easier comparisons across time with greater accuracy.

There are a number of reasons why hurricanes moving through this region may not have been recorded in historical records. First it must be noted, however that the major islands in this region were not settled until the early to mid-1600s, and colonists in the region might not have known about these storms. Second, prior to the early to mid-1600s, hurricanes that moved through the region were not recorded due to lack of permanent settlements. Third, a small percentage of North Atlantic hurricanes made landfall in only certain small sections of the region only, so therefore they were not recorded. Fourth, unless these storms produced excessive damage and/or loss of life, they were unlikely to be recorded in historical manuals or documents.

Fifth, during the 1700s, 1800s and early 1900s, wars in Europe and America with impact on the Caribbean were nearly constant during the colonial period. News of these events often dominated newspaper reports in the region and may have pre-empted reports of lesser scale weather events such as hurricanes, especially with the minor storms.

Furthermore, colonial affiliations impacted the sharing of news. Poor relations between the British and the French resulted in trade restrictions between the two colonies by extension this would inhibit the delivery of news of weather catastrophes to colonies with different affiliations. Sixth, it was estimated that as much as fifty-four percent of the hurricanes and tropical storms in the North Atlantic Ocean failed to make landfall in the Caribbean, so from a historical perspective, these storms would only be documented if a ship encountered a hurricane while in transit, survived, and then reported the incident after making port. For example, in the Bahamas, between 1784 and 1837, ships' captains filed twenty-two reports of storm damage after making port in Nassau.

Seventh, ship logs, newspaper records and weather dairies of plantation owners often reported these storms as 'gales' or 'severe gales' rather than hurricanes or tropical storms, so some of these storms might have gone unreported or under-reported. Finally, hurricanes that made their way through one island in the region after (or prior to) inflicting greater damage among those of other populated areas of the North Atlantic coast or the Caribbean may have gone unreported in the face of the greater damage reports from these more populated areas.

The investigation of historical hurricane activity in the North Atlantic Ocean has been limited to three primary authors. Ivan Tannehill (1950) provided the first comprehensive listing of historical hurricane activity in the region. Tannehill's pioneering work still serves as the basis from which later hurricane chronologies are derived. Tannehill compiled his chronology from a number of historical sources. He accessed a large number of ship's logs to help confirm reports of hurricane activity at sea and relied heavily on the works of Southey (1827), Reid (1850), Poey (1862), Redfield (1864), Alexander (1902) and Mitchell (1928). Ludlum (1963) and José Millas (1968) extended Tannehill's original work as they focused on specific regions and time periods. The two works are complementary. Millas concentrated on hurricane activity in the Caribbean, and Ludlum's work centered on the coastal areas of the United States.

Millas limited his efforts to the period 1492 to 1800 as he consulted previously untapped Spanish language resources from the colonial era. Millas added a number of hurricane events to the historical record. He also found several errors in the original Tannehill chronology and corrected them. Similarly, Ludlum used Tannehill as a base for compiling his chronology of hurricane events along the coast of the United States for the period 1492 to1870. Ludlum utilized archival newspaper holdings to further extend Tannehill's work, and he contributed additional hurricane events to the historical record. As with Millas, Ludlum discovered a number of errors in the original Tannehill Chronology and amended the record accordingly.[82]

Today, in the North Atlantic basin, there is a great deal of hurricane research going on with regards to correcting the errors of present day and past hurricanes using the HURDAT project from the National Hurricane Center located in

---

82 *The Bahamas Journal of Science Vol. 5 No.1-Historical Hurricane Impacts on the Bahamas, Part I: 1500-1749* Ronald V. Shaklee- Geography Department at Youngstown State University, Youngstown, OH, Media Publishing Ltd.

Florida. What is HURDAT, one may ask? In simplest terms, HURDAT is the "official" hurricane database that contains a detailed record of all tropical storms (TS) and hurricanes (H) known to have developed somewhere within the North Atlantic basin-which includes the Atlantic Ocean, Caribbean Sea, and the Gulf of Mexico-for the period of 1851 to the present day. It is also the official record for all landfalling tropical storms and hurricanes known to have impacted the United States (U.S.) coastlines as well. This database was initially created in support of the Apollo space program in the 1960's and contained six-hourly positions and intensities for all tropical cyclones that have been documented up until that time. Unfortunately, there were (and in some cases, still are) many systematic and random errors contained within the database that needed to be corrected before the final research on a particular storm is presented. Another issue that needed to be addressed were biases contained in the database resulting from a greater understanding of tropical cyclones that had developed over the years, and the enhanced analysis techniques used by NHC forecasters.

As a result, researchers with the Hurricane Research Division (HRD)-led by Science and Operations Officer NOAA/NCEP/National Hurricane Center Chris Landsea, undertook the work to correct these "errors" through a project called "The Atlantic Hurricane Database Re-analysis Project (HRP)." The stated "objective" of the HRP is an effort led by the Hurricane Research Division to extend and revise the North Atlantic hurricane database (or HURDAT). Going back as far as 1851 and revisiting storms in more recent years, information on tropical cyclones is revised using an enhanced collection of historical meteorological data in the context of today's scientific understanding of hurricane and analysis techniques.

These new technological advances have provided hurricane forecasters with new tools and data sources that has led to continued improvement in the detection, observation, and forecasting of tropical cyclones. These "new tools and data sources" include Quikscat, the advanced microwave sounding unit, and the cyclone phase space analysis. Without these, it is estimated that at least one tropical cyclone per season would've been "missed"-likely misidentified as an extra-tropical cyclone instead-during the past decade. Obviously, the same would be true for the entire historical record that preceded it.

The primary goal for this project is to provide an extended and corrected Atlantic hurricane database of individual tropical cyclone tracks and intensities for both the entire Atlantic basin, as well as U.S. landfalling storms. This fits in well with the goals of NOAA and HRD to better understand variability of extreme events, such as tropical storms. As result of these efforts, HURDAT has been extended back in time to 1851 (from its original starting point of 1886), and an extensive revision has been made to the database for all known tropical cyclones up to near present day storms in the North Atlantic basin hurricane season. The reanalysis project, for instance, determined that Hurricane Andrew in 1992 was a Category 5 storm at landfall rather than a Category 4 storm as the previous records indicated. As a result, ten years after its landfall in Florida, the official category for this storm in the official record books is now labeled as a Category 5 hurricane on the Saffir-Simpson Hurricane Wind Scale.

One may ask, 'Why do meteorologists and other scientists study, research, document or re-analyze historic hurricanes, and what purpose is there to dig up the past?' The best answer to that question was given by Dr. Christopher Landsea in an interview with *The Palm Beach Post* on April 2, 2015. Christopher W. Landsea (born 1965) is an American meteorologist, formerly a research meteorologist with Hurricane Research Division of Atlantic Oceanographic & Meteorological Laboratory at NOAA, and now the Science and Operations Officer at the National Hurricane Center. Over the years, Landsea's work has involved the general hurricane FAQ currently on the Atlantic Oceanographic and Meteorological Laboratory website and the North Atlantic reanalysis. Landsea has contributed to *Science, Bulletin of the American Meteorological Society, Journal of Climate,* and *Nature.* He has been vocal on the lack of evidence or lack of a link between global warming and current hurricane intensity change. Landsea has published a number of research papers on tropical cyclones and hurricanes. He is the author of *Hurricanes, Typhoons, and Tropical Cyclones: FAQ.* He also has been the lead scientist in the North Atlantic hurricane reanalysis since 1997. In this interview, he stated that:

"We re-analyze historic hurricanes for the purpose of getting as accurate a record as you can. Part of the reason for doing that is so that we know if a hurricane has hit in the past-it's going to hit again. A hurricane hitting one location is a rare event, so we want to be able to take a look at seeing when a historic storm has hit, knowing how strong it was, so that we can plan for future storms, and we use that as a guiding point. Another reason for investigating old storms is to better understand how climates have changed, because we know that there are cycles, trends and variations in climate, and if you don't have an accurate record for past hurricanes, you might have a misleading trend. Finally, we want to be able to have an accurate record for the folks doing the insurance rates, insurance companies want to be able to charge the accurate and justifiable rates, but to do that they need an accurate record going back as far as possible so that they can provide what the accurate rate should be."[83]

The Atlantic hurricane season is the period in a year when hurricanes usually form in the North Atlantic basin. Tropical cyclones in the North Atlantic are called hurricanes, tropical storms, or tropical depressions. In addition, there have been several storms over the years that have not been fully tropical which are categorized as subtropical depressions and subtropical storms. Worldwide, tropical cyclone activity peaks in late summer, when the difference between temperatures aloft and sea surface temperatures is the greatest. However, each particular basin has its own seasonal patterns. On a worldwide scale, the month of May is the least active month, while September is the most active. In the North Atlantic Basin, a clear and distinct hurricane season sharply peaks from late August through September; the season's climatological peak of activity occurs around September 10 each season.

Tropical disturbances that reach tropical storm intensity are named from a pre-determined list. On average, 12 named storms occur each season, with an average of 6 becoming hurricanes and 3 becoming major hurricanes (Category 3 or greater). The most active season was 2005, during which 28 tropical cyclones formed, of which a record 15 became hurricanes. The least active season was the 1914, with only one known tropical cyclone developing during that year. The North Atlantic hurricane season is a time when most tropical cyclones are expected to develop across the North Atlantic Ocean. During the season, regular tropical weather outlooks are issued by the National Hurricane Center, and coordination between the Hydro-Meteorological Prediction Center and National Hurricane Center occurs for systems which have not formed yet, but could develop during the next three to seven days.

The basic concept of a hurricane season began during 1935, when dedicated wire circuits known as hurricane circuits began to be set up along the Gulf and Atlantic coasts, a process completed by 1955. It was originally the time frame when the tropics were monitored routinely for tropical cyclone activity and was originally defined as from June 15 through October 31. Over the years, the beginning date was shifted back to June 1, while the end date was shifted to November 15, before settling at November 30 by 1965. This was when hurricane reconnaissance planes were sent out to fly across the Atlantic and Gulf of Mexico on a routine basis to look for potential tropical cyclones,

---

83 *The Palm Beach Post April 2, 2015, Video Interview: Hurricane historian Christopher Landsea: Lessons of studying old hurricanes,* Retrieved: 04-08-2015.

in the years prior to the continuous weather satellite era. Since regular satellite surveillance began, hurricane hunter aircraft fly only into storm areas which are first spotted by satellite imagery. When ranking hurricanes by strength, the obvious choice is to compare wind speeds. But since measurements of the most extreme winds are difficult to obtain, we instead compare hurricanes by their lowest central pressure, a measure that has a strong relationship to wind speed; generally, the lower the pressure in a hurricane, the stronger its winds.

The historical records of tropical cyclones over the North Atlantic region extends back more than half a millennium. Geological records provide clues to hurricane activity farther back still. This section of this book identifies some of the major hurricanes of the past and their impact on the various countries, and the region as a whole. From the perspective of European history, the first North Atlantic hurricane sighting was made by world famous explorer Christopher Columbus while sailing along the north coast of Cuba in June of 1494. The hurricane of July 1500 is the first known hurricane to affect the present day state of Florida in the United States. In these earlier times, storm accounts were kept by sailors and ships captions in their log books.

The post-World War II use of radar to track tropical cyclones near the coast further improved the forecasting capabilities of these storms. By the middle 1950s, radar systems were available at some U.S. Weather Bureau sites along the Gulf and Atlantic coasts, and by the early 1960s the Weather Bureau placed a network of radars all along the Gulf Coast and Eastern Seaboard sites. Radar is particularly useful as the hurricane approaches to within several hundred miles of the coast and can be used to detect sudden and often subtle shifts in the track of an approaching storm. Today, since 1988 new advanced and better resolution radars called Doppler radars are in use in many countries and weather offices across the region. Doppler radars can quickly show in great details the wind speed and direction within the storm's cells. The National Hurricane Center takes the information from radars and other sources and uses super computers to help forecast the path, speed, and strength of hurricanes. Today, it is fair to say that these radars are greatly improving hurricane forecasts in the process and providing advanced warnings to coastal regions of the North Atlantic, therefore saving many lives in the process. Perhaps the single most important technological advancement for hurricane detection and monitoring is the weather satellite. Satellites provide a global view of the weather, which is particularly essential in areas lacking in ground-based weather stations, such as over open waters of the North Atlantic Ocean and in the tropics in general.

When dealing with the greatest and deadliest storms of this region, there are several striking features about these storms. The first is that hurricanes are not evenly distributed around the region. That is to an extent a function of population density and location; because where there are more people, located in an area or country, it is fair to assume that there exists the potential for more lives to be lost. In fact, some countries or cities get more than their fair share of hurricanes. For example, Trinidad located in the southern Caribbean, rarely gets hit by a hurricane because of its close distance to the equator. Very few hurricanes with a few notable exceptions have struck Trinidad. The 1933 Trinidad hurricane was one of only three North Atlantic tropical cyclones on record to produce hurricane-force winds in Trinidad and Venezuela. The second tropical storm and first hurricane of the 1933 North Atlantic hurricane season, the system formed on June 24 to the east of the Lesser Antilles. It moved westward and attained hurricane status before striking Trinidad on June 27. The storm caused heavy damage on the island, estimated at around $3 million. The strong winds downed trees and destroyed hundreds of houses, leaving about 1,000 people homeless. Later, the hurricane crossed the northeastern portion of Venezuela, where power outages and damaged houses were reported.

On the other hand, Cape Hatteras, North Carolina gets brushed or hit by a tropical cyclone once every 1.36 years and remains in the number 1 position for the last two years within the North Atlantic region of cities and countries most frequently impacted by tropical cyclones. This city had more brushes or hits than any other cities or countries in the top 50 cities or countries with a considerable amount of recurvatures of many of the storms occurring just offshore in this city. There are also numerous back door systems from the Gulf of Mexico that have cut through Cape Hatteras on the way out to sea with some becoming extratropical. Overall, it is affected a whopping 105 times since 1871. Second on the list is Morehead City, North Carolina which is brushed or hit once every 1.54 years and has been affected 93 times since 1871. Third on the list is the island of Grand Bahama in the Bahamas which is brushed or hit once every 1.63 years and was affected 88 times since 1871. It is the most affected island in the Bahamas (Abaco and Andros are in the numbers 6 and 7th positions respectively). Located in the NW Bahamas, these three Bahamian islands experience many hurricanes from many of the various tropical cyclone tracks and formation zones within the North Atlantic. In the fourth spot is the Cayman Islands in the Caribbean and they are affected once every 1.68 years.[84]

---

84 *http://www.hurricanecity.com/rank.htm/Jim Williams.* Retrieved 11-10-2015.

A second striking feature is that many of the worst hurricanes happened in or before 1900 and one notable exception to this rule was Hurricane Mitch of 1998, which struck several Central American countries like Honduras, Nicaragua and Costa Rica killing over 10,000 persons. But the greatest and deadliest hurricane on record in the North Atlantic basin is one that we have almost completely blotted from our memory. This storm occurred in 1780 and it is simply called the 'Great Hurricane of 1780', which killed over 22,000 persons. The contributing factor of increased death toll prior to 1900 was the lack of warnings in those countries impacted by the hurricane. During this era, there were no satellites, radars, radios, reconnaissance aircrafts, computers, or televisions to warn the residents of an impending storm.

Finally, putting disasters behind us and forgetting them seems to be a very deep-seated human trait; maybe at some primeval level, we need to forget in order to get on with our lives, perhaps just to keep our sanity. The scale of human loss as presented here in this book is truly unbelievable and horrifying. The same or very similar hurricane disasters keep on happening in the same places, because if a location or country has been prone to flooding, it stands to reason that it will occur once again in the future with similar or greater occurrences. An alarming aspect of this patterning is that as coastal locations grow by staggering amounts, then devastation from these storms will grow as well. Because most hurricane disasters follow patterns and cycles, it is becoming increasingly possible to forecast the disasters of the future, thereby significantly reducing the death toll. But one long-anticipated and greatly feared future hurricane catastrophe may well not happen at all, so – against all expectations – this book will have a happy or fairytale ending.

CHAPTER EIGHT

The major North Atlantic hurricanes from 1494 – 1600

The Discovery of America most commonly referred to as Christopher Columbus' 1492 transatlantic maritime expedition or the First Voyage of Christopher Columbus, in which he became the first Christian European to make landfall in the Americas. Columbus, an Italian navigator sailing for the Spanish Crown, sought a westward route to Asia, which led him to coin the misnomer "West Indies" for the Antilles, where he made landfall. The newly discovered landmass came to be known in Europe as the New World. Ultimately, the two continents and collection of islands of the Western Hemisphere became known as the Americas, after Amerigo Vespucci. Vespucci, an Italian navigator, is credited with recognizing the Americas as newly discovered, previously unknown territory, as opposed to islands associated with Asia, as Columbus originally surmised. Over four voyages to the Americas between 1492 and 1502, Columbus set the stage for the European exploration and colonization of the Americas, ultimately leading to the Columbian Exchange. Considered an indicator of the start of modern history, the great significance of his voyages to the history of the world is uncontested.

At the time of the voyages, the Americas were inhabited by natives considered to be the descendants of Asians who crossed the Bering Strait to North America in prehistoric times. Vikings were the first Europeans to reach the Americas, establishing a short-lived colony in Newfoundland circa 1000. Columbus' voyages led to the widespread knowledge that a new continent existed west of Europe and east of Asia. This breakthrough in geographical science led to the exploration and colonization of the New World by major European superpowers and is sometimes cited as the start of the modern era.

Spain, Portugal and other European kingdoms sent expeditions and established colonies throughout the New World, converted the native inhabitants to Christianity, and built large trade networks across the Atlantic, which introduced new plants, animals, and food crops in both continents. The search for a westward route to Asia continued in 1513, when Nuñez de Balboa crossed Central America he became the first European to sight the Pacific Ocean. The search was completed in 1521, when the Spanish Magellan-Elcano expedition sailed across the Pacific and reached southeast Asia.

Observation data for years before 1492 is completely unavailable because most native Indian populations of the Caribbean, Central and North America lacked written languages to keep records in the pre-Columbian era, and most records in written Mesoamerican languages either did not survive or have not been deciphered and translated. Scientists now regard even data from the early years of the Columbian era as suspicious because Renaissance scientists and sailors made no distinction between tropical cyclones and extratropical systems and were incomplete because European exploration of North America and European colonization of the Americas reached only scattered areas in the 16th century.

After the Caribbean was visited by Christopher Columbus in 1492, Spain claimed the area, and its ships searched for treasure. With the Spanish discovery of the Pacific Ocean in 1513 the Caribbean became the main route of their expeditions, and later of convoys. Pirates and warships of rival powers preyed on Spanish ships in the Caribbean. Although Spain controlled most of the sea, Britain, France, the Netherlands, and Denmark established colonies on the islands along the eastern fringe of the Caribbean. From September 6th, when he left the Canary Islands, to that memorable day on October 12th, when he discovered and landed on the island of San Salvador in the Bahamas, he crossed the Atlantic Ocean unaware of the great danger that he could have encountered from a hurricane. There are some scholars who believe that the three ships of Columbus were very good and sturdy vessels that could have withstood the powerful winds and the extremely rough seas of any hurricane. On the other hand, others speculated that it would have been nearly impossible for these ships to survive intact, considering that many similar hurricanes caused complete fleets to go down in them.

After the discovery of the New World, initially by Christopher Columbus in 1492, and the eventual colonization of this New World by the Spanish at first and followed by the various European nations, hurricanes were a new meteorological phenomenon and hazard to them. Hurricanes are so important to the history of the Caribbean that the word itself has its origins here. The native Taíno Indians called these ferocious tropical cyclones passing through the Caribbean "Huracán", which is believed to have been derived from their god of evil spirits, weather and big winds. When the Spaniards arrived in the late 15th century, they had never encountered such a fierce and mighty storm, so they had no name for it in their own vocabulary. Thus, the native Indian word "Huracán" quickly became incorporated into the Spanish language. The Taíno Indians had no written language, so the Spaniards just sounded it out phonetically. The word "hurricane" is the anglicized spelling of the Spanish version of the word "Huracán."

A large number of ships came to the West Indies during the early and late 1500s, many of them in time became of no use to the Spanish explorers and were eventually dismantled to utilize on land or the wood salvaged to build or repair other ships because some of the timber was still in good condition. In these cases, the loss of the ship was considered normal and nothing said about it. The loss of a ship was mentioned in letters, judicial documents, royal correspondences, etc., and only when the ship was destroyed by a hurricane did that garner any kind of special attention. Therefore, the loss of a ship by a hurricane or it being shipwrecked is a very valuable indicator to the students of the history of hurricanes in the region during the early years of discovery and colonization about what obstacles they may have faced and how they dealt with them. The existence of a hurricane can also be inferred from the mention in shipping documents of an unavoidable arrival at the nearest port on account of a nearby storm.

The history of hurricanes plaguing the North Atlantic region goes back as far as there have been settlements to record their impact. Christopher Columbus was undoubtedly a very skilled mariner, but yet he was also an extremely lucky one. About ninety percent of all tropical storms and hurricanes in the North Atlantic form between the latitudes of 10°North and 35°North, but yet in September 1492, at the height of the hurricane season, Columbus during this voyage encountered exceptionally good weather en route to the Bahamas. He sailed along the main hurricane route but yet didn't experience any hurricanes. The first European encounter and observation with a hurricane occurred in 1494 on the island of Hispaniola (present-day Dominican Republic and Haiti). A "violent hurricane" struck Hispaniola near La Isabela from southwest. This storm occurred during Christopher Columbus Second Voyage to the New World. The fleet of his arrived at Hispaniola one day before the September eclipse on September 14th, and a storm occurred shortly thereafter this time.

Another hurricane also affected La Isabela, Hispaniola, in late October 1495, damaging some of the ships in the harbor.

In describing this hurricane, Columbus reported in his log book: "Groves were rent from the mountain precipices, with vast masses of earth and rock, tumbling into the valleys with terrific noise, and choking the course of rivers. The fearful sounds in the air and on the earth, the pealing thunder, the vivid lightning, the howling of the wind, the crash of falling trees and rocks, filled every one with affright; and many thought that the end of the world was at hand. Some fled to caverns for safety, for their frail houses were blown down, and the air was filled with the trunks and branches of trees, and even with fragments of rocks, carried along by the fury of the tempest. When the hurricane reached the harbor, it whirled the ships around as they lay at anchor, snapped their cables, and sank three of them with all who were on board. Others were driven about, dashed against each other, and tossed mere wrecks upon the shore by the swelling surges of the seas, which in some places rolled for three or four miles upon the land. The tempest lasted for three hours. When it was passed away, and the sun again appeared, the Indians regarded each other in mute astonishment and dismay. Never in their memory, nor in the traditions of their ancestors, that their island had been visited by such a storm. They believed that the Deity had sent this fearful ruin to punish the cruelties and crimes of the white men; and declared that this people had moved the very air, the water, and the earth, to disturb their tranquil life, and to desolate their island."[85]

---

[85] Irwing, W. *The Life and Voyages of Christopher Columbus, Vol IV*. (New York, G.P. Putnam, 1861), pgs. 75-76.

This image shows a powerful and unnamed storm in 1495 on the island of Hispaniola and is one of the earliest European images and experience of a hurricane. The foundering ships and fleeing Spanish explorers and native Taíno Indians emphasize the destruction, helplessness, and power of this storm. (From Johann Feyerabend and Theodor de Bry, *Americae pars quarta*, Frankfurt am Main; courtesy of the John Carter Brown Library at Brown University)

In this first European account of a Caribbean hurricane, we find intertwined three elements that often appear in the early observations based on providential or diabolic intervention, and the use of theoretical knowledge and practical experience to understand and survive the storms. The tension between theology, theory, and experience in the face of nature both fascinated and baffled European observers during the following three centuries. The first Europeans in the Caribbean naturally turned to their previous experiences as a guide.

During Christopher Columbus' fourth and final voyage to the New World, the explorer experienced the wrath of a powerful hurricane. He encountered the storm just off the coast of Hispaniola. On June 29, 1502, Columbus stopped at Hispaniola to send letters back to Spain and potentially trade one of his slower ships, *the Santiago de Palos.* However, Columbus suspected that a hurricane was approaching the area. During his earlier voyages, natives warned Columbus of bad storms which they called "horrible tempests", or "Huracán." Sensing one of these storms was near Columbus attempted to seek shelter in Santo Domingo on the southern side of Hispaniola. However, the explorer and his fleet were denied access to the port by Hispaniola's local governor, Don Nicolas de Oravando. With access to Santo Domingo denied, Columbus, strategically moved his 4 ships to the west side of the island. Columbus then noticed that the governor was preparing to send a "treasure fleet" with gold and slaves to Spain. Columbus warned de Oravando about the pending storm and advised him to keep the fleet in port. Orvando ignored Columbus' advice and sent the ships on their way, only to their own demise.

People didn't appreciate the politeness of hurricanes until scientists developed the technology to track them. Until recently, there were no satellite photos and no planes to fly into the hurricane's eye. The Taíno Indians described the hurricane's warning signs to Christopher Columbus, and he listened to them. On at least one occasion, this knowledge saved Columbus' fleet from a watery grave. Lesser Antilles Islanders came to know that hurricanes were likely to strike during August and September. They would watch closely for the signs — a hazy sun, a light drizzle, an upswing of wind, and most notably the erratic inland flight of the magnificent frigate bird, known on some islands as the hurricane bird. But telltale signs didn't always appear to tell their story and the results were great devastation along coastal areas and a very high death toll on the islands impacted by the hurricane. Today, the people of these islands in the Caribbean have developed a deep respect for the power of hurricanes.

An accurate record of historical weather patterns is essential as scientists attempt to understand how contemporary weather patterns relate to the weather and climate of the past with a view of affecting the weather of the future. When choosing these storms, I took into consideration such obvious factors as the event's magnitude, historical significance, meteorological uniqueness (low barometric pressure, catastrophic storm surge and high winds), records they created or shattered, economic impact, and death toll when devising this list. Based on these factors, these storms on the list have earned the title as the major North Atlantic storms.

The islands of the West Indies lie between North and South America, from Florida to the coast of Venezuela and separating the Caribbean Sea and the Gulf of Mexico from the Atlantic Ocean. The archipelago, sometimes called the Antilles, is divided into three groups: The Bahamas; the Greater Antilles (Cuba, Jamaica, Haiti, the Dominican Republic, and Puerto Rico), and the Lesser

Antilles (Leeward Islands, Windward Islands, Trinidad and Tobago, Barbados) and the islands off the northern coast of Venezuela. The British dependent territories are the Cayman Islands, the Turks and Caicos, Anguilla, Montserrat, and the British Virgin Islands. The Dutch territories are Aruba, Curacao, Bonaire, Saint Eustatius, Saba, and part of Saint Martin. The French territories are Guadeloupe and its dependencies, part of Saint Martin, and Martinique. Puerto Rico is a self-governing commonwealth associated with the United States, and the Virgin Islands of the United States are both U.S. territories. Margarita belongs to Venezuela. Many of the islands are mountainous, and some have partly active volcanoes. Hurricanes occur frequently, but the warm climate (tempered by northeast trade winds) and the clear tropical seas have made the West Indies a very popular mecca and a resort area. Some 34 million people live on the islands, and the majority of inhabitants are of black African descent.

Between 1492 and 1550, Spain extended its control over the large islands of the Caribbean, completing the conquest of Hispaniola, Cuba, Jamaica, and Puerto Rico, exploring, raiding, and slaving, but not occupying the Bahamas (the so-called "useless islands") and the Lesser Antilles. New Spain (Mexico) was brought under Spanish control in the 1520s and 1530s, for the most part. Yucatan took longer, but by the 1540s, despite isolated cases of Maya resistance, it too had been conquered, as had large sections of northern Mexico.

The history of the West Indies reveals the significant role the region played in the colonial struggles of the European powers since the 15th century. Soon after the voyages of Christopher Columbus to the Americas, both Portuguese and Spanish ships began claiming territories in Central and South America. These colonies brought in gold, and other European powers, most specifically England, the Netherlands, and France, hoped to establish profitable colonies of their own. Imperial rivalries made the Caribbean a highly contested area during European wars for centuries. During the first voyage of the explorer Christopher Columbus (mandated by the Spanish crown to conquer), contact was made with the Lucayans in the Bahamas and the Taíno in Cuba and the northern coast of Hispaniola, and a few of the native people were taken back to Spain. Small amounts of gold were found in their personal ornaments and other objects such as masks and belts. The Spanish, who came seeking wealth, enslaved the native population and rapidly drove them to near extinction. To supplement the Amerindian labor, the Spanish imported African slaves.

Although Spain claimed the entire Caribbean, they settled only the larger islands of Hispaniola (1493), Puerto Rico (1508), Jamaica (1509), Cuba (1511), and Trinidad (1530), although the Spanish made an exception in the case of the small 'pearl islands' of Cubagua and Margarita off the Venezuelan coast because of their valuable pearl beds, which were worked extensively between 1508 and 1530. The other European powers established a presence in the Caribbean after the Spanish Empire declined, partly due to the reduced native population of the area from European diseases. The Dutch, the French, and the British followed one another to the region and established a long-term presence. They brought with them millions of slaves imported from Africa to support the tropical plantation system that spread through the Caribbean islands.

This is a list of all known or suspected Atlantic hurricanes before 1600. Although most storms likely went unrecorded and many records have been lost, recollections of hurricane occurrences survive from some sufficiently populated coastal areas and rarely ships at sea that survived these tempests. Observation data for years before 1492 is completely unavailable because most natives of North America lacked written languages to keep records in the pre-Columbus era, and most records in written Mesoamerican languages either do not survive or have not been deciphered and translated. Scientists now regard even data from the early years of the Columbian era as suspicious because Renaissance scientists and sailors made no distinction between tropical cyclones and extratropical systems and incomplete because European exploration of North America and European colonization of the Americas reached only scattered areas in the 16th century.

The Hurricane of 1494--Christopher Columbus' fleet of ships after arriving on November 3, 1493, at an island in the Lesser Antilles that he named Dominica, Columbus crew sailed northward and later westward to Isabella, Hispaniola, the first city in the New World, at the end of January 1494. Then in June of this year, Isabella was struck by a "violent hurricane", the first time that European men had seen such a terrible storm. It was the first hurricane in the North Atlantic observed and reported by Europeans. Columbus was not there when the hurricane struck Isabella because he was sailing near the Isle of Pine. So his companions of the ships *Marigalante* and *Gallega* were the first white men that heard this speech sound that was applied to a phenomenon of the New World. Storm occurred during Christopher Columbus' second voyage to Hispaniola.

The Hurricane of 1495--In 1495, Christopher Columbus encountered a hurricane near Hispaniola. The earliest hurricane report comes from Christopher Columbus, who encountered a tropical storm on one of his voyages to the New World. He later declared that "nothing but the service of God and the extension of the monarchy" would induce him to expose himself to such a danger from a hurricane again. Columbus and his crew were the first Europeans to experience a hurricane, and it is from his accounts that information about storms and the word itself entered European consciousness and vocabularies. While sailing off Hispaniola in June of 1495 during his second voyage to the New World, Columbus encountered a "whirlwind" so strong that "it plucked up by the roots...great trees" and "beat down to the bottom of the sea three ships which lay at anchor." The local Indians, he wrote, called "these tempests of the air...Furacanes." "Furacanes" was a mistranscription of hurakán, the Taino word for a storm of wind and rain under control a supernatural force. All the Indian groups in the region had a similar word, and the Spanish quickly adopted it in their descriptions of powerful storms that routinely battered their early settlements. When the hurricane reached the harbor, it whirled the ships around as they lay at anchor, snapped their cables, and sank three of them with all who were on board, and the others were dashed against each other and driven to mere wrecks against the shore.[86]

The Hurricane of late June or early July of 1500 (sometimes referred to as the 'Christopher Columbus Hurricane of July 1500')--Christopher Columbus crew member Vicente Yáñez Pinzón lost two caravels with their crews near Xumeto (Jumeto) or Saometo, called by Columbus "La Isabela," or what we now know as 'Crooked Island', in the Bahamas. His other two vessels sustained damage but escaped to Hispaniola for repairs. This is the first hurricane known in the Bahamas, and probably Florida. Vicente Yáñez Pinzón (born in Palos de la Frontera, Spain, in 1462 – died 1514) was a Spanish navigator, explorer, and conquistador, the youngest of the Pinzón brothers. Along with his older brother Martin Alonso Pinzón, who captained the *Pinta*, he sailed with Christopher Columbus on the first voyage to the New World in 1492, as captain of the *Niña*. His was the first European expedition to explore the coast of Brazil and to provide a description of the Amazon River's mouth.

In 1500, there was a major hurricane to hit during the latter part of June or early July on Crooked Island in the Bahamas. This is the first documented hurricane known in the Bahamas. This case was first mentioned by Moreau de Jonnes in 1822 and other historians later on. According to another historian,

---

86 Rubillo, T. (2006) *Hurricane Destruction in South Carolina: Hell and High Water,* (USA, The History Press, 2006), pg.23.

Justin Winsor in 1891 wrote: "Vincent Pinzon (commander of the ship 'Nina' during Columbus' first voyage to the New World) had just came from discovering Brazil, crossed the Gulf of Paria, continued sailing onto the Caribbean Sea and the Gulf of Mexico, until he found himself in the Bahama Islands, and there he lost two of his caravels (ships) and two others badly damaged, on account of being shattered against some rocks in the vicinity of Crooked Island." In September of 1500 he went back to Palos in Spain after suffering the lost of two of his ships.

The following words about Vicente Pinzon are in Justin Winsor's book (1891, pg. 377): "Vicente Pinzon touched at Espanola (Hispaniola) in the latter part of June, 1500. Proceeding thence to the Lucayan Islands, two of his caravels were swallowed up in gale and the other two disabled. The remaining ships crossed to Espanola to refit, whence sailing once more reached Palos in September, 1500."[87]

The month of June 1495, most certainly caused Columbus to revise his opinion that "all weather is like May" in the West Indies. As his fleet was anchored in the harbor of Isabella on the northern coast of Hispaniola, there arose "a boisterous tempest of wind" which left the *San Juan*, the *Cardera*, and probably the *Gallega* destroyed. In the words of historian Peter Martyr: "When this whirlwind came to the haven of the city, it beat down to the bottom of the sea three ships which lay at anchor, and broke the cables in sunder: and that (which is the greater marvel) without any storm or roughness of the sea, only turning them three or four times about." The Island natives declared that neither they nor their great-grandfathers had ever seen "such violent and furious Furacanes, that plucked up great trees by the roots."

From Peter Martyr, again we have: "When in the month of July, they were overtaken by such a sudden and violent storm that, of the four caravels composing the squadron, two were engulfed before their eyes. The third was torn from its anchorage and disappeared; the fourth held good, but was so shattered that it seams almost burst. The crew of this fourth ship, in despair of saving it, landed. The Tempest ceased; the caravel which had been driven off by the fury of the elements returned with eighty of the crew, while the other ship, which held to her anchorage, was saved. It was with these ships that, after being tossed by the waves and losing many of their friends, they returned to

87 José C. Millas, Hurricanes of The Caribbean and Adjacent Regions 1492-1800, (Miami, Edward Brothers Inc/Academy of Arts and Sciences of the Americas, 1968), pg. 37.

Spain, landing at their native town of Palos, where their wives and children awaited them."[88]

Washington Irving, another historian in 1929 wrote: "He (Pinzon) reached the island of Hispaniola about June 23 from whence he sailed for the Bahamas. Here, in July, while at anchor, there came such a tremendous hurricane that two of the caravels were swallowed up with all their crews in sight of their terrified companions; a third parted her cables and was driven out to sea, while the fourth was so furiously beaten by the tempest that the crew threw themselves into the boats and made for shore...They again made sail for Spain and came to anchor in the river before Palos, about the end of September."[89]

The Hurricane of July 1502--In July of 1502, on his 4th voyage to the New World, Columbus noticed a veil of cirrostratus clouds developing, an oily swell coming from the southeast, and several other signs that he took for a hurricane approaching. As the hurricane passed, heavy rains and wind caused much of Columbus' fleet to break anchor, and all but the boat he captained were pulled out to sea. Despite these events, however, all of Columbus' ships survived and sustained only moderate damage. Orvando's fleet, on the other hand, did not fare as well. Shortly after his ships departed Hispaniola, the hurricane arrived. Twenty-five of de Orvando's ships sank, 4 turned back to Hispaniola, and only 1 ship actually made it to Spain. Approximately 500 of Orvando's men lost their lives during the hurricane. The only ship of de Orvando's to make it through the hurricane and reach Spain was the *Aguja*. Interestingly, this ship was only carrying Columbus' gold. The King and Queen of Spain allowed Columbus, in a post-arrest settlement, to appoint an accountant to tally his gold during his final voyage. Columbus chose Alonso Sanchez de Carvajal, who was an accountant, as well as a sea captain. Orvando had thought that the *Aguja* was the most pitiful ship in the fleet, so he assigned Carvajal and the gold of Columbus to it. This plan backfired on de Orvando as already noted, the *Aguja* was the only ship of de Orvando's fleet to survive the hurricane.

Just before the hurricane, he sent a message to Don Nicholas de Ovando, the Spanish Governor of Hispaniola, to warn him not to send out the Spanish fleet of 30 gold ships that were due to depart for Spain. He also asked for permission to dock his ships at the harbor of Santo Domingo until the hurricane had

---

88 *https://www.islandnet.com/~see/weather/history/columbus.html.* Retrieved: 15-04-2015.

89 José C. Millas, Hurricanes of The Caribbean and Adjacent Regions 1492-1800, (Miami, Edward Brothers Inc/Academy of Arts and Sciences of the Americas, 1968) pg. 37.

passed. Ovando was not a fan of Columbus and mocked his request and sent the fleet of 30 Spanish gold ships on their merry way. Ovando forced Columbus to anchor his ships in a nearby estuary and ignored his advice, sending the fleet of 30 ships on to Spain. A tremendous hurricane sank 24 of them: three returned, and only one – ironically, the one containing Columbus' personal effects that he wished to send to Spain – arrived safely.

The hurricane struck them as they were traversing the Mona Passage between the Dominican Republic and Puerto Rico. Santo Domingo and other Spanish colonies suffered extensive damage. With access to Santo Domingo denied, Columbus, strategically moved his 4 ships to the west side of the island. A few miles away, Columbus' ships were badly battered, but all of them remained afloat. Columbus and his men rode out the storm on the south side of Hispaniola, with the mountains to guard against the worst part of the storm, and survived it by the skin of their teeth. Historians believe this hurricane was likely a strong Category 3 or Category 4 hurricane. Some historians called it the "Columbus Hurricane" since he predicted it.

On the 5th December 1502, Columbus and his crew found themselves in a storm unlike any they had ever experienced. In his journal, Columbus writes:

"For nine days I was as one lost, without hope of life. Eyes never behold the sea so angry, so high, so covered with foam. The wind not only prevented our progress, but offered no opportunity to run behind any headland for shelter; hence we were forced to keep out in this bloody ocean, seething like a pot on a hot fire. Never did the sky look more terrible; for one whole day and night it blazed like a furnace, and the lightning broke with such violence that each time I wondered if it had carried off my spars and sails; the flashes came with such fury and frightfulness that we all thought that the ship would be blasted. All this time the water never ceased to fall from the sky; I do not say it rained, for it was like another deluge. The men were so worn out that they longed for death to end their dreadful suffering."[90]

[90] Samuel Morison, Admiral of the Ocean Sea: A Life of Christopher Columbus, (Boston, Little, Brown and Company, 1942), pg. 617.

'Hurricane strikes land, capsizing a ship and causing Spanish soldiers to flee. Includes guns or muskets, lightning, swords, and spears on the island of Santo Domingo (Dominican Republic).' The image describes a violent storm on the island of Hispaniola, which capsized Christopher Columbus's fleet. The image is derived from Theodor de Bry, America, Pt. 4, plate 11. This image follows the special title page for Antonio de Herrera y Tordesillas, Twee opmerklyke scheeps-togten afgevaardigd naar in West-Indian in 't jaar 1502, Leiden, 1706. (Image courtesy of the John Carter Brown Library at Brown University).

The Hurricane of August 1508--On the third day of August 1508, a severe hurricane visited Santo Domingo. All the thatched houses and several built of stone, and every house in Bonaventura, were destroyed. Twenty sailing vessels were wrecked. At first the gale blew from the north, according to the accounts, and then shifted suddenly to the south. To make matters worse, the following year on 29th July, 1509, another powerful hurricane hit the city of Santo Domingo and leveled the entire city.

The Hurricane of August 1511--A storm struck Panama with an unknown number of persons who died in this storm but was noted because of two castaways, Gerónimo de Aguilar and Gonzalo Guerrero, both of whom had been on an expedition with Balboa to visit Panama in 1510. Sailing from Panama in 1511, their ships were caught in a hurricane, and the crew members

Aguilar and Guerrero were among the survivors taken prisoner by the Yucatec Maya population. Eight years after his enslavement, Aguilar would later play an important role as a translator when he joined the Cortés expedition that arrived in Yucatan in 1519. Guerrero, however, married a Maya Indian and rose to a position of authority and prominence among his captors. He refused the opportunity to fight with the Spanish but instead died leading a Maya resistance against his conquering compatriots.

The Hurricanes of 1525--Hernán Cortés sent a vessel to Trinidad, Cuba. Juan de Avalos commanded a ship to Vercruz to supply his relative Hernán Cortés and the conquistadors. A "very severe" hurricane sunk the ship west of Havana, killing the captain, two Franciscan friars, and seventy seamen, but eight persons survived.

The Hurricanes of 1527--The Mississippi was almost discovered but for a hurricane. On October 23rd, a nemesis of Cortes was a man by the name of Panifo de Narvaez. His luck was always bad...this mission to Florida was no exception. When forced to leave due to hunger and hostile natives, his five boats of less than 250 men sailed westward, hugging the northern Gulf coast. As they were passing the Mouth of the Mississippi, a storm caught the barges and 'tossed them like driftwood.' This occurred near 155 years before La Salle made his historic trip down the Mississippi, its mouth doomed not to be rediscovered for decades. On November 1527, there is record of a hurricane destroying a merchant fleet on Galveston Island. Up to 200 lives were taken by the storm. This is the first record known of a hurricane along the Texas coastline, and also one of the most unusual...it struck during the month of November, only one other hurricane has ever struck during November (1839).

The Hurricanes of 1530--Hurricanes not only shaped individual destinies, but they also shaped the general environment of the islands. In Puerto Rico, a series of hurricanes in this year had left the island hungry, defenseless, and subject to attacks from the Caribs of the Lesser Antilles, whose own economy had also been disrupted by the storms. A Carib raid slaughtered what few cattle remained after the storms and killed or captured some thirty Spaniards, as well as Indians and black slaves, who were taken back to the Carib settlement on Dominica.

The Hurricane of 1553--A fleet of 20 ships of the New Spain Flota with five hundred soldiers, a thousand to eleven hundred civilians, 240 horses, and supplies, loaded with silver and gold along the Texas coast, were struck by a hurricane and 16 of them were lost and never heard from again. The three heaviest vessels sunk early in the storm. Most of the others were either scattered widely across the Western Gulf of Mexico, grounded, or capsized just offshore Padre Island. Only 300 of the original 2000 crew made it ashore on the four remaining ships. Unfortunately, the natives to the area known as 'the Karankawa' had a hostile relationship with the Spaniards. Thus, a battle ensued between the survivors, and the tribe and the Europeans tried valiantly to fight their way south into what is today known as Mexico. Only two of the original 2000 ever lived long enough to tell of their ordeal.

The Hurricane of 1559--This hurricane wrecked a Spanish expedition fleet and the first documented hurricane to strike Florida. A Spanish fleet sent to recapture Florida sailed into a hurricane. Most of the fleet was sunk, but one ship survived and founded a colony near Pensacola, Fla. This storm destroyed 7 of the 13 ships anchored in what is now called Pensacola Bay, the fleet of Spaniard Don Tristán de Luna y Arreland, who had been appointed to the task by the viceroy of New Spain, Luis de Velasco. The settlement at what is now known as Fort Barrancas was leveled. It was such a monumental disaster that Spain did not attempt to re-establish a colony in this area for another 139 years, and there is no written record of tropical cyclone activity in this area again until the early 18th century: though other storms came before, it was in 1559 that Spanish Explorers recorded the first hurricane in Florida, The Great Tempest, as it was called back then. Nature had gotten the better part of the small colony, and the Spanish did not return to colonize Pensacola until 1698.

The Hurricane of 1565--A powerful storm in 1565 destroyed the French fleet near Florida. The French, who had an outpost at Fort Carolina (near modern-day Jacksonville, Florida), lost their bid to control the Atlantic coast of North America when a storm destroyed their fleet, allowing the Spanish at St. Augustine to capture Fort Carolina, Florida.

The Hurricane of 1567--Six ships, carrying 3 million pesos were wrecked in a storm off Dominica. This storm is notable because the island's natives killed all the survivors.

The Hurricane of 1568--In early September, a British fleet of slave traders commanded by John Hawkins was blown off course by a hurricane in the Gulf of Mexico and straggles into the Spanish-controlled port of San Juan de Ulloa, near Vera Cruz, Mexico, on September 16. After an initial truce, the Spaniards launched a surprise attack on the English, sinking all but two ships and killing many men. Hawkins commanded one of the surviving ships; the other was captained by Francis Drake, whose bravery was brought to the attention of the queen of England, thereby launching his impressive career. Hawkins went on to preside over the English Naval Board and drew on his hurricane experiences to redesign the English galleon, which would prove instrumental in establishing Britain's superior naval power.

The Hurricane of 1586--Hurricane came ashore on Roanoke Island and was the first of many storms to hit the first colonial settlement. Also, nine ships were lost in the Bahamas, possibly related to the Roanoke Island hurricane.

The Hurricane of 1587--Hurricane once again came ashore on Roanoke Island on August 31st, and Sir Francis Drake took six days to regroup in Roanoke after the storm.

The Hurricane of 1588--Spain, which was at war with England and becoming more worried about the English sea power, dispatches the largest naval force in history, dubbed "The Invincible Fleet," to invade England. However, two weakening but still potent hurricanes (at the end of their life cycle) hit the Spanish Fleet in the summer, destroying half of the fleet. Spain lost control of the Caribbean Sea, and therefore its domination of the New World, to England.

The Hurricane of 1589--The 120-ton ship *Espíritu Santo* under captain Miguel Baltasar, transporting sugar and hides from Puerto Rico, joined the preceding flotilla convoy in Havana, Cuba. About 50 leagues from the Old Bahama Channel, a tempest struck the Spanish treasure fleet. Strong northeasterly winds lasted for four consecutive days. On the first day, the sea "swallowed" a total of ten ships, possibly including the *Espíritu Santo*. Some ships returned to Cuba; others proceeded to the Iberian Union.

The Hurricane of 1590--In early November a hurricane in the Gulf of Mexico caused one of the worst maritime disasters in the history of this region. Over 1000 people lost their lives at sea while aboard a ship.

The Hurricane of 1591--During mid-August of 1591 just off the Azores, over a hundred ships, galleons and merchants' ships were wrecked, their crews drowned and their riches lost.

CHAPTER NINE

The major North Atlantic hurricanes from 1600 – 1700

Before European settlement on the islands of the West Indies, they were inhabited by several different races of Indian people, but the major ones were the Taínos and the Caribs. These indigenous tribes were effectively wiped out by European colonists. Christopher Columbus was the first European to visit several of the islands, beginning with his first landfall on the island of San Salvador in the Bahamas in 1492. In 1496, the first permanent European settlement was made by the Spanish on Hispaniola. By the middle 1600s, the English, French, and Dutch had established settlements in the area, and in the following century there was constant warfare among the European colonial powers for control of the islands. Some islands flourished as trade centers and became targets for pirates. Large numbers of Africans were imported to provide slave labor for the sugarcane plantations that developed there in the later years of the 1600s.

The first English settlement on any island in the West Atlantic was the result of an accident. Castaways from an English vessel, wrecked on its way to Virginia in 1609, and found safety on Bermuda. When news of the island reached England, a party of sixty settlers was sent out in 1612 to rescue them. Three decades later, the religious friction in the Bermuda community caused a group of dissenters to seek a place of their own elsewhere. From 1648, they settled in the Bahamas, a chain of uninhabited islands forming the fringe of the northern Caribbean. This is where Columbus made his first landfall in 1492. In the intervening half-century, the Spanish shipped the natives (some 20,000-40,000 Taíno Indians) to work in the mines of Hispaniola.

Meanwhile, the eastern fringe of the Caribbean was also unprotected by the Spanish, apart from occasional raids in search of slaves. The British were the first to acquire valuable footholds in this region. They established settlements in St. Kitts (1623), Barbados (1627) and Antigua, Nevis and Montserrat (by 1636). The French, hard on their heels, occupied a part of St. Kitts (1627), Dominica (1632) and Martinique and Guadeloupe (1635). Later in the 17th century, Spain lost two large sections of the central Caribbean to her European enemies. An English fleet invaded and captured Jamaica in 1655. In 1664, France's West India Company occupied the western half of Hispaniola (the country now known as Haiti).

The 1600s was an era of piracy. Whether we think of buccaneers, corsairs, filibusters, pirates, they will always mean death and destruction, either on the high seas or in the lands bordering the Caribbean. It is known that many cities, towns, and villages were totally or partially burned by the pirates; therefore, many valuable records and official documents (including valuable information about hurricanes) must have been irretrievably lost by these stupid, horrid, and needless deeds. The knowledge that such terrible suffering could strike at any place at any time was the cause of a permanent fear in the minds of all settlers and travelers between the islands and the mainland, also those traveling between Europe and the New World. They certainly had to adapt their lives and their ways of thinking, this constant fear of possible danger, hanging over them as the sword of Damocles.

During the 1600s, war was a common occurrence in Europe and between European countries. One notable example was the Thirty Years' War, which had a significant impact on Spain and its possessions. The Thirty Years' War was a series of wars in Central Europe between 1618 and 1648. It was one of the longest, most destructive conflicts in European history. Initially, it was a war between Protestant and Catholic states in the fragmenting Holy Roman Empire, it gradually developed into a more general conflict involving most of the great powers of Europe, becoming less about religion and more a continuation of the France-Habsburg rivalry for European political pre-eminence. The Thirty Years' War saw the devastation of entire regions, with famine and disease significantly decreasing the population of the German and Italian states, the Kingdom of Bohemia, and the Low Countries. The war also bankrupted most of the combatant powers. Both mercenaries and soldiers in armies were expected to fund themselves by looting or extorting tribute, which imposed severe hardships on the inhabitants of occupied territories, including the Caribbean. During this century, there were numerous aggressive actions against Spain by the British and the French, and in a more passive way, the Spaniards. From a period of friendship, they turned enemies, to become friends again for a while and taking their battles to the Caribbean.

The list of the major North Atlantic hurricanes in the 17th century encompasses all known and suspected Atlantic tropical cyclones from 1600 to 1699. Although records of every storm that occurred do not survive, the information presented here originated in sufficiently populated coastal communities and ships at sea that survived the hurricanes. As the Caribbean colonies became more important to England economically as a number of hurricanes suffered by Barbados and the other islands of the Lesser Antilles in the 1670s caught the attention of the English reading public, interest in hurricanes and how to prepare for them expanded. The first barometers arrived in Barbados in 1677, and by 1680 they were in the hands of Colonial William Sharpe, an important sugar planter and former Speaker of the Barbados House of Assembly who eventually became acting governor of the island (1714-15). He began to keep a dairy of his weather observations in 1680, and when the island was hit in August by a storm that subsequently devastated the French island of Martinique and then damaged Santo Domingo, Sharpe was able to report his observations to the Royal Society. Those were the first barometer readings of a tropical depression made anywhere in the Caribbean.

In the fifteenth century, Italian artist and scientist Leonardo da Vinci (1452–1519) invented the hygrometer (pronounced hi-GROM-e-ter), an instrument that measures atmospheric humidity (moisture in the air). Around 1643, Italian physicist Evangelista Torricelli (1608–1647) created the barometer to measure air pressure differences. These instruments have been improved upon and refined many times since. Weather information has long been displayed in map form. In 1686, English astronomer Edmond Halley (1656–1742) drafted a map to explain regular winds, tradewinds, and monsoons. Nearly 200 years later, in 1863, French astronomer Edme Hippolyte Marie-Davy published the first isobar maps, which have lines (isobars) connecting places having the same barometric pressure.

Meanwhile, there were similar developments in the Spanish empire, but in much later years. In Cuba, beginning in 1782, advocates of science were suggesting such observations, and by 1791 the *Papel Periódico de La Habana* was regularly publishing the weekly wind, barometer, and thermometer readings. In 1794, it also published readings taken during a hurricane in Havana that year. This weather reporting was a tradition that continued and expanded in the early nineteenth century and helped paved the way for today's weather forecast and the recording of daily weather observations throughout the region and worldwide.

The Hurricane of 1601--A hurricane came ashore near Veracruz, Mexico, and killed over 1000 persons.

The Sea Venture Hurricane of 1609--The *Sea Venture* and a fleet of ships were bound for Virginia to relieve the starving Jamestown colonists when a powerful hurricane crippled their ships on July 28, 1609. The 150 men, women and children aboard found safety on the Bermuda Islands. Some of the ships were damaged in the hurricane on the surrounding coral reef, while others were destroyed and part of the fleet was grounded at Bermuda. For some time, it was called Somers Island after the ship's captain, Admiral Sir George Somers, who claimed the island for The British Crown and vowed to return. Also onboard the ship was Sir Thomas Gates, future governor of Virginia, who was on his way to England from Jamestown. The Spaniards, though shipwrecked on the island many times, had failed to colonize there. The passengers became Bermuda's first inhabitants, and their stories helped inspire William Shakespeare's writing of his final play, *The Tempest,* making it perhaps the most famous hurricane in early American history. In May 1610, they set forth for Jamestown, this time arriving at their destination.

The Hurricane of 1622--*Nuestra Señora de Atocha* ("Our Lady of Atocha") was the most famous of a fleet of Spanish ships that sank in 1622 off the Florida Keys while carrying copper, silver, gold, tobacco, gems, jewels and indigo from Spanish ports at Cartagena and Porto Bello in New Granada (modern day countries of Colombia and Panama, respectively) and Havana bound for Spain. The ship was named for the parish of 'Atocha' in Madrid. An ill-fated series of difficulties kept the *Atocha* in Veracruz before she could rendezvous in Havana with the vessels of the Tierra Firme (Mainland) Fleet. The treasure arriving by mule to Panama City was so immense that during the summer of 1622, it took 2 months to record and load the precious cargo on the *Atocha.* After still more delays in Havana, what was ultimately a 28-ship convoy did not manage to depart for Spain until 4 September 1622, six weeks behind schedule.

On 6 September, the *Atocha* was driven by a severe hurricane onto the coral reefs near the Dry Tortugas, about 35 miles west of Key West. With her hull badly damaged, the vessel quickly sank, drowning everyone on board except for three sailors and two slaves. This storm was reported having traversed the

Bahama Channel on September 15, 1622. This storm approaching from the east seemingly caught the Spanish Fleet (which was destroyed) by surprise as it came through the Bahama Channel. On September 6, 1622, at least six ships of the Spanish Terra Firme Fleet were wrecked by this hurricane, taking the lives of 550 persons. Perhaps the most famous of these ships was the *Atocha,* which treasure hunter Mel Fisher discovered back in 1985.

Spanish expansion in the New World was rapid and by the late 1500s Mexico City, Lima and Potosi had populations that exceeded the largest cities in Spain. It would be another half a century or more before the chief cities of colonial North America Boston, Philadelphia, and New York, were to be founded. Colonists were granted huge tracts of land to grow tobacco, coffee and other products for export to the European mainland. More important to the throne, however, was the region's great amount of mineral wealth of silver and gold, which were vital to Spain's continued growth and expansion in the New World. Trade with the colonies followed a well-established system. Beginning in 1561 and continuing until 1748, two fleets a year were sent to the New World. The ships brought supplies to the colonists and were then filled with silver, gold, and agricultural products for the return voyage back to Spain.

The fleets sailed from Cadiz, Spain, early in the year, following the approximate route that Columbus had taken years before. Upon arrival in the Caribbean, the two fleets would split up, the Nueva España Fleet continuing on to Veracruz, Mexico and the Tierra Firme Fleet to Portobello in Panama. Here, the ships were unloaded and the cargo of silver and gold brought aboard. For the return trip, the divided fleets reassembled in Havana, then rode the Gulf Stream and the Bahama Channel north along the coast of Florida before turning east when at the same latitude as Spain. The treasure fleets faced many obstacles the two greatest of which were pirates and weather, but more specifically the dreaded hurricanes of the region. It was well-known that the hurricane season began in late July, so for this reason the operation was timed for an earlier departure. For protection against pirates, each fleet was equipped with two heavily armed guard galleons. The lead ship was known as the *Capitaña.* The other galleon, called the *Almiranta,* was to bring up the rear. A recently constructed 110-foot galleon, the *Nuestra Señora de Atocha,* was designated the *Almiranta* of the Tierra Firme Fleet.

The fleet departed Spain on March 23, 1622, and after a brief stop at the Caribbean Island of Dominica, the *Atocha* and the Tierra Firme Fleet continued on to the Colombian port city of Cartagena, arriving in Portobello on May 24th. Treasure from Lima and Potosi was still arriving by mule train from Panama

City, a port on the pacific side of the Isthmus. It would take nearly 2 months to record and load the *Atocha's* cargo in preparation for departure. Finally, on July 22, the Tierra Firme Fleet set sail for Havana, via Cartagena, to meet the fleet returning from Veracruz. In Cartagena, the *Atocha* received an additional cargo load of treasure, much of it gold and rare first year production silver from the recently established mints there and at Santa Fe de Bogata. It was late August, well into the hurricane season, before the fleet arrived in Havana.

As a military escort, the *Atocha* carried an entire company of 82 infantrymen to defend the vessel from attack and possible enemy boarding. For this reason, she was the ship of choice for wealthy passengers and carried an extraordinarily large percentage of the fleet's treasure. Unfortunately, firepower could not save her from the forces of nature. On Sunday, September 4th, with the weather near perfect, the decision was made to set sail for Spain. The twenty-eight ships of the combined fleet raised anchor and in single file set a course due north towards the Florida Keys and the strong Gulf Stream current. The *Atocha*, sitting low from its heavy cargo, took up its assigned position in the rear. By evening, the wind started to pick up out of the northeast, growing stronger through the night. At daybreak, the seas were mountainous, and for safety most everyone was below deck seasick or in prayer. Throughout the next day, the wind shifted to the south, driving most of the fleet past the Dry Tortugas and into the relatively safe waters of the Gulf of Mexico.

The *Atocha, Santa Margarita, Nuestra Señora del Rosario* and two smaller vessels all at the tail end of the convoy received the full impact of the storm and were not so fortunate. With their sails and rigging reduced to shreds, and masts and tillers battered or broken, the ships drifted helplessly toward the reefs. All five ships were lost, the *Atocha* being lifted high on a wave and smashed violently on a coral reef. She sunk instantly, pulled to the bottom by her heavy cargo of treasure and cannon. The next day, a small merchant ship making its way through the debris rescued five *Atocha* survivors still clinging to the ship's mizzenmast. They were all that were left of 265 passengers and crew.

Salvage attempts began immediately. The *Atocha* was found in 55 feet of water with the top of its mast in plain view. Divers, limited to holding their breath, attempted recovery but were unable to break into the hatches. They marked the site and continued searching for the other wrecks. The *Rosario* was found in shallow waters and was relatively easy to salvage, but the other vessels could not be located. While the salvagers were in Havana obtaining the proper equipment to retrieve the *Atocha's* treasure, a second hurricane ravaged the area, tearing the upper hull structure and masts from the ship. When they returned, the wreck was nowhere to be found, and salvage attempts over the next 10 years proved futile. However, the *Santa Margarita* was discovered in 1626 and much of her cargo salvaged over the next few years. But time and events slowly erased memories of the *Atocha*. Copies of the ship's register and written events of the times eventually found their way into the Archives of the Indies in Seville, Spain. These documents, like the treasure itself, were to lay in obscurity, waiting for the right set of circumstances centuries later. Treasure hunter Mel Fisher discovered the *Santa Margarita* in 1980 and the *Atocha* on July 20, 1985, her hull lying in 55 feet of water, exactly as recorded by the first salvagers in 1622.

The Hurricane of 1623--This Hurricane destroyed the first tobacco crop planted on St. Kitts by the English on September 9 and then went on to hit Cuba. This storm was responsible for approximately 150 to 250 deaths.

The Hurricane of 1631--On October 21, a hurricane moved through the Gulf of Mexico, taking over 300 lives at sea.

The Colonial Hurricane of 1635--Was a powerful New England hurricane that struck the Massachusetts Bay Colony in 1635, some fifteen years after the Mayflower struck land at Plymouth Rock. This storm killed over 42 persons and reminded many of the pilgrims and settlers of past hurricanes that struck in the West Indies or Caribbean. Many of the pilgrims believed that this storm was apocalyptic. Many shipwrecks and several disasters occurred during the storm, one of which would give birth to a favorite New England legend surrounding Thatcher's Island. The eye passed between Boston and Plymouth, Mass., and caused a twenty-foot tide in Boston. Gov. William Bradford reported, "It blew down many hundred, thousands of trees," and many houses.

The Hurricane of 1640--Dutch fleet commanded by Cornelius Jol (called by the Spanish "Peg Leg the Pirate") suffered a hurricane on September 11, off Havana, while lying in wait for the yearly treasure fleet; 4 ships of his fleet were wrecked by the storm on the Cuban shore. This disaster helped the Spaniards secure control of Cuba.

The Hurricane of 1642--A hurricane came ashore on St. Kitts and Nevis, drowning a number of persons, and several ships containing prized tobacco ran aground and poisoned the water, killing thousands of fish.

The Hurricane of 1643--A fleet of thirty Spanish ships and galleons from Tierra Firme laden with treasure, and seven galleons bristling with guns, managed to get into Havana Harbor. Burdened with leaks, the great treasure ship, *Nuestra Señora de la Concepcion,* was unfit to go on. Over the protests of the captains, loaded to the waterline with treasure and 540 people, she was ordered to sail out, unrepaired. This fleet encountered a powerful hurricane near the Bahamas that forced the great treasure ship, *Nuestra Señora de la Concepcion,* onto a reef, and hundreds drowned. This was a blow to the Crown, and the reefs were named "The Silver Shoals" and the channel to the north of them was called "The Silver Passage" after the silver on the treasure laden ship that was lost.

The Hurricane of 1666--An intense hurricane struck the islands of St. Christopher, Guadeloupe, and Martinique. Every vessel and boat on the coasts of French Guadeloupe was dashed to pieces. A fleet of seventeen ships belonging to Lord Willoughby, British governor of Barbados, set sail with two thousand troops and it went down in the hurricane, and only two were ever heard from again. The French captured the remaining survivors, resulting in France's control of Guadeloupe through the twentieth century. The governor of the French half of St. Kitts wrote to Colbert, Louis the Fourteenth's able minister, that if peace was not made soon so that cassava could be brought in from nearby islands, both settlers and troops, stunned by disaster, "like men totally ruined," would die of hunger. After a series of back to back devastating hurricanes, many packed their bags and left for America. The French remembered this storm very well, and a fund was subsequently created by the French crown to have a *Te Deum* (The *Te Deum,* also known as 'Ambrosian Hymn' or 'A Song of the Church' is an early Christian hymn of praise) chanted each year on August 15, the Feast of the Assumption, to celebrate this victory given by the wind to French arms.

The Hurricane of 1667--This Hurricane affected St. Christopher, Nevis and Virginia between September 1-6 and killed an unknown number of persons. Over 10,000 houses were destroyed; massive crop damage (including corn and tobacco), major flooding, and nearly all buildings on Nevis were flattened. The inhabitants of the island sought shelter by throwing themselves on the ground in the fields. This storm is also referred to as the "Harry Cane of 1667." This hurricane is considered one of the most severe hurricanes to ever strike Virginia. Many cattle drowned in the area's rivers and bays by twelve-foot storm surge, and 'many people had to flee.' The foundations of the fort at Point

Comfort were swept into the river. A graveyard of the first Lynnhaven parish church tumbled into the waters. Twelve days of rain followed this storm across Virginia. This system is blamed for the widening of the Lynnhaven River.

The Hurricane of 1680--This hurricane came ashore on Martinique on August 3 and killed a number of persons, and 22 ships were lost. It then went on to hit The Dominican Republic on August 15 and killed an unknown number of persons and destroyed over 25 ships.

The Hurricane of 1683--A powerful hurricane occurred on September 5-10, 1683. William Dampier, a sailor and buccaneer, gave a "vivid account" of a hurricane in the North Atlantic, three days after leaving Virginia. He addressed it in his chapter titled *"Discourse of the Trade-Winds, Breezes, Storms, Seasons of the Year, Tides and Currents of the Torrid Zone throughout the World,"* published between 1703 and 1705. This writing became a classic of maritime literature.

The Hurricane of 1689--This hurricane killed over half of the inhabitants on the island of Nevis.

The Hurricane of 1692--This devastating hurricane destroyed over half of the sugar mills and much of the sugar cane crop in western Cuba. It left most of the poor in Havana without food or shelter. Governor Manzaneda issued orders mandating the owners of sugar mills, ranchers, and merchants to pay for the opening of roads and ordered all slaves who worked on the city streets and in the port to report for work details.

CHAPTER TEN

The major North Atlantic hurricanes from 1700 – 1800

This destructive era for hurricanes should be seen against a backdrop of the American Revolution. This war, which involved hostilities in the Caribbean by the fleets of Spain, France and the Dutch Republic operating against British fleets with the concomitant greater risk of loss of life due to increased exposure of warships and transports to hazardous weather conditions. This critical coincidence is at least partially responsible for the unprecedented losses of life inflicted, especially in the three fierce hurricanes that struck in quick succession during October. The high demand for slave labor in the Caribbean islands in the 1700s to the early 1800s led to the cultivation of sugarcane and other plantation or cash crops such as, coffee, tobacco and cotton caused what came to be known as the Triangle Trade. Ships leaving Europe en-route to the Caribbean made its first stop in Africa for African slave labor, where they traded weapons, ammunition, metal, liquor, and cloth for captives taken in wars or raids.

The ships then traveled to the Caribbean and America, where slaves were exchanged for sugar, rum, salt, and other island products. The ships returned home loaded with products such as, coffee, salt, sugar and rum popular with the European people, and ready to begin their journey again. An estimated 8 to 15 million Africans reached the Americas from the 16th through the 19th century. Only the strongest, youngest and healthiest persons were taken for what was called the Middle Passage of the Triangle Trade, partly because they would be worth more in America, and partly because they were the most likely to reach their destination alive. Conditions aboard the ship were terrible. Slaves were jammed into the hull chained to one another in order to stop revolts; as many as one in five passengers did not survive the journey. When one of the enslaved people was stricken with dysentery or smallpox, they were simply cast overboard, to avoid contaminating the entire slaves' population onboard the ship.

Those who survived the Middle Passage faced with even greater abuses on the plantations. Many of the plantation owners had returned to Europe, leaving their landholdings in America and the Caribbean to be managed by overseers who were often unstable or unsavory. In many cases, families were split up, and the Africans were not allowed to learn to read or write. African men, women, and children were forced to work with little to eat or drink. Gradually, the African slave population began to out-number the Europeans and Native Americans. The proportion of slaves ranged from about one-third in Cuba to more than ninety percent in many of the Caribbean islands such as, Barbados and Jamaica. As a result, slave rebellions were common. As slave rebellions became more frequent, European investors lost money.

The costs of maintaining slavery grew higher when the European governments sent in armed forces to quell the revolts. Many Europeans began to apply intense pressure to their governments to abolish slavery. The first organized opposition to slavery came in 1724 from the Quakers, a Christian sect also known as the Society of Friends. Great Britain banned slavery in all of their territories in 1833, but the practice continued for almost fifty years on some of the islands in the Caribbean. Once slavery was abolished, the plantation owners hired hundreds of thousands of people from India and other places in Asia. In Trinidad, about forty percent of the population is Asian. The slave ships from Africa brought a precious slave cargo to the region. They were transported from Africa and dropped off on various island plantations in the Caribbean, the Gulf of Mexico and finally on the southeastern coast of the United States. A hurricane is born in Africa over warm water and follows the same path that these ancestors did. As a result of these ships traversing the North Atlantic following the same routes as hurricanes, it stands to reason that some of them would encounter deadly hurricanes, and many of them did, and sometimes the entire slave ship and crew would be lost to the unforgiving Atlantic. One notable example was on 6th October, 1766, where twelve inbound slave ships from Africa to Isle de Saints, Guadeloupe, were lost at sea, with the entire crew of these ships perishing and the slave cargo lost in the Atlantic.

Sugar, slaves and shipping mainly dominated the history of the region in the 1700s. Shipping continued during this era, with the known sailing vessels being built larger, and their numbers increased significantly. The navigation also improved and was significantly more accurate in the second half of the century than in previous times. The first Spanish colonists in the Caribbean, in the 16th century, hoped primarily to grow rich by finding gold. The native Indians of the islands were put to work as slaves in the mines. Thereafter, when the limited supply of gold was exhausted, the Spanish West Indies survived primarily as part of the broader economy of Spanish America. The West Indian islands were both a gathering point and a staging area for the fleets bringing goods from Spain and taking back the wealth of Mexico and Peru. By contrast, the English and French who settled on the islands of the eastern Caribbean needed to rely on agriculture, but most notably plantation agriculture. At first they grew tobacco in small land holdings. But soon it became drastically clear that the most profitable agricultural produce was sugarcane, which was grown on large estates and cultivated by slave labor imported from Africa. By this time, the original inhabitants of the West Indies would have already been virtually wiped out by a combination of European diseases and physical exploitation.

The plantation owners were therefore forced to rely instead on slave labor from Africa. The slaves were at first imported mainly by the Dutch, who had seized many of the Portuguese slaving stations in West Africa, but later on the trade was dominated by the English. Jamaica, in English hands from 1655, became the major slave market of the region. The economic importance of the islands (with the exception of the Bahamas which lacked significant plantations because of the poor and rocky soils) brought in the Spanish, French and British fleets into often close proximity of each other, and this meant that the Caribbean was one of Europe's regular theatres of war. The smaller islands frequently change hands between France and Britain during the 18th century, in an ongoing conflict which reached its peak in the 1790s during the French Revolutionary War. The renewal of war between Britain and France in 1793 was a continuation of a century-long conflict between the two most aggressive imperial powers. In this war, the results favored Britain, particularly in Canada and India, during the Seven Years' War.

In the new conflict, the first arena of war was another rich colonial region, the West Indies. In 1794, the British seized several of the smaller French islands in the Caribbean, at an extremely heavy cost in terms of loss of lives when troops died of yellow fever. On the 1st June in 1794 (the Glorious First of June in British accounts), Richard Howe destroyed a French squadron in the Atlantic - but failed in his primary purpose of capturing the rich convoy which was being accompanied on its journey from America to France. The greatest damage to French interests in the West Indies was not caused by the British fleets, but by the ideals of the French Revolution.

By far, the most profitable French possession in the region, and indeed the most productive of all the Caribbean sugar-producing colonies, was the western half of Hispaniola, under French control from 1664 and known then as Saint Domingue. By the late 18th century, 90% of the people in the colony (numbering some 520,000 in all) were slaves from Africa. The liberty proclaimed in the French Revolution was to them an excellent idea. As a result, in 1791 they rose in revolt. By 1794, after considerable chaos, a capable leader had emerged and the colony was for the first time under black control.

Natural hazards were and had always been an endemic risk in the region, but the potential for catastrophic results was increased by the intersection of historical process and a shift in climatic conditions. It would appear that such a change took place in the mid-1760s as an intensive cycle of El Niño/La Niña events, beginning with the 1766 hurricane season, increased the frequency and intensity of storms and heavy rains in the North Atlantic that then alternated with extended periods of drought. The periods of drought produced poor harvests and worsened conditions of erosion; this in turn made the region vulnerable to flooding when the rains returned.

The fifteen hurricane landfalls of 1766 hit colonies of every single empire in the region. Martinique alone suffered a thousand casualties and lost eighty ships, and all of the French islands felt some impact. With France having lost to Britain and ceded Louisiana to Spain at the end of the Seven Years' War, the traditional sources of food supply were gone. But the French crown and local officials sought to subvert this process by allowing trade with foreigners in flour, salt, meat, and other foods despite the loud complaints of the merchants who controlled that commerce, and sadly, with the increased frequency of these hurricanes, it only exacerbated the problem.

In the decade of the 1780s, the impact of climatic conditions on war, reform, slavery, and politics became a matter of considerable public interest. The 1700s will always be remembered by an exceptional and horrific hurricane the one of 1780, so devastating that it was the benchmark for all hurricanes before and after it and is simply regarded as the Great Hurricane of 1780. It certainly deserves this name, as never before or after has such a tremendous storm been recorded. Another intense cycle of ENSO (El Niño-Southern Oscillation) events made this decade one of the most meteorologically active and destructive on record, and the social and political context of the North Atlantic intensified the storm- and drought-related effects they produced. The hurricane decade of 1780-1790 was extremely deadly, and in fact the deadliest decade in the history of the North Atlantic. The hurricane season of 1780 saw at least eight major storms which made landfalls in the Caribbean and on the Gulf Coast, affecting colonies of all the European empires. The American Revolution was already in progress. France and Spain had entered the war (respectively in 1778 and 1779) on the side of the rebellious colonies, and the entire Caribbean was on a wartime footing, overflowing with troops and ships, as you will see later on.

The Rising Sun Hurricane of 1700--On September 14, a hurricane struck the South Carolina coastline while the *Rising Sun*, a Scottish ship, was docked in Charleston Harbor. The ship was lunged up on the beach, broke up, and all aboard were drowned. The only surviving sailors from the ship had gone ashore earlier to look for provisions and ended up having to bury the dead on the beach the following day. The other ships docked there were also wrecked. Charleston was devastated and flooded by this ferocious hurricane. Known as the Rising Sun Hurricane of 1700, this hurricane killed 98 persons.

The Daniel Defoe Hurricane of 1703 (it is also often referred to as 'The Great Storm of 26 November 1703')--This hurricane occurred on the 26th November of 1703, which moved from the Atlantic across southern England and was made famous by an obscure political pamphleteer, English novelist, journalist and traveler Daniel Defoe. He was just out of prison for jibing at Whigs and Tories in the same article. It was six years before he wrote the world famous book Robinson Crusoe. At the time the hurricane struck, he needed money, so the storm gave him the idea of collecting eyewitness accounts of the storm and publishing it in a pamphlet. He printed and sold this pamphlet under the exceptionally strange and long title, 'The Storm or Collection of the Most Remarkable Casualties and Disasters which happened in the late Dreadful Tempest both by Sea and Land.' In his account in the pamphlet, he stated that "the bricks, tiles, and stones from the tops of the houses flew with such force and so thick in the streets…pieces of timber, iron and sheets of lead have from higher buildings been blown much farther…several ships that rode it out till now gave up all, for no anchor would hold. Even the ships in the River Thames were all blown away from their moorings and from Execution Dock to Limehouse Hall there was four ships that rid it out, the rest were…huddled together and drove on shore, heads and sterns, one upon another…There was a prodigious tide the next day but one…that brought up the sea raging that in some parts of England the water rising six or eight feet higher than it was ever known to do in the memory of man; by which ships were fleeted upon firm land...and an incredible number of cattle and people drowned."[91]

According to Defoe, people were afraid to go outdoors or to go to bed. Perhaps they were wise to remain alert, but they were not entirely safe indoors. The Bishop of Bath and Wells died in his bed when a chimney fell on him. Along the south coast, Eddystone Lighthouse, off Plymouth, was washed away and 12 warships were sunk, as well as hundreds of other vessels. In all, around 8,000 sailors lost their lives, untold numbers perished in the floods on shore, and 14,000 homes, 400 windmills and 16,000 sheep were destroyed. Some of the windmills burned down, because they turned so fast in the fierce winds that friction generated enough heat to set them on fire. The damage in London alone was estimated to have cost £2 million (at 18th century prices).

---

[91] Brown, P. (21 November 2010) *The Great Storm of 26 November 1703*, The Guardian Newspaper.

Image titled 'Capt. Edward Low in ye. Hurricane' (where he and his entire crew perished in this hurricane) by Daniel Defoe, 1661-1731(Image courtesy of the John Carter Brown Library at Brown University).

The Hurricane of 1715--This hurricane occurred on July 31st near the southeastern Bahamas and the Straits of Florida. The fleet of Spanish Admiral Don Juan de Ubilla suffered a hurricane in the Bahama Channel. Ten treasure laden ships were lost, and with them, the Admiral and one thousand persons. The Spanish Government sent a salvage crew to recover the sunken treasure, some of which they recovered. The Bahamian pirates recovered some, but the majority of the treasure remains unclaimed, even to this day. In fact, this area would later be named the 'Treasure Coast' for the millions in gold, silver, and jewels that those ships took down with them.

With end of the War of Spanish Succession in 1714, the Spanish Crown was in desperate need of monetary resources to fund their major undertakings around the world. No major shipment of goods from Spain's New World colonies had been undertaken during the war, so a fleet of galleons was organized to visit various ports of call around the Spanish Main to gather both royal and private treasure to be shipped to Cadiz. Since the majority of the goods consisted of silver coins and bullion, the venture was dubbed the Spanish Plata (Silver) Fleet. Due to numerous delays, the fleet of twelve ships didn't leave Havana Harbor until July 27, 1715, well into hurricane season, a decision they came to regret many times over.

The voyage began with pretty good weather, but that didn't last too long because once they turned north into the Bahama Channel the ships encountered contrary northeasterly winds. As the winds strengthened, the fleet was forced to a scuttle as it moved into the wind in the narrow Bahama Channel. A French ship, the *Grifon,* which was forced by security concerns to sail with the fleet, made good time and broke with the fleet to speed ahead to a rendezvous point off the Carolinas. But the heavy-laden Spanish ships were left to slowly sail on to Spain, and they began to experience the signs of an oncoming hurricane. But Captain General Don Juan Esteban de Ubilla found himself trapped between the uninhabited, reef-strewn Florida shore to his west and the shallow, English pirate-laden Bahama Bank to his east and had no choice but to try to clear the channel before the worst of the storm struck.

It was a race he lost, and the hurricane overtook the fleet just as it emerged from the channel. Three ships were sunk in deep water, the other eight were driven onto the Florida coast from present-day Fort Pierce to Wabasso (north of Vero Beach), where they wrecked upon rocks and reefs. Of the 2500 sailors and passengers, 1000 perished in the storm, including Ubilla. The rest struggled for survival on an inhospitable coast. Two boats were salvaged from the wrecks and were sent for help, one to St. Augustine, the other back to Havana. Most of the survivors were rescued, and salvage operations were begun almost immediately. Meanwhile, the *Grifon* made Brest, France, by September 2nd, unaware of the fate of the rest of the fleet. Much of the treasure was recovered and shipped on to Spain. But word of the disaster reached English ears, and Privateer Henry Jennings carried out a daring raid on the Spanish salvage camps, claiming what treasure they had stored for shipment home. Eventually, the Spanish abandoned salvage operations and English opportunists occupied their camps to claim what was left in the wrecks. When the pickings became slim, even the English left the site.

The Hurricane of 1722--The town of Port Royal, Jamaica, was devastated by a severe hurricane on August 28, 1722. During this storm, there were 26 merchant vessels which were wrecked, and four hundred persons lost their lives. The following month, September 22-24th, another hurricane struck New Orleans as they got a chance to test their new levee system during and after the hurricane. This is the first well documented hurricane to have hit Louisiana. It initially moved through the Lesser Antilles on September 11th, later making landfall west of the Mouth of the Mississippi on the 23rd, and then passing through Central Louisiana. This same storm most likely re-curved northeast into South Carolina, as they reported 3 days of flooding rains around the 27th. Hurricane force winds lasted 15 hours, beginning on the night of the 22nd. Storm surges were reported to be 3 feet at Bayou St. John and 8 feet in the Mississippi River. Thirty-six huts were destroyed during the storm, which included the area hospital. These buildings were hastily constructed in 1717-18, when New Orleans was initially selected to be the capital of the Louisiana Company. The St. Louis church was destroyed. This storm was responsible for moving the old site of Mobile from 27 miles north of the mouth of the Mobile River to its present-day site. Ships were reported to have been sunk in the harbor of New Orleans and the area lakes as well. Three pirogues loaded with fowl, corn, and other goods were lost up towards the Tensas.

In 1718, a 3-foot-high levee protected New Orleans from both river and tidal overflow. This proved inadequate, as older area settlements used the devastation of New Orleans in the "Great Hurricane of 1722" as final proof of that city's unsuitability as the capital of Louisiana, as it followed a great flood by only 3 years. A "rude little fort" was built in the marshes near the Mouth of the Mississippi, a location discovered by Sieur de la Salle in 1682 and inhabited by 1699. It was named La Balize, French for "The Seamark". In 1721, the first lighthouse-type structure, a wooden pyramid rising 62 feet out of the muck, was constructed. It is considered one of the oldest settlements within the current boundaries of Louisiana.

The Hurricane of 1725--During this year, many French ships in Martinique's Harbor, then called Fort Royal, ready to sail to Haiti, which had been given to France by the Treaty of Madrid, were destroyed in a hurricane that blasted up the mountain slope, and many lives were lost in this hurricane.

The Woodes Rodgers Hurricane of 1729--This hurricane reportedly did major damage to the city of Nassau, in the Bahamas during the first week of August, 1729. This provides the first report of a major storm damage at one of the settlements in the Bahamas, although there presumably would have been several such incidents by this point in the colony's history. It is dated by its occurrence three weeks prior to the arrival of the first Royal Governor of the Bahamas, Woodes Rogers in the colony. Upon his arrival in the colony on 25th August, 1729 he reported that this storm was very violent and that it had blown down the greatest part of the houses on the island. He further stated that the Royal Assembly had not been able to sit and conduct the business of the colony because of the extensive damage done by this hurricane. This storm has not been previously carried in any of the chronologies of hurricane activity in the North Atlantic.

The Hurricane of 1733--On July 15th a 22-ship Spanish treasure fleet was struck by hurricane trying to cross the Bahama Channel leaving 16 ships sunk or grounded in the 80 miles near Elliott Key Vaca in the Florida Keys. After the storm, perhaps a thousand people were left to survive for days on their sorry hulks or on the islets until help from Havana could arrive. One of North America's greatest maritime disasters, it was unknown in our history until 1938, when diver Art Mckee began his underwater and archival investigations of a "cannon wreck" shown to him by Islamorada fisherman Reggie Roberts. In fact, the remains of one of the ships, *The Pedro,* is located in 20 feet of water off Indian Key in the Florida Keys. This area where these ships sunk is now an official State of Florida underwater historic site.

The Hurricane of 1740--This hurricane struck another blow to Louisiana on September 23, just years after the 1722 storm. This hurricane came ashore at the mouth of the Mississippi River. It destroyed a large portion of the crops and left many colonists without shelter. The storm, along with others during the 1740s, removed all traces of the original habitation of La Balize. An island named San Carlos surfaced and became the new site of the Balize.

The Hurricane of October 1743--This storm affected the Northeastern United States and New England, brought gusty winds and rainy conditions as far as Philadelphia, and produced flooding in Boston. Central barometric pressure of the storm was measured to be 29.35 inches of Hg in Boston. This was the first hurricane to be measured accurately by scientific instruments. John Winthrop, a professor of natural philosophy at Harvard College, measured the pressure and tide during the storm passage. This storm, which wasn't particularly powerful, was memorable because it garnered the interest of future patriot and one of the founders of the United States, Benjamin Franklin, who believed the storm was coming in from Boston. However, it was going to Boston. Benjamin Franklin had planned to study a lunar eclipse one evening in September 1743, but the remnants of a hurricane ruined his evening. His curiosity aroused, Franklin gathered additional details and learned that the storm had moved up the Atlantic seaboard and against the surface winds. Thus science took the first step toward a basic understanding of hurricanes.

The Hurricane of 1752--This storm occurred on September 26 in the vicinity of Cuba, and sixteen ships were lost in this storm.

The Hurricanes of 1766--Martinique was hit by a hurricane on August 13. 440 people perished in this storm. Then on September 4, a hurricane hit Galveston, Texas. Five ships were destroyed, but the crew and items were saved. A Spanish mission named Nuestra Senora De la Luz and the presidio San Augustine de Ahumado on the lower Trinity River were destroyed. Constance Bayou in Louisiana was named after one of the wrecked ships from this storm. St. Christopher, Montserrat, was hit by a hurricane on September 13, destroying half of the town and many ships. Guadeloupe was hit by a hurricane on October 6, sinking twelve ships and killing all aboard. This hurricane also devastated Martinique, ruining its sugarcane business. Among the families affected was that of one Joseph Tascher, who was financially ruined by the storm. Distressed about the well-being of his family, he sent his daughter, Rose Tascher, to France. Rose later married Napoleon Bonaparte, who rechristened his new bride Josephine. Northwest Florida experienced a hurricane on October 23, sinking a ship and killing the entire crew except for three persons.

The Hurricane San Cayetano of 1767--On August 7th, the San Cayetano Hurricane passed to the south of the island of Puerto Rico, where it caused severe flooding and major damage to crops. On the island of Martinique, approximately 1,600 persons drowned in this storm.

The Hurricane of 1768--Havana, Cuba, was hit by a hurricane on October 15, destroying over 4,000 houses, including 93 public buildings and causing 1000 deaths. In the same year, a ship carrying convicts to Maryland was forced by the rage of the storm to seek shelter at Antigua. It was stated that there was much suffering among the convicts and eleven of them died and the survivors had to eat their shoes and the like to sustain life.

The Alexander Hamilton Hurricane of 1772--Alexander Hamilton in 1772 experienced a powerful hurricane while as a boy living in the Caribbean. He later on in life became the confidential aide to George Washington, and his greatness rests on his Federalist influence on the American Constitution, and much as on his financial genius as the first Secretary of the Treasury. A westward moving hurricane hit Puerto Rico on August 28. It continued through the Greater Antilles, hitting Hispaniola on the 30th and later Jamaica. It moved northwestward through the Gulf of Mexico and hit just west of Mobile, Alabama, on the 4th. Many ships were destroyed in the Mobile area, and its death toll is at least 280 persons. In Pensacola, it destroyed most of the wharves. The most devastation occurred in the vicinity of Mobile and the Pasca Oocola River. All shipping at the Mouth of the Mississippi was driven into the marshes; this included the ship *El Principe de Orange,* from which only 6 survived. This storm was famously described by Alexander Hamilton, who was living on the island of St. Croix at the time and wrote a letter about it to his father in St. Kitts. The letter was so dramatic and moving that it was published in newspapers locally and in New York, and locals raised money to have him brought to the American colonies to receive a formal education. The letter included:

Honored Sir:

I take up my pen, just to give you an imperfect account of one of the most dreadful hurricanes that memory or any records whatever can trace, which happened here on the 31st ultimo at night. It began about dusk, at north, and raged very violently till ten o'clock. Then ensued a sudden and unexpected interval which lasted about an hour. Meanwhile the wind was shifting around to the south west point, from whence it returned with redoubled fury and continued till nearly three in the morning. Good God! What horror and destruction-it's impossible for me to describe-or you to form any idea of it. It seemed as if a total dissolution of nature was taking place. The roaring of the sea and wind-fiery meteors flying about in the air-the prodigious glare of almost perpetual lightning-the crash of falling houses-and the ear-piercing shrieks of the distressed were sufficient to strike astonishment into Angels. A great part of the buildings throughout the island are leveled to the ground-almost all the rest very much shattered-several persons killed and numbers utterly ruined-whole families wandering about the streets, unknowing where to find a place of shelter-the sick exposed to the keenness of water and air-without a bed to lie upon-or a dry covering to their bodies-and our harbors entirely bare. In a word, misery, in its most hideous shapes, spread over the whole face of the country.[92]

This letter created such a sensation that some planters of St. Kitts, in the midst of the hurricane ruin, took up a collection to send him to America for better schooling because they saw in him great potential. By 1774, he was a student at King's College, now Columbia University, in New York. While the previous hurricane was moving through the Caribbean, a tropical storm was moving northward in the Western Atlantic, hitting North Carolina on September 1. It forced fourteen vessels ashore, and fifty people perished in the storm. Three hurricanes affected St. Kitts and Nevis in 1772. It is not known whether or not any of them were related to the above storms. Nevis had very little houses standing after the first storm, and the worst one, on August 31. On St. Kitts, the damage was considerable, and once again many houses were flattened, and there were several fatalities and many more injuries. Total damage from the storm was estimated at £500,000 on St. Kitts. The second storm struck just three days later.

The Hurricane of 1775--This hurricane hit the Newfoundland Banks between 9-12 September and was responsible for over 4,163 deaths, mainly sailors from England and Ireland. Strong winds in Virginia; a localized storm surge is reported to have reached heights of between 20 and 30 feet in Newfoundland, destroying many English ships. The storm surge from this storm was reported to have reached heights of between 20 to 30 feet. The hurricane, also known as the 'Independence Hurricane', is Canada's most tragic natural disaster, and the eighth deadliest North Atlantic hurricane in recorded history.

The Hurricane of November 2, 1775--A hurricane hit the Turks and Caicos Islands. During the hurricane, 11 merchant men and several English warships were lost in the Windward Passage near the Caicos Islands.

The Hurricane of 1776--A powerful hurricane hit Martinique on September 5, 1776. It hit Pointe-a-Pitre Bay, Guadeloupe, the next day and caused 6000 fatalities, more than any other known hurricane before it, and is currently the

92 *http://www.photolib.noaa.gov/historic/nws/hamilton.html*. Retrieved: 07-08-2015.

seventh deadliest North Atlantic hurricane on record. Maximum sustained winds were estimated to be at least 74 mph when it struck Guadeloupe. The storm also affected Antigua and Martinique early in its duration, and later it struck Louisiana on September 12. The storm struck a large convoy of French and Dutch merchant ships, sinking or running aground 60% of the vessels. The ships were transporting goods to Europe.

The Hurricane of 1778--On August 12, a hurricane prevented a naval battle between the British and French in the Revolutionary War, causing them to separate as the hurricane moved up the coast.

The Hurricane of 1779--On August 18th a hurricane made landfall at New Orleans. At that time, Spain had declared war on Great Britain. Almost all of Bernardo de Galvez's ships (governor of New Orleans) that were to be used to secretly seize the British post at Baton Rouge were grounded or destroyed, thus ruining his plans for invasion until the 27th. The only ship that escaped disaster was *El Volante*. Some of the ships were found in the middle of the woods after the storm. Wind and rain began on the night of the 17th. Full violence of the storm was attained by 3am. All houses, piroughs, barges, and boats were decimated; fields were leveled, and all crops, stock, and provisions were lost. These included an American Frigate, *The Morris*. During this storm, William Dunbar made observations that uncovered the true nature of tropical storms and hurricanes; that they had a progressive forward movement and that the winds revolved around a vortex at the center. His findings were presented to the American Philosophical Society in 1801.

The Great Hurricane of 1780

This image is titled "Ouragan aux Antilles," by Nicholas de Launay, which first appeared in the 1780 edition of Abbé Raynal's popular history of colonization and commerce in the West and East Indies. View of a hurricane in the Antilles or Caribbean. A woman clutches her baby and tries to protect her and the two children from a house blowing down on top of them. A body lies under the wreckage of some timber. Other people cower in the background. Images like this naturalized these storms as a dreaded but regular aspect of life in the Caribbean. (From Guillaume Thomas François Raynal, *Histoire philosophique et politique des éuropéens dans les deux Indies*, Geneva, 1783; Image courtesy of the John Carter Brown Library at Brown University).

In the American Revolution, not all its battles were fought between the American colonies and England. In the Atlantic and Caribbean, England, Spain and France fought for control of the island colonies. But in October 1780, they all faced the same vicious and formidable adversary- 'The Great Hurricane of 1780', which devastated many islands in the Caribbean and left these islands in total disarray. During this era, it was already a perilous area of the world for ships--it is estimated that about one of every 20 ships sent to the West Indies was lost at sea during this era, and hurricanes were one of the major reasons for this loss. This storm was one of several major hurricanes that struck that year, which was one of the worst hurricane seasons in the era prior to record taking.

This storm affected the southern Leeward and Windward Islands, including Barbados, St. Lucia (only two houses in all of St. Lucia remained standing), St. Vincent, Grenada, Tobago, Martinique, St. Eustatius, Antigua, Puerto Rico and Grand Turk Island between October 10th and October 16th and is responsible for over 22,000 deaths. Of that total, between 4,000 and 5,000 people were killed on St. Eustatius, Martinique had an estimated 9,000 people killed, including 1,000 in St. Pierre, which had all of its homes destroyed, and 4,326 people were killed in Barbados. The production of sugar and rum-vital to the local economies-was drastically curtailed, not recovering for another four years. To make matters worse, many settlers abandoned their plantations and returned to England, leaving these islands' economies even further depressed. For example, *The Barbados Mercury* reported that "in most of the plantations, all the buildings, the sugar mills excepted, are laid level with the earth, and that there is not a single estate on the island which has entirely escaped the violence of the tempest."[93]

The first news of the disaster was carried to England in a letter from Major General Vaughn, commander-in-chief of His Majesty's forces in the Leeward Island, dated October 30, 1780:

"I am much concerned to inform your Lordship, that this island was almost entirely destroyed by a most violent hurricane, which began on Tuesday the 10th instant. And continued almost without intermission for nearly forty-eight hours. It is impossible for me to attempt a description of the storm; suffice it to say, that few families have escaped the general ruin, and I do not believe that 10 houses are saved in the whole island: scarce a house is standing in Bridgetown; whole families were buried in the ruins of their habitations; and many, in attempting to escape, were maimed and disabled: a general convulsion of nature seemed to take place, and an universal destruction ensued. The strongest colors could not paint to your Lordship the miseries of the inhabitants: on one hand, the ground covered with mangled bodies of their friends and relations, and on the other, reputable families, wandering through the ruins, seeking for food

93 Kerry Emanuel, Divine Wind-The History and Science of Hurricanes, (Boston, Oxford University Press, 2005), pg. 65.

and shelter: in short, imagination can form but a faint idea of the horrors of this dreadful scene."

Admiral Rodney was in New York during the hurricane, and when he visited Barbados, he incorrectly concluded that the storm must have been accompanied by a massive earthquake to achieve such total destruction. Rodney writes: "The whole face of the country appears an entire ruin, and the most beautiful island in the world has the appearance of a country laid waste by fire, and sword, and appears to the imagination more dreadful than it is possible for me to find words to express."[94]

Throughout history, the islands in the Caribbean have had quite a few memorable hurricanes that made their impact on regional history, and The Great Hurricane of 1780 was definitely one of the most destructive and memorable hurricanes to ever hit this region. The 1780 Atlantic hurricane season was extraordinarily destructive and was the deadliest Atlantic hurricane season in recorded history, with over 22,000 deaths. Three separate hurricanes, all in October, caused at least 1,000 deaths, each during this hurricane season; this event was such a rare event that it has never been repeated, and only in the 1893 and 2005 seasons, where there were two such hurricanes. The 1780 hurricane season still holds the record for the deadliest North Atlantic hurricane of all time.

- On June 13, a hurricane "caused deaths and losses", mainly on the island of Puerto Rico.
- Louisiana experienced a hurricane on August 24, causing crop damage, flooding, and tornadoes.
- A hurricane hit Jamaica on October 5 and completely destroyed the settlement of Savanna-la-Mar. It continued its direction and hit Cuba and then moved over the Bahamas before entering the shipping lanes between Cape Hatteras and Bermuda. The storm caused an estimated 1,115 deaths and destroyed two British fleets, with one being the ship the *Monarch*, killing all of its crew, as well as several hundred Spanish prisoners onboard.
- The Great Hurricane of 1780 existed in early to mid-October, causing a record number of 22,000 deaths in the eastern Caribbean Sea.
- A powerful hurricane called *'Solano's Storm'* in the Eastern Gulf of Mexico from October 17 to the 21st killed 2,000 people. The final hurricane of

94 D.M. Ludlum, Early American Hurricanes 1492-1870. (Boston, MA., American Meteorological Society, 1849), pg. 198.

the season to hit the Caribbean pounded the 64-ship Spanish fleet of 64 warships, transport ships, and supply vessels carrying some four thousand soldiers, under Admiral Don José Solano and his friend Field Marshall Don Bernardo de Gálvez, off the western tip of Cuba as he was preparing to attack the English at Pensacola, Florida. As for Pensacola, the English under General Campbell, always fearful of a Spanish attack, did not know until much later how lucky they were and how the hurricane had saved them. Both Gálvez and Solano survived and returned to Cuba, but Gálvez returned to capture Pensacola the following May. "Have we so little constancy and tenacity that a single tropical storm suffices to halt us?" Gálvez wrote in a heated argument with the War Council in Havana, about another expedition against Pensacola.[95]

- He fought off a British attack on Mobile. The cautious War Council had to admit that the British were too weak to attack Havana. As a result of this hurricane, Cuba remained under the control of the Spanish, even to this day, rather than the British, who were strategically planning to grasp control and claiming this large island nation for the King of England. The next May, therefore, after great gallantry, Gálvez moved in on Pensacola again. The first Fleet Commander, Calbo, refused to cooperate, and it was not until Solano came up with a fleet which he put at Gálvez's orders that Pensacola finally fell and the British lost all of West Florida.
- This history-changing hurricane was always called 'Solano's Storm' because an English Ambassador at Madrid copied and translated Solano's log book from the Spanish records, should the full story be told it would show that Solano was only a latecomer and all of the credit should go to Gálvez. It should be rightfully called 'The last Hurricane of Bernardo de Gálvez,' or better yet 'Gálvez's Hurricane,' who endured much at the hands of this storm. It was during this storm that Dunbar noted that tornadoes form around tropical storms and seldom lasted more than 5 to 10 minutes. This was no comfort to the inhabitants of the area, who were distraught after these two storms and an excessively cold winter, followed by a very rainy summer. These residents wrote the Spanish sovereign not to abandon the country, regardless of the adverse blows of nature.
- The Spanish government, after the storms of 1780, followed its usual policy of permitting the purchase of foodstuffs from foreigners, especially now

95 *Publications of the University of California at Los Angeles in Social Sciences, Volumes 4-5*, University of California Press, 1934, pg. 197.

from its allies in North America, but it continued to restrict the extent to which tax exemptions were granted.

The 1780 hurricane season was the century's worst, and the deadliest. News of these hurricanes traveled far and wide and sealed the reputation of the Caribbean as a dangerous place for trade and habitation. The year was a turning point in Caribbean history, marking the end of a long period of economic boom and the beginning of an episode of economic and cultural decline. Eight different storms battered the West Indies and American coasts, including four killer storms in October. During that month, hurricanes killed more people than died in battle during the entire six-year war. Thousands of deaths also occurred offshore. The hurricane struck the Caribbean in the midst of the American Revolution and took a heavy toll on the British and French fleets contesting for the control of the area. The British Admiral George Rodney, sailing from New York to the West Indies, had his fleet scattered and damaged by the storm. Arriving at Barbados, he found eight of the 12 warships he'd left there a total loss and most of their crew drowned.

French ships were also heavily damaged. The British fleet in the Leeward Islands then numbered twenty-five ships, with a commensurate number of support vessels ready to do combat against the French. After this hurricane, the governor of Martinique caused the English soldiers who had become his prisoners to be set free, though the French and English were then at war. He declared that in such a disaster all men should feel as brothers. The Spaniards had assumed much the same attitude. In Bridgetown, Barbados, the Great Hurricane of 1780 had destroyed the prison building holding 800 Spanish prisoners of war. The immediate fear was that these men would join the island's slaves, who had already begun to loot damaged properties. A British troop was organized to meet the threat, but their fears of internal danger were allayed when they were assisted by the prisoner of war don Pedro de Santiago, a captain of the regiment of Argon, who organized the Spanish prisoners to help in the relief efforts and the control of the rebellious slaves. A later commentator wrote, "let it be remembered with gratitude, that laying aside all national animosity in that season of calamity, they omitted no service or labor for the relief of the distressed inhabitants and preservation of the public order.[96]

The death toll from the 1780 storm alone exceeds that for any other entire decade of Atlantic hurricanes. By contrast, the second deadliest North Atlantic

---

96 Poyer, J. History of Barbados, (London, J. Mawman Pub., 1808), pgs. 449-455.

hurricane on record was Hurricane Mitch in 1998. Due to its slow motion from October 29 to November 3, Hurricane Mitch dropped historic amounts of rainfall in Honduras, Guatemala, and Nicaragua, with unofficial reports of up to 75 inches. Deaths due to catastrophic flooding made it the second deadliest North Atlantic hurricane in history; nearly 11,000 people were killed, with over 11,000 left missing by the end of 1998.

Coke, a well-known early West Indian historian, in his 1808 book *'History of the West Indies'* said:

"To estimate, with accuracy, the damage which the colony received in all its departments would be an impossible task. The calculation which was made soon after the mournful occasion, estimated the loss at little less than one million and a half sterling."

- At St. Christopher's, many vessels were forced on shore.
- At St. Lucia, all the barracks and huts for His Majesty's troops and other buildings in the island were blown down, and the ships driven to sea; only two houses were left standing in the town.
- At Dominica, they suffered greatly.
- At. St. Vincent, every building was blown down and the town destroyed.
- At Grenada, nineteen sails ofloaded Dutch ships were stranded and beaten to pieces.
- At Martinique, all the ships that were bringing troops and provisions were blown off the island. In the town of St. Pierre, every house was blown down and more than 1000 people perished. The number of people who perished in Martinique was said to be 9000.
- At. St. Eustatius, the loss was very great. Between 4000 and 5000 persons are said to have lost their lives.[97]

Major-General Cunninghame, Governor of Barbados, in his account of the 1780 Hurricane at Barbados wrote: "the armory was leveled to the ground, and the arms scattered about. The buildings were all demolished; for so violent was the storm here, when assisted by the sea, that a 12-pounder gun was carried from the south to the north battery, a distance of 140 yards. The loss to this country is immense: many years will be required to retrieve it." The Editor

---

97 Extracted from, *NEMO remembers the Great Hurricane of 1780* by NEMO Secretariat/ Colin Depradine former Principal of the Caribbean Institute for Meteorology and Hydrology on the 225th anniversary of this storm, Friday October 7, 2005.

of "The West Indian" a Barbados paper, writing about the 1831 Hurricane, mentions the 1780 Hurricane. He wrote: "At the dawn of day (October 10th), the wind rushing with a mighty force from the northwest. Towards evening the storm increased, and at nine o' clock had attained its height, but it continued to rage till four the next morning, when there was a temporary lull. Before day-break, the castle and forts, the church, every public building and almost every house in Bridgetown, were leveled with the earth."[98]

The Great Hurricane of 1780 remained in the vicinity of Barbados for two days between the 10th thru 14th October, 1780 killing 4,326 persons in the process. The strong, powerful winds basically leveled practically every tree and structure on the island. To give some indication of the violence of the storm, some eyewitnesses said that many of the trees were stripped of their bark by the force of the wind. Dozens of fishing boats failed to return to port, their passengers drowned. Almost everyone living on the island lost a family member in the storm. The Barbados Mercury reported that "In most plantations all the buildings, the sugar mills excepted, are laid level with the earth, and that there is not a single estate in the island which has entirely escaped the violence of the tempest." John Poyer, a historian who survived the storm damage on Barbados, wrote that by the morning of October 11, "Far as the eye could reach one general scene of devastation presented itself to the sight." Poyer describes himself as "among the midnight wanderers, who traversed the deary waste in search of an uncertain place of shelter and repose." In the aftermath of the storm, officials ordered a survey of individual parishes to determine losses. The findings were staggering: the hurricane killed over two thousand slaves and six thousand head of cattle and caused total property damage of more than £1,300,000.[99]

---

98 Ibid.

99 Wayne Neely, The Great Hurricane of 1780: The Story of the Greatest and Deadliest Hurricane of the Caribbean and the Americas, (Bloomington, iUniverse, 2012), pg.2.

Top Ten Deadliest North Atlantic Hurricanes on Record

The 10 Deadliest Tropical Cyclones for the Atlantic RankName / Areas of Largest Loss		Dates	Deaths
1.	**"Great Hurricane of 1780": Martinique, Barbados, St. Eustatius**	**10-16 Oct 1780**	**22000**
2.	"Great Galveston Hurricane of 1900": Galveston Island	8 Sep 1900	8000-12000
3.	Mitch: Honduras, Nicaragua, Guatemala, El Salvador, Belize	10/22 - 11/5 1998	9086
4.	Fifi: Honduras	14-19 Sep 1974	8000-10000
5.	"The Dominican Republic Hurricane of 1930": Dominican Republic	1-6 Sep 1930	8000
6.	Flora: Haiti, Cuba	9/30-10/8 1963	8000
7.	"Pointe-a-Pitre Bay Hurricane": Guatemala	6 Sep 1776	6000
8.	"Newfoundland Banks": Newfoundland	9-12 Sep 1775	4000
9.	"Hurricane of San Ciriaco": Puerto Rico, Carolinas	8-19 Aug 1899	3433
10.	"Great Okeechobee-San Felipe II Hurricane": Florida, the Bahamas, Puerto Rico, Martinique, Guadeloupe, Turks & Caicos	12-17 Sep 1928	4118

Deadliest North Atlantic Hurricanes on record courtesy of:
1) 1995: Rappaport, Edward N. and Fernandez-Partagas, Jose; "The Deadliest Atlantic Tropical Cyclones, 1492-1994," NOAA Technical Memorandum NWS NHC-47, National Hurricane Center, pg. 41. 2) HURDAT, Hurricane Research Division-NOAA, 3) Weather Underground, American Red Cross/Individual Islands & Countries, 4) Wikipedia.

British Admiral George Rodney arrived from New York after the storm, finding eight of twelve warships left in Barbados totally destroyed and most of their crew drowned. One of the warships that was destroyed was the famous *74-gun HMS Cornwall* and over 100 British merchant ships. The storm also scattered and damaged most of the fleet under his command. A British scout was sent to survey the damage on Barbados but mistakenly thought that an earthquake had accompanied the hurricane because of the great devastation he had seen. The following quotation is from Sir George Rodney to Lady Rodney, dated at St. Lucia, December 10, 1780, on the effects of the storm on Barbados:

"The strongest buildings and the whole of the houses, most of which were stone, and remarkable for their solidity, gave way to the fury of the wind, and were torn up to their foundations; all the forts destroyed, and many of the heavy cannon carried upwards of a hundred feet from the forts. Had I not been an eyewitness, nothing could have induced me to have believed it. More than six thousand perished, and all the inhabitants are entirely ruined."[100]

The storm killed nine thousand persons on Martinique, where ships, towns, churches, houses, and a hospital were all demolished. While in the Lesser Antilles, this deadly hurricane also killed several thousand sailors of the Spanish, Dutch, British, and French fleets. The storm also took many lives on other islands, including St. Lucia, where it totally devastated that country. However, one good thing that came out of this storm was the fact that it drowned a plague of ants that had been eating and destroying the sugar cane. Ships were dismasted as far south as the islands of St. Vincent and Grenada, where fifteen Dutch ships were smashed against the rocks. The ships east of Martinique were also ravaged against the rocks. As stated before, the surviving Englishmen, dazed and water soaked, were taken prisoners by a gang of French slaves, but the Marquis de Bouillé, Governor of Martinique, refused to take them and lock them up but instead sent them back to St. Lucia, writing that he would not keep as prisoners' men who had suffered the same horror and misery that had significantly impacted them all. On the other hand, Admiral George Rodney hurried to seize St. Vincent, hearing that it had been destroyed, but the disgusted French on the island simply drove him away.

The following quotation from the book, 'The Ocean', by Élisée Reclus published in 1874, gives an approximate idea of the violence of this storm: "The most terrible cyclone of modern times is probably that of the 10th of October, 1780, which has been specially named the 'Great Hurricane.' Starting from Barbados, where neither trees nor dwellings were left standing, it caused the English fleet anchored off St. Lucia to disappear and completely ravaged this island, where 6000 persons were crushed under the ruins. After this, the whirlwind tending toward Martinique, enveloped a convoy of French transports, and sunk more than 40 ships carrying 4000 soldiers; on land, the town of St. Pierre and other places are completely razed by the rind, and 9000 persons perished there. More to the north, Dominique, St. Eustatius, St. Vincent and Porto Rico were likewise devastated and most of the vessels which were on the path of the cyclone foundered, with all their crews. Beyond Porto

---

[100] Extracted from an article by Dr. Colin Depradine, the former Principal of the Caribbean Institute for Meteorology and Hydrology (CIMH). The article was originally published in "The Advisory", The 35th Anniversary Edition of CIMH, 2002.

Rico, the tempest bent to the northeast, toward the Bermudas and though its violence had gradually diminished, it sunk several English warships returning to Europe. At Barbados, where the cyclone had commenced its terrible spiral, the wind was unchained with such fury, that the inhabitants hiding in their cellars did not hear their houses falling above their heads; they did not feel the shocks of earthquake which, according to Rodney, accompanied the storm."[101]

Four to five thousand lives were lost on the island of Saint Eustatius. The storm then moved over the southwestern corner of Puerto Rico on a northwestward track, and it probably ranked as the most devastating storm in the history of the island at the time. The hurricane passed just east and north of Hispaniola sometime on the 16th October and apparently approached Florida on 17 October. It continued to produce strong northerly gale force winds off Charleston, South Carolina, as it passed to the east of the coast. Some sources say its center recurved (ceased to make westward progress and turned east of due north) at the Tropic of Cancer north of Haiti around 16-18 October; others, however, suggest that the storm came much closer to Florida, and then its center, then passed about fifty miles southeast of Bermuda, driving fifty British Navy ships aground, including some that had been hit by the month's first hurricane, east of present-day Daytona Beach.

There was a very interesting and fascinating folklore tale attached to this storm, and it involved a slave locally referred to as 'Plato the Wizard.' Jamaican folklore attached the devastation of this western town as the work of the runaway slave known as Plato the Wizard, from beyond the grave. Just before his 1780 execution in Jamaica, the renowned obeah man pronounced a curse on Jamaica - predicting that his death would be avenged by a terrible storm set to befall the island before the end of that same year. It is said that Plato and his band of other runaways kept the parish of Westmoreland in a state of continuous apprehension from his stronghold in the Moreland Mountains. Plato warned that whoever dared to lay a finger on him would suffer spiritual torments. It is not surprising that no slave would set traps for Plato, even though the reward for his capture was great.

Plato was an example of the type of spirit slavery could not hold. However, he did have one weakness, and that was the uncontrollable desire to consume Jamaican rum. It was proved to be his downfall. At the time, Plato's usual supplies were curtailed as a result of a massive hunt conducted for his arrest. He arranged with a watchman he knew well to go out and get him some rum.

---

101 E. Reclus, E. The Ocean, (London, Harper and Brothers, 1873).

The watchman decided to use the rum as a lure to have him captured. It was easier than he expected. Soon after he handed Plato the rum, he fell into a drunken stupor, and right into the watchman's trap. Plato was captured, tried and immediately sentenced to death in the town of Montego Bay. As a dreadful power was said to have descended upon him, Plato calmly cursed any and everything in sight, stating that a great tempest would come and the sea would rise to seek retribution for his death.

He terrified the jailor who tied him to the stake by announcing that he had cast an obeah spell on him and he did not have long to live. Soon after Plato's death, the jailor left Jamaica, but before he did, it was said that he was plagued by bad dreams and visions and eventually fell ill and died. Before the year was over, Plato's other curse came true - the island was hit by what was described as the most terrible hurricane to ever spread death and destruction in the seas of the West Indies. The region where Plato the Wizard had roamed free and died in betrayal was hardest hit. To make matters worse, Jamaica was ravaged again by another massive and devastating hurricane in the following year. Over a hundred ships were driven ashore and all newly-planted provision grounds destroyed. Thirty years later, the 'duppy' or ghost of Plato was said to still stalk the Moreland Mountains and the area of Montego Bay. The story may be apocryphal, but it at least provides a window into the slaves' own narratives of survival, resistance, and divine intervention in the face of hurricanes. The Jamaica hurricane of 1780 had become Plato's storm.

The Central Atlantic Hurricane of 1782--This hurricane was one of the deadliest hurricanes in the North Atlantic. It struck the fleet of Admiral Thomas Graves as it sailed across the North Atlantic in September 1782. It is believed to have killed some 3,000 people.

The Hurricane of 1785--On August 24, an eastward moving hurricane hit St. Croix. It continued to hit Puerto Rico, Jamaica, and Cuba before last being seen on the 29th. It caused 142 deaths.

The Hurricane of 1788--Martinique was hit by a hurricane on August 14. It continued, hitting Dominica, and later the Bahamas. It moved northward and hit New England on the 19th. 600-700 people lost their lives because of this hurricane.

The Hurricane of 1791--On June 21st and 22nd a powerful storm occurred at Havana, killing 3,000 people, and 11,700 head of cattle perished on the island, most of them killed mainly by flood waters. Also, a hurricane struck the Lower Texas Coast. Padre Island and the mainland nearby were submerged. A herd of 50,000 cattle belonging to a Spanish cattle baron drowned in the storm surge.

Image shows a view of the town of Léogane, under the ravages of a hurricane in 1791 (present-day Haiti). Includes key for the town, the embankment, anchorage site, and the Port la Pointe. Also includes a depiction of a hurricane or severe storm with a ship wrecked on the waters. Description topographique, physique, civile, politique et historique de la partie française de l'isle Saint-Domingue by M.L.E. (Médéric Louis Elie) Moreau de Saint-Méry, Paris, 1784-90. Author Ponce, Nicolas, 1746-1831. Image courtesy of the John Carter Brown Library at Brown University.

The Hurricane of 1794--The so called "dreadful" hurricane on August 25th struck Havana, and 100 bodies were recovered in the harbor the day after. In the Florida Keys, two vessels were wrecked and the crew of the *Vigilant* stayed on their water-filled hulk for 48 hours without food or water until they were rescued by Bahamian wreckers.

CHAPTER ELEVEN

The major North Atlantic hurricanes from 1800 – 1900

If the turbulent decades of the Circum-Caribbean from the period of 1790 to 1840 could be characterized by a single change, it would surely be the transformation of its labor system. The violent and abrupt end to slavery in the western section of Santo Domingo, finally resulting in the creation of an independent Haiti in 1804, the growth and intensification of slavery as export agriculture in the Spanish colonies of Cuba and Puerto Rico, and the abolition of the slave trade followed by the emancipation of slaves in the British West Indies overshadowed all other events. The concepts of property rights lay at the heart of the issue of slavery. The "great slave question" had not so long been an issue in the American Revolution and had plagued the signers of the Constitution, and it was, from a different perspective, the principal concern in the Haitian Revolution and an issue during the revolutionary fervor in the other French Caribbean colonies.

During this period of intense political change revolutionary ideologies provoked slave unrest and expectations all over the Circum-Caribbean region. Beginning in the 1780s and intensifying in the following decades, from Bahia, Brazil, to Coro, Venezuela, to Barbados (1816), Demerara (1823), Jamaica (1831), and Virginia (1831), slave uprisings tested the limits and strength of the colonial institutions in the region and the colonial powers in Europe. At the same time, the abolitionist movement, missionary activity, and slave rebelliousness were creating a transnational community of pro slavery interests that sought to maintain the institution or to control any changes within it. The major hurricanes of the region in the early 1800s came at a pivotal point in the history of the region. When the Whigs, led by an abolitionist as Lord

Chancellor, won control of the British Parliament in 1830, it was clear that the anti-slave movement and a move towards emancipation had gained the upper hand. Planters in Barbados were the most reluctant to relinquish the institution of slavery. With the emancipation of slavery in the British West Indies in 1834 and the abolition of slavery in the North Atlantic, it became concentrated in the United States' southern states and the Spanish islands of the Caribbean. In the British and French West Indies, the transition to free labor had followed a number of different paths influenced by political conditions, land availability, and world market prices.

It is simply a curious coincidence that 1831, the year of the Great Barbados Hurricane, was also the year that a major advancement in the understanding and analysis of hurricanes were set in motion and the early crude but modern era of the understanding of hurricanes came to an end. The early 'weather watchers' or 'armchair meteorologists' of the previous century had in a Baconian fashion gathered a great amount of data, often by compulsive and fastidious recording of weather, barometer readings, rainfall, or other meteorological phenomena. Some of these storm watchers had by experience, study, and intuition begun to unravel the structure of the tropical storms. The mariner William Dampier in the late seventeenth century and Benjamin Franklin in the eighteenth century had by different paths come to realize that hurricanes were 'whirlwinds,' that is, storms in which the winds moved in a circular fashion in a manner equivalent to a whirlpool.

Scientists began to understand hurricanes during the 1800s, and forecasters were able to issue warnings as storms approached. Despite this growing knowledge, hurricanes continued to cause incredible destruction throughout the century. The century of the 1800s was a very busy and destructive one. While data is not available for every single storm that occurred, some parts of the coastline were populated enough to give data of hurricane occurrences. Information is sparse for earlier years of the 1800s, due in part to limitations in tropical cyclone observation, though as coastlines became more populated, more data became available. The National Hurricane Center recognizes the uncertainty in the death tolls, lack of meteorological information and the dates of the events. The 1800s brought U.S. ships into the Caribbean, especially after 1848, when many gold-seekers crossed the sea to reach California via Panama. After unsuccessful French attempts in the late 1800s to build a canal across Panama, the United States, in 1903, assumed control of the project.

The mid-nineteenth-century advances in communication brought about by the telegraph now made possible the dream of the weather watchers:

simultaneous observations over widely separated distances and the creation of synoptic weather maps. These visions seemed to promise predictability. States could see the utility for agriculture, maritime commerce, and war that such a promise implied.

In 1815, the "Great September Gale" made landfall first in Long Island, NY, and then onto hit the Connecticut coast, causing significant damage across the entire New England region. A Harvard professor produced an article in 1819, concluding that hurricanes where a "moving vortex" and establishing them as a counter-clockwise spinning cyclone. William Redfield concluded, several years later, that a hurricane is a "progressive whirlwind" when he published an article in the American Journal of Science. Throughout the 1800s, hurricanes continued to wreak havoc along the Eastern and Gulf Coasts of the United States, including:

- The Great Hurricane of 1831 arrived at a particularly pivotal moment in the eastern Caribbean, where the British islands were in the midst of the transition that had been set in motion first by the Leeward Islands' Act of Amelioration of 1798, limiting brutality in the treatment of slaves, followed by the abolition of the slave trade in 1807. Both of these measures had origins in the activities of abolitionist in Parliament but also were a response to the rise in slave rebelliousness in the 1790s, and to a growing anti-slavery sentiment of free traders who could observe that as British exports were doubling, the slave-based West Indies were absorbing a declining percentage of them. As Britain became the dominant maritime nation and the hub of world finance and commerce, the power of the West Indies interests in Parliament and their ability to protect the institution of slavery declined.
- 1837: "Racer's Storm" creates a 2,000-mile path of destruction through Jamaica, the Yucatan, the Gulf Coast of Texas, and then moved over Louisiana, Mississippi, Alabama, Georgia and South Carolina before leaving the North Carolina coast.
- 1848: Two Hurricanes hit within a month of each other near Tampa, Florida (then known as Fort Brooke).
- 1873: U.S. Army Signal Corps warned of an approaching hurricane off the coast of Cape May, New Jersey and Connecticut, creating the first Hurricane Warning. However, the storm never made landfall.
- 1881: A massive hurricane hits Georgia and South Carolina, killing 700 people and submerging several of barrier islands with its storm surge.

- 1893: Two different hurricanes kill approximately 2,000 people each. One hit the coast of South Carolina and left that state's barrier islands completely under water. The other hit Louisiana, flooding a prominent and populated bayou area.

The Hurricanes of 1806--A tropical cyclone was tracked near the northeastern Lesser Antilles on August 17. Moving west-northwest, the cyclone strengthened into a major hurricane which hit the southern North Carolina coast on August 23 and led to 42 deaths. It moved out to sea, disrupting British and French ships involved in the Napoleonic Wars. Another hurricane hit Dominica on September 9, resulting in 457 casualties. The cyclone subsequently moved through the Caribbean Sea and Gulf of Mexico, striking Mississippi by September 18. In addition, on September 20, another hurricane hit Dominica, causing an additional 165 deaths.

The Hurricane of 1812--A tropical cyclone was sighted east of Jamaica on August 14. By August 19, it struck southeast Louisiana as a major hurricane after grazing the Caribbean Islands. It passed just to the west of New Orleans, almost destroying the levee north of town. The hurricane caused severe flooding, damaged 53 boats, caused $6,000,000 in damage, and 100 deaths. The British fleet in the War of 1812 was disrupted.

The Hurricane of 1813--A powerful hurricane hit Dominica and Martinique beginning August 25, causing 3000 deaths. The cyclone moved south of Jamaica by August 28.

The Great September Gale of 1815--"The Great September Gale" hit New England in September of 1815. It first made landfall on Long Island, N.Y., and then again in Connecticut. The storm flooded Providence, Rhode Island, and caused extensive damage throughout the region.

In 1819, the concept of hurricanes as a 'moving vortex' was published--Harvard professor John Farrar concluded in an 1819 article that a hurricane is a cyclone and spins in a counter-clockwise direction "appears to have been a moving vortex and not the rushing forward of a great body of the atmosphere."[102] Several years later,

[102] John Farrar (1819) *An account of the violent and destructive storm of the 23rd of September, 1815,* The Quarterly Journal of Literature, Science and the Arts, pg. 104.

William C. Redfield published an account in the American Journal of Science identifying a hurricane as a progressive whirlwind. Redfield made the observation after studying trees and other objects scattered by a storm. Redfield suggested that hurricanes form east of the Leeward Islands and then travel west at a moderate speed. In Barbados, Lt. Col. William Reid of the Royal Engineers built on Redfield's theories by studying logs of ships struck by the Great Hurricane of 1780.

The Bay St. Louis Hurricane of 1819--The exact origin of this category 3 or 4 strength hurricane is unknown, but it likely formed off the coast of Cuba before heading on a west-northwest track towards the Gulf Coast. It made landfall on July 27 in southeastern Louisiana, and a second landfall in Bay St. Louis, Mississippi, before dissipating inland. This hurricane caused severe damage across Alabama, Louisiana, and Mississippi. One ship that was destroyed in the storm was the U.S. warship *Firebrand,* drowning 39 sailors. There were also reports of people being attacked by alligators, snapping turtles, and snakes, which further added to the death toll.

The Hurricane of 1821--The Norfolk and Long Island Hurricane was a deadly hurricane that rapidly moved up the Atlantic coast during the first few days of September. It included a hurricane landfall within the modern borders of New York City, the only recorded case of a hurricane eyewall moving directly over the city. It caused 200 deaths and is estimated to have been a Category 4 hurricane.

The Hurricane of 1825--On July 26, a powerful hurricane hit near Guadeloupe, and it continued west-northwestward to hit Puerto Rico, causing 1,300 deaths before moving to the west of Bermuda by August 2. This hurricane is also known as the Hurricane of Santa Ana.

The Great Caribbean Hurricane of 1831--Also known as 'The Great Barbados Hurricane', was an intense Category 4 hurricane that left cataclysmic damage across the Caribbean and Louisiana in 1831. A possible Cape Verde type hurricane, the storm slammed into Barbados, destroying the capital of Bridgetown. Some 1,500 to 2,500 persons died, either drowned by the 17 feet storm surge that the hurricane brought or crushed beneath collapsed buildings, leaving the island desolate. The storm then proceeded westward, striking St. Vincent the following day, damaging virtually every sugar estate on that island. At the time, it was the third largest producer of sugar in the British West Indies, behind only Jamaica and Trinidad.

The hurricane moved past Haiti and Cuba and then crossed the entire length of Cuba (Hurricane Georges of 1998 had a similar track). Its estimated Category 4 winds brought ships ashore at Guantanamo Bay, causing mudslides, damaging wharves, many ships and resulted in major structural damage. It turned to the northwest, where it made landfall near Last Island, Louisiana, as a Category 3 hurricane. There, it flooded parts of New Orleans from 7 to 10 feet storm surge in Lake Pontchartrain, and also causing hail. The Great Barbados Hurricane left 2,500 people dead and $7 million dollars (1831 dollars) in property damage. The damage from this storm was surveyed by British engineer William Reid and is instrumental in confirming William Redfield's theory that hurricanes are vortical.

The Padre Ruiz Hurricane of 1834--A hurricane struck the island of Dominica on September 20, bringing heavy winds and a 12ft storm surge that devastated the capital of Roseau; 230 people are believed to have been killed by the hurricane's onslaught. Then the hurricane made its second landfall at Santo Domingo, Dominican Republic, on the 23rd. About 170 sailors died when their ship sank in the Ozama River. On land, the hurricane disrupted the funeral service of Padre Ruiz, a Roman Catholic priest, hence this hurricane was named after him. There were 400 persons who were killed in this hurricane.

The "Racer's Storm" of 1837--This storm left a 2,000-mile path of destruction. Racer's Storm, named for a British warship which encountered the storm in the northwest Caribbean, was one of the most destructive storms of the 19th century. The British ship *'Racer'* survived the storm and went to Havana, Cuba, for repairs and provided valuable information about the storm to William Reid. It formed near Jamaica, crossed the Yucatan, struck the Gulf coast of Texas, and moved over Louisiana, Mississippi, Alabama, Georgia, and South Carolina before arriving off the North Carolina coast on October 9. It caused destruction all over the Gulf Coast, wiped out the Mexican Navy, and destroyed several U.S. ships. During this storm, a new paddle-wheel steamer, *Home* was coming south on her third trip from New York to Charleston, crowded with more than ninety passengers when she ran head on into this hurricane off Cape Hatteras. On the boat, there were only two life preservers, so most of the women and children herded together on the boat, but sadly they all drowned when the vessel sunk and began to break up during the storm. Only forty people from the ship survived. Because of this hurricane wreck, it caused Congress to pass the new law that required every vessel to carry a life preserver for every passenger. This hurricane caused 105 deaths on a 2,000-mile track from Caribbean to Texas to North Carolina.

The Hurricane of 1839--This cyclone is known as 'Reid's Hurricane.' This storm moved from east of the West Indies into the southwest Atlantic. Swells were noted as early as September 9 at Bermuda. During late on September 11 and early September 12, this hurricane struck Bermuda. The storm tide was measured as 11 feet. Thousands of trees were blown down, and the Tower Hill was leveled. Damage done to private property totaled 8000 pounds sterling (1839 pounds). This cyclone later swept western Ireland as an extratropical storm, which they called 'The Great Wind of 1839.' This was one of the first hurricanes to be studied by William Reid in person, in this case as governor of the island the year after his publication of "The Law of Storms."

The Hurricane of 1841--An intense hurricane remained offshore of the Carolinas in early October. It moved northeastward, entraining cold air into its circulation. It became an extratropical storm and hit New England on October 3. It led to a storm of snow and sleet in Connecticut, bringing drifts of up to 18 feet of snow in some areas. The storm wrecked the Georges Bank fishing fleet, which drowned 81 fishermen and knocked down trees, tore roofs off houses and forced boats to go up on shore. The storm also destroyed a saltworks factory along Cape Cod, sending the economy to a slump. In 1842, a monument was erected to remember the sailors and fishermen lost at sea to the "October Gale" of 1841.

Antje's Hurricane of 1942--This low-intensity Category 2 (estimated) hurricane crossed the Caribbean Sea between August 30 and September 8, 1842. Named for the schooner *Antje*, which it dismasted in the eastern Caribbean, just north of Puerto Rico on August 30, the hurricane followed an unusual straight-line track west across the Caribbean before making landfall near the town of Victoria, Mexico. Closely traced via ship's logs and weather reports by one of history's earliest hurricane watchers, William Redfield, the storm did not follow the curving northward track normally taken by late-season hurricanes, but instead it sailed directly over the Bahamas before brushing past Havana, Cuba, and Key West, Florida, on September 4. While Antje's Hurricane was of only minor intensity at Key West, in nearby Dove Key its swelling storm surge carried away a small lighthouse and destroyed several outbuildings.

Sources indicate that when the hurricane finally collided head-on with the Mexican coast on the afternoon of September 8, its hefty storm surge flooded the shore as far north as the mouth of the Rio Grande. Its lowest barometric pressure, 28.93 inches (979 mb), was recorded by a weather station in Havana, while observers in Mexico noted that the calm passage of its eye, which was apparently of small diameter, lasted no more than five minutes. Because of a lack of weather maps that show synoptic conditions over North America for the year 1842, it is nearly impossible to say with any certainty why Antje's Hurricane followed the unusual course that it did. However, the better-tracked San Ciprian Hurricane of September 1932 followed a similar straight-line route west across Puerto Rico and Hispaniola and into Mexico's Yucatán Peninsula. This-equally unusual course was caused by an intense high-pressure system that blanketed much of North America. With this scenario in mind, it is possible to see how Antje's Hurricane could have found itself near a similar high-pressure area in 1842, one that firmly kept it from swinging northward.

The Great Havana Hurricane of 1846--This hurricane was a powerful late-season hurricane that caused extensive damage and 163 deaths as it moved across Cuba, Florida, and the eastern United States before dissipating over the Canadian Maritimes. The damage from the storm is mostly unknown, but likely severe. Key West reportedly had $200,000 (1846 USD) in damage. Two major inlets on the Outer Banks of North Carolina were cut by this hurricane in September 1846. Some experts say this hurricane was probably a Category 5 on the Saffir-Simpson Hurricane Wind Scale. The hurricane wrecked 85 merchant ships with 30-foot seas near Cuba. Nearly every building in Havana was demolished, and coastal villages were wiped out in a matter of hours. Some disputed reports say 600 people died; the official death toll in Cuba is 163. In the Florida Keys, 20 boats and ships were sunk, dismasted or grounded by the storm. The twin lighthouses at Sand Key and Key West collapsed, drowning people who'd taken refuge in them. The large Naval hospital in Key West was severely damaged, and 594 of the island's 600 buildings were either damaged or destroyed. There were 50 persons who were reportedly killed in Key West.

The Hurricane of 1848--This hurricane pushes a 15-foot tide through Tampa, Florida. Fort Brooke, site of the present-day city of Tampa, was nearly destroyed by two hurricanes that hit the area within a month of each other.

The Hurricane of 1856--A Category 4 hurricane hit the resort island town of Last Island, causing 200 deaths, and perhaps as many as 400.

The Hurricane of 1857--A tropical storm was first observed north-northeast of the Dominican Republic on September 9. It moved northwestward, strengthening to a hurricane on September 10 and a Category 2 hurricane on September 12. It passed over the Outer Banks of North Carolina on September 13, and shortly thereafter, it weakened and then went out to sea on September 14. It caused 424 deaths, all from a ship named the *SS Central America,* which sank during the storm. Also on the ship was 30,000 pounds of gold, which contributed to the 'Panic of 1857.'

The Great Bahamas Hurricane of 1866--A powerful hurricane struck the islands of the Bahamas, causing widespread devastation and killing approximately 387 persons. It must be noted that some local accounts put the unofficial death toll figure much higher than that, due to the lack of proper documentation after the storm. Also, known as the Great Nassau Hurricane of 1866, the sixth hurricane of the season was also the longest-lasting. The brig *Jarien* encountered the hurricane on September 24 to the west-southwest of the Cape Verde Islands. The track is unknown for the following five days, until another ship reported a hurricane about 20 miles north of Anegada in the British Virgin Islands. The hurricane affected the Leeward Islands, washing several ships ashore and destroying a pier in St. Thomas. On September 30 through the following day, the cyclone moved through the Turks and Caicos Islands, becoming what was considered "one of the most terrific hurricanes ever known." About 75% (about 3,000 persons) of the population was left homeless and moneyless after the island's main revenue earner-the harvesting sea salt was destroyed by the rain and winds of the storm.

After affecting the Turks and Caicos Islands, the hurricane passed through the Bahamas, where damages were described as "extremely devastating." The eye crossed over Nassau, where a barometric pressure of 938 mbar (27.70 inHg) was reported. Based on this observation, the hurricane was estimated to have sustained winds of 140 mph. The hurricane killed approximately 386 persons in the Bahamas. A total of 1,034 persons were rendered homeless (out of a total population in Nassau of 11,503 persons). It destroyed 612 homes and numerous shops and other buildings in Nassau. The hurricane struck without warning in the Bahamas, either washing ashore or sinking every ship but one in Nassau Harbor. Although a Bahamian topographical map in 1839 showed the connection or joining between the island of New Providence and Lyford Cay, where it was linked with shallow tide covered flats. It was only until 1866 that this hurricane changed the appearance of this area. The Great Bahamas

Hurricane of 1866 moved vast amounts of sand to build up the isthmus which would eventually be covered with vegetation and then stabilized to where the isthmus has survived all other great storms.

One of the ships destroyed was a boat called *The General Clinch*, the last of the blockade runners remaining in the harbor. In addition, the strong winds downed trees and destroyed roofs. Every building in Nassau was damaged or destroyed, including all of the churches such as Trinity Methodist, Bethel Baptist, and St. Anne's Churches. On the island of Long Island, there were 230 houses destroyed, 112 dwelling houses were destroyed on Exuma, 240 homes and 831 persons were left homeless on Eleuthera. After moving through the islands, the hurricane curved northeastward, affecting dozens of other ships and wrecking four. On October 4, it passed to the north of Bermuda, where it produced Force 11 winds on the Beaufort scale. The hurricane was last observed on October 5 to the southeast of Atlantic Canada.[103]

The Illustrated view of the Damaged ruins of the Trinity Methodist Church after the Great Bahamas Hurricane of 1866. This building was built for the Trinity Methodists, at a cost of nearly £8000, one fourth of which was contributed by a grant from the local government. It was opened for public worship in April, 1865 (Courtesy of Jonathon Ramsey, Balmain Antiques).

103 Wayne Neely, *The Great Bahamas Hurricane of 1866*, (Bloomington, iUniverse Publishing, 2011), pgs. 306-342.

The Hurricane of 1867--One of the really great hurricanes of that era and it impacted the Virgin Islands and Puerto Rico on October 29, 1867. At St. Thomas, the barometer reading felled as low as 27.95 inches just prior to the calm, which occurred shortly after noon. More than six hundred persons were drowned at St. Thomas, and many more were killed on shore by falling houses. In Puerto Rico, this storm is known as "The Hurricane of San Narciso", where over 1,000 persons lost their lives.

"Ouragan", a sailing vessel laboring under hurricane conditions. In: "Les Meteores", Margolle et Zurcher, 3rd Edition, 1869, pg. 140. Image courtesy of the John Carter Brown Library at Brown University.

The Hurricane of October 1870--On October 5, a tropical storm developed south of Haiti. It moved west-northwest, becoming a hurricane south of Cuba, on the 6th. The hurricane rapidly strengthened to its peak of 115 mph prior to hitting Matanzas, Cuba, on the 7th. After crossing the island, it then moved over the northwest Bahamas and then slowly over the Florida Keys, causing an additional 1200 deaths there. It moved out to sea, last being seen on the 14th. The hurricane, known as the 'Hurricane of San Marcos' or the 'Straits of Florida Hurricane,' caused massive flooding in Cuba and South Florida, resulting in 2000 casualties and leaving behind $12 million USD in damage.

The Hurricane of August 1873--This hurricane is significant because this was the first hurricane where a warning was issued in the United States. On August

13, a tropical storm formed in the central Atlantic. It followed the track of a Cape Verde-type hurricane, becoming a hurricane on the 17th. It recurved to the north and northeast as it reached its peak of 115 mph. As it passed to the south of Nova Scotia, it slowed down and drifted towards the coast of Newfoundland and destroyed more than 1,200 ships in the Canadian Maritimes. The U.S. Army Signal Corps warned of a storm approaching the coast between Cape May, N.J., and New London, Conn. The storm never made landfall but caused $3.5 million in damage (1873 USD) and 600 deaths.

The Hurricane of September 1874--Struck the Carolinas around the end of September 1874. This storm is remembered for being the first such hurricane to be shown on a weather map by the Weather Bureau. At the time it was shown, the hurricane was located off the southeast coast between Jacksonville, Florida, and Savannah, Georgia.

The Hurricane of September, 1875--On September 8, 1875, a hurricane was first observed east of Barbados. It moved past the islands and through the Caribbean, hitting Cuba on the 13th. It weakened while over Cuba to a tropical storm, but in the Gulf of Mexico, it restrengthened to a peak of 115 mph. It hit Indianola, Texas, at that intensity on the 16th. It turned northeastward, dissipating over Mississippi. The storm brought strong storm surge to the Texas coast, causing heavy damage and a total of 800 deaths. The storm was the first of two hurricanes to devastate Indianola, the other being the 'Indianola Hurricane of 1886.' This was an intense hurricane that struck the southern coast of Cuba, as predicted by Father Benito Vines, who began to develop a tremendous reputation for accurately predicting when and where a hurricane would strike. His studies of tropical storms and hurricanes during the latter portion of the 19th century made the Cuban forecasters some of the best hurricane forecasters in the world at the time.

The San Felipe Hurricane of 1876--This hurricane was first observed east of the Windward Islands on September 12 and hit the islands that night. It strengthened to become a Category 3 hurricane and hit Puerto Rico at that intensity on the 13th. It crossed over Hispaniola and Cuba before turning northward, avoiding Florida on the way. The weakened tropical storm headed towards the Carolinas, where it strengthened to a minimal hurricane before hitting near Wilmington, North Carolina, on the 17th. It continued through the interior of the United States, dissipating on the 19th near Cape Cod. There were 19 deaths reported, but historians suspected the Spanish Government withheld actual damage and death toll data. The storm was remembered as the "San Felipe Hurricane" because it struck on September 13, the feast day of Saint Philip.

The Hurricane of 1878--This hurricane is notable because it is one of the very few hurricanes which remained over Florida for three days. A slow-moving hurricane made landfall in the Florida Keys and slowly made its way up the center of the state.

The Hurricane of 1878--Also known as the 'Gale of 1878' and was an intense Category 2 hurricane that caused extensive damage from Cuba to New England. A tropical storm formed off the coast of Jamaica on October 18, 1878, and moved nearly due north. On October 20, the storm reached hurricane status, and on October 21 the hurricane struck Cuba. The damage in Cuba was only minor, and three schooners sank. The hurricane continued moving northwest and made landfall in North Carolina, where it wrecked a schooner and several steamers. The storm later continued inland, moving at speeds between 40-50 mph, carrying hurricane force winds as far as Richmond, Virginia, before merging with an extratropical storm over New England. The hurricane killed 71 people and left $2 million dollars in damage (1878 USD). The hurricane killed 71 people and left $2 million dollars in damage (1878 USD).

The Hurricane of 1881--This hurricane killed 700 in Georgia and South Carolina. A westward moving tropical storm moved through the northeastern Lesser Antilles on August 22. It reached hurricane strength on the 24th and continued its slow northwestward movement until its Savannah and Augusta, Georgia, landfalls on the 27th as a Category 2 hurricane. Several barrier islands were completely submerged by the storm surge. It moved inland, dissipating on the 29th over northwestern Mississippi, resulting in around 700 deaths.

The Hurricane of 1882--On October 5, a tropical storm formed in the western Caribbean Sea. It drifted northward, and as it approached the coast of Cuba, it rapidly intensified to a 140-mph major hurricane. It weakened greatly over the island, never recovering while moving northward over the Gulf of Mexico. It crossed Florida and went out to sea, dissipating on the 15th. Its remnants brought heavy rainfall to Labrador and left 140 casualties in its path.

The Indianola Hurricane of 1886--The 1886 Indianola Hurricane destroyed the town of Indianola, Texas and as such had a significant impact on the history and economic development of Texas. It was the fifth hurricane of the 1886 Atlantic hurricane season and one of the most intense hurricanes ever to hit the United States.This storm dumped 21.4 inches of rain on Alexandria, Louisiana. After flooding the Louisiana coast, the storm moved into Texas, where it completely destroyed the city of Indianola and as a result of this storm Indianola was never rebuilt. It was the fifth most intense hurricane to ever to hit the United States. The areas affected included the Lesser Antilles, Dominican Republic, Cuba, Texas. The hurricane obliterated the town that was only just recovering from a powerful hurricane in 1875 in the same location. This storm caused fewer fatalities (46 in Indianola, compared to 400 in the 1875 storm) than the 1875 storm, mainly because the storm struck during the day and residents had time to seek safe shelter.

The following excerpt is taken from an account in the Monthly Weather Review of August 1886: "The appearance of the town after the storm was one of universal wreck. Not a house remained uninjured, and most of those that were left standing were in an unsafe condition. Many were washed away completely and scattered over the plains back of the town; others were lifted from their foundations and moved bodily over considerable distances. Over all this strip of low ground, as far as could be seen, were the wrecks of houses, carriages, personal property of all kinds, and a great many dead animals. Very few people were able to save anything whatever, and as the houses which were left were scarcely habitable, the town was deserted as fast as possible."[104]

The Hurricane #10 of 1886--A tropical storm was observed in the northwest Caribbean Sea on October 8. It moved to the northwest, reaching major hurricane strength in the Gulf of Mexico on the 11th. Late on the 12th, the hurricane made landfall near the border between Louisiana and Texas. It caused 175-200 deaths due to heavy rainfall and storm surge, with $250,000 in damage occurring.

The Hurricane of 1888--On August 31, a tropical storm was observed northeast of the Lesser Antilles. It moved westward, strengthening to a hurricane later that day. As it continued to strengthen, it brought heavy rain over Puerto Rico, Great Inagua, the Turks and Caicos Islands, and Cuba. On

---

104 *docs.lib.noaa.gov/rescue/mwr/014/mwr-014-08-0230.pdf.* Retrieved: 11-11-2015.

the 3rd, it reached its peak of 130 mph, but land interaction with Cuba weakened to a minimal hurricane. It crossed the island and the Yucatán Channel, reaching the northeast coast of the Yucatán Peninsula on the 6th. After weakening to a tropical storm, it restrengthened to a Category 2 hurricane while moving southwestward in the Bay of Campeche, but it dissipated after its Veracruz landfall on the 8th. It caused 921 deaths.

The Hurricane of 1891--A powerful storm struck Martinique and killed between 700 and 1,000 persons and injured a thousand more. The storm also devastated the agricultural sector and sunk or damaged all the shipping in the two harbors of St. Pierre and Fort de France. This storm focused France's attention on the vulnerability of the islands. In 1892, Henri Monet published a book describing the storm in order to raise money for the victims.

The Sea Islands Hurricane of 1893--A major hurricane of Category 3 strength that made landfall in Savannah, Georgia, on August 27th, but its northeast quadrant hammered Sea Islands in Beaufort County, South Carolina. As a result, approximately 2,000 to 2,500 people were killed and upwards of 30,000 people were left homeless. The destruction at Charleston was reported in the press as terrific. "Hundreds of corpses were strewn among the farms, unknown except to the vultures which flocked about them. Whole families are wiped out in some places. The coroner has sworn in an army of deputies, and these are hunting for the dead."[105]

The 1893 Chenier Caminanda Hurricane--The 10th storm of the season, also known as the Great October Hurricane of 1893, formed on September 27 in the western Caribbean Sea. After hitting the northeastern coast of the Yucatán Peninsula as a Category 2 hurricane, it moved through the Gulf of Mexico. As it approached the southeast coast of Louisiana near Cheniere Caminada, just west of Grand Isle, it rapidly strengthened to a Category 4 hurricane with sustained winds of 135 mph, and hit land on October 2, Louisiana. There were 779 people who died out of the town's 1500 residents from the high winds and flooding from the storm surge. The surge was up to 16 feet, with heavy surf above it. The hurricane caused about 2000 fatalities in total, making it among the deadliest American hurricanes. In the city of New Orleans, Louisiana, the

---

105 Jay Barnes, *Florida's Hurricane History*, Chapel Hill, The University of North Carolina Press, 2007), pg. 74.

most active months for a tropical cyclone to occur here is usually mid-August through early October. This city gets a serious brush on average once every 2.29 years. It is averaged that this U.S. city gets a direct hit once every 6.00 years. In the city of Grand Isle, Louisiana, the most active months for a tropical cyclone to occur here is usually mid-August through early October. This city gets a serious brush on average once every 2.25 years. It is averaged that this U.S. city gets a direct hit once every 6.00 years.[106]

The Gulf States were greatly affected by the hurricane. There were significant losses to the orange and rice crops, and combined with destruction of the wind, the hurricane caused about $5 million in damage (1893 USD, $128.3 million in 2016 USD). It moved through Alabama, Georgia, and the Carolinas before dissipating at sea. This storm was one of the first hurricanes to receive Category 4 strength on the modern Saffir-Simpson Hurricane Wind Scale. There was tremendous loss to the shipping of the area and caused widespread property damage. This hurricane was appropriately named after a Spanish sugar planter, Francisco Caminada, various sources give the name of the village as Caminadaville, Chenier Caminada, Cheniere Caminada, or Chenier Caminanda. The island and village were nearly destroyed. Today the town of Cheniere Caminada is located in Jefferson Parish, Louisiana.

The Hurricane #4 of 1896--The fourth storm on September 22 and lasted until September 30. It formed directly over the Lesser Antilles and hit Cuba, Florida, South and North Carolina, Virginia, Washington, D.C., and Pennsylvania. Its maximum sustained winds were at 130 mph. This storm was responsible for an estimated 130 deaths and $1.5 million in damage (1896 dollars).

106 *http://www.hurricanecity.com/city/neworleans/grandisle.html.* Retrieved: 07-09-2015.

Workers gather among the rubbles to look for survivors at Fernandina Beach, Florida, after The Great Hurricane of 1896 (Florida Photographic Collection, courtesy of the State Library and Archives of Florida).

The Privy Hurricane of 1898--In 1898, Cuba was part of the oppressive Spanish empire. After the USS Maine was sunk under mysterious circumstances in Havana, Cuba, the Americans declared war on Spain. An American regiment called the 'Rough Riders' under Lt. Col. Theodore Roosevelt quickly overwhelmed the Spanish garrison and liberated Cuba. Lookout posts were established along the Cuban coastline to watch for a Spanish counterattack, but by August 12 the war was over and Cuba was free. The U.S. weather service saw great potential for the Cuban lookout posts and took them over as part of a hurricane early warning system. They were dismayed to find the outdoor privy (or in other words, an outhouse) was stolen from one of the stations. This caused such uproar that the local who had stolen it for his own personal use returned it. Very shortly afterward, on October 2, both the observation post and its privy were destroyed by a hurricane.

The 1899 Hurricane of San Ciriaco--This storm was the first hurricane to hit Puerto Rico under the control of USA and was known as the Hurricane of San Ciriaco, which formed on August 3 halfway between Africa and the Leeward and Windward Islands in the Atlantic. It continued westward, striking the Lesser Antilles, and passed directly across the entire length of Puerto Rico as a 150 mph Category 4 hurricane on August 8, on the feast day of San Ciriaco. The storm surge from this storm destroyed almost all of the houses at the port of Humacao, and more than eighty lives were lost there. Property damage at Arroyo and Humacao exceeded $2,000,000. This hurricane was the fifth most intense hurricane ever to hit the United States. The hurricane was tied with Hurricane Ginger for the longest lasting hurricane on record, lasting for 31 days, 28 of which it displayed tropical characteristics. In all, more than 3,433 lives were lost in Puerto Rico, mostly from drowning. Total property loss on the island was estimated at about $20,000,000 (1899 USD). In the city of San Juan, Puerto Rico, the most active months for a tropical cyclone to occur here is usually mid-August through early October. This city gets a serious brush on average every 3.51 years. It is averaged that this US territory gets a direct hit once every 13.09 years.[107]

In the Bahamas, the storm brought widespread catastrophic damage throughout the island chain and a death toll of at least 334 persons, comprising mostly of Bahamian sponge fishermen near Andros and Exuma, who were caught at sea during the hurricane. Some 50 spongers in the vicinity of Exuma drowned. Many other schooners and sloops were destroyed, sunk or badly damaged. On Inagua, three vessels were lost and a schooner *Vivid* was left beached at Lantern Head, while other boats that were hauled up on the bay, suffered severe damage. About a third of the year's total output (50,000 to 60,000 bushels) of the harvested sea salt was destroyed. The public school house was destroyed on Ragged Island, though the dwellings escaped with only minor damages. Plantain and banana plantations were completely flattened at Deadman's Cay on Long Island. Three vessels were beached on Rum Cay, but only one was considerably damaged. About 10 bushels of salt were lost. Two churches and a number of private homes were damaged on San Salvador Island. A few ships and vessels were destroyed, damaged, or lost on Eleuthera, leaving a several persons dead or missing. On Cat Island, several persons were lost at sea on a schooner called *Choir* however, a boy crew member was later found alive stranded on the island, naked and there for several days.[108]

---

107 *http://www.hurricanecity.com/city/sanjuan.html/**. Retrieved: 07-09-2015.

108 Wayne Neely, The Great Bahamian Hurricane of 1899 And 1932-The Story of Two of the Greatest and Deadliest Hurricanes to Impact the Bahamas, (Bloomington, iUniverse Publishing, 2012), pgs. 304-333.

CHAPTER TWELVE

The major North Atlantic hurricanes from 1900 – 2000

The century's first major hurricane-The Great Galveston Hurricane in 1900 hit the coast of Texas at Galveston Island with almost no warning, creating the deadliest natural disaster in United States. This hurricane came ashore with 15 feet storm tides and was responsible for at least 8,000 deaths, with some estimates as high as 12,000. In 1926, the storm known as "The Great Miami Hurricane" came ashore in Florida as a Category 4 hurricane, causing massive destruction with its 15-foot storm surge and deadly winds. This hurricane killed more than 350 people and eventually led to the invention of the first building codes in Miami, which was subsequently replicated in more than 5000 cities. In 1969, Hurricane Camille came ashore with a 24 ½-foot storm surge, which along with heavy rains and winds, killed 143 in Mississippi and Camille would later kill 113 persons while flooding Virginia. 1992's Hurricane Andrew caused massive destruction in South Florida and Louisiana. Andrew only killed 23, but caused up to $26.5 billion in damage, $25 billion in Florida alone, becoming the costliest storm in U.S. history until Katrina hit in 2005.

Other notable hurricane dates or events that change the way we observe and forecast hurricanes during the 1900s include:

- Bjerknes organized a nationwide weather-observing system in their native Norway. With the data available, they formulated the theory of polar fronts: the atmosphere is made up of cold air masses near the poles and warm air masses near the tropics, and fronts exist where these air masses meet.
- During World War II (1939–45), American military pilots flying above the Pacific Ocean discovered a strong stream of air rapidly flowing from west

to east, which became known as the jet stream, and this since then has had a significant impact on the aviation industry.

- The development of radar, rockets, and satellites greatly improved data collection and saved many lives in the process because meteorologist were now able to track and follow a hurricane as it came of the African coast until it made landfall somewhere in the North Atlantic. Weather radar first came into use in the United States in 1949 with the efforts of Horace Byers (1906–1998) and Roscoe R. Braham. Conventional weather radar shows the location and intensity of precipitation. In the 1990s, the more advanced Doppler radar, which can continuously measure wind speed and precipitation, came into wide use.
- 1928: The Great Okeechobee Hurricane-A storm originating due east of the Leeward Islands and devastated these islands and then moving on to Puerto Rico and then continued its fury as it went through the Bahamas and onto Palm Beach, Florida, and killed a total of 3,411 people as it tracked through the Caribbean, Bahamas and Florida.
- 1943: Colonel Joseph Duckworth is the first pilot to fly into the eye of a hurricane (intentionally).
- 1944: A hurricane off the East Coast of the U.S. sunk a Navy destroyer, Minesweeper, 2 U.S. Coast Guard Cutters and another light vessel, disrupting World War II shipping and killing 344 people.
- 1950: Hurricanes were given formal military alphabet names.
- 1953: Hurricane naming begins with the storms receiving female names.
- 1954: Back-to-back hurricanes (Carol and Edna) pummel the New England area, specifically Long Island, NY, Connecticut and Cape Cod. The 2 storms had very similar paths and formed only a few days apart. The storms killed more than 80 people.
- 1963: Hurricane Flora hits Haiti and Cuba, killing more than 7,000 people.
- 1971: Hurricane Ginger spins through the North Atlantic, the Bermuda Triangle and the coasts of both North Carolina and Virginia for 31 days, setting a hurricane endurance record. Twenty of those days recorded hurricane force winds.
- 1974: Hurricane Fifi kills more than 10,000 people in the Honduras.
- 1975: The Saffir-Simpson Hurricane Wind Scale which was created in 1971 by a meteorologist and a civil engineer developing a way to measure hurricanes and saw its widespread use in 1975 after Neil Frank replaced Simpson at the helm as the Director of the National Hurricane Center in 1974.
- 1979: Officials begin using male names for Hurricanes.

- 1983: Category 3 Hurricane Alicia hits Texas through Galveston and Houston, causing $2 billion in damage.
- Hurricane Gilbert devastated the country of Jamaica and became the most intense hurricane in the North Atlantic in 1988 with a surface pressure of 888 mbar, but it was only recently broken by Hurricane Wilma of 2005 which attained a pressure of 882 mbar.
- 1989: Hurricane Hugo caused $7 billion damage to the mainland U.S. after making landfall in Charleston, S.C. The storm killed 21 with storm surge that reached 20 feet.
- 1998: Hurricane Mitch kills over 10,000 in Honduras.

The Great Galveston Hurricane of 1900 — The Deadliest Disaster in American History

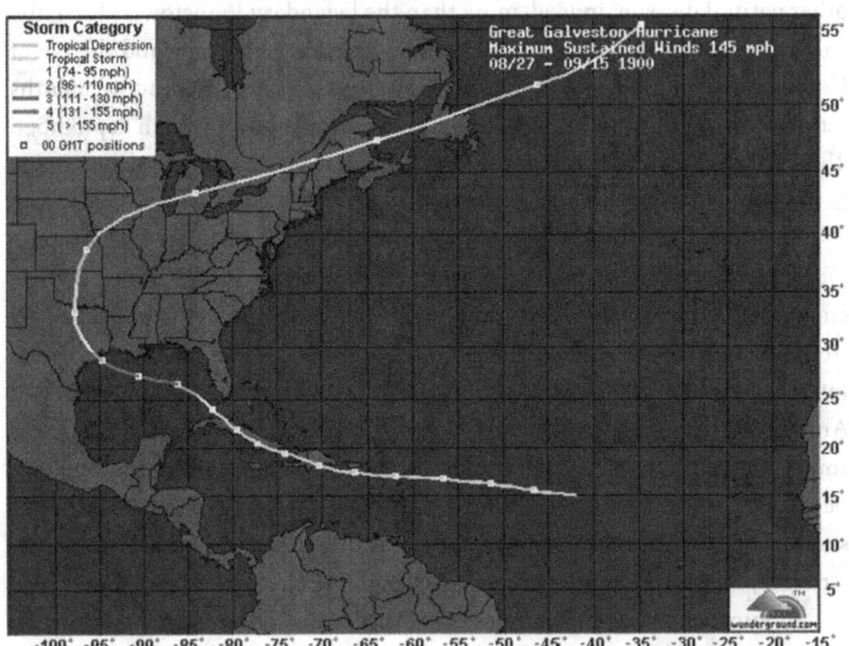

This map shows the track of the Great Galveston of 1900 as it moved through the Leeward Islands, Puerto Rico, Dominican Republic, USA and Canada (Information courtesy of the Weather Underground Inc.).

The dawn of the 20th century ushered in many remarkable changes in the United States. The Wright Brothers were making great strides in the aviation sector when they conducted flight experiments at Kitty Hawk, North Carolina.

The U.S. population was 76 million in 1900, compared to 321,216,397 today.[109] The U.S. government took in $567 million in 1900, and at the end of the 20th century it took in $1.7 trillion. In 1900 there were no weather satellites, no Doppler radars or computers to give residents any kind of advanced warnings against these powerful storms. However, some warnings were issued by the U.S. Weather Bureau, the predecessor of NOAA's National Weather Service. People were advised to seek higher ground. Many didn't heed the warnings, preferring instead to watch the huge waves generated by the storm-a decision many of them came to regret.

On September 8, 1900, a killer hurricane struck the Texas coastal city of Galveston. This hurricane would become the greatest natural disaster, by number of deaths, in United States history: 8,000 by accepted figures, perhaps as many as 12,000. Of that total, 6,000 perished in Galveston alone (about 20% of the city's population). The tragedy killed more Americans than any other natural disaster, indeed, more than the legendary Johnstown Flood, the San Francisco Earthquake, the 1938 New England Hurricane and the Great Chicago Fire combined. In the city of Galveston, Texas, the most active months for a tropical cyclone to occur here is usually mid-August through September. This city gets a serious brush on average every 2.71 years. It is averaged that this U.S. city gets a direct hit once every 9.00 years.[110]

The storm first became organized in the warm equatorial mid-Atlantic Ocean west of the Cape Verde Islands about August 27, 1900. A ship encountered the tropical depression on the 28th, noting in its log book: "winds from the south-southwest at Beaufort force 6, about 25-31 mph." As the system intensified, it moved due westward toward the Leeward Islands of the Lesser Antilles. By the morning of August 31, its position was located about 200 miles southeast of Puerto Rico and headed directly for Hispaniola. As September began, the storm center was located in the Caribbean Sea about 200 miles south of Santo Domingo City, Hispaniola. While its winds were still gathering strength, the storm's rains showered the islands of the Greater Antilles.

In Jamaica, for example, miles of railway roadbed were washed out when heavy rains flooded the island. Then the rains began in Cuba, and the director of the Belen Observatory in Havana, Father Gangoite, saw the approach of the storm and became a little worried. This observatory was one of only two main

---

109 *http://*www.census.gov/popclock (Courtesy *of the* United States Census Bureau). Retrieved: 08-08-2015.

110 *http://www.hurricanecity.com/city/galveston.htm.* Retrieved: 08-08-2015.

centers for observing and forecasting the movement of hurricanes of the North Atlantic, the other being the U.S. Weather Bureau in the United States. At this time, the center of the storm was believed to be about 175 miles south of mid-island Cuba. He wrote: "This kind of storm sometimes produces heavy rain over this island, and acquires greater strength as it moves out over the Atlantic."[111] On Monday, September 3rd, Santiago, Cuba, was inundated by 10 inches of rain in just eight hours, 12.58 inches in 24 hours, and before it finally stopped raining, 24.35 inches over two days. The storm crossed Cuba on the 4th and then left the northern island early on the 5th. Father Gangoite's words had been correct about the rain, and now he was correct about the increase in strength.

The storm, which would soon become known as the Great Galveston Hurricane, intensified to hurricane force as it approached the Florida Keys. But Gangoite was dead wrong about its track. The hurricane continued northwestward, reaching a point midway between Havana and Key West, Florida, by the morning of the 5th. The hurricane continued to move northwestward, passing the Florida Keys and bringing high winds to southern Florida. Observations from Jupiter, Florida, at the southeast tip of the state reported sustained NE winds at 48 mph. Forecasters at the U.S. Weather Bureau office in Washington DC examined the maps and, using their knowledge of past hurricanes behavior, expected the storm would curve along a northeasterly track across Florida and then northward along the U.S. east coast. The office telegraphed a forecast to New Orleans at midday on September 5, stating the storm "probably will be felt as far north as Norfolk, Virginia, by Thursday night September 6 and is likely to extend over the middle Atlantic and South New England states by Friday."[112]

The Galveston Hurricane, however, had other ideas than follow its forecast track. Rather than follow the more likely path which would recurve back toward the Atlantic, it continued on its west-northwest course. As it moved into the Gulf of Mexico, it gave gale force winds to Tampa on Florida's west coast, Key West, and Jupiter on Florida's east coast, assuring weather forecasters in Washington that it was moving over the state. But a region of high pressure located to the east blocked this path, and the storm was forced to move into the Gulf of Mexico and toward the coastal Texas city of Galveston, while significantly strengthening over the warm Loop Current and the sheltered

111 *http://askville.amazon.com/find-map-Galveston-Texas-1900.* Retrieved: 11-11-2015.

112 Ibid.

but warm waters of the Gulf of Mexico. A general west-northwestward motion occurred over the Gulf of Mexico.

By the time the storm reached the Texas coast south of Galveston late on September 8th, it was already a Category 4 hurricane. After landfall, the cyclone made a northward track through the Great Plains. It became extratropical and turned east-northeastward on September 11th, passing across the Great Lakes, New England, and southeastern Canada. It was last spotted over the north Atlantic on September 15th. This hurricane was the deadliest hurricane on record to ever hit the United States. Storm surges of 8 to 15 feet inundated the whole Galveston Island, as well as other portions of the nearby Texas coast. These storm surges were largely responsible for the 6,000 to 12,000 deaths attributed to the storm. The damage to property was estimated at $30 million (1900 USD).

The Great Galveston Hurricane of 1900 made landfall on the city of Galveston, Texas, on September 8, 1900. It had estimated winds of 135 miles per hour at the time of landfall, making it a Category 4 storm on the Saffir-Simpson Hurricane Wind Scale. The hurricane caused widespread devastation and great loss of life. The persons who died in this storm were estimated to be approximately 6,000 to 12,000 persons, depending on whether one counts casualties from the city of Galveston itself, the larger island, or the region as a whole. The number most cited in official damage reports is 8,000, giving the storm the third-highest number of casualties of any North Atlantic hurricane, after the Great Hurricane of 1780 and 1998's Hurricane Mitch. The Galveston Hurricane of 1900 is to date the deadliest natural disaster ever to hit the United States. By contrast, the second-deadliest storm to strike the United States, the Great Lake Okeechobee Hurricane in 1928, caused at least 2,500 deaths.

This hurricane has no official name and is referred to under various descriptive, unofficial names because the naming system as we know it today was not in existence at the time. Common names for the storm include the 'Galveston Hurricane of 1900', the 'Great Galveston Hurricane', and in older documentation, the 'Galveston Flood.' It is often locally known in the Galveston area as the 'Great Storm of 1900.' The city of Galveston at the end of the 19th century was a thriving metropolis with a population of 42,000. In the years prior to the great storm of Sept. 8, 1900 Galveston had grown from a small but busy seaside city on the Texas coast into one of the wealthiest cities in the country. Its position on the natural harbor of Galveston Bay along the Gulf of Mexico made it the center of trade and the biggest city in the state of Texas.

Galveston was the hub of a booming cotton export trade because it had the only deep-water port in Texas at the time. Its natural deepwater channel made Galveston the most important seaport in Texas. Trains carried cargo to and from the port, and ships traveled across the seas. In fact, more than 70 percent of the country's cotton crop at the time passed through the port of Galveston, and some 1,000 ships called on the port annually. This loss of the cotton crop also caused severe problems in the textile industries in Europe for several years after the storm, because they depended heavily on Galveston's cotton. Unfortunately, with this prosperity came a false sense of complacency as the residents felt they were immune to hurricanes, even if they lived on a coastal city. Regrettably, it was built on a barrier island along the Gulf Coast, the worst place to be during a hurricane of any strength, let alone a major Category 4 hurricane with its powerful winds and deadly storm surge.

A quarter of a century earlier, the nearby town of Indianola on Matagorda Bay was undergoing its own boom period and was the second busiest town right below Galveston among Texas ports. Then in 1875, a powerful hurricane blew through, nearly destroying the town. Indianola was rebuilt, but a second hurricane in 1886 caused residents to simply give up and move elsewhere. Many Galveston residents took the destruction of Indianola as an object lesson on the threat posed by hurricanes. Galveston was a low, flat island, little more than a giant sandbar along the Gulf Coast. They called for a seawall to be constructed to protect the city, but their concerns were dismissed by the majority of the population and the city's government.

Since its formal founding in 1839, the city of Galveston had weathered numerous storms, which the city survived with ease. So the residents had a false sense of security because residents believed any future storms would be no worse than previous events or that they were immune from powerful storms. In order to provide an official meteorological statement on the threat of hurricanes, Galveston Weather Bureau section director Isaac Cline wrote an 1891 article in the *Galveston News* in which he argued not only that a seawall was not needed to protect the city, but that it would be impossible for a hurricane of significant strength to strike the island. To make a long story short, the seawall was not built, and development activities on the island actively increased its vulnerability to storms. Sand dunes along the shore were removed to be used to fill low-lying areas in the city, removing what little natural barrier there was to the Gulf of Mexico.

The storm's origins are unclear, due to the limited observation ability at the end of the 19th century. At the time without satellite technology, ship reports were the only reliable tool for observing hurricanes at sea, and because the telegraph was in its infancy, these reports were not available until the ships came into the harbor. Like most powerful Atlantic hurricanes, the 1900 storm is believed to have begun as a Cape Verde-type hurricane—a tropical wave moving off the western coast of Africa. The first formal sighting of the hurricane's precursor occurred on August 27, about one thousand miles east of the Windward Islands, when a ship recorded an area of "unsettled weather." Three days later, Antigua reported a severe thunderstorm passing over, followed by the hot, humid calmness that often occurs after the passage of a tropical cyclone. By September 1, the U.S. Weather Bureau observers were reporting on a "storm of moderate intensity (not a hurricane)" southeast of Cuba. On September 4, the Galveston office of the U.S. Weather Bureau began receiving warnings from the Bureau's central office in Washington, D.C., that a "tropical storm" had moved northward over Cuba. The Weather Bureau forecasters had no way of knowing where the storm was or where it was going without satellite technology.

At the time, conditions in the Gulf of Mexico were conducive for further strengthening of the storm. The Gulf had seen little cloud cover for several weeks, and the seas were very warm. The storm was reported to be north of Key West, Florida, on September 6, and in the early morning hours of Friday, September 7, the Weather Bureau office in New Orleans, Louisiana, issued a report of heavy damage along the Louisiana and Mississippi coasts. Details of the storm were not widespread; damage to telegraph lines limited communication. The Bureau's central office in Washington, D.C., ordered storm warnings raised from Pensacola, Florida, to Galveston.

By the afternoon of the 7th, large swells were being propagated from the southeast and were being observed in the Gulf, and clouds at all altitudes began moving in from the northeast. Both of these observations are consistent with a hurricane approaching from the east. The Galveston Weather Bureau office raised its double square flags; a hurricane warning was in effect. The ship *Louisiana* encountered the hurricane at 1 p.m. that day after departing New Orleans. The ship's Captain Halsey estimated wind speeds of 150 mph. Early the next morning, the swells continued despite only partly cloudy skies. Mainly because of the typical or ordinary September-like weather, few residents took the storm warnings seriously enough to evacuate. Few people evacuated across Galveston's bridges to the mainland, and the majority of the population was unconcerned by the rain clouds that had begun rolling in by mid-morning. Most residents reasoned that even if a storm was on its way, they had weathered storms before. As a relative of one victim later recalled: "Mama didn't want to leave. She'd been through it before and said she wasn't worried. It had never been that bad." However, Galveston had never seen a storm like this one. In fact, this storm would go down in history as one of the greatest, deadliest and enduring hurricanes of the North Atlantic.[113]

Isaac Cline, the controversial local forecast official with the U.S. Weather Bureau who lost his wife when their home collapsed in the onslaught of the storm, claimed that he took it upon himself to travel along the beach and other low-lying areas, warning people personally of the storm's approach. This is based on Cline's own reports and has been called into question in recent years, as no other survivors corroborated his account. Cline's role in the disaster is the subject of some controversy. Supporters point to Cline's issuing a hurricane warning without permission from the Bureau's central office. Detractors (including author Erik Larson, who wrote the bestselling book *'Isaac's Storm'*) point to Cline's earlier insistence that a seawall was unnecessary and his belief that an intense hurricane could not strike the island. Isaac was U.S. Weather Bureau climatologist Isaac Cline, who dismissed as absurd the notion that a hurricane could devastate Galveston. As stated earlier, his stance discouraged the town from building a sea wall. The day before the hurricane arrived, warning flags were raised as huge waves pounded the shores, barometric pressure dropped rapidly and high fish-scale-shaped clouds moved inland.

Before dawn on September 8, the water crept ashore and kept rising, despite strengthening north winds that should have repelled the storm. By now, Cline was worried. "Unusually heavy swells from the southeast.... Such high water with opposing winds never observed previously," he wrote in a telegram to the bureau's headquarters in Washington.[114] But less than half the population evacuated the island, and some sightseers even came over from Houston to view the spectacle of the huge and powerful surf. Cline rode down the beach in a horse-drawn buggy, warning people to get to the mainland. But for most part it was too late, and his warning fell on deaf ears. A steamship broke free of its moorings and destroyed three bridges to the mainland. As people fled to higher ground, waves raged inward from both the gulf and the bay. Homes disintegrated, and rushing waters swept people away. Cline's aides measured speeds of 100 mph before their anemometer was blown away, and the wind would eventually peak at 150 mph.

---

113 *http://www.eyewitnesstohistory.com/galveston.html*. Retrieved: 11-11-2015.

114 *http://www.galvestonghost.com/1900storm.html*. Retrieved: 11-11-2015.

Cline's own home was battered by the waves and heavy debris and eventually collapsed. "My residence went down with about 50 persons who had sought it out for safety, and all but 18 were hurled into eternity. Among the lost was my wife, who never rose above the water after the wreck of the building," Cline wrote in his report. Almost a month would pass before Cora May Cline's body was found among the mounds of debris that littered the city. Cline saw his wife and baby daughter sink and were sucked down into blackness and unconsciousness. Cline himself nearly drowned but recovered and when he found himself clinging to his youngest child. His brother Joseph had grabbed Cline's other two children, and they managed to keep afloat for three hours on wreckage until the worst of the storm had passed. "The roofs of the houses and timbers were flying through the streets as though they were paper, and it appeared suicidal to attempt a journey through the flying timbers," Cline wrote later that month in a report to his superiors.[115]

St. Mary's Orphanage, home to 93 children and 10 Catholic nuns, stood near the beach and was one of the first buildings to succumb to the storm. The sisters also operated St. Mary's Infirmary in Galveston. It was the first Catholic hospital in the state, established in 1867. The sisters were called to Galveston by Catholic Bishop Claude M. Dubuis in 1866 to care for the many sick and infirm in what was the major port of entry for Texas. They were also charged with caring for orphaned children, most of whom had lost their parents during yellow fever epidemics, which were prevalent during this time period. At first the Sisters of Charity opened an orphanage within the hospital, but later moved it three miles to the west on beachfront property on the former estate of Captain Farnifalia Green. The location seemed ideal because it was far away from the town and the threat of yellow fever. The ten sisters in her order who ran St. Mary's Orphanage back then and 90 of the children they cared for perished when the hurricane demolished the building complex that evening.

The dormitories had sat on a piece of ground called Green's Bayou on the outskirts of the island town of Galveston. But as the 1900 hurricane approached, the waters of the Gulf and the bayou swelled and came ashore to surround the orphanage. The sister moved all the children to the newer girl's dormitory. As they looked out, they saw the boys building disintegrate in the storm. So to ease the fears of the children, the nuns led them in prayers and hymns. One in particular was called 'Queen of the Waves', and this was a hymn traditionally sung by French fishermen during storms. By nightfall, 140 miles an hour winds

---

115 Ibid.

howled around the orphanage, and the sisters took desperate measures. They had cut the clothesline down, and each sister had about six or eight children tied to her side like mountain climbers to keep them from separating from each other during the ferocious storm. In this way, they had hoped to hold on to the children and lead them to safety. Unfortunately, their efforts were to no avail.

Eventually, the girl's dormitory gave way and collapsed, dumping the 93 children and 10 sisters into the raging waters and powerful winds of the storm. When the bodies of the children and sisters were later discovered, many of them were still tied together with the sisters' hand still tightly holding the children's hand (according to the three survivors the Catholic sisters had promised the children that they would not let them go-a promise they kept even in death). Days after the storm, in a strange but sad twist of fate, the searchers found a child dead on the beach, when they lifted the toddler, the body of another child and then another emerged from the sand. The only survivors were three boys, William Murney, Frank Madera and Albert Campbell, who miraculously managed to cling to an uprooted tree as it was tossed around by the rising floodwaters. After floating for more than a day, they were eventually able to make their way into town, where they told the other sisters what had happened at St Mary's Orphanage. Firmly committed to the healing ministry of Jesus Christ, the Sisters repaired St. Mary's Orphanage and one year later opened a new orphanage. Today the sisters have extended their ministry to other states and foreign countries.

Carrying out bodies just removed from the wreckage; on the city of Galveston (Courtesy of Wikipedia).

Water continued to rise until the whole island was submerged by 3 p.m., and by midnight waves 15 feet high tore buildings apart with contemptuous ease. "Some of them were on rooftops, while some of them were in trees, some of them were hanging on to logs and other stuff in the water," recalled a survivor, Maybelle Doolin. Doolin's father and his three stepbrothers spent hours in a row boat pulling people from the debris filled water; they are credited with saving 200 lives. Historians don't know exactly how many people perished, but they believe it could have been as many as 12,000, but the official total is about 6,000 persons in Galveston. This exact total is not known and perhaps will never, ever be known because no one really knows how many non-residents were in the busy city at the time of the disaster or how many were lost at sea. Sadly, nearly everyone in Galveston lost family and friends.[116]

Milton Elford was a young man living in Galveston with his mother, father and a young nephew, Dwight. Milton was the only one of his family to survive the storm. He described his experience in a letter to his brothers in North

116 *http://www.galvestonghost.com/1900storm.html.* Retrieved: 12-12-2015.

Dakota. We join his story as the rising water and intensity of the storm persuade the family to leave their home for a sturdier brick house across the street:

"We left our house about 4 o'clock, thinking we would be safer in a larger house, not dreaming that even that house would be washed away. We went across the street to a fine large house, built on a brick foundation high off the ground. About 5, it grew worse and began to break up the fence, and the wreckage of other houses was coming against us.

"We had arranged that if the house showed signs of breaking up, I would take the lead and Pa would come next, with Dwight and Ma next. In this way, I could make a safe place to walk, as we would have to depend on floating debris for rafts. There were about fifteen or sixteen in the house besides us. They were confident the house would stand anything; if not for that, we would probably have left on rafts before the house went down. We all gathered in one room; all at once the house went from its foundation and the water came in waist-deep, and we all made a break for the door but could not get it open. We then smashed out the window, and I led the way. I had only got part way out when the house fell on us.

"I was hit on the head with something, and it knocked me out and into the water head first. I do not know how long I was down, as I must have been stunned. I came up and got hold of some wreckage on the other side of the house. I could see one man on some wreckage to my left and another on my right. I went back to the door that we could not open. It was broken, and I could go part way in, as one side of the ceiling was not within four or five feet, I think, of water. There was not a thing in sight. I went back and got on the other side, but no one ever came up that I could see. We must all have gone down at the same time, but I cannot tell what they did not come up.

"I then started to leave by partly running and swimming from one lot of debris to another. The street was full of tops and sides of houses, and the air was full of flying boards. I think I gained about a block on the debris in this way and got in the shelter of some buildings, but they were fast going down, and I was afraid of getting buried. Just then, the part I was on started down the street, and I stuck my head and shoulders in an old tool chest that was lying in the debris that I was on. I could hardly hold this down on its side from being blown away, but that is what saved my life again. When the water went down about 3 a.m., I was about five blocks from where I started. My head was bruised and legs and hands cut a little, which I did not find until Monday, and then I could hardly get my hat on.... As soon as it was light enough, I went back to the location of the house, and not a sign of it could be found, and not a sign any house within two blocks, where before there was scarcely a vacant lot. I then went to the City Hall to see the chief of police, to get some help to recover the corpses, thinking, I guess, that I was the only one in that fix.

"The firemen and others started before noon to bring in corpses; they brought them in in wagon loads of about a dozen at a time, laid them down in rows to be identified, and the next day they were badly decomposed and were loaded on boats and taken to sea, only to wash back on the beach. They then started to bury them wherever they were found, but yesterday (Wednesday) the corpses were ordered burned. Men started removing the debris and burning it, and when they came upon a corpse, it is just thrown on the pile."[117]

Wrecked Negro High School Building, Galveston, Texas after the Great Galveston Hurricane of 1900 (Courtesy of Wikipedia)

[117] Milton Elford's account appears in: Halstead, Murat, Galveston: The Horrors of a Stricken City (1900); Bixell, Patricia, Galveston and the 1900 Storm (2000); Larson, Erick, *Isaac's Storm* (1999).

The next account of this storm is the account of Isaac M. Cline, the Senior Weather Bureau employee present at Galveston, of the events leading up to the storm, his personal experiences in the storm, and the aftermath. The horror of Galveston is only partly described in this work. He was probably somewhat still in shock when he wrote this report, as he lost his wife when his house collapsed during the storm, and virtually all of his possessions. In a later biographical work, he referred to the shooting of hundreds of looters by vigilantes in the aftermath of the storm and the cremation of hundreds of unknown storm victims who otherwise would have decomposed where they lay. This particular report is excerpted from the NOAA's *Monthly Weather Review* for September 1900.

SPECIAL REPORT ON THE GALVESTON HURRICANE OF SEPTEMBER 8, 1900

By Isaac M. Cline, Local Forecast Official and Section Director

"The hurricane which visited Galveston Island on Saturday, September 8, 1900, was no doubt one of the most important meteorological events in the world's history. The ruin which it wrought beggars' description, and conservative estimates place the loss of life at the appalling figure, 6,000.

"A brief description of Galveston Island will not be out of place as introductory to the details of this disaster. It is a sand island about thirty miles in length and one and one-half to three miles in width. The course of the island is southwest to northeast, parallel with the southeast coast of the State. The City of Galveston is located on the east end of the island. To the northeast of Galveston is Bolivar Peninsula, a sand spit about twenty miles in length and varying in width from one-fourth of a mile to about three miles. Inside of Galveston Island and Bolivar Peninsula is Galveston Bay, a shallow body of water with an area of nearly five hundred square miles. The length of the bay along shore is about fifty miles, and its greatest distance from the Gulf coast is about twenty-five miles. The greater portion of the bay lies due north of Galveston. That portion of the bay which separates the island west of Galveston from the mainland is very narrow, being only about two miles in width in places, and discharges into the Gulf of Mexico through San Louis Pass.

"The main bay discharges into the Gulf between the jetties; the south one being built out from the northeast end of Galveston Island and the north one from the most southerly point of Bolivar Peninsula. The channel between the jetties is twenty-seven to thirty feet in depth at different stages of the tide. There are channels in the harbor with a depth of thirty to thirty-five feet, and there is an area of nearly two thousand acres with an anchorage depth of eighteen feet or more. The mainland for several miles in the back of the bay is very low, in fact much of it is lower than Galveston Island, and it is so frequently overflowed by high tide that large areas present a marshy appearance. These are in brief the physical conditions of the territory devastated by the hurricane.

"The usual signs which herald the approach of hurricanes were not present in this case. The brick-dust sky was not in evidence to the smallest degree. This feature, which has been distinctly observed in other storms that have occurred in this section, was carefully watched for, both on the evening of the 7th and the morning of the 8th. There were cirrus clouds moving from the southeast during the forenoon of the 7th, but by noon only alto-stratus from the northeast were observed. About the middle of the afternoon, the clouds were divided between cirrus, alto-stratus, and cumulus, moving from the northeast.

"A heavy swell from the southeast made its appearance in the Gulf of Mexico during the afternoon of the 7th. The swell continued during the night without diminishing, and the tide rose to an unusual height when it is considered that the wind was from the north and northwest. About 5 a.m. of the 8th, Mr. J. L. Cline, Observer, called me and stated that the tide was well up in the low parts of the city and that we might be able to telegraph important information to Washington. He having been on duty until nearly midnight was told to retire, and I would look into conditions. I drove to the Gulf, where I timed the swells, and then proceeded to the office and found that the barometer was only one-tenth of an inch lower than it was at the 8 p.m. observation of the 7th. I then returned to the Gulf, made more detailed observations of the tide and swells, and filed the following telegram addressed to the Central Office in Washington:

"Unusually heavy swells from the southeast, intervals of one to five minutes, overflowing in the low places to the south portion of city, three to four blocks from beach. Such high water with opposing winds never observed previously. Broken stratus and strato-cumulus clouds predominated during the early forenoon of the 8th, with the blue sky visible here and there. Showery weather commenced at 8:45 a.m., but dense clouds and heavy rain were not in evidence until about noon, after which dense clouds with rain prevailed.

"The winds during the forenoon of the 8th was generally north, but oscillated, at intervals of five to ten minutes, between northwest and northeast, and continued so up to 1 p.m. After 1 p.m. the wind was mostly northeast, although as late as 6:30 p.m. it would occasionally back to the northwest for one or two minutes at a time. The prevailing wind was from the northeast until 8:30 p.m., when it shifted to the east, continuing from this direction until about 10 p.m. After 10 p.m. the wind was from the southeast, and after about 11 p.m., the prevailing direction was from the south or southwest. The directions after 11 p.m. are from personal observations. A storm velocity was not attained until about 1 p.m. after which the wind increased steadily and reached a hurricane velocity about 5 p.m. The greatest velocity for five minutes was 84 miles per hour at 6:15 p.m. With two minutes at the rate of 100 miles per hour. The anemometer blew away at this time, and it is estimated that prior to 8 p.m. the wind attained a velocity of at least 120 miles per hour. For a short time, about 8 p.m., just before the wind shifted to the east, there was a distinct lull, but when it came out from the east and southeast it appeared to come with greater fury than before. After shifting to the south at about 11 p.m., the wind steadily diminished in velocity, and at 8 a.m. on the morning of the 9th was blowing at the rate of 20 miles per hour from the south.

"The barometer commenced falling on the afternoon of the 6th and continued falling steadily but slowly up to noon of the 8th, when it read 29.42 inches. The barometer fell rapidly from noon until 8:30 p.m. of the 8th, when it registered 28.48 inches, a fall of pressure of about one inch in eight and one-half hours. After 8:30 p.m. the barometer rose at the same rapid rate that had characterized the fall. The barograph trace sheet during this storm, from noon September 6 to noon September 10, is enclosed as fig. 1. On account of the rapid fall in pressure, Mr. John d. Blagden, Observer, took readings of the mercurial barometer as a check on the barograph, and readings are as follows:

Time.	Readings.	Time.	Readings.
5:00 p.m.............	29.05	6:40 p.m............	28.75
5:11 p.m.............	29.00	6:48 p.m............	28.70
5:30 p.m.............	28.95	7:15 p.m............	28.69
5:50 p.m.............	28.90	7:40 p.m............	28.62
6:06 p.m.............	28.86	8:00 p.m............	28.55
6:20 p.m.............	28.82	8:10 p.m............	28.53

"These readings confirm the low pressure shown by barograph and indicate the great intensity of the hurricane. Mr. Blagden looked after the instruments during the hurricane in a heroic and commendable manner. He kept the wires of the self-registering apparatus intact as long as it was possible for him to reach the roof. The rain gauge blew away about 6 p.m., and the thermometer shelter soon followed. All the instruments in the thermometer shelter were broken, except the thermograph which was found damaged but has been put in working order.

"Storm warnings were timely and received a wide distribution, not only in Galveston, but throughout the coast region. Warning messages were received from the Central Office at Washington on September 4, 5, 6, 7, and 8. The high tide on the morning of the 8th, with storm warning flying, made it necessary to keep one man constantly at the telephone giving out information. Hundreds of people who could not reach us by telephone came to the Weather Bureau office seeking advice. I went down on Strand Street and advised some wholesale commission merchants who had perishable goods on their floors to place them 3 feet above the floor. One gentleman has informed me that he carried out my instructions, but the wind blew his goods down. The public was warned, over the telephone and verbally, that the wind would go by the east to the south and that the worst was yet to come. People were advised to seek secure places for the night. As a result, thousands of people who lived near the beach or in small houses moved their families into the center of the city and were thus saved.

"Those who lived in large strong buildings, a few blocks from the beach, one of whom was the writer of this report, thought that they could weather the wind and tide. Soon after 3 p.m., conditions became so threatening that it was deemed essential that a special report be sent at once to Washington. Mr. J. L. Cline, Observer, took the instrumental readings while I drove first to the bay and then to the Gulf, and finding that half the streets of the city were under water added the following to the special observation at 3:30 p.m.: "Gulf rising, water covers streets of about half of city." Having been on duty since 5 a.m., after giving this message to the observer, I went home to lunch. Mr. J. L. Cline went to the telegraph offices through water from two to four feet deep and found that the telegraph wires had all gone down; he then returned to the office, and by inquiry learned that the long distance telephone had one wire still working to Houston, over which he gave the message to the Western Union telegraph office at Houston to be forwarded to the Central Office at Washington.

"I reached home and found the water around my residence waist deep. I at once went to work assisting people, who were not securely located, into my residence, until forty or fifty persons were housed therein. About 6:30 p.m. Mr. J. L. Cline, who had left Mr. Blagden at the office to look after the instruments, reached my residence, where he found the water neck deep. He informed me that the barometer had fallen below 29.00 inches that no further messages could be gotten off on account of all wires being down, and that he had advised everyone he could see to go to the center of the city; also, that he thought we had better make an attempt in that direction. At this time, however, the roofs of houses and timbers were flying through the streets as though they were paper, and it appeared suicidal to attempt a journey through the flying timbers. Many people were killed by flying timbers about this time while endeavoring to escape to town.

"The water rose at a steady rate from 3 p.m. until about 7:30 p.m., when there was a sudden rise of about four feet in as many seconds. I was standing at my front door, which was partly open, watching the water, which was flowing with great rapidity from east to west. The water at this time was about eight inches deep in my residence, and the sudden rise of 4 feet brought it above my waist before I could change my position. The water had now reached a stage 10 feet above the ground at Rosenberg Avenue (Twenty-fifth Street) and Q Street, where my residence stood. The ground was 5.2 feet elevation, which made the tide 15.2 feet. The tide rose the next hour, between 7:30 and 8:30 p.m., nearly five feet additional, making a total tide in that locality of about twenty feet. These observations were carefully taken and represent to within a few tenths of a foot the true conditions. Other personal observations in my vicinity confirm these estimates. The tide, however, on the bay or north side of the city did not obtain a height of more than 15 feet. It is possible that there was 5 feet of backwater on the Gulf side as a result of debris accumulating four to six blocks inland. The debris is piled eight to fifteen feet in height.

By 8 p.m. a number of houses had drifted up and lodged to the east and southeast of my residence, and these with the force of the waves acted as a battering ram against which it was impossible for any building to stand for any length of time, and at 8:30 p.m. my residence went down with about fifty persons who had sought it for safety, and all but eighteen were hurled into eternity.

"Among the lost was my wife, who never rose above the water after the wreck of the building. I was nearly drowned and became unconscious but recovered through being crushed by timbers and found myself clinging to my youngest child, who had gone down with me and my wife. Mr. J. L. Cline joined me five minutes later with my other two children and with them and a woman and child we picked up from the raging waters; we drifted for three hours, landing 300 yards from where we started. There were two hours that we did not see a house nor any person, and from the swell we inferred that we were drifting to sea, which, in view of the northeast wind then blowing, was more than probable.

"During the last hour that we were drifting, which was with southeast and south winds, the wreckage on which we were floating knocked several residences to pieces. When we landed about 11:30 p.m., by climbing over floating debris to a residence on Twenty-eighth Street and Avenue P, the water had fallen about 4 feet. It continued falling, and on the following morning the Gulf was nearly normal. While we were drifting, we had to protect ourselves from the flying timbers by holding planks between us and the wind, and with this protection we were frequently knocked great distances. Many persons were killed on top of the drifting debris by flying timbers after they had escaped from their wrecked homes. In order to keep on the top of the floating masses of wrecked buildings, one had to be constantly on the lookout and continually climbing from drift to drift. Hundreds of people had similar experiences.

"Sunday, September 9, 1900, revealed one of the most horrible sights that ever a civilized people looked upon. About three thousand homes, nearly half of the residences portion of Galveston, had been completely swept out of existence, and probably more than six thousand persons had passed from life to death during that dreadful night. The correct number of those who perished will probably never be known, for many entire families are missing. Where 20,000 people lived on the 8th, not a house remained on the 9th, and who occupied the houses may, in many instances, never be known. On account of the pleasant Gulf breezes, many strangers were residing temporarily near the beach, and the number of these that were lost cannot yet be estimated. I enclose a chart, fig. 2, which shows, by shading, the area of total destruction. Two charts of this area have been drawn independently; one by Mr. A. G. Youens, inspector for the local board of underwriters, and the other by myself and Mr. J. L. Cline. The two charts agree in nearly all particulars, and it is believed that the chart enclosed represents the true conditions as nearly as it is possible to show them. That portion of the city west of Forty-Fifth Street was sparsely settled, but there were several splendid residences in the southern part of it.

"Many truck farmers and dairy men resided on the west end of the island, and it is estimated that half of these were lost, as but very few residences remain standing down the island. For two blocks, inside the shaded area, the damage amounts to at least fifty percent of the property. There is not a house in Galveston that escaped injury, and there are houses totally wrecked in all parts of the city. All goods and supplies not over eight feet above floor were badly injured, and much was totally lost. The damage to buildings, personal, and other property in Galveston County is estimated at above thirty million dollars. The insurance inspector for Galveston states that there were 2,636 residences located prior to the hurricane in the area of total destruction, and he estimates 1,000 houses totally destroyed in other portions of the city, making a total of 3,636 houses totally destroyed. The value of these buildings alone is estimated at $5,500,000.

"The grain elevators which were full of grain suffered the smallest damage. Ships have resumed loading and work is being rushed day and night. The railroad bridges across the bay were washed away, but one of these has been repaired and direct rail communication with the outside world was established within eleven days after the disaster. Repairs and extensions of wharves are now being pushed forward with great rapidity. Notwithstanding the fact that the streets are not yet clean and dead bodies are being discovered daily among the drifted debris, the people appear to have confidence in the place and are determined to rebuild and re-establish themselves here.

"Galveston being one of the richest cities of its size in the United States, there is no question but that business will soon regain its normal condition and the city will grow and prosper as she did before the disaster. Cotton is now coming in by rail from different parts of the State, and by barge from Houston. The wheels of commerce are already moving in a manner which gives assurance for the future. Improvements will be made stronger and more judiciously; for the past twenty-five years, they have been made with the hurricane of 1875 in mind, but no one ever dreamed that the water would reach the height observed in the present case. The railroad bridges are to be built ten feet higher than they were before. The engineer of the Southern Pacific Company has informed me that they will construct their wharves so that they will withstand even such a hurricane as the one we have just experienced. I believe that a sea wall, which would have broken the swells, would have saved much loss of both life and property. I base this view upon observations which I have made in the extreme northeastern portion of the city, which is practically protected by the south jetty; this part of the city did not suffer more than half the damage that other similarly located districts, without protection, sustained.

From the officers of the U.S. Engineer tug *Anna*, I learned that the wind at the mouth of the Brazos River went from north to southwest by way of west. This shows that the center of the hurricane was near Galveston, probably not more than 30 miles to the westward. The following towns have suffered great damage, both in the loss of life and property: Texas City, Dickinson, Lamarque, Hitchcock, Arcadia, Alvin, Manvel, Brazoria, Columbia, and Wharton. Other towns further inland have suffered, but not so seriously. The exact damage at these places cannot be ascertained. A list of those lost in Galveston, whose names have been ascertained up to the present time, contains 3,536 names."[118]

DR. ISAAC. M. CLINE,
Local Forecast Official and Section Director,
Weather Bureau, Galveston, Texas.

At the time of the 1900 storm, the highest point in the city of Galveston was only about 9 feet above mean sea level. The hurricane had brought with it a storm surge of over 15 feet, which washed over the entire island. The surge knocked buildings off their foundations, and the surf pounded them to pieces. Over 3,600 homes were destroyed, and a wall of debris faced the ocean.

The few buildings that survived, mostly solidly built mansions and houses along the Strand, are today maintained as tourist attractions. As terrible as the damage to the city's buildings was, the human cost was even greater. Due to the destruction of the bridges to the mainland and the telegraph lines, no word of the city's destruction was able to reach the mainland. At 11 a.m. on September 9, one of the few ships at the Galveston wharfs to survive the storm, the *Pherabe*, arrived in Texas City on the western side of Galveston Bay. It carried six messengers from the city. When they reached the telegraph office in Houston at 3 a.m. on September 10, a short message was sent to Texas Governor Joseph D. Sayers and President William McKinley: "I have been deputized by the mayor and Citizen's Committee of Galveston to inform you that the city of Galveston is in ruins." The messengers reported an estimated five hundred dead. This was considered to be an exaggeration at the time.[119]

---

118 The United States Weather Bureau Office, *Special Report on the Galveston Hurricane of September 8, 1900,* Monthly Weather Review Vol. XXVIII No. 9, pgs. 371-377. This account was courtesy of the United States Weather Bureau Office. Galveston, Texas, September 23, 1900. After the storm the United States Government honored Isaac Cline for his "Heroic devotion to duty" during the storm.

119 *https://en.wikipedia.org/wiki/1900_Galveston_hurricane.* Retrieved: 12-12-2015.

Three young men walking among the ruins of St. Patrick's Church, after the Great Galveston Hurricane (Courtesy of www.wikipedia.org).

The city of Houston knew a powerful storm had blown through and had made preparations to provide assistance. Workers set out by rail and ship for the island almost immediately. Rescuers arrived to find a city completely devastated. About six to eight thousand people had lost their lives, a fifth of the island's population. Most had drowned or been crushed as the waves pounded the debris that had been their homes hours earlier. Many survived the storm itself but died after several days trapped under the wreckage of the city, with rescuers unable to reach them. The rescuers could hear the screams of the survivors as they walked on the debris trying to rescue those they could. They realized that there was no hope.

The bodies were so numerous that burial was not a viable option because of the fear of spreading of diseases and contamination. Initially, the dead were taken out to sea and weighted down and dumped into the Gulf of Mexico. However, the currents of the Gulf simply washed the bodies back onto the beach, leaving even more treacherous work for the cleanup crews, so a new solution was needed. So funeral pyres were set up to burn the bodies or buried in mass graves wherever the dead were found. In the aftermath of the storm, pyres burned for weeks and the city reeked with burnt and rotting flesh. Authorities had to pass out free strong whiskey to the work crews that had to throw the bodies of their wives and children on the burn piles. It is said that the stench from the dead bodies could be smelled as far as 50 miles out at sea. To make matters worse, bodies were scattered everywhere after the storm. A hundred victims hung from a grove of cedar trees, deposited in branches by the 20-foot storm surge that swept shattered buildings and houses into a pile of debris three stories high. No one knows how many bodies never emerged from the sea, but many residents refused to eat scavenging shrimp and crabs for years afterward. Interestingly enough, more people were killed in this single storm than have been killed in the over the top ten deadliest hurricanes that have struck the United States combined, and that includes the recent Hurricane Katrina.

Deadliest North Atlantic Hurricanes on Record

The 10 Deadliest Tropical Cyclones for the Atlantic Rank, Name, Areas of Largest Loss		Dates	Deaths
1.	"Great Hurricane of 1780": Martinique, Barbados, St. Eustatius	10-16 Oct 1780	22000
2.	**"Great Galveston Hurricane of 1900": Galveston Island**	**8 Sep 1900**	**8000-12000**
3.	Mitch: Honduras, Nicaragua, Guatemala, El Salvador, Belize	10/22 - 11/5 1998	9086
4.	Fifi: Honduras	14-19 Sep 1974	8000-10000
5.	"The Dominican Republic Hurricane of 1930": Dominican Republic	1-6 Sep 1930	8000
6.	Flora: Haiti, Cuba	9/30-10/8 1963	8000
7.	"Pointe-a-Pitre Bay Hurricane": Guatemala	6 Sep 1776	6000
8.	"Newfoundland Banks": Newfoundland	9-12 Sep 1775	4000
9.	"Hurricane of San Ciriaco": Puerto Rico, Carolinas	8-19 Aug 1899	3433
10.	"Great Okeechobee-San Felipe II Hurricane": Florida, Puerto Rico, Martinique, Guadeloupe, Turks & Caicos	12-17 Sep 1928	3411

Deadliest North Atlantic Hurricanes on Record-Courtesy of: 1995: Rappaport, Edward N. and Fernandez-Partagas, Jose; "The Deadliest Atlantic Tropical Cyclones, 1492-1994," NOAA Technical Memorandum NWS NHC-47, National Hurricane Center 2) Wikipedia Encyclopedia

Survivors set up temporary shelters in surplus U.S. Army tents along the shore. They were so numerous that observers began referring to it as the "White City on the Beach." Others constructed so-called "storm lumber" homes, using salvageable material from the debris to build shelter. By September 12, the first post-storm mail was received at Galveston. The next day, basic water service was restored, and Western Union began providing minimal telegraph service. Within three weeks, cotton was again being shipped out of the port. Prior to the Galveston Hurricane of 1900, Galveston was considered to be a beautiful and prestigious city and was known as "the New York of the South." Many people say that had it not been for the hurricane, Galveston would today be one of the nation's largest and most beautiful cities. The same proximity to the sea that had made the city of Galveston grow and prosper as a port city was to change Galveston, Texas, forever. However, after the hurricane, development shifted north to Houston, which was enjoying the benefits of the oil boom.

The dredging of the Houston Ship Channel in 1909 and 1914 ended Galveston's hopes of returning to its former state as a major commercial emporium. To prevent future storms from causing destruction like that of the 1900 hurricane, many improvements to the island were made. The first three miles of the 17-foot-high Galveston Seawall were built beginning in 1902, under the direction of Henry Martyn Robert. Phase one of the projects cost $1.6 million dollars, an astronomical amount at the time but considered a small price to pay for peace of mind and security from future hurricanes. In addition, an all-weather bridge was constructed to the mainland to replace the ones destroyed in the storm. Civil engineers also raised Galveston's elevation, the highest point of which before the storm was less than nine feet above sea level.

Thousands of homes and buildings were propped up so earth could be filled in underneath, a method that raised some structures as high as 17 feet. The most dramatic effort to protect the city was this raising. Dredged sand was used to raise the city of Galveston by as much as 17 feet above its previous elevation. Over 2,100 buildings were raised in the process, including the 3,000-ton St. Patrick's Church. The seawall and rising of the island were jointly named a National Historical Civil Engineering Landmark by the American Society of Civil Engineers in 2001. In 1915, a storm of similar strength and track to the 1900 hurricane struck Galveston. The 1915 storm brought a 12-foot storm surge, which tested the new seawall. Although 275 people lost their lives in the 1915 storm, this was a great reduction from the thousands that died in the 1900 hurricane.

The Galveston city government was reorganized into a commission government, a newly devised structure where the government consisted of a small group of commissioners, each responsible for one aspect of governance. This was prompted by fears that the existing city council would be unable to handle the problem of rebuilding the city. While Galveston succeeded in rebuilding after the storm, it would never regain its former prominence as one of the wealthiest communities in the nation. As a major Texas city, it was soon overshadowed by the emergence of nearby Houston as a center for the Texas oil industry and as a major port following the completion in 1914 of a ship channel that linked it directly to the Gulf of Mexico.

Today, Galveston is home to a major cruise port, two universities, and a major insurance corporation. Homes and other buildings that survived the hurricane have been preserved and give much of the city a Victorian look. The seawall, since extended to ten miles, is now an attraction itself, as hotels and tourist attractions have been built along its length in seeming defiance of future storms. Interestingly enough, the last reported survivor of the Galveston Hurricane of 1900, Mrs. Maude Conic of Wharton, Texas, died November 14, 2004, at the claimed age of 116 (census records indicate she was younger than that). A tradition that still goes on to this day is that from 1901, each year the city of Galveston holds a wreath-laying ceremony and a time of prayer in remembrance to those lost in this deadly storm. Modern observation and forecasting help ensure that if another storm of similar strength threatens Galveston, the city will not be caught by surprise.

The "Hurricane" of 1903--The storm was indicated to be a hurricane by many in the media at the time, but it wasn't, in fact, a tropical storm with 70 mph winds along the coast. It was the first such tropical storm or hurricane to impact the Jersey shore in one hundred years. It was also called the "Vagabond Hurricane" since it caused such a stir in media outlets such as Philadelphia and New York, which had people covering the storm for the various newspapers in those cities.

The Major Hurricane of 1906--In the early morning hours of October 17, a major Hurricane swept through the Upper Florida Keys from the southwest. Please note that many October hurricanes approach from the southwest mainly from the southern Caribbean Sea. Two large houseboats firmly moored on the Gulf side of Long Key were torn loose. One with 150 men aboard washed into the Atlantic, of which only 83 survived. The other houseboat washed into the bay and back to shore with no causalities. The *St. Lucie* sank off Elliot Key, killing 25. On Lower Matecumbe Key, two houseboats with 45 men were carried out to sea, never to be heard from again. As with powerful hurricanes, the number of lives lost varies, however 160 is a good estimate.

The Hurricane of 1909--As many as 2,000 persons died when a hurricane hit northeast Mexico.

The Atlantic-Gulf Hurricane of 1919--This fearsome cyclone was first detected near the Lesser Antilles on September 2. It moved generally west-northwestward for several days, passing near the Dominican Republic on September 4 and into the southeastern Bahamas on the 5th and 6th. At that time, it became a hurricane. A westward turn on September 7 took the center across the central Bahamas on the 7th and 8th and into the Straits of Florida on the 9th. The now large hurricane was of Category 4 intensity as the eye passed just south of Key West, Florida, and the Dry Tortugas on September 10. A continued west to west-northwestward motion brought the center to the Texas coast south of Corpus Christi as a Category 3 hurricane on September 14. The cyclone dissipated over northern Mexico and southern Texas the next day.

Although hurricane-force winds occurred over the Florida Keys and the central and south Texas coast, no reliable wind measurements are available from near the center. A storm surge of up to 12 feet inundated Corpus Christi, Texas, causing major damage to the coastal areas. A ship moored near the Dry Tortugas measured a pressure of 27.37 inches as the center passed, and based on this, the storm is ranked as one of the most intense hurricanes to hit the United States. The death toll was estimated at 600 to 900 people. Of these, more than 500 were lost on ten ships that either sunk or were reported missing. In fact, the steamer *Valbanera* was found sunken between Key West and the Dry Tortugas, with 488 persons onboard perishing. Damage in the United States was estimated at $22 million.

The Great Nassau Hurricane of 1926--According to Hurricane City Database, on average, Nassau is brushed or hit by a hurricane every 2.40 years and gets a direct hit once every 5.76 years. Being a very tiny island, it has the surrounding larger Bahamian Islands like Abaco, Andros and Grand Bahama having more affects and ranked higher and was impacted by a hurricane 60 times since 1871 when reliable data became available.[120] Part of the 1926 North Atlantic hurricane season, the Nassau Hurricane of 1926, as it was called in the *Monthly Weather Review,* was a destructive Category 4 hurricane on the Saffir-Simpson Hurricane Scale.

Although it weakened considerably before its Florida landfall, it was reported as one of the most severe storms to affect Nassau in the Bahamas in several years until the 1928 Lake Okeechobee Hurricane, which occurred just two years later. It decimated the entire Bahamas and impacted the sea-sponging industry (the number one industry in the Bahamas at the time) for years to follow. The storm also delivered flooding rains and loss of crops to the southeastern United States and Florida and the Bahamas. The system was first spotted east of the Lesser Antilles as a tropical disturbance on July 22. Moving northwest, the tropical storm passed near Dominica with moderate intensity, then passed just south of Puerto Rico on the 23rd with a gradual increase in intensity. San Juan, Puerto Rico, recorded maximum winds of around 66 mph

[120] *http://www.hurricanecity.com/rank.hmtl.* Retrieved: 12-12-2015.

and a low barometric pressure of 29.70 inches as the storm's center passed near the extreme southwest corner of Puerto Rico. The storm continued northwest and tracked over Hispaniola while strengthening to hurricane status.

The totally destroyed warehouse (showing barrels of rum for the illegal trans-shipment into the United States during the bootlegging era) of James Alvin Haugh in Nassau, Bahamas after the Great Nassau Hurricane of 1926 (Courtesy of Charles.J. Whelbell Collection, the Department of Archives, Nassau, Bahamas).

The storm continued strengthening, and by the time it reached the central Bahamas, it was at full Category 4 intensity with 140 mph winds. On July 26, while still moving northwest, the storm's eye passed directly over Nassau, where winds were unofficially estimated at 135 mph. Hundreds of schooners and men and boys were lost at sea in the Bahamas. Most of them were Bahamian men engaged in collecting sea sponges from the sea bottom on the various islands of the Bahamas to sell in the major cites of Paris, London and New York, where there was a great demand for them at the time. In the capital of Nassau alone, some 4,300 buildings were destroyed and far exceeded £250,000 to shipping in Nassau alone. The death toll in the Bahamas is often unclear, but approximately 258-268 persons lost their lives in the Bahamas from this storm.[121] Although damage reports are not clear, the storm was reported to

121 Wayne Neely, The *Great Bahamian Hurricanes of 1926: The Story of Three of the Greatest Hurricanes to Affect the Bahamas,* (Bloomington, iUniverse Publishing, 2007), pgs. 234, 248-294. Based on personal recollections from various storm survivors, Colonial Office files (CO23), local newspapers accounts, Out Island Commissioners' Reports, the Bahamas House of Assembly Reports and the Bahamas birth/death records.

be destructive around Nassau, where "some roofs were torn off entirely" and that the storm was "more fearful and devastating than any most people can remember", according to an eyewitness account posted in the July issue of the NWS Monthly Weather Review. Heavy damage was reported, and residents said it was the most severe storm there in many years. Trees, power poles, and various debris littered streets, and many people were left homeless. Automobiles at Nassau were also reported damaged by the storm, and flooding was reported.

Moving slowly, the storm weakened to Category 2 status while sliding up the Florida coast, making final landfall near Melbourne, Florida, on July 27 as a Category 1 hurricane. In Florida, the storm's lowest barometric pressure of 975 mbar (28.79 inches) was observed. The storm weakened rapidly as it moved inland, weakening to a tropical storm and eventually a depression as it moved across Georgia and Alabama while dumping heavy rains, resulting in serious flooding. It continued across the southeastern United States while losing tropical characteristics, gradually beginning to curve northeastward over Arkansas, Missouri, and the Ohio Valley, becoming extratropical on August 1. It finally dissipated the following day as it moved northeastward over Lake Ontario.

More than 287 people were killed in Puerto Rico, the Dominican Republic, and Florida by the storm. Prior to the record-breaking 2005 Atlantic hurricane season, this was the most intense hurricane ever recorded in July (with 140 mph winds) until Hurricane Emily of 2005, a Category 5 hurricane which had top sustained winds of 160 mph and a pressure of 929 mbar, broke the record set by the July 1926 Nassau Hurricane. Hurricane Dennis, also from 2005, was also still more intense in barometric pressure and wind strength than the Nassau Hurricane of July 1926. It must be noted that Hurricane Audrey was also more intense and occurred even earlier in the season in June.

The Great Miami Hurricane of 1926--According to Hurricane City Database, on average, Miami, Florida is brushed or hit by a hurricane every 2.00 years and gets a direct hit once every 2.00 years. Being a very exposed state, it is the state in the USA most frequently impacted by a hurricane and was impacted by a hurricane 72 times since 1871 when reliable data became available.[122] The "Great Miami" (or the Big Blow) Hurricane was first spotted as a tropical wave located 1,000 miles east of the Lesser Antilles on September 11th. The system moved quickly westward and intensified to hurricane strength as it moved to

---

122 *http://www.hurricanecity.com/rank.hmtl.* Retrieved: 12-12-2015.

the north of Puerto Rico on the 15th. Winds were reported to be nearly 150 mph as the hurricane passed over the Turks Islands on the 16th and through the Bahamas on the 17th. Little in the way of meteorological information on the approaching hurricane was available to the Weather Bureau in Miami. As a result, hurricane warnings were not issued until midnight on September 18th, which gave the booming population of South Florida little notice of the impending disaster. The Category 4 hurricane's eye moved directly over Miami Beach and downtown Miami during the morning hours of the 18th. This cyclone produced the highest sustained winds ever recorded in the United States at the time, and the barometric pressure fell to 27.61 inches or 935 mbar, and winds peaked at 128 mph in Miami as the eye passed over that city. A storm surge of nearly 15 feet was reported in Coconut Grove.

The Pelicaus Sponge Warehouse in the background-totally destroyed in the Great Miami Hurricane of 1926 and workers in the foreground gathering the natural sea sponges after the hurricane had scattered them throughout the yard in Nassau, Bahamas. Collecting and selling natural sea sponges on the world markets in New York, Paris and London was the number one industry in the Bahamas during this era (Courtesy of the Charles. J. Whelbell Collection, the Department of Archives, Nassau, Bahamas).

Many casualties resulted as people ventured outdoors during the half-hour lull in the storm as the eye passed overhead. Most residents, having not experienced a hurricane, believed that the storm had passed and ventured outside during the lull. They were suddenly trapped and exposed to the eastern half of the hurricane shortly thereafter. Every building in the downtown district of Miami was damaged or destroyed. The town of Moore Haven on the south side of Lake Okeechobee was completely flooded by lake surge from the hurricane. Hundreds of people in Moore Haven alone were killed by this surge, which left behind floodwaters in the town for weeks afterward. This storm hit at the worst possible time for the fledgling city. Incorporated in 1896 following the extension of the Florida East Coast Railway by Henry Flagler, the city of Miami was at the end of its first boom period early in 1926.

As described in Galbraith's (1955) *The Great Crash: 1929*, the Great Miami Hurricane of 1926 was one of several factors that cooled the Jazz-Age speculative frenzy in Miami real-estate boom and brought the depression to South Florida three years before equity values collapsed worldwide in the great stock market crash of 1929 and the Great Depression of 1929. The storm also served as a lesson for those wishing to go outside during the eye's passage. The storm surge ranged from eight to fifteen feet and caused $150 million dollars in damage then, or $1.7 billion today. If a similar storm hit the Miami area today, it would cause an astronomical $90 billion in damage. The hurricane continued northwestward across the Gulf of Mexico and approached Pensacola on September 20th. The storm nearly stalled to the south of Pensacola later that day and buffeted the central Gulf Coast with 24 hours of heavy rainfall, hurricane force winds, and storm surge. The hurricane weakened as it moved inland over Louisiana later on September 21. Nearly every pier, warehouse, and vessel on Pensacola Bay was destroyed.

The Great Miami Hurricane of 1926 ended the economic boom in South Florida. Florida's economy didn't recover until the 1950s. With a highly transient population across southeastern Florida during the 1920s, the death toll is uncertain since more than 800 people were missing in the aftermath of the cyclone. A Red Cross report lists 373 deaths and 6,381 injuries as a result of the hurricane. However, the NWS reported that this storm was responsible for damages totaling well over $100 million dollars and approximately 550 deaths.

The University of Miami was founded in 1925 and opened its doors for the first time just days after the hurricane hit Florida on October 17, 1926, with 560 students. During the next two decades, it struggled through the Great Depression and came close to folding, at one-point filing for bankruptcy protection. When the school's football team took to the field for the first time in the fall of 1926, a team member suggested a nickname inspired by the great storm; the Hurricanes. The team adopted as its mascot the ibis, the bird that according folklore is the first to return after a hurricane passes. So the

University of Miami Hurricanes sports football team was named in memory of this catastrophe, and a name that is still used even to this day.

Great devastation in the city of Miami after the Great Miami Hurricane of 1926 (Courtesy of NOAA-NHC)

Hurricane #10 of the 1926 hurricane season--On October 14, a tropical storm developed in the southwest Caribbean Sea. It moved northward, becoming a major hurricane on the 20th before crossing Cuba and southeast Florida. It headed northeastward and strengthened into a Category 4 before hitting Bermuda on October 22. It became extratropical on the 23rd. The hurricane's impact caused severe damage in Cuba and 650 deaths. After the two earlier hurricanes, the Governor of the Bahamas requested assistance from the King of England to send a British ship to take hurricane relief supplies to the various islands throughout the Bahamas impacted by the storm. A frequent visitor to the Caribbean in the 1920's, the *HMS Valerian* sank when it was hit by this powerful hurricane leaving the Bahamas en-route to Bermuda on 22nd October, 1926. There was a loss of 88 of the crew of 115, it became one of the greatest peacetime losses for a British warship. Also sunk in this storm was the *HMS Eastway* with some 22 crew perishing in the general vicinity of HMS Valerian in the vicinity of Bermuda. The hurricane then passed directly over Bermuda, where it sank two British Naval warships (*HMS Valerian* and *HMS Eastway*), drowning 88 of 115 British sailors on the *HMS Valerian* and 22 on the *HMS Eastway*. The *HMS Valerian* was returning from the Bahamas after rendering assistance to the residents of the various islands in the Bahamas after two storms (Great Nassau Hurricane of 1926 and Great Miami Hurricane of 1926) decimated the Bahamas. Overall, the hurricane left 760 people dead and over $100 million dollars (1926 USD) in damage.

The Great Okeechobee Hurricane or Hurricane San Felipe Segundo of 1928

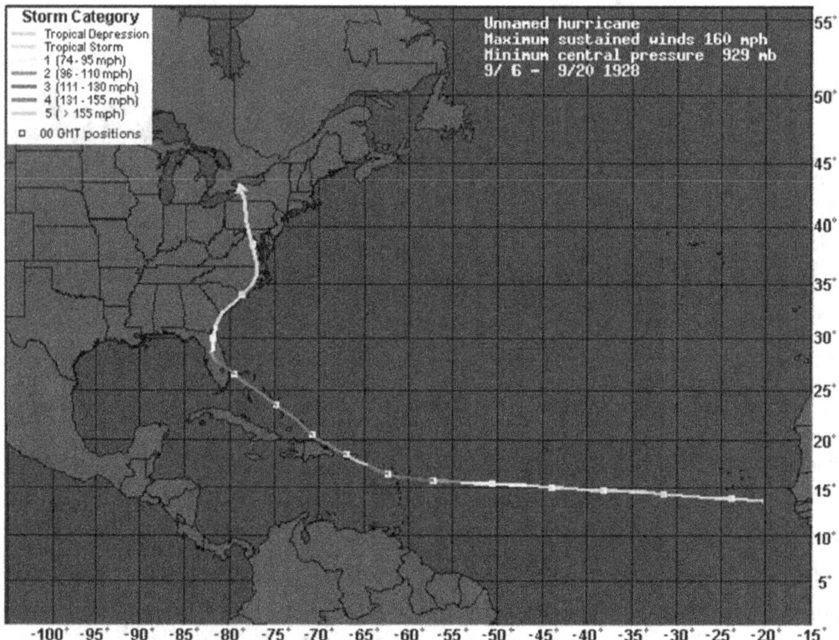

This map shows the track of the Great Okeechobee Hurricane of 1928 as it moved through the Leeward Islands, Puerto Rico, Dominican Republic, the Bahamas and the USA (Information courtesy of The Weather Underground Inc.)

The Great Okeechobee Hurricane of 1928 or Hurricane San Felipe Segundo, as it is called, was a powerful and deadly hurricane that struck the Leeward Islands, Puerto Rico, the Bahamas, and south-central Florida in September of the 1928 Atlantic hurricane season. On September 17, 1928, one of the worst hurricane of the twentieth century came unannounced into the lives of people of the Greater and Lesser Antilles, Puerto Ricans, Bahamians and Floridians, leaving utter devastation in its wake. The Great Okeechobee Hurricane, or Saint (San) Felipe Segundo (Spanish for 'second') Hurricane of 1928, as it came to be known, changed everything, from the landscape and its inhabitants' lives, to the Weather Bureau and U.S. Army Corps of Engineers' practices, to the measure and kinds of relief Floridians would receive during this great storm and the resulting pace of regional economic recovery. Over the years, Florida, the Bahamas and the rest of the Caribbean have experienced many great storms. Some have been not very deadly or destructive, while others have left horrendous damage and a significant amount of deaths, but all have tested the spirit, strength, and resolve of the people they affected. Some have passed namelessly and uneventfully into meteorological history, while others on the other hand made their presence felt in a significant way.

Each storm has brought its own distinctive wrath, though at times only in a limited region, like the Lake Okeechobee region in 1928, which felt the full effects of the storm. We can indeed say that Floridians over the years have proved that they can adapt and recover from any and everything that Mother Nature can throw at them. The importance of our appreciation of the power of these storms was made very clear during the devastating 1928 hurricane season. The Great Okeechobee Hurricane of 1928, or Saint Felipe (Phillip) Segundo Hurricane, was one of the most destructive and powerful storms to strike South Florida.

Today, it remains the only recorded hurricane to strike Puerto Rico at Category 5 strength, and the seventh most intense hurricane on record to make landfall in the United States. The San Felipe-Great Okeechobee Hurricane, as it is commonly called, was a classic Cape Verde type hurricane that was first detected over the tropical Atlantic on September 10, 1928, although it likely formed several days earlier. It moved westward through the Leeward Islands on the 12th. It then turned west-northwestward, making a direct hit on the island of Puerto Rico on the 13th (on the day of the feast of San-Felipe, hence the name San Felipe) as a Category 4 hurricane. It was remembered as the San Felipe Hurricane because the eye of the hurricane made landfall on the Christian feast day of Saint Phillip; the Latin American custom, since the Spanish colonial era began in 1492, was to name these storms upon their arrival after Catholic religious feast days. It was named "Segundo" (Spanish for "the Second") because of the eerie similarity in devastation with another hurricane which made landfall in Puerto Rico on that very same day 52 years earlier.

The hurricane caused devastation throughout its path. As many as 1,200 people were killed on the island of Guadeloupe. Puerto Rico was struck directly by this powerful storm at peak strength, killing at least 300 and leaving hundreds of thousands homeless. In South Florida, at least 2,500 persons were killed when storm surge from Lake Okeechobee breached the dike surrounding the lake, flooding an area covering hundreds of square miles. The lake itself holds enough water in it to give 300 gallons to every living person on Earth. In total, the hurricane killed at least 4,118 people and caused around $100 million in damages over the course of its path from the Caribbean to the United States.[123]

The exact number of those who perished in Florida in the Lake Okeechobee region can never be determined, because the Miami Daily News on September 25, 1928 gave a total of 2300 persons died, the Red Cross gave a total of 1810 persons killed and many other newspapers gave totals ranging from 1800 to 2350 persons who died from this hurricane. The official National Weather Service death toll was 1836 persons, and in 2003 this was revised up to 'at least 2,500', making the Okeechobee Hurricane the second-deadliest natural disaster in United States history, a record that still stands even to this day. However, the exact number of those who perished in the Okeechobee storm can never be confirmed because approximately 75% of the dead victims were blacks, and 75% of those blacks who perished were Bahamian migrant workers. Furthermore, it was complicated by the fact that most of them were known, even to their friends, only by a nickname. This was because most of these Bahamian migrants came in, worked, got paid, and went back home to their families after their work tenure had ended, and they were paid in cash, so there was little or no paperwork for them. If someone died, he might not be counted if no relative was looking for him.

Another reason the number cannot be determined was because of the fact that many persons were carried by the flood waters far into the sawgrass wastes. Furthermore, immediately after the storm, a considerable amount of time, money and effort was made to return this region back to some degree of normalcy and recover financially in the aftermath. As a result, rather than making an effort in obtaining an 'official' death toll and the names of those who perished in this hurricane they simply began the clean-up and rebuilding process as quickly as possible. This resulted in many bodies and skeletons were simply buried without any kind of documentation in makeshift mass graves. This was because they were too many to count, too decomposed to identify, and rotting so quickly that they had to be burned in mass graves so as to prevent the outbreak of diseases and contamination. As a result, many didn't get a decent funeral. Furthermore, many bodies and skeletons were also discovered years later, thereby increasing the death toll even more.

---

[123] Wayne Neely, *The Great Okeechobee Hurricane of 1928-The Story of the Second Deadliest Hurricane in US History and the Deadliest Hurricane in Bahamian History*, Bloomington, iUniverse Publishing, 2014), pg. 123.

The storm was first detected about 900 miles to the east of Guadeloupe on September 10, 1928, by the ship *S.S. Commack*. At the time, this was the most easterly report of a tropical cyclone ever received through a ship's radio. A Cape Verde-type hurricane, a post-hurricane analysis in the 1990s determined the storm likely formed about four days' prior between the Cape Verde Islands and the west coast of Africa. As the storm approached the eastern Caribbean, it was already a Category 3 hurricane on the Saffir-Simpson Scale. On September 12, the storm passed over Guadeloupe and then south of the other Leeward Islands; Guadeloupe reported a pressure of 27.76 inches (940 mbar), and a ship just south of St. Croix in the United States Virgin Islands reported it as an even stronger storm, with a pressure of 27.50 inches (931 mbar).

On the 13th, the storm made a direct passage over the island of Puerto Rico directly as a Category 5 hurricane, allegedly packing winds of 160 mph; reliable reports from San Juan placed the wind speed at 125 knots (145 mph), and a report from Guayama placed the pressure at 27.65 inches. The 160 mph wind speed measurement from Puerto Rico was taken by a cup anemometer in San Juan, 30 miles north of the storm's center, which measured 160 mph sustained winds three hours before the peak wind speed was reached; however, the instrument was destroyed soon after and could not be verified. This unverified reading was the strongest wind measurement ever reported for an Atlantic hurricane up until that time; not until Hurricane Dog of the 1950 hurricane season were stronger winds officially measured in an Atlantic storm, although some unmeasured storms like the Great Labor Day Hurricane of 1935 may have been stronger. Because of this measurement, the Okeechobee storm is considered to be the first hurricane in the Atlantic basin ever to reach Category 5 intensity, the highest possible rating on the Saffir-Simpson Hurricane Scale; although it is virtually certain that earlier hurricanes had achieved this strength (a likely candidate is the 'Great Havana Hurricane of 1846'), none had ever had their winds or pressure recorded properly.

The hurricane was also extremely large as it crossed Puerto Rico. Hurricane-force winds were measured in Guayama for 18 hours; since the storm was estimated to have been moving at 13 mph, the diameter of the storm's hurricane winds was estimated very roughly to be 234 miles. After leaving the Caribbean, the hurricane moved across the Turks and Caicos Islands and the Bahamas as a strong Category 4 hurricane, where it left great devastation and 21 persons dead. It continued to the west-northwest and made landfall in southern Florida on the evening of September 16. Atmospheric pressure at landfall was measured at 929 mbar, and winds "in excess" of 150 mph. The eye passed ashore in Palm Beach County near West Palm Beach, then moved directly over Lake Okeechobee. The hurricane's path turned northeast as it crossed Florida, taking it across northern Florida, eastern Georgia, and the Carolinas on September 19. It then moved inland and merged with a low-pressure system around Toronto on the 20th.

The hurricane moved directly over the Leeward Islands in the Caribbean, strengthening as it did so. On the island of Dominica, winds were clocked at 24 mph; there were no reports of damages. In Martinique, even further south of the storm's path, there were three fatalities. Guadeloupe received a near-direct hit from the storm, apparently with little warning; the death toll there was 600–1200, and damage reports relayed through Paris indicated "great destruction" on the island. Montserrat, just north of the storm's center, was warned in advance of the storm but still suffered £150,000 (1928 UKP) in damages and 42 deaths; Plymouth and Salem were devastated, and crop losses caused near-starvation conditions before relief could arrive. The storm passed to the south of the islands of St. Kitts and St. Croix, which suffered heavy damages to property and crops, but no reported fatalities. Damage reports from elsewhere in the Leeward Islands are not available.

The island of Puerto Rico received the worst of the storm's winds when the hurricane moved directly across the island at Category 5 strength. The island knew of the storm's approach well ahead of time; by about 36 hours in advance, all police districts were warned and radio broadcasts provided constant warnings to ships. Effective preparation is credited for the relatively low death toll of 312, and amazingly not a single ship was lost at sea in the vicinity of Puerto Rico. By comparison, the weaker 1899 Hurricane of San Ciriaco killed approximately 3,000 people. Property damage on the island from winds and rain, however, was catastrophic. The northeast half of the island received winds in excess of Category 3 strength, with hurricane-force winds lasting for as long as 18 hours. At least 10 inches (250 mm) of rain was dropped over the entire island, with much greater amounts of nearly 30 inches (750 mm) being received in some areas. Official reports stated that "several hundred thousand" people were left homeless, and property damages were significant and were estimated at $50 million ($698,000,000 million in 2015 U.S. dollars).[124]

The storm is remembered in Puerto Rico as the Hurricane of San Felipe because the eye of the cyclone made landfall on the Christian feast day of Saint Philip; the Latin American custom, since the Spanish colonial era began in

[124] *http://www.usinflationcalculator.com*. Retrieved: 12-12-2015.

1492, was to name hurricanes upon their arrival after Catholic religious feast days. It was named "Segundo", Spanish for "the Second", because of another destructive "Hurricane San Felipe" which struck Puerto Rico on that very same day 52 years earlier. The eye of the hurricane passed just south of Grand Bahama as a strong Category 4 hurricane, again causing very heavy damage. According to a firsthand account from the island, it was the worst storm in memory to strike the area.

As in Puerto Rico, however, authorities in the Bahamas were well aware of the hurricane's passage well ahead of time, and preparations minimized the loss of life in the islands. Furthermore, the number one industry in the Bahamas at the time was the gathering and selling of sea sponges, which required Bahamian men and boys to go out to several selected areas around the country to harvest these sponges. Sadly, the vast majority of these ships were caught in the three hurricanes in 1926, and as a result, many of these sponge schooners were lost and the casualty count very great in these three hurricanes. As a result, in the 1928 hurricane season, very little sponge schooners were at sea simply because they were still being rebuilt or new ones constructed, so the casualty level was minimal. The only report of fatalities was from a sloop lost at sea in the vicinity of Ambergris Cay, which went down with 18 persons on board and three other persons on land.

Loading bodies of those who perished in the Everglades into a truck at Belle Glade after the 1928 Great Okeechobee Hurricane (Florida Photographic Collection, Courtesy of the State Library and Archives of Florida).

The Lake Okeechobee (a Seminole word meaning 'Big Water') region in Florida in the late 1920s was a new and sparsely populated frontier. Only within 10 years or so had the Everglades region near Lake Okeechobee (the second largest body of fresh water that is entirely contained within U.S. borders) been drained to expose the fertile black muck soil for agriculture. Many Bahamian blacks and other nonwhite persons had come to or were brought to the Lake Okeechobee region to live and provide field labor. The lake itself, a large but very shallow lake on average less than 15 feet deep, was partially surrounded by a levee from 5 to 9 feet above the ground. Normally, the water level in the lake was maintained slightly above the level of the surrounding farmland so that the water could be drained off as needed. In the weeks before the hurricane, heavy rains had kept the lake level high and filled the ditches and canals around the lake. When the intense hurricane-force winds finally hit the lake, they lifted the waters out of Lake Okeechobee and tossed them southward, completely washing away entire communities and the dams that were built to protect them. Few were able to survive this gigantic wall of water.

The hurricane moved ashore in Palm Beach County on the evening of 16 September 1928, only two years after the Great Miami Hurricane of 1926 had devastated Miami, Florida. The damage sustained from this hurricane was estimated around $25 million, which when normalized for population, wealth, and inflation, would be around $338,000,000 today.[125] It passed over the eastern shore of Lake Okeechobee, causing terrible flooding in the towns of Pahokee, Canal Point, Chosen, Belle Glade, and South Bay and killing thousands. To this day, the number of people who lost their lives on the shores of Okeechobee is known only by a rough estimate because the majority of migrant workers were not included in censuses, and at the time state politics were dominated by northern Floridians, many of whom took a dim view to the immigrants in the south. This lack of sympathy toward the welfare of the migrant workers, most of whom were foreign born blacks, contributed to the lack of an accurate death toll.

Coastal damage in Florida near the point of landfall was catastrophic. Miami, well south of the point of landfall, escaped with very little damage; Hollywood and Fort Lauderdale suffered only slight damages. Northward, from Pompano Beach to Jupiter, buildings suffered serious damage from the heavy winds and 10-feet storm surge, which was heaviest in the vicinity of Palm Beach; total coastal damages were estimated at "several million" dollars.

---

125 *http://www.usinflationcalculator.com*. Retrieved: 12-12-2015.

Because of well-issued hurricane warnings, residents were prepared for the storm, and the loss of life in the coastal Palm Beach area was only 26.

Inland, the hurricane wreaked much more widespread destruction along the more heavily populated coast of Lake Okeechobee. Residents had been warned to evacuate the low ground earlier in the day, but after the hurricane did not arrive on schedule, many thought it had missed them and some people returned to their homes with deadly consequences. When the worst of the storm crossed the lake-with winds measured on the ground at around 140 mph-the south-blowing wind caused a storm surge to overflow the small dike that had been built at the south end of the lake. The resulting flood covered an area of hundreds of square miles, with water that in some places was over 20 feet deep. Houses were floated off their foundations and dashed to pieces against any obstacle they encountered. Most survivors and bodies were washed out into the Everglades, where many of the bodies were never found.

During the hurricane, there was a compelling story of a young girl who was tossed into the flood waters after her family's home was destroyed but was saved from sure death by an alligator who grabbed onto her arm and held her up above the flood waters to prevent her from drowning until help had arrived. She believed the reason she survived was because she prayed to God that he would keep her alive and he did. Furthermore, she believed that the frightened alligator did this to keep both her and him alive.

As the rear eyewall passed over the area, the flood reversed itself, breaking the dikes along the northern coast of the lake and causing a similar but smaller flood. Floodwaters persisted for several weeks, greatly impeding attempts to clean up the devastation. Burial services were quickly overwhelmed, and many of the bodies were placed into mass graves. Around 75% of the fatalities were migrant farm workers, making identification of both dead and missing bodies very difficult because most of them were only known by only their nicknames; as a result of this, the count of the dead is not very accurate. The Red Cross estimated the number of fatalities as 1,836 (coincidentally, the same total as Hurricane Katrina in 2005), which was taken as the official count by the National Weather Service for many years. However, in the summer of 2003 this was revised as "at least 2,500", making the Okeechobee hurricane the second-deadliest natural disaster in United States history. This was not as a result of any new evidence, but reflecting a need to have a more accurate number in time for the storm's seventy-fifth anniversary. The storm would then be officially classified as the second deadliest disaster in American history, behind only the Galveston Hurricane of 1900 and surpassing the Johnstown, Pennsylvania, flood of 1889, which killed 2,209 persons. Today, a levee breach of this kind is unlikely to occur again because of the much larger Herbert Hoover Dike that now contains the waters of Lake Okeechobee.

The Great Bahamas Hurricane of 1929--(also called **The 1929 Florida Hurricane**, and also known in the Bahamas as **The Great Andros Island Hurricane**) was the second hurricane and the only major hurricane during the very inactive 1929 Atlantic hurricane season. The hurricane was the only hurricane to cause any significant damage, resulting in $676,000 (1929 USD, $8.9 million 2016 USD) in damage in Florida. The total damage in the Bahamas is unknown, but the estimates seem to suggest several million dollars. Only a year after the Great Lake Okeechobee Hurricane, the hurricane caused only three deaths in southern Florida, a low number due to well-executed preparations.

The hurricane was much more severe in the Bahamas, where damage was near extreme due to the hurricane stalling over the area for well over three days. There, the hurricane caused well over 134 deaths (some historians claimed that this total is much higher than the official count, because some of the bodies were never found and were never included in the overall total). In Nassau, 456 houses were destroyed and 640 were badly damaged and 73% of the houses and about 95% of the churches (including, Salem Union Baptist Church, St. Ann's Church, St. Matthews Church, the Shirley Street Seven Day Adventist Church, Zion Baptist Church, St. Agnes Church, Wesley Methodist and Trinity Methodist Churches and others) in Nassau were destroyed. There were 64 sponging vessels were destroyed in Nassau Harbor including, *The Priscilla* and *Ollie Forde*. The American freighter *Wisconsin Bridge* with a crew of 34 persons was sunk near Abaco at Hole-in-the-Wall Lighthouse with all of the crew perishing. In Andros, the majority of the sponging fleet were destroyed. The majority of the houses, churches and fishing wharfs on the island of Andros were destroyed.

This storm was partly (or some may argue a major factor) responsible for ending the number one industry in the Bahamas at the time--the sea sponging industry. This industry, along with over-sponging and a fungus disease destroyed the Bahamian sponges in the late 1930s. It also destroyed the majority of the sponging schooners, the boats used to harvest the sponges and transfer them to Nassau, where they would be sold by auction. A very fascinating story that came out of this hurricane was the fact that a dog and his temporary master by the name of Prince Rolle were saved from death during this storm. This happened when the hurricane destroyed the sponging schooner they were on got destroyed in the hurricane. They were forced to swim from out to sea, back to the Andros mainland, but Prince was saved from sure death by the dog when he became too tired to swim any further. His dog companion by the name of 'Speak Your Mind' rescued him by swimming him on his back into the land, and when he got on the deserted mainland, the dog once again came to his rescue by catching a live land crab, and they survived by eating the uncooked crab.

The tragedy of this hurricane pierced the national memory, poems, songs and short stories were written about it, and those who survived. The most popular song 'Run Come See Jerusalem' is sung in most schools throughout the Bahamas and just about every Bahamian know the words of this song and can sing this popular song made famous by a popular Bahamian folk artist called Blind Blake, about the tragedy of three ships caught at sea during this hurricane.[126]

Total roof damage to the St. Agnes Church in Nassau, Bahamas after the Great Bahamas Hurricane of 1929. The cross of Jesus in the background was one of the few things that remained standing in this church building (Courtesy of the Charles Whelbell Collection, Department of Archives, Nassau, Bahamas).

The Great Dominican Republic Hurricane (Hurricane San Zenon) of 1930--The 1930 hurricane season was one of the least active seasons on record,

126 Wayne Neely, *The Great Bahamas Hurricane of 1929-The Story of the Greatest Bahamian Hurricane of the Twentieth Century*, (Bloomington, iUniverse Publishing, 2011).

with only two tropical cyclones known to have formed during the season. However, both reached hurricane strength, and the second of the two remains to this day one of the deadliest Atlantic hurricanes in recorded history. In Dominican Republic, the most active months for a cyclone is usually mid-August through September. This island gets a serious brush on average every 5.03 years. It is averaged that this country gets a direct hit once every 22.66 years. They had 22 hurricanes that have impacted this coast from 1871 to 2004 of which 5 were very devastating. The September 3, 1930: Hurricane San Zenón (4,500 (some accounts say more than 8,000) lives lost. This was one of the top five most devastating Caribbean cyclones); October 3, 1963: Hurricane Flora (400 lives lost); September 26, 1966: Hurricane Inez (60 lives lost); August 31, 1979: Hurricane David (1,000+ lives lost); September 22, 1988: Hurricane Georges (247 lives lost).

The very controversial President of the Dominican Republic at the time, Rafael Trujillo made a dramatic speech to the Dominican people after the hurricane said, "Given the enormous catastrophe that destroyed the city of Santo Domingo and its environs, I am deeply moved. The terrifying picture that has been offered to my eyes as soon as the fury of the wind allowed me to throw myself into the street, has left the most profound wound on my heart as both a citizen and president. At first, under the distress caused by such a fatal event, tears filled my eyes that I never dreamed would spill; however, aware of my responsibilities, I recovered quickly and have concentrated all my energy and all my activity in the task of providing relief to the people crushed by this terrible disaster."[127]

The 1930 Dominican Republic Hurricane was a small but intense Category 4 hurricane during the 1930 Atlantic hurricane season. This tropical cyclone killed as many as 8,000 people when it crossed Hispaniola, making it the fifth deadliest Atlantic hurricane on record. While crossing the Lesser Antilles, the hurricane had a relatively minor effect, bringing flooding and shipping delays. The city of Santo Domingo, Dominican Republic was nearly wiped away from the hurricane's strong winds. There, damage was estimated at $50 million (1930 USD). The death toll is estimated between 2,000 to 8,000 people. The rest of Hispaniola fared well during the storm, with little damage or flooding being seen. This is due to the small nature of the storm, as well as the effect the mountainous terrain had at rapidly weakening the hurricane.

---

127 *"El ciclón San Zenón deja miles de muertos y destrucción,"* El Diari Dominicano. Retrieved: 03-10- 2015.

The Hurricane of 1931--On September 6-10, a powerful storm devastated the Central American country of Belize, killing between 1,500-2,500 persons.

The Great Abaco Island Hurricane of 1932--The 1932 Bahamas hurricane, also known as the Great Abaco hurricane of 1932, was a large and powerful Category 5 hurricane that struck the Bahamas at peak intensity. The fourth tropical storm and third hurricane in the 1932 Atlantic hurricane season, it was also one of two Category 5 hurricanes in the Atlantic Ocean that year, the other being the 1932 Cuba hurricane. The 1932 Bahamas hurricane originated north of the Virgin Islands, became a strong hurricane, and passed over the northern Bahamas before recurving. The storm never made landfall on the continental United States, but its effects were felt in the northeast part of the country and in the Bahamas, especially on the Abaco Islands, where damage was very great. As of 2015, it is one of only three Category 5 Atlantic hurricanes to make landfall in the Bahamas at that intensity, the others having occurred in 1933 (The Treasure Coast Hurricane) and 1992 (Hurricane Andrew).

There were 18 people were reported killed on the island of Abaco, along with an additional 300 injured. This entire toll occurred in the Bahamas, notably on and around Abaco Island; damage estimates in dollars, however, were not released. Despite the large size and great intensity of the hurricane, ample warnings prevented loss of life and commerce at sea. As the storm passed north of the island of Cat Island, it caused a pressure of 29.47 inHg (998.0 mbar) and a wind of 20 mph from the north. Although the hurricane passed within 65 miles of the Bahamian capital Nassau, the storm only caused winds up to 50 mph and no significant damage there.

Great damage and devastation in Green Turtle Cay in Abaco after the Great Abaco Hurricane of 1932 as workers gather amongst the ruins looking for survivors, including two girls looking for their father who was later found dead under the rubbles. (Courtesy of Marysa Malone, Nassau, Bahamas).

The storm was very destructive on Abaco Island, where the reported barometric pressure was below 27.50 inHg (931.3 mbar). At Hope Town, strong winds shifting from northeast to southeast destroyed 83 homes and severely damaged 63. Food supplies ran low and salt contaminated the drinking supply. All public buildings along with the radio station were destroyed. The lowest pressure at Hope Town was 27.20 inHg (921.1 mbar) around 1500 UTC on September 5. At nearby settlement of Marsh Harbor, northeast winds shifted to the southwest at 2000 UTC and calm conditions occurred for 15 minutes as the eye passed. The barometer dropped as low as 27.60 inHg (934.6 mbar). There were 12 homes destroyed and most of the remainder severely damaged in this settlement.

On Green Turtle Cay, near Abaco Island, north and northwest winds coincided with the worst conditions; a large storm surge inundated the island, all buildings and the graveyard were destroyed, and at least six people died with 25 injuries reported. At nearby Coopers Town, just six homes survived the storm. Only four homes were still standing on Great Guana Cay. On Green Turtle Cay, two large brick churches with stone walls 3 feet (0.91 m) thick were destroyed by the storm and winds were estimated by one resident to have exceeded 200 mph; some of the stone blocks from the churches were reportedly carried ½ miles from where they were originally located. Newspaper reports and photos helped to establish estimated prevailing winds on Green Turtle Cay that possibly exceeded 150 mph during the hurricane.

At Governor's Harbor in Eleuthera, the sustained winds were measured at 75 miles per hour from the northwest and then later from the southwest with the peak of the winds occurring between noon and midnight on Monday. Major damages were reported to the roads and to the tomato crops on the island. A large portion of the stone part of the Government Wharf was demolished and the foreshore near the Wharf was washed away. There was significant damage reported to the island crops and other plants. The hurricane passed over Grand Bahama, destroying a few houses and wrecking several vessels. Many of the crops were destroyed. The Commissioner who was stationed at Sweeting's Cay during the storm, reported that several houses were blown down and that there was a shortage of food from there to Eight Mile Rock. At Water Cay the sloop *Regulator* and the schooners *Relief* and *Increase* were totally destroyed and considerable damage was done to many of the other remaining boats. The water was said to have risen to a height of 9 feet in Hawksbill Creek on the north side. At West End, there was considerable damage to the citrus crop. Entire roofs were blown off several houses and many others were well shaken up. The fields were badly damaged and several people were slightly injured.[128]

After the storm passed Abaco on September 6 and 7, several vessels were caught in the storm and recorded winds of Force 12 (Beaufort Wind Scale) and low barometric pressures; the steamship *Yankee Arrow* recorded a pressure of 27.65 inHg (936.3 mbar) on September 7, while the nearby steamship *Deer Lodge* reported a lower pressure of 27.58 inHg (934.0 mbar).

[128] Wayne Neely, The Great Bahamian Hurricane of 1899 And 1932-The Story of Two of the Greatest and Deadliest Hurricanes to Impact the Bahamas, (Bloomington, iUniverse Publishing, 2014), pgs. 304-333.

Great damage and devastation in Green Turtle Cay in Abaco after the Great Abaco Hurricane of 1932 as workers gather amongst the ruins looking for survivors. (Courtesy of Bob Davies, Nassau, Bahamas).

The Santa Cruz del Sur Hurricane of 1932--A powerful and deadly hurricane struck the town of Santa Cruz del Sur, Cuba in November of 1932, killing approximately 2,500 persons. In Havana, Cuba the most active months for a tropical cyclone is usually mid-August through October. This city gets a serious brush on average every 3.00 years. It is averaged that this country gets a direct hit once every 9.00 years. The director of the Havana National Observatory, José Carlos Millas, one of the most prominent and extraordinary lineage of Cuban meteorologists who held that position, wrote an excellent report on the storm. His remarkable description of the storm not only included the normal physical descriptions but the scientific details as well:

"On the morning of Wednesday, November 9, 1932, a Cuban town disappeared. It was noble, industrious town that played an important role in the first turbulent years of the history of our fatherland and then later knew how to maintain its virtues so that battles of a different type never detracted in the least from its noble tradition. This town was Santa Cruz del Sur."[129] The town was rebuilt at a different location, and a monument was constructed in

[129] Stuart, B. Schwartz, Sea of Storms-The History of Hurricanes in the Greater Caribbean from Columbus to Katrina, (New Jersey, Princeton University Press, 2015), pgs. 252-253.

the cemetery for those lost on November 9. The event is still commemorated each year. The tragedy pierced the national memory, poems and short stories were written about it, and those who survived, the *cicloneros,* bore witness to the disaster. The death of Santa Cruz del Sur eventually became part of a nationalist, and later socialist, critique of the failure of capitalism, or even a tale of its role in the creation of national catastrophe.

The Treasure Coast Hurricane of 1933--The 1933 hurricane season was a very active year for tropical storms and hurricanes with 21 named storms, and 10 of them becoming hurricanes. In addition to the Great Chesapeake Hurricane of 1933, the Mid-Atlantic was hit by another hurricane almost exactly a month to the day later when a Category 3 hurricane emerged from a disturbance in the Bahamas, and came up the coast to make landfall at Cape Lookout, North Carolina. The 1933 Treasure Coast Hurricane was the second-most intense tropical cyclone to strike the United States during the very active 1933 Atlantic hurricane season. The eleventh tropical storm, fifth hurricane, and the third major hurricane of the season, it formed east-northeast of the Leeward Islands on August 31. The tropical storm moved rapidly west-northwestward, steadily intensifying to a hurricane. It acquired peak winds of 140 miles per hour and passed over portions of the Bahamas on September 3, including Eleuthera and notably Governor's Harbor and Harbor Island, causing severe damage to crops, buildings, and infrastructure. Winds over 100 mph affected many islands in its path, especially those that encountered its center, and many docks and other infrastructures were ruined.

This hurricane remains one of the strongest and most destructive hurricanes to impact the Bahamas. This powerful hurricane moved over or near several islands in the Bahamas. Sustained winds on Eleuthera, notably the settlements of Spanish Wells and Harbor Island were both estimated at around 140 mph. Winds reached 110 mph at Governor's Harbor, 100 mph on Eleuthera, and 120 mph on the island of Abaco. The storm was farther away from Nassau, where winds reached 61 mph. The hurricane damaged a lumber mill on Abaco, washing away a dock. Heavy damage occurred on Harbor Island, including to several roofs, the walls of government buildings, and the water system. The hurricane destroyed four churches and 37 houses, leaving 100 people homeless. A 1.5 miles' road on Eleuthera was destroyed. Several islands sustained damage to farms, including the total loss of various fruit trees on Russell Island. Despite Category 4 winds on Spanish Wells, only five houses were destroyed, although most of the remaining dwellings lost their roofs. Collectively between North

Point, James Cistern, and Gregory Town on Eleuthera, the storm destroyed 55 houses and damaged many others. On Grand Bahama, where a 9 to 12 feet storm surge was reported, half of the houses were destroyed, as were 13 boats and two planes, and most docks were wrecked.[130]

The Great Cuba–Brownsville Hurricane of 1933--The Cuba–Brownsville hurricane was one of two storms in the 1933 Atlantic hurricane season to reach the intensity of a Category 5 strength on the Saffir-Simpson Hurricane Wind Scale. It formed on August 22 just off the west coast of Africa, and for much of its duration it maintained a west-northwest track. The system intensified into a tropical storm on August 26 and into a hurricane on August 28. Passing north of the Lesser Antilles, the hurricane rapidly intensified as it approached the Turks and Caicos Islands. It reached Category 5 status and its peak winds of 160 mph on August 31. Subsequently, it weakened before striking northern Cuba on September 1 with winds of 120 mph. In the country, the hurricane left about 100,000 people homeless and killed over 70 people. However, throughout its path, the hurricane killed at least 179 people collectively in the Turks and Caicos Islands, Cuba, and south Texas. Damage was heaviest near the storm's path, and the strong winds destroyed houses and left areas without power. Damage was estimated at $11 million.

On August 29, the hurricane passed north of the Lesser Antilles as it approached the islands of the southeastern Bahamas. It underwent rapid deepening: in a 24-hour period beginning late on August 29, the winds increased from 105 mph to 150 mph. It also became a small storm, as Grand Turk Island reported winds of 56 mph while the hurricane passed slightly to the north on August 30. At 0130 UTC the next day, a ship near Mayaguana reported a barometric pressure of 930 mbar (27 inHg) and hurricane-force winds. Mayaguana is the most easterly island of the Bahamas. It is one of only a few Bahamian islands which retain their native Lucayan Indian names. The pressure would ordinarily suggest winds of 152 mph, but because it was not reported in the eye and the storm was smaller than normal, the winds were estimated at 160 mph. The hurricane's winds rank as a Category 5 on the Saffir-Simpson Hurricane Scale, one of two such storms in the 1933 season.[131] This

[130] Wayne Neely, *The Major Hurricanes to Affect the Bahamas-Personal Recollections of Some of the Greatest Hurricanes to Affect the Bahamas*, (Bloomington, AuthorHouse Publishing, 2006).

[131] Chris Landsea; et al. (May 2012). *Documentation of Atlantic Tropical Cyclones Changes in HURDAT (1933) (Report). Hurricane Research Division*. Retrieved 03-03-2016.

storm remains one of only three storms (The Great Abaco Hurricane of 1932 and Hurricane Andrew in 1992 were the other two) to hit the Bahamas at Category 5 intensity on the Saffir-Simpson Hurricane Wind Scale.

After maintaining peak winds for about 12 hours, the hurricane began weakening as it passed through the southeastern Bahamas. At around 1200 UTC on September 1, the hurricane made landfall on northern Cuba near Sagua La Grande, with winds of about 120 mph. The eye moved along the northern coast of Cuba, crossing over Matanzas. Shortly thereafter the storm exited into the Straits of Florida, and late on September 1 the hurricane passed about 16 miles north of Havana. After entering the Gulf of Mexico, the hurricane restrengthened, and a ship reported a pressure of 948 mbar (28.0 inHg) late on September 2; this suggested winds of about 140 mph. The hurricane turned more to the west on September 3, and as it approached southern Texas it weakened slightly as it decelerated. At 0400 UTC on September 5, the hurricane made its final landfall on South Padre Island in southern Texas, with winds estimated at 125 mph. It quickly weakened over land as it crossed into northeastern Mexico, and the storm dissipated late on September 5.[132]

The Hurricane of June 1934--On June 4-8, between 2,000 and 3,000 persons died in a hurricane in Honduras and El Salvador.

The Great Labor Day Hurricane of 1935--In 1935, on the federal holiday that recognizes U.S. workers, a group of World War I veterans striving to improve the quality of their life on the Florida Keys lost their lives in one of the great workplace disasters in the history of the United States. In the Florida Keys, the most active months for a tropical cyclone is usually mid-August through September. The Florida Keys gets a serious brush on average every 2.77 years. It is averaged that this chain of islands gets a direct hit once every 6.00 years. Simply referred to as "The Great Labor Day Hurricane of 1935", it became one of the greatest, deadliest and impactful hurricanes to strike the United States. At the time, it was the strongest landfalling hurricane on record in the North Atlantic before Hurricane Gilbert in 1988 (888 mbar) and Hurricane Wilma in 2005 (882 mbar) eclipsed this record, but it still remains the strongest landfalling hurricane within the United States. It brought Category 5 winds and a terrifying storm surge to the upper Florida Keys on the late evening of Monday, September 2, 1935. The compact Great Labor Day Hurricane of 1935

---

132 Ibid. Retrieved 03-03-2016.

developed very rapidly from a system that was classified as a tropical storm less than two days before landfall in the Keys. Brushing the south end of Andros Island, it headed toward the north coast of Cuba before angling unexpectedly rightward and intensifying with astonishing speed as it approached the Keys, passing over the very warm waters of the Florida Straits.

"As the hurricane moved rapidly across the Keys on that fateful Monday night, local weather observer Ivar Olsen measured 26.35" (892 mbar) with a barometer that was later tested and proven reliable at the Weather Bureau. This remains the lowest value ever measured by a ground-based station in a tropical cyclone in the Western Hemisphere (Dropsondes released by reconnaissance aircraft produced sea-level pressure measurements of 882 mb on October 19, 2005, during Hurricane Wilma, and 870 mb on October 12, 1979, during Typhoon Tip). The 1935 hurricane went on to brush the west coast of the Florida peninsula before accelerating northeastward, reentering the Atlantic off the Virginia coastline and producing rains that topped 16" in Maryland."[133]

This was the most powerful hurricane in 1935 to make landfall in the United States. A very small storm, this Category 5 hurricane tore through the Florida Keys with 180 mph sustained winds and a low barometric pressure of 26.35 inches. The lure of the Keys, further enhanced by author Ernest Hemingway's presence in Key West, drew an increasing number of settlers and tourists. The main transportation route linking the Florida Keys to mainland Florida was a single railroad line, the Florida, Overseas Railroad portion of the Florida East Coast Railway. A 10-car evacuation train, sent down from Homestead, was washed off the track by the storm surge and high winds on Upper Matecumbe Key.

The train was supposed to rescue a group of World War I veterans, who as part of a government relief program, were building a new road bridge in the Upper Keys. Three years earlier, 20,000 vets, calling themselves the 'Bonus Expeditionary Forces,' had marched on Washington to complain that they had not been paid the bonus they had been promised. Partly to employ them, and partly to get them out of the spotlight, President Roosevelt put some of them to work on a new highway linking the keys, beginning in 1934. The engineer taking these workers to and from the Keys chose to back the train down the single track line, in hopes of saving time on the outward trip, and was unable to reach the waiting veterans before the storm did. Only a small part of the

133 *Remembering the Labor Day Hurricane of 1935 in the Florida Keys*-Jeff Master's Blog-*http://www.wunderground.com/blog/JeffMasters*, written by Bob Henson. Retrieved: 07-09-2015.

locomotive remained upright on the rails and had to be barged back to Miami several months later.

In total, at least 423 people (164 residents and 259 veterans employed on the road project) were killed by the hurricane. It must be noted that the official National Hurricane Service estimate remains at 408 deaths. Bodies were recovered as far away as Flamingo and Cape Sable on the southwest tip of the Florida mainland. In a fortuitous coincidence, about 350 of the 718 veterans living in the Keys work camps were in Miami to attend a Labor Day baseball game when the storm hit. If not for this outing, many more of the men, whose barracks in the Keys were flimsy, temporary wooden shacks on the lower Matecumbe and Windley Keys, might have been killed by the storm. This hurricane still has the lowest barometric pressure ever recorded over land in North America of 26.35 inches or 892 mbar. Wilma in 2005 still has the lowest central pressure of 882 mbar, and therefore the most intense hurricane in the North Atlantic hurricane history.

Religious officials, including a Catholic priest, a rabbi and a Protestant minister, held a funeral ceremony on Matecumbe Key prior to cremating the victims by setting fire to the wooden caskets. Servicemen stand ready for a final salute to veterans who perished in the 1935 storm. After the storm, active Army units were assigned to search the shoreline, tidal creeks, and other likely areas where bodies might have been blown or washed up in the final stages of the hurricane. The crude boxes are makeshift caskets, containing bodies for cremation (Florida Photographic Collection, Courtesy of the State Library and Archives of Florida).

Long Island Express of 1938--A classic east coast hurricane, this Category 3 storm in 1938 moved rapidly from Cape Hatteras, North Carolina, into New England in a matter of just six hours, killing 600 people. This hurricane hit the United States, particularly the Northeast, at a vulnerable time. The region, tied as it was to industries and economies of big cities, was just beginning to regroup after the Great Depression and the stock market crash of 1929. In September 1938, the country was weathering two very different types of storms: the first was the Great Depression, now in its ninth year, and the second was the gathering storm in Europe, soon to overwhelm the whole world. Worryingly, on September 20, 1938, one of the headline stories of *The New York Times* read:

"BRITAIN AND FRANCE TELL CZECHS TO ACCEPT HITLER'S TERMS TODAY, OR FACE LOSS OF WHOLE COUNTRY."

As serious as those economic and political storms were, within 24 hours it would be another kind of storm that would totally consume and dominate the attention of Long Islanders and New Englanders. That day's *Times* alluded to it: tucked away on an inside page was a 'small' and inconspicuous story that read, in part:

"A SEVERE TROPICAL HURRICANE WHICH GAVE CONCERN TO [BUT SPARED] RESIDENTS OF FLORIDA'S EAST COAST...... TURNED IN A WIDE NORTHWARD ARC TODAY AND IS APPARENTLY HEADING OUT TO SEA."

It was a statement, no doubt, prompted by dispatches from (the then) U.S. Weather Bureau, which would echo those same words for more than another 24 hours. Even the next day, as the storm turned northward after sideswiping the Carolinas and New Jersey, there was still no hurricane warning. Only at the last minute, about 2:00 p.m. on September 21, when Hurricane No. 3* (sequence controversial) of 1938 was just off the New Jersey Coast, did the forecaster issue a final advisory to include "whole gale force winds" (up to 73 mph). By that time, the storm was racing northward at forward speeds of up to 70 mph.

That morning, the *New York Times* Newspaper editorial entitled "Hurricane" concluded, "Every year an average of three such whirlwinds sweep the tropical North Atlantic between June and November. In 1933, there was an all-time record of twenty-one. If New York and the rest of the world have been so well informed about the cyclone, it is because of an admirable organized meteorological service." Except for Charlie Pierce, a junior forecaster in the U.S. Weather Bureau who predicted the storm but was overruled by the chief forecaster, the Weather Bureau experts and the general public never saw it coming. Later that day, the greatest weather disaster ever to hit Long Island and New England struck in the form of a Category 3 hurricane. Long Island, New York and New England were changed forever by a hurricane simply known as The Long Island Express Hurricane of 1938.[134] In Long Island, New York the most active months for a cyclone is usually mid-August through October. This city gets a serious brush on average every 2.72 years. It is averaged that this country gets a direct hit once every 8.47 years.

The immediate effect of this powerful hurricane was to decimate many Long Island communities in terms of human and economic losses however, the long term effects linger today. The '38 Hurricane created the Shinnecock Inlet and widened Moriches Inlet which, to this day, are changing the landscape of the south shore due to their influence on the natural littoral sand transport. History has shown that these powerful storms are rare but do in fact occur with long-term frequency. Case studies have shown that the next time a storm like the Long Island Express roars through, it might be the greatest disaster in U.S. history.

Known simply as the "Long Island Express," because this powerful storm crashed into New York's Long Island and then went on to batter southern New England. This hurricane struck with little warning, which was one of the reasons why the death toll was so high. Since Europeans settled New England in the 1600s, three hurricanes stand out for their destructiveness. The first struck Aug. 14, 1635; the second, on Sept. 23, 1815. The most recent pounded the area Sept. 21, 1938, and took an estimated 600 lives and seriously injured another 1,750.

More than 93,000 families suffered major property losses, including nearly 7,000 summer dwellings, 2,000 other dwellings, 2,600 boats, and 2,300 barns. About 26,000 automobiles were destroyed. Somewhere between 500,000 and 750,000 chickens were killed, as well as 1,675 head of livestock. Many small coastal towns, fishing villages and beach residents were completely unprepared for the hurricane that hit with 100-mile winds and tidal waves of

---

134 September 20, 1938, *The New York Times*: *"A severe tropical hurricane which gave concern to [but spared] residents of Florida's east coast... ... turned in a wide northward arc today and is apparently heading out to sea." Pg.2. Retrieved: 10-09-2014.*

astounding force. The hurricane demolished buildings, isolated communities and marooned thousands of people. It tore up highways, bridges and railroads, ripped down telephone and light wires, and flooded hundreds of square miles of land. Connecticut, soaked by several days of torrential rain, was hard hit, as were Massachusetts, New York and Rhode Island. In addition, to the hurricane there were several large fires which compounded the hurricane's fury. A 300,000-cubic-foot gas tank exploded in Providence, Rhode Island, and six blazes erupted in New London, Conn., threatening the entire city for 10 hours. Swirling flood waters hampered firemen. Everything told, the storm did more than $300 million worth of damage in 1938 dollars, or about $5.1 billion in 2015 dollars.

The central portion of the bathing pavilion at Bailey's Beach, Rhode Island, transported to the middle of the road. The New England Hurricane of 1938 traveled 600 miles in 12 hours, surprising southern New England and causing widespread destruction (Courtesy of NOAA-NHC).

The Joseph P. Duckworth Hurricane of 1943--Joseph B. Duckworth (September 8, 1902 – July 26, 1964) was a colonel in the United States Air Force and was regarded as the "father" of modern instrument flight. He is also noted in the record books as being the first person to fly intentionally through the eye of a hurricane in 1943, in the Gulf of Mexico. This flight was unplanned and unauthorized. On July 27, 1943, Army Air Force Lt. Col. Joseph P. Duckworth flew his single-engine AT-6 trainer airplane into the eye of a Category 1 hurricane bearing down on the Texas coast. His purpose: to win a crazy bet against some British pilots on the base to prove it could be done, and to defend the quality workmanship of his single-engine AT-6 aircraft. In his report, he stated, "The only embarrassing episode would have been engine failure, which, with the strong ground winds, would probably have prevented a landing, and certainly would have made descent via parachute highly inconvenient." Today, NOAA hurricane-hunter planes, and similar propeller-driven models flown by a special Air Force unit out of Mississippi, are flown directly into storms of all strength and category.[135]

To monitor and track the development and movement of a hurricane, we rely on remote sensing by satellites and radars, as well as data gathered by reconnaissance aircrafts (or sometimes called Hurricane Hunters). The reconnaissance aircraft was a major advancement in the field of meteorology. The reconnaissance aircraft flying into the eye of a hurricane has been a great success for both meteorologists and the public at large. This idea of flying into hurricanes to gather vital information about a hurricane was also a recent development. On July 27th, 1943, during the height of World War II, brave pioneers Joseph P. Duckworth, a flight instructor, and navigator Ralph O'Hair took an AT-6 aircraft from the United States Bryan Air Force Base in Texas without permission to find out what it was like to fly inside the eye of a hurricane that was nearing Galveston, Texas, at the time, which they did with remarkable success. When they got back to the base, their base supervisor bitterly complained not because they had removed an aircraft without permission but that they had not taken him along. As a result, Duckworth was forced to take him back into the hurricane. This flight was the spark that initiated the process and allowed for the introduction of planes flying into hurricanes to gather vital information about the storm, which in turn resulted in saving many lives in the process.

The Great Hurricane Atlantic Hurricane of 1944--Is perhaps a forgotten storm in light of the Great Labor Day Hurricane of 1935, and the Long Island Express of 1938. However, this was a memorable storm in its own right. This large and powerful hurricane was first detected northeast of the Leeward Islands on September 9, 1944. It moved west-northwestward through the 12th, then turned northward on a track that brought the center of the hurricane

135 *http://www.chicagotribune.com/sns-hc-history-1943-story.html.* Retrieved: 08-08-2014.

near Cape Hatteras, North Carolina, on the 14th. The hurricane accelerated north-northeastward, moving across eastern New England and into Canada by September 15. The storm became extratropical over Canada and finally merged with a larger low near Greenland on September 16. This hurricane was of Category 3 intensity at landfalls at Cape Hatteras, Long Island, and Point Judith, Rhode Island, and Category 2 as far north as the coast of Maine. Cape Henry, VA, reported 134 mph sustained winds (measured 90 feet above the ground), with estimated gusts to 150 mph. Hurricane-force winds were reported elsewhere along the storm's track from North Carolina to Massachusetts, with a maximum reported gust of 109 mph at Hartford, Connecticut.

Rainfall totals of between 6 to 11 inches accompanied the storm. While this hurricane caused 46 deaths and $100 million in damage in the United States, including $25 million in New Jersey alone, where some 300 homes were destroyed on Long Beach Island. However, the worst effects occurred at sea, where it wreaked havoc on World War II shipping. Five ships, including a U. S. Navy destroyer and minesweeper, two U.S. Coast Guard cutters, and a light vessel sank due to the storm and caused 344 deaths. The powerful storm caused tremendous damage along the coast from North Carolina to New England, with some 41,000 buildings damaged, and a death toll of 390 people.

The Great Hurricane of 1945--The September 15, 1945, hurricane did severe damage to the Homestead-Miami area. Homestead reported gusts up to 196 mph. Carysfort Lighthouse in Florida measured a 138 mph gust. The Richmond blimp base in south Dade, Florida, lost 25 blimps. However, the Upper Keys reported minimal hurricane damage, just as it did in Hurricane Andrew. Being on the left side of a hurricane was a definite advantage.

Hurricane Dog of 1950--This marked the official naming of hurricanes using the military alphabet, but the terms 'major', 'great' and 'extreme' to describe hurricanes continued until the Saffir-Simpson Scale was adopted. Hurricane Dog was the fourth named storm of the 1950 Atlantic hurricane season, and it was a strong Category 5 hurricane that reached its peak intensity of 185 mph over the open Atlantic after delivering extensive damage to the Leeward Islands as a tropical storm and, eventually, a major hurricane; however, the storm never made landfall on the continental United States. Several deaths were reported from Dog, including 11 deaths off New England when the storm capsized several boats. The islands of Antigua and Barbuda reported $1 million in damage to houses, roads, trees, and power lines. 2 people were killed when their boat sank. Though it never made landfall in New England, passing over 100 miles away, its strong winds still caused 12 casualties, 11 by sinking boats as Nantucket Island, MA recorded gusts to 70 mph. Damage amounted to $2 million.

Hurricanes Carol and Edna of 1954--Carol formed near the Central Bahamas Islands on August 25, 1954, and moved slowly northward and north-northwestward. By August 30th, it was a hurricane about 100-150 miles east of Charleston, South Carolina. It then speeded up while maintaining a north to northeastward track, where it made landfall as a Category 3 hurricane over Long Island, New York and Connecticut on the 31st. The cyclone became extratropical later that day as it crossed the remainder of New England and southeastern Canada. Sustained winds of 80 to 100 mph were reported over much of eastern Connecticut, all of Rhode Island, and eastern Massachusetts. A peak gust of 130 mph was reported at Block Island, Rhode Island, while gusts of 100 to 125 mph occurred over much of the rest of the affected area. Storm surge flooding occurred along the New England coast from Long Island northward, with water depths of 8 to 10 feet reported in downtown Providence, Rhode Island. Carol was responsible for 60 deaths and $461 million in damage in the United States.

No discussion of Carol is complete without the mention of the remarkably similar Hurricane Edna. This storm first formed east of the Windward Islands on September 2. It moved northwestward, and by September 7 it was a hurricane very near where Carol had formed two weeks before. From this point, Edna followed a path just east of Carol's. It accelerated past Cape Hatteras, North Carolina, on September 10 and made landfall over Cape Cod as a Category 3 hurricane the next day. Edna moved across Maine into eastern Canada later on the 11th as it became extratropical. Martha's Vineyard, Massachusetts, reported a peak wind gust of 120 mph during Edna, and much of the rest of the affected area had gusts of 80 to 100 mph. The storm was responsible for 20 deaths and $40 million in damage in the United States.

Hurricane Hazel of 1954--Hazel was first spotted east of the Windward Islands on October 5, 1954. It traversed through the islands later that day as a hurricane, then it moved westward over the southern Caribbean Sea through October 8. A slow turn to the north-northeast occurred from October 9-12, with Hazel crossing western Haiti as a hurricane on the 12th. The hurricane turned northward and crossed the southeastern Bahamas on the 13th, followed by a northwestward turn on the 14th. Hazel turned north and accelerated on October 15, making landfall as a Category 4 hurricane near the North Carolina-South Carolina border. Subsequent rapid motion over the next 12 hours took the storm from the coast across the eastern United States into southeastern Canada as it became extratropical.

Hazel was a Category 4 hurricane that came ashore in North Carolina in October, 1954, and then brought hurricane force winds as far inland as Canada. Passing 95 miles to the east of Charleston, South Carolina, Hazel made landfall very near the North Carolina and South Carolina border and brought a record 18 feet storm surge at Calabash, North Carolina. Wind gusts of 150 mph were felt in Holden Beach, Calabash, and Little River Inlet, 100 mph gusts were felt farther inland at Virginia, Maryland, Pennsylvania, Delaware, New Jersey, and New York. High winds occurred over large portions of the eastern United States. Myrtle Beach, South Carolina, reported a peak wind gust of 106 mph, and winds were estimated at 130 to 150 mph along the coast between Myrtle Beach and Cape Fear, North Carolina. Washington, D.C., reported 78 mph sustained winds, and peak gusts of over 90 mph occurred as far northward as inland New York State. A storm surge of up to 18 feet inundated portions of the North Carolina coast. Heavy rains of up to 11 inches occurred as far northward as Toronto, Canada, resulting in severe flooding. Hazel was responsible for 95 deaths and $281 million in damage in the United States, 100 deaths and $100 million in damage in Canada, and an estimated 400 to 1000 deaths in Haiti.

Hurricanes Alice in the 1954 & 1955 hurricane seasons--Hurricanes Alice from both the 1954-55 seasons are interesting cases in themselves. Hurricane Alice #1 was the second-strongest North Atlantic hurricane to make landfall in the month of June since reliable records began in the 1850s. While not a major hurricane, the storm was linked to catastrophic flooding in southern Texas and northern Mexico, especially along the Rio Grande and its tributaries. The third tropical cyclone and first hurricane of the 1954 Atlantic hurricane season, Alice was one of two storms to receive the same name that year, the other being an unusual post-season hurricane that persisted into the new year of 1955, becoming one of only two January hurricanes on record (the other having formed in 1938). The first Alice developed rather suddenly on June 24 over the Bay of Campeche, though it may well have formed earlier but went undetected due to limited surface weather observations. Moving northwestward, Alice strengthened rapidly as it neared the Mexican coastline, becoming a hurricane early the next day. By midday on June 25, the hurricane reached peak winds of

110 miles per hour before moving inland well south of the U.S.–Mexico border. The storm struck an area with few inhabitants and caused relatively minimal impacts from wind near the point of landfall and in southern Texas.

Hurricane Alice #2 was originally recognized as a hurricane and named Alice on January 2, 1955. At that point, the same lists were being used from year to year, and there had already been a deadly Hurricane Alice in June 1954, so the 1954 North Atlantic hurricane season has two named hurricanes called Alice and is the first time this occurred. However, post-storm analysis determined that the latter Alice #2 had been a hurricane on December 31, 1954. Hurricane Alice is the only known Atlantic hurricane to span two calendar years and one of only two named Atlantic tropical cyclones, along with Tropical Storm Zeta of 2005, to do so. The twelfth tropical cyclone and the eighth hurricane of the 1954 Atlantic hurricane season, Alice developed on December 30, 1954 from a trough of low pressure in the central Atlantic Ocean in an area of unusually favorable conditions. The storm moved southwestward and gradually strengthened to reach hurricane status. After passing through the Leeward Islands on January 2, 1955, Alice reached peak winds of 90 mph before encountering cold air and turning to the southeast. It dissipated on January 6 over the southeastern Caribbean Sea.

Alice produced heavy rainfall and moderately strong winds across several islands along its path. Saba and Anguilla were affected the most, with total damage amounting to $623,500 (1955 USD). There was an earlier hurricane named Alice in the season. Operationally, the lack of definitive data prevented the U.S. Weather Bureau from declaring the system a hurricane until January 2. It received the name Alice in early 1955, though re-analysis of the data supported extending its track to the previous year, resulting in two tropical cyclones of the same name in one season.

Hurricanes Connie and Diane of 1955--These two hurricanes must be mentioned together. They struck the North Carolina coast only five days apart, and the rains from Connie set the stage for the devastating floods caused by Diane. Connie was first detected as a tropical storm over the tropical Atlantic on August 3, 1955. It moved just north of west for several days, reaching hurricane strength several hundred miles' northeast of the Leeward Islands on the 5th. After passing north of the Leeward Islands on the 6th, Connie turned northwestward - a motion that continued until the 10th. An erratic, generally north-northwestward motion then brought Connie to the North Carolina coast on August 12 as a Category 3 hurricane. This was followed by a gradual northwestward turn through August 14, when Connie dissipated over the eastern Great Lakes. Fort Macon, North Carolina, reported 75 mph sustained winds with gusts to 100 mph, while a storm surge of up to 8 feet occurred along the coast. There were no reported deaths, and the damage in the United States was $40 million. However, the most significant aspect of Connie was the rainfall of up to 12 inches that affected the northeastern United States.

Diane was first detected over the tropical Atlantic on August 7. Moving generally west-northwestward, the cyclone became a tropical storm on the 9th. Diane became a hurricane on August 11, by which time it was moving northwestward. A northward turn occurred on the 12th, followed by a westward turn on the 13th and a west-northwestward motion on the 14th. This motion brought Diane to the North Carolina coast on August 17 as a Category 1 hurricane. At its peak, Diane produced winds of 125 mph, but at landfall winds were down 50 mph in Cape Hatteras, while Wilmington had a gust of minimal hurricane force. The storm turned northward across Virginia, then it turned northeastward and moved back into the Atlantic near Long Island, New York, on August 19. Diane became extratropical over the North Atlantic on the 21st.

Hurricane conditions affected only a small part of the North Carolina coast, and the damage from winds and tides was relatively minor. The main impact was heavy rains. Diane poured 10 to 20 inches of rain on areas soaked by Connie just a few days before, producing widespread, severe flooding from North Carolina to Massachusetts. The floods proved more devastating and were responsible for about 200 deaths and $832 million in damage, creating a new benchmark for damage at the time. The havoc wreaked by Diane brought out 'Presidential Commission on Storm Modification' that eventually led to Project Stormfury.

Hurricane Janet of 1955--Hurricane Janet was the most powerful hurricane of the 1955 North Atlantic hurricane season, and the 10th strongest Atlantic hurricane on record. It made landfall as a Category 5 hurricane on the Saffir-Simpson Hurricane Wind Scale, causing catastrophic damage and up to 681 deaths in the Yucatán Peninsula. Janet caused extensive destruction in British Honduras (on June 1, 1973, 'British Honduras' was officially renamed Belize) amounting to 680 deaths and nearly $50 million ($516 million in 2016 USD) in damage. Janet was the only North Atlantic hurricane to cause the loss of a Hurricane Hunter aircraft, a P2V Neptune under the command of Navy Lieutenant Commander Grover B. Windham. This Hurricane Hunter was lost when the aircraft flew from the airfield at Guantanamo Bay, Cuba, and disappeared after signaling that it was entering the Category 5 hurricane. Janet also destroyed a U.S. Weather Post on Swan Island. Janet added to the severe flooding caused by Gladys and Hilda and caused $47,800,000 in damage through its path of destruction. In addition, Janet caused 681 deaths (538 according to some sources).

From the Naval Helicopter, Historical Society Collection - The fury of Hurricane Janet left Chetumal, Mexico 90% demolished when it swept through that city. This photo was taken on Friday, September 30, 1955 by a Navy P5M Marlin from Coco Solo, Canal Zone, which took relief of medical supplies, food and doctors to the devastated area. Hurricane Janet's eye passed just a few miles south of Chetumal during the night. (Courtesy of Wikimedia. Commons).

Hurricane Hilda of 1955--Hurricane Hilda developed from a tropical wave on September 10, 1955, over the northern Lesser Antilles. It moved northwestward and gradually strengthening to a 95-mph hurricane before hitting eastern Cuba on the 14th. Hilda weakened to a tropical storm while moving across the island but quickly re-strengthened to a 115-mph hurricane while over the Caribbean Sea before hitting the sparsely populated eastern Yucatán Peninsula between Chetumal and Cozumel. After weakening over land, Hilda rapidly intensified to a 130 mph Category 3 hurricane in the Gulf of Mexico and hit Tampico, Mexico, as a weakened Category 2 hurricane on the 19th, dissipating the next day over Mexico. Hilda killed 300 people and caused $120 million in damage (1955 USD), mostly from flooding. Despite its destruction, Hilda was one of the rare storms that was not retired after causing tremendous damage and destruction along its path, though the name was later retired in the Hurricane Hilda of 1964.

Hurricane Audrey of 1957--Audrey was first detected over the southwestern Gulf of Mexico on June 24, 1957. It moved slowly northward as it became a tropical storm and a hurricane the next day. A faster northward motion brought the center to the coast near the Texas-Louisiana border on the 27th. Rapid strengthening in the last six hours before landfall meant Audrey made landfall as a Category 4 hurricane. The cyclone turned northeastward after landfall, becoming extratropical over northern Mississippi on June 28 and merging with another low over the Great Lakes the next day. The combined system was responsible for strong winds and heavy rains over portions of the eastern United States and Canada. No reliable wind or pressure measurements are available from Audrey's core at landfall. The main impact was from an 8 to 12 feet storm surge that penetrated as far inland as 25 miles over portions of low-lying southwestern Louisiana. These surges were responsible for the vast majority of the 390 deaths from Audrey. Damage in the United States was estimated at $150 million.

Hurricane Donna of 1960--One of the all-time great hurricanes, Donna was first detected as a tropical wave moving off the African coast on August 29, 1960. It became a tropical storm over the tropical Atlantic the next day, and a hurricane on September 1. Donna followed a general west-northwestward track for the following five days, passing over the northern Leeward Islands on the 4th and 5th as a Category 4 hurricane, and then to the north of Puerto Rico later on the 5th. Donna turned westward on September 7 and passed through the southeastern Bahamas. A northwestward turn on the 9th brought the hurricane to the middle Florida Keys the next day at Category 4 intensity. Donna then curved northeastward, crossing the Florida Peninsula on September 11, followed by eastern North Carolina (Category 3) on the 12th, and the New England states (Category 3 on Long Island and Categories 1 to 2 elsewhere) on the 12th and 13th. The storm became extratropical over eastern Canada on the 13th.

Hurricane Donna ripped through the southeastern islands of the Bahamas with torrential rains, storm surge and mighty winds leaving widespread destruction in its wake. Among the hardest hit islands were, Mayaguana, Long Cay, Exuma, Crooked Island, Acklins and Long Island. A Special Committee was appointed by the Governor to oversee Hurricane Relief and to raise funds for the people affected by the hurricane. At Mayaguana, three settlements, Abraham's Bay, Pirates Well and Betsy Bay were reportedly flattened. Ninety-five percent of Abrahams Bay, ninety-five percent of Pirates Wells, and an estimated fifty percent of Betsy Bay residents were left homeless after the hurricane. The Mayaguana Auxiliary Air Force Base and the missile tracking station was hard hit.

Acklins suffered considerable damage because about 90% of the houses were totally wiped out. At Pine Field 22 houses were destroyed and 13 others were badly damaged, at Hard Hill 13 houses were destroyed and 16 others badly damaged, at Anderson Hill, 10 houses were destroyed and two others badly damaged. At Snug Corner, 30 houses were destroyed and 12 others were badly damaged, and at Mason's Bay, 18 houses were destroyed and 15 others badly damaged. Long Island did not receive the full force of the hurricane; however, the southern and central parts of the island did suffer considerable damage. Many houses were totally destroyed while many others suffered considerable damage. Most of the farms throughout the island were wiped away by the storm, causing considerable hardship to the people who were dependent upon farming for their livelihood. The communications lines were in total disrepair. After the hurricane the government sent food, clothing, lumber and medicine to the people of long island to ease their pain.

Donna is the only hurricane of record to produce hurricane-force winds in Florida, the Mid-Atlantic States, and New England. Sombrero Key, Florida, reported 128 mph sustained winds, with gusts to 150 mph. In the Mid-Atlantic States, Elizabeth City, North Carolina, reported 83 mph sustained winds, while Manteo, North Carolina, reported a 120 mph gust. In New England, Block Island, Rhode Island, reported 95 mph sustained winds, with gusts to 130 mph. Donna caused storm surge of up to 13 feet in the Florida Keys and 11 feet surge along the southwest coast of Florida. Four to eight feet surge were reported along portions of the North Carolina coast, with 5 to 10 feet surge along portions of the New England coast. Heavy rainfalls of 10 to 15 inches occurred in Puerto Rico, 6 to 12 inches in Florida, and 4 to 8 inches elsewhere along the path of the hurricane. The landfall pressure of 27.46 inches makes Donna the eighth strongest hurricane on record to hit the United States. It was responsible for 50 deaths in the United States. Hurricane Donna was a very destructive hurricane that caused extensive damage from the Lesser Antilles to New England. At least 364 people were killed by the hurricane, and property damage was estimated at $900 million (1960 USD).

Hurricane Carla of 1961--This was one of two Category 5 hurricanes to develop during the 1961 Atlantic hurricane. This storm struck between the Port O'Connor and Port Lavaca area of Texas back in September, 1961, as a Category 4 hurricane, becoming one of the most powerful storms to ever strike the United States. It was the most powerful storm to hit the Texas Coast in about 40 years. It winds were in excess of 150 mph, and gusts went up to 170 mph. Tides near Port Lavaca were 18.5 feet above normal, and the barometric pressure was 27.62 inches of Hg. Estimated damage from the storm was $408 million dollars (over $3.3 billion in 2016 U.S. dollars), while the death toll hit 43 persons, but due to a massive evacuation, the death toll was extremely low. Today, the cost would have been far greater.

Hurricane Hattie of 1961--Hurricane Hattie was a powerful Category 5 hurricane that pounded Central America on Halloween during the 1961 North Atlantic hurricane season. Hattie is the only hurricane on record to have earned three names (Hattie, Simone, Inga) while crossing into different basins twice. Hattie swept across the Caribbean and came ashore in the town of Belize City, British Honduras (now called Belize), on October 31. It was a strong Category 4 hurricane at landfall, having weakened from a Category 5 just offshore. The country of Belize, at the time known as British Honduras, sustained the worst damage from the hurricane. The former capital, Belize City, was buffeted by strong winds and flooded by a powerful storm surge. The territory governor estimated that 70% of the buildings in the city had been damaged, leaving more than 10,000 people homeless. Hurricane Hattie moved ashore in British Honduras, with a storm tide of up to 14 feet near Belize City, a city of 31,000 people located at sea-level; its only defenses against the storm surge were a small seawall and a strip of swamp lands. The capital experienced high waves and a 10 feet storm surge along its waterfront that reached the third story of some buildings. A trained observer estimated winds of over 150 mph, and winds in the territory were unofficially estimated as strong as 200 mph.

The destruction caused by the storm was so severe that the government had to relocate inland to a new city, Belmopan. Overall, Hattie caused about $60 million in losses and 307 deaths in the territory. Although damage was heavier in Hattie than a hurricane in 1931 that killed 2,000 people, the death toll from Hattie was less due to advance warnings. Elsewhere in Central America, Hattie killed 11 people in Guatemala and one in Honduras. Hattie is the only hurricane on record to have earned three names (Hattie, Simone, Inga) while crossing into different basins twice. After making landfall, its remnants crossed over into the Pacific and attained tropical storm status again under the name Simone. In a remarkable turn of events, after Simone itself made landfall, its remnants crossed back over to the Gulf of Mexico, where the storm became Tropical Storm Inga before dissipating. However, it is debatable whether Inga in fact formed from the remnants of Simone at all.

Hurricane Flora of 1963--This storm blasted through the Caribbean in September and October 1963. Flora was one of the deadliest hurricanes in history, killing over 7,211 persons. Flora left 7,193 people dead in Haiti and Cuba, making it one of the deadliest hurricanes in the North Atlantic history. The passage of Hurricane Flora destroyed 2,750 of Tobago's 7,500 houses and damaged 3,500 others. The hurricane killed 18 on the island and resulted in $30 million in crop and property damage (1963 USD). In addition, Flora caused a total of $528,500,000 in damage (1963 dollars) along its entire path of destruction. It is estimated that if a hurricane like Flora struck in 1998, it would cause over 12,000 casualties.

Hurricane Cleo of 1964--The first hurricane to strike the Miami area since Hurricane King in 1950, this 1964 storm produced wind gusts of 138 mph and knee-deep water that produced some $125 million dollars in damage ($962 million 2016 USD). With this hurricane, the U.S. Weather Bureau, using satellite technology for the first time, used cloud images from a space satellite as a hurricane tracking aid.

Hurricane Dora of 1964--Within a few weeks after Cleo in September 1964, this hurricane hit the Northeastern coast of Florida at a right angle. It was the first storm ever to do this since the Great Hurricane of 1880. Dora had winds of 125 mph at St. Augustine and produced a 12 feet storm surge.

Hurricane Betsy of 1965--A Category 3 hurricane that struck the Bahamas, South Florida and Louisiana in September 1965. Hurricane Betsy in 1965 moved across the Atlantic, executing 2 loops before moving across the Bahamas and South Florida, the last major hurricane to affect South Florida until Hurricane Andrew in 1992. Residents of the Bahamas were warned of the hurricane on the evening of the 5th and Betsy continued through the Northern Bahamas, with the eye passing just to the north of Nassau. The highest winds were measured in Abaco at 147 miles per hour on the evening of the 6th and hurricane force winds battered Abaco for a grueling 20 hours. In New Providence, there was one loss of life and damage to businesses and homes were said to be minimal, which was attributed to the fact that the people in New Providence took care to secure and batten down their houses and stay at home.

All around the island of Nassau, there were downed power lines and fallen trees. At the old Winsor Field Airport, many planes were broken away from their holdings and smashed into each other, crushed, and some damaged beyond repairs. There was one known fatality on the island of New Providence. He died aboard his ship during the hurricane, which was wrecked in Nassau Harbor during the storm. But compared to the islands of Eleuthera and Abaco, Nassau suffered considerably far less damage. Therefore, most of the Bahamas Government's resources were diverted to Eleuthera and Abaco-the two hardest hit islands. Total overall losses in the Bahamas were estimated at £5 million pounds, and much of the losses sustained were from crop losses. It was estimated that £150,000 to £200,000 was spent by the Bahamas Government and charitable organizations to repair the damages caused by Hurricane Betsy. Insurance claims were estimated at £1.4 million.[136]

---

[136] Wayne Neely, *The Major Hurricanes to Affect the Bahamas-Personal Recollections of some of the Greatest Hurricanes to Affect the Bahamas,* (Bloomington, AuthorHouse, 2006).

Two airplanes damaged by Hurricane Betsy at the old Windsor Airfield in the Bahamas, and the one in the foreground was tied to the ground, but that was no match for Betsy's strong winds (Courtesy of Wayne Neely).

After leaving the Bahamas, Betsy moved on a westerly course and passed over the Florida Keys. It then passed over Louisiana on September 9, 1965, as a Category 4 hurricane. The eye passed to the southwest of New Orleans, killing several dozen persons, though the eyewall covered much of southeast Louisiana for an 8-hour period. Four parishes in New Orleans sustained significant flooding. "God, it was like one giant swimming pool as far as the eye could see," one resident of Chalmette recalled. "A woman who lives down the block floated past me, with her two children beside her." Betsy and a second hurricane of 1935 are the only two American hurricanes recorded made landfall from the northeast. The effects of Hurricane Betsy were far-reaching and unprecedented damage inflicted on the areas impacted by the hurricane. Though the extents of impacts were limited to the Bahamas and portions of the United States, the damage in these respective regions was extensive. According to the Hurricane Research Division of the Atlantic Oceanographic and Meteorological Laboratory, Betsy produced Category 3 winds (111 mph or greater) in southeastern Florida and southeastern Louisiana. However, winds of such intensity were also reported in the Bahamas. The final enumerated damage figure of $1.425 billion in damage costs made Betsy the first hurricane in the United States to accrue more than $1 billion in damage, unadjusted for inflation. For this reason, the tropical cyclone was nicknamed

"Billion Dollar Betsy." The damage cost remained unsurpassed for 4 years, until Hurricane Camille struck similar regions in 1969. Betsy remains the 27th costliest hurricane in the history of the United States.

Bahamian resident Bertram Mills and his family were victims of Hurricane Betsy. This sad picture shows him standing with his children amid the ruins of his totally demolished home on the island of Abaco, in the Bahamas.

Hurricane Inez of 1966--Known as "The Crazy One," this powerful Cape Verde-type hurricane carved an erratic path of death and destruction from the Caribbean to Florida, and to Mexico in October 1966. It left some 1,500 people dead and produced millions of dollars in damage, with top winds of approximately 190 mph. The minimum central pressure in Inez was recorded as low as 27.38 inches during the peak of the storm. Inez is among the deadliest hurricanes on record in the North Atlantic, with an approximate death toll of over 1,000 people across several Caribbean countries. In addition to being exceptionally deadly and intense, Inez was the first solitary storm on record to affect the West Indies, Bahamas, Florida, and Mexico, all on one track. Overall, damage was estimated to be about $200 million. The total was less than expected, possibly due to the small, compact size of the storm. In small storms, rain is not as big of a threat, as it normally is in big ones.

Hurricane Alma of 1966--This was a rare major hurricane in June of the 1966 North Atlantic hurricane season. It was the earliest continental U.S. hurricane to strike within any season since 1825. While drifting over northeastern Central America as a tropical depression, Alma dropped torrential rains, resulting in 30 inches of rain in some locations. The Honduran town of San Rafael was nearly destroyed, killing 73 of the town's population. In Cuba, the storm brought heavy flooding, causing nearly $200 million in damage and 11 deaths. In Florida, Alma caused strong wind damage, flooding, and spawned 9 tornadoes, amounting to $10 million and 6 deaths. In all, Hurricane Alma caused over $210.1 million in damage (1966 USD), with 90 deaths related to the storm.

Hurricane Beulah of 1967--Hurricane Beulah was a Category 4 hurricane on the Saffir-Simpson Hurricane Wind Scale that hit Texas in 1967 and spawned some 150 tornadoes after making landfall, the most ever produced on record by a tropical system. Hurricane Frances in 2004 spawned half that number, which is still quite a bit in its own right.

Hurricane Camille of 1969--This powerful, deadly, and destructive hurricane formed just west of the Cayman Islands on August 14, 1969. It rapidly intensified, and by the time it reached western Cuba the next day, it was a Category 3 hurricane. Camille tracked north-northwestward across the Gulf of Mexico and became a Category 5 hurricane on August 16. This was the last Category 5 hurricane to make landfall over the United States before Hurricane Andrew did in August 1992. Today, it ranks as the second most intense hurricane to hit the United States (including Katrina in 2005), behind the powerful Great Labor Day Hurricane of 1935. The hurricane maintained this intensity until it made landfall along the Mississippi coast late on the 17th.

Camille weakened to a tropical depression as it crossed Mississippi into western Tennessee and Kentucky, then it turned eastward across West Virginia and Virginia. The cyclone moved into the North Atlantic on August 20 and regained tropical storm strength before becoming extratropical on the 22nd. A minimum pressure of 26.84 inches was reported in Bay St. Louis, Mississippi, which makes Camille the second most intense hurricane on record to hit the United States. The actual maximum sustained winds will never be known, as the hurricane destroyed all of the wind-recording instruments in the landfall area, and it is typical for powerful storms of this category to have the wind instruments be blown away. The estimates at the coast are near 200 mph. Columbia, Mississippi, located 75 miles inland, reported 120 mph sustained winds.

A storm surge of 24.6 feet occurred at Pass Christian, Mississippi. The heaviest rains along the Gulf Coast were about 10 inches. However, as Camille passed over the Virginias, it produced a burst of 12 to 20 inches of torrential rainfall, with local totals of up to 31 inches. Most of this rain occurred in 3 to 5 hours and caused catastrophic flash flooding. The combination of sustained winds, massive storm surge, and torrential rainfall played a significant factor in the high death toll of 256 deaths (143 on the Gulf Coast and 113 in the Virginia floods) and $1.421 billion in damage. Three deaths were reported in Cuba. In the aftermath of the storm came a compelling story of regret in the midst of a serious tragedy. On the night of August 17, it was told, a group of 23 friends gathered at the Richeilieu Apartments in Pass Christian, Mississippi, to mark the arrival of Camille with a "hurricane party." The group had lived through hurricanes before and thought they knew what to expect from Camille. As Camille struck the coast, water rushed into the building, rising from the first floor to the second floor within minutes. The hurricane tore through the apartments, supposedly killing all but one survivor, Mary Ann Gerlach.

Hurricane Celia of 1970--A powerful Category 3 hurricane that came ashore in the Corpus Christi area during the 1970 season. Sustained winds were 130 mph, which made it a strong Category 3 hurricane. Winds gusted as high as 161 mph, and it ended up being the costliest storm at the time. Some other areas received wind gusts as high as 180 mph. Celia became the third major hurricane to strike the Texas Gulf Coast, behind Hurricane Carla (1961) and Hurricane Beulah (1967). Today, it still ranks quite high, as the National Hurricane Center places it 24th on the all-time list, with $453 billion dollars in damage. The silver lining in all of this was the fact that only 11 people died from the storm, even though 466 people were injured, 9,000 homes were destroyed, 14,000 homes were significantly damaged, and another 41,000 suffered minor damage.

Hurricane Ginger of 1971--Hurricane Ginger was the eighth tropical cyclone and fifth hurricane of the 1971 Atlantic hurricane season. Ginger sets the endurance record by spending 27.25 days as a tropical cyclone (20 of them with hurricane force winds). Ginger is the second longest-lasting North Atlantic hurricane on record. The hurricane, which lasted from September 5 to October 3, spent most of its life over the western Atlantic Ocean. Ginger ultimately struck North Carolina and the coast of Virginia, causing $10 million in damage (1971 USD) due to severe flooding. Because damage was relatively light, the name Ginger was not retired. However, due to a change in the list of hurricane names in 1979, the name Ginger was not used to name an Atlantic storm again.

Ginger was a tropical cyclone from September 5 to October 3, a total of 27.25 days. This makes Ginger the second longest-duration storm in the Atlantic Ocean, behind only 1899's Hurricane San Ciriaco. Ginger spent 20 days as a hurricane (of at least Category 1 strength), from September 11 to September 30, one of the longest durations on record. On September 11, there was a record of 4 active tropical cyclones at once: Hurricane Edith, Hurricane Fern, Hurricane Ginger and Tropical Storm Heidi. For the scientists of Project Stormfury, Ginger became a very good candidate for cloud seeding, so it was one of the first hurricanes that were seeded in the Project Stormfury program.

Hurricane Agnes of 1972--The large disturbance that became Agnes was first detected over the Yucatan Peninsula of Mexico on June 14, 1972. The system drifted eastward and became a tropical depression later that day and a tropical storm over the northwestern Caribbean on the 16th. Agnes turned northward on June 17 and became a hurricane over the southeastern Gulf of Mexico the next day. A continued northward motion brought Agnes to the Florida Panhandle coast on June 19 as a Category 1 hurricane. Agnes turned northeastward after landfall and weakened to a depression over Georgia. However, it regained tropical storm strength over eastern North Carolina on June 21 and moved into the Atlantic later that day. A northwestward turn followed, and a just-under-hurricane-strength Agnes made a final landfall on the 22nd near New York, New York.

The storm merged with a non-tropical low on June 23rd, with the combined system affecting the northeastern United States until the 25th. Agnes was barely a hurricane at landfall in Florida, and the effects of the winds and storm surge were relatively minor. The major impact was over the northeastern United States, where Agnes combined with the non-tropical low to produce widespread rainfall of 6 to 12 inches, with local amounts of 14 to 19 inches. These rains produced widespread severe flooding from Virginia northward to New York, with other flooding occurring over the western portions of the Carolinas. Agnes caused 122 deaths in the United States and left well over 330,000 persons homeless. Nine of these were in Florida (mainly from severe thunderstorms), while the remainder were associated with the flooding. The storm was responsible for $2.1 billion in damage in the United States, the vast majority of which came from the flooding. Agnes also affected western Cuba, where seven additional deaths occurred.

Hurricane Fifi (or Hurricane Fifi-Orlene) of 1974--This was a catastrophic storm during the 1974 North Atlantic hurricane season which made landfall in Belize. Fifi was one of the costliest hurricanes in history, causing $3.7 billion in damages. It was also one of the deadliest North Atlantic hurricanes, killing as many as 10,000 people and rendering over 100,000 persons homeless. Fifi was one of the rare storms that crossed from the Atlantic into the Pacific Ocean. A tropical wave that moved off the coast of Africa on September 8 became a tropical depression in the eastern Caribbean Sea on September 14. It moved westward, slowly strengthening to a tropical storm on the 16th. Conditions became favorable for further development, and Fifi became a hurricane on the 17th. Fifi reached a peak of 110 mph winds, just before skimming the northern coast of Honduras on the September 18 and 19. The hurricane made landfall as a Category 2 storm in Belize on the 19th, and continued through Guatemala and Mexico as a tropical system. After weakening to a depression, Fifi emerged into the Pacific Ocean, becoming the first crossover storm since Hurricane Irene-Olivia in 1971.

Fifi, for a long time was considered a Category 3 hurricane but was finally classified as a Category 2 hurricane, skirted the north coast of Honduras, causing massive flooding from the inflow of southerly winds. It was reported that 24 inches of rain fell in 36 hours across northeast Honduras. The rains collected in rivers, which caused enormous amounts of physical and economic damage to poor villages, small towns, and commercial banana plantations when it skimmed Honduras. Most of the country's fishing fleet was destroyed. Roughly half of food crops, including up to 95% of the banana crop, was wiped out. Fourteen bridges were washed away. The cities of Choloma, Omoa, and Tujillo and the island of Roatan were virtually destroyed. The Ulúa river valley became a lake about 20 miles wide for several days following Fifi. About 20% of railroad lines survived the cyclone. Although estimates of the number killed range from 3,000 to 10,000, a figure of 8,000 dead is generally accepted, ranking it as the fourth deadliest North Atlantic hurricane on record. Most deaths appear to have been caused by flash flooding from the rainfall that accompanied the hurricane.

This enormous amount of rainfall triggered mudslides and flash floods and caused rivers and streams to swell which, coupled with the winds, destroyed 182 towns and villages in just 24 hours. Resultant inland flooding caused an incredible amount of damage. The Ulua River Valley was transformed into a lake 20 miles wide. In the market town of Choloma, 2,300 people were killed when a natural dam created by landslides eventually gave way into a nearby river. About half of Honduras' food crops were destroyed by the winds and flooding, including coffee crops and 95% of the total banana crop, a major product accounting for some 50% of the country's exports. The fishing industry also suffered, as moorings were destroyed and ships grounded. Along its path, Fifi impacted nine countries, causing over 8,000 fatalities and $1.8 billion (1974 USD; $8.7 billion 2016 USD) in damage. Most of the loss of life and damage occurred in Honduras.[137]

Hurricane Eloise of 1975--A powerful hurricane which formed in September 1975, Eloise was a Category 3 hurricane with sustained winds of 125 mph, and gusts of up to 156 mph. It produced a 12 to 16 feet storm surge along the Florida Coast from Ft. Walton Beach to Panama City, Florida. With a minimum central pressure of 28.20 inches, Eloise was the first major hurricane to make a direct hit on this area in the 20th century and caused some $1 billion dollars in damage, as well as 21 deaths.

Hurricane Belle of 1976--A Category 3 hurricane at one point with 120 mph winds, Belle was the second named storm of the 1976 Atlantic Hurricane Season. The storm would eventually weaken, though; to just a tropical storm by the time it came ashore on Long Island. Shortly afterwards, it became extratropical.

Tropical Storm Claudette of 1979--Claudette was first detected as a tropical wave that moved off the African coast on July 11, 1979. The wave strengthened into a tropical depression on July 16 that briefly became a tropical storm the next day as it approached the Leeward and Virgin Islands. Claudette weakened to a tropical depression and then a tropical wave while passing near Puerto Rico on the 18th, and little re-development occurred until the system moved into the southeastern Gulf of Mexico on the 21st. Claudette regained tropical storm strength over the western Gulf on July 23 and made landfall the next day near the Louisiana-Texas border. The hurricane made a slow loop over southeastern Texas on the 24th and 25th, followed by a northward motion into Oklahoma on the 27th.

The remnants of Claudette turned eastward and merged with a frontal system over West Virginia on July 29. Claudette produced tropical storm conditions along portions of the Texas and Louisiana coasts, but the storm will

137 *http://www.hurricanescience.org/history/storms/1970s/fifi.* Retrieved: 12-12-2015.

be most remembered for its record breaking amounts of rainfall. Widespread amounts in excess of 10 inches occurred over portions of southeastern Texas and southwestern Louisiana, with several local amounts in excess of 30 inches. An observer west of Alvin, Texas, reported 43 inches in 24 hours, which is a United States record for 24 hours' rainfall amount. The storm total at that location was 45 inches. The rains produced severe flooding that was responsible for one death and $400 million in damage. The storm also produced heavy rains over portions of Puerto Rico that was responsible for one death.

Hurricane David of 1979--At the time, David was ranked as one of the strongest and deadliest Atlantic hurricanes on record. It formed from a tropical wave in the central Atlantic, east of the Windward Islands. The storm headed west, steadily strengthening. By the time David reached the Leeward Islands, it was a Category 4 hurricane. This storm also totally destroyed the island of Dominica, where the losses from this hurricane amounted to more than 100% of the island's gross domestic product and left over 80,000 persons homeless. David continued strengthening and reached Category 5 status south of Puerto Rico.

A twin engine C-46 aircraft lies atop an aircraft hangar at Las Americas Airport in the Dominican Republic, Sept. 2, 1979, after Hurricane David hit the capital Santo Domingo.[138]

[138] Wayne Neely, Rediscovering Hurricanes-The Major Hurricanes of the North Atlantic, (Bloomington, AuthorHouse Publishing, 2007).

The storm spent nearly two days at Category 5 intensity, storming through Santo Domingo, the capital of the Dominican Republic. Crossing the mountains of Hispaniola greatly weakened the storm nonetheless, David still exited the island as a weak Category 1 hurricane. This storm, according to most experts, set this country's economy back a staggering ten years. In the Bahamas, heavy rainfall fell on most islands causing widespread flooding and in one day alone, Long Island reported 9.35 inches, Long Cay 13.04 inches and Bimini 8.16 inches of rainfall. Fallen trees, downed power and communication lines and damage were done to the roofs, roads and docks. Considerable damage was done to the agriculture sector, but it was said to be mild in comparison to other countries of the Caribbean. The total damage to the Bahamas was estimated at U.S. $1.74 million (1979 USD) of which U.S. $1.41 or 81 percent was inflicted on agriculture. In addition, a further U.S. $400,000.00 in damage was done to a warehouse, a home and a hotel in New Providence by several tornadoes, which formed on the Monday afternoon of 03rd of September in the wake of Hurricane David.

David then strengthened into a Category 2 hurricane just off the South Florida coast. The western eyewall crossed the shoreline near Fort Lauderdale and continued up the entire length of the coast. The beach erosion was severe. David made landfall near Savannah, Georgia, as a Category 1 hurricane on September 4, 1979, and dissipated inland. David remains the only storm of Category 5 intensity to make landfall on the Dominican Republic in the 20th century and the deadliest since the 1930 Dominican Republic Hurricane. Also, the hurricane was the strongest to hit Dominica in the 20th century, and was the deadliest Dominican tropical cyclone since a hurricane killed over 200 in September of the 1834 season. David killed over 2,000 people in Hispaniola, 56 people on the island of Dominica, and 12 people in the U.S., as well as causing $1.54 billion (1979 USD) in damage. However, overall David is believed to have been responsible for 2,068 deaths, making it one of the deadliest hurricanes of the modern era. It caused torrential damage across its path, most of which occurred in the Dominican Republic where the hurricane made landfall as a Category 5 hurricane.

The devastation caused by Hurricane David in Dominica (Courtesy of Joyette Bruno).

Hurricane Frederic of 1979--Frederic in 1979 was a long-lived Cape Verde-type hurricane. It first became a hurricane in the central Atlantic east of the Windward Islands but soon weakened back into a tropical storm. Frederic crossed the rugged mountainous terrain of Hispaniola and weakened into a tropical depression. Frederic then crossed Cuba and regained tropical storm strength before entering the Gulf of Mexico. It was then that Frederic started to strengthen rapidly. By the time it reached a point just east of the Mississippi River Delta, Frederic was a Category 4 hurricane. It made landfall near the Alabama/Mississippi border with 125 mph winds. Due to prior warning, the death toll was minimal, with only five people losing their lives; however, damages soared to $2.3 billion (1979 dollars ($7.6 billion 2016 dollars)) in damage.

Hurricane Allen of 1980--The first named storm of the 1980 North Atlantic hurricane season, Allen became a Category 5 hurricane on three separate occasions and is ranked as one of the strongest storms ever recorded in the North Atlantic. Allen's eye didn't touch land from the time it crossed the Windward Islands, including St. Lucia, until it came ashore near Port Mansfield, Texas. Allen killed roughly 250 people, mostly in Haiti. Property damage was estimated at over $1 billion (1980 USD), mostly in the United States and Haiti.

Hurricane Alicia of 1983--A strong Category 3 hurricane with winds of 125 mph, Alicia was the last hurricane to make landfall in the Galveston, Texas, area back in August 1983. Alicia killed 22 people, and estimated damage from this storm was $2 billion dollars. Alicia was the first storm for which the National Hurricane Center issued numeric landfall probabilities. Probabilities had been calculated for prior storms for use in the issuing of hurricane watches and warnings, but this was the first time the raw numeric probabilities were released to the public. The probabilities issued were accurate, indicating that Galveston and surrounding portions of the upper Texas coast were the most likely areas, to be struck.

Hurricane Elena of 1985--A very fickle storm, Elena stayed away from land in the Gulf of Mexico for about a week as upper level winds broke weakened above the storm. As a result, it strengthened from a Category 1 to a Category 3 hurricane with 125 mph winds as it came ashore in Biloxi, Mississippi, in September 1985. Estimated damage as a result of this storm was $1.25 billion.

Hurricane Gloria of 1985--The first storm to be termed the 'Storm of the Century' at one point in its life. Gloria was one of the most destructive storms and the strongest hurricane of the 1985 hurricane season. This Category 3 hurricane made landfall over the Outer Banks of North Carolina, and then moved up the East Coast of the United States on September 27, 1985. Estimated damage from this storm was $900 million ($2.0 billion in 2016 USD) and killed eleven.

Hurricane Kate of 1985--An unusually strong late season hurricane, Kate was a Category 2 hurricane that struck the Port St. Joe area of the Florida Panhandle in November 1985. It was the latest hurricane ever recorded in a season to strike that far north in Florida. It ended up causing some $300 million in damage.

Hurricane Gilbert of 1988--A tropical wave exiting the African coastline on September 3rd developed into the 12th tropical depression of the season on September 8th while approaching the Windward Islands. The cyclone rapidly strengthened to hurricane status on September 10, 1988, as a west-northwest motion brought Gilbert into the eastern Caribbean Sea. Gilbert passed directly over Jamaica on September 12th as a major hurricane, becoming the first direct impact for the island from a hurricane since 1951. Winds gusts to nearly 150 mph were recorded as Gilbert produced a 9-foot storm surge along Jamaica's northeast coast. Jamaica was devastated as the eyewall traversed the entire length of the island. During this period, the eye contracted from 25 miles to only 12 miles upon exiting Jamaica. Gilbert emerged off the western coastline of Jamaica and began a period of extraordinarily rapid intensification.

The ferocious hurricane strengthened to Category 4 status as its northern eyewall pounded Grand Cayman Island with 155 mph wind gusts early on September 13th. Gilbert's remarkable intensification trend continued as the cyclone reached Category 5 status on the afternoon of the 13th and eventually reached peak winds of 185 mph. The minimum central pressure of the cyclone plummeted to 888 mbar (at the time becoming the most intense hurricane on record, but this was surpassed by Hurricane Wilma in 2005), which represented a 70- mbar drop in only a 24-hour period. This minimum central pressure recorded by NOAA aircraft remains the second lowest pressure ever recorded in the western hemisphere, second only to Hurricane Wilma of 2005. Gilbert crossed the northeast coast of Mexico's Yucatan peninsula on September 14th, becoming the first Category 5 hurricane in the Atlantic basin to strike land since Camille in 1969. Gilbert weakened over the Yucatan peninsula and emerged into the western Gulf of Mexico as a Category 2 hurricane.

Gilbert's large circulation regained major hurricane status as the hurricane continued on a west-northwest course on the 16th. The hurricane made its final landfall near the town of La Pesca on the Mexican Gulf Coast on the evening of September 16th as a strong Category 3 hurricane. Gilbert's remnants spawned 29 tornadoes over Texas on September 18th, with flooding spreading to the Midwest as the remnants merged with a frontal boundary over Missouri on September 19th. Although no reliable measurements of storm surge exist from Gilbert's two Mexican landfalls, estimates are that Gilbert produced between 15 and 20 feet of surge along the Yucatan, and 8 to 13 feet at landfall in mainland Mexico. Gilbert's large size and impacts were felt over much of the Caribbean, Central America, as well as portions of the United States.

Hurricane Gilbert blew this airplane from several yards away up into the trees at the Norman Manley International Airport, Jamaica (Courtesy of Edmundo Jenez)

The death toll of 318 gives an idea of the scope of Gilbert's impacts in the region: Mexico 202, Jamaica 45, Haiti 30, Guatemala 12, Honduras 12, Dominican Republic 5, Venezuela 5, United States 3, Costa Rica 2, and Nicaragua 2. The deaths from Costa Rica, Guatemala, Honduras, Nicaragua, and Venezuela were caused by inland flash flooding from the outer rain bands. Hurricane Gilbert made a direct hit over the country of Jamaica and destroyed that country's economy and left well over $1.2 billion in damage, mainly to tourism and agriculture in that country. It also left 45 people dead and well over 500,000 homeless on that island and left about four-fifths of the island's houses badly damaged or destroyed. According to The Organization of American States, Gilbert's losses amounted to 65% of the gross domestic product (GDP) of Jamaica. Hurricane Gilbert directly and indirectly impacted the island nation of Jamaica to such an extent that it brought their tourism industry to a virtual standstill for almost 2 years. Fortunately, local and international aid was able to bring some degree of stability to that country.

Hurricane Hugo of 1989--This classic Cape Verde type hurricane was first detected as a tropical wave emerging from the coast of Africa on September 9, 1989. Moving steadily westward, the system became a tropical depression the next day, a tropical storm on the 11th, and a hurricane on the 13th. Hugo turned west-northwest on September 15 as it became a Category 5 hurricane. It was still a Category 4 hurricane when the center moved through the Leeward Islands and St. Croix, United States Virgin Islands, and the 18th. Turning northwestward, the center passed across the eastern end of Puerto Rico on

September 19. This general motion would continue with some acceleration until Hugo made landfall just north of Charleston, South Carolina, on 22 September. Strengthening in the last twelve hours before landfall made Hugo a Category 4 hurricane at the coast. After landfall, the storm gradually recurved northeastward, becoming extratropical over southeastern Canada on September 23.

Hurricane Hugo totally destroyed the island of St. Lucia and other Windward and Leeward Islands and their main agricultural crops of banana and sugar cane. Before 1989, the economy of St. Lucia was almost totally dependent on agriculture as a main revenue earner, but after Hurricane Hugo it forced the government of St. Lucia to change its main dependence from banana and sugar cane to tourism as the main revenue earner, and so far it has worked out tremendously well for that country.

The Naval Air Station at Roosevelt Roads, Puerto Rico, reported sustained winds of 104 mph with gusts to 120 mph, which were the highest winds reported from the Caribbean. A ship moored in the Sampit River in South Carolina measured sustained winds of 120 mph. At one point in its lifetime, Hugo reached Category 5 intensity with 160 mph winds, and a minimum central pressure of 27.11 inches. High winds associated with Hugo extended far inland, with Shaw Air Force Base, South Carolina, reporting 67 mph sustained winds with gusts to 110 mph and Charlotte, North Carolina, reporting 69 mph sustained winds and gusts to 99 mph. Storm surge from Hugo inundated the South Carolina Coast from Charleston to Myrtle Beach, with maximum storm surge of 20 feet observed in the Cape Romain-Bulls Bay area. Hurricane Hugo caused 34 fatalities (most by electrocution or drowning) in the Caribbean and 27 in South Carolina, left nearly 100,000 homeless, and resulted in $10 billion (1989 USD) in damage overall, making it the most damaging hurricane ever recorded at the time. Of this total, $7 billion was from the United States and Puerto Rico, ranking it as the costliest storm to impact the country at the time. Since 1989, however, it has been surpassed by multiple storms (including Sandy in 2012) and now ranks as the eleventh costliest hurricane in the United States.

A Florida road completely destroyed after Hurricane Hugo (Florida Photographic Collection, Courtesy of the State Library and Archives of Florida).

Hurricane Bob of 1991--This Category 2 hurricane was one of the more memorable storms of the 1991 hurricane season, besides the "Perfect" Halloween Storm later that year. It moved up the East Coast before making landfall in New England. The 1991 hurricane season experienced relatively low activity, with just eight named storms, likely as the result of a strong El Niño that lasted from 1991 to 1994. Hurricane Bob was the most damaging storm of the season. The hurricane traveled up the East Coast of the United States, making landfall in Rhode Island. It was responsible for 17 deaths and an estimated $1.5 billion (1991 USD) in damage.

Hurricane Grace of 1991--Contrary to what was said in the movie *The Perfect Storm*, (staring George Clooney and Mark Walberg) Hurricane Grace was only a Category 1 storm, but it would combine with a mid-latitude cyclone to form what would be known as the "Perfect Storm" in meteorological terms during the final days of October 1991. In meteorology, as in nature, the weather elements always try to achieve a perfect balance, but thankfully they never do. But the week of October 27th to November 1st 1991, perfection to an extent was achieved in meteorology with what has come to be known as "The Perfect Storm." The

Perfect Storm is infamous for its powerful combination of multiple weather elements, something that had never happened before in recorded history. This storm was later made into a major motion picture several years later and was based on the bestselling novel by Sebastian Junger and the movie starring George Clooney and Mark Walberg.

The effects or repercussions of 'The Perfect Storm', or 'The Halloween Storm' as it was called by the meteorologists at the National Hurricane Center in Miami, were definitely felt from Northeast Canada to as far south as Puerto Rico, with large north and northeasterly swells from Tuesday 28th October, 1991, to Saturday, 02nd November, 1991. On Sunday 27th October, 1991, a late season hurricane called Hurricane Grace formed just southwest of Bermuda in the temperate Mid-Atlantic waters. Hurricane Grace moved northwestward toward North Carolina while a strong migratory high-pressure system over eastern Canada moved southeast towards the United States, with its leading edge marked by a vigorous cold front. The front exited the East Coast and forced Hurricane Grace northwards as an area of low pressure formed along the front about 700 miles to the north of Hurricane Grace. The high pressure in the east forced Hurricane Grace to head directly north along the front toward the stalling low-pressure area. The low pressure system absorbed Hurricane Grace into its circulation by undercutting and destroying Grace's low-level circulation.

It then developed into a massive extra-tropical cyclone which fed off the cold, dry air to its northwest and Grace's warmth and humidity. This extremely rare and unusual combination greatly enhanced and strengthened this extra-tropical storm, causing it to quickly intensify from 988 mbar to a very low pressure of 972 mbar within just 24 hours. During this process, it in turn transferred considerable energy from the winds to the waves, which resulted in progressively larger swells over the eastern shores of the United States, Canada, the Bahamas and Puerto Rico during this period. The main reason why it was called "The Perfect Storm" was because of these rare and unusual sequences of events which was involved in the process or evolution of this storm. Remarkably, it also earned the name "The Halloween Storm" as well because of two reasons, first, because of the time of year it occurred, and second, but most importantly, it donned a masterful disguise and the meteorologists and hurricane specialists at the National Hurricane Center had to 'unmask' it, so to speak, to reveal a tropical cyclone, or a 'hybrid storm.'

Meteorologists call them hybrid storms and find them very interesting to study, forecast and monitor because they aren't easy to categorize or explain because normally they don't fit into any particular weather mold or simply fit into more than one particular weather mold where the characteristics are quite opposite each other. A hybrid is anything of mixed origin, and the offspring produced by crossing two individuals of unlike constitutions forms an offspring, which have the characteristics of both regions from where they were formed. The image of an eye became apparent on the satellite pictures as the intensity of the storm increased or re-intensified. The discovery of an eye was a sure sign that the storm was developing a tropical structure and was of hurricane intensity.

The National Hurricane Center sent out a reconnaissance aircraft into the storm to investigate this storm, and when they got into the storm they found a cluster of hurricane hallmarks: winds of nearly 100 mph at flight level, a temperature increase of seven degrees in the storm's core (indicating a warm core system), a well defined center with convective activity around the center, and an extrapolated surface pressure of 981 mbar. Although the formation of a hurricane in the center of a large extratropical low is unusual, it has happened before in this region. For example, Hurricane Karl formed in the center of a deep layer non-tropical cyclone in the central Atlantic on November 25th 1980. With this hurricane, it met all the meteorological standards to be designated or categorized as a hurricane, but yet still it became one of a rare few cases where it went unnamed (the extremely busy and very active 2005 season was another storm-hurricane #28 which went unnamed) in the North Atlantic basin since the modern naming process began in 1950.

This decision to allow this storm to go unnamed was made by a consortium of National Weather Service forecasters (including National Oceanic Atmospheric Administration (NOAA) National Meteorological Center, the U.S. Navy, the Maritimes Weather Center of the Atmospheric Environment Service of Canada and other selected national weather service forecast offices). The reason for this was simple, at the time of the hurricane most of the news media attention was focused on the massive damage incurred along the coastal United States from the large oceanic swells, so they decided against it to avoid unnecessarily confusion and alarming the public. In addition, these meteorologists at the time felt that this unnamed hurricane was only a threat to maritime interests and was no threat to land area, so they decided against naming it. Up until 1995, this was a heated debate and a very controversial topic within the meteorological community as to whether this hybrid storm was indeed a hurricane, but eventually the majority of the meteorologists came to the conclusion that it was indeed a hurricane. In terms of damage to these areas, this storm reached its climatic peak on Thursday, 31st October, 1991. This storm generated large ocean swells, high surf and associated coastal flooding conditions from the coastal United States all the way down to Puerto Rico in the south, causing hundreds of millions of dollars in damage.

Hurricane Andrew of 1992

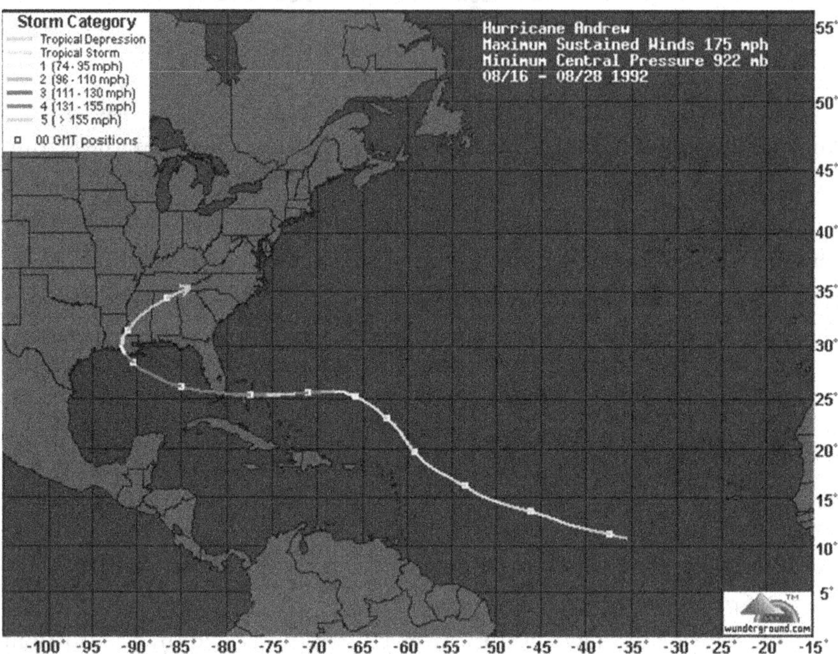

This map shows the track of Hurricane Andrew in 1992 as it moved through the Bahamas, Florida and the Gulf States in the USA (Information courtesy of the Weather Underground Inc.).

Every fifty to one hundred years, there comes a hurricane that redefines and reintroduces hurricanes on a level or platform that had never been experienced or done before with any previous hurricane, and Hurricane Andrew was definitely that defining storm. Furthermore, there is a hurricane that comes along and changes a country and a region so drastically that it will be remembered for generations to come, Hurricane Andrew was definitely that storm. Hurricane Andrew was one of the most destructive hurricanes to affect this region. Hurricane Andrew was, at the time of its occurrence in August 1992, the costliest hurricane in United States history. This hurricane forced South Florida to re-evaluate and change its building codes and upgraded these codes to withstand future storms like Hurricane Andrew or stronger. This hurricane is probably one of three most recent memorable destructive hurricanes in modern history. After struggling to develop in the Atlantic, this Category 5 hurricane quickly developed over the Gulf Stream and devastated the Bahamas, South Florida and South Central Louisiana with strong winds of 165 mph on August 23rd thru 26th 1992. Today, it remains the fifth costliest hurricane disaster on record in U.S. history, with some $26.5 billion in damage, fifth only to the recent 1) Hurricane Katrina (2005), 2) Sandy (2012), 3) Ike (2008), and 4) Wilma (2005).

Striking as the first named storm of the 1992 Atlantic hurricane season in August 1992, Andrew caused great damage in the northwestern Bahamas, southern Florida south of Miami, and south-central Louisiana. The storm caused 65 deaths. More than 80,000 homes were destroyed, and another 55,000 were badly damaged in Florida alone. The storm destroyed about 63,000 of Dade County's 528,000 residences and damaged another 110,000. Nine public schools were reduced to rubbles and 23 heavily damaged. More than 9 out of every 10 mobiles homes were obliterated in south Dade County, and only 1 percent of the city of Homestead's mobile homes survived intact.[139]

The storm virtually obliterated South Florida's lime, avocado, tropical fruit, and nursery industries. The hurricane flattened an area the size of Chicago. The people of Florida were not really concerned about hurricanes. There had been no serious hurricanes to hit land since the 1950s, and for decades the suburbs of Miami expanded and developed with little regard to any disaster that could strike. Even when Hurricane Andrew began to form out in the Atlantic, there was no sense of urgency. Initial reports suggested that the hurricane would move up the eastern seaboard. But it changed direction, leaving the people of Florida with little time to prepare.

After the hurricane, desperate survivors, upon returning to their Florida homes, found no infrastructure left. Electricity and running water were gone. An influx of 16,000 troops helped to maintain order while relief workers from all over the country began to restore normality to the region. Before Hurricane

---

[139] Edward Rappaport (10-12-1993). *Hurricane Andrew. National Hurricane Center (Preliminary Report)* (Miami, Florida: United States National Oceanic and Atmospheric Administration's National Weather Service). Retrieved: 06-06-2015. Max Mayfield (1992-08-17). *Tropical Depression Three Discussion One (TXT). National Hurricane Center (Report).* Hurricane Andrew, Hurricane Wallet Digital Archives (Miami, Florida: United States National Oceanic and Atmospheric Administration's National Weather Service). Retrieved: 06-06-2015.

Andrew, Florida was regarded as one of the best places in the United States to live. The destruction caused by the Hurricane showed just how vulnerable the state really was to natural disasters. About 25,000 people left the area and never returned.

Hurricane Andrew devastated this Homestead, Florida, community (Courtesy of NOAA-NHC).

Andrew started modestly as a tropical wave that emerged from the west coast of Africa on August 14 and passed south of the Cape Verde islands. The wave morphed into a tropical depression on August 16, which became Tropical Storm Andrew the next day. Further development was slow, as the west-northwestward moving Andrew encountered an unfavorable upper-level trough. The storm almost dissipated on August 20, due to strong vertical wind shear. By August 21, Andrew was midway between Bermuda and Puerto Rico and then began turning westward into a more favorable environment. Rapid strengthening occurred, with Andrew reaching hurricane strength on the 22nd and Category 5 status on the Saffir-Simpson Hurricane Wind Scale on the 23, peaking with 175 mph winds and a minimum pressure of 922 mbar. The storm was extremely small, however, with gale-force (35 mph) winds extending outwards only 90 miles from the center.[140]

Andrew was the first major hurricane to affect the Bahamas since Hurricane Betsy in 1965. It caused $250 million in damage (1992 USD, $425 million 2016 USD), with damage heaviest on Eleuthera and Cat Cay. Four deaths occurred due to the storm, of which one was indirectly related to the hurricane. Andrew made landfall twice while moving through the Bahamas, crossing the island of Eleuthera with sustained winds of 160 mph and passing through the Berry Islands at Great Harbor Cay with sustained winds of 150 mph. The storm weakened after its second landfall, maintaining strong winds, but with the pressure rising to 937 mbar. While crossing the Gulf Stream, however, Andrew quickly regained its strength and briefly regained Category 5 status as it made landfall over South Florida on August 24 with 165 mph winds and pressure of 922 mbar.

The hurricane continued westward into the Gulf of Mexico as a Category 4 hurricane, where it gradually turned northward. This motion brought Andrew to the central Louisiana coast (near Morgan City) August 26 as a Category 3 hurricane, with sustained winds near 115mph. By noon on August 26, Hurricane Andrew was downgraded to tropical storm status for the first time since August 22. The system was in eastern Tennessee by the morning of August 28th where the system merged with a cold front, the remains of the Pacific Hurricane Lester. Andrew finally died out in Pennsylvania on August 29th 1992.[141]

---

140 Edward Rappaport (1993-12-10). *Hurricane Andrew. National Hurricane Center (Preliminary Report)* (Miami, Florida: United States National Oceanic and Atmospheric Administration's National Weather Service). Retrieved: 06-06-2015. Max Mayfield (1992-08-17). *Tropical Depression Three Discussion One (TXT). National Hurricane Center (Report)*. Hurricane Andrew, Hurricane Wallet Digital Archives (Miami, Florida: United States National Oceanic and Atmospheric Administration's National Weather Service). Retrieved: 06-06-2015.

141 Arthur Rolle, *The Effects of Hurricane Andrew in the Bahamas*-(Nassau, The Bahamas Department of Meteorology Official Hurricane Andrew Report, 1992), pgs-1-10.

Hurricane Andrew devastated this South Florida community (Courtesy of NOAA-NHC).

Reports from private barometers helped establish that Andrew's central pressure at landfall in Homestead, Florida, was 27.23 inches (922 mbar), which at the time made it the third most intense hurricane on record to hit the United States (it has since fallen to fourth, as of 2015). Andrew was only the third Category 5 hurricane to hit the United States, the previous ones being Hurricane Camille (which hit Mississippi and Louisiana in August 1969) and the Great Labor Day Hurricane of 1935 (which struck the Florida Keys in September 1935).

Amazingly, Hurricane Andrew's peak winds in South Florida were not directly measured due to destruction of the measuring instruments. An automated station at Fowey Rocks reported 142 mph sustained winds with gusts to 169 mph (measured 144 ft above the ground), and higher values may have occurred after the station was damaged and stopped reporting. The National Hurricane Center had a peak gust of 164 mph (measured 130 feet above the ground), while a 177 mph gust was measured at a private home. No Category 5 hurricane in the North Atlantic has struck the United States at that intensity since. Andrew was responsible for 23 deaths in the United States, and three more in the Bahamas. There were 65 (26 direct, 39 indirect) total deaths attributed to Andrew.[142]

Unlike most hurricanes, surprisingly, the vast majority of the damage in Florida was due to the winds. The agricultural loss in Florida was $1.04 billion alone. Hurricane Andrew was reclassified as a Category 5 hurricane, with winds estimated to be about 165 mph. Initially, the maximum winds at landfall were reported to be 145 mph, but a panel convened in 2002 to assess Andrew's intensity concluded, based mostly on engineering analyses of the damage, that the highest sustained winds were about 165 mph. The reason for the reclassification was a better mathematical model which estimated surface winds based on the data gathered by the Reconnaissance Aircrafts. This improved model produced a wind speed higher than previously thought. Hurricane experts agreed and upgraded Andrew from a Category 4 hurricane to a Category 5 storm, one of the rare times this has happened where a hurricane was upgraded and reclassified after the hurricane season had ended. Hurricane Andrew was interesting because it actually had what hurricane experts call a 'double eyewall.' This is literally one eye about 8 miles wide inside larger one about 25 miles wide. The strongest winds were in the inner eye wall that surrounds the calm center of the storm. The outer eyewall has weaker winds than the inner wall, but stronger winds than those found in the space between the outer and inner walls.

Tropical Storm Alberto of 1994--Alberto was first detected as a tropical wave that moved off the African coast on June 18, 1994. The wave moved into the western Caribbean by late June and formed into a tropical depression near the western tip of Cuba on June 30. The cyclone moved northwest through July 1 as it became a tropical storm, then it turned northward. This motion continued until the cyclone made landfall in the western Florida Panhandle on the 4th. Alberto then moved north-northeastward into western Georgia, where it did a loop on the 5th and 6th. The cyclone finally dissipated over central Alabama on July 7. Tropical Storm Alberto was a strong tropical storm at landfall in early July

---

142 Edward Rappaport (1993-12-10). *Hurricane Andrew. National Hurricane Center (Preliminary Report)* (Miami, Florida: United States National Oceanic and Atmospheric Administration's National Weather Service). Retrieved: 06-06-2015. Max Mayfield (1992-08-17). *Tropical Depression Three Discussion One (TXT). National Hurricane Center (Report)*. Hurricane Andrew, Hurricane Wallet Digital Archives (Miami, Florida: United States National Oceanic and Atmospheric Administration's National Weather Service). Retrieved: 06-06-2015.

1994, but it would end up being one of the most memorable tropical storms as it proceeded to meander over northwest Florida and southern Georgia. Alberto's winds and tides produced only minor damage at the coast, but the excessive rains that fell in Georgia, Alabama, and western Florida were another story. Amounts exceeded 10 inches in many locations, with the maximum being the 27.61 inches, with the maximum amount of rainfall occurring at Americus, GA (including 21 inches in 24 hours). Severe flooding resulted over large portions of southern Georgia, western Alabama, and the western Florida Panhandle. The floods were responsible for 30 deaths and $500 million in damage.

Hurricane Gordon of 1994--One of the most unusual, erratic moving and long-lived hurricanes, and still one of the deadliest hurricanes in the last 21 years. Starting out in the western Caribbean off the coast of Honduras and Nicaragua, Gordon made its way through the Caribbean and Florida before making its first landfall as a Category 1 hurricane along the Outer Banks of North Carolina. It then turned southwestward again and moved over Florida, where it finally dissipated. Gordon was a catastrophic storm in Haiti, killing an estimated 1,122 people. Although Gordon was a tropical storm for most of its existence, it caused enormous damage and loss of life.

Haiti, unfortunately, often suffers great death tolls from many hurricanes or tropical storms over the years simply because of the majority of the hills are devoid of trees or vegetation. In most cases, the trees were removed for firewood or cooking, leading to exacerbated deadly flash floods. Hurricane Gordon killed 1,122 in the impoverished nation in 1994. It has been argued that the damage caused by Hurricane Gordon, among other storms, are in part human-induced disasters or climate change. Massive deforestation has left Haiti with about 1.4% of its forests, leaving denuded mountain slopes that rainwater washes down unimpeded. The lack of tree cover contributed to the devastating floods that caused a majority of the deaths resulting from Hurricane Gordon.

Six deaths were reported in Costa Rica, five in the Dominican Republic, two in Jamaica, two in Cuba, and eight in Florida. Property damage to the United States was estimated at $400 million (1994 dollars). Property damage statistics for the other affected areas are not available but were reportedly severe in both Haiti and Cuba. Interestingly enough, despite the devastation in Haiti and the extensive damage in Cuba and Florida, Gordon was not retired in 1994. The World Meteorological Organization issued an official statement crediting Jamaica and Cuba's warning infrastructure for the low loss of life there and blaming Haiti's lack of such a system for the large number of deaths there. The name Gordon was used for the first time in 1994 (replacing 1988's Gilbert) and was used again in the 2000 and 2006 seasons. The storm left some $400 million dollars in damage and 1145 people dead in November 1994.

Hurricane Erin of 1995--The 1995 season was extremely active, largely due to favorable environmental conditions, including a La Niña event and very warm sea surface temperatures. Erin was the first hurricane to hit the U.S. since Hurricane Andrew in 1992. Nineteen named storms formed during the season, making it the third most active on record, behind the 2005 and 1933 seasons and tied with 1887 season. There were also eleven storms that reached hurricane strength, again the third most hurricanes in one season after the 1969 and 2005 seasons. Heavy rains occurred in Jamaica, which caused a plane crash that killed 5 people. The plane was a Cessna 310 twin-engine aircraft, owned by Region Air, a subsidiary of the Guardsman Group. The aircraft contained four employees of Brinks Jamaica, who were due to testify in a court hearing, and a pilot. The plane departed from the Tinson Pen Aerodome in Kingston, Jamaica, and was bound for Montego Bay, St. James. Two teenagers were also killed on a football field in Braeton, Saint Catherine Parish, when lightning associated with Erin struck them dead.

Erin actually made two landfalls over Florida. The first occurred on August 2nd at Vero Beach, and the second a few days later over Pensacola as a strong Category 1 hurricane with 90 mph winds. Rain from this system was felt as far north as Illinois, and the storm caused some $700 million ($1.1 billion 2016 USD) in damage. The cruise ship Club Royale sank, causing three of the deaths. Another ship was also sunk due to Erin. More than one million people lost power due to the hurricane. Six drowning deaths are attributed to Erin off the coasts of Florida and the Bahamas.

Hurricane Luis of 1995--Luis was one of the most powerful hurricanes of the 1995 season. This storm devastated the Leeward Islands, as well as parts of Puerto Rico and the Virgin Islands, with sustained winds of 150 mph before turning out to sea in September 1995. This storm caused approximately $2.5 billion in damage and killed 17 people.

Hurricane Marilyn of 1995--Formed on the heels of Hurricane Luis in the Western Atlantic back in September 1995 and brought Category 3 hurricane force winds to parts of the Leeward Islands and the Virgin Islands before turning out to sea. Caused approximately $1.5 billion in damage and left 8 people dead.

Many homes and businesses in Puerto Rico were destroyed when Hurricane Marilyn destroyed many homes and businesses on this island, Sunday September 17, 1995 (Courtesy of NOAA/FEMA).

Hurricane Opal of 1995--Opal was first detected as a tropical wave moving off the African coast on September 11. The waved moved westward through the Atlantic and Caribbean and merged with a broad low pressure area over the western Caribbean on September 23. The combined system then developed into a tropical depression near the east coast of the Yucatan Peninsula on September 27. The depression drifted slowly northward, becoming Tropical Storm Opal as it reached the north coast of Yucatan on the 30th. Opal then moved slowly westward into the Bay of Campeche, where it became a hurricane on October 2. A gradual north-northeastward turn started later on the 2nd, with acceleration on the 3rd and 4th. Opal continued to strengthen, and a period of rapid strengthening late of the 3rd and early on the 4th made it a Category 4 hurricane. Weakening followed, and Opal was a Category 3 hurricane when it made landfall near Pensacola Beach, Florida, late on the 4th.

Opal continued quickly north-northeastward and became extratropical over the Ohio Valley on the 5th. The hurricane was last seen over the eastern Great Lakes on October 6. Hurlbert Field, Florida, reported sustained winds of 84 mph with a peak gust of 144 mph, and gusts to 70 mph occurred as far inland as northwest Georgia. However, the main impact from Opal was from storm surge. A combination of storm surge and breaking waves inundated portions of the western Florida Panhandle coast to a depth of 10 to 20 feet. The surge was responsible for the bulk of the $3 billion in damage attributed to Opal in the United States. Opal was responsible for 9 deaths in the United States, including 8 from falling trees and one from a tornado. Opal was responsible for 50 deaths in Mexico and Guatemala due to flooding caused by heavy rains.

Hurricane Roxanne of 1995--Formed in the Bay of Campeche region of Mexico in the weeks following Hurricane Opal's landfall near Panama City, Florida. The storm was a Category 3 hurricane with sustained winds of 115 mph, and a minimum central pressure of 28.23 inches of Hg. The storm left 14 people dead and some $1.5 billion in damage.

Hurricane Bertha of 1996--This was one of the earliest hurricanes to form in the Eastern Atlantic during the 1996 hurricane season. Developed just west of the Cape Verde islands in the last week of June 1996 and made landfall as a Category 2 hurricane over Wilmington, North Carolina, on July 12, 1996. Killed 12 people and caused some $275 million in damage.

Hurricane Fran of 1996--This was the most powerful hurricane to make landfall in the United States during the 1996 hurricane season. It made landfall over North Carolina with sustained winds of 115 mph in September of that year and caused some $3.2 billion in damage at the time. Damage estimates are even higher today.

Hurricane Hortense of 1996--Was a hurricane that formed during the Labor Day weekend of the 1996 hurricane season. While the storm didn't make landfall in the United States, it ravaged parts of the Caribbean, including Puerto Rico, with torrential rains. Damage estimates from this storm amounted to approximately $500 million. Hortense reached tropical storm status on September 7, while east of the Lesser Antilles. It moved west over Guadeloupe, and once in the Caribbean Sea it reached hurricane strength. Hortense turned northward and crossed southwestern Puerto Rico near Guánica on September 10. Hortense then grazed the eastern coast of the Dominican Republic and headed north. Hortense then brought hurricane force winds to the Turks and Caicos Islands. The storm continued strengthening and briefly peaked at Category 4 strength. Its northward motion accelerated, and a weakened Hortense became extratropical near Newfoundland on September 15. There were 21 people killed, and another 21 reported missing. Damage in Puerto Rico was estimated at $127 million.

Hurricane Georges of 1998--This hurricane was indeed a very powerful and long-lived classic Cape Verde-type Category 4 hurricane. It caused severe destruction as it passed through the Caribbean and Gulf of Mexico in September 1998, making seven landfalls along its path. Georges was the seventh tropical storm, fourth hurricane, and second major hurricane of the 1998 North Atlantic hurricane season. It became the second most destructive storm of the season after Hurricane Mitch and the costliest North Atlantic since Hurricane Andrew in 1992. Georges killed 604 people, mainly on the island of Hispaniola, and caused extensive damage resulting at just under $10 billion (1998 US dollars, $14.1 billion 2016 USD) in damage mostly in St. Kitts and Nevis, Puerto Rico and Hispaniola. The hurricane made landfall in at least seven different countries (Antigua and Barbuda, St. Kitts and Nevis, Haiti, the Dominican Republic, Cuba and the United States) and Puerto Rico, a Commonwealth of the United States — more than any other hurricane since Hurricane Inez of the 1966 season.

A large and long-lasting hurricane, Hurricane Georges brought torrential rainfall, flashfloods and mudslides along much of its path through the Greater Antilles. In all, the hurricane caused $9.72 billion (1998 USD) in damage to the United States and its possessions and resulted in 604 fatalities, with the most of them occurring in the Dominican Republic. In the two months after Georges' final landfall, the American Red Cross spent $104 million (1998 USD, $152 million 2015 USD) on relief aid through Puerto Rico, the U.S. Virgin Islands, Florida, Louisiana, Alabama, and Mississippi, making Georges the costliest disaster aid in the program's 125-year history.

This Category 4 hurricane ripped through the Leeward Islands and Caribbean with sustained winds of 150 mph. It then hit the Florida Keys before making landfall in Mississippi. In the Dominican Republic, it left an estimated 100,000 persons homeless, and approximately 70 percent of the bridges on this island were badly damaged or totally destroyed. Approximately 90 percent of all plantation crops were ruined. In Puerto Rico, more than 33,000 homes were destroyed and 50,000 more suffered major or minor damage. Georges destroyed 75 percent of the coffee crop in Puerto Rico and 95 percent of its plantation crops.[143]

143 *http://www.nhc.noaa.gov/data- "NHC Hurricane Georges Report Archived October 5, 2009"*. Retrieved: 08-08-2015.

Hurricane Mitch in 1998

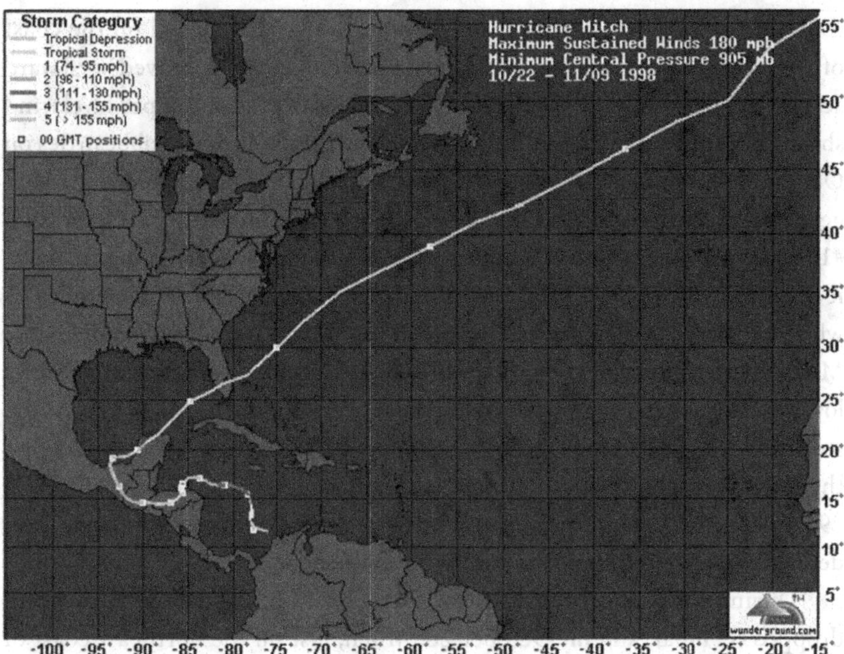

This map shows the track of Hurricane Mitch in 1998 as it moved through Central America and South Florida (Information courtesy of The Weather Underground Inc.).

Hurricane Mitch, a very large hurricane, formed in the western Caribbean Sea on October 22, 1998, and after moving into extremely favorable environmental conditions, it rapidly strengthened to peak at Category 5 status, the highest possible rating on the Saffir-Simpson Hurricane Wind Scale. After drifting southwestward and weakening, the hurricane struck Honduras only as a minimal hurricane. It gradually drifted through Central America, reformed in the Bay of Campeche, and eventually struck Florida as a strong tropical storm. Due to its slow movement from October 29 to November 3, Hurricane Mitch released record breaking amounts of rainfall in the countries of Honduras and Nicaragua, with unofficial reports of up to 75 inches being reported in some areas. The results remain unofficial because most of the recording instruments and records were simply destroyed or washed away in the storm. Deaths due to catastrophic flash flooding made it the second deadliest North Atlantic hurricane in history; nearly 11,000 people were killed, with over 8,000 left missing by the end of 1998. The flooding caused extreme damage, estimated at over $6.2 billion.[144]

Hurricane Mitch formed from a tropical wave that moved off the coast of Africa near the Cape Verde Islands, on October 10. It moved westward across the North Atlantic Ocean under the influence of strong upper-level wind shear, and remained relatively disorganized until entering the Caribbean Sea on October 18. Upon entering the western Caribbean Sea, the system started to get better organized, and on October 21, the wave became Tropical Depression #13 while 415 miles south of Kingston, Jamaica. Under weak steering currents, it drifted slowly westward and intensified into a tropical storm on October 23 while 260 miles east-southeast of San Andrés Island and was given the name Mitch. At first, intensification was limited due to interaction with an upper-level low which caused strong vertical wind shear over Tropical Storm Mitch. As the storm made a small loop to the north, the upper-level shear weakened, allowing the system to strengthen. Mitch attained hurricane status on October 24 while 295 miles south of Jamaica and with warm sea surface temperatures and well-defined outflow, the hurricane rapidly strengthened.[145]

During a 24-hour period from October 24-25, the central pressure dropped 52 mbar, and on October 26, Mitch, just off the northeast coast of Honduras, reached peak intensity with 180 mph and gusts well over 200 mph winds and a pressure of 905 mbar, one of the lowest pressures ever recorded in a North Atlantic hurricane. Mitch thus became tied for the fourth strongest North Atlantic hurricane on record based upon barometric pressure values. Though the pressure began rising six hours later, Mitch remained at Category 5 status for a continuous period of 33 hours - the longest continuous period for a Category 5 storm since the 36 consecutive hours by Hurricane David in 1979. In addition, Mitch maintained sustained winds of 155 mph for 15 hours - the third longest period of such winds on record after the continuous 18 hours of 155 mph winds or higher by Hurricane Camille in 1969 and Hurricane Dog in 1950. Though exact comparisons are suspect due to differing frequencies in observation times (3-hourly versus 6-hourly observations) and a bias in earlier years toward higher estimated wind speeds, it is quite apparent that Mitch was one of the stronger storms ever recorded in the North Atlantic. The hurricane

144 John L. Guiney; Miles B. Lawrence (1999-01-28). *Hurricane Mitch Preliminary Report (PDF) (Report)*. National Hurricane Center. Retrieved: 15-03-2015.

145 Ibid. Retrieved: 15-03-2015.

matched the fourth most intense Atlantic hurricane on record (it has since dropped to seventh).

A strong ridge of high pressure forced the hurricane westward, resulting in its land interaction with Honduras. This weakened Mitch slightly, and after passing over the Swan Islands on October 27, the hurricane steadily weakened. The ridge of high pressure built further, forcing the hurricane to drift southward along the Honduran coastline. Mitch made landfall 80 miles east of La Ceiba in Honduras on October 29 as a Category 1 hurricane on the Saffir-Simpson Hurricane Wind Scale, with 80 mph winds. It continued to weaken over land, drifting westward through Central America, and its low-level circulation dissipated on November 1 near the Guatemala-Mexico border. The remnant area of low pressure drifted northward into the Bay of Campeche and reorganized on November 3 into a tropical storm while 150 miles southwest of Mérida, Yucatán.

Mitch moved to the northeast, making landfall on the Yucatán Peninsula near Campeche on November 4. It weakened to a tropical depression over land but re-strengthened to a tropical storm over the southeastern Gulf of Mexico. As Mitch moved rapidly to the northeast in combination with a cold front that was extending into Gulf, it gradually intensified and made landfall near Naples, Florida, on November 5 as a tropical storm with 65 mph winds. One person was killed in the U.S. near Dry Tortugas, when a fisherman died from a capsized boat. A second person was missing. Another person died as a result of an auto accident on a slick highway. Mitch passed through the Bahamas and finally became extratropical later that day on November 5, but it continued to persist for several days before losing its identity just north of Great Britain on November 9.

Hurricane Mitch resulted in nearly eleven thousand people being confirmed dead, and almost as many reported missing. Deaths were mostly from flooding and mudslides in Central America, where the slow-moving hurricane and then tropical storm dropped nearly 3 feet of rain. The resulting floods and mudslides virtually destroyed the entire infrastructure of Honduras and devastated parts of Nicaragua, Guatemala, Belize, and El Salvador. Whole villages and their inhabitants were swept away in the torrents of flood waters and deep mud that came rushing down the mountainsides. The flooding and mudslides damaged or destroyed tens of thousands of homes, with total damage amounting to over $5 billion, most of which was in Honduras and Nicaragua. Prior to Hurricane Mitch, the deadliest hurricane in Central America was Hurricane Fifi in 1974, which killed an estimated 8,000 to 10,000 persons.

Prior to hitting Honduras, Hurricane Mitch sent waves of up to 22 feet in height to the coast. Upon making landfall, it diminished in intensity but still caused a strong storm surge and waves of 12 feet in height. While the storm was drifting over the country, it provided an excessive amount of rainfall with nearly 36 inches in Choluteca, where over 18 inches of that total amount of rain fell in one day. The rainfall in Choluteca was equivalent to the average rainfall total in 212 days that normally occurs in that city. In addition, there were estimates of as high as 75 inches in the mountainous regions. Mitch caused such massive and widespread damage that Honduran President Carlos Roberto Flores said that it destroyed fifty years of progress in that country. Mitch destroyed about 70% of the crops, totaling to about $1 billion in losses. An estimated 70-80% of the transportation infrastructure of the entire country was wiped out, including nearly all bridges and secondary roads; the damage was so great that existing maps were rendered obsolete. About 25 small villages were reported to have been entirely destroyed by the massive landslides caused by the storm. Damages to the transportation and communication networks totaled to $671. Across the country, the storm destroyed 33,000 houses and damaged 50,000 others. In addition, it downed numerous trees, leaving mountainsides bare and more vulnerable to future mudslides.

Village ravaged by Hurricane Mitch on Guanaja, Bahia Islands, Honduras (Courtesy of NOAA-NHC).

Mitch's rainfall resulted in severe agricultural losses in the country, affecting more than 300 sq. miles or 29% of the country's arable land. The flooding led to severe losses in food crops, including 58% of the corn output, 24% of sorghum, 14% of rice, and 6% of the bean crop. Several important export crops faced similar losses, including 85% of banana, 60% of sugar cane, 29% of melons, 28% of African palms, and 18% of coffee. Crop damage alone totaled to more than $1.97 billion. Large amounts of animal losses occurred as well, including the death of 50,000 bovines and the losses of 60% of the fowl population. Shrimp production, which had become an important export, faced nearly complete destruction. Total animal losses amounted to $348 million and was estimated that damage inflicted to agriculture will take years to recover.[146]

The extreme flooding and mudslides killed over 6,500, with up to 11,000 missing. Many of the unidentified bodies were buried in mass graves or cremated, resulting in great uncertainty over the final death toll. Tegucigalpa Mayor Cesar Castellanos, a likely candidate for Honduras' presidency in elections in 2001, and three others were killed when their helicopter crashed while surveying the hurricane and flood damage on Sunday, November 1. Over 20% of the country's population, possibly as many as 1.5 million people were left homeless. The severe crop shortages left many villages on the brink of starvation, while lack of sanitation led to outbreaks of malaria, dengue fever, and cholera.

Two million people in Nicaragua were directly affected by Hurricane Mitch. Across the country, Mitch's heavy rains damaged 17,600 houses and destroyed 23,900, leaving 368,300 homeless. 340 schools and 90 health centers were severely damaged or destroyed. Sewage systems and the electricity sub sector were severely damaged, and, combined with property, damage totaled $348 million. Transportation was greatly affected by the hurricane as well. The rainfall left 70% to 80% of the roads unusable and destroyed or greatly damaged 71 bridges.[147]

---

146 *Central America After Hurricane Mitch: The Challenge of Turning a Disaster into an Opportunity* (Report). Inter-American Development Bank. 2000. Archived from the original on April 19, 2013. Retrieved: 22-05-2013.

147 *Mitch: The Deadliest Atlantic Hurricane Since 1780* (Report). National Climatic Data Center. 2009-01-23. Retrieved: 20-06-2015.

Most intense North Atlantic hurricanes Intensity is measured solely by minimal central pressure			
Rank	**Hurricane**	**Season**	**Min. pressure**
1	Wilma	2005	882 mb (hPa)
2	Gilbert	1988	888 mbar (hPa)
3	The Great Labour Day Hurricane	1935	892 mbar (hPa)
4	Rita	2005	895 mbar (hPa)
5	Allen	1980	899 mbar (hPa)
6	Katrina	2005	902 mbar (hPa)
7	Camille	1969	900 mbar (hPa)
	Mitch	**1998**	**905 mbar (hPa)**
8	Dean	2007	905 mbar (hPa)
10	Cuba	1924	910 mbar (hPa)
10	Ivan	2004	910mbar (hPa)

The most intense North Atlantic hurricanes (Courtesy of HURDAT and wikipedia.org)[148]

A ridge of high pressure forced the hurricane westward, resulting in land interaction with Honduras. This weakened Mitch slightly, and after passing over the Swan Islands on October 27, the hurricane steadily weakened. The ridge of high pressure built further, forcing the hurricane to drift southward along the Honduran coastline. Mitch made landfall 80 miles east of La Ceiba in Honduras on October 29 as a Category 1 hurricane on the Saffir-Simpson Hurricane Wind Scale, with 80 mph winds. It continued to weaken over land, drifting westward through Central America, and its low-level circulation dissipated on November 1 near the Guatemala-Mexico border.

148 *https://en.wikipedia.org/wiki/List_of_Atlantic_hurricane_records/HURDAT.* Retrieved: 08-08-2015.

Several residents walking among the ruins to salvage some of their personal effects and major flood damage along the Choluteca River caused by Hurricane Mitch in 1998 in Tegucigalpa, Honduras.

Due to the threat, the Government of Honduras evacuated some of the 45,000 citizens on the Bay Islands and deployed all air and naval resources throughout the country. The Government of Belize issued a red alert and asked for citizens on offshore islands to leave for the mainland. Because the hurricane threatened to strike near Belize City as a Category 4 hurricane, much of the city was evacuated in fear of a repeat of Hurricane Hattie 37 years earlier. The destruction from Hurricane Hattie was so severe that it prompted the government to relocate inland to a new city, Belmopan. Overall, Hattie caused about $60 million in losses and 307 deaths in Belize (then British Honduras). It caused 307 fatalities in Belize and devastated the then city of Belmopan. Guatemala issued a red alert as well, recommending boats to stay in port, telling people to prepare or seek shelter, and warning of potential overflowing rivers. By the time Mitch made landfall, numerous people were evacuated along the western Caribbean coastline, including 100,000 in Honduras, 10,000 in Guatemala, and 20,000 in the Mexican state of Quintana Roo.

Hurricane Mitch Impact by Region

Region:	Deaths:	Damages:
Belize	11	$50 thousand
Costa Rica	7	$92 million
El Salvador	240	$400 million
Guatemala	268	$748 million
Honduras	14,600	$3.8 billion
Jamaica	3	
Mexico	9	$1 million
Nicaragua	3,800	$1 billion
Panama	3	$50 thousand
United States	2	$40 million
Offshore	31	
Total:	**18,974**	**$6.08 billion**[1]

Hurricane Mitch impact by region

In all, Hurricane Mitch caused at least 3,800 fatalities in Nicaragua, of which more than 2,000 were killed from the mudslide of the Casitas volcano when the walls of the crater collapsed. The mudslide buried at least four villages completely in several feet of mud. Throughout the entire country, the hurricane left between 500,000 and 800,000 homeless. In all, damage in Nicaragua was estimated at around $1 billion. Mitch was also responsible for the loss of the *Fantome* windjammer sailing ship, owned by Windjammer Barefoot Cruises; sadly, all 31 of the crew perished. The ship, which was sailing south of Guanaja Island, experienced up to 50 foot waves and over 100 mph winds, causing the *Fantome* to sink just off the coast of Honduras.

In Jamaica, Mitch killed three people and left many others homeless. Due to Mitch's large size, it dropped heavy precipitation as far south as Panama, especially in the Darién and Chiriquí provinces. The flooding washed away a few roads and bridges and damaged numerous houses and schools, leaving thousands homeless. The hurricane left three casualties in Panama. In Costa Rica, Mitch dumped heavy rains, causing flash flooding and mudslides across the country, mostly in the northeastern part of the country. The storm impacted 2,135 homes to some degree, of which 242 were destroyed, leaving 4,000 homeless. Throughout the country, the rainfall and mudslides affected 126 bridges and 800 miles of roads, mostly on the Inter-American Highway, which was affected by Hurricane Cesar two years earlier. Mitch affected 115 sq.

miles of crop lands, causing damage to both export and domestic crops. In all, Hurricane Mitch caused $92 million in damage and seven deaths.

While drifting through El Salvador, the hurricane dropped tremendous amounts of precipitation, resulting in flash flooding and mudslides through the country. Multiple rivers, including the Río Grande de San Miguel and the Lempa River, overflowed, contributing to overall damage. The flooding damaged more than 10,000 houses, leaving around 59,000 homeless and forcing 500,000 to evacuate. Crop damage was severe, with serious flooding occurring on 386 sq. miles of pasture or crop land. The flooding destroyed 37% of the bean production, 80% of the maize production, and 20% losses in sugar canes. There were heavy losses in livestock as well, including the deaths of 10,000 cattle. Total agricultural and livestock damaged amounted to $154 million. In addition, the flooding destroyed two bridges and damaged 1,200 miles of unpaved roads. In all, Mitch caused nearly $400 million in damage and 240 deaths.

Similar to the rest of Central America, Mitch's heavy rains caused mudslides and severe flooding over Guatemala. The flooding destroyed 6,000 houses and damaged 20,000 others, displacing over 730,000 and forcing over 100,000 to evacuate. In addition, the flooding destroyed 27 schools and damaged 286 others, 175 severely. Flooding caused major damage to crops, while landslides destroyed crop land across the country. The most severely affected crops for domestic consumption were tomatoes, bananas, corn, other vegetables, and beans, with damaged totaling to $48 million. Export crops such as bananas or coffee were greatly damaged as well, with damage amounting to $325 million. Damage to plantations and soil totaled to $121 million. The flooding also caused severe damage to the transportation infrastructure, including the loss of 37 bridges. Across the country, flooding damaged or destroyed 840 miles of roads, of which nearly 400 miles were sections of major highways. In all, Hurricane Mitch caused $748 million and 268 deaths in Guatemala. In addition, Mitch caused 11 indirect deaths when a plane crashed during the storm.[149]

In Belize, the hurricane was less severe than initially predicted, though Mitch still caused heavy rainfall across the country. Most of Belize City evacuated on October 28 as Mitch threatened to hit the city as at least a Category 4 storm. Had this occurred, it might have been similar to the Hurricane Hattie

---

[149] John L. Guiney; Miles B. Lawrence (1999-01-28), <u>*www.nhc.noaa.gov/ noaa.gov/ nhc-Hurricane Mitch Preliminary Report (PDF) (Report). National Hurricane Center*</u>. Retrieved: 08-08-2015.

disaster of October 31, 1961, when Belize City was virtually destroyed, and as a result the capital was moved inland to Belmopan. Numerous rivers exceeded their crests, though the rainfall was beneficial to trees in mountainous areas. The flooding caused extensive crop damage and destroyed many roads. Throughout the country, eleven people died because of the hurricane. In Mexico, Mitch produced gusty winds and heavy rains on the Yucatán Peninsula, with Cancún on the Quintana Roo coast being the worst hit. Nine people were killed from the flooding, though damage was relatively minimal. Five died near Tapachula in southern Mexico near the Guatemalan border when their car was washed from the road. A U.S. citizen was killed near Cancun in a boating accident. Though ocean swells hit the Mexican tourist cities of Cancun and Cozumel, they were largely unaffected.

Countries around the world helped those countries affected by Mitch by donating significant relief aid in the amount of $6.3 billion. Former Presidents George W. Bush and Jimmy Carter visited the region and called for re-structuring and scaling back of international debt owed by Honduras and Nicaragua. As a direct result of the disaster, the International Monetary Fund began considering the formation of an emergency fund to help countries hit by natural disasters. The United States announced on Thursday, November 5, that it would supply $70 million in aid for Central America, and on November 10, an additional $10 million was added. Spain reported it would provide $105 million in aid, and Sweden announced it would provide $100 -$200 million over a three-year period. In addition, tons of food and grain were flown in by humanitarian organizations. Mexico provided an airlift of urgently needed supplies, and European countries donated $8 million. Canada supplied over $7 million in assistance. Additional help came from Japan and other countries. Throughout Central America, which was recovering from an economic crisis that occurred in 1996, many wished to continue the growth of the infrastructure and economy. In addition, after witnessing the vulnerability to hurricanes, the affected governments endeavored to prevent such a disaster from occurring again.[150]

Hundreds of thousands of people lost their homes, but many took this as an opportunity to rebuild stronger houses. With a new, structurally improved foundation, homes were redesigned to be able to withstand another

---

150 John L. Guiney; Miles B. Lawrence (1999-01-28), _www.nhc.noaa.gov/ noaa.gov/ nhc-Hurricane Mitch Preliminary Report (PDF) (Report). National Hurricane Center._ Retrieved: 08-08-2015.

hurricane. However, lack of arable crop land took away the jobs from many, decreasing an already low income even lower. Following the passage of Mitch, disease outbreaks occurred throughout Central America, including cholera, leptospirosis, and dengue fever. Over 2,328 cases of cholera were reported, killing 34 people. Guatemala was most affected by the virus, where most of the deaths occurred from contaminated food. 450 cases of leptospirosis were reported in Nicaragua, killing seven people. There were over 1,357 cases of dengue reported, though no deaths were reported from the disease.

Honduras, the country most affected by the hurricane, received significant aid for the millions impacted by the hurricane. Mexico quickly gave help, sending 700 tons of food, 11 tons of medicine, four rescue planes, rescue personnel, and trained search dogs. Cuba also volunteered, sending a contingent of physicians to the country. The U.S. administration offered at first troops stationed in Honduras, and then withdrew them a few days after the storm. They also at first offered only $2 million in aid, which came as a shock to residents and President Carlos Roberto Flores alike. The U.S. later increased their offer to $70 million. The Honduran government distributed food, water, and medical services to the hurricane victims, including the more than 4 million without water. In addition, the country initially experienced a sharp increase in the unemployment rate, largely due to the destruction of crop lands. However, rebuilding provided jobs in the following years. In Costa Rica, reconstruction after the hurricane increased the number of jobs by 5.9%, lowering the unemployment rate slightly.[151] In an awesome display of power and destruction, Hurricane Mitch will be remembered as one of the region's most notable, enduring and deadliest hurricanes to strike the North Atlantic in the last two centuries.

Hurricane Floyd of 1999--Also termed 'The Storm of the Century' at one point, at the time Floyd caused the largest peacetime evacuation in history that involved 3,000,000 people from South Florida to Cape Hatteras, North Carolina, as it bore down on the southeast coast in September 1999. It later made landfall as a Category 3 hurricane over North Carolina and would bring up to 30 inches of rain from North Carolina to New Jersey spawning terrible floods. Floyd ranks as one of the costliest hurricanes of all time in damage with an estimated $4.5 billion dollars in damage, although some estimates run as

151 Inter-American Development Bank Hurricane Mitch Report. *Central America after Hurricane Mitch- Costa Rica, December 1998.*

high as $6 billion. These floods also were responsible for 50 of the 56 deaths caused by Floyd in the United States. Floyd also caused moderate damage in the Bahamas, with one death reported.

Hurricane Irene of 1999--Is an often-forgotten storm from the 1999 North Atlantic hurricane season, except for those in Florida. Forming during the middle of October, Irene became a Category 2 hurricane with sustained winds of 100 mph, and higher gusts. The storm also produced some 10 to 20 inches of rain across South Florida while causing 8 deaths by electrocution and $800 million in damage.

Hurricane Lenny of 1999--Known by those in the Caribbean as "El Zorito", or "the Lefty", Lenny was the first storm on record to strike the Lesser Antilles from the west in November 1999. The 1999 North Atlantic hurricane season set a record by having five storms reach Category 4 strength, which was later tied by the 2005 season. Hurricane Lenny was the 12th tropical storm, eighth hurricane, and fifth major hurricane in the 1999 North Atlantic hurricane season. Lenny spent its entire lifespan (November 13-23) traveling in a west-to-east fashion from the central Caribbean to the Atlantic, which was unprecedented in the history of North Atlantic tropical cyclone record-keeping. Tropical systems are typically guided westward from the Atlantic to the Caribbean by high pressure anchored over the Atlantic, then may curve to the northeast if they encounter a dip in the jet stream over or emerging from North America. In Lenny's case, a large dip in the jet stream was in place over the western Atlantic and put the hurricane on its eastward track and on a collision course with the northern Leeward Islands.

Lenny was the strongest North Atlantic hurricane ever recorded in November and quite unusual in that it moved west-to-east across the Caribbean. Hurricane Lenny was unusual in several respects. First, it traversed the Caribbean from west to east, the reverse of typical hurricane paths. It was the first time such a trajectory had been seen in 113 years of hurricane observations in the North Atlantic/Caribbean basin. The last hurricane to strike the western portion of the Lesser Antilles was Hurricane Klaus from the 1984 season. Second, Lenny's Lenny reached its peak intensity on November 17 as it slammed into St. Croix of the U.S. Virgin Islands with maximum sustained winds of 155 mph peak, just under Category 5 intensity on the Saffir-Simpson Hurricane Wind Scale, making it the strongest November hurricane on record in the North Atlantic basin. Finally, Lenny was also the fifth Category 4 hurricane of the 1999 North Atlantic hurricane season, breaking the record for the number of storms of that strength in one season. This record was tied with the 2005 season. In all, 17 deaths were attributed to Hurricane Lenny. Its Category 4 winds caused widespread destruction across the northeastern Caribbean, amounting to $330 million ($472 million in 2016 USD) in damage to U.S. territories.

CHAPTER THIRTEEN

The Major Hurricanes from 2000 – Present

Hurricane Keith of 2000--Powerful Category 4 hurricane that struck the Central American country of Belize in the first week of October 2000. Making landfall near the area of Belize City, the storm caused some two million dollars in damage and left 11 people dead.

Tropical Storm Leslie of 2000--This storm started out as a subtropical depression in the Florida Straits and brought some 15 to 20 inches of rain to parts of South Florida. It caused about $1,000,000 in damage and killed two people. After flooding South Florida, it gained more tropical characteristics and became a minimal tropical storm in October, 2000.

Hurricane Michael of 2000--Formed in the Western Atlantic in the third week of October, 2000 and eventually headed northward into the Canadian Maritimes, where it brought 100 mph winds to parts of Newfoundland in Canada. Because it was unknown that Michael became extratropical before landfall, it was the initially considered the first tropical cyclone to strike Newfoundland since Hurricane Luis in 1995. Furthermore, Michael was also considered the first hurricane to make landfall in Canada since Hurricane Hortense in 1996. When the Meteorological Service of Canada and the National Research Council flew a Convair research flight into Michael on October 19, it was the first successful research flight made into a tropical cyclone by those agencies. Later flights have been made into Tropical Storm Karen, Hurricane Isabel (while inland), Hurricane Juan, and Hurricane Ophelia.

Tropical Storm Allison of 2001--Became the first tropical storm to get its name retired in June of 2001. However, the greatest legacy of the cyclone was the widespread heavy rains and resulting floods along the entire path of the cyclone. Houston, Texas, was the worst affected area, as the Port of Houston reported 36.99 inches and several other locations reported more than 30 inches. The storm also spawned 23 tornadoes. Allison was responsible for 41 deaths, 27 of whom drown and at least $9 billion (2001 USD, $12.1 2016 USD) in damage in the United States, making it the deadliest and costliest United States tropical storm of record. This ties Allison with a tropical storm in 1917 as the second-deadliest tropical storm to impact the U.S. only surpassed by the 1925 Florida tropical storm which killed 73 people. Due to extreme destruction, the name Allison was retired in spring 2002 and will never again be used in the North Atlantic Basin; the 2001 incarnation of Allison is the only Atlantic tropical system to have its name retired without reaching hurricane strength. The name was replaced with Andrea in the 2007 season.

Hurricane Iris of 2001--A very small and narrow hurricane that brought 145 mph winds to the central portion of Belize in October 2001. The winds and storm surge of Iris caused severe damage over portions of the southern Belize coast. The storm was responsible for millions of dollars in damage and for 31 deaths, including 20 in Belize, 8 in Guatemala, and 3 in the Dominican Republic. The deaths in Belize occurred when the M/V Wave Dancer capsized in port, killing 20 of the 28 people on board.

Hurricane Michelle of 2001--Hurricane Michelle, a Category 4 hurricane on the Saffir Simpson Hurricane Wind Scale, at its peak brought torrential rainfall along its path through the western Caribbean Sea, causing extensive damage in Central America, Cuba, and the Bahamas and killing 22 people. A powerful late season hurricane, Michelle brought 135 mph winds to portions of western Cuba and the Isle of Youth before turning east and avoiding South Florida by going out to sea in November 2001. At the time, Michelle was the costliest hurricane in Cuban history, with an estimated $1.8 billion in damage; this figure was greatly surpassed by Hurricane Ike nearly seven years later. As a weakening system, Michelle moved past Florida and the Bahamas. Hurricane Michelle was one of the wettest hurricanes on record here in the Bahamas, with 12.64 inches falling during its passage at Lynden Pindling International Airport. Strong waves caused severe beach erosion and wind-damaged property. Throughout the entirety of Michelle's track, 22 people were killed, and damage was estimated at roughly $2 billion (2001 USD; $2.66 billion 2016 USD). After the season, the name Michelle was retired and was replaced with Melissa for the 2007 North Atlantic hurricane season.

Hurricane Isidore of 2002--Isidore was a powerful Category 3 hurricane that originally developed in the Caribbean, Isidore made landfall over the Yucatan Peninsula with 125 mph but only made landfall over Louisiana as a tropical storm in September 2002.

Hurricane Lili of 2002--Another powerful hurricane that formed in the Caribbean on the heels of Isidore, Lili grew to Category 4 strength with sustained winds of 140 mph. Threatening Louisiana as a major hurricane, Lili encountered hostile upper level conditions just before landfall and weakened to just a Category 2 hurricane when it came ashore over Louisiana in October 2002.

Tropical Storm Ana of 2003--Usually, nothing much would be said about a minimal strength tropical storm that emerges from a subtropical depression, but Ana, which formed over the Easter weekend in 2003, was an exception since it became the first ever recorded storm to form in April.

Hurricane Fabian of 2003--A hurricane that last for about a week, and a tropical system that lasted for nearly two weeks, Fabian was a Category 4 hurricane at one point with winds of 145 mph in September 2003. Responsible for eight deaths and $300 million dollars in damage, Fabian went down as the worst hurricane to strike the tiny resort island of Bermuda since 1926.

Hurricane Isabel of 2003--A very rare and powerful Category 5 hurricane and the most intense hurricane of the 2003 season, Isabel underwent rapid intensification and was able to stay at the highest level a hurricane can reach for over 30 hours, which made it one of the longest lasting Category 5 storms on record. Maximum sustained winds recorded were 160 mph, but gusts were as high as 234 mph. Although it eventually weakened, Isabel came ashore along the Outer Banks of North Carolina as a Category 2 hurricane and was responsible for 17 deaths and $3.37 billion in damage.

Hurricane Juan of 2003--Was the first hurricane to make landfall near Halifax, Nova Scotia, in Canada in over a century in September 29, 2003. A Category 2 hurricane, Juan was responsible for four deaths, numerous power outages, tree damage, and went down as the most damaging hurricane in the history of Halifax.

Hurricane Alex of 2004--Was the first hurricane of the 2004 North Atlantic hurricane season, and even became the season's first major hurricane as well. Alex brushed the Outer Banks of North Carolina before turning out to sea in early August 2004. With sustained winds of 120 mph, it was a solid Category 3 hurricane.

Hurricane Charley of 2004--It was the third named storm, the second hurricane, and the second major hurricane of the 2004 North Atlantic hurricane season. Charley lasted from August 9 to August 15, and at its peak intensity it attained 150 mph winds, making it a strong Category 4 hurricane on the Saffir-Simpson Hurricane Wind Scale. It made landfall in southwestern Florida at maximum strength. When it was all said and done, Hurricane Charley went down as the most devastating hurricane to hit anywhere in Florida since Hurricane Andrew in August 1992. At the time, it also ended up being the second costliest hurricane in U.S. history, behind Hurricane Andrew in 1992, but that record was broken several times over with Hurricane Sandy in 2012, Hurricane Ike in 2008, Hurricane Katrina in 2005 and a few others (it has since dropped to 8th). Charley fooled forecasters by not only rapidly intensifying, but also making a turn to the north and east much sooner than anticipated, which spared the city of Tampa but devastated the Port Charlotte area on August 13, 2004. The storm left at least 35 people dead and $15.4 billion in damage. Casualties were remarkably low, given the strength of the hurricane and the destruction that resulted.

Hurricane Frances of 2004--This storm was not as devastating as Charley, but still a very destructive storm due to its slow motion. Moving between 5 to 10 mph across the Florida Peninsula, Frances pounded just about all of the Sunshine State with tropical storm and hurricane force winds for at least 24 hours on the Labor Day Weekend of 2004. Prior to that, the third major hurricane of the 2004 season rolled through the Bahamas with 145 mph winds. According to the then Prime Minister of the Bahamas, Perry Christie, Hurricane Frances cost the Bahamas 8% of the GDP, and that some $200 million was sustained in direct losses and $300 million in insured infrastructure damage. The storm forced the evacuation of 2.8 million people in Florida, as well as knocking out power to about 6 million there as well. Frances was also responsible for producing 100 tornadoes. Final damage estimate is $9 billion dollars for the storm. Eight deaths resulted from the forces of the storm - seven in the United States and one in the Bahamas. U.S. damage is estimated to be near $8.9 billion, over 90% of which occurred in Florida.

Hurricane Ivan of 2004--A classic Cape Verde type storm that formed at unusually low latitude, Ivan rapidly developed into a Category 4 hurricane during the Labor Day Weekend of 2004 before briefly weakening to a Category 2 hurricane for a period. However, as it moved through the extreme southern Windward Islands of Barbados and Grenada, the storm strengthened back to a major hurricane status and destroyed 75 to 90 percent of all buildings on the island of Grenada. The storm then continued to re-energize and reach Category 5 status. It was the second Category 5 storm in as many years after almost a five-year drought following Mitch in October 1998.

It would eventually weaken somewhat, but it still made landfall near Gulf Shores, Alabama, as a strong Category 3 hurricane, packing sustained winds of 130 mph. Moving farther inland, Ivan's remains sparked torrential rains, flooding, and 123 tornadoes, which is second to Hurricane Beulah's 150 in 1967. Ivan's storm surge completely over-washed the island of Grand Cayman, where an estimated 95% of the buildings were damaged or destroyed, and in Grenada it was estimated that 90% of the homes were destroyed. Surge heights of 10-15 feet occurred along the Gulf Coast states during Ivan's first U.S. landfall. Peak rainfall amounts in the Caribbean and United States were generally 10-15 inches. The death toll from Ivan stands at 92 - 39 in Grenada, 25 in the United States, 17 in Jamaica, 4 in Dominican Republic, 3 in Venezuela, 2 in the Cayman Islands, and 1 each in Tobago and Barbados. U.S. damage is estimated to be near $14.2 billion, the fifth largest total on record.

The roof of this church was blown off by Hurricane Ivan in 2004 and totally destroyed in Grenada, where 90% of the homes were destroyed. When this photo was taken, the locals were still using it for their church services, even without the roof, and the hurricane had done so much damage to the church that it would cost thousands to rectify it. The children (not pictured) were outside of the church selling Christmas cards of the church as it was prior to the hurricane to try and raise funds towards the renovation of the church (Courtesy of Nigel Storer).

Hurricane Jeanne of 2004--Originally not a powerful storm, Jeanne carved a path of death and destruction from Puerto Rico into Hispaniola with 80 mph winds and heavy rains on September 18, 2004. The torrential rainfall produced deadly flashfloods and mudslides in Haiti, which left an estimated 2,400 people dead and 300,000 persons homeless in Haiti and 31 persons were killed in Puerto Rico and the Dominican Republic and 1 in the Bahamas. The storm has also been known for its erratic motion taking an eastward turn away from the United States after going through the Bahamas, and then turning southward and westward back toward land. Jeanne finally made landfall in the United States along the south-central coast of Florida near Stuart, with sustained winds of 120 mph. It was the fifth storm, fourth hurricane, and third major hurricane to impact the Sunshine State and the Bahamas in 2004. The worst damage occurred in Haiti, where over 3,000 people died as a result of flooding and mudslides caused by this storm.

In the Bahamas, 6,682 houses suffered damage during the passage of this hurricane. Of that amount, 4,100 suffered minor damage but were usable, while 1,851 suffered major damage in excess of $10,000 per house but were usable. Some 671 houses (in value of over $110,000 per house) were destroyed while some 2,000 homes might fall into the category of major repairs and rebuilds. The severity of the winds and sea surges resulted in the worst damages being done to the housing sector, where the damage assessment exceeded $99 million. After impacting Florida and the Bahamas, the storm spread northward into the southeast, Mid-Atlantic, and northeast, where it produced flooding rains and tornadoes. Total death toll was estimated to be over 3,000, and the final damage total is estimated to be $6.9 billion.

Cyclone Caterina in 2004--The extremely unusual Hurricane Catarina (officially, it is called Cyclone Catarina, because the term cyclone is the southern hemispheric term for a hurricane, but for uniformity I will use the term 'hurricane'), which even though it did not occur in the North Atlantic, it amazed and baffled meteorologists from every corner of the Earth. My book includes tropical cyclones of "The Americas" so I decided to include this storm in the list of storms. Hurricane Catarina was an extremely rare South Atlantic tropical cyclone that hit southeastern Brazil in late March 2004. Typically, tropical cyclones do not form in the South Atlantic Ocean, due to strong upper level shear, cool water temperatures, and the lack of a convergence zone of convection. Occasionally, though, as seen in 1991 and early 2004, conditions can become slightly more favorable. For Catarina, it was a combination of climatic and atmospheric anomalies. Water temperatures on Catarina's path ranged from 24 to 25 °C, slightly less than the 26.5 °C threshold temperature of a normal tropical cyclone to form, but sufficient for a storm of baroclinic origin.

The storm developed out of a stationary cold-core upper-level trough on March 12. Almost a week later, on March 19, a disturbance developed along the trough and traveled towards the east-southeast until March 22, when a ridge stopped the forward motion of the disturbance. The disturbance was in an unusually favorable environment, with below average wind shear and above average sea surface temperatures. The combination of the two led to a slow transition from an extratropical cyclone to a subtropical cyclone by March 24. The storm continued to obtain tropical characteristics and became a tropical storm the next day while the winds steadily increased. The storm reached winds of 75 mph—equivalent to a low-end Category 1 hurricane on the Saffir-Simpson Hurricane Wind Scale—on March 26. At this time, it was unofficially named Catarina and was also the first hurricane-intensity tropical cyclone ever recorded in the Southern Atlantic Ocean. Unusually favorable conditions persisted, and Catarina continued to intensify and was estimated to have peaked with winds of 100 mph on March 28. The center of the storm made landfall later that day at the time between the cities of Passo de Torres and Balneário Gaivota, Santa Catarina. Catarina rapidly weakened upon landfall and dissipated the next day.

To this day, Catarina is the only hurricane strength tropical cyclone ever observed in the South Atlantic Ocean since 1970. Other systems have been observed in this region; however, none have reached hurricane strength, and no eyes ever have been seen on imagery or radar. While Catarina formed in an unusual area, its relation to global warming or any other type of global climatic change is still up for debate. Former U.S. Vice-President Al Gore in his book, An Inconvenient Truth, used this storm as an indicator for or the direct result of global warming. The Brazilian Society of Meteorology attributed it to "climatic changes and atmospheric anomalies," while other researchers have indicated that it could be the result of the Southern Annular Mode or other seasonal variations in weather within the southern hemisphere, again linked to global changes in climate. However, more research in the area is still needed to make a definite conclusion.

Since Catarina was the first tropical cyclone to make landfall in Brazil since the first creation of reliable records, the damage was quite severe. Although the storm was an unprecedented event, Brazilian officials took the appropriate actions and warned the public about the approaching storm. Residents heeded the warnings and prepared for the storm by either evacuating or by riding it out in their homes. Catarina ended up destroying 1,500 homes and damaging around 40,000 others. Agricultural products were severely damaged. Approximately 85% of the banana crops and 40% of the rice crops were lost in the storm. Despite the warnings posted for the storm, three people were confirmed to have perished in the storm, and 75 others were injured. Damages from the storm amounted to $350 million (2004 USD $438 million 2016 USD).

Hurricane Dennis of 2005--Was a rare powerful July hurricane that formed in the southeastern Caribbean a few hundred miles to the west-northwest of Grenada on the evening of July 4th, 2005. Gradually strengthening in the days that followed, Dennis brought heavy rains and flooding to Jamaica, the Cayman Islands, and Hispaniola, but Cuba bore the brunt of its assault on Cienfuegos, Cuba, with sustained winds of 150 mph. The coastal Cuban community was devastated as telephone poles and wires were knocked down. Just missing Category 5 strength on the Saffir-Simpson Hurricane Wind Scale, Dennis cross the narrow, but rugged terrain of Cuba and re-emerged in the Gulf of Mexico as a Category 1 storm before rapidly intensifying to a Category 4 hurricane in the early morning hours of July 10th, 2005. Dennis eventually made landfall near Pensacola, Florida, on the afternoon of July 10th. Dennis caused 42 deaths - 22 in Haiti, 16 in Cuba, 3 in the United States, and 1 in Jamaica. The hurricane caused considerable damage across central and eastern Cuba, as well as the western Florida Panhandle, including widespread utility and communications outages. Considerable storm surge-related damage also occurred near St. Marks, Florida, well to the east of the landfall location. The damage associated with Dennis in the United States is estimated at $2.23 billion. Damage in Jamaica was estimated at $31.7 million.

Hurricane Emily of 2005--Was another rare powerful July hurricane that formed in the Atlantic on the heels of Hurricane Dennis during the week of July 10th, 2005. The storm became the most powerful hurricane ever recorded in the month of July after its winds reached a peak speed of 160 mph and its minimum central pressure dropped to 929 mbar, or 27.43 inches of Hg. This just surpassed the levels previously established by Dennis and made it the first Category 5 hurricane of the 2005 season. Three more Category 5 hurricanes would follow. Although Emily ransacked the island of Grenada, which was still recovering from Hurricane Ivan's impact in September, 2004, the storm mercifully spared the islands of Jamaica and the Caymans, as well as weakened before making landfall in the Yucatan. The storm did regain some steam after losing its punch over the plateau of the Yucatan Peninsula and made a final landfall as a major hurricane in Northeastern Mexico, with winds of 125 mph. The storm was responsible for 64 deaths and initially $300,000,000 in damage. It also contributed to the rise in oil prices by forcing the evacuation of employees of Mexico's primary oil company, PEMEX, from their offshore rigs in the Gulf of Mexico.

Hurricane Katrina in 2005

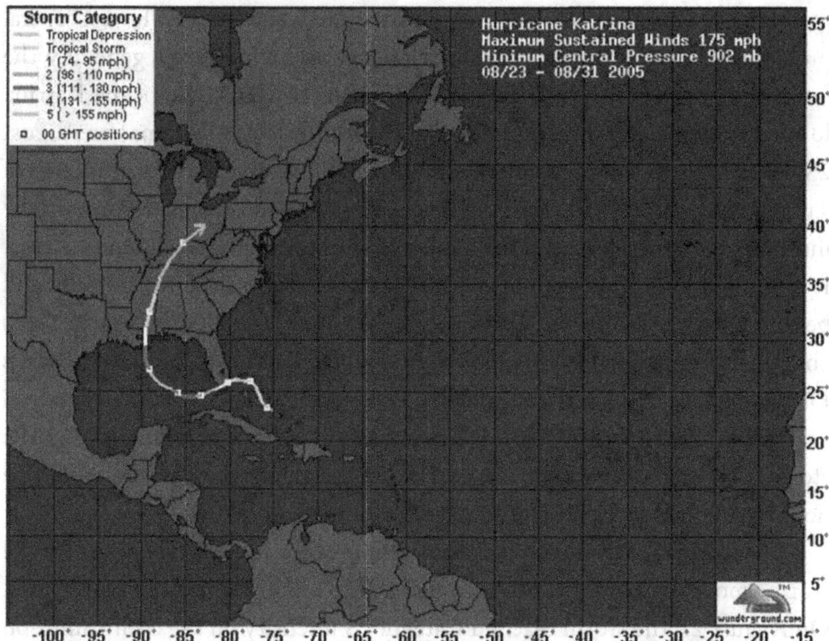

This map shows the track of Hurricane Katrina in 2005 as it moved through the Bahamas, South Florida, Mississippi and Louisiana in the USA (Information courtesy of the Weather Underground Inc.)

The storm surge caused severe and catastrophic damage along the Gulf Coast States, devastating the cities of Mobile, Alabama, Waveland and Biloxi/ Gulfport in Mississippi, and New Orleans and other towns in Louisiana. Levees (built in 1722 from the French word 'lever', meaning "to raise") separating Lake Pontchartrain and several canals from New Orleans were breached by the surge, subsequently flooding 80% of the city and many areas of neighboring parishes for weeks. Severe wind damage was reported well inland. Criticism of the federal, state and local governments' reaction to the storm was widespread and resulted in an investigation by the United States Congress and the resignation of FEMA director Michael Brown.[152]

---

[152] Richard Knabb, Rhome, R. Jamie; Daniel Brown, National Hurricane Center (December 20, 2005). Hurricane Katrina: August 23 – 30, 2005 (PDF) (Tropical Cyclone Report). United States National Oceanic and Atmospheric Administration's National Weather Service. Retrieved: 03-04-2015.

When ranking hurricanes by strength, the obvious choice is to compare wind speeds. But since measurements of the most extreme winds are difficult to obtain, as a result meteorologists compare hurricanes by their lowest central pressure, a measure that has a strong relationship to wind speed; generally, the lower the pressure in a hurricane, the stronger its winds. Hurricane Katrina formed as Tropical Depression #12 over the southeastern Bahamas on August 23, 2005 as the result of an interaction of a tropical wave and the remnants of Tropical Depression #10. The system was upgraded to a tropical storm on the morning of August 24, and at this point the storm was given the name Katrina. It became the fifth most intense hurricane of all time ahead of Camille and behind Hurricane Gilbert (1988), the Great Labor Day of Hurricane of 1935, and Hurricane Allen (1980). The tropical storm continued to move towards Florida and became a hurricane only two hours before it made landfall between Hallandale Beach and Aventura, Florida on the morning of August 25. The storm weakened over land, but it quickly regained hurricane status about one hour after entering the Gulf of Mexico.

The storm rapidly intensified after entering the Gulf, partly because of the storm's movement over the warm waters of the Gulf of Mexico's Loop Current. On August 27, the storm reached Category 3 intensity on the Saffir-Simpson Hurricane Wind Scale, becoming the third major hurricane of the season. An eyewall replacement cycle disrupted the intensification but caused the storm to nearly double in size. Katrina again rapidly intensified, attaining Category 5 status on the morning of August 28 and reached its maximum strength at 1:00 p.m. CDT that day, with maximum sustained winds of 175 mph and a minimum central pressure of 902 mbar. The pressure measurement made Katrina the fourth most intense Atlantic hurricane on record at the time, ahead of Hurricane Camille and behind Hurricane Gilbert (1988), the Great Labor Day of Hurricane of 1935, and Hurricane Allen (1980), only to be surpassed by Hurricanes Rita and Wilma later in the season; it was also the strongest hurricane ever recorded in the Gulf of Mexico at the time (a record also later broken by Rita). On August 29, Katrina's storm surge caused several breaches in levees around New Orleans. Most of the city was subsequently flooded, as the breached drainage and navigation canals allowed water to flow from the lake into low areas of the city and Saint Bernard Parish.

Katrina made its second landfall at 6:10 a.m. CDT on August 29 as a Category 3 hurricane, with sustained winds of 125 mph near Buras-Triumph, Louisiana. At landfall, hurricane-force winds extended outward up to 120 miles from the center, and the storm's central pressure was 920 mbar. After moving over southeastern Louisiana and Breton Sound, it made its third landfall near the Louisiana/Mississippi border, with 120 mph sustained winds, still at Category 3 intensity. Katrina maintained hurricane strength well into Mississippi but weakened thereafter, finally losing hurricane strength more than 150 miles inland near Meridian, Mississippi. It was downgraded to a tropical depression near Clarksville, Tennessee, but its remnants were last distinguishable in the eastern Great Lakes region on August 31, when it was absorbed by a frontal boundary. The resulting extratropical storm moved rapidly to the northeast and affected Ontario and Quebec.

The confirmed death toll (total of direct and indirect deaths) stood at 1,836, mainly from Louisiana (1,577) and Mississippi (238). However, it is important to note that 705 people remain categorized as missing in Louisiana, so this number is not final, even after 11 years since the storm has passed. Many of the deaths are indirect, but it is almost impossible to determine the exact cause of some of the fatalities. Federal disaster declarations covered 90,000 square miles of the United States, an area almost as large as the United Kingdom. The hurricane left an estimated three million people without electricity. On September 3, 2005, Homeland Security Secretary Michael Chertoff described the aftermath of Hurricane Katrina as "probably the worst catastrophe, or set of catastrophes," in the country's history, referring to the hurricane itself plus the flooding of New Orleans.

Hurricane Katrina first made landfall on August 25 in South Florida, where it hit as a Category 1 hurricane, with 80 mph winds. Rainfall was heavy in places and exceeded 14 inches in Homestead, Florida, and a storm surge of 3–5 feet was measured in parts of Monroe County. More than 1 million customers were left without electricity, and damage in Florida was estimated at between $1 and $2 billion, with most of the damage coming from flooding and fallen trees. There were 11 fatalities reported in Florida as a result of Hurricane Katrina. Most of the Florida Keys experienced tropical-storm force winds from Katrina as the storm's center passed to the north, with hurricane force winds reported in the Dry Tortugas. Rainfall was also high in the islands, with 10 inches falling on Key West. On August 26, a strong F1 tornado formed from an outer rain band of Katrina and struck Marathon, Florida. The tornado damaged a hangar at the airport there and caused an estimated $5 million in damage.

Although Hurricane Katrina stayed well to the north of Cuba, on August 29 it brought tropical-storm force winds and rainfall of over 8 inches to western regions of the island. Telephone and power lines were damaged and around 8,000 people were evacuated in the Pinar del Rio Province. According to

Cuban television reports, the coastal city of Surgidero de Batabano was 90% underwater.

On August 29, Hurricane Katrina made landfall near Buras, Louisiana, with 125 mph winds, as a strong Category 3 storm. However, as it had only just weakened from Category 4 strength and the radius of maximum winds was large, it is possible that sustained winds of Category 4 strength briefly impacted extreme southeastern Louisiana. Although the storm surge to the east of the path of the eye in Mississippi was higher, a very significant surge affected the Louisiana coast. The height of the surge is uncertain because of a lack of data, although a tide gauge in Plaquemines Parish indicated a storm tide in excess of 14 feet and a 12-foot storm surge was recorded in Grand Isle, Louisiana.

Views of inundated areas in New Orleans following breaking of the levees surrounding the city as a direct result of Hurricane Katrina. New Orleans, Louisiana, on September 11, 2005 (Courtesy of NOAA-NHC).

Hurricane Katrina also brought record-breaking rainfall to the U.S. State of Louisiana, with 8-10 inches falling on a wide swath of the eastern part of the state. In the area around Slidell, the rainfall was even higher, and the highest rainfall recorded in the state was approximately 15 inches. As a result of the rainfall and storm surge, the level of Lake Pontchartrain rose and caused significant flooding along its northeastern shore, affecting communities from Slidell to Mandeville. Several bridges were destroyed, including the I-10 Twin Span Bridge connecting Slidell to New Orleans. Almost 900,000 people in

Louisiana lost power as a result of Hurricane Katrina. As the eye of Hurricane Katrina moved to the northeast, it subjected the city to hurricane conditions for hours. Although power failures prevented accurate measurement of wind speeds in New Orleans, there were a few measurements of hurricane-force winds. From this, the NHC concluded that it is likely that much of the city experienced sustained winds of Category 1 or Category 2 strength. However, wind speeds increase with height, and therefore the winds experienced on upper floors of high rise structures were likely to have been significantly higher.

The heavy winds and storm surges from Katrina severely weakened the city's levee system, and there were reports of extensive failures of the levees and flood walls protecting New Orleans, Louisiana and surrounding communities. The Mississippi River Gulf Outlet (MR-GO) breached its levees in approximately 20 places, flooding much of east New Orleans (East Side), most of Saint Bernard Parish and the East Bank of Plaquemines Parish. The major levee breaches in the city included breaches at the 17th Street Canal levee, the London Avenue Canal, and the wide, navigable Industrial Canal, which left approximately 80% of the city flooded. Most of the major roads traveling into and out of the city were damaged. The only routes out of the city were the westbound Crescent City Connection and the Huey P. Long Bridge, as the I-10 Twin Span Bridge traveling eastbound towards Slidell, Louisiana, had collapsed. The Lake Pontchartrain Causeway only carried emergency traffic. On August 29, at 7:40 a.m. CDT, it was reported that most of the windows on the north side of the Hyatt Regency New Orleans had been blown out, and many other high rise buildings had extensive window damage. The Hyatt was the most severely damaged hotel in the city, with beds reported to be flying out of the windows. Insulation tubes were exposed as the hotel's glass exterior was completely sheared off.[153]

The Superdome, which was sheltering a large number of people who had not evacuated, sustained significant damage. Two sections of the Superdome's roof were severely damaged and the dome's waterproof membrane had essentially been peeled off. Louis Armstrong New Orleans International Airport was closed before the storm but did not flood. On August 30, it was reopened to humanitarian and rescue operations. Limited commercial passenger service resumed at the airport on September 13, and regular carrier operations

---

153 Christine A. Anderson; et al. (June 1, 2007). The New Orleans Hurricane Protection System: What Went Wrong and Why (PDF). American Society of Civil Engineers. Archived from the original (PDF) on November 26, 2007. Retrieved: 12-02-2016.

resumed in early October. Katrina also caused widespread loss of life, with over 700 bodies recovered in New Orleans by October 23. Some survivors and evacuees reported seeing dead bodies lying in city streets and floating in still-flooded sections, especially in the east of the city. Due to the advanced state of decomposition of many of the corpses, some of which were actually left in the water or sun festering for days before being collected, it hindered efforts by coroners to identify many of the dead. The first deaths reported from the city were reported shortly before midnight on August 28, as three nursing home patients died during an evacuation to Baton Rouge, most likely from dehydration. While there were also early reports of numerous fatalities amid the mayhem at the Superdome, only six deaths were confirmed there, with four of these originating from natural causes, one from a drug overdose and one a suicide. At the Convention Center, four bodies were recovered. One of the four is believed to be the result of a homicide.

The Gulf Coast of Mississippi suffered massive damage from the impact of Hurricane Katrina on August 29, leaving 238 people dead, 67 missing, and billions of dollars in damages. Afterwards, the lower 47 counties in Mississippi were declared disaster areas for federal assistance. After making a brief initial landfall in Louisiana, Katrina made its final landfall near the state line and the eyewall passed over the cities of Bay St. Louis and Waveland as a Category 3 hurricane, with sustained winds of 120 mph. Katrina's powerful right-front quadrant passed over the west and central Mississippi coast causing a powerful 27 foot storm surge, which penetrated 6 miles inland in many areas and up to 12 miles inland along bays and rivers; in some areas, the surge crossed Interstate 10 for several miles. Hurricane Katrina brought strong winds to Mississippi, which caused significant tree damage throughout the state. The highest unofficial reported wind gusts recorded from Katrina was one of 135 mph in Poplarville, in Pearl River County. The storm was also responsible for 8-10 inches of rain falling in the southwestern Mississippi area and rainfall in excess of 4 inches falling throughout the majority of the state.

Costliest North Atlantic Hurricanes (Cost refers to the total estimated property damage)[154]

Rank	Hurricane	Year	Damage
1	**Katrina**	**2005**	**$125 billion**
2	Sandy	2012	$75 billion
3	Ike	2008	$37.5 billion
4	Wilma	2005	$29.3 billion
5	Andrew	1992	$26.5 billion
6	Ivan	2004	$18.8 billion
7	Irene	2011	$15.6 billion
8	Charley	2004	$15.1 billion
9	Rita	2005	$12 billion
10	Frances	2004	$9.51 billion

Costliest North Atlantic Hurricanes

Hurricane Katrina weakened as it moved inland, but tropical-storm force gusts were recorded as far north as Fort Campbell, Kentucky, on August 30, and the winds damaged trees in New York. The remnants of the storm brought high levels of rainfall to a wide swath of the eastern United States, and rainfall in excess of 2 inches fell in parts of 20 states. A number of tornadoes associated with Katrina formed on August 30 and August 31, which caused minor damages in several regions. In total, 62 tornadoes formed in eight states as a result of Katrina. Eastern Arkansas received light rain from the passage of Katrina. The strong winds of Katrina downed some trees and power lines, although the damage was minimal. In Kentucky, a storm that had moved through the weekend before had already produced flooding, and the rainfall from Katrina added to this. As a result of the flooding, Kentucky's Governor Ernie Fletcher declared 3 counties disaster areas and a statewide state of emergency.

One person was killed in Hopkinsville, Kentucky, and part of a high school collapsed. Flooding also prompted a number of evacuations in West Virginia and Ohio, the rainfall in Ohio leading to two indirect deaths. Katrina also caused a number of power outages in many areas, with over 100,000 customers affected in Tennessee, primarily in the Memphis and Nashville areas. The remnants of Katrina merged with a frontal system over Ohio, but the moisture continued north and affected Canada on August 31. In Ontario, there were a

154 *Courtesy of the National Hurricane Center and Wikipedia.* Retrieved: 09-08-2015.

few isolated reports of rain in excess of 100 mm, and there were a few reports of damage from fallen trees. Flooding also occurred both in Ontario and Quebec, cutting off a number of isolated villages in Quebec.

The economic effects of Hurricane Katrina were far-reaching. In 2006, the Bush Administration sought $105 billion for repairs and reconstruction in the region, and this does not account for damage to the economy caused by potential interruption of the oil supply, destruction of the Gulf Coast's highway infrastructure, and exports of commodities such as grain. Katrina damaged or destroyed 30 oil platforms and caused the closure of nine refineries; the total shut-in oil production from the Gulf of Mexico in the six-month period following Katrina was approximately 24% of the annual production, and the shut-in gas production for the same period was about 18%. The forestry industry in Mississippi was also affected, as 1.3 million acres of forest lands were destroyed. The total loss to the forestry industry from Katrina is calculated to rise to about $5 billion. Furthermore, hundreds of thousands of local residents were left unemployed, which will have a trickle-down effect as fewer taxes are paid to local governments. Before the hurricane, the region supported approximately one million non-farm jobs, with 600,000 of them in New Orleans.

Katrina redistributed New Orleans' population across the southern United States. Houston, Texas, had an increase of 35,000 people; Mobile, Alabama, gained over 24,000; Baton Rouge, Louisiana, over 15,000; and Hammond, Louisiana received over 10,000, nearly doubling its size. Chicago received over 6,000 people, the most of any non-southern city. By late January 2006, about 200,000 people were once again living in New Orleans, less than half of the pre-storm population. By July 1, 2006, when new population estimates were calculated by the U.S. Census Bureau, the state of Louisiana showed a population decline of 219,563, or 4.87%. Additionally, insurance companies have stopped insuring the area because of the high costs from Hurricanes Katrina and Rita or have raised insurance premiums to cover their risk.

Katrina also had a tremendous impact on the environment. The storm surge caused substantial beach erosion, in some cases completely devastating coastal areas. In Dauphin Island, approximately 90 miles to the east of the point where the hurricane made landfall, the sand that comprised the barrier island was transported across the island into the Mississippi Sound, pushing the island towards land. The storm surge and waves from Katrina also obliterated the Chandeleur Islands, which had been affected by Hurricane Ivan the previous year. The lands that were lost were also breeding grounds for marine mammals, brown pelicans, turtles, and fish, as well as migratory species such as redhead ducks. Overall, about 20% of the local marshes were permanently overrun by water as a result of the storm.

Katrina also forced the closure of 16 National Wildlife Refuges, of which Breton National Wildlife Refuge received the worst damage, as half of its area was swept off. As a result, the hurricane affected the habitats of sea turtles, Mississippi sandhill cranes, Red-cockaded woodpeckers and Alabama Beach mice. Finally, as part of the cleanup effort, the flood waters that covered New Orleans were pumped into Lake Pontchartrain, a process that took 43 days to complete. These residual waters contained a mix of raw sewage, bacteria, heavy metals, pesticides, toxic chemicals, and about 6.5 million U.S. gallons of oil, which has sparked fears in the scientific community of massive numbers of fish dying.

Over seventy countries pledged monetary donations or other assistance. Kuwait made the largest single pledge, $500 million; other large donations were made by Qatar ($100 million), South Korea ($30 million), India, China (both $5 million), Pakistan ($1.5 million), and Bangladesh ($1 million). Israel sent an IDF delegation to New Orleans to transport aid equipment, including 80 tons of food, disposable diapers, beds, blankets, generators and additional equipment which were donated from different governmental institutions, civilian institutions and the IDF. The Bush Administration announced in mid-September that it did not need Israeli divers and physicians to come to the United States for search and rescue missions, but a small team landed in New Orleans on September 10 to give assistance to operations already under way. The team administered first aid to survivors, rescued abandoned pets and discovered hurricane victims.

Cuba and Venezuela were the first countries to offer aid, in the form of $1 million, 1,100 doctors, 26.4 metric tons of medicine, two mobile hospitals, 10 water purifying plants, 18 generators, 20 tons of bottled water, 50 tons of canned food and 66,000 barrels of heating oil. Their offers were refused by the U.S. government. Countries like Sri Lanka, which was still recovering from the massive Indian Ocean Tsunami, also offered to help. Countries including Canada, Mexico, Singapore, and Germany sent supplies, relief personnel, troops, ships and water pumps to aid in the disaster recovery. Britain's donation of 350,000 emergency meals did not reach victims because of laws regarding mad cow disease. Russia's initial offer of two jets was declined by the U.S. State Department but accepted later. The French offer was also declined and requested later. As a result of the large loss of life and property along the Gulf Coast, the name Katrina was officially retired on April 6, 2006, by the World

Meteorological Organization at the request of the U.S. government. It was replaced by Katia in the North Atlantic hurricane naming lists, which was used in the 2011 North Atlantic hurricane season.

Hurricane Rita of 2005--was the fourth-most intense North Atlantic hurricane ever recorded and the most intense tropical cyclone ever observed in the Gulf of Mexico. Part of the record-breaking 2005 North Atlantic hurricane season, which included three of the six most intense North Atlantic hurricanes ever recorded (along with #1 Wilma, #2 Gilbert and #6 Katrina), Rita was the eighteenth named storm, tenth hurricane, and fifth major hurricane of the 2005 season. The seventeenth named storm and fifth major hurricane of the 2005 North Atlantic hurricane season, Rita began near the Turks and Caicos Islands as a tropical depression on September 17th, 2005. However, as it passed near the Florida Keys and South Florida, Rita blossomed into the season's tenth hurricane, and brought sustained winds of Category 2 strength with gusts over 100 mph.

As it continued to strengthen, Hurricane Rita became a major hurricane on September 21st, 2005, as its eye experienced a 77 mbar drop in just 39 hours. The storm, which followed a similar track to the devastating Hurricane Katrina, which struck New Orleans and the Mississippi Gulf Coast on August 29th, 2005, became the third Category 5 hurricane to emerge in 2005 with 175 mph winds, and a minimum central pressure of 897 mbar, or 26.49 inches of Hg. Hurricane Hunters also found wind gusts as high as 235 mph. The approach of Rita to the western Gulf Coast prompted the evacuation of some 2.7 million people. Poor planning led to traffic jams and cars running out of gas in Texas. A usual four-hour trip from Houston to Dallas ended up taking as long as 18 hours.

Prior to making landfall, the storm had already caused problems, including the deaths of 107 people trying to flee the storm, flooding in Galveston, and breeches in the New Orleans levee system that was severely damaged by Hurricane Katrina a month earlier. Twenty-four of those people that died during evacuation were in a bus that had a fire and explosion on Interstate 45 south of Dallas, Texas. Rita finally made landfall in the Sabine Pass area of the Texas/Louisiana border in the early morning hours of September 24th, bringing with it wind gusts as high as 111 mph in Cameron, Louisiana, and heavy damage in Lake Charles and Vermillion Parish. Approximately 1.1 million people were initially without power in Texas and Louisiana. Damage estimates from the storm are currently $12 billion (2005 USD), and 120 people were directly killed by the storm including five who lost their lives in an apartment complex in Beaumont, Texas, a man, who lost his life when a tornado struck in Northern Mississippi, and an East Texas man who died at the hands of a fallen tree.[155]

Hurricane Stan of 2005--The eighteenth named storm and tenth hurricane of the 2005 North Atlantic hurricane season started out modestly and only was a Category 1 hurricane on the Saffir-Simpson Hurricane Wind Scale when it made landfall over southern Mexico, but the heavy rains it produced resulted in a deadly toll. Overall, Stan caused at least 1,668 deaths across six countries, Guatemala, Mexico, El Salvador, Honduras, Nicaragua, and Costa Rica. Most of these fatalities occurred in Guatemala and were mostly caused by mudslides triggered by torrential rainfall. The floods in Guatemala destroyed entire towns and disrupted exportation of petroleum.

In Mexico, the heavy rains triggered additional mudslides and caused the rivers to overflow their banks, flooding nearby villages. Despite being relatively far from Stan as opposed to other countries, El Salvador was also severely affected by the hurricane. The Santa Ana Volcano erupted while Stan was producing heavy rains in the country, which contributed to the damage already wrought by mudslides. Across the region, Stan caused $3.9 billion in damages, primarily due to torrential rainfall. In addition, the Mexican Government estimated that damage from Stan cost approximately $1.9 billion (2005 USD). While crop damage in El Salvador was estimated to be about $10 million. The great death toll reported from Hurricane Stan makes this storm among the deadliest of all time in the North Atlantic. Rainfall amounts ranging between 15 to 20 inches were reported in the region.

Hurricane Vince of 2005--Vince developed from an extratropical system on October 8, becoming a subtropical storm southeast of the Azores. The National Hurricane Center (NHC) did not officially name the storm until the next day, shortly before Vince became a hurricane. The storm weakened at sea and made landfall on the Iberian Peninsula as a tropical depression on October 11. Vince was the first tropical system to do so since the 1842 Spain Hurricane. It dissipated over Spain, bringing much needed rain to the region, and its remnants passed into the Mediterranean Sea. Well...OK, you probably think that this storm was nothing special, but it actually was for several reasons. Forming in the second full week of October 2005, Vince not only became the

---

155 *https://en.wikipedia.org/wiki/Hurricane_Rita.* Retrieved: 08-08-2014.

20th named storm and 11th hurricane of the busy 2005 season, but it also marked the first time since the naming of storms began in 1950 that a season reached the "V" named storm. The previous mark was set in 1995 when that season reached the "T" named storm. It also set history in a couple more ways as well. Forming in the vicinity of the Madiera Islands in the Northeastern Atlantic, Hurricane Vince was the first hurricane on record to form in this region. In addition, Vince became the first tropical cyclone of any kind to make landfall in Spain since 1842 as it made landfall in the southwestern portion of western Europe near Huelva on October 11, 2005, as a tropical depression with 35 mph winds and a minimum central pressure of 1002 mbar, or 29.59 inches.

Although Hurricane Vince developed in an unusual location in the northeastern Atlantic, well away from where tropical cyclones are usually found, it is neither the most northerly-forming nor the most easterly-forming Atlantic tropical storm; these records are held by Alberto of the 1988 season at 41.5° N, and Ginger of the 1967 season at 18.1° W, respectively. Hurricane Vince developed into a hurricane farther east than any other known storm at 18.9°W. Vince's record north was broken by Tropical Storm Grace in 2009. When Subtropical Storm Vince formed on October 8, it was the earliest in the season that the twenty-first tropical or subtropical storm had ever developed, 38 days ahead of the previous record held by Tropical Storm Twenty-one of the 1933 North Atlantic hurricane season. Hurricane Vince was also the first named "V" storm in the Atlantic since naming began in 1950. Because the storm did not cause significant damage, the name Vince was not retired by the World Meteorological Organization and was on the list of names for the 2011 season.[156]

Hurricane Wilma of 2005--This storm set the record for the most intense hurricane recorded in the North Atlantic basin. It devastated parts of the Yucatán Peninsula and southern Florida during October in the 2005 North Atlantic hurricane season. There is no question about this one being on the list. Wilma was not only a very memorable storm, but it also set numerous records for both strength and seasonal activity. Wilma was only the third Category 5 ever to develop in the month of October, and with the formation of Hurricane Wilma, the 2005 season became the most active on record, exceeding the 21 storms of the 1933 season. Wilma was the twenty-second storm (including the

---

[156] James L. Franklin (2006-02-22), *Tropical Cyclone Report: Hurricane Vince" (PDF)*. National Hurricane Center. Retrieved: 10-04-2015.

subtropical storm discovered in reanalysis), thirteenth hurricane, sixth major hurricane, and fourth Category 5 hurricane of the record-breaking season. Wilma made several landfalls, with the most destructive effects felt in the Yucatán Peninsula of Mexico, Cuba, and the U.S. state of Florida. At least 87 deaths were reported, and damage was estimated at over $29.4 billion (2005 USD), ranking Wilma among the top 10 costliest hurricanes ever recorded in the North Atlantic and ranks in the top ten costliest hurricanes in U.S. history. Wilma also affected eleven countries with winds or rainfall, more than any other hurricane in recent history.

Hurricane Wilma tore the roof of this church in Freeport, Grand Bahama, in the Bahamas.

Wilma started out impressively as the 24th depression of the 2005 North Atlantic hurricane season on Saturday, October 15th, and battled some ups and downs that weekend, but over time the storm would become a monster. In a span of 36 hours from Tuesday morning, October 18th, to Wednesday afternoon, October 19th, rapid intensification occurred as the barometric pressure in the storm dropped some 102 mbar to an all-time low for pressure in the Atlantic Basin of 882 mbar, or 26.05 inches of Hg. Maximum sustained winds increased to 175 mph. Wilma is now the strongest storm all time in the North Atlantic, surpassing the mark set by Hurricane Gilbert in 1988 (888 mbar). It also was the 21st named storm, 12th hurricane, and 6th major hurricane of 2005, which equaled marks for storms in 1933 and hurricanes in 1969. Wilma was the fourth Category 5 hurricane to form in the season as well, joining Katrina and Rita, which are also among the five or six strongest storms on record.

After reaching its peak, Wilma gradually decreased in intensity to a strong Category 4 hurricane with sustained winds of 140 mph before making its first landfall over Cozumel, Mexico, on Friday, October 21, 2005. Six hours later on Friday night, Wilma slowly moved over the Yucatan as it made a second landfall in Cancun. After bringing hurricane-force winds to the Yucatan for over 24 hours, the storm gradually departed and moved out over the southern Gulf of Mexico, where it was picked up by a trough over the eastern United States and carried across Florida. Moving as fast as 25 miles per hour to the northeast, Wilma made a third landfall over Cape Romano, Florida, some 22 miles to the south of Naples and brought with it winds of Category 3 strength at 125 mph.

Battening up for Hurricane Wilma with a twist of humor in South Florida (Florida Photographic Collection, Courtesy of the State Library and Archives of Florida).

Wilma had a devastating effect on much of the east coast of South Florida, including Fort Lauderdale, which experienced its worst hurricane in 55 years. Nearby in Key Biscayne, wind gusts were as high as 116 mph, while they were 95 mph at Opa Locka Airport, outside Miami. Between three and six million people were left without power in the hours after the storm. There were waves as high as 45 feet, which came over the sea wall and battered the capital of Havana in Cuba. The storm was responsible for 87 deaths, with most of the fatalities occurring in Florida, Mexico and throughout the Caribbean. Damage estimates are said to be about $29.4 billion (2005 USD).

Tropical Storm Alpha of 2005--Not too many tropical storms get mentioned in this list unless they are record breakers, or what we call notable or extraordinary storms. Alpha does meet these criteria, as it was the 23rd named storm to form in the tropical Atlantic during the 2005 Atlantic Hurricane season, which broke the record previously set in 1933 with 21 storms. It also marked the first time since names have been used in the North Atlantic (since 1950) that a second list of storm names was used for the same season. Alpha was the first tropical storm to be assigned a Greek-alphabet name after the list of hurricane names was exhausted. There have also been 12 hurricanes in 2005, which equaled the mark set in 1969, and 6 major hurricanes, including three Category 5 storms, which is also a record.

Alpha dumped torrential rain on the island of Hispaniola, making it the eighth wettest storm to impact poverty-stricken Haiti. It caused 26 deaths, 17 of them in Haiti and all of them caused by floods and rain-related landslides. Roads were blocked for weeks and hundreds of houses were destroyed. It must be noted that the name 'Alpha' had been used before in the North Atlantic for a subtropical storm but it was not truly tropical in nature, but 2005 was the first season to have a truly tropical storm Alpha. At the time it was thought that Alpha was the twenty-second storm of the season, and so was the storm which broke the 1933 season's record for most storms in a single season. However, in post-season analysis by the National Hurricane Center, it was revealed that there was also a previously unnoticed subtropical storm on October 4, which made Alpha the twenty-third storm of the season. The name 'Alpha of 2005' was retired in the spring of 2006 by Region IV Hurricane Naming Committee of the World Meteorological Organization, making it the first time ever a Greek lettering storm was retired by the WMO.

Hurricane Beta of 2005--Like Alpha, Beta is an historic storm for different reasons. Only a Category 1 hurricane on the Saffir-Simpson Hurricane Wind Scale on October 28th, 2005, Beta originally developed in the extreme southwestern Caribbean on October 26th, 2005. It became the 24th named storm of the season, and then strengthened to the 14th hurricane of the season as well. Packing winds of 90 mph and a minimum central pressure of 28.79

inches of Hg, Beta became a record-breaking hurricane by placing 2005 in the history books again with the most hurricanes in a single season. 2005 broke the previous mark set in 1969 with 12 hurricanes. On the morning of October 29th, Beta strengthened to its peak intensity as a major hurricane with 115 mph winds and a minimum central pressure of 28.35 inches of Hg. It made Beta the eight-major hurricane of the 2005 season. That tied the season for second all time for most major hurricanes with 1961, which also had seven major storms. The 1950 North Atlantic hurricane season had the most major hurricanes with eight. The storm would finally make landfall in Nicaragua some 50 miles to the north of Bluefields on October 29th.

When Tropical Depression Twenty-six was upgraded to Tropical Storm Beta, it was the first time that the second letter of the Greek alphabet was used for a tropical cyclone. Upon being named, it was the first time that a North Atlantic hurricane season had produced 24 tropical or subtropical cyclones. Operationally, Beta was the record-breaking 13th hurricane, surpassing the 12 hurricanes produced in 1969. In the post-season analysis by the National Hurricane Center, Tropical Storm Cindy was upgraded to a hurricane, thus making Beta the 14th hurricane of 2005. Due to the relatively low impact caused by Beta, the name was not retired by the WMO in the spring of 2006 and remains on the auxiliary list of names in the event that another Atlantic hurricane season produces more than 21 storms. Hurricane Beta caused 9 deaths, 3 in Panama and 6 in Nicaragua, and caused $15.5 million (2005 USD) in damages.

Hurricane Dean of 2007--This storm was the fourth named storm, third tropical cyclone, first hurricane and first major hurricane of the 2007 North Atlantic hurricane season, the most intense tropical cyclone in the North Atlantic Basin since Hurricane Wilma of 2005 and the most intense tropical cyclone to threaten Jamaica since Hurricane Ivan of 2004. Dean was the first hurricane to make landfall in the North Atlantic basin at Category 5 intensity since Hurricane Andrew on August 24, 1992. Additionally, it made the third most intense North Atlantic hurricane landfall. A Cape Verde-type hurricane, Dean took a west-northwest path through the Caribbean Sea and passed just to the south of Jamaica on August 20. Hurricane Dean was a very destructive hurricane and caused an estimated damage of $1.66 billion (2007 USD).

Hurricane Dean was a Category 5 storm, but it missed major population centers in Mexico and its exceptional Category 5 strength landfall caused no deaths there and less damage than in the Caribbean islands it passed as a

Category 2 hurricane. The hurricane's intense winds, waves, rains and storm surge were responsible for at least 45 deaths (40 direct and 5 indirect) across ten countries. Throughout the affected regions, clean up and repairs took months to complete. Donations solicited by international aid organizations joined national funds in clearing roads, rebuilding houses, and replanting destroyed crops. In Jamaica, where the damage was worst, banana production did not return to pre-storm levels for over a year. Mexico's tourist industry, too, took almost a year to rebuild its damaged cruise ship infrastructure.

Hurricane Gustav of 2008--This storm was the second most destructive hurricane of the 2008 North Atlantic hurricane season. The storm was the seventh tropical cyclone, third hurricane, and second major hurricane of the season. Gustav caused serious damage and casualties in Haiti, the Dominican Republic, Jamaica, the Cayman Islands, Cuba and the United States. Gustav caused at least $6.6 billion (2008 USD) in damage and 153 deaths. A tropical wave formed in the coast of Africa on August 18. It intensified into a disturbance, which developed in the deep tropical Atlantic in the fourth week of August. It tracked westward into the Caribbean Sea, where it encountered more favorable atmospheric conditions and became a tropical depression on the morning of August 25, west of the Windward Islands. It rapidly intensified into Tropical Storm Gustav early that afternoon, and into Hurricane Gustav early on August 26. Striking southwest Haiti, it weakened into a tropical storm on the evening of August 27 due to land interaction and slowed down considerably. It re-organized further south into a strong tropical storm once again on August 28 before speeding up and hitting Jamaica. Gustav killed 92 people in Haiti, the Dominican Republic, and Jamaica.

It then was upgraded to a hurricane again during the late afternoon of August 29. On the morning of August 30, Gustav was upgraded to a major Category 3 hurricane on the Saffir Simpson Hurricane Wind Scale. After intensification slowed for a few hours, another round of rapid intensification occurred and Gustav was upgraded to a Category 4 hurricane. Continuing to intensify, it became a 155 mph storm that afternoon before landfall. Soon after Gustav made landfall in Cuba, firstly on the island of Isla de la Juventud and later on the mainland near Los Palacios in Pinar del Río Province, causing catastrophic damage, although it was difficult to estimate it; damage was later estimated at $3 billion (2008 USD). On September 4, Gustav was absorbed by a cold front while over the Ozarks.

Hurricane Ike of 2008--A tropical disturbance developed off the coast of Africa near the end of August. It tracked south of the Cape Verde Islands and slowly developed. On September 1, it became Tropical Depression # 9 while just west of the Cape Verde Islands and intensified into a tropical storm later that day, when it was given the name Ike. Ike developed an eye late on September 3 as it underwent explosive intensification, as it strengthened from a tropical storm to a Category 4 hurricane in twelve hours with an estimated pressure drop of 43 mbar (1.3 inHg), from 991 to 948 mbars (29.3 to 28.0 inHg) and a 24-hour pressure drop of 61 mbars (1.8 inHg), from 996 to 935 mbars (29.4 to 27.6 inHg), making it one of the more rapidly intensifying hurricanes on record in the North Atlantic. The most rapidly intensifying hurricane in the North Atlantic still belongs to Hurricane Wilma of 2005. It also reached its 882 mbar (26.0 inHg) pressure in a span of 24 hours, making it the fastest pressure drop of any storm in the North Atlantic Hurricane basin.

Fearing that the new forecast tracks would come to fruition, residents in South Florida prepared for a direct strike from a strong hurricane, with forecasts measuring the storm to be stronger than Hurricane Wilma, which had struck the region three years earlier. Fortunately for Floridians, whose state had endured eight hurricanes strikes in the period 2004 - 2005, a strong Bermuda high pressure system pushed Ike toward a more southerly track. Ike weakened to a Category 2 hurricane before re-intensifying back to Category 4. It ripped across the Bahamas near the island of Inagua and Grand Turk in the Turks and Caicos Islands, where 80% of the buildings on Grand Turk were severely damaged or completely destroyed. It weakened to a strong Category 3 and then re-strengthened to Category 4 late in the afternoon of September 7 as it headed for the northeastern coast of Cuba that evening. In addition, Hurricane Ike killed at least 74 people in Haiti and 2 people in the Dominican Republic.

As Ike crossed Cuba on September 8, it weakened to Category 1 and emerged into the Caribbean Sea, where it moved along the southern coast. Ike killed 7 people in Cuba, having traversed nearly the entirety of the island nation. It crossed into the Gulf of Mexico on September 9 and ballooned in size. Ike maintained a double eyewall structure across most of the Gulf of Mexico and continued to expand in size. It made landfall on Galveston Island on September 13 as a strong Category 2 hurricane, but its large size brought a storm surge of over 15 feet (4.6 m) from Galveston Island eastward into southern Louisiana. The Bolivar Peninsula was worst affected by the surge, while Galveston Island (where waves topped the seawall) and the Port Arthur areas also saw extensive damage. Power was knocked out to most of the Houston area, and windows were blown out of skyscrapers in downtown Houston. As Ike moved inland, it brought extensive flooding and wind damage throughout the Midwest and as far north as Pennsylvania. Ike was categorized extratropical on September 14.

Damage from Ike is estimated at $37.5 billion (2008 USD), of which $29.5 billion was in the U.S., the third most destructive U.S. hurricane on record, behind Sandy of 2012 and Katrina in 2005. At least 195 fatalities have been blamed on Ike, of which 112 were in the United States. It was the most destructive hurricane in Texas history. Ike was an extremely large and powerful storm. At one point, the diameter of Ike's tropical storm and hurricane force winds were 600 and 240 miles (965 and 390 km), respectively. Ike also had the highest Integrated Kinetic Energy (IKE) of any North Atlantic storm. IKE is a measure of storm surge destructive potential, similar to the Saffir-Simpson Hurricane Wind Scale, though it is more complex and in many ways, more accurate. On a scale that ranges from 1 to 6, with 6 being highest destructive potential, Ike registered 5.6. Ike crossed the U.S. northward into southern Ontario, Canada, releasing abundant rainfall which broke records dating back many years, in several cities. It was noted as the second most active tropical storm to have reached the Canadian mainland since Hazel in 1954. Like Ike, Hazel had also affected southern Ontario. The storm dissipated as it reached southern Québec on September 14.

Hurricane Paloma of 2008--An area of low pressure became stationary in the Caribbean Sea without showing tropical development for several days at the beginning of November. Finally, on November 5 the low-pressure system organized and became Tropical Depression #17 just east of Nicaragua. The next day, it strengthened to become Tropical Storm Paloma, then later Hurricane Paloma. The following days proved to be a rarity in terms of tropical cyclone intensity in the month of November. This was seen when Paloma was upgraded to a Category 2, then later a Category 3 major hurricane, making it the first 'P' named storm to reach major hurricane status in the North Atlantic Basin. On November 8, the system attained was upgraded to a Category 4 and reached its peak intensity with sustained winds of 145 mph. Thereafter, Paloma began a period of rapid weakening before making landfall as a Category 2 hurricane near Santa Cruz del Sur, Cuba. On November 9, Paloma was downgraded to a tropical storm, and then a depression. Later that evening, the storm finally met its demise as it transformed into a remnant low. Paloma caused up to $300 million (2008 USD) in damage to Cuba, and $15 million in damage to the Cayman Islands.

Tropical Storm Matthew of 2010--Tropical Storm Matthew was the fourth and deadliest tropical cyclone to make landfall in Central America during the 2010 North Atlantic hurricane season. Matthew, despite being just a tropical storm, proved to be extremely deadly and very destructive nonetheless. The fifteenth tropical cyclone and thirteenth named storm of the year, Matthew formed on September 23 and lost its tropical cyclone characteristics in the morning of September 26. However, its remnants continued to produce life-threatening rainfalls over parts of Central America as it dissipated.

Throughout Central and South America, torrential rain produced by Matthew triggered widespread flooding and landslides. Eight people were killed by the storm in Venezuela, and at least 100 people have been confirmed dead throughout Central America and southern Mexico. In Mexico, a massive landslide, roughly 200 ft. (61 m) long, buried nearly 300 homes. Initially, officials feared hundreds of casualties, but the impact was much less fatal than expected. This storm was responsible for 126 deaths and a damage total of $171.2 million (2010 USD).

Hurricane Tomas of 2010--The 2010 North Atlantic hurricane season was the third most active North Atlantic hurricane season on record, tying with the 1887, 1995, 2011, and 2012 Atlantic hurricane seasons. It had the most number of named storms since the 2005 season and also ties with the 1969 North Atlantic hurricane season for the second largest number of hurricanes. In addition, the activity in the north Atlantic in 2010 exceeded the activity in the northwest Pacific Typhoon season. The only other known time this event happened was in 2005.

A tropical wave developed into Tropical Storm Tomas late on October 29, about 200 miles southeast of Barbados. Tomas become the twelfth hurricane of the season and crossed the Windward Islands as a Category 1 hurricane. After that, southwesterly shear and dry air weakened Tomas to a tropical storm. Tomas continued to weaken slowly until midnight on November 2. Early on November 2, Tropical Storm Tomas re-intensified slightly, but later weakened to a tropical depression. Then on the evening of November 3, Tomas re-strengthened into a tropical storm. Early on November 5, it became a hurricane again as it neared Haiti and Cuba. Late on November 7, the NHC issued its last advisory on Tomas as it became an extratropical cyclone. Early on November 10, the extratropical remnants of Hurricane Tomas were absorbed by another extratropical storm southeast of Nova Scotia. It caused $741 million in damages and killed 71 people, of which 14 were in St. Lucia.

Hurricane Irene of 2011--The 2011 North Atlantic hurricane season is tied with 1887, 1995, 2010, and the following 2012 season for the third highest number of named storms since record-keeping began in 1851. Forming on August 20, Irene was the second earliest ninth North Atlantic tropical cyclone on record, along with an unnamed tropical storm from the 1936 season. A total of 56 people were confirmed dead across the Caribbean, 10 U.S. and Canada, in the aftermath and damage from Hurricane Irene totaled $19 billion (2011 USD), making it the fifth costliest hurricane in the North Atlantic basin.

Hurricane Irene's impacts by individual countries

Country/Region	Deaths	Damage (USD)
The Bahamas	0	$40 million
Canada	1	$130 million
Dominican Republic	4	$30 million
Haiti	3	$260 million
United States	49	~$15.6 billion
Puerto Rico	1	$500 million
Other islands	0	Unknown
Total	**56**	**~$16.56 billion**

Hurricane Irene's impacts by individual countries (Courtesy of Wikipedia, NHC & Wunderground).

Throughout its path, Irene caused widespread destruction and at least 56 deaths. Damage estimates throughout the United States are estimated near $15.6 billion, which made it the seventh costliest hurricane in United States history, only behind Hurricane Andrew of 1992, Hurricane Ivan of 2004, Hurricanes Wilma and Katrina of 2005, Hurricane Ike of 2008, and Hurricane Sandy in 2012. In addition, monetary losses in the Caribbean and Canada were $830 million and $130 million respectively for a total of nearly $16.6 billion in damage. In the evening of August 20, a large low pressure area became organized enough to be classified as Tropical Storm Irene. It passed over the Leeward Islands early on August 21. Early on August 22, Irene strengthened into a Category 1 hurricane, with winds of 75 mph and a central pressure of 987 mbar (29.1 inHg), becoming the first hurricane of the season. This broke a streak of eight consecutive tropical cyclones to start the 2011 season, all of which did not strengthen beyond tropical storm force.

Early on August 24, Irene became a Category 3 major hurricane, with winds of 120 mph. Irene went through a partial eyewall replacement cycle, which weakened it slightly but caused its wind field to greatly expand. On August 26, New York mayor Michael Bloomberg told coastal residents to 'get moving, now.' The next day, Irene made landfall on Cape Lookout, North Carolina as a Category 1 hurricane with 85 mph winds with an unusually low pressure for a Category 1 hurricane. After weakening to a tropical storm, Irene made a second U.S. landfall at Brigantine Island in New Jersey at 5:35 a.m. On August 28, still a strong tropical storm, Irene made its third U.S. landfall in the Coney Island area of Brooklyn, New York, at approximately 9:00 a.m. on August 28. Irene became a post-tropical storm over Quebec and Atlantic Canada late on August 28.

In Washington, D.C., the forecast arrival of Hurricane Irene caused postponement of the planned August 28 dedication ceremony for the Martin Luther King, Jr. National Memorial. In anticipation of the storm, thousands of sandbags were prepared for placement at flood-prone Washington Metro station entrances. Amtrak service from Washington's Union Station southward was cancelled from August 26 until August 28.

Hurricane Isaac of 2012--The 2012 North Atlantic hurricane season was extremely active, tied with 1887, 1995, 2010, and 2011, for having the third-most named storms on record. A tropical wave developed into Tropical Depression # 9 at 0600 UTC on August 21, while located about 720 miles east of the Lesser Antilles. The depression headed just north of due west and twelve hours later strengthened into Tropical Storm Isaac. After intensifying somewhat further, Isaac passed through the Leeward Islands on August 22. A few islands reported tropical storm force winds and light rainfall, but no damage occurred. Unfavorable conditions, primarily dry air, as well as a reformation of the center, caused Isaac to remain disorganized in the eastern Caribbean Sea.

Early on August 25, it made landfall near Jacmel, Haiti as a strong tropical storm. Strong winds and heavy rain impacted numerous camps set up after the 2010 Haiti earthquake, with about 6,000 people losing shelter. Approximately 1,000 houses were destroyed, resulting in about $8 million in damage; there were 24 deaths confirmed. In neighboring Dominican Republic, 864 houses were damaged and cross losses reached approximately $30 million; five deaths were reported. Isaac became slightly disorganized over Haiti and re-emerged into the Caribbean Sea later on August 25, hours before striking Guantánamo Province, Cuba, with winds of 60 mph. There, 6 homes were destroyed and 91 sustained damage.

Later on August 25, Isaac emerged into the southwestern Atlantic Ocean over the Great Bahama Banks. Initially, the storm posed a threat to Florida and the 2012 Republican National Convention, but passed to the southwest late on August 26. However, its outer bands spawned tornadoes and dropped isolated areas of heavy rainfall, causing severe local flooding, especially in Palm Beach County. Neighborhoods in The Acreage, Loxahatchee, Royal Palm Beach and Wellington were left stranded for up to several days. Tornadoes in the state destroyed 1 structure and caused damage to at least 102 others. Isaac reached the Gulf of Mexico and began a strengthening trend, reaching hurricane status on August 28. At 0000 UTC on the following day, the storm made landfall near the mouth of the Mississippi River in Louisiana with winds of 80 mph. Throughout the United States, damage reached about $2.35 billion and there were 9 fatalities, most of which was incurred within the state of Louisiana. Overall, Isaac caused $2.39 billion (2012 USD) in damage and led to 41 fatalities.

Hurricane Sandy of 2012--Hurricane Sandy (unofficially known as "Superstorm Sandy") was the deadliest and most destructive hurricane of the 2012 North Atlantic hurricane season, and the second-costliest hurricane in United States history. Classified as the eighteenth named storm, tenth hurricane and second major hurricane of the year, Sandy was a Category 3 storm at its peak intensity when it made landfall in Cuba. While it was a Category 2 storm off the coast of the Northeastern United States, the storm became the largest North Atlantic hurricane on record (as measured by diameter, with winds spanning 1,100 miles). Experts assessed damage to have been over $75 billion (2015 USD), a total surpassed only by Hurricane Katrina. At least 233 people were killed along the path of the storm in eight countries.

A tropical wave developed into Tropical Depression #18 at 1200 UTC on October 22, while located about 350 miles south-southwest of Kingston, Jamaica. Six hours later, it strengthened into Tropical Storm Sandy. Initially, the storm headed southwestward, but re-curved to the north-northeast due to a mid to upper-level trough in the northwestern Caribbean Sea. A gradual increase in organization and deepening occurred, with Sandy becoming a hurricane on October 24. Several hours later, it made landfall near Bull Bay, Jamaica, as a moderate Category 1 hurricane. In that country, there was 1 fatality and damage to thousands of homes, resulting in about $100 million in losses. After clearing Jamaica, Sandy began to strengthen significantly. At 0525 UTC on October 25, it struck near Santiago de Cuba in Cuba, with winds of 115 mph; this made Sandy the second major hurricane of the season. In the province of Santiago de Cuba alone, 132,733 homes were damaged, of which 15,322 were destroyed and 43,426 lost their roofs. The storm resulted in 11 deaths and $2 billion in damage in Cuba. It also produced widespread devastation in Haiti, where over 27,000 homes were flooded, damaged, or destroyed, and 40% of the corn, beans, rice, banana, and coffee crops were lost. The storm left $750 million in damage, 54 deaths, and 21 people missing.

The storm weakened slightly while crossing Cuba and emerged into the southwestern Atlantic Ocean as a Category 2 hurricane late on October 25. Shortly thereafter, it moved through the central Bahamas, where three fatalities and $300 million in damage were reported. Early on October 27, it briefly weakened to a tropical storm, before re-acquiring hurricane intensity later that day. In the Southeastern United States, impact was limited to gusty winds, light rainfall, and rough surf. The outerbands of Sandy impacted the island of Bermuda, with a tornado in Sandys Parish damaging a few homes and businesses. Movement over the Gulf Stream and baroclinic processes caused the storm to deepen, with the storm becoming a Category 2 hurricane again at 1200 UTC on October 29. Although it soon weakened to a Category 1 hurricane, the barometric pressure decreased to 940 mbar (28 inHg).

At 2100 UTC, Sandy became extratropical, while located just offshore New Jersey. The center of the now extratropical storm moved inland near Brigantine late on October 29. In the Northeastern United States, damage was most severe in New Jersey and New York. Within the former, 346,000 houses were damaged or destroyed, while nearly 19,000 businesses suffered severe losses. In New York, an estimated 305,000 homes were destroyed. Severe coastal flooding occurred in New York City, with the hardest hit areas being New Dorp Beach, Red Hook, and the Rockaways; eight tunnels of the subway system were inundated. Heavy snowfall was also reported, peaking at 36 inches (910 mm) in West Virginia. Additionally, the remnants of Sandy left 2 deaths and $100 million in damage in Canada, with Ontario and Quebec being the worst impacted. Overall, 286 fatalities were attributed to Sandy. Damages totaled $65 billion in the United States and $68 billion overall, making Sandy the second-costliest Atlantic hurricane in recorded history, behind only Hurricane Katrina in 2005.

Costliest U.S. North Atlantic Hurricanes

Rank	Hurricane	Season	Damage
1	Katrina	2005	$108 billion
2	**Sandy**	**2012**	**$65 billion**
3	Ike	2008	$29.5 billion
4	Andrew	1992	$26.5 billion
5	Wilma	2005	$21 billion
6	Ivan	2004	$18.8 billion
7	Irene	2011	$15.6 billion
8	Charley	2004	$15.1 billion
9	Rita	2005	$12 billion
10	Frances	2004	$9.51 billion

Costliest U.S. North Atlantic Hurricanes (Courtesy of the National Hurricane Center/ Wikipedia-Costs refer to total estimated property losses).

According to The U.S. National Center for Atmospheric Research NCAR senior climatologist Kevin E. Trenberth, "The answer to the oft-asked question of whether an event is caused by climate change is that it is the wrong question. All weather events are affected by climate change because the environment in which they occur is warmer and moister than it used to be." Although NOAA meteorologist Martin Hoerling attributes Sandy to "little more than the coincidental alignment of a tropical storm with an extratropical storm," Trenberth does agree that the storm was caused by "natural variability" but adds that it was "enhanced by global warming." One factor contributing to the storm's strength was abnormally warm sea surface temperatures offshore the East Coast of the United States—more than 3 °C (5 °F) above normal, to which global warming had contributed 0.6 °C (1 °F). As the temperature of the atmosphere increases, the capacity to hold water increases, leading to stronger storms and higher rainfall amounts.

The effects of Hurricane Sandy in the Greater Antilles were spread over five countries and included at least 120 deaths, primarily on October 24 and 25, 2012. Sandy formed in the central Caribbean Sea south of Jamaica on October 22 as part of the 2012 North Atlantic hurricane season. In Jamaica, approximately 70 percent of the island lost power because of Sandy, and schools in the Kingston area were closed for a week. In Haiti, which was still recovering from the effects of the 2010 earthquake, at least 104 people have died, and an estimated 200,000 were left homeless as of October 29, as a result of four days of ongoing rain from Hurricane Sandy. In the Dominican Republic, two people were killed and 8,755 people evacuated as officials said the rains were expected to continue until at least October 27.

Hurricane Sandy strengthened into a Category 3 hurricane before hitting Cuba. In Cuba, at least 55,000 people had been evacuated principally because of expected flooding from rains that could total up to 20 inches (500 mm) in some places and a storm surge the Cuban weather service said was already beginning along the southeastern coast around midnight EDT. State media has said at least 11 people in Cuba were killed as a result of the storm, and Raúl Castro planned to visit Santiago de Cuba in the coming days. Nine of the deaths were in Santigo de Cuba Province, and two were in Guantánamo Province, and most of the victims were trapped in destroyed houses. This makes Sandy the deadliest hurricane to hit Cuba since 2005, when Hurricane Dennis killed 16 people. In the Bahamas, a NOAA automated weather station at Settlement Point on Grand Bahama Island reported sustained winds of 49 mph and a wind gust of 63 mph. One person died from falling off his roof while attempting to fix a window shutter in the Lyford Cay area on New Providence. Another died in the Queen's Cove area on Grand Bahama Island, where he drowned after the sea surge trapped him in his apartment. Portions of the Bahamas lost power or cellular service, including an island wide power outage on Bimini. Five homes were severely damaged near Williams' Town. Overall damage in the Bahamas was about $700 million (2012 USD), with the most severe damage on Cat Island and Exuma, where many houses were heavily damaged by wind and storm surge.[157]

A total of 24 U.S. states were in some way affected by Sandy. The hurricane caused tens of billions of dollars in damage in the United States, destroyed thousands of homes, left millions without electric service, and caused 71 direct deaths in nine states, including 49 in New York, 10 in New Jersey, 3 in Connecticut, 2 each in Pennsylvania and Maryland, and 1 each in New Hampshire, Virginia and West Virginia. There were also 2 direct deaths from Sandy in U.S. coastal waters in the Atlantic Ocean, about 90 miles off the North Carolina coast, which are not counted in the U.S. total. In addition, the storm resulted in 87 indirect deaths. In all, a total of 160 people were killed due to the storm, making Sandy the deadliest hurricane to hit the United States mainland since Hurricane Katrina in 2005, and the deadliest to hit the U.S. East Coast since Hurricane Agnes in 1972.

---

[157] *Haiti raises death toll from Hurricane Sandy to 54; regional deaths up to 71*, *Turnquest, Ava* (Ellington). January 21, 2013. Retrieved: 15-02-2015.

As Hurricane Sandy approached the United States, forecasters and journalists gave it several different unofficial names, at first related to its projected snow content, then to its proximity to Halloween, and eventually to the overall size of the storm. Early nicknames included "Snowicane Sandy" and "Snor'eastercane Sandy." The most popular Halloween-related nickname was "Frankenstorm", coined by Jim Cisco, a forecaster at the Hydrometeorological Prediction Center. CNN banned the use of the term, saying it trivialized the destruction. The severe and widespread damage the storm caused in the United States, as well as its unusual merge with a frontal system, resulted in the nicknaming of the hurricane "Superstorm Sandy" by the media, public officials, and several organizations, including U.S. government agencies. This persisted as the most common nickname well into 2013. The term was also embraced by climate change proponents as a term for the new type of storms caused by global warming, while other writers used the term but maintained that it was too soon to blame the storm on climate change. Meanwhile, Popular Science called it "an imaginary scare-term that exists exclusively for shock value.

Hurricane Sandy damage on Long Beach Island, New Jersey (Courtesy of Wikipedia-Public Domain).

Due to flooding and other storm-related problems, Amtrak cancelled all Acela Express, Northeast Regional, Keystone, and Shuttle services for October 29 and 30. More than 13,000 flights were cancelled across the U.S. on October

29, and more than 3,500 were called off October 30. From October 27 through early November 1, airlines cancelled a total of 19,729 flights, according to Flight Aware.

On October 31, over 6 million customers were still without power in 15 states and the District of Columbia. The states with the most customers without power were New Jersey with 2,040,195 customers; New York with 1,933,147; Pennsylvania with 852,458; and Connecticut with 486,927.[158] The New York Stock Exchange was closed on both October 29 and 30 as a result of Hurricane Sandy, due to power outages and flooding in the area. Such a closure for weather-related reasons had not happened since 1888. The markets reopened on October 31, and to the relief of investors, closed relatively flat that day. A week later, the National Association of Insurance Commissioners Capital Markets Bureau noted a slight uptick in the market (0.8%) and suggested that the negative economic impact of Hurricane Sandy was offset by the expected positive impacts of rebuilding. The New York Stock Exchange and Nasdaq reopened on October 31 after a two-day closure for storm. More than 1,500 FEMA personnel were along the East Coast working to support disaster preparedness and response operations, including search and rescue, situational awareness, communications and logistical support.

On November 2, the American Red Cross announced they have 4,000 disaster workers across storm damaged areas, with thousands more en route from other states. Nearly 7,000 people spent the night in emergency shelters across the region. *Hurricane Sandy: Coming Together,* a live telethon on November 2 that featured rock and pop stars such as Bruce Springsteen, Billy Joel, Jon Bon Jovi, Mary J. Blige, Sting and Christina Aguilera, raised around $23 million for American Red Cross hurricane relief efforts.[159] The National Hurricane Center ranks Hurricane Sandy as the second costliest U.S. hurricane since 1900, and the sixth costliest after adjusting for inflation, population and property values. Their report also states that due to global warming the number of future hurricanes will "either decrease or remain essentially unchanged" overall, but the ones that do form will likely be stronger, with fiercer winds and

---

158 *Hurricane Sandy Situation Report #6 (PDF).* United States Department of Energy Office of Electricity Delivery & Energy Reliability. October 31, 2012. Retrieved: 03-06-2015.

159 *Concert to Help Hurricane Sandy Victims Raises $23 Million.* RIA NOVOSTI WEBSITE GROUP. Retrieved: 04-11-2012.

heavier rains. Scientists at the University of Utah reported the energy generated by Sandy was equivalent to "small earthquakes between magnitudes 2 and 3."[160]

New York Governor Andrew Cuomo called National Guard members to help in the state. Storm impacts in Upstate New York were much more limited than in New York City; there was some flooding and a few downed trees. Rochester area utilities reported slightly fewer than 19,000 customers without power, in seven counties. In the state as a whole, however, more than 2,000,000 customers were without power at the peak of the storm. Hurricane Sandy sparked much political commentary. Many scientists say warming oceans and greater atmospheric moisture are intensifying storms while rising sea levels are worsening coastal effects. Representative Henry Waxman of California, the top Democrat of the House Energy and Commerce Committee, requested a hearing in the lame duck session on links between climate change and Hurricane Sandy. Some news outlets labeled the storm the October surprise of the 2012 United States presidential election, while Democrats and Republicans accused each other of politicizing the storm.

Major flood damage from Hurricane Sandy on the New Jersey shoreline (Courtesy of Wikipedia-Public Domain).

160 Superstorm Sandy jolted United States. *3 News NZ*. April 19, 2013. Retrieved: 04-11-2012.

The storm, which hit the United States one week before its general election, affected the presidential campaign, as well as local and state campaigns in storm-damaged areas. New Jersey Governor Chris Christie, one of Mitt Romney's leading supporters, praised President Barack Obama and his reaction to the hurricane and toured storm-damaged areas of his state with the president. It was reported at the time that Sandy might affect elections in several states, especially by curtailing early voting. *The Economist* said, "In this case, the weather is supposed to clear up well ahead of Election Day, but the impact could be felt in the turnout of early voters."[161] On the other hand, ABC News said this might be offset by a tendency to clear roads and restore power more quickly in urban areas. The storm ignited a debate over whether Republican presidential nominee Mitt Romney in 2011 proposed to eliminate the Federal Emergency Management Agency (FEMA). The Romney campaign eventually issued a statement promising to keep FEMA funded but did not explain what other parts of the federal budget he would cut to pay for it. Beyond the election, *National Defense Magazine* said Sandy "might cause a rethinking (in the USA) of how climate change threatens national security."

Because of the exceptional damage and deaths caused by the storm in many countries, the name *Sandy* was later retired by the World Meteorological Organization and will never be used again for a North Atlantic hurricane. The name was replaced with *Sara* for the 2018 Atlantic hurricane season.

Tropical Storm Erika in 2015--Tropical Storm Erika of August 2015 was the deadliest natural disaster in Dominica since Hurricane David in 1979. The fifth tropical cyclone and fifth named storm of the season, Erika developed from a westward-moving tropical wave while well east of the Lesser Antilles. Despite favorable conditions, the system failed to intensify significantly and continued to move generally westward. Erika instead became disorganized over the next few days, prior to encountering stronger wind shear. Contrary to predictions of a northwesterly recurvature, the cyclone persisted on a westerly course and passed through the Leeward Islands just north of Guadeloupe on August 27. Unfavorable conditions in the Caribbean Sea prevented Erika's intensity from attaining maximum sustained winds higher than 50 mph. Late on August 28, the storm made landfall in Dominican Republic near the border of Barahona and Pedernales provinces. Although the cyclone re-emerged into the Caribbean

161 The politics of Hurricane Sandy. The Economist. Retrieved: 29-10-2012.

early the following morning, Erika did not re-organize, and after crossing the Guantánamo Province of Cuba, it degenerated into a trough of low pressure.

Major damage to cars and homes from the floodwaters in the area of Coulibistire, in Dominica, after Tropical Storm Erika (Courtesy of Joyette Bruno).

Several Leeward Islands experienced heavy rainfall during the passage of Erika, especially Dominica. There, 15 in. (380 mm) of precipitation fell at Canefield Airport, causing catastrophic mudslides and flooding. Hundreds of homes were left uninhabitable, and entire villages were flattened. With at least 30 deaths, Erika is regarded as the deadliest natural disaster in Dominica since the passage of Hurricane David in 1979. Overall, the island nation was left with hundreds of millions in damage and was set back approximately 20 years in terms of development. In Guadeloupe, heavy rainfall in the vicinity of Basse-Terre caused flooding and mudslides, forcing roads to temporarily close. Approximately 200,000 people in Puerto Rico were left without electricity. The island experienced at least $20 million in agricultural damage. In the Dominican Republic, a weather station in Barahona measured 24.26 in (616 mm) of rain, including 8.8 in (220 mm) in a single hour. About 823 homes suffered damage, and 7,345 people were displaced. Five people died in Haiti, four from a weather-related traffic accident and one from a landslide. Total damage from Erika is estimated to be over $9 billion (2016 USD), with $482.8 million in Dominica alone.[162]

[162] *Storms' damage to roads, bridges pegged at $226M.* Press Reader. The Columbus Dispatch/ Wikipedia. Retrieved: 07-09-2015.

Torrential rains fell across Dominica, amounting to at least 15 in. (380 mm) at Canefield Airport. That airport and Douglas–Charles Airport were both flooded, with water rising above a small airplane at the latter. At least 20 homes were destroyed, and 80 percent of the island was left without power. The main river running through Roseau, the nation's capital, burst its banks during the overnight of August 26–August 27, flooding surrounding areas. One person was killed during a mudslide, and one building collapsed in the city.

Major damage to this SUV with dangling damaged telephone and electricity wires from the floodwaters in the area of Coulibistire, in Dominica, after Tropical Storm Erika (Courtesy of Joyette Bruno).

Dominica Prime Minister Roosevelt Skerrit stated that 31 fatalities have been confirmed, with at least 14 bodies recovered in the mountain community of Petite Savanne. A total of 35 people remains missing across the island, including two French citizens. Reports from The Dominican newspaper indicate at least 27 deaths in Petite Savanne, which was devastated by mudslides. The agency also reported eight deaths elsewhere on the island: three in Good Hope, two in Bath Estate, and one in each Castle Bruce, Delices, and Marigot. If confirmed, this would make Erika among the deadliest natural disasters in recent history on the island, comparable to Hurricane David in 1979.[163]

According to Prime Minister Skerrit, damage to Dominica was expected to total tens of millions of dollars and set the country back 20 years in terms of

[163] Paul J. Hebert (July 1, 1980). Atlantic Hurricane Season of 1979 (PDF). *Monthly Weather Review (American Meteorological Society)*, Wikipedia. Retrieved: 07-09-2015.

development. Preliminary surveys of the damage done in Dominica indicated that Erika wrought over $374 million in damage to the infrastructure and economy across Dominica; including $226 million in damage to roads and $87 million to the housing sector. This accounts for over half of the country's GDP of $500 million. A total of 890 homes were destroyed or left uninhabitable, while 14,291 people were rendered homeless. In the final analysis, the damage from the storm amounted to $482.8 million. When the storm was over, The Caribbean Disaster Emergency Management Agency pledged assistance to Dominica, offering two helicopters with supplies and medics from Trinidad. China and the Caribbean Development Bank offered U.S. $300,000 and U.S. $200,000 in aid, respectively, to the nation.[164]

Tropical Storm Erika of 2015, which lashed the Caribbean in August, killing 30, is only the second tropical storm to have its name retired. Tropical Storm Allison in 2001 was the only other retiree never to attain hurricane status. Allison, which caused $9 billion in damages, spurred one of the worst floods on record in Houston, according to the Weather Channel. The World Meteorological Organization on Monday 23rd April, 2016, retired the name 'Erika' from its rotating list used for hurricanes and tropical storms in light of the death and destruction caused by the storm last year. Tropical Storm Erika, which lashed the Caribbean in August, killing 30, is only the second tropical storm to have its name retired without reaching a hurricane status. Tropical Storm Allison in 2001 was the only other retiree never to attain hurricane status. Allison, which caused $9 billion in damages, spurred one of the worst floods on record in Houston, according to the Weather Channel. Including Erika and Joaquin, 80 Atlantic hurricane and tropical storm names have now been retired. The WMO replaced Erika with "Elsa", when the 2015 lists are reused in 2021.

Hurricane Joaquin in 2015--Hurricane Joaquin was a powerful Category 4 tropical cyclone that devastated several islands of the Bahamas and caused damage in the Turks and Caicos Islands, parts of the Greater Antilles, and Bermuda. The tenth named storm, third hurricane, and second major hurricane of the 2015 North Atlantic hurricane season, Joaquin evolved from a non-tropical low to become a tropical depression on September 28, well southwest of Bermuda. Tempered by unfavorable atmospheric wind shear, the depression

164 <u>*China offers $300,000 in aid to storm-hit Dominica,*</u> Beijing, China: *The Economic Times*. Agence France-Presse. August 29, 2015. Retrieved: 07-09-2015.

drifted southwestward. After becoming a tropical storm, the next day Joaquin underwent rapid intensification, reaching hurricane status on September 30 and Category 3 major hurricane strength on the Saffir-Simpson Hurricane Wind Scale on October 1. Meandering over the southeastern Bahamas, Joaquin's eye passed near or over several islands for a few days. On October 3, the hurricane weakened somewhat and accelerated to the northeast. Abrupt re-intensification ensued later that day, and Joaquin acquired sustained winds of 155 mph; this made it the strongest North Atlantic hurricane since 2010's Igor.

Roof damage at Club Med in San Salvador in the Bahamas after Hurricane Joaquin

Hurricane warnings were hoisted across most of the Bahamas as the hurricane threatened the country. Battering the nation's southern islands for over two days, Joaquin caused extensive devastation, most notably on Acklins, Crooked Island, Cat Island, Long Island, Rum Cay, and San Salvador Island. Severe storm surge inundated many communities, trapping hundreds of people in their homes; flooding persisted for days after the hurricane's departure.

Prolonged, intense winds brought down trees and power lines and unroofed homes throughout the affected region. As airstrips were submerged in floodwaters and heavily damaged, relief workers were limited in their ability to quickly help affected residents. Joaquin was one of the strongest storms on record to affect the nation, and the strongest to hit this island nation since Category 5 Hurricane Andrew in 1992.[165] Offshore, the American cargo ship *El Faro* and her 33 crew members were lost to the hurricane near the island of Crooked Island in the Bahamas.

Coastal flooding also impacted the nearby Turks and Caicos, washing out roadways, compromising seawalls, and damaging homes. Strong winds and heavy rainfall caused some property damage in eastern Cuba. One fisherman died when heavy seas capsized a small boat along the coast of Haiti. Storm tides resulted in severe flooding in several of Haiti's departments, forcing families from their homes and destroying crops. The weakening hurricane passed just west of Bermuda on October 4, attended by strong winds that cut power to 15,000 electric subscribers. Damage on Bermuda was minor. Although Joaquin steered clear of the mainland United States, another large storm system over the southeastern states drew tremendous moisture from the hurricane, resulting in catastrophic flooding in South Carolina.

Large swells ahead of the storm's arrival in the Bahamas washed out a main road on San Salvador Island. Widespread power outages affected several islands as the hurricane closed in. Reports of flooding and people in need of assistance were received from Acklins, Crooked Island, Rum Cay, San Salvador Exuma, and Long Island. Prolonged power and communication failures overwhelmed the nation's southeastern islands, leaving several islands effectively isolated in the immediate aftermath of Joaquin. The hurricane took all 59 of the Bahamas Telecommunications Company's cell sites in the central and southeastern Bahamas offline, most of them being returned to service within two weeks. By October 21, the Bahamas Electricity Corporation had remedied about 80% of its power outages, aided by crews from New Providence and the Caribbean Association of Electric Utilities group. Early aerial surveys revealed that Acklins, Rum Cay, Crooked Island, and San Salvador Island were "completely devastated."

---

[165] Ian Livingston (October 2, 2015). *Hurricane Joaquin among the strongest storms on record in the Bahamas.* Capital Weather Gang. The Washington Post. Retrieved: 04-10-2015.

A view of the significant structural and roof damage to this Landrail Point-Seven Day Adventist Church and the adjacent pastor's residence after Hurricane Joaquin hit Crooked Island in the Bahamas.

Throughout the archipelago, flooding from the hurricane trapped over 500 residents. Floodwaters up to 5 feet deep submerged at least 70% of nearby Crooked Island, where the storm left widespread structural damage. The hurricane "completely destroyed" a Bahamas Electricity Corporation power plant, where two large diesel tanks were shifted off their bases, allowing more than 10,000 gallons of fuel to leak into the ground. In the days following the storm, about 100 evacuees—including 46 from Crooked Island—were flown to New Providence, where several of them sought medical attention. On Long Island and Crooked Island, septic tank seepage contaminated residential wells, leaving residents without clean drinking water. Both areas still had extensive standing water on October 7. Acklins endured severe flooding, with many homes inundated and numerous calls for rescue; the island's sea barrier was breached by 9:00 a.m. local time. Some residents reported the entire island to be under water. A bridge in Lovely Bay was completely destroyed.[166]

Long Island was subject to an immense 18 feet storm surge that flooded homes with up to 12 feet of water. Southern areas of the island suffered considerable devastation; the surge washed out coastal roadways and drove

---

166 Sean Breslin (October 1, 2015). *Hurricane Joaquin's Bahamas Impacts: More Than 500 Residents Trapped in Their Homes, Excessive Power Outages*. The Weather Channel. Associated Press. R+etrieved: 02-10-2015.

numerous fishing boats ashore. The Member of Parliament for Long Island, Loretta Butler-Turner, estimated that 75% of all fishing vessels there were destroyed. This, combined with heavy losses to farms and crops, threatened the livelihoods of many residents. About 20 individuals required rescue on Long Island, while some hurricane shelters became compromised by water entrance. The bodies of dead animals were seen floating in the water. Strong winds unroofed dozens of homes, and many structures were fully destroyed. Northern parts of the island fared better in comparison. The winds and flooding took a large toll on native vegetation, even well inland.[167] In an amazing spirit of community organization, many former residents from Long Island and presently living in the capital of Nassau organized many clothing, food and other charity drives as well to assist the storm-ravaged island. This was also very true for other storm ravaged islands like Acklins and Crooked Island as well.

Several weeks after the storm, the Bahamas national disaster agency NEMA officials estimated that 836 residences had been destroyed, including 413 on Long Island, 227 on San Salvador, 123 on Acklins, 50 on Crooked Island, and 23 on Rum Cay. The storm's effects were considered comparable to the destruction wrought by Hurricane Andrew in 1992, which struck the northwestern Bahamas as a Category 5. Initial claims of numerous casualties throughout the island chain proved unsubstantiated, and although one man died during the storm on Long Island, his death was unrelated to the hurricane.[168] In the aftermath of the hurricane, one person was reported missing on Ragged Island, which escaped with relatively minor effects. Initially, Prime Minister of the Bahamas, Rt. Hon. Perry Christie, estimated that damages from Joaquin would exceed $60 million, but he increased this damage total to over $100 million while addressing a climate change conference for world leaders in Paris, France, on December 1, 2015.[169] Joaquin was replaced with "Julian" in 2021 hurricane season.

Hurricane Alex in 2016--Hurricane Alex was the first North Atlantic hurricane in January since the Alice in the 1954/1955 seasons and the first to form in the month of January since 1938. Alex originated as an extratropical cyclone near

167 Sancheska Brown (October 15, 2015). *Fishing and Farming Industries Are 'Completely Devastated.'* The Tribune. Retrieved: 16-10-2015.

168 Krishna Virgil (October 22, 2015). *Hurricane Wiped Out 836 Homes.* The Tribune. Retrieved: 26-10- 2015.

169 Neil Hartnell (December 2, 2015). *Joaquin Damages Grow to $100 million.* The Tribune. Retrieved: 02-12-2015.

the Bahamas on January 7, 2016. The system initially traveled northeast, passing Bermuda on January 8 before turning southeast. It subsequently deepened and acquired hurricane-force winds by January 10. Slight weakening took place thereafter, and the system eventually turned east and northeast as it acquired tropical characteristics. On January 13, it developed into a subtropical cyclone well south of the Azores, becoming the first tropical or subtropical system during January in the North Atlantic since an unnamed storm in 1978.

The National Hurricane Center in Miami categorized it as a subtropical storm on Wednesday, January 16, Alex took on a surprisingly healthy structure, with a symmetric core of showers and thunderstorms around its clearly defined eye. According to Bob Henson and Dr. Jeff Masters of the private weather company Weather Underground in the United States, "sea-surface temperatures beneath Alex are only around 20-22°C (68-72°F). Although these are up to 1°C above average for this time of year, they are far cooler than usually required for tropical cyclone development. However, upper-level temperatures near Alex were unusually cold for the latitude, which means that instability--driven by the contrast between warm, moist lower levels and cold, drier upper levels--is higher than it would otherwise be. That instability allowed showers and thunderstorms to blossom and consolidate, strengthening the warm core that makes Alex a hurricane as opposed to an extratropical or subtropical storm."[170]

As it turned north-northeast, Alex transitioned into a full-fledged tropical cyclone on January 14 and became a hurricane. The storm peaked as a Category 1 on the Saffir–Simpson Hurricane Wind Scale with maximum sustained winds of 85 mph and a barometric pressure of 981 mbar (hPa; 28.97 inHg). After weakening slightly, Alex made landfall on Terceira Island as a tropical storm the next day. Simultaneously, Alex began transitioning back into an extratropical cyclone; it completed this cycle hour after moving away from the Azores. The system ultimately merged with another extratropical cyclone over the Labrador Sea on January 17.

In records going back to 1851, only two hurricanes are known to have existed in the North Atlantic during the month of January: an unnamed tropical storm that became Hurricane #1 on January 4, 1938, and Hurricane Alice, which maintained hurricane strength from December 31, 1954, to January 4, 1955.

---

170 Jeff Masters (January 13, 2016). *Unprecedented: Simultaneous January Named Storms in the Atlantic and Central Pacific*. Weather Underground. Retrieved: 15-01-2016. Henson, Bob. *Astounding Alex Hits the Azores: January's First Atlantic Landfall in 61 Years.* Weather Underground. Retrieved: 16-01-2016.

Alice topped out at 80 mph, so Alex is officially the strongest January hurricane on record in the North Atlantic. Much like Alice, another tropical cyclone called Tropical Storm Zeta of the very active 2005/06 hurricane seasons--formed in December and extended into January, and a tropical storm was recorded in early January 1951. There was also a subtropical storm in January 1978.[171]

The hurricane prompted the issuance of hurricane and tropical storm warnings for the Azores and the closure of schools and businesses. Alex ultimately brought gusty winds and heavy rain to the archipelago, causing generally minor damage. One person died from a heart attack when the inclement weather prevented a helicopter from transporting them to a hospital.

The World Meteorological Organization reuses storm names every six years for both the North Atlantic and eastern Pacific basins. The nation hardest hit by a storm can request its name be removed because the storm was so deadly or costly that future use of the name would be insensitive or cause confusion among persons in the region. The removal also avoids confusion caused by a future storm having the same name. North Atlantic storm names can be either French, Dutch, Spanish or English, reflecting the languages of the various countries they can hit.

Tropical Storm Bonnie in 2016--On May 24, the National Hurricane Center began monitoring an area of disturbed weather resultant from the interaction of a weakening cold front and an upper-level trough near the Bahamas. A surface area of low pressure formed late the next day, eventually gaining sufficient organization to be declared a tropical depression at 3pm on May 27. It moved west-northwest within an only marginally conducive environment, the depression slowly intensified into Tropical Storm Bonnie a day later. The continued effects of high wind shear and dry air caused the cyclone's appearance to degenerate early on May 29, and Bonnie weakened back to tropical depression strength less than an hour prior to its landfall just east of Charleston, South Carolina. The depression meandered over South Carolina for over a day before regressing to a remnant low over the northeastern portion of the state at 11am on May 30. Upon formation, a Tropical Storm Warning was posted from the Savannah River to the Little River Inlet. Heavy rains associated with Bonnie led to localized flooding, prompting the South Carolina Highway Patrol to close the southbound lanes of Interstate 95 in Jasper County, South

171 Neely, Wayne, *The very unusual Subtropical Storm Alex/Hurricane Alex,* The Nassau Guardian, January 15, 2016. Retrieved: 16-01-2016.

Carolina. Rip currents along the coastline of the southeast United States led to dozens of water rescues; the body of one 20-year-old man was recovered in Brevard County, Florida after he drowned, while a 21-year-old man in New Hanover County, North Carolina went missing during storm.

Tropical Storm Colin in 2016--The 2016 Atlantic hurricane season is a current event in the annual tropical cyclone season in the North Atlantic. At the time of printing of this book, this was the third storm to form this year. These dates historically describe the period each year when most tropical cyclones form in the Atlantic basin. However, as demonstrated by Hurricane Alex which formed in January and Tropical Storm Bonnie which formed in May, the formation of tropical cyclones is possible at any time of the year. This season started exceptionally early, nearly five months before the official start, with Hurricane Alex forming in the Northeastern Atlantic in mid-January. Tropical Storm Bonnie followed in late May, which was the first occurrence of two pre-season Atlantic storms since 2012 and only the third occurrence since 1951. On June 5th, Tropical Storm Colin formed, making it the earliest third named storm in the North Atlantic in recorded history, beating the season of 1887. It's the earliest that three named storms have hit the region, besting the previous record -- which was set in 1887 -- by about a week.

Hurricane Earl in 2016—Hurricane Earl was the fifth named storm of the 2016 North Atlantic hurricane season, Earl formed on August 2 just to the southwest of Jamaica. It had previously passed just south of the island as a tropical wave. When it formed, it was designated Tropical Storm Earl and watches and warnings were posted across many countries including Mexico, Belize, the Cayman Islands, and Honduras. Earl strengthened into a hurricane on August 3. The next day, on August 4, Earl made landfall as a hurricane near Belize City, Belize, and started to weaken back to a tropical storm as it affected northern Guatemala.

Earl was responsible for several fatalities, along the Dominican Republic's northern coast near Nagua, the precursor wave produced strong winds that knocked a power line onto a bus, which caused a fire that killed six people and injured 12. A boat crash in Samaná Bay and killed another seven people. After Earl formed, the government of Honduras issued a tropical storm warning for its entire northern coastline, from Cape Gracias a Dios westward to the border with Guatemala. Despite early warnings, a lobster boat capsized with 83 people aboard. Only two of these people are missing, and the Navy went searching for them. The governments of Belize, and Mexico also issued a tropical storm warning and a hurricane watch from Belize's border with Guatemala northward to Punta Allen. Landslides in Mexico following the storm's second landfall resulted in an additional 54 deaths.

Hurricane Hermine in 2016—Hurricane Hermine was the first hurricane to make landfall in the state of Florida since Hurricane Wilma in 2005, and the first to develop in the Gulf of Mexico since Hurricane Ingrid in 2013. This hurricane was the ninth tropical depression, eighth named storm, and fourth hurricane of the 2016 Atlantic hurricane season, Hermine developed from a long-tracked tropical wave that had produced torrential rainfall in parts of the Caribbean. After being designated on August 29, Hermine shifted northeastwards due to a trough over Georgia and gradually intensified into an 80-mph hurricane just before making landfall in the Florida Panhandle during September 2. Rapid weakening followed as the storm weakened into a post-tropical cyclone before leaving the coast near the Outer Banks of North Carolina. The remnants of Hermine continued to bring heavy rain and rip-currents to the East Coast of the United States, before the National Hurricane Center discontinued advisories on the system, while it was situated east of the Delmarva Peninsula. Hermine caused 4 direct and 1 indirect fatalities and caused an estimated total of $500 million (2016 USD) in damage.

Hurricane Matthew in 2016—Hurricane Matthew was a very large, strong and destructive hurricane which impacted several islands in the Caribbean and the countries of Venezuela and Columbia on northern parts of the South American coast. It then skirted the southeastern most seaboard states in the United States. It was one of the weaker Category 5 (wind speeds of 157 mph or greater on the Saffir-Simpson Hurricane Wind Scale) hurricanes to strike the North Atlantic within the last 10 to 15 years. In fact, it was the first Category 5 hurricane (Matthew had sustained winds of 160 mph) since Hurricanes Dean (175 mph) and Felix (175 mph) of 2007. Matthew inflicted widespread destruction and catastrophic loss of life during its journey across the Western Atlantic, including parts of Haiti, Cuba, Dominican Republic, the Bahamas, the southeastern United States, and the Canadian Maritimes. At least 1,655+ estimated deaths have been attributed to the storm, including about 1000 to 1600 in Haiti, 1 in Colombia, 4 in the Dominican Republic, 1 in Saint Vincent and the Grenadines and 43 in the United States, making it the deadliest North Atlantic hurricane since Stan in 2005, which killed more than 1,600 in Central America and Mexico. The death toll in some countries within the region like

Jamaica, the Dominican Republic, the Leeward Islands and the Bahamas was relatively low due to well executed warnings and timely evacuations.

With the storm causing damages estimated in excess of US $8.1 billion, it was also the costliest North Atlantic hurricane since Hurricane Sandy in 2012. It was the fourteenth tropical cyclone, thirteenth named storm, fifth hurricane and second major hurricane of the very busy 2016 North Atlantic hurricane season. Matthew was a very active storm which impacted many countries within the Caribbean including, Grenada, St. Vincent, St. Lucia, Dominica, Aruba, Bonaire, Curaçao, Cuba, Haiti, the Dominican Republic, Jamaica, the Bahamas and Cuba. It also impacted Colombia and Venezuela on the South American continent and the southeastern United States on the North American continent.

On September 29, the circulation of Matthew became exposed from the convection due to an increase in wind shear in the upper atmosphere attacking the system. Even with that circumstances, the winds continued to increase. Both the Hurricane Hunters and a Special Sensor Microwave Imager/Sounder (SSMIS) satellite pass revealed an eye feature had developed by early morning of September 30. Close to Matthew's peak intensity, a rare phenomenon known as 'lightning sprites' were observed above the storm in Puerto Rico. In spite of the northwesterly wind shear, Matthew began to undergo a period of explosive intensification, doubling its wind speed from 80 mph to 160 mph over a period of 24 hours. Hence, Matthew intensified from a Category 1 hurricane on the Saffir-Simpson Hurricane Wind Scale to a Category 5 hurricane in just 24 hours. Matthew became a Category 5 hurricane at 13.3 degrees north, surpassing Hurricane Ivan as the southernmost hurricane of this intensity on record in the North Atlantic basin.

Heavy rains and strong winds battered the Lesser Antilles as Matthew entered the Caribbean Sea as a strong tropical storm. The winds caused significant and widespread power outages and damaged crops, particularly in St. Lucia where it destroyed 85% of the banana crop, while flooding and landslides caused by the rainfall damaged many homes and roads. The storm's unusually low latitude resulted in widespread flash flooding on the Guajira Peninsula, which saw its first heavy rain event in three years. Extensive preparations took place in Cuba, Jamaica, and Hispaniola as the strong hurricane approached, including the opening of numerous shelters and the evacuation of roughly 1 million people in Cuba. Although Jamaica avoided significant impacts, Haiti on-the-other-hand, experienced major impacts, including more than US$1 billion in damage and at least 1,000 deaths. The bad combination of flooding particularly flash flooding and high winds interrupted and crippled telecommunications and destroyed extensive areas of land; around 80% of Jérémie sustained significant damage. Heavy rainfall spread eastward across the Dominican Republic, where only four persons were killed. Effects in Cuba were most severe along the coast, where storm surge caused extensive damage in Guantánamo Province.

Passing through the Bahamas as a major hurricane, Matthew inflicted severe impacts across several islands, particularly Grand Bahama, where an estimated 95% of homes sustained damage in the townships of Eight Mile Rock and Holmes Rock. The capital city of Nassau and the northern section of Andros were totally devastated, due to substantial flooding, fallen trees everywhere, numerous downed utility lines, significant crop failure mainly in North Andros- the agricultural belt of the Bahamas. In the settlement of Lowe Sound in North Andros, the majority of the homes suffered from severe flooding and the majority of them were destroyed either by the strong winds or the floodwaters. Power outages in some hurricane ravaged areas lasted for over two weeks before the electricity was restored. The Prime Minister Perry Christie in a speech given in the Bahamian Parliament, estimated that to bring the Bahamas back to a state of normalcy, it will cost well over $600 million. This makes this storm the costliest hurricane in Bahamian history and eclipsing the previous record holder Hurricane Andrew in 1992 with $250 million in damage.

Preparations began in earnest across the southeastern United States as Matthew approached, with several states declaring a state of emergency for either entire states or coastal counties; widespread evacuations were ordered for extensive areas along the coast. In Florida, over 1 million lost power as the storm passed to the east, with 478,000 losing power in Georgia and South Carolina. While damage was primarily confined to the coast in the Florida and Georgia, torrential rains spread inland in the Carolinas and Virginia, causing widespread flooding. At around 11:00 a.m. EDT on October 8, Matthew made landfall at Cape Romain National Wildlife Refuge, near McClellanville, South Carolina as a Category 1 hurricane with winds of 75 mph. This made Matthew the first hurricane to make landfall in the United States north of Florida in the month of October since Hurricane Hazel in 1954. As it moved away from the coast, Matthew began to undergo a period of extratropical transition, with most of the convection becoming displaced to the north, and the hurricane became post-tropical on October 9 while situated to the east of the Outer Banks of North Carolina. The remnants persisted for another day before dissipating on October 10 as it merged with another low over Atlantic Canada.

CONCLUSION

Hurricanes have been menacing the North Atlantic for as long as anyone can remember; in fact, world famous explorer Christopher Columbus encountered his first hurricane in the New World as early as 1495, when he encountered this hurricane on the island of Hispaniola. It is fair to say these storms have been coming relentlessly from time immemorial, but the monetary damages these storms have inflicted on this region has increased in recent years, as this book clearly shows. The devastation from Hurricane Sandy in 2012 — later dubbed a "Superstorm" — damage total came in at $75 billion, leaving 233 people (direct and indirect) dead and more than 6 million homeless.

Does that mean hurricanes are getting more powerful or more common? Not necessarily. While many atmospheric scientists believe that climate change may strengthen tropical cyclones—higher temperatures at the ocean tend to feed hurricanes—the power of the storm isn't the only factor in the extent of the damage. Far more important, at least for now, is the increase in the number of people and the value of the property in coastal areas that are perennially vulnerable to major hurricanes. Hurricane Katrina was so expensive not just because it was powerful, but because it landed directly on top of a major American city—and one that was clearly unprepared for a storm of that magnitude. The more people and property we put in harm's way, the greater the damage any storm will cause. If climate change really does give hurricanes an extra kick as some claim—and if we do nothing to slow global warming or prepare for the effects—damage will be incalculably greater.

A hurricane is a type of tropical cyclone, which is a generic term for a low pressure system that generally forms in the tropics. A hurricane is an intense, rotating oceanic weather system that possesses maximum sustained winds exceeding 74 mph. It forms and intensifies over warm tropical oceanic regions. The cyclone is accompanied by thunderstorms and, in the northern hemisphere, a counterclockwise circulation of winds near the Earth's surface.

Hurricanes cause devastation all over the world, but they are all born in the same latitudes-the tropics. Yet while all the ingredients for hurricanes to exist and thrive for much of the summer in tropical climates, they do not always result in deadly storms. The catalyst needed for these conditions to become a hurricane is an atmospheric disturbance. When making landfall along the coastline, a hurricane brings more than its intensely powerful and destructive winds ashore. Hurricanes also are responsible for a range of weather impacts, from storm surge and flooding caused by heavy rains to tornadoes.

The size of the countries of the North Atlantic and their particular geographical and societal conditions make them susceptible to influences associated with hurricanes. Hurricanes have always accounted for a great deal of death and destruction, and as populations continue to move into areas prone to hurricanes, we will inherently become more vulnerable to future devastating hurricanes. Of all nature's deadly extremes, hurricanes seem the most personal. Landslides, floods, earthquakes and volcanoes may kill, yet they never seem more than the vast, impersonal rumblings of a living planet. But the big spiral storms seek people out and test their determination and resolve in personal combat. Perhaps it all goes back to the 1950 decision by the U.S. Weather Bureau in the United States to begin publicly referring to the big storms by the alphabetical nicknames used informally by staff meteorologists. Suddenly, hurricanes were no longer unknowable forces of nature, but clearly identifiable villains: Katrina, Mitch, Gilbert, Andrew, Sandy and the Great Hurricane of 1780 all made this point so clear here in the North Atlantic. Even most reporters trained to avoid attributing human emotions to nature events commonly refer to "Andrew's fury," "Katrina's malevolence" or "Mitch's wrath," and readers nod their heads. Since the early 1500s, the region has sustained thousands of hurricanes in which overall damages exceeded well over $500 billion, and with the rapid development of coastal areas here in the region, perhaps we will soon see the first 'billion-dollar hurricane' every single season.

Thanks to advancing technology, scientists have learned much about hurricanes in the past 150 years. Today, we know that one takes shape when large low-pressure systems draw in air and begin to spin in a counterclockwise direction, creating a spiral pattern around a central calm eye. The storm's power is fed as its winds draw warm ocean water, which helps generate gradually intensifying thunderstorms. When it makes landfall, a hurricane hammers land dwellers with two mighty fists: it's howling winds, which have been recorded as gusting to over 200 mph, and the mighty storm surge it drives before it, which can elevate ocean levels by more than 20 feet, sending floodwaters cascading over beaches, breakwaters and seawalls.

The storm surge generated by Hurricane Katrina in 2005 in Louisiana and Mississippi in the United States was over twenty-five to twenty-eight feet high and it was reported that the floodwaters were up to the rafters in many houses, and some even covered the roofs when the levee failed, which resulted in hundreds of persons drowning. Yet with all of our knowledge of how hurricanes form, it hasn't helped us fight them; man's current tools are powerless against such vast weather phenomena. As a result, scientists work desperately to improve our ability to predict their movement, in hopes of providing early, accurate warnings to imperiled coastal residents, which in turn would lessen the chances of fatalities and reduce the costs associated with them.

Every year hurricanes threaten the Eastern and Gulf Coast states of the United States, Mexico, Central America and the Caribbean. The inhabitants of southeast Asia name them *"Typhoons."* In Australia, they are called *"Willy-Willies,"* and in the Indian Ocean they are simply known as *"Cyclones."* No matter what name they may go by, these storms are a nightmare for everyone who lives in a tropical region. Hurricanes wreak havoc when they make landfall, and they can kill thousands of people and cause billions of dollars of property damage when they hit heavily populated areas. Hurricanes are severe tropical cyclones, which, though not nearly so frequent as mid-latitude cyclones, receive a great deal of attention from lay people and scientists alike, mainly because of their awesome intensity, strength and their great destructive powers. Abundant, even torrential rainfall and winds of great speeds characterize hurricanes.

Though these storms develop over the warm oceanic waters and often can spend their entire lives there at times their tracks do take them over islands and coastal lands. The results can be devastating by causing the destruction of property and sometimes even death. It is not just the rainfall and raging winds that can produce such tremendous damages to people and their surroundings, for accompanying the hurricane are unusually high seas, called storm surges, which can flood entire coastal communities. The hurricane challenge facing mankind in the twenty-first century involves several components. Although we cannot control hurricanes, we can encourage better preparation in these countries impacted by hurricanes so that similar tragedies can be avoided in the future. It would seem clear that people should avoid living in low coastal areas that are subjected to hurricanes, but the sad fact remains that people will always remain attracted to the coast for the many benefits that attract them there. As a consequence, property damage costs due to hurricanes have skyrocketed, placing the insurance industry on the brink of financial chaos when a major hurricane hits a metropolitan area. In fact, many coastal residents are now finding it difficult to obtain insurance now.

Hurricanes are one of the most dangerous and unpredictable of all the natural forces at work on our planet. Thanks to weather satellites, reconnaissance aircrafts and radars, scientists can track hurricanes and try to predict where and when they might make landfall. Earth's chaotic atmosphere can and often does strike at random with little or no warning, and the end result is total devastation, and these hurricanes that struck this region proved this certainly beyond a shadow of a doubt. The weather may very well be mankind's most widely discussed topic. Its effects are all pervasive, ranging from the trivial issue whether of we should wear a sweater to an outdoor function or whether we should take an umbrella to work, to tragedies that unfold during extreme weather events such as hurricanes. The weather dictates the kind of life we live, the way we build our homes, the way we dress and what we eat. In conjunction with the geological forces at work on our planet, the weather has shaped the landforms around us, and the variety of life here on Earth reflects nature's myriad solutions to the range of meteorological conditions that have occurred throughout history.

There is nothing like them in the atmosphere. Born in warm tropical waters, these spiraling cloud masses require a complex combination of atmospheric processes to grow, mature, and then die. They are not the largest storm systems in our atmosphere or the most violent, but they combine these qualities as no other weather phenomenon does. In the Atlantic Basin, they are called hurricanes, a term that echoes a colonial Spanish and Caribbean Indians word for evil spirits and big winds. These awesome storms have been a deadly problem for residents and sailors ever since the early days of colonization.

Today, hurricane damage costs billions of dollars, but fortunately, people injured or killed during tropical cyclones have been steadily declining due in part to enhanced and improved weather technology such as satellites and ground-based radars. However, our risk from hurricanes is increasing, because with population and development continuing to increase along coastal areas, greater numbers of people and property are vulnerable to hurricane threats. Large numbers of tourists also favor coastal locations, adding greatly to the problems of emergency managers and local decision makers during a hurricane threat.

It is important to add that hurricanes can't be controlled, but our vulnerability can be reduced through preparedness and education. This region's geographic location persuades us to be more aware of the past hurricanes since history guarantees that they will come again with the same or greater fury than in the past. We can identify patterns and commonalities between storms just as human history helps us learn from our society's disasters, and hopefully with this knowledge we can better prepare and adapt to the next big hurricane. People are now much more aware of hurricanes than they were ever before. When a hurricane threatens any country within this region, it becomes big news. Nowadays, forecasts, combined with timely warnings about hurricane dangers, are saving lives. The more we learn about hurricanes, the better our chances are of staying safe and secure from them.

Over the last years and centuries in the North Atlantic, hurricanes and their aftermath have had a bigger impact on your family and friends and all of humanity than the Internet has had. Imagine if you knew a quarter-century ago how information technology and the Internet were going to revolutionize so many aspects of our lives? Not only that but save so many lives in the process with the use of recent valuable cutting-edge weather tools like, hurricane hunters aircrafts, satellite and radar imageries and computer modelling systems. Imagine how valuable that knowledge would have been to you, your family and the many residents of this region. Thankfully, today it turns out that we have such advanced knowledge of how hurricanes will play out over the next quarter-century and beyond. The purpose of this book is to provide you with that knowledge. Hurricanes and their great impact on societies not only here in this region but worldwide, are now an existential issue for humanity to deal with. Serious hurricanes impacts have already been observed on almost all of the countries within this region and worldwide, often costing the battered countries millions of dollars to get their lives and countries back to some degree of normalcy. Today, thanks to climate change and the alarming more persons living on or near the hurricane prone coastlines, it is fair to say that the cost and damage factors from these storms will inevitably rise.

REFERENCES

- *"HURRICANE!" A Familiarization Booklet by NOAA, April, 1993.*
- Chris Landsea, et al. (2003). *"Documentation of Atlantic Tropical Cyclones Changes in HURDAT: 1900-1930"*. NHC-Hurricane Research Division. http://www.aoml.noaa.gov/hrd/hurdat/metadata_1928-30.htm#1928_3.
- http://www.aoml.noaa.gov/hrd/tcfaq/costliesttable.html.
- http://www.reliefweb.org.
- http://www.wunderground.com/hurricane/haiti.asp.
- *National Weather Service, Weather Forecast Office, Miami Florida, Memorial Web Page for the 1928 Okeechobee Hurricane.*
- *The Monthly Weather Review, Special Report on The Galveston Hurricane of September 8, 1900 Isaac M. Cline.*
- The Hurricane Photographic Collection, State Library and Archives of Florida
- *Duke University News and Communications: 'Hurricanes bring benefits to Barrier Islands and Beaches' Monday, September 13th 2004, Orrin Pilkey, Brad Murray and Andrew Coburn, Duke University Press.*
- *Link Between Climate Change and Tropical Cyclone Activity: More Research Necessary*, WMO-Press Release No. 766, Geneva, 11 December 2006.
- O'Neil A. (2005) *It's a new era' of Hurricanes-Experts: String of intense storms is part of normal cycle*, CNN-September 23, 2005.
- P.J. Webster, G.J. Holland, J.A. Curry and H.R. Chang, *Journal Science-Changes in Tropical Cyclone Number, Duration, and Intensity in a Global Warming Environment*, Vol 309 no 5742 pg. 1844-1846
- *2014 Breaks Heat Record, Challenging Global Warming Skeptics*, by Justin Gillis, January 16th 2015, New York Times.
- *2014 warmest year on record, say US researchers*, by Mark Kinver-Environment reporter, BBC News. Retrieved: 10-11-2015.

- *2014 Hottest Year on Record by weather.com Jan 16 2015.*
- *NOAA: 2014 is shaping up as hottest year on record* by Shelby Lin Erdman-CNN, November 30, 2014.
- *Hurricanes growing fiercer with global warming* by Elizabeth A. Thomson-MIT July 31, 2005.
- *Frequency of Atlantic Hurricanes Doubled Over Last Century; Climate Change Suspected* by NCAR & UCAR News Release, July 29, 2007.
- Hurricanes Are Getting Stronger, NCAR & UCAR Study Says-NCAR & UCAR-*The University Corporation for Atmospheric News Release,* September 15, 2005.
- *Counting Atlantic Tropical Cyclones Back to 1900*-pgs. 197, 202 Eos, Vol. 88, No. 18, May 1, 2007 by Chris Landsea.
- *NOAA Model Projects Fewer, But More Intense Hurricanes Late This Century-Greenhouse Gases Have Little Impact in Tropical Storm and Hurricane Numbers,* NOAA, May 19, 2008.
- *The Bahamas Journal of Science Vol. 5 No1 Historical Hurricane Impacts on the Bahamas, Part I: 1500-1749* Ronald V. Shaklee, Media Publishing Ltd.
- *Miami Daily News, Monday, September 24, 1928, Miami Public Library*
- *Miami Herald, Monday, October 1, 1928, University of Miami, Fla. Otto G. Richter Library.*
- *Florida Historical Society: The Florida Historical Quarterly volume 65 issue 3*
- *U.S. Department of Commerce, Sept. 15th 1965 'Hurricane Betsy-Preliminary Report with Advisories and Bulletins Issued'*
- *"Weathering the Storms: Hurricanes and Risk in the British Greater Caribbean."* Business History Review, Vol. 78, No. 4, Winter 2004.
- Knabb, Richard D; Rhome, Jamie R; Brown, Daniel P; National Hurricane Center (December 20, 2005). *Hurricane Katrina: August 23 – 30, 2005 (PDF) (Tropical Cyclone Report).* United States National Oceanic and Atmospheric Administration's National Weather Service.
- Blake, Eric S; Kimberlain, Todd B; Berg, Robert J; Cangialosi, John P; Beven II, John L; National Hurricane Center (February 12, 2013). *Hurricane Sandy: October 22 – 29, 2012 (PDF) (Tropical Cyclone Report).* United States National Oceanic and Atmospheric Administration's National Weather Service. Archived from the original on February 17, 2013. Retrieved February 17, 2013.
- *Hurricane/Post-Tropical Cyclone Sandy, October 22 – 29, 2012 (Service Assessment).* United States National Oceanic and Atmospheric

Administration's National Weather Service. May 2013, pg. 10. Archived from the original on June 2, 2013. Retrieved June 2, 2013.

- Chris Landsea, et al. (2011). *"Documentation of Atlantic Tropical Cyclones Changes in HURDAT: 1928 Hurricane Season"*. NHC-Hurricane Research Division.
- *Votes of the House of Assembly-1917-1930-*The Department of Archives-Nassau, Bahamas.
- *The Sponging Industry Booklet-Bahamas Department of Archives Exhibition 18-22 February, 1974. Pgs. 1-31.*
- Wxeltv-Heritage, Episode 10: *Hurricane of 1928.*
- *The Bahamas Journal of Science Vol. 6 No. 1. Historic Weather at Nassau-* Ronald V. Shaklee, Media Publishing Ltd.
- *The Bahamas Journal of Science Vol. 5 No. 1 Historical Hurricane Impacts on The Bahamas, Part I: 1500-1749* Ronald V. Shaklee, Media Publishing Ltd.
- *The Bahamas Journal of Science Vol. 5 No. 2 Historical Hurricane Impacts on The Bahamas, Part II: 1750-1799* Ronald V. Shaklee, Media Publishing Ltd.
- *The Bahamas Journal of Science Vol. 8 No. 1 Historical Hurricane Impacts on The Bahamas: Floyd on San Salvador & Early Nineteenth Century Hurricanes 1800-1850 Ronald* V. Shaklee, Media Publishing Ltd.
- *Harper's Weekly-A Journal of Civilization Vol. X-No. 516, Saturday, 17th 1866 'Hurricane in The Bahamas.'*
- *Bahamas Gazette 1784-1815. John Wells, editor. Nassau, Bahamas.*
- *Miami Daily News, Monday, September 24, 1928, Miami Public Library*
- *Miami Daily News, Monday, September 25, 1928, Miami Public Library*
- *Miami Herald, Monday, October 1, 1928, University of Miami, Fla. Otto G. Richter Library.*
- *A Columbus Casebook-A Supplement to "Where Columbus Found the New World" National Geographic Magazine, November 1986.*
- *Annual Colonial Reports (CO-23-Governor's Dispatches) for the Bahamas, 1917-1929-*The Bahamas Department of Archives-Nassau, Bahamas.
- *Censuses of the Bahama Islands, 1891, 1901, 1911, 1921.Department of Archives-Nassau, Bahamas.*
- *"Hurricanes and the Shaping of Caribbean Societies,"* Florida Historical Quarterly, 83:4 (2005), pgs. 381-409.
- *Miami Daily News, Monday, September 24, 1928, Miami Public Library*
- *Miami Daily News, Monday, September 25, 1928, Miami Public Library*
- *Miami Herald, Monday, October 1, 1928, University of Miami, Fla. Otto G. Richter Library.*

- *The Palm Beach Post*, September 13th 1928.
- *The Palm Beach Post*, September 20th 1928.
- *The Tribune*, Wednesday, September 19th 1928 pgs.1 & 2 'Extraordinary Hurricane Hits Bahamas.'
- National Weather Service, *Weather Forecast Office, Miami Florida, Memorial Web Page for the 1928 Okeechobee Hurricane.*
- *The Florida Historical Quarterly*, January 1987. Published by the Florida Historical Society.
- Mitchell, Charles L. *"The West Indian Hurricane of September 10-20, 1928."* Monthly Weather Review Vol. 56, No. 9. Weather Bureau. 1928. pgs. 347-350.
- Saunders, Gail (1985) *The Social History of the Bahamas 1890-1953*, A thesis presented to the University of Waterloo in fulfillment of the thesis requirement for the degree of Doctor of Philosophy in History.
- *The Nassau Daily Tribune, Saturday, September 28, 1929 pgs. 1&2-'Courage.'*
- Blake, Eric S., E. N. Rappaport, J. D. Jarrell, and C.W. Landsea, 2005: *The Deadliest, Costliest, and Most Intense United States Tropical Cyclones from 1851 to 2004 (And Other Frequently Requested Hurricane Facts)*. NOAA Technical Memorandum NWS TPC-4, Tropical Prediction Center, Miami, FL. Landsea, Christopher W., 2002: personal communication.
- *McNoldy, Brian "When is the 'peak' of hurricane season? It's more complicated than you think." The Washington Post, 9th September, 2016. Retrieved: 11-09-2016.*
- Gross, Eric L., 1995: *Somebody Got Drowned, Lord: Florida and the Great Okeechobee Hurricane Disaster of 1928, Vol. I and II*, Dissertation submitted to the Department of History in partial fulfillment of the requirements for a doctoral degree, College of Arts and Sciences, Florida State University, Tallahassee, FL.
- "*Millions in Hurricane insurance claims in the Bahamas*". Caribbean360. October 7, 2011. Retrieved January 21, 2015.
- *Miami Daily News*, Friday, September 14, 1928, Miami Public Library.
- *Miami Daily News*, Monday, September 24, 1928, Miami Public Library.
- *Miami Daily News*, Tuesday, September 25, 1928, Miami Public Library.
- *Miami Herald*, Monday, October 1, 1928, University of Miami, Fla. Otto G. Richter Library.
- *Palm Beach Hurricane 92 Views*, American Autochrome Company, Chicago, IL, 1928.

- Pfost, Russell, 2003: Reassessing the Impact of Two Historical Florida Hurricanes. *Bulletin of the American Meteorological Society*, 84, Issue 10 (October 2003) pgs. 1367–1372.
- Pielke, Roger A., and C. W. Landsea, 1998: Normalized Hurricane Damages in the United States: 1925-95. *Weather Forecasting*, pgs. 13, 621-631.
- Ahrens, D., *Meteorology Today, An Introduction to Weather, Climate, and The Environment*, New Jersey, Brooks/Cole Publishing, 2005.
- Albury, P., *The Story of the Bahamas*, London, Macmillan Education Ltd., 1975.
- Allaby, M. (2000), *DK Guide to Weather-A Photographic Journey Through the Skies*, London, Dorling Kindersley Ltd., 2000.
- Baquedano, E., *Eyewitness Aztec*, London, Dorling Kindersley Ltd. 2006.
- Barnes, Jay., *Florida's Hurricane History*, Chapel Hill, The University of North Carolina Press, 2007.
- Barratt, Peter., *Bahama Saga-The Epic Story of the Bahama Islands*, Bloomington, AuthorHouse, 2006.
- Bergreen, L., *Columbus-The Four Voyages*, New York, The Penguin Group Inc., 2011.
- Biel, S., *American Disaster*, New York, New York University Press, 2001.
- Braasch, G., *Earth Under Fire-How Global Warming is Changing the World*, California, University of California Press, Ltd., 2007.
- Burroughs, Crowder, Robertson, *The Nature Company Guides to Weather*, San Francisco, Time-Life Publishing Inc., 2007.
- Butler, K., *The History of Bahamian Boat Builders from 1800-2000*, Unpublished.
- Butler, E., *Natural Disasters*, Australia, Heinemann Educational Books Ltd., 1980.
- Carrier, J., *The Ship and the Storm-Hurricane Mitch and the Loss of the Fantome*, New York, Harvest Book/Harcourt, Inc., 2001.
- Castleden, R., *Natural Disasters that Changed the World*, New Jersey, Chartwell Books, Inc., 2007.
- Challoner, J., *Hurricane and Tornado*, Great Britain, Dorling Kindersley Publishing, 2000.
- Clarke, P., Smith, A., *Usborne Spotter's Guide to Weather*, England, Usborne Publishing Ltd., 2001.
- Craton, M., *A History of the Bahamas*, Canada, San Salvador Press., 1986.
- Davis, K. *Don't Know Much About Geography*, New York, William Morrow and Company Publishers, 1992.

- Davis, K. *Don't Know Much About World Myths*, New York, HarperCollins Publishers, 2005.
- Day, F., Downs, R., *National Geographic Almanac of Geography*, Washington, D.C., National Geographic Society, 2003.
- Domenici, D. *The Aztecs-History and Treasures of an Ancient Civilization*, Italy, White Star Publishing, 2008.
- Douglas, S.M., *Hurricane*, New York, Rinehart and Company Inc., 1958.
- Drye, Willie., *Storm of the Century-The Labor Day Hurricane of 1938*, Washington, National Geographic Society, 2002.
- DuBois, B., *Memories of the '28 Hurricane*, Florida, self-published by *Bessie* DuBois, 1968.
- Duggard, M., *The Last Voyage of Columbus*, New York, Little Brown and Company, 2005.
- Duedall, I., Williams, J., *Florida Hurricanes and Tropical Storms 1871-2001*, Florida, University Press of Florida, 2002.
- Durschmied, E., *The Weather Factor-How Nature has changed History*, New York, Arcade Publishing, Inc., 2001.
- Elsner, J., Kara, B., *Hurricanes of The North Atlantic-Climate and Society*, New York, Oxford University Press, 1999.
- Emanuel, K., *Divine Wind-The History and Science of Hurricanes*, New York, Oxford University Press, 2005.
- Fitzpatrick, J.P., *Natural Disasters-Hurricanes*, USA, ABC-CLIO, Inc., 1999.
- Gore, A., *An Inconvenient Truth-The Planetary Emergency of Global Warming and What We Can Do About It*, New York, Rodale Publishing, 2006.
- Goudsouzian, A., *The Hurricane of 1938*, Massachusetts, Commonwealth Editions, 2004.
- Green, J., MacDonald, F., Steele, P. & Stotter, M., *The Encyclopedia of the Ancient Americas*, London, South Water Publishing, 2001.
- Green, J., *Disasters-Hurricane Andrew*, Wisconsin, Gareth Stevens Publishing, 2005.
- Hairr, J., *The Great Hurricanes of North Carolina*, United Kingdom, The History Press. 2008.
- Hile, K., *The Handy Weather Answer Book 2nd Edition*, Michigan, Visible Ink Press, 2009.
- Horvitz, A.L., *The Essential Book of Weather Lore*, New York, The Reader's Digest Association, Inc., 2007.

- J.D. Jarrell, Max Mayfield, Edward Rappaport, & Chris Landsea *NOAA Technical Memorandum NWS TPC-1 The Deadliest, Costliest, and Most Intense United States Hurricanes from 1900 to 2000 (And Other Frequently Requested Hurricane Facts).*
- Johnson, H., *Bahamian Labor Migration to Florida in the Late Nineteenth and Early Twentieth Centuries" from International Migration Review, vol. 22, No.1* (Spring 1998) pgs. 84-102.
- Johnson, H., *The Bahamas in Slavery and Freedom,* Jamaica, Ian Randle Publishers Limited, 1991.
- Jones W., *Hurricane-A Force of Nature,* Bahamas, Jones Communications Publication Ltd. 2005.
- Kahl, J., *National Audubon Society First Field Guide to Weather,* Hong Kong, Scholastic Inc., 1998.
- Keegan, W., *The People Who Discovered Columbus-The Prehistory of the Bahamas,* Tallahassee, University Press of Florida, 1992.
- Kieffer, S., *The Dynamics of Disaster,* New York, W.W. Norton & Company Ltd., 2013.
- Kindersley, D., *Eyewitness Weather,* London, Dorling Kindersley Ltd, 2002.
- Kleinberg, E., *Black Cloud-The Deadly Hurricane of 1928,* New York, Carroll & Graf Publishers, 2004.
- Lauber, P., *Hurricanes: Earth's Mightiest Storms,* Singapore, Scholastic Press, 1996.
- Lawlor, J & A., *The Harbour Island Story,* Oxford, Macmillan Caribbean Publishers Ltd, 2008.
- Linden, E., *The Winds of Change,* New York, Simon & Schuster, 2006.
- Lightbourn, G. R., *Reminiscing I & II-Photographs of Old Nassau,* Nassau, Ronald Lightbourn Publisher, 2005.
- Lloyd, J., *Weather-The Forces of Nature that Shape Our World.* United Kingdom, Parragon Publishing, 2007.
- Ludlum, D. M., *Early American Hurricanes 1492-1870.* Boston, MA: American Meteorological Society, 1989.
- Lyons, A.W., *The Handy Science Weather Answer Book,* Detroit, Visible Ink Press, 1997.
- MacPherson, J., *Caribbean Lands-A Geography of the West Indies, 2nd Edition,* London, Longmans, Green and Co Ltd, 1967.
- Martin, J., *Introduction to Weather and Climate Science,* Wisconsin, Cognella Academic Publishing Inc., 2013.

- McQuaid, J. and Schleifstein, M., *Path of Destruction-The Devastation of New Orleans and the Coming Age of Superstorms*, New York, Little, Brown and Company, 2006.
- Millas C.J., *Hurricanes of The Caribbean and Adjacent Regions 1492-1800*, Miami, Edward Brothers Inc./Academy of the Arts and Sciences of the Americas, 1968.
- Mulcahy, Matthew, *Hurricanes and Society in the British Greater Caribbean, 1624-1783*, Baltimore, The Johns Hopkins University Press, 2006.
- Mykle, R., *Killer 'Cane-The Deadly Hurricane of 1928*, Maryland, Taylor Trade Publishing, 2002.
- Neely, Wayne, *The Major Hurricanes to Affect the Bahamas-Personal Recollections of Some of the Greatest Hurricanes to Affect the Bahamas*, Bloomington, Authorhouse Publishing Inc., 2006.
- Neely, Wayne, *Rediscovering Hurricanes-The Major Hurricanes of the North Atlantic*, Bloomington, Authorhouse Publishing Inc., 2007.
- Neely, Wayne, *The Great Bahamian Hurricanes of 1926-The Story of Three of the Greatest Hurricanes to Ever Affect the Bahamas*, Bloomington, iUniverse Publishing Inc., 2009.
- Neely, Wayne, *The Great Bahamas Hurricane of 1866-The Story of One of the Greatest and Deadliest Hurricanes to Ever Impact the Bahamas*, Bloomington, iUniverse Publishing Inc., 2011.
- Neely, Wayne, *The Great Bahamian Hurricanes of 1899 and 1932: The Story of Two of the Greatest and Deadliest Hurricanes to Impact the Bahamas*, Bloomington, iUniverse Publishing Inc., 2012.
- Neely, Wayne, *The Great Hurricane of 1780: The Story of the Greatest and Deadliest Hurricane of the Caribbean and the Americas*, Bloomington, iUniverse Publishing Inc., 2012.
- Neely, Wayne, *The Great Bahamas Hurricane of 1929: The Story of the Greatest Bahamian Hurricane of the Twentieth Century*, Bloomington, iUniverse Publishing Inc., 2013.
- Neely, Wayne, *The Great Okeechobee Hurricane of 1928: The Story of the Second Deadliest Hurricane in American History and the Deadliest Hurricane in Bahamian History*, Bloomington, iUniverse Publishing Inc., 2014.
- Norcross, B., *Hurricane Almanac 2006-The Essential Guide to Storms Past, Present, and Future Vol. 1*, New York, St Martin's Griffin, 2006.
- Norcross, B., *Hurricane Almanac 2007-The Essential Guide to Storms Past, Present, and Future Vol. 2*, New York, St Martin's Griffin, 2007.

- Pearce, A.E., Smith G.C., *The Hutchinson World Weather Guide,* Great Britain, Helicon Publishing Ltd., 1998.
- Peters, K., *The Whole Story of Climate-What Science Reveals About the Nature of Endless Change,* New York, Prometheus Books, 2012.
- Phillips, C., *The illustrated Encyclopedia of the Aztec & Maya,* London, Lorenz Books, 2007.
- Redfield; W.C., *On Three Several Hurricanes of the Atlantic and their relations to the Northers of Mexico and Central America,* USA, New Haven, 1846.
- Reynolds, R., *Philip's Guide to Weather,* London, Octopus Publishing Group Ltd., 2000.
- Robinson, J., *Historic Osceola County: An Illustrated History,* Florida, Historical Publishing Network, 2009.
- Rose, S., *El Niño and La Niña,* USA, Simon Spotlight, 1999.
- Rouse, I., *The Taínos-The Rise and Decline of the People Who Greeted Columbus,* New Haven, Yale University Press, 1992.
- Saunders, A., *History of Bimini Volume 2,* Nassau, New World Press, 2006.
- Saunders, G, and Craton, M., *Islanders in the Stream: A History of the Bahamian People Volume 2,* Georgia, University of Georgia Press, 1998.
- Schwartz, S., *Sea of Storms-A History of Hurricanes in the Greater Caribbean from Columbus to Katrina,* New Jersey, Princeton University Press, 2015.
- Scott, Phil., *Hemingway's Hurricane-The Great Florida Keys Storm of 1935,* New York, McGraw-Hill, 2006.
- Scotti, R., *Sudden Sea-The Great Hurricane of 1938,* New York, Chapter and Verse Ink, 2003.
- Sharer, C., *The Population Growth of the Bahamas Islands,* Michigan, University of Michigan, 1955.
- Sheets, B., Williams, J., *Hurricane Watch-Forecasting the Deadliest Storms on Earth,* New York, Vintage Books, 2001.
- Simpson, R., Riehl, *The Hurricane and Its Impact,* Louisiana, Louisiana State University Press, 1981.
- Simon, S., *Hurricanes,* New York, Harper Collins, 2007.
- Steinberg, T., *Acts of God-The Unnatural History of Natural Disaster in America,* New York, Oxford University Press, 2000.
- Stevens K.W., *The Change in The Weather: People, Weather, and the Science of Climate,* New York, Random House Inc., 1999.
- Tannehill, I., *Hurricanes-Their Nature and History-Particularly those of the West Indies and the Southern Coasts of the United States,* New Jersey, Princeton University Press, 1950.

- Tennesen, M., The Complete Idiot's Guide to Global Warming, Indianapolis, Penguin Group Inc., 2004.
- Thompson, C., Home from The Contract-The 50th Anniversary of The Contract. Nassau, 1998.
- Treaster, J., Hurricane Force-In the Path of America's Storms, Boston, King Fisher, 2007.
- Triana, P., San Salvador-The Forgotten Island, Spain, Ediciones Beramar, 1997.
- Tucker, T. Beware the Hurricane! The Story of the Gyratory Tropical Storms That Have Struck Bermuda. Bermuda: Hamilton Press.
- Underwood, L., The Greatest Disaster Stories Ever Told, Connecticut, The Lyons Press, 2002.
- Wade, N., The New York Times Book of Natural Disasters, Connecticut, The Lyons Press, 2001.
- Will, L., Okeechobee Hurricane and the Hoover Dike 3rd Edition, The Florida, Glades Historical Society, 1961.
- Williams, J., The Weather Book, New York, Vintage Books Ltd., 1997.
- Williams, P., Chronological Highlights in the History of the Bahamas 600 to 1900, Nassau, Bahamas Historical Society, 1999.
- Williams, T., Hurricane of Independence-The Untold Story of the Deciding Moment of the American Revolution, Illinois, Sourcebooks, Inc., 2008.
- Withington, John, Disaster! A History of Earthquakes, Floods, Plagues, and Other Catastrophes, New York, Skyhorse Publishing, 2010.
- Wood, D., Bahamian Migration to Florida 1898 to 1940, Florida, Florida International University, 1987.
- www.enchantedlearning.com
- www.aoml.noaa.gov
- www.noaa.gov
- www.nasa.gov
- www.nhc.noaa.gov
- www.wmo.ch
- www.ocala.com
- www.weather.unisys.com
- www.sun-sentinel.com
- www.weathernotebook.org
- www.rumler.com
- www.hurricaneville.com
- www.mcguinnessonline.com

- www.deadlystorms.com
- www.1900storm.com
- www.snapshotsofthepast.com
- www.hbs.edu
- www.novalynx.com
- www.pewclimate.org
- www.stormcarib.com
- www.bbc.co.uk
- www.sky-chaser.com
- www.cnn.com
- www.pbs.org
- www.answers.com
- www.weather.com
- www.marine.usgs.gov
- www.wxresearch.org
- www.history.com
- www.weathernotebook.org
- www.wunderground.com
- www.usatoday.com
- www.keyshistory.org
- www.ihrc.fiu.edu
- www.palmbeachpost.com
- www.thedominican.net
- www.wikipedia.org
- www.colorado.edu
- www.iri.columbia.edu
- www.weatherexplained.com
- www.publicaffairs.noaa.gov
- www.nationalgeographic.com
- www.weathersavvy.com
- www.usaid.gov
- www.caribbeannetnews.com
- www.oii.net
- www.cidi.org

ACKNOWLEDGEMENTS

The good people of the region, scientists, researchers, librarians, historians and meteorologists who opened their doors, hearts and minds to assist me with this project and provided me with overwhelming research materials, and many others too numerous to mention who gave me their take on these devastating hurricanes. But most of all, I would also like to thank the many sponsors who made this book possible. The writing of this book has been a highly satisfying project, made so not only by the subject itself, but also by the people who have helped and assisted me in some way or the other, so here are the persons I wish to thank:

My Father and Mother Lofton and Francita Neely
My Uncle and Aunt Coleman and Diana Andrews and family
My Grandmother the late Mrs. Joanna Gibson
Ms. Inger Simms
Mr. Wendall Jones
Mr. Rupert Roberts
Mr. Kerry Emanuel
Mr. Michel Davison
Mrs. Stephanie Hanna
Mr. Kevin Hudson
Mr. Dwayne Swaby
Mr. Ray Duncombe
Mrs. Shelley Moree
Mr. Ethric Bowe
Mr. Curtis Baker
Ms. Elisa Montalvo
Ms. Ashleigh Payne
The late Mr. William Holowesko

The Hon. Glenys Hanna-Martin
Mr. Murrio Ducille
Mr. Charles and Eddie Carter
Dr. Gail Saunders
Mr. Joshua Taylor and family
Mrs. Patrice Wells
Mrs. Betty Thompson-Moss
The late Professor William Gray
My uncles the Late Glenwood and Theophilus Neely
Mr. Bryan Norcross
Dr. Steve Lyons
Dr. Phil Klotzbach
Dr. Christopher Landsea
Mrs. Jan Roberts
Mrs. Nancy Saunders
Ms. Carole Balla
Mrs. Shavaughn Moss
Mr. Juan and Paige McCartney
Mr. Michael and Phillip Stubbs
Mr. John Minichiello
Mr. Orson Nixon
Mr. Neil Sealey
The late Dr. Myles Munroe
Dr. Timothy Barrett
Mr. Jack and Karen Andrews
Rev. Theo and Blooming Neely and family
Staff and Management of Logos Bookstore
Staff and Management of Ghostwriter Extraordinaire(GWE)
Staff and Management of The Nassau Guardian Newspaper and NB12 News
Staff and Management of Media Enterprises and Publishing Co.
Staff and Management of The Tribune Newspaper
Staff and Management of Island 102.9fm Radio Station
Staff and Management of Jones Communications Network
Staff and Management of Guardian Radio 96.9fm
Staff and Management of Star Radio 106.9fm
Staff and Management of the Broadcasting Corporation of the Bahamas (ZNS)
Staff of the Bahamas Department of Archives
Staff of the Bahamas Department of Meteorology

Staff of NOAA and National Hurricane Center in Miami
Staff and Management of The Counsellors and Bahamas At Sunrise

For Booking and Speaking Arrangements here is my Contact Information: -

Mr. Wayne Neely
P.O. Box EE-16637
Nassau, Bahamas
E-Mail: wayneneely@hotmail.com
or wayneneely@yahoo.com

I would like to sincerely thank each one of the sponsors, both individual and corporate, who assisted me financially and in other ways in making this book project a reality, and without them this book would have not been possible, so from the bottom of my heart I thank each and every one of you:

J.S. JOHNSON
PEACE OF MIND
INSURANCE AGENTS & BROKERS

BAHAMAS FIRST

FIRST IN INSURANCE. TODAY. TOMORROW.

32 Collins Avenue
P.O. Box SS-6238
Nassau, Bahamas
Telephone: 242-302-3900
Fax: 242-302-3901
Email: info@bahamasfirst.com
Website: www.bahamasfirst.com

Royal Star House
John F. Kennedy Drive
P.O. Box N-4391
Nassau, Bahamas
Tel: (242) 328-7888 / 677-2221
Fax: (242) 325-3151
Website: rsabahamas.com

Your Bahamian Supermarkets
SUPER
VALUE
&
QUALITY
SUPERMARKETS

Branch Store #3-Nassau & Meadow Street
P.O. Box N-3039
Nassau, Bahamas
Phone: 242-323-4861/323-4862
Fax: 242-326-4874
E-Mail: svfsltd@batelnet.bs

Branch Store #6-Prince Charles Drive
P.O. Box N-3039
Nassau, Bahamas
Phone: 242-393-0116/393-5229/393-6266
Fax: 242-394-6526
E-Mail: svfsltd@batelnet.bs

Branch Store #7-Mackey Street (Top of the Hill)
P.O. Box N-3039
Nassau, Bahamas
Phone: 242-393-4533/393-4534
Fax: 242-394-2991
E-Mail: svfsltd@batelnet.bs

Branch Store #8-Wulf Road & Montrose Avenue
P.O. Box N-3039
Nassau, Bahamas
Phone: 242-325-5903/325-7794
Fax: 242-325-37794
E-Mail: svfsltd@batelnet.bs

Branch Store #9-Robinson Road & East Street
P.O. Box N-3039
Nassau, Bahamas
Phone: 242-325-4564/325-4492
Fax: 242-326-4886
E-Mail: svfsltd@batelnet.bs

Branch Store #10-Cable Beach Shopping Centre
P.O. Box N-3039
Nassau, Bahamas
Phone: 242-327-8879
Fax: 242-327-3494
E-Mail: svfsltd@batelnet.bs

Branch Store #11-Winton Shopping Centre
P.O. Box N-3039
Nassau, Bahamas
Phone: 242-324-2186/324-2172
Fax: 242-364-6492
E-Mail: svfsltd@batelnet.bs

ABOUT THE AUTHOR

Wayne Neely attended the Caribbean Meteorological Institute in Barbados, where he majored and specialized in weather forecasting. He is an international speaker, best-selling author, educator, and meteorologist at the Department of Meteorology in Nassau, Bahamas, where he has worked for more than twenty-six years. He has written ten books on hurricanes and regularly speaks at schools, colleges, and universities about the history and impact of hurricanes.

INDEX

D

E

F

G

H

T

U

W

Printed in the United States
by Baker & Taylor Publisher Services